Key studies in psychology

Key studies in psychology

RICHARD D. GROSS

Hodder & Stoughton

LONDON SYDNEY AUCKLAND TORONTO

To Jan, Tanya and Joelle, for once again
enabling me to achieve this goal.

British Library Cataloguing in Publication Data

Gross, Richard D.
  Key studies in psychology.
  1. Psychology
  I. Title
  150

  ISBN 0 340 51837 5

First published 1990
Third impression 1991

Printed in Great Britain for the educational division of Hodder and
Stoughton Ltd, Mill Road, Dunton Green, Sevenoaks, Kent by
Clays Ltd, St Ives plc

Contents

Introduction

A major reason for writing this book was the wish to do what is impossible in a general textbook of Psychology (such as *Psychology: The Science of Mind and Behaviour*), namely to look at a number of individual studies in depth. Invariably, students want to know much more about a particular study than a textbook trying to cover the whole A-level syllabus can provide and, very often, more than a teacher can provide in the classroom situation. This means that students either have to search for and read the original article, which can be impractical and time-consuming (especially for A- and AS-level students), or simply get by with what they can extract from teacher and textbooks.

While it is very important that students (at all levels) get used to reading original sources, how to make efficient use of the material may be far from obvious. The commentaries at the end of each summary are intended to provide students with a framework in which to read *any* original material, so as to make the best use of reading time.

Please note that the articles are (with the exception of Chapter 3) *not* reprints of the original, but highly detailed *summaries*; the aim was to retain the substantial character of the original (not possible in a general textbook), and at the same time to cut down on unnecessary bulk. The following points indicate how the originals were summarised:

1 I have retained all the section headings as they were used in the original (and in their original order). Note that not all journals adopt the same format, e.g. some have a summary or abstract at the beginning, while others have none, and yet others put it at the end.

2 Most tables, figures, etc. have been retained, but not all; where there have been omissions, those retained appear in sequence within the summary (and so not in their original sequence).

3 The summaries comprise a combination of paraphrasing (i.e. re-wording) and reproduction of the original; however, nothing appears in quotation marks because this would seriously break up the continuity, making the summary more difficult to read.

4 Difficult or obscure language has been replaced by simpler or more familiar language. (Hopefully the reader will not notice where this has occurred.)

5 English spelling has been used at all times (even though many of the articles are American).

It is also worth noting that the references given at the back of the book contain only those works referred to in the commentaries, as it would have proved impractical to include all the references from the summaries themselves.

Finally, we come to the (arguably) most crucial question: namely, how did I choose the studies to be included? This was definitely the single most difficult feature of the whole book for me. The main criteria were:

1 The need to sample all the major areas of Psychology: cognitive, social, comparative, bio, developmental and individual differences (using the AEB A-level syllabus as the framework).

2 The need to sample a wide range of empirical methods: experiments (laboratory, field and natural), correlational studies, case studies, surveys, questionnaire construction, observation and content analysis. The selection also includes review articles and those which offer conceptual reinterpretation of previous research.

3 The wish to include studies which would (probably) feature in every students' and teachers' 'top ten famous studies of all time', alongside some less well known, but equally influential studies (including some recent ones).

I recognise that a hundred different authors would choose a hundred different combinations of 31 'key studies', but I hope (and believe) that I have achieved a selection which will satisfy the majority of readers.

Acknowledgements

I would like to thank everyone directly, or indirectly, involved in the production of this book: Maggie Tulloch, for typing the manuscript so expertly (despite all kinds of hardships), Hugh Coolican, for giving valuable feedback on the Exercises and Answers (and who is innocent of any errors which may still remain), Tim Gregson-Williams, for all his support throughout this project, Catriona Dawson, for her thorough checking of the manuscript, and Linda Claris, for having helped to initiate the project. I would also like to thank Professor Peter Bryant for his help regarding Chapter 25, and, similarly, Dr Martin Skuse regarding Chapter 23. John Gammon (AEB A-level Chief Examiner) provided useful comments and encouragement regarding the original proposal and sample material.

The publishers would like to thank the following for permission to reproduce material in this volume:

Academic Press Inc. for 'Levels of Processing: A Framework for Memory Research' by Fergus I. M. Craik and Robert S. Lockhart from the *Journal of Verbal Learning and Verbal Behaviour* Vol. 11, 1972 and 'Imprinting and perceptual learning' by W. Sluckin and E. A. Salzen from the *Quarterly Journal of Experimental Psychology* 13, 1961; The American Psychological Association for extracts from 'Hemisphere Deconnections and Unity in Conscious Awareness' by R. W. Sperry fron *American Psychologist* 23, 1968, 'Emotionality and perceptual defence' by Elliot McGinnies from *Psychology Review* 56, 1969, 'Psychology as a means of Promoting Human Welfare' by G. A. Miller from *Amerian Psychologist*, 1969, 'Good Samaritanism' by Irving M. Piliavin, Judith Rodin and Jane Allyn Piliavin from the *Journal of Personality and Social Psychology* 13, 1969, 'Physical Attractiveness' by Bernard I. Murstein from the *Journal of Personality and Social Psychology* 22, 'Semanatic integration of vectal information into a visual memory' by Elisabeth F. Loftus, David G. Miller and Helen J. Burns from the *Journal of Experimenal Psychology* 4, 'The measurement of psychological androgyny' by Sandra L. Bem from the *Journal of Consulting and Clinical Psychology* 42, 'Cognitive social and physiological determinants' by Stanley Schachter and Jerome E. Singer from the *Psychology Review* 69, 'Positive Reinforcement produced by electrical stimulation of the septal area and other regions of the rat brain' by James Olds and Peter Milner from the *Journal of Comparative and Physiological Psychology* 47, 1954, 'Cognitive consequences of forced compliance' by Leon Festinger and James M. Carlsmith from the *Journal of Abnormal and Social Psychology* 58, 1959, 'A case of multiple personality' by Corbett H. Thigpen and Hervey M. Cleckley from the *Journal of Abnormal and Social Psychology* 49, 1954, 'Behavioural study of obedience' by Stanley Milgram from the *Journal of Abnormal and Social Psychology* 67, 1963; The British Medical Association for 'The hallucinations of widowhood' by W. Dewi Rees from the *British Medical Journal* 4, 1971; The British Psychological Society for 'Sex-role stereotyping in British television advertisements' by A. S. R. Manstead and Caroline McCulloch and 'Fear of Animals: What is Prepared?' By Jamie Bennett-Levy and Theresa Marteau both from the *British Journal of Psychology* 75, 1984; David Cornwell and Sandy Hobbs for the extract from *The Strange Saga of Little Albert*; Sigmund Freud Copyrights Ltd, The Institute of Psycho-Analysis and The Hogarth Press for 'Analysis of phobia in a five-year-old boy' from, *The Standard Edition of the Complete Psychological Works of Sigmund Freud* translated and edited by James Strachey; John Garcia for 'Learning with prolonged delay of reinforcement' by John Garcia, Frank R. Ervin and Robert Koelling; *New Scientist* for 'Forty years of rhesus research' by Richard Rawlins, 12 April 1979; Martin T. Orne for his article 'Hypnosis, motivation and compliance from the *American Journal of Psychiatry* 122; Pergamon Press for 'IQ and behavioural adjustments of ex-institutional adolescents' and 'Social and family relationships of ex-institutional adolescents' both by Jill Hodges and Barbara Tizard from the *Journal of Child Psychology and Psychiatry* Vol. 30, No. 1, 1989 and 'Asking only one question in the conservation experiment' by Judith Samuel and Peter Bryant from the *Journal of Child Psychology and Psychiatry* Vol. 23, No. 2, 1984; Routledge for 'Minds, Brains and Programs' by John R. Searle from *Artificial Intelligence – The Case Against* by Rainer Born (1987); Science for 'Teaching sign language to a chimpanzee' by R. A. Gardner and B. T. Gardner from *Science* Vol. 165, No. 3894, 1969, 'Familial studies of intelligence – a review' by Thomas J. Bouchard Jr and Matthew McGue from *Science* Vol. 212, 1981, 'On being sane in insane places' by D. L. Rosenhan from *Science* Vol. 179, 1973; Scientific American Inc. for 'Pictorial perception and culture' by Jan B. Deregowski from *Scientific American* 227, 1972.

G. A. MILLER (1969)

Psychology as a means of promoting human welfare*

American Psychologist, 24, pp. 1063–75

The most urgent problems we face today are not produced by nature or imposed as punishment by God but are those we have made for ourselves, and to solve them we must change our behaviour and our social institutions. Psychology is a science directly concerned with behavioural and social processes and so it might be expected to lead the way in the search for new and better personal and social arrangements.

However, psychologists have contributed relatively little of real importance – even less than their rather modest understanding of behaviour might justify. They have not used all the knowledge they do have and the challenge for psychologists is not only to extend and deepen their understanding of mental and behavioural phenomena but to apply this knowledge more effectively to the vast social changes that lie ahead. This doesn't mean that psychologists are failing in the task set them by society or that psychological theories are scientifically invalid. As scientists we are obliged to communicate what we know, but we have no special obligation to solve social problems.

However, psychologists are also citizens and our obligations as citizens are far broader than our obligations as scientists. Most American psychologists do accept this broader interpretation of their responsibilities and most are engaged full time in trying to solve social problems, and with a certain degree of success.

Role of the American Psychological Association

The first article of our Bylaws states that the Association shall have as its object to promote human welfare, a goal that is echoed in our statement of the *Ethical Standards of Psychologists*.

But I am very sceptical about how this goal can be translated into objective action for two major reasons.

*Presidential address to the *American Psychological Association*.

First, there is the problem of defining human welfare and deciding which group's welfare is being promoted (which may conflict with that of another).

Second, there has been much debate in recent years about the appropriate role for individual psychologists to play in the initiation of social reforms: should they remain expert advisers or should they play a more active part in determining public policy? Those who favour the latter believe that the APA should also become directly involved in advocating particular social policies. However, although the APA's failure to reform society does *not* mean that it approves the social/political status quo, there is relatively little such an association can do and its attitude towards major and urgent human problems is largely irrelevant.

The important question, to my mind, is not what the APA is doing, but what psychologists are doing. What psychology can do as an associaton depends directly on the base provided by psychology as a science. It is our science that provides our real means for promoting human welfare.

Revolutionary potential of psychology

In my opinion, scientific psychology is potentially one of the most revolutionary intellectual enterprises ever conceived by the mind of man. If we were ever to achieve substantial progress toward our stated aim – toward the understanding, prediction and control of mental and behavioural phenomena – the implications for every aspect of society would make brave men tremble.

If this revolutionary potential has been played down in the past, there are probably two major reasons; firstly, the achievements of psychology so far are rather modest: scientific colleagues will admit that psychometric tests, psychoanalysis, conditioned reflexes, sensory thresholds, implanted electrodes and factor analysis are all quite admirable, but they can scarcely be compared to gunpowder, the steam engine, organic chemistry, radio-telephony, computers, atom bombs, or genetic surgery in their revolutionary consequences for society.

However, I do not believe the psychological revolution is still pie in the sky, but that it has already begun.

This leads on to the second reason, namely that we have been looking for it in the wrong place. We have assumed that psychology should provide new technological options, and that a psychological revolution will not occur until somebody in authority exercises these options to attain socially desirable goals. One reason for this assumption, perhaps, is that it follows the model we have inherited from previous applications of science to practical problems. An applied scientist is supposed to provide instrumentalities for modifying the environment; instrumentalities that can then, under public regulation, be used by wealthy and powerful interests to achieve certain goals. The psychological revolution, when it comes, may follow a very different course, at least in its initial stages.

An important difference between applied social science and applied natural science is that:

'when the science is concerned with human beings – not just as organisms but as goal-seeking individuals and members of groups – then it cannot be instrumental in this way [in the way that applied natural science is, by finding a means to an end which is the attainment of human goals], because the object of observation has a say in what is going on and, above all, is not willing to be treated as a pure instrumentality.'(Davis, 1966)

More important, however, I believe that the real impact of psychology will be felt, not through the technological products it places in the hands of powerful men, but through its effects on the public at large, through a new and different public conception of what is humanly possible and what is humanly desirable.

I believe that any broad and successful application of psychological knowledge to human problems will necessarily entail a change in our conception of ourselves and of how we live and love and work together. Instead of inventing some new technique for modifying the environment, or some new product for society to adapt itself to however it can, we are proposing to tamper with the adaptive process itself. Such an innovation is quite different from a 'technological fix'. I see little reason to believe that the traditional model for scientific revolutions should be appropriate.

Consider, for example, the effect that Freudian psychology has already had on Western society. It is obvious that its effects, though limited to certain segments of society, have been profound. Yet I do not believe that one can argue that those effects were achieved by providing new instrumentalities for achieving goals socially agreed upon. As a method of therapy, psychoanalysis has had limited success even for those who can afford it. It has been more successful as a method of investigation, perhaps, but even there it has been only one of several available methods. The impact of Freud's thought has been due far less to the instrumentalities he provided than to the changed conception of ourselves that he inspired. The wide range of psychological problems that Freud opened up for professional psychologists is only part of his contribution. More important in the scale of history has been his effect on the broader intellectual community and, through it, on the public at large. Today we are much more aware of the irrational components of human nature and much better able to accept the reality of our unconscious impulses. The importance of Freudian psychology derives far less from its scientific validity than from the effects it has had on our image of man himself.

It may be true that other scientific advances have also changed our conception of man and society (such as Darwin's discovery that our remote ancestors lived in trees) but such new conceptions can have little effect on the way we behave in our daily affairs and in our institutional contexts. A new conception of man based on psychology, however, would have immediate implications for the most intimate details of our social and personal lives.

The heart of the psychological revolution will be a new and

scientifically-based conception of man as an individual and as a social creature. When I say that the psychological revolution is already upon us, what I mean is that we have already begun to change man's self-conception. If we want to further that revolution, not only must we strengthen its scientific base, but we must also try to communicate it to our students and to the public. It is not the industrialist or the politician who should exploit it, but everyman, everday.

Control of behaviour

One major message that many scientific psychologists are trying to communicate to the public is the truism that some stimuli can serve to reinforce the behaviour that produces them. The practical significance of this principle is that by controlling the occurrence of these reinforcing stimuli you thereby control behaviour. Since control is the practical pay-off from other sciences, the public is prepared to believe that psychology too is about control.

Closely related to this emphasis on control is the frequently reported claim that living organisms are nothing but machines. Personally, I believe there is a better way to advertise psychology and to relate it to social problems. Reinforcement is only one of many important ideas that we have to offer. Instead of repeating constantly that reinforcement leads to control, I would prefer to emphasise that reinforcement can lead to satisfaction and competence. And I would prefer to speak of understanding and prediction as our major scientific goals.

Understanding and prediction are better goals for psychology and for the promotion of human welfare because they lead us to think, not in terms of coercion by a powerful elite, but in terms of the diagnosis of problems and the development of programmes that can enrich the lives of every citizen.

Public psychology: two paradigms

It is possible to identify two alternative images of human nature as influenced by scientific advances in psychology which are similar to McGregor's (1960) Theory X and Theory Y, meant to explain why people work. Theory X (the traditional theory) states that because people dislike work, they must be coerced, controlled, directed and threatened with punishment before they will do it; people have little ambition and want to avoid responsibility and so will tolerate – and may actually prefer – being directed. The alternative Theory Y (based on social science) maintains that work is as natural as play or rest, so that people exercise self-direction and self-control in order to achieve goals to which they are committed: their commitment is a function of the rewards associated with the achievement of their goals. People may actually seek responsibility and many display imagination, ingenuity and creativity, despite the conditions of modern industrial life.

McGregor's theories are rival theories held by industrial managers about how best to achieve their institutional goals. A broader view of the social nature of human beings is taken by Varela, a Uruguayan engineer, who describes two conceptions of man or 'paradigms' (based on Kuhn, 1962). The first of these is a set of assumptions on which our social institutions are currently based:

> All men are created equal, most behaviour is created by econo-mic competition and conflict is inevitable. When things go wrong, there is always someone who is to blame and the guilty person, who is responsible for his own misbehaviour and rehabi-litation, must be found and punished.

The second paradigm is based on psychological research and main-tains that there are large individual differences between people, both in ability and pesonality. Human motivation is complex and we never act as we do for any single reason, but positive incentives are generally more effective than threats or punishments. Conflict is not inevitable and can be prevented. A person's perception of the situation is more important to them than 'the true facts' when something goes wrong, and to be able to reason about the situation, their irrational feeling must first be toned down. Social problems are solved by correcting causes, not symptoms, and this can be done more effectively in groups than individually. Teachers and supervisors must be experts in social science because they are responsible for the co-operation and indi-vidual improvement of their students or subordinates.

Here, then, is the real challenge: how can we foster a social climate in which some such new public conception of man based on psycholo-gy can take root and flourish? In my opinion, this is the proper translation of our more familiar question about how psychology might contribute to the promotion of human welfare.

Part of the answer is that psychology must be practiced by non-psychologists. We are not physicians, the secrets of our trade need not be reserved for highly-trained specialists. Psychological facts should be passed out freely to all who need and can use them. And from successful applications of psychological principles the public may gain a better appreciation of the power of the new conception of man that is emerging from our science.

There are not enough psychologists (including non-professionals) to meet every need for psychological services. Our scientific results will have to be instilled in 'the public consciousness' in a practical and usable form so that what we know can be applied by ordinary people. The people at large will have to be their own psychologists, and make their own applications of the principles that we establish. Of course, everyone practices psychology. I am not suggesting any radical departure when I say that non-psychologists must practice psycholo-gy. I am simply proposing that we should teach them to practice it better, to make use self-consciously of what we believe to be scien-tifically valid principles. Our responsibility is less to assume the role of experts and try to apply psychology ourselves than to give it away to the people who really need it, and that includes everyone. The practice of valid psychology by non-psychologists will inevitably change people's conception of themselves and what they can do. When we have accomplished that, we will really have caused a psychological revolution.

How to give psychology away

This is no easy matter and there is much resistance to change and new ways of doing things; man's attempts to introduce sound psychological practices into schools, clinics, hospitals, prisons or industries have failed. One problem is that the innovation may be piecemeal, not taking the whole 'culture' of the institution into account. But if you understand the system as a whole, you don't need to control it: relatively minor changes can then have extensive consequences throughout the entire organisation. There is no possibility of legislating the changes I have in mind. Passing laws that people must change their 'conceptions' of themselves and others is precisely the opposite of what we need. Education would seem to be our only possibility. This does not mean only education in the schoolroom. I have in mind a more ambitious programme of educating the general public.

In order to get started, we must begin where they are, not assume we know where they should be. If a supervisor is having trouble with his men, perhaps we should teach him how to write a job description and how to evaluate the abilities and personalities of those who fill the job; perhaps we should teach him the art of persuasion or the time and place for positive reinforcement. If a ghetto mother is not giving her children sufficient intellectual challenge, perhaps we should teach her how to encourage their motor, perceptual and linguistic skills. The techniques involved are not some esoteric branch of witchcraft that must be reserved for those with PhD degrees in psychology. When the ideas are made sufficiently concrete and explicit, the scientific foundations of psychology can be grasped by sixth-grade children [12-year-olds].

Psychological principles and techniques can usefully be applied by everyone, not just specialist professionals. We must, however, give people something whose value they recognise, which is valid for them, not give them something which we think is important. Take the example of teaching children to read. The conventional method is for experts to provide teachers with reading schemes which are then used with children. But an alternative method is that developed by Ashton-Warner (1963), a teacher in New Zealand. She begins by asking a child what words (s)he wants and which are bound up with the child's own loves and fears. The words, are written on a large card which is given to the child who learns to read them almost immediately: it is *their* word.

These are not dead words of an expert's choosing, but words that live in a child's own experience. Under this regimen, a word is not an imposed task to be learned with reinforcement borrowed from some external source of motivation. Learning the word is itself reinforcing. Each child decides where he wants to start, and each child receives something whose value he can recognise.

This technique for teaching children to read is related to White's (1959) concept of competence motivation – the urge to feel more effective. Psychology can be used to help people feel more effective especially about personal problems in their own life. From this start, some people may want to learn more about the science that helped them increase their competence and then things could become more abstract.

But in the beginning we must try to diagnose and solve the problems people think they have, not the problems we experts think they ought to have, and we must learn to understand those problems in the social and institutional contexts that define them. With this approach we might do something practical for nurses, policemen, prison guards, salesmen – for people in many different walks of life. That, I believe, is what we should mean when we talk about applying psychology to the promotion of human welfare. I can imagine nothing we could do that would be more relevant to human welfare, and nothing that could pose a greater challenge to the next generation of psychologists, than to discover how best to give psychology away.

Commentary

Aim and nature

As the footnote indicates, the article is in fact Miller's Presidential address to the American Psychological Association. In it, he sets out the role which he believes Psychology should play in society, namely 'a means of promoting human welfare' by 'giving psychology away', i.e. encouraging non-psychologists ('ordinary people') to practise psychology, to be their own psychologists, helping them to do better what they already do through familiarising them with (scientific) psychological knowledge. Psychology should not be the 'property' of the scientific/professional experts – psychological principles and techniques can usefully be applied by everyone. 'The techniques involved are not some esoteric branch of witchcraft that must be reserved for those with PhD degrees in psychology. When the ideas are made sufficiently concrete and explicit, the scientific foundations of psychology can be grasped by sixth-grade children'.

Background and context

According to Murphy *et al.* (1984), Miller's Presidential address captures the turmoil that psychology was experiencing during the late 1960s and, although it is too soon to judge whether Miller's words have influenced the way psychologists go about their work, his paper has been quoted many times since 1969 and many psychologists have endorsed his sentiments, including Shotter (*Images of Man in Psychological Research*, 1975) and Kay in his 1972 Presidential address to the British Psychological Society.

Murphy *et al.* believe that Miller seems to have drawn attention to two particular issues which had been raised by the radical critics of psychology in the late 1960s, namely, (*i*) the accusation that psychology has created a dehumanising image of human beings and (*ii*) the accusation that psychology has ignored the real-world setting within which human beings live their lives. As far as (i) is concerned, this centres on the notion of behavioural *control*, discussed at length by Miller. What makes it dehumanising is that people are capable of *self*-control, controlling their own behaviour, so that imposing a behavioural technology of control removes a basic human freedom, as well as conveying the impression that people are machine-like. This is discussed in detail by Heather (1976).

Control, along with understanding (explanation) and prediction, is usually taken to be one of the major aims of science (including psychology) and is, as you might expect, the one emphasised by Skinner. (Indeed, Skinner sees understanding as irrelevant, since this is the job of theory and he claims that his work on operant conditioning is atheoretical.) Miller takes the opposite view, and sees understanding and prediction as the appropriate aims of psychology; to this extent he is agreeing with radical critics, such as Shotter and Heather, for whom Skinner's represents the ultimate kind of mechanistic, dehumanising, approach. [When you consider that operant conditioning, as applied to people, is based on work with rats and pigeons in the highly controlled environment of the Skinner box, it is little wonder that radical critics should select Skinner as a prime target.]

As far as (ii) is concerned, Miller advocates that we must start with what people themselves believe their problems to be; this is reminiscent of the view taken by Joynson (1974) in which he attacks the behaviourists for looking at people as objects, from the outside, while ignoring their experience and rejecting the validity of their attempts to explain their own behaviour. Radical psychologists would regard any attempt to study people as objects as both unethical and scientifically unsound, since people can and do choose courses of action – any theory or system which ignores this feature of human beings must be presenting only a partial or inaccurate account. In Davis's (1966) terms, human beings are 'goal-seeking individuals and members of groups'; this makes the subject-matter of psychology *qualitatively* different from that of the natural sciences.

Another facet of this second issue is the importance that the *experiment* has assumed: while it may be the method of investigation which affords the greatest degree of control, it also, to the same extent, studies behaviour in artificial, contrived, situations, often far removed from real-life situations. This criticism of the experimental method (which applies mainly to laboratory as against field experiments) is another made at length by Heather (1976) but is not directly raised by Miller's address.

Evaluation

1 When discussing giving psychology away, Miller seems to be talking mainly about helping people to solve their personal – and professional – problems and so is advocating a problem-centred approach. But surely the promotion of human welfare means more than this? Surely it also involves a much more positive approach, whereby people can realise their potential as human beings. (Of course, this may be much harder to achieve when the person faces problems, particularly those to do with basic survival needs – see Maslow (1954).) But positive growth may also occur through the process of trying to overcome problems and hardships and this perhaps deserves more emphasis.

2 Throughout the address, Miller talks of psychology as a *science* without ever actually defining what a science is. However, he argues that a science of human beings is qualitatively different from a science of the natural world – through influencing our image of ourselves, what we think is achievable and important to achieve (i.e. changing the goals and not just moving the goal-posts!), scientific psychology can help to change the very subject matter it is trying to study! This, surely, means that psychology can never be objective in the way the natural sciences aspire to be, since psychological theories and principles can actually transform the 'things' they are meant to explain: chemicals are not affected by what chemists say about them, but psychologists are part of their own subject matter and this is another sense in which total objectivity is impossible.

Miller believes that changing how we see ourselves is a more appropriate model for psychology than developing a technology which has always been the measure of the effectiveness of natural science; the latter is more tangible than the former and the effects of applications of Skinner's operant conditioning, for example, may be much easier to quantify than the effects of Freud's view of people as irrational and driven by unconscious forces. However, Miller believes that it is precisely the impact on our conception of ourselves and *not* technological applications of psychological principles, which makes psychology (potentially) revolutionary.

Exercises

1 In what ways can we all (already) be thought of as psychologists?

2 What are 'demand characteristics' (Orne, 1962) and how do they make experiments using human subjects less objective?

3 In the case of psychology, what is 'common sense' knowledge and how does this relate to 'scientific' (or 'expert') knowledge?

4 Do you agree with Skinner that the major aim of psychology should be the control of behaviour? Or is Miller right when he says the appropriate goals are understanding and prediction?

Emotionality and perceptual defence

Psychological Review, 56, pp. 244–51

During the past decade a number of experimental investigations have progressively revealed the so-called 'dynamic' or motivational aspects of perceptual behaviour. No longer do we view perception as organized solely in terms of the structural characteristics of stimulus objects or the frequency with which the individual has been exposed to these objects (i.e. the limiting stimulus conditions) but also with regard to the possibilities of reward (Proshansky & Murphy, 1942; Schafer & Murphy, 1943), need fulfilment (Bruner & Goodman, 1947; Levine *et al.*, 1942), attitudinal orientation (Postman *et al.*, 1948), potential anxiety (Bruner, 1948), symbolic value (Bruner, 1948) and release from tension (Bruner & Postman, 1947), to mention just a few. In order to describe such facts as the perceptual selection and accentuation of valued objects and the elimination or distortion of harmful stimulus objects, it has been found convenient to invoke mechanisms of *sensitization, defence and value resonance* (Postman *et al.*, 1948), *vigilance* (Bruner & Postman, 1947) and *primitivation* (Bruner, 1948). Finally, playing host to these varied and intrinsic functions, is the 'ego', in whose service, presumably, the various perceptual adjustments operate.

It seems well established, then, that the perceptual 'filtering' of visual stimuli often serves to protect the observer as long as possible from an awareness of objects which have unpleasant emotional significance. But does this process entirely insulate from the emotion-provoking qualities of the stimulus situation?

If we view emotion essentially as a motivating condition of the individual (Leeper, 1948), the critical nature of the relationship between emotion and perception becomes apparent. Emotion does appear to represent a highly organized and directed state of the organism, such that emotion-inducing stimuli may be expected to initiate those perceptual responses consistent with the general picture of emotional adaptation. Several exploratory studies have indicated that the individual both perceives and reacts in a way consistent with his emotional response to stimulation. Bruner and Postman (1947) demonstrated that tension (defined as reactivity to threat, deprivation or thwarting) will induce perceptual 'accentuation' of objects previously associated with the anxiety-producing stimulation. Postman *et al.* (1948) have shown that frustration (induced by sarcasm and criticism) will raise the perceptual thresholds of observers to tachistos-copically-presented words. Recognition thresholds are also raised when individuals are faced with stimulus objects which, while not actually threatening, are of little relevance or about which they feel some dislike. This process of perceptual 'screening' apparently is acquired by the individual as a technique for organizing perceptions around value expectancies so as to produce maximum reinforcement of these expectancies.

One question which is repeatedly raised by these experimental findings is: 'How is a raised or lowered recognition threshold for harmful stimulus objects achieved before the observer discriminates them and becomes aware of their threatening character?' While the answer will follow eventually only from fuller knowledge of the neurophysiological processes underlying perceptual responses, detection of any one aspect of physiological reaction accompanying perceptual behaviour should throw some light on the processes by which perceptual defence is effected. For example, we might hypothesize that stimuli of an appropriate sort will arouse autonomic reactions characteristic of anxiety or pleasure *prior* to conscious awareness of the nature of the stimulus; if so, we might expect to find a change in galvanic skin response (GSR) in reaction to visually-presented stimuli with emotion-provoking connotations before the subject is able to report the exact nature of the stimulus. So, autonomic reactivity may have a lower threshold to threat than do those neural systems which mediate consciousness. Study of such reactions should hold significant possibilities for adding to our understanding of the process by which discriminatory evaluation of visually sensed objects is achieved before accurate perception occurs.

The experiment

Because it can be measured easily and precisely, the GSR was chosen as an index of emotionality (i.e. autonomic response independent of any phenomenological content) in response to affectively-charged verbal symbols. A list of 11 neutral and seven critical (emotionally-toned) words was made (see table 2.1). The words were presented via a Gerbrand's Mirror Tachistoscope, which allowed controlled variation of exposure time, starting at 0.01 seconds.

The subjects were eight male and eight female undergraduates from an elementary psychology class at Alabama University, all naïve as to the purpose of the experiment. The subject sat in front of the tachistoscope and had electrodes strapped to both palms for measuring GSR; a 32 cm scale microammeter accurate to 0.5 per cent allowed precise readings of current changes of 1 microampere. Each subject's threshold was first determined for four trial words in order to accustom him to the apparatus and to allow his level of resistance to stabilize. In all cases, thresholds were determined by exposing the word once at 0.01 seconds, once at 0.02 seconds, etc., until it was correctly reported.

Table 2.1   Stimulus words used in the experiment in order of their presentation to each observer

Critical or emotional words are in bold

apple	**kotex**★
dance	broom
raped	stove
child	**penis**
belly	music
glass	trade
river	**filth**
whore	clear
sleep	**bitch**

★ a form of sanitary towel

Prior to experimentation, subjects were told that they would be shown words which they might not be able to recognize at first. They were instructed to report whatever they saw or thought they saw on each exposure, regardless of what it was. They were also asked to withhold stating their hypothesis until they received a signal from the experimenter; in this way, we could expose the stimulus word, note the maximum deflection of the microammeter pointer during the six-second period following exposure, and then record the subject's response. One experimenter operated the tachistoscope, another recorded GSR and re-set the current through the subject to 40 microamperes after recognition of each word.

Experimental findings

Emotionality   Since we were interested primarily in subjects' GSR during the period *preceding correct recognition* of the stimulus words, we have based our analysis upon just those readings taken on exposure trials up to, but not including, the trial on which recognition finally occurred. Assuming that the GSR is a valid measure of 'emotionality', we have succeeded in measuring emotional, or autonomic, reactivity to verbal symbols during the period preceding accurate recognition of the stimulus. Statistical analysis confirms that emotionality is signi-

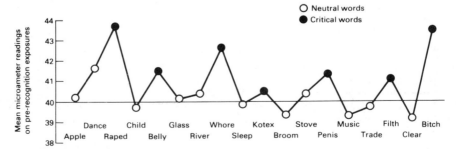

Figure 2.1   Group averages of galvanic skin response to neutral and critical words during pre-recognition exposures.

ficantly greater during pre-recognition exposures of the critical than of the neutral words. Testing the null hypothesis that no differences other than those attributable to random fluctuations in the data would exist between mean GSRs of observers to the neutral and critical words, we found a *t*-value of 5.10 for 15 degrees of freedom, significant at the 0.01 level of significance. The null hypothesis can, therefore, be rejected. The results are presented graphically in figure 2.1 and summarized in table 2.2.

Thresholds Figure 2.2 shows that, without exception, the mean thresholds were greater for the critical than for the neutral words and table 2.2 shows that the difference was significant ($t = 3.96$, *d.f.* $= 15$, $p < 0.01$).

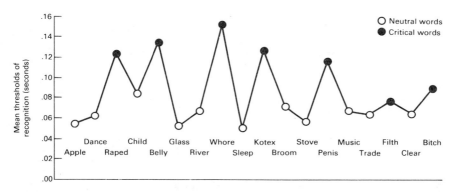

Figure 2.2   Mean thresholds of recognition of the observers to the neutral and emotionally-charged words.

A breakdown of the data with respect to sex showed that, on average, male subjects had significantly lowe thresholds for both neutral and critical words. However, since individual differences in visual acuity was not controlled, these results cannot be accepted as more than suggestive of a sex difference in threshold of visual recognition. There was no significant difference between thresholds for neutral and critical words for male and female subjects, i.e. neither group showed greater perceptual defence than the other. Also, no significant sex differences were found in absolute size of GSR to the critical and neutral words or to differential GSR to the two types of words, i.e. emotionality during the pre-recognition period was of equal degree in both sexes.

Content analysis Since subjects were instructed to report whatever they saw, they typically volunteered a number of pre-recognition 'hypotheses' before recognition occurred. Four content categories were used to code the subjects' perceptual 'guesses':

1 *Structurally similar* The guesses resembled the structure of the stimulus word, e.g. 'trace' for 'trade', 'whose' for 'whore'.

2 *Structurally unlike* The guesses were dissimilar in structure to the stimulus word, e.g. 'roared' for 'belly', 'ideal' for 'glass'.

Table 2.2 Summary of raw data and statistical tests for all observers for both GSR and thresholds of recognition for neutral and critical stimulus words

Observer	Mean microammeter readings during pre-recognition exposures		Mean thresholds of recognition	
	Neutral words	Critical words	Neutral words	Critical words
1	37.80	40.46	0.055	0.184
2	40.96	41.53	0.044	0.094
3	39.31	42.06	0.054	0.080
4	38.34	40.80	0.103	0.126
5	41.48	43.76	0.040	0.064
6	41.41	47.08	0.070	0.130
7	40.75	39.94	0.057	0.104
8	39.98	42.85	0.063	0.076
9	39.44	42.68	0.059	0.130
10	40.02	42.71	0.049	0.223
11	39.88	41.55	0.046	0.077
12	41.27	44.02	0.057	0.091
13	40.56	41.37	0.033	0.037
14	40.19	41.42	0.034	0.054
15	40.85	40.63	0.046	0.056
16	40.83	41.84	0.036	0.046

	Mean difference = 1.98, $t = 5.10, p < 0.01$	Mean difference = 0.045, $t = 3.96, p < 0.01$

3 *Nonsense* The guesses simply had no dictionary meanings, e.g. 'egtry' for 'kotex', 'widge' for 'stove'.

4 *Part* These guesses were fractional or incomplete, consisting of any disconnected group of letters.

Figure 2.3 shows the percentage of responses in each content category made to neutral and critical stimulus words for all 16 subjects. A Chi-square test of independence between type of hypothesis and meaning of the stimulus words shows a significant relationship ($\chi^2 = 31.26$, $p < 0.01$) (see table 2.3). The subjects made proportionately more *unlike* and *nonsense* responses to the critical words.

The subjects were asked after the experiment whether they had reported their perceptions of the words promptly and accurately. In all cases they assured the experimenters that, with the occasional exception of the first critical words, they did not withhold or modify their verbal response because of reluctance to say the word. It seems then, that the GSR was recording genuine pre-recognition reactions to the stimulus words.

Implications for perceptual theory

It seems clear that emotional reactivity, as measured by the GSR, does accompany perceptual defence. Murray (1933) states that '.... certain features of the object which the subject does not consciously

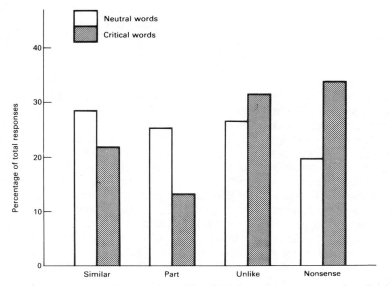

Figure 2.3 Percentage frequencies with which hypotheses to neutral and critical stimulus words appeared in the response categories.

Table 2.3 Chi-square test of independence between stimulus words and response categories
(theoretical frequencies are in brackets)

	Neutral	**Critical**	
Similar	89	93	182
	(76.36)	(105.64)	
Part	79	57	136
	(57.06)	(78.94)	
Unlike	83	136	219
	(91.89)	(127.11)	
Nonsense	62	147	209
	(87.69)	(121.31)	
	313	433	746

$\chi^2 = 31.26, p < 0.01$

perceive are nevertheless physically affecting his body, and though he may be unable to report upon these internal happenings, they are nevertheless affecting his conscious appraisal of the object'. Although this statement was not based on laboratory evidence, his account of emotional conditioning is essentially correct.

Early in life, most people learn that words like 'whore' and 'bitch' are socially taboo. If a child uses such words, they will generally be punished by the parent and a conditioned emotional reaction to these verbal symbols is soon established. This pattern of conditioned emotional response is one of fear or anxiety aroused by symbols having sexual, excretory or otherwise unpleasant or 'immoral' connotations.

Despite the fact that these words may be used frequently at a later age, especially in the company of members of one's own sex, the early emotional reaction persists, as revealed by the GSR, even when overt signs of anxiety or embarrassment are not observable.

Despite evidence of unconscious emotional arousal, perceptual defence against those anxiety-arousing symbols still occurs. This poses a problem for neurophysiological explanation. Is the GSR preceding recognition of critical words a result of 'feedback' from the cortical association centres, or is autonomic response initiated as the visual impulses reach the optic thalamus? If the latter is true, then we might speculate that 're-routing' of afferent activity then takes place in the various visual centres so that cortical integration is effectively modified in the direction of phenomenological distortion. Evidence for this hypothesis is found in the greater frequency of *nonsense* and *unlike* hypotheses in response to the critical words. Formulation of these pre-recognition perceptions represents tactics designed to delay accurate recognition of the stimulus word. On the other hand, relatively higher frequency of *part* responses to the neutral words suggests an effort towards recognition, based on whatever fractional discriminations the subject can make.

Dr Jerome Bruner has suggested an alternative explanation: 'critical' words appear less often in print and the greater threshold for these words is a function of their unfamiliarity – greater 'effort' is required to recognize them which, in turn, causes an increased GSR. However, (i) the critical words are, in fact, quite common in conversational usage despite their infrequent appearance in print; (ii) there is no reason why unfamiliarity should generate a greater number of *nonsense* and *structurally-unlike* hypotheses; (iii) if GSR merely accompanies increased effort spent in recognizing words with higher thresholds, there should be a correlation between mean GSRs and mean thresholds for both the neutral and critical words; using Pearsons r test, correlations of -0.002 and $+0.077$ were found for the neutral and critical words respectively, clearly insignificant. The results, therefore, may be viewed as reflecting genuine emotional response rather than mere autonomic reactivity accompanying effort at recognition.

Perceptual defence appears to be based on conditioned avoidance of unpleasant or dangerous stimuli. It is clear from the increased emotionality before recognition that the individual actually discriminates the stimulus before fully perceiving it ('discrimination without awareness'). Threatening stimuli, then, may serve as cues which are appropriately evaluated by the central nervous system even though integration of the afferent impulse is such as to delay recognition, either through distortion or an increase in threshold or both. The subjects' GSR was almost always greatest following the final exposure of the critical words, i.e. the one during which recognition occurred. Clearly, perceptual defence is designed to delay the greater anxiety which accompanies actual recognition of the stimulus.

Summary

Recognition thresholds and GSRs during the pre-recognition period were measured for 16 subjects presented tachistoscopically with 11 neutral and seven emotionally-toned words, presented in random order. GSRs were significantly greater during the pre-recognition presentation of the critical words as were recognition thresholds, compared with the neutral words. Hypotheses made before recognition of the critical words indicated resistance to recognizing these words and the overall findings are interpreted as representing conditioned avoidance of verbal symbols having unpleasant meanings. The stimulus word acts as a cue to deeply-rooted anxiety which is revealed in the GSR. Avoidance of further anxiety is simultaneously aroused in the form of perceptual defence against recognition of the stimulus object.

Commentary

Aim and nature

The study is a laboratory experiment aimed at establishing the existence of the process of perceptual defence as a pre-conscious response to anxiety-producing stimuli. Taking GSR as a measure of autonomic arrousal (physiological arousal beyond the subject's conscious control), McGinnies hypothesizes (*i*) that there will be a significant change in GSR in reaction to visually presented stimuli (words) with emotive connotations before the subject is able to report the exact nature of the stimulus, compared with stimuli without such connotations, and (*ii*) that the mean recognition threshold for the former will be significantly higher than that for the latter (i.e. it will take longer to recognize the former). It is the reference to the higher recognition threshold which represents the concept of perceptual defence. The design is a repeated measures design, since all the subjects are presented with all 18 words (11 neutral, seven emotionally-toned). The words (neutral or emotive) represent the independent variable and the dependent variable is measured as (*i*) mean GSR and (*ii*) mean recognition threshold.

Background and context

A commonly held view of perception is that it is an active process, influenced by motivational, emotional and cognitive processes (as opposed to a passive receipt of sensory information from and about the external world). Allport (1955) distinguished six types of motivational-emotional influence on perception: bodily needs, reward and punishment, emotional connotation, individual values, personality and the value of objects.

The third and the last of these are the most directly related to the McGinnies study and in fact represent the converse of each other: the value of objects is to do with the phenomenon of perceptual accentuation (or sensitization), whereby things that are relevant or salient for us are perceived as larger/brighter/more attractive/more valuable etc. (than things which are not and compared with objective size). Perceptual defence (coined by Postman *et al.*, 1948; McGinnies, 1949) is related to Freud's concept of repression, whereby dangerous or threatening memories, ideas or feelings are forced out of consciousness and made unconscious and thus inaccessible to the conscious mind. Clearly, this has a very important defensive function (both in the child and adult) and is one of several ego defence mechanisms described by Freud (see chapter 24). Perceptual defence is, in turn, linked to the more general- – and less defence- – oriented concept of subliminal perception, i.e. recognition below the threshold of consciousness. A number of studies have shown that recognition can occur before perception enters conscious awareness ('autonomic discrimination without awareness'/the 'subception effect'): somehow, enough information about the stimulus is transmitted to the autonomic nervous system to determine different levels of GSR but not enough reaches the brain centres responsible for correct verbal identification. Note that changes in GSR are being used as an index of pre-conscious recognition, thus physiological changes are taken as (indirect) indicators of an essentially psychological process. (This suggests that any hard-and-fast distinction between mind and body is artificial.)

Dixon (1971) reviewed a number of studies which showed that verbal stimuli which are too quick or too dim to be consciously perceived, will nonetheless affect the subject's associative processes. It has been found that (*i*) associations following the subliminal perception of a word were linked to its meaning (Marcel & Patterson, 1978), (*ii*) subjects' self-ratings of anxiety increased following the subliminal presentations of unpleasant words, such as 'cancer' (Tyrer *et al.*, 1978), and (*iii*) GSRs increase to the subliminal presentation of emotive picture stimuli, such as a 'breast' (O'Grady, 1977).

Evaluation

1 A number of studies have challenged McGinnies' conclusions regarding perceptual defence. Howes and Solomon (1950) argued that subjects' higher threshold for taboo words was due to their greater reluctance to say them out loud without more confidence in their guesses. Some support for this criticism comes from a study by Aronfreed *et al.* (1953) in which female subjects were tested by a male experimenter: higher recognition thresholds and greater GSRs were produced for the taboo words compared with those produced when other combinations of subject and experimenter were used. (Note that McGinnies found no significant sex difference either in perceptual defence or emotionality during the pre-recognition period.) Support also comes from Bitterman and Kniffin (1953) who found that there was no perceptual defence effect if subjects were allowed to write down their answers instead of saying them aloud. Also the perceptual defence effect could be eliminated by warning subjects that taboo words would be shown (Lacy *et al.*, 1953; Postman *et al.*, 1953).

However, Beier and Cowen (1953) found that even when subjects were warned about sexual words, most still perceived them more slowly and they also reported that they did *not* consciously stop themselves from uttering them.

2 Another criticism is to do with the lower frequency of occurrence of the taboo words in written English, i.e. they are less familiar than the neutral words and this *alone* could explain the differences in recognition threshold (Solomon & Howes, 1951). They obtained a list of the frequency of about 30,000 words in print and chose 60 (all non-taboo) of varying frequencies and determined their recognition thresholds. Using a similar procedure to McGinnies, they found a high negative correlation (-0.79) between frequency of word in print and recognition threshold. In a more direct test of the word-frequency explanation, Postman *et al.* (1952) determined how frequent the taboo words were in print and matched them with neutral words of the same frequency; they found no support for perceptual defence: in fact, the threshold for the taboo words was significantly *lower* (probably due to underestimation of the taboo word frequency).

However, none of these studies measured GSR. Cowen and Beier (1954), on the other hand, demonstrated the emotional effects of sexual words *independently* of their frequency. Again, it is difficult to estimate the actual familiarity of individual subjects with taboo words just from their frequency in written English; several words used in these various experiments are sexual slang ('balls', 'screw') and how familiar subjects are will depend on their particular social experience (Vernon, 1962).

To get around these criticisms, Lazarus and McCleary (1951) created traumatic or neutral stimuli by pairing five nonsense syllables with shock during a training period (while another five were not). After a sufficient number of trials, the shock-paired syllables became threatening to the subjects but there was no threat involved in their being uttered. (This got round the problem of response-withholding.) Also, all the nonsense syllables (by definition) were equally unfamiliar. Following training, recognition thresholds were measured in the usual way, plus GSR. On those trials when subjects made incorrect guesses, there was a higher GSR to shock-paired than neutral syllables, strongly supporting the idea of autonomic discrimination without awareness (and so, indirectly, of perceptual defence).

3 Is perceptual defence a truly *perceptual* phenomenon or is the increased recognition threshold for taboo words due to some kind of *response bias* (Eysenck, 1984)? Hardy and Legge (1968) asked subjects to detect the presence of a faint auditory stimulus while watching a screen on which emotive or neutral words were presented subliminally. Though nearly all failed to notice that any words had been presented, the auditory threshold was *higher* when emotive words were being presented. This effect was due to reduction in sensitivity to stimulation as opposed to a shift in response bias: the experimental design effectively precluded any report suppression. Hardy and Legge concluded that perceptual defence is a genuine perceptual phenomenon.

4 However, there remains a paradox. According to Howie (1952), when we talk about perceptual defence we are speaking of 'perceptual processing as somehow being both a process of knowing and a process of avoiding knowing', i.e. how is it that the perceiver can selectively defend him/herself against an emotional stimulus *unless* (s)he has already perceived and identified it (Eysenck, 1984)?

The concept of subliminal perception in general, and perceptual defence in particular, becomes more acceptable if perception is thought of *not* as a unitary process but one involving multiple processing stages and mechanisms, with consciousness perhaps representing just the final level of processing (Dixon, 1981; Erdelyi, 1974). Put another way, consciousness may not be essential to cognition (Eysenck, 1984).

Exercises

1 Which statistical test was used for recognition thresholds and GSR (in table 2.2)?

2 Why was it important to have an equal number of male and female subjects?

3 Why was it important to determine each subject's GSR threshold for four trial words?

4 How was the order of the words determined and why is it an important thing to control for in this kind of experimental design?

5 If the independent variable was the neutrality/emotionality of the words, what other characteristics of the words should have been controlled?

6 (*i*) How many degrees of freedom (d.f.) are there in table 2.3?
(*ii*) What is the more familiar term for 'theoretical' frequencies?

7 Why was it a good idea to have two experimenters (one to operate the tachistoscope and one to measure the subject's GSR)?

3

JAN B. DEREGOWSKI (1972)

Pictorial perception and culture

Scientific American, 227, pp. 82–8

Do people of one culture perceive a picture differently from people of another? Experiments in Africa show that such differences exist, and that the perception of pictures calls for some form of learning

A picture is a pattern of lines and shaded areas on a flat surface that depicts some aspect of the real world. The ability to recognize objects in pictures is so common in most cultures that it is often taken for granted that such recognition is universal in man. Although children do not learn to read until they are about six years old, they are able to recognize objects in pictures long before that; indeed, it has been shown that a 19-month-old child is capable of such recognition. If pictorial recognition is universal, do pictures offer us a lingua franca for intercultural communication? There is evidence that they do not: cross-cultural studies have shown that there are persistent differences in the way pictorial information is interpreted by people of various cultures. These differences merit investigation not only because improvement in communication may be achieved by a fuller understanding of them but also because they may provide us with a better insight into the nature of human perceptual mechanisms.

Reports of difficulty in pictorial perception by members of remote, illiterate tribes have periodically been made by missionaries, explorers and anthropologists. Robert Laws, a Scottish missionary active in Nyasaland (now Malawi) at the end of the 19th century, reported: 'Take a picture in black and white and the natives cannot see it. You may tell the natives, "This is a picture of an ox and a dog," and the people will look at it and look at you and that look says that they consider you a liar. Perhaps you say again, "Yes, that is a picture of an ox and a dog." Well, perhaps they will tell you what they think this time. If there are a few boys about, you say: "This is really a picture of an ox and a dog. Look at the horn of the ox, and there is his tail" And the boy will say: "Oh! yes and there is the dog's nose and eyes and ears!" Then the old people will look again and clasp their hands and say, "Oh! yes, it is a dog." When a man has seen a picture for the first time, his book education has begun.'

Mrs Donald Fraser, who taught health care to Africans in the 1920s, had similar experiences. This is her description of an African woman slowly discovering that a picture she was looking at portrayed a human head in profile: 'She discovered in turn the nose, the mouth, the eye, but where was the other eye? I tried by turning my profile to explain why she could only see one eye but she hopped round to my other side to point out that I possessed a second eye which the other lacked.'

There were also, however, reports of vivid and instant responses to pictures: 'When all the people were quickly seated, the first picture flashed on the sheet was that of an elephant. The wildest excitement immediately prevailed, many of the people jumping up and shouting, fearing the beast must be alive, while those nearest to the sheet sprang up and fled. The chief himself crept stealthily forward and peeped behind the sheet to see if the animal had a body, and when he discovered that the animal's body was only the thickness of the sheet, a great roar broke the stillness of the night.'

Thus the evidence gleaned from the insightful but unsystematic observations quoted is ambiguous. The laborious way some of these Africans pieced together a picture suggests that some form of learning is required to recognize pictures. Inability to perceive that a pattern of lines and shaded areas on a flat surface represents a real object would render all pictorial material incomprehensible. All drawings would be perceived as being meaningless, abstract patterns until the viewer had learned to interpret and organize the symbolic elements. On the other hand, one could also argue that pictorial recognition is largely independent of learning, and that even people from cultures where pictorial materials are uncommon will recognize items in pictures, provided that the pictures show familiar objects. It has been shown that an unsophisticated adult African from a remote village is unlikely to choose the wrong toy animal when asked to match the toy to a picture of, say, a lion. Given a photograph of a kangaroo, however, he is likely to choose at random from the array of toys. Yet one can argue that this sample was not as culturally remote as those described above. It is therefore probably safer to assume that utter incomprehension of pictorial material may be observed only in extremely isolated human populations.

Conventions for depicting the spatial arrangement of three-dimensional objects in a flat picture can also give rise to difficulties in perception. These conventions give the observer depth cues that tell

---

Figure 3.1   Pictorial depth perception is tested by showing subjects a picture such as the top illustration in figure 3.1. A correct interpretation is that the hunter is trying to spear the antelope, which is nearer to him than the elephant. An incorrect interpretation is that the elephant is nearer and is about to be speared. The picture contains two depth cues: overlapping objects and known size of objects. The bottom illustration depicts the man, elephant and antelope in true size ratios when all are the same distance from the observer.

him the objects are not all the same distance from him. Inability to interpret such cues is bound to lead to misunderstanding of the meaning of the picture as a whole. William Hudson, who was then working at the National Institute for Personnel Research in Johannesburg, stumbled on such a difficulty in testing South African Bantu workers. His discovery led him to construct a pictorial perception test and to carry out much of the pioneering work in cross-cultural studies of perception.

Hudson's test consists of a series of pictures in which there are various combinations of three pictorial depth cues. The first cue is familiar size, which calls for the larger of two known objects to be drawn considerably smaller to indicate that it is farther away. The second cue is overlap, in which portions of nearer objects overlap and obscure portions of objects that are farther away; a hill is partly obscured by another hill that is closer to the viewer. The third cue is perspective, the convergence of lines known to be parallel to suggest distance; lines representing the edges of a road converge in the distance. In all but one of his tests Hudson omitted an entire group of powerful depth cues: density gradients. Density gradients are provided by any elements of uniform size: bricks in a wall or pebbles on a beach. The elements are drawn larger or smaller depending on whether they are nearer to the viewer or farther away from him.

Hudson's test has been applied in many parts of Africa with subjects drawn from a variety of tribal and linguistic groups. The subjects were shown one picture at a time and asked to name all the objects in the picture in order to determine whether or not the elements were correctly recognized. Then they were asked about the relation between the objects. (What is the man doing? What is closer to the man?) If the subject takes note of the depth cues and makes the 'correct' interpretations, he is classified as having three-dimensional perception. If the depth cues are not taken into account by the subject, he is said to have two-dimensional perception (see figure 3.1). The results from African tribal subjects were unequivocal: both children and adults found it difficult to perceive depth in the pictorial material. The difficulty varied in extent but appeared to persist through most educational and social levels.

Further experimentation revealed that the phenomenon was not simply the result of the pictorial material used in the test. Subjects were shown a drawing of two squares, one behind the other and connected by a single rod (see figure 3.2)]. They were also given sticks and modeling clay and asked to build a model of what they saw. If Hudson's test is valid, people designated as two-dimensional perceivers should build flat models when they are shown the drawing, whereas those designated as three-dimensional perceivers should build a cubelike object. When primary school boys and unskilled workers in Zambia were given Hudson's test and then asked to build models, a few of the subjects who had been classified as three-dimensional responders by the test made flat models. A substantial number of the subjects classified as two-dimensional perceivers built three-dimensional models. Thus Hudson's test, although it is more severe than the construction task, appears to measure the same variable.

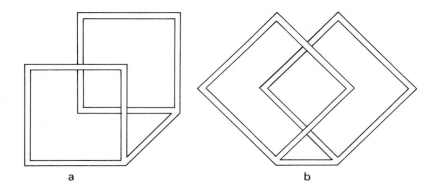

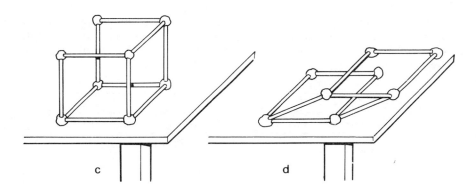

Figure 3.2 Construction-task figures consist of two squares connected by a single rod. Most subjects from Western cultures see the figure (a) as a three-dimensional object, but when the figure is rotated 45 degrees (b), they see it as being flat. Africans from a variety of tribes almost always see both figures as being flat, with the two squares on the same plane.

Stick-and-clay models of figure (a) in the top illustration were made by test subjects. Almost all the three-dimensional perceivers built a three-dimensional object (c). Subjects who did not readily perceive depth in pictures tended to build a flat model (d).

'Split' drawing was preferred by two-dimensional perceivers when shown a model like figure (c) and given a choice between the split drawing and figure (a).

The finding was checked in another experiment. A group of Zambian primary school children were classified into three-dimensional and two-dimensional perceivers on the basis of the model-building test. They were then asked to copy a 'two-pronged trident,' a tantalizing drawing that confuses many people. The confusion is a direct result of attempting to interpret the drawing as a three-dimensional object (see figure 3.3). One would expect that those who are confused by the trident would find it difficult to recall and draw. The students actually made copies of two tridents: the ambiguous one and a control figure that had three simple prongs. To view the figure the student had to lift a flap, which actuated a timer that measured how long the flap was held up. The student could view the figure for as long as he wanted to, but he could not copy it while the flap was open. After the flap was closed the student had to wait 10 seconds before he began to draw. The delay was introduced to increase the difficulty of copying the figure. The results confirmed that the students who were three-dimensional perceivers spent more time looking at the ambiguous trident than at the control trident, whereas the two-dimensional perceivers did not differ significantly in the time spent viewing each of the two tridents.

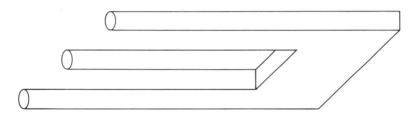

Figure 3.3 Ambiguous trident is confusing to observers who attempt to see it as a three-dimensional object. Two-dimensional perceivers see the pattern as being flat, and are not confused.

Do people who perceive pictorial depth really see depth in the picture or are they merely interpreting symbolic depth cues in the same way that we learn to interpret the set of symbols in 'horse' to mean a certain quadruped? An ingenious apparatus for studying perceived depth helped us to obtain an answer. This is how the apparatus is described by its designer, Richard L. Gregory of the University of Bristol:

'The figure is presented back-illuminated, to avoid texture, and it is viewed through a sheet of Polaroid. A second sheet of Polaroid is placed over one eye crossed with the first so that no light from the

Figure 3.4 Apparatus for studying perceived depth enables the subject to adjust a spot of light so that it appears to lie at the same depth as an object in the picture. The light is seen stereoscopically with both eyes, but the picture is seen with only one eye. Africans unfamiliar with pictorial depth cues set the light at the same depth on all parts of the picture.

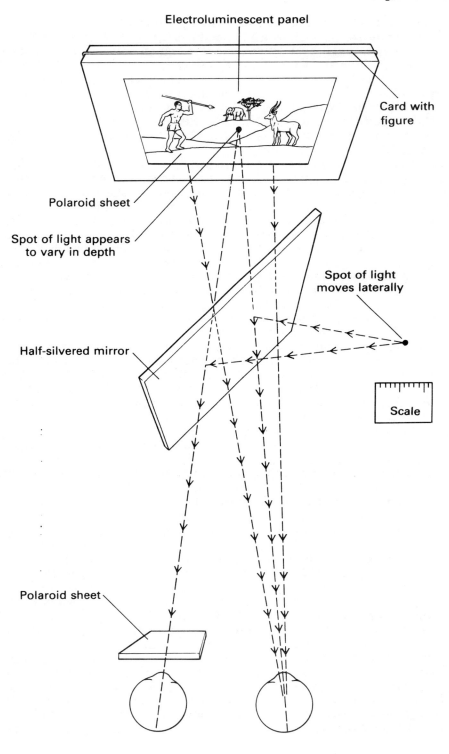

Electroluminescent panel

Card with figure

Polaroid sheet

Spot of light appears to vary in depth

Spot of light moves laterally

Half-silvered mirror

Scale

Polaroid sheet

figure reaches this eye. Between the eyes and the figure is a half-silvered mirror through which the figure is seen but which also reflects one or more small light sources mounted on an optical bench. These appear to lie in the figure; indeed, optically they *do* lie in the figure provided the path length of the lights to the eyes is the same as that of the figure to the eyes. But the small light sources are seen with both eyes while the figure is seen with only *one* eye because of the crossed Polaroids. By moving the lights along their optical bench, they may be placed so as to lie at the same distance as any selected part of the figure.'

A Hudson-test picture that embodied both familiar-size and overlap depth cues was presented in the apparatus to a group of unskilled African workers, who for the most part do not show perception of pictorial depth in the Hudson test and in the construction test (see figure 3.4). The test picture showed a hunter and an antelope in the foreground and an elephant in the distance. The subjects set the movable light at the same apparent depth regardless of whether they were asked to place it above the hunter, the antelope or the elephant. In contrast, when three-dimensional perceivers were tested, they set the light farther away from themselves when placing it on the elephant than when setting it on the figures in the foreground. The result shows that they were not simply interpreting symbolic depth cues but were actually seeing depth in the picture.

When only familiar size was used as the depth cue, neither group of subjects placed the movable light farther back for the elephant. The result should not be surprising, since other studies have shown that familiar-size cues alone do not enable people even in Western cultures to see actual depth in a picture, even though they may interpret the picture three-dimensionally.

The fact that depth was seen in the picture only in the presence of overlap cues is of theoretical interest because it had been postulated that a perceptual mechanism for seeing depth cues where none are intended is responsible for certain geometric illusions, for example overestimating the length of the vertical limb of the letter *L*. If the mechanism is the same as the one for the perception of pictorial depth in Hudson's tests, then one would expect a decrease in the perception of geometric illusions in people who have low three-dimensional scores.

Do people who find pictures of the perspective type difficult to interpret tend to prefer pictures that depict the essential characteristics of an object even if all those characteristics cannot be seen from a single viewpoint? Here again the first systematic cross-cultural observations were carried out by Hudson. He showed African children and adults pictures of an elephant. One view was like a photograph of an elephant seen from above; the other was a top view of an elephant with its legs unnaturally split to the sides. With only one exception all the subjects preferred the drawing of the split elephant (see figure 3.5). The one person who did not prefer the drawing said that it was because the elephant was jumping about dangerously.

Other studies have shown that preference for drawings of the split

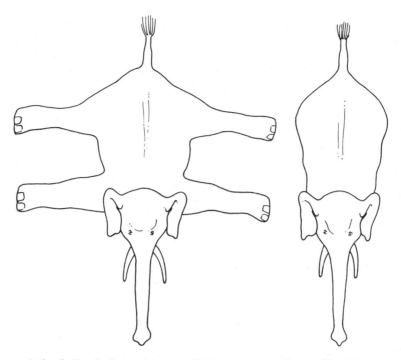

Figure 3.5   Split-elephant drawing (left) was generally preferred by African children and adults to the top-view perspective drawing (right). One person, however, did not like the split drawing because he thought the elephant was jumping around in a dangerous manner.

type is not confined to meaningful pictures but also applies to geometric representations. Unskilled Zambian workers were shown a wire model and were asked to make a drawing of it. Only an insignificant proportion of them drew a figure that had pictorial depth; most drew a flat figure of the split type (see figure 3.2). They also preferred the split drawing when they were shown the model and were asked to choose between it and a perspective drawing. Then the process was reversed, and the subjects were asked to choose the appropriate wire model after looking at a drawing. Only a few chose the three-dimensional mode after looking at the split drawing; instead they chose a flat wire model that resembled the drawing. Paradoxically the split drawing had proved to be less efficient than the less preferred perspective drawing when an actual object had to be identified.

Although preference for drawings of the split type has only recently been studied systematically, indications of such a preference have long been apparent in the artistic styles of certain cultures, for example the Indians of the northwestern coast of North America. Other instances of the split style in art are rock paintings in the caves of the Sahara and primitive art found in Siberia and New Zealand. What art historians often fail to note is that the style is universal. It can be found in the drawings of children in all cultures, even in those cultures where the style is considered manifestly wrong by adults.

Perspective drawings and drawings of the split type are not equally easy to interpret. Even industrial draftsmen with a great deal of experience in interpreting engineerng drawings, which are essentially of the split type, find it more difficult to assemble simple models from engineering drawings than from perspective drawings.

One theory of the origin of the split style was put forward by the anthropologist Franz Boas. His hypothesis postulated the following sequence of events. Solid sculpture was gradually adapted to the ornamentation of objects such as boxes or bracelets. In order to make a box or a bracelet the artist had to reduce the sculpture to a surface pattern and include an opening in the solid form, so that when the sculptured object was flattened out, it became a picture of the split type. It is possible that this development led to the beginnings of split drawings and that the natural preference of the style ensured its acceptance. There is no historical evidence that this evolution actually took place, however, and it does seem that the hypothesis is unnecessarily complicated.

The anthropologist Claude Lévi-Strauss has proposed a theory in which the split style has social origins. According to him, split representation can be explored as a function of a sociological theory of split personality. This trait is common in 'mask cultures,' where privileges, emblems and degrees of prestige are displayed by means of elaborate masks. The use of these mask symbols apparently generates a great deal of personality stress. Personalities are torn asunder, and this finds its reflection in split-style art.

Both Boas' and Lévi-Strauss's hypotheses ignore the universality of the phenomenon. If one acccepts the existence of a fundamental identity of perceptual processes in all human beings and extrapolates from the data I have described, one is led to postulate the following. In all societies children have an aesthetic preference for drawings of the split type. In most societies this preference is suppressed because the drawings do not convey information about the depicted objects as accurately as perspective drawings do. Therefore aesthetic preference is sacrificed on the altar of efficiency in communication.

Some societies, however, have developed the split drawing to a high artistic level. This development occurs if the drawings are not regarded as a means of communication about objects or if the drawings incorporate cues that compensate for the loss of communication value due to the adoption of the split style. Both of these provisions are found in the art of the Indians of the Pacific Northwest. These pictures were intended to serve primarily as ornaments. They also incorporate symbolic elements that enable the viewer to interpret the artist's intention. Every such code, however, carries the penalty that communication is confined to people familiar with the code. Highly stylized art is not likely to be easily understood outside of its specific culture. Thus whereas the same psychological processes under the influence of different cultural forces may lead to widely different artistic styles, the styles arrived at are not equally efficient in

Figure 3.6 Stylized bear rendered by the Tsimshian Indians on the Pacific coast of British Columbia is an example of split drawing developed to a high artistic level. According to anthropologist Franz Boas, the drawings are ornamental, and not intended to convey what an object looks like. The elements represent specific characteristics of the object.

conveying the correct description of objects and evoking the perception of pictorial depth.

What are the forces responsible for the lack of perception of pictorial depth in pictures drawn in accordance with the efficacious conventions of the West? At present we can only speculate. Perhaps the basic difficulty lies in the observers' inability to integrate the pictorial elements. They see individual symbols and cues but are incapable of linking all the elements into a consolidated whole. To the purely pragmatic question 'Do drawings offer us a universal lingua franca?' a more precise answer is available. The answer is no. There are significant differences in the way pictures can be interpreted. The task of mapping out these differences in various cultures is only beginning.

Commentary

Aim and nature

The aim of the article is to present a summary of some of the findings from studies of pictorial perception in different cultural groups, including the author's own research and that of others (e.g. Hudson, 1960, 1962). It is often not clear when he is referring to his own (and that of his co-workers) rather than someone else's and it is only through reading other sources (e.g. Serpell, 1976) that this can be achieved. The overall nature of the studies discussed is *cross-cultural*, since a comparison is being made between the interpretation of 3-D pictures by members of Western cultures (unspecified) and various African countries (e.g. Zambia). However, the method used to actually collect the data is a kind of experiment in which either the independent variable is the nationality of the subjects or it is the characteristic of being a 3-D or 2-D perceiver (based on, say, Hudson's picture tests). In both cases, the investigator is, of course, unable to manipulate the independent variable: it is a characteristic the subject already possesses and is selected accordingly. This method is sometimes referred to as a *quasi-experiment*, sometimes as *ex post facto* experimentation (see Coolican, 1990). (Note that cross-cultural studies as such represent *not* a method of collecting data but an overall approach to the study of human behaviour, just as cross-sectional and longitudinal approaches do in developmental psychology. Exactly how data is collected will depend on the purpose of the study, the age of the subjects, the kind of behaviour under investigation, etc., and the overall approach may involve the use of experiments, observation or some combination of different methods.) Deregowski also considers some explanations which have been put forward for cultural differences in perception but no empirical support is provided.

Background and context

A major advantage of cross-cultural studies is that they act as a buffer against generalizing from a comparatively small sample of the earth's population (Price-Williams, 1966); i.e. unless we study a particular process in different cultures, we cannot be sure what the contributory influences are on that process, in particular, heredity and environment. If we find consistent differences between different cultural groups then, unless we have good, independent reasons for believing that these differences are biologically caused, then we are forced to attribute them to environmental factors, be they social customs, ecological, linguistic, etc., or some combination of these.

Relating this to perception, cross-cultural studies enable us to discover the extent to which perceiving is structured by the nervous system (and so common to all human beings) and to what extent by experience. These factors are what are emphasized, respectively, by the Nativists and Empiricists.

A common method is to present members of different cultural groups with visual illusions, such as the Müller–Lyer and Horizontal–Vertical. The pioneering study by the Cambridge Anthropological Expedition to the Torres Straits (Rivers *et al.*, 1901) found that, compared with English adults and children, the Murray Islanders were less prone to the Müller–Lyer. This was attributed to the fact that the natives limited their attention strictly to the task they were asked to perform (i.e. judge the length of the arrow shafts), while European subjects tended to regard the figure as a whole (including the arrowheads). By contrast, the Horizontal–Vertical illusion was *more* marked among the Murray Island men; this, combined with the pronounced character of the illusion in children, led Rivers *et al.* to conclude that it was due to some physiological condition or, at least, to some simple and primitive psychological condition (Price-Williams, 1966)

A later and more extensive study (Segall, Campbell & Herskovits, 1963; Campbell, 1964) presented illusions to samples of non-European children and adults, mainly African, but including the Philippines. Their findings regarding the Müller–Lyer largely confirmed those of Rivers *et al.* (if all the Europeans are compared with all the non-Europeans) However, the Horizontal–Vertical has a different cultural distribution: the Batoro and Bayankole peoples of Africa, who both live in high open country, are at the top of the susceptibility scale while the Bete, who live in a jungle environment, are at the bottom. Europeans and Zulus fall somewhere in between.

Allport and Pettigrew (1957) used a very different illusion, the Rotating Trapezoid, produced by a figure cut in the form of a trapezoid which, when attached to a motor, revolves in a circle. Horizontal and vertical lines attached give the impression of a window (to those familiar with windows!) and it is usually reported by Western subjects as oscillating to and fro (not revolving in a complete circle, which is objectively what it does), particularly if it is seen through one eye only and from a greater distance. Zulus, however, who are not used to conventional windows and also have a bias towards circularity (not rectangularity) in their culture, are likely to report the illusion less often, especially if it is seen binocularly and from a shorter distance.

How can such cultural differences be explained? Campbell (1964) proposed the 'carpentered-world' hypothesis, whereby the visual world of Western culture is largely man-made, consisting of straight lines and in which there is a bias towards interpreting acute and obtuse angles as right angles extended in space. Since we tend to interpret illusion figures, which are 2-D drawings, in terms of our past experience, we 'add' the third dimension (depth) which is not actually present in the drawing. This misleads us as to the true nature of the stimulus, resulting in what we call an illusion. Members of non-carpentered environments will be much less prone to making such mistakes.

However, a number of studies failed to support the carpentered-world hypothesis (e.g. Mundy-Castle & Nelson, 1962; Gregor & McPherson, 1965; Jahoda, 1966) and there was a subsequent move away from environmental or ecological explanations of cultural differences towards considering 2-D pictures as cultural products in their own right. The interpretation of pictures came to be seen as an acquired skill of considerable complexity.

Evaluation

Perhaps it is not a simple matter of cultural differences in the ability to identify 2-D pictorial representations of the real, 3-D world, but the conditions under which the recognition of things depicted is made: (*i*) do the studies Deregowski describes make it difficult for the African subjects to give 'correct' responses? Is learning to 'read' pictures as necessary as it appears to be? (*ii*) could it be that the drawings used by Hudson emphasize certain depth cues while ignoring others, thus putting non-Western perceivers at a double disadvantage? (*iii*) is it also possible that what is taken as a difference in perception is really a matter of stylistic preference? Serpell (1976) provides answers to all three questions.

(*i*) Deregowski *et al.* (1972) studied the Me'en tribe of Ethiopia, living in a remote area and still largely unaffected by Western culture. Members of the tribe were shown drawings of animals and they responded by feeling, smelling, tasting or rustling the paper, showing no interest in the visual content of the picture itself.

However, when the unfamiliar paper was replaced by pictures painted on (familiar) cloth, they responded to the drawing of the animal. These animals were 30 cm high (compared with only 5 cm on the paper) and, without exception, despite almost certainly not having seen a picture before, seven out of ten correctly identified the first cloth picture as a buck, and ten out of ten the second as a leopard. As Serpell says,

> Given a sufficiently salient stimulus, with distracting cues removed such as the novelty of paper or the distinct white band of the border, immediate recognition may be possible simply by stimulus generalization, one of the most basic characteristics of learning.

At the same time, several subjects misidentified the buck and leopard as other four-legged animals and, in some cases, recognition seems to have been built up gradually, by helping the subject to trace the outline of the animal with a finger. Deregowski *et al.* note the similarity in this respect of their subjects' verbal responses to those of young American children in a task presenting successively clearer images for identification, starting with a completely blurred image (Potter, 1966).

Another way of simplifying the task is to ask the subject to recognize an object without having to identify it by name. Deregowski (1968b) gave a recognition task to boys and men in a 'relatively pictureless' Bisa community (a region of Zambia remote from main roads). They had to select from an array of 18 model animals the one depicted in a black-and-white photo. Six were commonly seen in the area, the rest were very exotic. The boys were better at finding the strange animals than were the men (they had received more schooling) but the men (mainly hunters) were better with familiar animals.

Under optimal conditions, pictures do seem to be recognizable without any prior learning; unlike words, most pictures are not entirely arbitrary representations of the real world; their arbitrariness 'lies in what features they choose to stress and what features to leave out and it is these conventions governing this choice which the experienced picture perceiver must learn' (Serpell, 1976).

(*ii*) [Before reading on, try to identify *pictorial depth cues* which are missing from the Hudson pictures. What about non-pictorial depth cues? See Exercises.]

One of the things the experienced picture perceiver has learned is the Western artist's use of *relative size* to represent distance. So in Hudson's pictures, a major cue to the relationship between the man, elephant and antelope is their relative size against the background knowledge of their normal sizes. Hudson also uses the cues of overlap (or superimposition) and linear perspective, e.g. in one drawing the elephant and a tree were shown near the apex of a pair of converging straight lines representing a road. Since the laws of perspective were a late discovery in European art (Gombrich, 1960) and the assumption of parallel edges to a road is promoted by a 'carpentered' environment, it is not too surprising that African children seldom understand this cue. Hudson (1960) found overlap (if noticed) to be the most effective of his three cues (confirmed by Kilbride *et al.* 1968, with a sample of Ugandan schoolchildren).

Also, there is a contradiction between these depth cues and others in the real world, namely *binocular disparity* and *motion parallax*, both of which are missing from Hudson's pictures (and, indeed, from *all* pictures). Also missing is *gradient of density* (or texture gradient). Gibson (1950) and Wohlwill (1965) found these all to be more important as depth cues in pictures than in 3-D displays for Western subjects over a wide age-range. Serpell refers to an unpublished report by Kingsley *et al.* in which they got an artist to redraw one of Hudson's pictures adding pebbles on the road and grass in open terrain, each surface showing a gradient of density while everything else remained unchanged. 12-year-old Zambian children gave 64 per cent 3-D answers under these conditions compared with 54 per cent on Hudson's original. When colour and haze around distant hills etc. were added, the figure rose to 76 per cent.

(*iii*) Much of the research seems to imply a belief that the Western style of pictorial art represents the real world in an objectively correct fashion; by implication, the subject who does not understand it is 'deficient' in some way. But since 'artistic excellence' is not identical with 'photographic accuracy' (Gombrich, 1960), Serpell (1976) asks if it may be possible that subjects in different cultures 'reject' Western art forms on aesthetic grounds and that all the research has mistakenly described a stylistic preference as a difference in perception.

Hudson (1962) and Deregowski (1969b, 1970) found that African subjects with limited Western education slightly preferred unfolded, 'split', 'developed' or 'chain-type' drawings (as in the left-hand elephant) to 'orthogonal' or perspective drawings (as in the right-hand elephant). Why? Often it is because the latter fails to show some of the important features (recall the African woman shown the photograph by Mrs Donald Fraser).

The importance of artistic convention increases the more symbolic and abstract the art is; the convention is part of the fund of common experience shared by the artist and the audience. Duncan *et al.* (1973) point out that the small lines used by cartoonists to imply motion are the least understood of all the pictorial conventions which have been shown to rural African schoolchildren. And where the artist had drawn a boy's head in three different positions above the same trunk to indicate the head was turning around half the children thought he was deformed.

Likewise, Western observers require guidance from an anthropologist to understand the art forms of American Indians (Boas, 1927) or Nuba personal art in the Sudan (Faris, 1972).

Exercises

1 Hudson's pictures include the depth cues of relative size, overlap (superimposition) and linear perspective. Deregowski also refers to gradient of density (texture gradient). Serpell says that (*i*) binocular (retinal) disparity and (*ii*) motion parallax are missing. Briefly explain what is meant by each of these.

2 Briefly describe three other depth cues.

3 Most depth cues are both pictorial and monocular. What do you understand by this statement?

4 In Hudson's study, how was 3-D perception operationalized?

5 How was the validity of Hudson's test of 3-D perception established?

6 What kind of validity does this represent?

7 What would be the hypothesis which predicts that Hudson's test is valid (i.e. a one-tailed hypothesis)?

JOHN R. SEARLE (1980)

Minds, brains and programs

The Behavioural and Brain Sciences, 3, pp. 417–57

I distinguish between strong and weak Artificial Intelligence (AI). According to strong AI, appropriately programmed computers literally have cognitive states, and therefore the programs are psychological theories. I argue that strong AI must be false, since a human agent could run the program and still not have the appropriate mental states. I examine some arguments against this claim, and I explore some consequences of the fact that human and animal brains are the causal bases of existing mental phenomena.

What psychological and philosophical significance should we attach to recent efforts at computer simulations of human cognitive capacities? In answering this question I find it useful to distinguish *strong* AI from *weak* AI (or *cautious* AI). According to weak AI, the main value of the computer in the study of the mind is that it gives us a very powerful tool, e.g. it enables us to formulate and test hypotheses in a more rigorous and precise fashion than before. But according to strong AI the computer is not merely a tool; rather the appropriately program-med computer really is a mind in the sense that computers given the right programs can be literally said to *understand* and have other cognitive states. Further, because the programmed computer has cognitive states, the programs are not mere tools that enable us to test psychological explanations but the programs are themselves explana-tions. The article will be directed to the claims of strong AI, and whenever AI is referred to, it is the strong version that is intended.

I will consider the work of Schank and his colleagues at Yale (e.g. Schank & Abelson, 1977) because it provides a clear example of the sort of work I wish to examine. But all the arguments that follow would apply to Winograd's (1972) SHRDLU, Weizenbaum's (1965) ELIZA and, indeed, any Turing machine simulation of human mental phenomena.

In essence, Schank's program is intended to simulate the human ability to understand stories, a characteristic of which is to answer questions about the story even though the information given was not explicitly stated in the story. For example, 'a man went into a restaurant and ordered a hamburger. When the hamburger arrived it was burned to a crisp, and the man stormed out of the restaurant angrily, without paying for the hamburger or leaving a tip'. If you are asked 'Did the man eat the hamburger?' you will presumably say 'No, he did not'. Similarly, if the story runs 'A man went into a restaurant and ordered a hamburger. When the hamburger came he was very pleased with it and as he left the restaurant, he gave the waitress a large tip before paying his bill' and you are asked the same question, this time you will presumably say 'Yes, he ate the hamburger'. Schank's machines can similarly answer questions about restaurants in this way. In order to do so, they have a 'representation' of the sort of information which human beings have about restaurants: when given the story and then asked the question, the machine will print out answers like those we would expect people to give if told similar stories.

Supporters of strong AI claim that the machine is not only simulating a human ability but also (*i*) it can literally be said to *understand* the story and provide answers to questions, and (*ii*) what it and its program do *explains* the human ability to understand stories and answer questions about them. Are these claims justified?

A way of testing any theory of mind is to ask oneself what it would be like if one's own mind actually worked on the principles which the theory says all minds work on. Let us apply this test to the Schank program with the following *Gedanken experiment*. Suppose that I am locked in a room and am given a large batch of Chinese writing. Suppose that I know no Chinese, either written or spoken, and that I am not even confident that I could recognise Chinese writing as Chinese writing distinct from, say, Japanese writing or meaningless squiggles. After this first batch of Chinese writing, I am given a second batch together with a set of rules for correlating the second batch with the first batch. The rules are in English and I understand them as well as any other English native speaker. They enable me to correlate one set of formal symbols with another set of formal symbols and all that 'formal' means here is that I can identify the symbols entirely by their shapes. I am then given a third batch of Chinese symbols together with some instructions, again in English, which enable me to correlate elements of this third batch with the first two batches and these rules instruct me how to give back certain Chinese symbols with certain sorts of shapes in response to certain sorts of shapes provided in the third batch. Unknown to me, the people giving me all these symbols call the first batch a 'script', the second batch a 'story', the third batch 'questions', the symbols I give back in response to the third batch, 'answers to the questions' and the set of Engish rules 'the program'. I am also given stories in English which I understand, questions in English about these stories and I give back answers in English.

After a while I get so good at following the instructions for manipulating the Chinese symbols and the programmers get so good at writing the program that, from the point of view of somebody outside the room, my answers are indistinguishable from those of native Chinese speakers, just as my answers to the English questions are indistinguishable from those of other native English speakers. However, although from the external point of view my answers to the Chinese and the English questions are equally good, in the English case this is because I am a native speaker of English while in the Chinese case this is because I am manipulating uninterpreted formal symbols and in this respect I am simply behaving like a computer, i.e. performing computational operations on formally specified elements. For the purposes of the Chinese, I am simply a realisation of the computer program.

How does this thought experiment bear on the two claims made by strong AI?

(*i*) It seems obvious that I do not understand a word of the Chinese stories. I have inputs and outputs which are indistinguishable from those of native Chinese speakers and I can have any formal program you like, but I still understand nothing.

(*ii*) Since the computer and the program are functioning but there is still no understanding, they clearly do not provide sufficient conditions of human understanding (i.e. the program does not explain human understanding). But does it even provide a necessary condition or a significant contribution to understanding? Supporters of strong AI claim that when I understand a story in English I am simply manipulating formal symbols (just as I am doing with the Chinese). If the claim has any plausibility, it is based on the two assumptions that we can construct a program which will have the same inputs and outputs as native speakers, and that speakers have some level of description where they are also the realisation of a program. Although these represent empirical possibilities, there is not the slightest reason to suppose that Schank's program tells us anything about human understanding. What the Chinese room example suggests (though does not demonstrate) is that the computer program is irrelevant to my understanding of the story: I have everything that AI can put into me by way of a program but I still understand nothing about Chinese, while I understand everything in the English case and there is so far no reason at all to suppose that my understanding has anything to do with computer programs, i.e. with computational operations on purely formally specified elements. As long as the program is defined in terms of computational operations on purely formally defined elements, what the example suggests is that these by themselves have no interesting connection with understanding.

What is it, then, that I have in the case of English sentences which I lack in the case of Chinese? Why couldn't we give it to a machine, whatever it is?

The word 'understanding' is open to interpretation but there are clear cases where 'understanding' does and clear cases where it does not apply and such cases are all I need for my argument. I understand stories in English, to a lesser degree stories in French, stories in German to a lesser degree still and in Chinese, not at all. My car and adding machine, however, understand nothing; we often attribute 'understanding' and other cognitive predicates to such things by metaphor and analogy (e.g. 'the adding machine *knows how* (*understands how, is able*) to do addition and subtraction but not division'). Our tools are extensions of our purposes and so we find it natural to attribute them, metaphorically, with mental states. But if this were the sense in which Schank's programmed computers are supposed to be able to understand stories, the issue would not be worth discussing. Newell and Simon state that the sense of 'understanding' they claim for computers is exactly the same as for human beings, i.e. it is literal (not metaphorical). But I will argue that in the literal sense, the programmed computer (like the car and adding machine) understands nothing: its understanding is not just partial or incomplete (like my understanding of German) but is zero.

The most common replies to the Chinese room example are now discussed (with their geographical origins given in brackets):

1 The systems reply (Berkeley)

'While it is true that the individual person who is locked in the room does not understand the story, the fact is that he is merely part of a whole system and the system does understand the story. The person has a large ledger in front of him in which are written the rules, he has a lot of scrap paper and pencils for doing calculations, he has "data banks" of sets of Chinese symbols. Now, understanding is not being ascribed to the mere individual, rather it is being ascribed to this whole system of which he is a part'.

Let the individual internalise all these elements of the system, memorising the rules in the ledger and the data banks of Chinese symbols and doing all the calculations in his head. The individual then incorporates the entire system – there isn't anything at all in the system which he does not encompass. We can even get rid of the room and suppose he works outdoors. All the same, he understands no Chinese and this is all the more true of the system, because there is nothing in the system which is not in him. It is clearly implausible to believe that while a person does not understand Chinese, somehow the *conjunction* of that person and bits of paper might do so. But people who are committed to the ideology of strong AI might claim that there are really two sub-systems in the man: one understands English, the other Chinese and 'it's just that the two systems have little to do with each other'. But we can go much further than this and argue that they are not even remotely alike. The 'sub-system' which understands English knows that the stories are about restaurants and eating hamburgers etc., knows that he is being asked questions about restaurants and answering questions by making inferences from the content of the story, etc. But the Chinese system knows none of this, while the English sub-system knows that 'hamburgers' refers to hamburgers, the Chinese sub-system knows only that 'squiggle-squiggle' is followed by 'squoggle-squoggle'. All he knows is that various formal symbols are being introduced at one end and are manipulated according to rules written in English, and that other symbols are going out at the other end. The whole point of the original example was to argue that such symbol manipulation by itself could not be sufficient for understanding Chinese in any literal sense because the man could write 'squoggle-squoggle' after 'squiggle-squiggle' without understanding anything in Chinese.

The only motivation for saying there *must* be a sub-system in me which understands Chinese is that I have a program and I can pass the Turing test, i.e. I can fool native Chinese speakers (Turing, 1950). But the adequacy of the Turing test is precisely one of the points at issue: the example shows that there could be two 'systems' both of which pass the Turing test but only one of which understands. In short, the systems reply simply begs the question by insisting without argument that the system must understand Chinese.

Further, if we are to conclude that there must be cognition in me because I have a certain sort of input and output and a program in between, then it could be argued that my stomach is a cognitive system: it has a level of description where it does information processing and it operates according to any number of computer programs. But surely we do not want to say our stomach has any understanding?

If strong AI is to be a branch of psychology, it must be able to distinguish systems which are genuinely mental from those which are not, i.e. to distinguish the principles on which the mind works from those on which non-mental systems work. But quite often in the AI literature the distinction is blurred, e.g. McCarthy (1979) says: 'Machines as simple as thermostats can be said to have beliefs, and having beliefs seems to be a characteristic of most machines capable of problem-solving performances'. We normally think of the study of the mind as starting with such facts as that human beings have beliefs while thermostats, telephones and adding machines do not and this, therefore, would contradict McCarthy's claim. However, if the claim were true, it would be fatal to the claim of strong AI to be a science of the mind, for now the mind is everywhere.

2 The robot reply (Yale)

'Suppose we wrote a different kind of program from Schank's and put a computer inside a robot. This computer would not just take in formal symbols as input and give out formal symbols as output, but rather it would actually operate the robot in such a way that the robot does something very much like perceiving, walking, moving about, hammering nails, eating, drinking – anything you like. The robot might have a TV camera attached to it which enabled it to see, arms and legs which enabled it to act and all this would be controlled by its computer brain. Such a robot, unlike Schank's computer, would have genuine understanding and other mental states'.

This reply implicitly concedes that cognition is not solely a matter of formal symbol manipulation since it adds a set of causal relations with the outside world. But the addition of such 'perceptual' and 'motor' capacities adds nothing by way of understanding, in particular, or mental states in general, to Schank's original program. Suppose that instead of the computer inside the robot, you put me inside the Chinese room, as in the original example, and that, unknown to me, some of the Chinese symbols that come to me come from a TV camera attached to the robot and other symbols which I give out serve to make the motors inside the robot move its arms or legs. All I am doing is manipulating formal symbols, receiving information from the robot's 'perceptual' apparatus and giving out 'instructions' to its motor apparatus without knowing either of these facts. I am the robot's homunculus, but unlike the traditional homunculus, I don't know what's going on, I only understand the rules for symbol manipulation and all the robot is doing is moving about as a result of its electrical wiring and its program.

3   The brain simulator reply (Berkeley and MIT)

'Suppose we design a program which does not represent information about the world, as in Schank's scripts, but simulates the actual sequence of neuron firings at the synapses of the brain of a native Chinese speaker when he understands stories in Chinese and gives answers to them. The machine takes in Chinese stories and questions about them as input, simulates the formal structure of actual Chinese brains in processing these stories, and gives out Chinese answers as outputs. We can even imagine that the machine operates with a whole set of programs operating in parallel, as actual human brains are believed to do when processing natural language. At the level of the synapses what would or could be different about the program of the computer and that of the Chinese brain?'.

The whole idea of strong AI is that we do not need to know how the brain works to know how the mind works; the basic hypothesis is that there is a level of mental operations which comprises computational processes over formal elements which constitute the essence of the mental and can be realised in all sorts of different brain processes in the same way that any computer program can be realised in different computer hardwares: the mind is to the brain as the program is to the hardware and thus we can understand the mind without doing neuro-physiology. However, even getting this close to the operation of the brain is still not sufficient to produce understanding. Instead of a monolingual man in a room shuffling symbols, imagine the man operating an elaborate set of water pipes with valves connecting them, when he receives Chinese symbols he looks up in the program, written in English, which valves he must turn on and off. Each water connection corresponds to a synapse in the Chinese brain and the whole system is rigged up so that after doing all the right firings, i.e. turning on all the right taps, the Chinese answers pop out at the output end of the series of pipes.

Now where is the understanding in this system? The man certainly does not understand Chinese and neither do the water pipes. The problem with the brain simulator is that it is simulating the wrong things about the brain: it is not the formal structure that matters but its causal properties, i.e. its ability to produce mental states. And the water-pipes example shows that the formal properties are not sufficient for the causal properties.

4 The combination reply (Berkeley and Stanford)

'If you take the first three replies together, they are collectively much more convincing and even decisive than any one on its own. Imagine a robot with a brain-shaped computer in its cranial cavity, programmed with all the synapses of a human brain and with behaviour indistinguishable from human behaviour. If we think of the whole thing as a unified system and not just as a computer with inputs and outputs, surely we would have to attribute intentionality to the system'.

It seems difficult not to agree with this reply but does it really help the claims of strong AI? According to strong AI, running a formal program with the right input and output is a sufficient condition of, indeed is constitutive of, intentionality. As Newell (1980) puts it, the essence of the mental is the operation of a physical symbol system. But the attributions of intentionality we make to the robot in this example have nothing to do with formal programs: they are simply based on the assumption that if the robot looks and behaves sufficiently like us, we would suppose until proven otherwise that it must have mental states like ours which cause and are expressed by its behaviour, and it must have an inner mechanism capable of producing such mental states. If we knew independently how to account for its behaviour without such assumptions, we would not attribute it with intentionality, espcially if we knew it had a formal program (see the discussion of reply 2).

By contrast, when we find it completely natural to attribute intentionality to apes and monkeys and dogs, it is for two reasons: (*i*) we cannot make sense of the animal's behaviour without doing so and (*ii*) we can see that the animals are made of stuff similar to ourselves: eyes, nose, skin, etc. We go on to assume that the animal must have mental states underlying its behaviour and that the mental states must be produced by mechanisms made from stuff like our stuff. We would certainly make similar assumptions about the robot unless we had some reason not to, but as soon as we knew that the behaviour was the result of a formal program, and that the actual causal properties of the physical substance were irrelevant, we would abandon the assumption of intentionality.

5 The other minds reply (Yale)

'How do you know that other people understand Chinese or anything else? Only by their behaviour. Now the computer can pass the behavioural tests as well as they can (in principle), so if you are going to attribute cognition to other people, you must in principle also attribute it to computers'.

The real issue is not how I know that other people have cognitive states but rather what it is that I am attributing to them when I do so. It could not be just computational processes and their output because these can occur without the cognitive state; and in 'cognitive science' one presupposes the reality and knowability of the mental in the same way that in physical science one presupposes the reality and knowability of physical objects.

6   The many mansions reply (Berkeley)

'Your whole argument presupposes that AI is only about analogue and digital computers. But that just happens to be the present state of technology. Eventually it will be possible to build devices which have the causal processes you say are necessary for intentionality and that will be artificial intelligence. So your arguments are in no way directed at the ability of AI to produce and explain cognition'.

This reply seems to trivialize strong AI by redefining it as whatever artificially produces and explains cognition. The original claims were that AI regards mental processes as computational processes over formally defined elements and all the above objections are directed against this thesis.

Returning to an earlier question, why could we not give a machine that certain something which enables me to understand English (and which I lack when I fail to understand Chinese)? I see no reason in principle why this should not be possible, since in an important sense our bodies with our brains are precisely such machines. But this is not so where the operation of the machine is defined solely in terms of computational processes over formally defined elements, i.e. where the operation of the machine is defined as the realisation of a computer program. It is not because I am the realisation of a computer program that I am able to understand English, but as far as we know it is because I am a certain sort of organism, with a certain biological (i.e. chemical and physical) structure, and this structure under certain conditions is causally capable of producing perception, action, understanding, learning and other intentional phenomena. And part of the point of the present argument is that only something with such causal powers could have that intentionality. It is an empirical question as to whether other biological processes could produce exactly these effects, e.g. Martians may also have intentionality but their brains may be made of different stuff.

However, the main point here is that no purely formal model will ever by itself be sufficient for intentionality, because the formal properties do not by themselves constitute intentionality and have no causal powers except that, when realised, to produce the next stage of the formalisation when the machine is running. What matters about brain operation is not the formal shadow cast by the sequence of synapses but the actual properties of the sequences.

'Could a machine think?'
Obviously, yes. We are precisely such machines.
'Yes, but could an artefact, a man-made machine, think?'
If we could artificially produce a machine with a nervous system, neurons with axons and dendrites, etc. sufficiently like ours, then 'yes'. If you can exactly duplicate the causes you could duplicate the effects.
'OK, but could a digital computer think?'
If 'digital computer' means anything at all which can correctly be described as the realisation of a computer program, then again, the answer is, of course, 'yes', since we are the realisation of any number of programs and we can think.

'But could something understand, think, etc., *solely* by virtue of being a computer with the right sort of program?'

No.

'Why not?'

Because the formal symbol manipulations by themselves don't have any intentionality, they are meaningless and aren't even *symbol* manipulations, since the symbols don't symbolize anything (they have syntax but no semantics). In the Chinese room example, the formal program carries no additional intentionality: it adds nothing to the man's ability to understand Chinese.

The most appealing feature of AI, namely the distinction between the program and its realisation in the hardware is precisely the one which proves fatal to the claim that simulation could be duplication. This distinction seems to parallel that between level of mental operations and level of brain operations. But the equation 'Mind is to brain as program is to hardware' breaks down at several points, including the following:

(*i*) The program-realisation distinction has the consequence that the same program could have all sorts of crazy realisations with no form of intentionality. Weizenbaum (1976), for example shows in detail how to construct a computer using a toilet roll and a pile of small stones. Similarly, the Chinese story: understanding program can be programmed into a sequence of water pipes, a set of wind machines or a monolingual English speaker, none of which thereby acquires an understanding of Chinese.

(*ii*) The program is purely formal but the intentional states (e.g. the belief that it is raining) are not in that way formal, i.e. they are defined by their content, not their form.

(*iii*) Mental states and events are a product of the operation of the brain, but the program is not in that way a product of the computer.

'So how can we explain why so many people have believed that computers can think?' I don't know. No one supposes that computer simulations of a rainstorm will leave us all drenched so why should anyone suppose that a computer simulation of understanding actually understood anything? For simulation, all you need is the right input and output and a program in between which transforms the former into the latter: that is all a computer has for anything it does and to confuse simulation with duplicaton is the same mistake, whether it is pain, love, cognition, or rainstorms.

Perhaps the confusion over the term 'information processing' is partly responsible. Many people believe that the essence of the mental is information processing and so, if a computer can be programmed appropriately, then it is doing what people are doing when they, say, think about arithmetical problems, or read, or answer questions about stories. However, the computer does not process information in these ways, but manipulates formal symbols: the fact that the programmer and the interpreter of the computer output use the symbols to stand for objects in the world is totally beyond the scope of the computer. If you type in 'two plus two equals?' it will type out 'four' but it has no idea that 'four' means four or that it means anything at all.

Another reason for the belief in strong AI is that in much of AI there is a residual behaviourism or operationalism. Since appropriately programmed computers can have input/output patterns similar to human beings, we are tempted to attribute mental states to the computer similar to human mental states. The Turing test is typical in being unashamedly behaviouristic and operationalistic, and this gives rise to much of the confusion between simulation and duplication. This is linked to a residual form of dualism; namely, that programs are independent of their realisation in machines: it is programs which matter and the same program could be realised by an electronic machine, a Cartesian mental substance or a Hegelian World Spirit. Many AI workers are shocked by the idea that actual human mental phenomena might be dependent on actual physical–chemical properties of actual human brains. For strong AI, the mind has to be conceptually and empirically independent of the brain because its aim is to reproduce and explain the mental by designing programs which must be independent of brains or any other particular form of realisation. If mental operations consist of computational operations on formal symbols, it follows that they have no interesting connection with the brain, which just happens to be one of the infinitely many types of machines capable of realising the program. This is Cartesian dualism in the sense that it insists that what is specifically mental about the mind has no intrinsic connection with the actual properties of the brain.

Only a machine could think, and then only very special kinds of machines, namely brains and machines with the *same causal powers* as brains. Strong AI is, by its own definition, about programs and programs are not machines. Whatever else intentionality is, it is a biological phenomenon and it is as likely to be as causally dependent on the specific biochemistry of its origins as any other biological phenomenon. Whatever the brain does to produce intentionality, it cannot consist of realising a program, since no program by itself is sufficient for intentionality.

Commentary

Aim and nature

The article is intended to (*i*) distinguish between strong and weak AI, and (*ii*) to challenge the claims of strong AI by discussing the implications of the Chinese room. This is an example of a *Gedanken* experiment; from the German 'to think', the 'thought experiment' is a common 'method' of philosophy, especially the philosophy of mind and epistemology (the philosophy of knowledge). Although it is in itself non-empirical (i.e. it does not involve collecting, measuring or recording data) it still makes use of possible states of affairs as a way of trying to clarify certain concepts, in the present case, the concept of understanding language. So, if such-and-such a state of affairs were to exist, what light would this throw on the issue being discussed? To the extent that philosophy is part of *cognitive science* (see below), such 'thought experiments' have an important role to play in the attempt to further our understanding of the human mind.

Background and context

AI represents a major meeting point between what were, previously, two unrelated disciplines, psychology and computer science. Cognitive psychology, in particular, has been very much influenced by computer science, since the 1950s, largely in the form of the 'information-processing' approach to understanding human mental processes. According to Garnham (1988), the uneasy relationship between the two disciplines lasted until the late 1970s when the new discipline of *Cognitive Science* emerged, borne out of cognitive psychology, AI, philosophy, linguistics, anthropology and neuroscience (see Gardner, 1985).

According to Dreyfus (1987), 'the basic project of AI research is to produce genuine intelligence by means of a programmed digital computer'. This requires, in effect, that human knowledge and understanding be defined in terms of formally specified elements and sequences of rule-governed operations. Computer programs comprise formal systems, 'a set of basic elements or pieces and a set of rules for forming and transforming the elements or pieces' (Flanagan, 1984). For example, a computer programmed to play noughts and crosses is an automatic formal system and every modern computer is just such an automated, self-regulating, imitator of some formal system or other (Flanagan, 1984).

Advocates of strong AI (e.g. Haugeland, Newell, Simon, Minsky) believe that people and computers turn out to be merely different manifestations of the same underlying phenomenon, namely automatic formal systems (the *Computational Theory of Mind*). It is precisely this equation and the *reduction* of human intelligence to 'formal systems' which Searle is trying to refute in his Chinese room example.

A way of discussing 'mentality' or 'the mind' in the context of AI is through the notion of *Intentionality*, which Searle claims humans have but computers do not and which he (and others) believes is an essential characteristic of genuine mentality or consciousness. The term is misleading because intentions are only one kind of mental state; others include beliefs, desires, perceptions, wishes and fears. What they have in common is that they are all *about* things and states in the world apart from themselves, i.e. they have an external reference to something outside themselves and this is (part of) what we mean by saying that the world is meaningful to us and that we understand it.

By contrast, according to Searle and other critics of strong AI, the symbols a computer manipulates or transforms or produces are meaningless to the computer: the formal system which is imitated by every modern computer is meaningless, consisting of pure syntax (a set of rules for manipulating symbols) and devoid of semantic content (reference to anything in the world). Meaning is assigned *by* the programmer who interprets the computations carried out by the computer. When we use and understand a language we do not just shuffle uninterpreted formal symbols, we actually know what they mean; if we try to *give* the computer an interpretation of the symbols, all we can do is give it more formal symbols. By definition, the program is syntactical and syntax by itself is never sufficient for semantics (Searle, 1987). The Chinese room is intended to demonstrate precisely this point, namely that manipulating symbols does not – and cannot – amount to understanding.

Evaluation

In order to evaluate the Chinese room thought experiment, we need to ask whether or not it succeeds in disproving four major claims of strong AI, namely that:

(*i*) Mental processes are nothing but sequences of rule-governed operations;

(*ii*) These operations are performed on determinate bits of data (symbols) which represent facts about the world (information, in the technical sense);

(*iii*) The mind is to the brain as the computer program (software) is to the computer hardware, i.e. all there is to having a mind is having the right program ('functionalism');

(*iv*) The computer, fed the right program, does not merely simulate the corresponding human behaviour or mental process (e.g. understanding stories) but actually duplicates it (is an *instance* of it).

1 According to Newton (1988), when we say we understand a word, this usually implies two things; (*i*) We can perform various operations involving the word, such as using it appropriately and acting appropriately when it is used; it has an objective meaning comprising rules for its use which constitutes the *formal* aspect of the word and is currently programmable; (*ii*) the word is meaningful for us in ways going beyond (*i*) because it produces 'feelings and echoes' in us which are different from the operations we perform on the symbol. (This distinction corresponds to that between *denotation* and *connotation* respectively.) Newton calls (*i*) the *Formal Component* (relating to external behaviour) and (*ii*) the *Intentional Component* (relating to internal state). It is understanding in this *second sense* which Searle exploits in his Chinese room example: when he says (in discussing reply 2) that his homunculus ('little man' inside the – in this case – computer's head) does not understand the restaurant story, no one could argue with this. However, Newton believes that the disagreement between Searle and Schank and Abelson stems from the ambiguity of the term 'understanding': while humans normally understand in both senses (formal and intentional, thus supporting Searle), we do sometimes consider understanding to be going on when only the formal component is involved (supporting Schank and Abelson). If understanding is equated with the intentional component only, the nature of the disagreement becomes obscured. So the critical question becomes: could a machine realize the intentional component?

Newton's answer is a qualified 'yes'. While agreeing with Searle that Schank and Abelson's (1977) SAM program (and others designed simply to pass the Turing test – see below) lacks understanding, she does not agree with Searle's *reasons*: it is not that understanding is not computational but that, if computations are to constitute understanding, they must occur within a certain sort or structure of architecture which is missing in Searle's examples. In all Searle's examples intentionality is missing because it must begin with something *familiar*.

A symbol is meaningful to a person if (s)he makes a connection between the symbol and something already meaningful; new things come to be understood (in the intentional sense) in terms of what is already understood, and what is most fundamentally meaningful is our repeatable goal-directed actions. But can we ascribe *action* to a machine? Machine actions refer to those movements it is programmed to perform under certain circumstances and which are designed to achieve goals as part of a plan. In these terms, any programmable robot can be described as conforming to an action-pattern. However, could a robot *represent* (take as an 'object') all or part of the program which constitutes its action pattern? Yes, in the sense that a computer can operate *on* its instructions as well as in accordance with them.

In her own *Gedanken* experiment, Newton imagines a robot, operating on two levels: **1** *action:* it performs an intentional action, i.e. its movements conform to its action plan, part of its program. It is battery-operated with forward and backward mobility, designed to move forward in circles in the centre of a maze till its battery becomes low, at which point it seeks an outlet to recharge itself. **2** *function:* it answers questions about a story for which it possesses a script (independent of its Level 1 actions). Here it corresponds roughly to the Chinese room. It is more limited than SAM and can only answer 'yes' or 'no'.

It is instructed to select from its Level 1 program parts to serve as interpretations for the symbols 'Yes' and 'No' for answering the questions; the criterion is that the selected parts should, as far as possible, be isomorphic (i.e. having the same form) with the Level 2 operations which it performs when it answers 'Yes' or 'No'. For example whenever on Level 2 it reads or prints the symbol for 'No' it simultaneously represents the part of its Level 1 program which instructs it to reverse or turn away from a negative outlet, or the sign of one. This representation *refers*, for the machine, to part of its action pattern and so it is making a connection between a symbol ('No') and one of its repeatable goal-directed actions (reversing or turning away) which, according to the criteria discussed above regarding familiarity, makes the symbol meaningful to the robot.

Newton claims to have demonstrated that the robot understands the symbol for 'No' in both the intentional and the formal senses. However, she points out that the conclusion only applies to a single symbol used in connection with other symbols which remain meaningless to the robot: it understands nothing of the subject matter of the story or what it is negating by 'No' or even what a question is (all this in agreement with Searle).

> In a primtive way, however, it understands *what it is doing* when it answers 'No': it is rejecting an initiated set of possible movements. I hold that this is 'real', artificial and limited but not simulated, understanding. (Newton, 1988)

This understanding robot of Newton's is directly relevant, of course, to Searle's discussion of the 'Robot Reply'. The meaning of the symbol ('No') is at least partially something internal to and familiar to the machine, something undeniably within its 'experience' and it is this meaning which the machine understands. The Robot Reply criticized by Searle lacks this structural feature.

However, Newton recognizes that it may be mistaken to speak of 'understanding' in such a restricted context: how can you claim to understand 'No' as a response to questions unless you also understand what questions and answers are, and something of the subject matter of the story? This seems to be much more in line with what is usually meant by 'intentionality' than can be claimed for (or by!) Newton's robot.

2 Searle is trying to refute the major *methodological* presupposition of strong AI which is the Turing Test. This was proposed by Alan Turing (1950) as an objective way of deciding whether a computer could validly be said to have been programmed to 'think'. The idea is that a computer and a human subject are both hidden from the view of a perceptive experimenter who can communicate with either of the two subjects (human or electronic) but is not told which is which. The questions and answers are typed into a keyboard and displayed on a screen. The experimenter has to decide which subject is which and if unable to do so reliably, the computer('s program) has passed the test.

According to Penrose (1987), part of the skill involved in getting the computer to pass the test would be to make it *suppress* the kind of answers a computer could easily provide but which an ordinary human subject could not; also it would sometimes have to 'lie' (e.g. when asked 'Are you a human being?') But that is the easy part: the hard part is to get the computer to give convincing answers that could be answered easily in a 'common sense' way by an ordinary human subject.

Supporters of strong AI claim that it is only a matter of time before computers will pass the Turing Test and once they do so, terms such as thought, understanding, awareness, happiness, pain, etc. could be applied equally to computers and human subjects. Clearly, the Turing Test represents an operational, behaviouristic definition of 'thinking' because it is defined as an appropriate kind of 'output', or performance, regardless of what may be going on 'inside'. Yet this is precisely the definition which the Chinese room is aiming to show is invalid.

But isn't the Chinese room a highly restricted and artificial environment? Gregory (1987a) argues that, like us, AI programs must have knowledge of the world in order to deal with the world. Imagine rearing a baby in the Chinese room: how could it learn the meaning of the Chinese (or any other) symbols in such a restricted environment? Years of active exploration in infancy are essential for us to learn to read meanings in the neural signals from our senses; extended to perception as a whole, the Chinese-room environment would prevent correlations between symbols and events developing as it has no view of the outside world, provides no opportunity for exploration as a way of building up a store of knowledge and relating these to Chinese (or other) symbols.

> The Chinese Room parable does not show that computer-based robots cannot be intelligent as we are – because *we* wouldn't be intelligent from this school either. (Gregory, 1987a)

However, isn't Searle's rejection of the Turing Test still valid in relation to the distinction between simulation and duplication (of mental processes)? In discussing the Robot Reply, he says that our willingness to accept the robot's understanding depends on its *behaviour*, not the fact that it runs a certain type of program; once we have discovered that its behaviour can be explained by a program, we will withdraw our belief that it understands. In other words, 'the robot has mental states' (duplication) and 'a program is running inside this robot' (simulation) are alternative – and incompatible – explanations of the robot's behaviour not allowed for by the Turing Test.

Garnham (1988) criticizes Searle for not allowing that these two explanations might operate at different levels and so be compatible. The idea that computers only simulate thought processes is suggested by the analogy between AI programs and certain other types of program, e.g. those which can simulate a country's economy or weather system. The latter don't take out billion-dollar loans or blow from the south-west: they simulate these economic/meteorological phenomena without realizing them. The input for those non-AI programs is a *representation* of aspects of the economy or weather, but language-understanding programs, for example, might eventually be expected to process *real* sentences.

In a way, this begs the whole question of the Chinese room, but Garnham suggests that a solution to the dilemma might be found in what the program is *being used for*: if used as part of a research project, it might only *simulate* language understanding but one answering questions about train times in a railway station, and thus guiding people's actions, might truly be said to understand (certain aspects of) language.

3 According to Searle, when we attribute intelligence to people we do so based on all sorts of evidence: behavioural (they act the right way), biological (they have the right sort of bodies) and phenomenological (they have the right sort of experiences). But computers only have to *behave* appropriately in order to pass the Turing Test. However, some of his critics argue that the Turing Test does not discriminate in this way because, in fact, we use exclusively behavioural evidence in the case of people too. (Indeed, the whole of cognitive psychology can be seen as relying upon inferences drawn from behaviour.)

By this same argument, supporters of strong AI, by analogy with the computer, analyze human intelligence in terms of the possession and operation of appropriate programs (a form of 'machinomorphism'). Thus, our bodies – including our brains – are seen as in no way necessary to our intelligence. This is a form of functionalism which represents a solution to the mind–body (mind–brain) problem: it is the program (software) that matters (the computational theory of mind) with the brain (hardware) being incidental.

Flanagan (1984) believes that, while Searle may not have *proved* the impossibility of strong AI, he is certainly correct that merely running a computer program is *not* sufficient for our kind of mentality. So what else is needed?

He finds it implausible that our evolutionary history, genes, biochemistry, anatomy and neurophysiology have nothing essential to do with our defining features (even though it remains *logically* possible). Would an inorganic device which formally operated according to all known biochemical laws about plants be expected to undergo photosynthesis (Flanagan, 1984)?

Searle (1987) believes that mental states and processes are real biological phenomena in the world, as real as digestion, photosynthesis, lactation, etc., that they are 'caused by processes going on in the brain' which are entirely internal to the brain. Again, the intrinsically *mental* features of the universe are just higher-level physical features of brains.

Penrose (1987) agrees that there is more to understanding than just carrying out some appropriate program (software) and that the actual physical construction of the brain (hardware) is also important. He argues that a computer designed to follow the logical operations of every detail of the workings of the human brain would itself *not* achieve 'understanding' even though the person whose brain is being considered would claim to understand.

Searle's view has been referred to as *carbon/protoplasm* chauvinism (Torrance, 1986), i.e. his only basis for denying that robots think is that they are not made of flesh and blood. His views about the causal properties of the brain have been attacked by many as obscure. Is he proposing that intentionality is a substance secreted by the brain? (Gardner, 1985). Gardner argues that if Searle is claiming that, by definition, *only* the human brain or brain-like mechanisms can display intentionality/ understanding, then there is no point to the controversy and the Chinese room loses its force.

A major problem is that we simply do not know what makes the brain conscious and so we cannot design a conscious machine, one that would exactly duplicate its physical nature. Still, the brain *is* a physical entity and it *is* conscious, so it must have some design features (presumably physical) which make it conscious (McGinn, 1987). This does not mean that a machine could *not* be conscious: only that it would have to be the same kind of machine the brain is, whatever that kind is. In support of Searle, Teichman (1988) states that while we know that the computer hardware does *not* produce (initiate) the program, it is highly probable that the brain does help to produce mental states.

Gregory (1987a) believes that intelligence isn't necessarily embodied in living organisms or protoplasm but may occur in a computer system based on silicon (or any other material). The emphasis here is on the process as opposed to the substance: though there must be physical mechanisms to carry out the processes, strong AI claims that *any* physical system capable of carrying out the necessary processes can be described as intelligent, even if it is 'made of old beer cans', in Searle's words.

Exercises

1 How does Searle distinguish between weak and strong AI?

2 Do you believe that the Turing Test is an adequate test of intelligence?

3 Do you think there is any *empirical* way of trying to choose between Searle's arguments and the claims of strong AI, or is it a purely logical/philosophical debate involving the analysis of concepts such as 'understanding', 'intentionality', etc.?

4 Are there any ethical issues raised by AI in general (weak or strong)?

FERGUS I. M. CRAIK AND ROBERT S. LOCKHART (1972)

Levels of processing: a framework for memory research

Journal of Verbal Learning and Verbal Behaviour, 11, pp. 671–84

This paper briefly reviews the evidence for multistore theories of memory and points out some difficulties with the approach. An alternative framework for human memory research is then outlined in terms of depth or levels of processing. Some current data and arguments are re-examined in the light of this alternative framework and implications for further research considered.

Over the past decade, models of human memory have been dominated by the concept of stores and the transfer of information among them. One major criterion for distinguishing between stores has been their different retention characteristics. The temporal properties of stored information have, thus, played a dual role: besides constituting the basic phenomenon to be explained, they have also been used to generate the theoretical constructs in terms of which the explanation is formulated. The apparent circularity has been avoided by the specification of additional properties of the stores (such as their capacity and coding characteristics), thereby characterizing them independently of the phenomenon to be explained. The essential concept underlying this approach is that of information being transferred from one store to another, and the store-to-store transfer models may be distinguished, at least in terms of emphasis, from explanations which associate different retention characteristics with qualitative changes in the memory code.

In this paper we will (*i*) examine the reasons for proposing multistore models, (*ii*) question their adequacy and (*iii*) propose an alternative framework in terms of levels of processing. The memory trace can be understood as a by-product of perceptual analysis, and trace persistence is a positive function of the depth to which the stimulus has been analysed. Stimuli may also be retained over short intervals by continued processing at a constant depth. These views offer a new way to interpret existing data and provide a heuristic framework for further research.

Multistore models

The case in favour

When humans are viewed as information processors (Miller, 1956; Broadbent, 1958) it seems necessary to propose holding mechanisms or memory stores at various points in the system. For example, on the basis of his dichotic listening studies, Broadbent (1958) proposed that information must be held transiently before entering the limited-capacity processing channel; items could be held over the short term by recycling them, after perception, through the same transient storage system and from there, information could be transferred into and retained in a more permanent long-term store. Broadbent's ideas have been extended by Waugh and Norman (1965), Peterson (1966) and Atkinson and Shiffrin (1968). According to the modal model (Murdock, 1967), it is now widely accepted that memory can be classified into three levels of storage: sensory stores, short-term memory (STM) and long-term memory (LTM). These terms will be used to refer to experimental situations, while 'short-term store' (STS) and 'long-term store' (LTS) will be used to refer to the two relevant storage systems.

Stimuli can enter the sensory stores regardless of whether the subject is paying attention to that source (i.e. they are 'preattentive' (Neisser, 1967)). The input is represented in a rather literal form and can be replaced by further inputs in the same modality (Neisser, 1967, Crowder & Morton, 1969). This modality-specific nature, moderately large capacity and transcience of their contents, distinguish the sensory registers from later stores.

Attention to the material in a sensory register is equivalent to reading it out and transferring it to STS, where verbal items are coded in a phonemic way (Schulman, 1971) or in auditory-verbal-linguistic terms (Atkinson & Shiffrin, 1968). STS also has a limited capacity (Miller, 1956; Broadbent, 1958), as indicated by loss of information mainly through displacement (Waugh & Norman, 1965) and by the slower rate of forgetting from STS: 5 to 20 seconds compared with the $\frac{1}{4}$ to 2-second estimates for sensory storage.

The STS–LTS distinctions are well documented. LTS has no known capacity limit, compared with the limited capacity of STS: verbal items are usually coded phonemically in STS but mainly semantically in LTS (Baddeley, 1966); forgetting from STS is complete within 30 seconds or less while forgetting from LTS is either very slow or material is not forgotten at all (Shiffrin & Atkinson, 1969). In free-recall exepriments, the last few items are supposedly, retrieved from STS and the early items are retrieved from LTS and it is now known that several variables affect one of these retrieval components without affecting the other (Glanzer, 1972). Further evidence for the STS/LTS distinction comes from clinical studies (Milner, 1970, Warrington, 1971). The differences between the three storage levels are summarized in table 5.1.

Such multistore models are apparently specific and concrete; information flows in well-regulated paths between stores whose characteristics

Table 5.1 Commonly accepted differences between the three stages of verbal memory

Feature	Sensory registers	Short-term store	Long-term store
Entry of information	Preattentive	Requires attention	Rehearsal
Maintenance of information	Not possible	Continued attention Rehearsal	Repetition Organisation
Format of information	Literal copy of input	Phonemic Probably visual Possibly Semantic	Largely semantic Some auditory and visual
Capacity	Large	Small	No known limit
Information loss	Decay	Displacement Possibly decay	Possibly no loss Loss of accessibility or discriminability by interference
Trace duration	¼–2 seconds	Up to 30 seconds	Minutes to years
Retrieval	Readout	Probably automatic Items in consciousness Temporal/ phonemic cues	Retrieval cues Possibly search process

have intuitive appeal and their properties may be elicited experimentally and described either behaviourally or mathematically. Despite these obvious attractions, when the evidence is examined in greater detail, the stores become less tangible.

The case against

General critics include Melton (1963) and Murdock (1972); others have objected to particular aspects, e.g. Tulving and Patterson (1968) argued against the notions of information being transferred from one store to another and, similarly, Shallice and Warrington (1970) presented evidence against the idea that information must necessarily 'pass through' STS to enter LTS. In our view, the criteria listed above do not justify distinguishing between different stores.

Capacity Although limited capacity has been a major feature of the information flow approach, and especially of STS in multistore models, its exact nature is rather obscure; in particular, is the limitation one of processing capacity, storage capacity or some interaction between the two? In terms of the computer analogy on which such models are based, does the limitation refer to the storage capacity of a memory register or to the rate at which the processor can perform certain operations? The action of a limited-capacity channel

(Broadbent, 1958) seems to emphasize the latter while later models (e.g. Waugh & Norman, 1965) seem to emphasize the former; both are present in Miller's (1956) interpretation, although the relationship between them is not explicitly worked out.

Attempts to measure STS capacity have leant towards the storage interpretation, with number of items being the appropriate scale of measurement, but the research offers a range of values. For example, Baddeley (1970) and Murdock (1972) have found values of two to four words; typically five to nine items are given for memory span (depending on whether the items are words, letters or digits) and if the words in a span list form a sentence, young subjects can accurately reproduce strings of up to 20 words (Craik & Masani, 1969). So, if capacity is a critical feature of STM operation, a box model has to account for this very wide range of capacity estimates.

The most widely accepted explanation is that capacity is limited in terms of chunks and that few or many items can be recoded into a chunk depending on the meaningfulness of the material. But how can a chunk be defined independently of its memorial consequences? And this view sees STS as a very flexible storage compartment which can accept a variety of codes from simple physical features to complex semantic ones.

We see capacity in terms of a limitation on processing: storage limitations are seen as a direct consequence of this more fundamental limitation.

Coding Based on studies with verbal material, Conrad (1964) and Baddeley (1966) concluded that information in STS is coded acoustically but predominantly semantically in LTS. However, (*i*) STS coding can be either acoustic or articulatory (Levy, 1971; Peterson & Johnson, 1971); (*ii*) even with verbal material, STS can sometimes be visual (Kroll *et al.*, 1970).

Can STS also hold semantic information? When traditional STM paradigms are used, the answer seems to be 'no' (Kintsch & Buschke, 1969; Craik & Levy, 1970), although Schulman (1970, 1972) believes it can.

Coding no longer seems to be a satisfactory basis for distinguishing STS/LTS. Although it could be argued that STS coding is flexible, this position removes an important characteristic by which one store is distinguished from another. We see the coding question as more appropriately formulated in terms of the processing demands imposed by the experimental design and the material to be remembered (see below).

Forgetting characteristics If this is to be used as a way of distinguishing STS/LTS, the retention function should be constant across different designs and experimental conditions. But there are cases where this clearly breaks down. For example, in paired-associate learning, STS retention extends over as many as 20 intervening items, while in free-recall and probe experiments (Waugh & Norman, 1965) STS information is lost much more quickly. Again, according to Neisser (1967), the icon (durability of the memory trace for visual stimuli) lasts one second or less, Posner (1969) gives an estimate of up to one to five seconds, while Murdock (1971), Phillips and Baddeley (1971) and Kroll *et al.* (1970) give estimates of six, ten and 25 seconds, respectively. Estimates of recognition memory for pictures are even longer (Shepard, 1967; Haber, 1970). Given that we recognise pictures, faces, melodies and voices after long periods of time, we clearly have LTM for relatively literal non-verbal information, making it difficult to draw a line between 'sensory memory' and 'representational' or 'pictorial' memory.

Whatever the limitations of the multistore model may be, obviously there are some basic findings which any model must accommodate. It seems certain that stimuli are encoded in different ways within the memory system, differently encoded representations seem to last for different lengths of time, and limited capacity at some points in the system seems real enough.

Levels of processing

Many theorists now agree that perception involves the rapid analysis of stimuli at a number of levels or stages (Selfridge & Neisser, 1960; Treisman, 1964; Sutherland, 1968). Earlier stages are concerned with analysis of such physical or sensory features as lines, angles, brightness, pitch and loudness, while later stages are more concerned with matching the input against stored abstractions from past learning, i.e. pattern recognition and the extractions of meaning. This conception of a series or hierarchy of processing stages is often referred to as 'depth of processing' where greater 'depth' implies a greater degree of semantic or cognitive analysis. After the stimulus has been recognised, it may be further processed by enrichment or elaboration; e.g. a word may trigger associations, images or stores based on the subject's past experience of the word. Such 'elaboration coding' (Tulving & Madigan, 1970) is not restricted to verbal material. We believe that it applies to sounds, sights, smells and so on.

One of the results of this perceptual analysis is the memory trace: its coding characteristics and persistence arise as by-products of perceptual processing (Morton, 1970). Specifically, trace persistence is a function of depth of analysis, with deeper levels of analysis associated with more elaborate, longer-lasting and stronger traces. It is advantageous to store the products of deep analyses since the organism is normally concerned only with extracting meaning from the stimulus.

Highly familiar, meaningful stimuli are, by definition, compatible with existing cognitive structures. So pictures and sentences will be processed to a deep level more quickly than less meaningful material, and will be well retained. Retention is a function of depth, not speed of analysis; various factors such as the amount of attention given to a stimulus, its compatibility with the analyzing structures and the processing time available, will determine the depth to which it is processed.

Thus, we prefer to think of memory as tied to levels of perceptual processing; although these levels may be grouped into stages (e.g.

sensory analyses, pattern recognition, stimulus elaboration), they are more usefully thought of as a continuum. Similarly, memory is viewed as a continuum from the transient products of sensory analyses to the highly durable products of semantic-associative operations. Superimposed upon this basic memory system is a second way of retaining stimuli, namely through recirculating information at one level of processing, which is otherwise referred to as 'keeping the items in consciousness', 'holding the items in the rehearsal buffer' or 'retention of the items in primary memory'.

We accept Moray's (1967) notion of a limited-capacity central processor which may be used in several different ways. If it is used to maintain information at one level, the phenomena of STM will appear. The processor itself is neutral with regard to coding characteristics and the observed primary memory (PM) code will depend on the processing modality within which the processor is operating. Further, while limited capacity is a function of the processor itself, the number of items held will depend on the level at which the processor is operating: at deeper levels, the subject can make greater use of learned rules and past knowledge, with more efficient handling of material and more material retained. Some types of information (e.g. phonemic features of words) are particularly easy to maintain within PM while others (e.g. early visual analyses – the 'icon') are apparently impossible.

Our notion of PM is identical with that of James (1890) in that PM items are still in consciousness, still being processed or attended to; when attention is diverted, information will be lost at the rate appropriate to its level of processing: slower rates for deeper levels. However, continued processing (i.e. repetition of analyses already carried out – Type I) merely prolongs an item's high accessibility without leading to formation of a more permanent memory trace; Type II processing, by contrast, which involves deeper analysis, should lead to improved memory performance.

Existing data re-examined

Incidental learning

An important feature of the incidental learning paradigm is that the subject processes the material in a way compatible with, or determined by, the orienting task. Therefore, comparison of retention across different orienting tasks provides a relatively pure measure of the memorial consequences of different processing activities. We agree with Postman (1964) that the instruction to learn facilitates performance only in so far as it leads the subject to process the material in a more effective way than the processing induced by the orienting task in the incidental condition. It is, therefore, possible, that with an appropriate orienting task and an inappropriate intentional strategy, learning under incidental conditions could be superior to that under intentional conditions.

So the Levels of Processing approach is interested in systematically studying retention following different orienting tasks within the incidental condition, rather than comparing incidental with intentional learning. Under incidental conditions, the experimenter has a control over the processing the subject applies to the material, which is missing when the subject is merely instructed to learn and uses an unknown coding strategy.

Tresselt and Mayzner (1960) tested free recall after incidental learning under three different orienting tasks: crossing out vowels, copying the words and judging how far the word was an instance of the concept 'economic'. Under the last condition, four times as many words were recalled than under the first, and twice as many as under the second condition. Similar results were found by Hyde and Jenkins (1969) and Johnston and Jenkins (1971), who showed that, with lists of highly-associated word pairs, free recall and organisation resulting from an orienting task requiring the use of the word as a semantic unit, was equivalent to that of an intentional control group with no incidental task, but both were substantially superior to that of an intentional group whose task was to treat the word structurally (checking for certain letters or estimating the number of letters in the word). Again, Mandler (1967) showed that incidental learning during categorisation of words produced similar recall level to that of a group who performed the same task but who knew their recall would be tested.

Bobrow and Bower (1969) and Rosenberg and Schiller (1971) found that recall after an orienting task which required processing a sentence to a semantic level was substantially superior to recall of words from equivalently exposed sentences processed non-semantically.

Schulman (1971) had subjects scan a list of words for targets defined either structurally (e.g. words containing the letter 'a') or semantically (e.g. words denoting living things). On an unexpected test of recognition, performance of the 'semantic' group was significantly better than that of the 'structural' group, even though scanning time per word was approximately the same in most cases.

These findings support the general conclusion that memory performance is a positive function of the level of processing required by the orienting task. However, beyond a certain point, how effective a form of processing is depends on how the memory is tested. For example, Eagle and Leiter (1964) found that whereas free recall in an unhindered intentional condition was superior to that of an incidental group and a second intentional group who had also to perform the orienting task, these latter two groups were superior on a test of recognition.

Selective attention and sensory storage

Moray (1959) showed that words presented to the non-attended channel in a dichotic listening test were not recognised in a later memory test, and Neisser (1964) found that non-target items in a visual search task left no recognisable trace. So, if stimuli are only partially analysed, or processed only superficially, they do not stay in memory very long. In a neat demonstration of this, Treisman (1964) played the same prose passage to both ears dichotically, but staggered in time with the unattended ear leading: the lag had to be reduced to 1.5 seconds before the subject realised that the messages were identical. When the attended (shadowed) ear led, subjects noticed the similarity at a mean lag of 4.5 seconds. Thus, even though the subjects were not trying to remember the material in either case the further processing required by shadowing was sufficient to treble the durability of the memory trace. She also found that meaningfulness of the material (reversed speech versus normal speech, random words versus prose) affected the lag needed for recognition, but only when the attended channel was leading.

Many studies of sensory memory are also consistent with the Levels of Processing approach. For example, Neisser (1967) concluded that 'longer exposures lead to longer-lasting icons' and studies by Norman (1969), Glucksberg and Cowen (1970) and Peterson and Kroener (1964) all show that non-attended material is lost within a few seconds. Massaro (1970) suggested that memory for an item is directly related to the amount of perceptual processing, but his (1972) claim that echoic memory inevitably lasts only 250 milliseconds is probably an overgeneralisation.

The STS/LTS distinction

The phenomenon of a limited-capacity holding mechanism in memory (Miller, 1956; Broadbent, 1958) is handled in the present framework by assuming that a flexible central processor can be used at one of several levels in one of several encoding dimensions, and that it can only deal with a limited number of items at a time, i.e. items are kept in consciousness or in PM by continuing to rehearse them at a fixed level of processing. The nature of the items will depend upon the encoding dimension and the level within it: at deeper levels, the subject can make more use of learned cognitive structures, making the item more complex and semantic. The depth of PM will depend both upon the usefulness to the subject of continuing to process at that level and also upon how easily the material can be more deeply processed. For example, if the subject's task is merely to reproduce a few words seconds after hearing them, phonemic analysis will be sufficient, but if the words form a meaningful sentence, deeper levels are needed, and longer units can be dealt with. It seems that PM deals at any level with units or 'chunks' rather than with information (Kintsch, 1970), i.e. we rehearse a sound, letter, word, idea or image in the same way that we perceive objects, not collections of attributes.

Regarding the claimed differences in coding between STS and LTS, we argue that acoustic errors will predominate only in so far as analysis has not proceeded to a semantic level. Much of the data on acoustic confusions in STM is based on material such as letters and digits which have relatively little semantic content, so the nature of the material itself tends to constrain processing to a structural level of analysis, and, not surprisingly, structural errors result.

The finding that presentation rate and word frequency can affect LT but not ST retention (Glanzer, 1972) can be interpreted thus:

increasing presentation rate, or using unfamiliar words, inhibits processing to those levels necessary to support LT retention but not ST retention. Conversely, manipulating processing at a structural level (e.g. modality differences – Murdock, 1966) should have transitory, but no long-term, effects.

The serial position curve

In free recall, the recency effect has been taken to reflect output from STS and the primacy effect, output from LTS (Glanzer & Cunitz, 1966). Perhaps the most plausible explanation is that initial items receive more rehearsals and so are better registered in LTS (Atkinson & Shiffrin, 1968; Bruce & Papay, 1970). In Levels of Processing terms, since the subject knows he must stop attending to initial items in order to perceive and rehearse subsequent ones, he subjects the first items to Type II processing, i.e. deeper semantic processing, while late items can survive on phonemic encoding. It would follow that in a subsequent recall test, final items should be recalled least well of all list items (i.e. negative recency) and this has in fact been found (Craik, 1970). But recency items were rehearsed fewer times than earlier items (Rundus, 1971). However, Jacoby and Bartz (1972), Watkins (1972) and Craik (1972) have all shown that it is the type – rather than the amount – of processing which determines the subsequent recall of the last few items in a list.

Repetition and rehearsal effects

The effects of repeated presentation depend on whether the repeated stimulus is merely processed to the same level or encoded differently on its further presentations. There is evidence, both in audition (Moray, 1959; Norman, 1969) and in vision (Turvey, 1967) that repetition of an item encoded only at a sensory level, does not improve memory performance. Tulving (1966) has also shown that repetition without intention to learn does not facilitate learning. His experiment, together with one by Glanzer and Meinzer (1967), show that the suggestion that rehearsal both maintains information in PM and transfers it to LTM (Waugh & Norman, 1965; Atkinson & Shiffrin, 1968) is not necessarily so.

Concluding comments

The Levels of Processing approach has much in common with that of Cermak (1972), Bower (1967) and Norman and Rumelhart (1970). Similarly, Posner (1969) advocates stages of processing with different characteristics associated with each stage.

If the memory trace is viewed as the by-product of perceptual analysis, an important goal of future research will be to specify the memorial consequences of various types of perceptual operations. Since deeper analysis will usually involve longer processing time, it will be crucial to disentangle such variables as study time and amount of effort from depth as such.

Our approach does not constitute a theory of memory, but a conceptual framework within which memory research might proceed. Multistore models have been useful but are often taken too literally. Our approach is speculative and incomplete: memory has been looked at purely from the input or encoding end, and no attempt has been made to specify either how items are grouped together and organised or how they are retrieved. Our approach provides an appropriate framework within which these processes can be understood.

Commentary

Aim and nature

This is a review paper, i.e. it summarizes and discusses the theory and research of other investigators rather than reporting the findings of the authors' own or most recent research. The purpose is to propose an alternative theoretical framework, namely Levels of Processing, to that which had been dominant during the previous ten to 15 years in memory research (the multistore model). The paper represents a landmark in how memory has been conceptualized and was the stimulus for a great deal of research and theorizing during the 1970s especially.

Background and context

The view that memory comprises a number of separate stores, between which information passes, has a long history. It was James (1890) who originally distinguished between *primary memory* and *secondary memory*, although Ebbinghaus (1885), one of the pioneers of memory research, would have accepted such a distinction. Hebb (1949), Broadbent (1958) and Waugh and Norman (1965), amongst others, have also made the distinction, but probably the most discussed and most elaborate multistore model is Atkinson and Shiffrin's 'Two Process Model' (1968, 1971), so named because it emphasizes STM (or STS) and LTM (LTS). This is where stored information has been coded or processed, i.e. transformed in a way which allows retention, although in fact there is a third component or store (which is prior to STS or LTS). This is *sensory memory* (or *sensory storage*), which holds information from the environment in roughly its original 'raw' (sensory) form for a very brief period.

In the model, STM and LTM are referred to as permanent *structural components* of the memory system and represent intrinsic features of the information-processing system of humans. In addition, the memory system comprises relatively transient processes (*control processes*), a major one being *rehearsal*; this serves two main functions; (*i*) to act as a buffer between sensory memory and LTS by maintaining incoming information within STS (*ii*) to transfer information to LTS.

The Levels of Processing approach represented the first major challenge to the multistore model: while the latter emphasizes the sequence of stages information passes through as it moves from one structural component to another while being processed, Craik and Lockhart's model *begins* with hypothesized processes and sees 'memory' as essentially a by-product of information processing. This is really a reversal of the logic of the multistore model. Again, instead of regarding rehearsal itself as being important, Craik and Lockhart argue that it is what is done with or to the material during rehearsal which determines the durability of memory (or trace persistence); specifically, it is a direct function of the depth of processing.

Evaluation

1 According to Eysenck (1984, 1986), the Levels of Processing (LOP) approach was probably the most influential theoretical approach in memory during the 1970s, but it rapidly went out of favour after that. He says that most psychologists believe it contains a grain of truth, but is a substantial over-simplification. We should note, though, that Craik and Lockhart themselves claim (in the final paragraph) that their approach does *not* constitute a *theory* of memory, but a conceptual framework for memory research; earlier in the article they refer to it as offering a new way of interpreting existing data, and as providing a heuristic framework for further research (i.e. a strategy, empirical rule or 'rule of thumb' which drastically reduces the amount of 'work' that must be done when trying to solve a problem).

According to Parkin (1987), LOP has made a significant contribution to our understanding of memory. Earlier models over-simplified the psychological factors involved in the formation of new memories; recognizing that acquisition is not a rigid process, and that variations in how information is handled can affect how well it is remembered, has had an important impact on how psychologists study memory. 'In attempting to explain a wide range of memory phenomena, it is now accepted that changes in the *processing strategy* adopted by the subject may provide the basis for an explanation' (Parkin, 1987).

2 Eysenck (1984, 1986) believes that Craik and Lockhart were absolutely right to argue that perception, attention and memory are interdependent: once it is recognized that memory traces are formed as a result of perceptual and attentional processes, it becomes necessary for memory research to focus on these processes. At this general level, LOP has made a major contribution. Prior to 1972, remarkably few experiments compared the effects on memory of different kinds of processing; it had been implicitly assumed that any particular stimulus will typically be processed in a very similar way by all subjects on all occasions.

3 Probably the most serious problem with LOP is the difficulty of measuring or defining depth *independently* of the actual retention score, i.e. if 'depth' is defined as 'how many words are remembered', and if 'how many words are remembered' is taken as a measure of 'depth', we are faced with a *circular* definition. Even when the circle is broken into via the kind of orienting task used, the problem may still remain. For example, in a famous experiment taken to support the LOP model (Hyde & Jenkins, 1973) five orienting tasks were used, meant to vary in the amount of processing of meaning involved. These were: (*i*) rating words for pleasantness; (*ii*) estimating the frequency with which the words are used in English; (*iii*) detecting the number of 'e's and 'g's in the words; (*iv*) deciding the part of speech appropriate to each word (noun/verb/adjective/'some other') and (*v*) deciding whether or not the word fitted various sentence frames ('it is the . . . . . .'/'it is . . . . . .'). Hyde and Jenkins defined (i) and (ii) as involving semantic (deep) processing, and (iii), (iv) and (v) as involving non-semantic (shallow) processing. The prediction, of course, was that (i) and (ii) would produce significantly higher retention, and this was, indeed, found. However, the assumption that (i) and (ii) involved thinking of the word's meaning while (iv) did not, has been challenged. If it is *no more* than an assumption, we are again faced with the lack of an adequate, independent, measure of 'depth'.

4 Eysenck (1984, 1986) argues that the original theory focused too narrowly on the processing activities occurring at the point of acquisition (operationally defined as the kind of orienting task involved) and virtually ignored all the other determinants of LTM. More specifically, learning and memory are affected by at least four factors: (*i*) nature of the task; (*ii*) the kind of stimulus material used; (*iii*) individual characteristics of the subjects (e.g. idiosyncratic knowledge) and (*iv*) the nature of the retention test used to measure memory. In many LOP experiments, several orienting tasks are used but only one kind of stimulus material (usually words), one fairly homogeneous set of subjects and one kind of retention test (e.g. Hyde & Jenkins, 1973 used only free recall).

However, there are often large interactions between the four factors, and an important demonstration of this is the study by Morris *et al.* (1977). They predicted (based on the transfer-appropriate processing view of memory) that stored information (whether deep or shallow) will be remembered only to the extent that it is *relevant* to the memory test used; so deep or semantic information would be of little use if the memory test involved learning a list of words and later selecting words that *rhymed* with the stored words, while shallow rhyme information would be very relevant. As an initial orienting task, the experimenter read aloud 32 sentences with one word missing from each. Each sentence was followed by vocal presentation of the target word. The subject had to say 'yes' if the target word could appropriately be inserted into the preceding sentence and 'no' if it couldn't (half the target words could, half could not). For half the sentences, the input-orienting task was semantic and for the other half it was a rhyme-orienting task. All subjects heard all the sentences.

Half the subjects were given a standard recognition test (the 32 original targets were mixed with 32 distractors: subjects had to say 'yes' to the targets and 'no' to the distractors), and the other half a rhyming recognition test (new words were presented and subjects had to say 'yes' to the new words which rhymed with the original targets and 'no' to those that didn't). The usual LOP effect was found (i.e. better retention) in the standard recognition test but the reverse was true for the rhyming recognition test.

This finding represents an experimental disproof of LOP, specifically the idea that deep processing is *intrinsically* more memorable than shallow processing. The results also demonstrate that how memory is tested must be taken into account when we are trying to predict the consequences of some processing activity: LTM is determined by the relevance of stored information to any given retention test.

5 The over-emphasis on the processing activities is based on the assumption that the subject's processing of stimuli is determined exclusively by the particular orienting task. However, there is an ever-present danger that the subject will engage in extraneous processing unrelated to the orienting task. For example, one of Hyde and Jenkin's (1973) orienting tasks involved checking for the letter 'e' or 'g' in the word (shallow processing) but they were still able to recall an average of seven words in a subsequent retention test. It seems difficult to explain this just in terms of the orienting task; some additional processing *must* have occurred. It is impossible to completely control subjects' processing activities (Eysenck, 1984, 1986).

6 While the original LOP model was attractively simple, it always seemed unlikely that depth was the only major factor influencing LTM. Another major problem is that it is more of a description than an explanation: we are not told *why* semantic processing usually produces better retention. More recent attempts have been made to extend and modify (or even replace) the original model, using the concepts of *elaboration* and *distinctiveness*. Anderson and Reder (1979), for example, assume that deep/semantic encodings tend to be more elaborate than shallow/non-semantic ones, making more information available to be stored, and thus making the stimulus or events easier to locate in the memory system. Craik and Tulving (1975) had found evidence that the elaboration of processing needs to be considered in addition to – or even instead of – processing depth; i.e. even when the same deep/semantic level is involved in two conditions, retention is better in a more, compared with a less, elaborate condition.

However, is it the sheer number of elaborations or their precise nature that is important? Bransford *et al.* (1979) found clear evidence for the importance of the nature of the elaboration (e.g. 'A mosquito is like a doctor because they both draw blood') rather than the number of elaborations (e.g. 'A mosquito is like a racoon because they both have heads, legs and jaws'). The former is better remembered because it 'stands out'. Such findings led Eysenck (1979), Jacoby and Craik (1979) and others to argue that it is encodings which are distinctive or unique in some way which are more likely to be remembered. This represents an alternative way of conceptualizing the basic concept of depth: it may be the non-distinctiveness of shallow encodings (as opposed to their shallowness *per se*) which leads to their poor retention (Eysenck, 1984, 1986). Is there a proper operational definition of distinctiveness? This is difficult because it depends, at least partly, on the context in which a particular stimulus is processed, and may vary between individuals due to experience.

Eysenck (1984, 1986) believes it is often difficult to choose between LOP, elaboration and distinctiveness because they tend to co-vary (i.e. occur together). We know retention cannot be predicted solely on the basis of LOP, because more elaborate or distinctive semantic encodings are usually better remembered than non-elaborate or non-distinctive semantic encodings. It is possible that all three make separate contributions to LTM, but distinctiveness, which relates to the *nature* of processing and takes account of relationships between encodings, is likely to prove more important than elaboration, which is only a measure of the *amount* of processing.

7 Finally, Eysenck (1984) criticizes the assumption that semanticity/depth of processing are directly related, with semantic being more meaningful, as too narrow a view of what constitutes meaningful processing. He quotes Stein, Morris and Bransford (1978) who argue that:

> Rather than emphasize the superiority of semantic over non-semantic processing, it may be more useful to ask how people use what they know (whether this knowledge is non-semantic, semantic, etc.) to more precisely encode and retain information.

Exercises

1 What is the difference between a heuristic and an algorithm?

2 In STS, what other theories of forgetting are there apart from displacement?

3 In LTS, what other theories of forgetting are there, apart from displacement?

4 What is meant by 'chunking' (as a way of increasing STS capacity)?

5 What kind of retention is being tested in
(*i*)   essay-based exams;
(*ii*) multiple-choice tests?

6 Give two examples of an orienting task used to study LOP.

7 Distinguish between incidental and intentional learning. Why is it important for subjects in LOP experiments to be tested under the former conditions?

ELIZABETH F. LOFTUS, DAVID G. MILLER AND HELEN J. BURNS (1978)

Semantic integration of verbal information into a visual memory

Journal of Experimental Psychology: Human Learning and Memory, 4(1), pp. 19–31

A total of 1242 subjects, in five experiments plus a pilot study, saw a series of slides depicting a single auto-pedestrian accident. The purpose of these experiments was to investigate how information supplied after an event influences a witness's memory for that event. Subjects were exposed to either consistent, misleading, or irrelevant information after the accident event. Misleading information produced less accurate responses on both a 'yes–no' and a 'two-alternative' forced choice recognition test. Furthermore, misleading information had a larger impact if introduced just prior to a final test rather than immediately after the initial event. The effects of misleading information cannot be accounted for by a simple demand-characteristics explanation. Overall, the results suggest that information to which a witness is exposed after an event, whether that information is consistent or misleading, is integrated into the witness's memory of the event.

Almost two centuries ago, Kant (1781) spoke of the human tendency to merge different experiences to form new concepts and ideas. That tendency has crucial implications for one's ability to report his/her experiences accurately. When one has witnessed a crime or an accident, one is occasionally exposed to subsequent information that can influence the memory of that event, even when the initial event is largely visual and the additional information is verbal in nature (Loftus, 1975; Pezdek, 1977). For example, in a previous study, *Ss* saw films of complex fast-moving events such as automobile accidents or classroom disruptions (Loftus 1975). Immediately afterward, *Ss* were asked a series of questions, some designed to present accurate, consistent information (e.g. suggesting the existence of an object which was in the scene) and others designed to mislead (e.g. suggesting the existence of an object which was not in the original scene). Thus a *S* might have been asked, 'How fast was the car going when it ran the stop sign?', when a stop sign actually existed (experiment 1), or 'How fast was the white sports car going when it passed the barn while travelling along the country road?', when no barn existed (experiment 3). These *Ss* were later asked whether they had seen the presupposed objects, and it was found that such questions increased the likelihood that *Ss* would later report having seen them. It was argued that the questions were effective because they contained information (consistent or misleading) which was integrated into the memorial representation of the event, thereby causing a reconstruction or alteration of the actual information stored in memory.

In these earlier experiments, the original event was presented visually, the subsequent information was introduced verbally via questionnaires, and the final test was also verbal. In the present experiments, *Ss* saw a series of slides depicting a complex event and afterwards were given verbal information about it (study phase). They were then given a recognition test in which target pictures, identical to ones seen before, plus distractor pictures altered in some way, were presented. Why this change? If one believes that verbal and visual information are stored separately, then perhaps Loftus' (1975) final test, being verbal in nature, helped *Ss* access the subsequent verbal information, thereby producing an incorrect response. If, however, recognition is assumed to be a relatively passive and simple process of matching stimuli to specific locations in a content-addressable storage system, one would expect a representation of the actual scene to result in a match, whereas an alteration would fail to match.

Pilot experiment

A series of 30 colour slides, depicting successive stages in an auto-pedestrian accident, were shown to 129 *Ss*. The car was a red Datsun, seen travelling along a side street toward an intersection having a stop sign for half the *Ss* and a give-way sign for the other half (see figure 6.1).

The remaining slides show the Datsun turning right and knocking

Figure 6.1   Critical slides used in the acquisition series.

down a pedestrian who is crossing at the crosswalk. Immediately after viewing the slides, *Ss* answered a series of 20 questions. For half the *Ss*, question 17 was 'Did another car pass the red Datsun while it was stopped at the stop sign?'; the other half were asked the same question with the words 'stop sign' replaced by 'give-way sign'. For half of each group of *Ss* the question contained consistent or correct information, for the other half, misleading or incorrect information. All *Ss* then performed a 20-minute filler activity (reading an unrelated short story and answering questions about it). Finally, a 'yes–no' recognition test was given, either immediately or one week later. The two critical slides (in figure 6.1) were randomly placed in the recognition series in different positions for different groups of *Ss*.

The results indicated that compared with consistent information, misleading information resulted in significantly less recognition of the slide actually seen and sightly more false recognitions. However, most *Ss* said 'yes' to the slide shown first in the recognition series, even though the opposite sign had been seen and mentioned in the questionnaire. This indicates that the two critical slides are so similar that *Ss* failed to distinguish between them. So it was felt necessary to use a forced choice recognition test, since it eliminates the problem of successive recognition tests, and forces *Ss* to discriminate between the two critical slides.

Overview of the experiments

In experiment 1, *Ss* were presented with the acquisition series of slides, an intervening questionnaire, and a final forced-choice recognition test. It was found that misleading information resulted in substantially less accurate responses than consistent information. Experiment 2 was designed to show that the results of experiment 1 cannot be explained simply by the demand characteristics of the procedure. In experiment 3, we asked whether information presented verbally has a different effect, depending on whether it is introduced immediately after the initial event (i.e. at the beginning of the retention interval) or just prior to the final test (i.e. at the end of the retention interval). It was found that misleading information has a greater impact when presented just prior to a recognition test. Finally, we wanted to know whether the verbally-presented information actually produces a transformation of an existing representation or whether it is simply a supplementation phenomenon. To answer this, we need to know whether the original sign entered memory initially, if not, then the subsequent verbal information may simply introduce a sign where non existed, supplementing the existing memorial representation. Experiment 4, in conjunction with experiment 3, indicates that the traffic sign is encoded by most *Ss* when viewing the series of slides. Experiment 5 shows the generality of the findings with other materials.

Experiment 1

Method

Ss were 195 students from Washington University who participated in groups of various sizes. With a few exceptions, the procedure was similar to that used in the pilot experiment. *Ss* saw the same series of 30 colour slides, seeing each slide for approximately three seconds. Approximately half the *Ss* saw a slide depicting a small red Datsun stopped at a stop sign, while the others saw the car stopped at a give-way sign. Immediately after viewing the acquisition slides, *Ss* filled out a questionnaire of 20 questions. For half the *Ss*, question 17 was, 'Did another car pass the red Datsun while it was stopped at the stop sign?', and for the other half, the same question was asked with the words 'stop sign' replaced with 'give-way sign'. Thus, for 95 *Ss*, the sign mentioned in the question was the one that had actually been seen (i.e. consistent information); for the other 100 *Ss* the question contained misleading information.

After completing the questionnaire, *Ss* performed a filler activity (as in the pilot study). Finally, a forced-choice recognition test was given. Using two slide projectors, 15 pairs of slides were shown, each pair for approximately eight seconds. One member of each pair was old, the other new, and for each pair, *Ss* were asked to select the one they had seen earlier. The critical pair was a slide depicting the red Datsun at either a stop sign or a give-way sign. The slides which *Ss* actually saw varied in the left and right positions.

Results

Ss correctly selected the slide they had seen before 75 per cent of the time when the intervening question contained consistent information and 41 per cent of the time when it contained misleading information ($z = 4.72$, $p < 0.001$). If 50 per cent correct selection is taken to represent chance guessing, *Ss* given consistent information performed significantly better than chance ($z = 5.10$, $p < 0.001$), while those given misleading information performed significantly worse ($z = 1.80$, $p < 0.05$, one-tailed tests).

Experiment 2

Orne (1962) proposed that certain aspects of any psychological experiment may provide clues, or *demand characteristics*, which allow observant *Ss* to work out the experimental hypothesis. Obliging *Ss* may then try to confirm the hypothesis. It is possible here that some or all the *Ss* not only remembered what traffic sign they saw, but also remembered what sign was presupposed on their questionnaire and then 'went along' with what they believed to be the experimental hypothesis and chose the sign from their questionnaire. A slightly different version of this position would argue that at the time of the final test, *Ss* said to themselves, 'I think I saw a stop sign, but my questionnaire said "give-way sign", so I guess it must have been a give-way sign'. Experiment 2 was designed to investigate this possibility.

Method

This was similar to that of experiment 1 with a few exceptions. 90 *Ss* saw the slide series. Half saw a stop sign, half a give-way sign. Immediately after the slides, *Ss* filled out the questionnaire. For 30 *Ss*, the critical question was, 'Did another car pass the red Datsun while it was stopped at the intersection?' (i.e. it did not mention a sign), for 30 other *Ss*, the critical question mentioned a stop sign, and for the remaining 30 *Ss* it mentioned a give-way sign. A 20-minute filler activity was followed by a forced-choice recognition test.

Finally, *Ss* were given a 'debriefing questionnaire'. It stated

The study in which you have just been involved was designed to determine the effects of subsequent information on eye-witness testimony. In the beginning, you saw a series of slides which depicted an accident. One of the slides contained either a stop sign or a give-way sign. Later you were given a questionnaire. One of the questions was worded to assume that you had seen either a stop sign or a give-way sign or else it contained no information about what kind of sign you saw.

Please indicate which sign you think you saw and what was assumed on your questionnaire.

I saw	*My questionnaire mentioned*
A stop sign	A stop sign
A give-way sign	A give-way sign
	No sign

This final debriefing questionnaire allowed a *S* to claim, e.g. that he/she had seen a stop sign but that the questionnaire had mentioned a give-way sign, i.e. it gave *Ss* an opportunity to be completely 'insightful' about their condition in the experiment.

Table 6.1 Data from experiment 2

Information given	Incorrect subjects on forced-choice test		Correct subjects on forced-choice test	
	n	% correct on debriefing questionnaire	*n*	% correct on debriefing questionnaire
Consistent	9	22	21	52
Misleading	17	12	13	31
None	11	9	19	42
Weighted *M*		14		43

Results

Of the 90 *Ss* who took the forced-choice recognition test, 53 chose the correct sign, 37 the incorrect sign. As in experiment 1, accuracy depended on whether *S* had been given consistent, misleading or no information on the intervening questionnaire. *Ss* who chose the correct sign on the forced-choice test were more than three times as likely as incorrect *Ss* to be completely correct on the debriefing questionnaire (43 per cent versus 14 per cent; $z = 2.96$, $p < 0.01$). Again, whether *Ss* responded accurately to the debriefing questionnaire depended on what kind of information they had been given on their intervening questionnaires. Of central concern were *Ss* who had received misleading information and who had subsequently chosen incorrectly on their forced-choice test, e.g. they saw a stop sign, read that it was a give-way sign, and subsequently chose the give-way sign on the forced-choice test. These were the *Ss* who may have been acting the way *E* wanted them to, i.e. they may have been deliberately choosing the sign mentioned on their questionnaire although fully remembering what they saw. Yet, when given the debriefing questionnaire which provided the opportunity to say 'I think I saw the stop sign, but my questionnaire said give-way', only 12 per cent did so.

Experiment 3

Does the information introduced subsequent to an event have a different impact when it is introduced immediately after the event than when it is introduced just prior to the final test?

Method

648 University of Washington students either participated for course credit or were paid. Groups were of various sizes. The procedure was almost identical to that used in experiments 1 and 2, the major variations being the retention interval and the time of the intervening questionnaire. The forced-choice test occurred after a retention interval of either 20 minutes one day, two days, or one week, with 133 *Ss* tested at each interval. Half the *Ss* at each retention interval answered the questionnaire immediately after viewing the acquisition slides (immediate questionnaire), and the other half just before the final forced-choice test (delayed questionnaire). In addition, 72 *Ss* saw the slides, received the questionnaire immediately afterward, and immediately after that were given the forced-choice test (representing a retention interval of zero). This last group was the only one not to do the 20 minute 'filler' task. *Ss* given the immediate questionnaire completed the filler activity after answering the questionnaire, while those given the delayed questionnaire did so after viewing the acquisition slides.

As before, question 17 was the critical one, mentioning either a stop sign, give-way sign, or no sign at all (i.e. consistent, misleading or no relevant information). Equal numbers of *Ss* received each version. In the final forced-choice recognition test, *Ss* were asked to choose the slide they had seen before and give a confidence rating from 1 (very confident) to 3 (a guess).

Results and discussion

Proportions of correct responses as a function of retention interval for the three conditions are shown in figure 6.2.

For both the immediate and delayed questionnaire, longer retention intervals led to worse performance. Also, relative to a control in which *Ss* received no information, consistent information improved their performance and misleading information hindered it. The control *Ss* showed the usual forgetting over time: by two days, they were performing at chance level.

For immediate questionnaire data only, a 5 (retention intervals) × 3 (types of information) analysis of variance (ANOVA) was carried out. It showed that longer retention intervals led to less accurate performance ($F = 5.67$). Furthermore, the type of information given affected accuracy ($F = 50.19$) and there was an interaction between these factors ($F = 5.19$). All results were significant at $p < 0.01$.

For delayed questionnaire data only, a 5×3 ANOVA was again carried out, and showed that longer retention intervals led to less accurate performance ($F = 13.37$); type of information ($F = 90.91$) and the interaction ($F = 2.98$) were also significant. All results were signficant at $p < 0.05$.

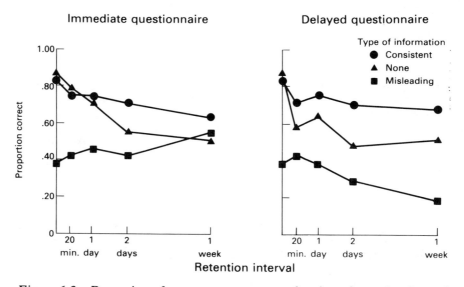

Figure 6.2 Proportion of correct responses as a function of retention interval displayed separately for subjects given an immediate questionnaire and subjects given a delayed questionnaire in Experiment 3. (The curve parameter is type of information the subject received during the retention interval.)

Consistent information   Not surprisingly, a S exposed to information which essentially repeats information previously encoded will recognise more accurately. With an immediate questionnaire, the visual and verbal repetitions are massed, whereas with a delayed questionnaire they are spaced. It seems that the S may have paid more attention to the second occurrence when it closely followed the first, (the opposite of what happens in most memory tasks – Hintzman, 1976), producing enhanced memory able to survive longer retention intervals.

Misleading information   On intuitive grounds, we would expect that when false information is introduced immediately after an event, it has its greatest impact soon after. So when the test was immediate, Ss performed well below chance. But after an interval of, say, one week, both the event and the misleading information apparently had faded such that the S performed near chance levels. By contrast, when the misleading information was delayed, it was able to influence Ss' choice more effectively as the delay increased. Presumably, the weaker the original trace, the easier it is to alter.

Confidence ratings

A $3 \times 2 \times 2$ ANOVA was performed on all but the zero-retention interval data (type of information × immediate vs. delayed questionnaire × correct vs. incorrect responses). Type of information affected confidence ($F = 9.15$), as did whether S responded correctly or not ($F = 23.64$), i.e. Ss were more confident if correct than if incorrect ($p < 0.01$). The effect of timing (immediate or delayed questionnaire) was not significant. The response accuracy × type of information interaction was marginally significant ($F - 2.71$, $0.05 < p < 0.10$) while the other two-way interactions were not. Finally, the triple interaction reached significance ($F = 5.01$). Clearly, a S's confidence is boosted by being told anything, whether true or not, and delaying misleading information raises confidence in incorrect responses above the corresponding value associated with correct response.

Experiment 4

Loftus (1975) argued that the information in a questionnaire influences subsequent choices because it is integrated into an existing memorial representation and thereby causes an alteration of that representation. This assumes that when S sees the initial event, the items of interest are actually encoded at the time of viewing; here this would mean that when S sees a stop sign, the sign gets into memory (i.e. is encoded). If a subsequent questionnaire reports that the sign was a give-way sign, that information might enter the memory system and change the original representation. We can now assume S has a give-way sign incorporated into his memorial representation of the event.

Part of the data from experiment 3 suggest that Ss do indeed attend to and/or encode the sign in the first place: when no information is contained in the questonnaire, *Ss* show some ability to discriminate the sign they saw from the one they did not, up to and including a retention interval of one day. They must have encoded the sign, otherwise performance would have been at chance level. Experiment 4 was designed to further test this issue.

Method

90 *Ss* were shown the same series of slides as described above, after which they were given a sheet of paper with a diagram on it similar to that in either figure 6.3a or 6.3b.

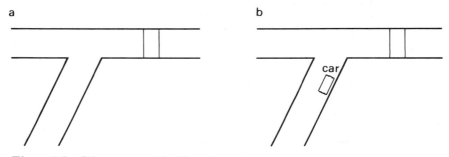

a   b

Figure 6.3   Diagrams used in Experiment 4.

45 *Ss* saw (a), 45 saw (b), and they were instructed to fill in as many details as they could remember. If the diagram contains no sketch of the car (a), *Ss* tend to concentrate their attention on details at the crosswalk, which is where the accident took place. They may have seen the sign at the corner but do not draw it, since it does not seem important to the accident. What is needed is a way to focus their attention on the intersection, and the placing of a car near it (b) seemed to be a way of achieving this.

Results

If a *S* either drew the sign he/she had seen, or wrote its name, the drawing was counted as correct. Overall, 45 per cent indicated the correct sign. Of those shown (a), 36 per cent correctly drew the stop sign and 32 per cent the give-way sign; of those shown (b), the figures were 60 per cent and 52 per cent respectively. An ANOVA showed that more *Ss* depicted a sign when a car was used to direct their attention to the intersection (b) than when there was no car (a). Whether *S* had actually seen a stop or a give-way sign did not significantly affect the likelihood of drawing the correct sign.

These results indicate that when *Ss* view the slides, at least half (and perhaps more) do encode the correct sign. Data for *Ss* shown (b) (with a car to focus their attention on the intersection) show that over half have encoded the sign to the point of including it in their diagrams. Others may have also encoded it but this was not revealed by the present procedure.

Experiment 5

This was designed to show the generality of our studies beyond the single-stimulus pair used in the previous studies.

Method

A new series of 20 colour slides depicting an auto-pedestrian accident was shown to 80 *Ss*. A male pedestrian is seen carrying some items in one hand and munching on an apple held with the other. He leaves a building and strolls toward a parking lot, where a maroon Triumph backs out of a parking space and hits him.

There were four critical slides. One version of each critical slide contained a particular object (e.g pair of skis leaning against a tree), while the other version contained a changed detail (e.g. a shovel leaning against a tree). Each *S* saw only one version of the critical slides and each critical slide was seen equally often across *Ss*.

After the slides there was a ten-minute filler activity and they read a three-paragraph description of the slide series supposedly written by another person who had been given much more time to view them. The description contained four critical sentences which either did or did not mention the incorrect critical object. The mention or non-mention of a critical incorrect detail was counter-balanced over *Ss* for the four critical items.

After ten minutes *Ss* were given a forced-choice recognition test, in which the four critical pairs were randomly intermixed with six other filler pairs; one member of each pair had, and one had not been seen before. Those which had been seen before varied in the left and right positions.

Results

There was 55.3 per cent correct selection when the intervening statement contained misleading information and 70.8 per cent when it contained no information. A related *t*-test indicated that these mean percentages were significantly different ($t = 9.43$).

Discussion

These results allow us to generalize beyond the single stop sign–giveway sign stimulus pair. But note that even with misleading information, *Ss* were correct about 55 per cent of the time, compared with the 42 per cent found in experiment 3 after a comparable retention interval. Why? Any particular object (e.g. a shovel) can assume many forms and there may be discrepancy between the form imagined while reading the story and that shown during the recognition test. With common traffic signs, such a discrepancy is much less likely to happen.

General discussion

When a person witnesses an important event, he/she is often exposed to related information some time later. How can this subsequent information influence memory for the original event?

In the pilot study, misleading subsequent information caused less accurate responses on a subsequent yes–no recognition test. The same occurred in experiment 1 on a forced-choice recognition test. Experiment 2 showed that when *Ss* were told that they might have been exposed to misleading information and were asked to say whether they thought they had, most persisted in claiming that they had seen the incorrect item. This rules out the demand-characteristics explanation of the results from the pilot study and experiment 1.

Experiment 4 showed that at least half the *Ss* encoded the initial sign sufficiently to be able to include it in a drawing they made of the incident. This suggests that subsequent information changes the original memory or creates a newer, stronger representation which competes with the original representation, rather than supplements it.

Experiment 3 showed that misleading information had a larger impact if presented just prior to a recognition test rather than just after the initial event.

The present work bears some resemblance to earlier work on the influence of verbal labels on memory for visually presented stimuli. Much of the earlier work was designed to test the Gestalt hypothesis that progressive memory-changes in the direction of a 'better' figure occur autonomously. Riley (1962), in a review of that earlier literature, concluded that the hypothesis of autonomous change is probably not testable. But despite this, the work on verbal labels was useful in revealing that reproductions and recognition memory (Carmichael *et al.*, 1932; Daniel, 1972) of simple forms were affected by the labels applied to those forms. The present work represents a much needed extension in that it reveals that these effects occur not only with artificial forms but also with highly naturalistic scenes under conditions which have a high degree of ecological validity. Further, the present work convincingly demonstrates both the integration of information from more than one source into memory, and the use of that information to reconstruct a 'memory' that was never actually experienced.

Commentary

Aim and nature

The article is an account of five separate, but related, laboratory experiments, all intended to investigate how information supplied after an event (in this case, seeing slides of a single auto-pedestrian accident) influences a witness's memory for that event. Specifically, the independent variables being manipulated were: experiment 1 – the nature of the information (whether consistent or misleading); experiment 2 – the nature of the information (consistent, misleading or irrelevant); experiment 3 – the same as experiment 2 plus (*i*) retention interval (20 minutes, one, two or seven days), and (*ii*) time of intervening questionnaire (immediately after the slides [immediate] or just before the final forced-choice test [delayed]); experiment 4 – the kind of diagram of a road shown to subjects after seeing the slides (either with or without car); experiment 5 – two versions each of four critical slides (different from those used in experiments 1 – 4, each containing a particular object which varied between the two versions and a description of the slide including four critical sentences which either did or did not mention the incorrect critical object.

As for the dependent variables: experiment 1 – correct identification of the road sign (stop or give-way) as measured by a forced-choice recognition test; experiment 2 – same as experiment 1 but with a 'debriefing questionnaire' which gave subjects the opportunity to state that their questionnaire had mentioned a different road sign from the one they had seen in the slide; experiment 3 – same as experiment 1; experiment 4 – filling in details on one of the two diagrams, in particular, the road sign; experiment 5 – same as experiments 1 and 3.

Background and context

The general theoretical framework of Loftus *et al.*'s experiments is originally that of Bartlett (1932), who, in contrast to those models of memory based on stimulus-response theory (associationist models), saw memory as involving interpretation and reconstruction of the past. We try to fit past events into our existing schemata (mental models or representations of the world), making them more logical, coherent and generally 'sensible', drawing inferences or deductions about what might or should have happened (all this being part of our 'efforts after meaning'). So, rather than human beings being computer-like, with the output matching the input, Bartlett saw human memory as an active attempt to understand, an 'imaginative reconstruction' of experience.

What is now referred to as 'schema theory' (e.g. Rumelhart & Norman, 1983) regards what we already know about the world as a major influence on what we remember. According to Cohen (1986), 'the use of past experience to deal with new experience is a fundamental feature of the way the human mind works'. The knowledge we have stored in memory is organized as a set of schemas, each incorporating all the knowledge of a given type of object or event, acquired from past experience. Schemas operate in a 'top-down' direction to help interpret the 'bottom-up' flow of information from the world. New experiences are not just passively 'copied' or recorded into memory; rather 'a memory representation is actively constructed by processes that are strongly influenced by schemas' (Cohen, 1986).

As interesing as this may be academically, when applied to real-life situations such as eye-witness testimony, these ideas about the reconstructive and interpretative nature of memory assume critical importance: the greater the unreliability (inaccuracy) of human memory and the greater the importance of eye-witness testimony in cases of crimes and accidents (as against other kinds of evidence), the greater the likelihood that people will be wrongly accused and convicted (a false positive error) and that the guilty will not come to justice (a false negative error).

Loftus is a pioneer – and still a leading figure – in the field of eye-witness testimony research, which represents an application of cognitive psychology to real-world, social phenomena. Her basic procedure has been to manipulate the questions subjects are asked about a film or slides of an automobile accident in order to see how these can affect what the subject remembers of the accident and is an attempt to simulate real-world events in which witnesses are asked questions (often very misleading ones) by police and lawyers.

In an early study (Loftus & Palmer, 1974) subjects were asked 'about how fast were the cars going when they . . . . . . ?', with the final word being either 'smashed', 'collided', 'bumped', 'hit' or 'contacted'. As predicted, the average estimate was higher depending on how 'serious' the term used to describe the kind of contact, ranging from 41 mph for 'smashed' to 32 mph for 'contacted'. A different group of subjects was asked to estimate the speed of cars for just 'hit' or 'smashed' with a control group not asked about speed at all. A week later, when asked 'did you see any broken glass?', 32 per cent of the 'smashed' subjects answered 'yes' compared with 14 per cent and 12 per cent of the 'hit' and controls respectively.

Loftus and Zanni (1975) asked subjects if they saw 'a broken headlight' or 'the broken headlight'. Of those whose film did not, in fact, feature a broken headlight, 7 per cent asked the former question said 'yes' compared with 15 per cent asked the latter. (The former question was also more likely to elicit a 'don't know' answer, regardless of whether one had been present or not.)

So there would seem to be a good deal of support for the reconstructive hypothesis: eye-witness testimony can be easily distorted, and modified, by information (in the form of questions) which becomes available *subsequent* to the actual event – even to the extent of 'remembering' things which were not actually seen in the original event. This new information becomes incorporated into the memory, updating it and erasing any of the original information which is inconsistent with it. Once this has occurred, the eye-witness cannot distinguish its source: (s)he believes it is what actually happened.

Recollection of an event seems to be more fragile and susceptible to modification than might have been expected and this discovery lends weight to attempts by the police and by lawyers to make as little use as possible of leading questions (i.e. questions suggesting to the witness the desired answer. (Eysenck, 1984)

Evaluation

1 The present (1978) study can be seen as a continuation of this research programme but testing a number of specific hypotheses (see the *Aim and nature* section above).

2 However, despite the repeated support for the basic idea of misleading information being integrated into the original memory, witnesses cannot always be misled so easily. For example, Loftus (1979) reports that integration does not happen if the misleading information is 'blatantly incorrect'. In one experiment, subjects saw colour slides of a man stealing a red purse from a woman's bag. 98 per cent correctly remembered the colour of the purse. When they read a narrative description of the event containing a 'brown purse', all but two continued to remember it as red.

'Thus, memory for obviously important information which is accurately perceived at the time is not easily distorted' (Cohen, 1986). In the above example, the colour of the purse is the focus of the whole incident, not a peripheral detail. Cohen (1986) points out that the experiment also showed that once subjects recognized one piece of misleading information as false, they were more distrustful and less likely to be misled by any subsequent false information. She summarizes the findings by saying that people are more likely to be misled if (*i*) the false information concerns insignificant details which are peripheral to the main event; (*ii*) the false information is given after a delay, when the memory of the actual event has had time to fade (consistent with the findings of experiment 3 in the Loftus *et al.* study); (*iii*) subjects are not aware that they may be deliberately misinformed and so have no reason to distrust the information.

She believes that eye-witness testimony research has concentrated on the fallibility of memory and so gives a rather one-sided picture.

3 Does the eye-witness testimony research lend support to schema theory? According to Alba and Hasher (1983), it does. But according to Cohen (1986), Loftus's misled witnesses are not only integrating prior knowledge from internal schemas about car accidents etc. with knowledge derived from recent observed events, they are also combining information from two *different external sources*: the observed event and subsequent verbal information about the event.

While Loftus claims that integration takes place with the original memory being modified by the new information, others (e.g. Bekerian & Bowers, 1983) have shown that the original memory may remain unintegrated, and, under the right circumstances, can be elicited intact. Clearly, memories are not simple copies of events, 'but may sometimes be composites based on different sources of information' (Cohen, 1986).

4 From a rather different theoretical angle, Fiske and Taylor (1984) believe that the distinction between episodic and semantic memory (Tulving, 1972) is useful in understanding eye-witness testimony. A 'leading' question might refer to things which were not actually present at the scene of the crime (episodic) but which would be a quite reasonable inference to make in these circumstances (semantic, which includes all our schemas and stereotyped beliefs about the world). It is easy to see how a witness could confuse the mention of something in a question with its actual presence at the scene of the crime if that something is commonly found in such situations. Similarly, if a witness examines a preliminary identity parade, (s)he may later remember having seen one of the suspects before, but *not* distinguish between the identity parade and the scene of the crime: the innocent suspect may be misidentified as the criminal because (s)he is familiar!

5 According to Loftus *et al.* (1970), laboratory studies on the accuracy of face-recognition (which show very high accuracy, e.g. Hochberg & Galper, 1967; Yin, 1969) are contradicted by real-world research on eye-witness testimony: people often do little better than guess when trying to identify an alleged criminal in an identity parade. It is evidence such as this which led to the publication of the Devlin Report (1976), which recommends that the trial judge be required to instruct the jury that it is not safe to convict on a single eye-witness testimony *alone*, except in exceptional circumstances (e.g. the witness is a close friend or relative) or when there is substantial corroborative evidence. The safeguards recommended are much stronger than those of the US Supreme Court but are similar to those of American legal experts. (Brown, 1986).

According to Brown (1986), in the US, England and Wales (but *not* Scotland), a person accused under the criminal law *can* be convicted on eye-witness identification alone, which means that there must be a substantial number of miscarriages of justice; more than is generally realized. He points out the paradox of eye-witness testimony, namely that while judges, defence lawyers and psychologists regard it as about the least trustworthy kind of evidence of guilt under the criminal law, jurors have always found it to be more persuasive than any other sort of evidence.

Exercises

1 In experiments 1 and 5, why was it necessary to vary the position of the slides subjects actually saw in the forced-choice recognition test?

2 Who were the subjects for the various experiments?

3 In experiment 3, for the immediate questionnaire or delayed questionnaire separately, a 5 (retention intervals) × 3 (type of information) ANOVA was performed, and for
the confidence ratings, a 3 (type of information) × 2 (immediate versus delayed
questionnaire) × 2 (correct versus incorrect responses) ANOVA was performed.
What is the ANOVA?

4 In experiment 5, the description contained four critical sentences which either did or
did not mention the incorrect critical object. Why was the mention/non-mention of a
critical incorrect detail counterbalanced across subjects for the four critical items?

5 In the final paragraph, what is meant by 'ecological validity'?

BERNARD I. MURSTEIN (1972)

Physical attractiveness and marital choice

Journal of Personality & Social Psychology, Vol. 22, No. 1, pp. 8–12

The stimulus-value-role theory of marital choice holds that individuals tend to choose marital partners of comparable physical attractiveness to themselves. Physical attractiveness was measured by self-perception, perception of the partner, and appearance judged from photos. Actual couples were hypothesized to be significantly less discrepant on these variables than a control group contrived by randomly pairing the scores of men and women. The two samples consisted of 99 and 98 college couples, respectively, who were going together or were engaged. Results support the hypothesis for self-percepts and photo-attractiveness but not for perception of the partner. The results support stimulus-value-role theory and the concept of marital choice as an exchange-market phenomenon.

The relationship of physical attractiveness to interpersonal attraction has recently been the subject of a considerable number of investigations. One focus of attention has been on whether, in a heterosexual encounter, individuals are attracted to those of a similar level of attractiveness to themselves. The results have been equivocal.

In the first of the recent series of studies, Walster *et al.* (1966) found no evidence of similarity of physical attractiveness leading to interpersonal attraction; instead, college freshmen, randomly matched at a computer dance, tended to be most attracted to physically attractive partners regardless of their own physical attractiveness. Failure to support the 'similarity' hypothesis has also been reported by Brislin and Lewis (1968) and Byrne and Ervin (1970).

However, Dion and Bersheid (1970) and Walster and Walster (1970) have reported positive results, and they explain the contradiction between their recent work and the earlier studies in terms of different demands of the situation. In the studies which did not support the 'similarity' hypothesis, subjects were already assured of a date before interacting with their partners, but they expressed their preference after having dated; in those which do support it, subjects chose their dates *before* spending any time with them.

In short, a 'similarity' hypothesis might be more effective when one has to *attain* a relationship because the possibility of fear of failure and rejection tends to dampen the aspirations of the unattractive. However, once assured of a 'date', since the possibility of immediate rejection, at least, is negligible, the individual focuses on what rewards the other can offer. Because associating with an attractive person may be taken to be more rewarding than associating with a less attractive person, the individual assured of a date tends to appreciate his partner as a function of her attractivess regardless of his own.

Although this explanation seems logical, it should be noted that the studies cited above have tested interpersonal attraction based on periods of interaction ranging from no interaction to a few hours; none has dealt with couples who have demonstrated attraction to each other over a period of months or years.

A recent theory of interpersonal attraction in marital choice (Murstein, 1970) deals with this kind of situation. This theory, called stimulus-value-role, holds that, in initial encounters in which individuals are not forced to interact with each other, attraction is a function of the individual's perception of the other's physical, social, mental or reputational attributes and his perception of his own qualities as he thinks these will be perceived by the other person. Because initial movement is influenced primarily by perceptual, non-interactional cues, the first stage of the theory is called the 'stimulus' stage.

Many stimulus variables, such as religion, race, professional aspiration, status and education do not directly influence the initial encounter: either they may be unknown at first (religion, professional aspiration) or they may be selected out in the circumstances that allow the couple to meet, e.g. level of education and status are unlikely to be very influential in determining attraction on a college campus. However, one potent stimulus variable in our culture which is not highly filtered out in interpersonal encounters is physical attraction.

Most individuals have a common standard of physical beauty, at least as far as facial features are concerned (Udry, 1965). Physical beauty is rewarding for both sexes (although more so for men in our culture), both as individual experience and for the status it brings to oneself in the eyes of others: if A's partner is handsome or beautiful, A is believed to possess certain qualities which earned him such a desirable partner. Unfortunately, the supply of physically-attractive partners is limited, whereas the desire to marry is experienced by well over 90 per cent of the population. The fact that we do not have a largely unmarried population, therefore, necessitates that we conceive of marital choice as a kind of exchange-market phenomenon.

Blau (1964), Homans (1961) and Thibaut and Kelley (1959) have all used some elementary economic concepts for explaining social behaviour; essentially, they maintain that each person tries to make social interaction as profitable as possible, *profit* being defined as the *rewards* gained from the interaction minus the *costs*. Rewards are the pleasures, benefits and gratifications gained from a relationship, while costs are factors which inhibit or deter the performance of more preferred behaviours, e.g. a two-hour ride across New York to date someone you met while on holiday at a resort.

Closely related to rewards and costs are assets and liabilities. *Assets* are the commodities (behaviours or qualities) which the individual possesses which are capable of rewarding others, and, in return, causing others to reciprocate by rewarding the individual. *Liabilities* are the behaviours or qualities of an individual which are costly to others and this, by reciprocity, costly also to the self. For example, a physically unattractive man (liability) desires a beautiful woman (asset); assuming, however, that his non-physical qualities are no more rewarding than hers she gains less profit than he does from the relationship and so he is likely to be rejected. Rejection is costly to him (i.e. it might lower his self-esteem and increase his fear of failure in future encounters) so he may decide to avoid approaching women whom he perceives as much above him in attractiveness.

Conversely, he is likely to feel highly confident of success if he tries to date a woman who is even less attractive than himself where there is little risk of rejection (low cost); however, her reward value is quite low, and so the profitability of such a move is quite low. Consequently, an experienced individual is likely to express a maximum degree of effort and also obtain the greatest reward at the least cost when he directs his efforts towards someone of approximately equal physical attraction (assuming all other variables are constant).

It is hypothesized, therefore, that premarital couples will show greater than chance similarity with respect to physical attraction. Physical attraction in the present research was measured in a number of different ways in two separate studies.

Study 1

Method

99 couples, who were either engaged or 'going steady', volunteered for a study on marital choice conducted simultaneously at Connecticut College, University of Connecticut and Yale University. The subjects received $15 each for participating and the testing procedure took several hours and involved a series of personality and person-perception tests.

Two of the questions subjects had to answer dealt with physical attraction: (i) how physically attractive do you find your partner? and (ii) how do you rate your own physical attraction? Each question was evaluated on a five-point scale, ranging from 'extremely good looking' (score of 5) to 'considerably below average in looks' (score of 1).

In addition, during the general testing procedure, each couple was called to another room and photographed twice using a Polaroid camera; one photo was taken with the couple in a natural pose looking directly at the camera, the other with the couple smiling. These photos were evaluated by eight judges (young professors and graduate students, four men and four women) on a five-point scale. The judges were instructed that, in the general population, a score of 5 (extremely good looking) would be obtained by about 8 per cent of the population, 4 (better looking than average) by about 17 per cent, 3 (average) by about 50 per cent, 2 (somewhat below average) by about 17 per cent, and 1 (considerably below average) by about 8 per cent. Comparison of the average of the male and female judged scores produced a Pearson r of 0.80, suggesting that no marked sex differences were present; so to determine interjudge reliability, the scores of all eight judges were pooled, and then separated into two random halves. The mean scores of each half were correlated using the Spearman–Brown formula, resulting in an r of 0.91, a reliability value sufficiently high for the purposes of the study.

Results

To test the hypothesis, a control group was formed by randomly pairing the physical attraction scores of the 99 men and women with each other. (This was repeated five times in order to ensure stability).

The absolute discrepancies between members of each of the actual couples were computed and a cut made as close to the median as possible; using this cut, the discrepancies of each random group were examined to determine the number of discrepancies above the cutting point of the real couples. The median discrepancy (third in size) of the five random groups was chosen as most representative of the 'true' random couple distribution and served as the control group to compare against the discrepancies of the actual group.

For example, for the photo judgements, the mean of the ratings of the eight judges served as the attractiveness score of each subject. (Judges did not know which partners belonged together.) The cut closest to the median for the actual subjects showed a discrepancy between the partners of 0.5 or less units for 60 cases and 0.5 or more units for the other 39 cases. The probability of getting a discrepancy score greater than 0.5 for the actual group is therefore 0.39 (39/99). What was the frequency of cases where the discrepancy was greater than 0.5 for the most typical random group? The distribution of the five random groups is shown in table 7.1; random group 4 possessed the median value of frequency of discrepancies greater than 0.5 (50) for all five random groups. So what's the probablity of getting 50 or

Table 7.1 Comparison of discrepancy scores for photo attractiveness between actual and randomly-paired couples

Couples	Frequency of discrepancy >0.5	p for median random couples (Trial 4)
Actual	39	
Random		
Trial 1	55	
Trial 2	47	
Trial 3	45	
Trial 4	50	0.01
Trial 5	60	

more cases with discrepancies greater than 0.5, where $n = 99$, and the probability of a discrepancy greater than 0.5 is 0.39 (for the actual couples)? The answer is found in a table of binomials (Romig, 1953); for the present example, it is $p < 0.01$. It is concluded, therefore, that the photo attractiveness of real couples was significantly less discrepant than those of artificially-paired couples. The same procedure was used to test the discrepancy between each subject's perception of his partner and between the self-concepts for physical attractiveness of the couple. The former comparison was clearly non-significant, whereas the latter was of marginal significance ($p = 0.06$), thus in accordance with the hypothesis, i.e. the self-concepts of actual couples were less discrepant than those of randomly paired couples and this difference approached significance ($p < 0.06$).

Study 2

Method

Essentially the same study was replicated with 98 new couples, except that photo attractiveness, which had been clearly significant in the first study, was omitted, and only three random couples instead of five were used.

Results

Again, discrepancy between the partners' perception of each other's physical attractiveness was not significantly smaller for actual couples than for artificial ones. However, as far as self-concepts were concerned, the discrepancy was highly significant ($p < 0.001$), thus supporting the hypothesis. After the intended analysis had been completed, it was realised that the best measure of equality of physical attractiveness might be an intraperceptual one, in which the subject compared his perception of the partner with his perception of himself. According to the hypothesis, a significant positive correlation should be found between each subject's self-concept for attraction and perception of his partner. The results confirmed this expectation, the correlation for men's perceptions being 0.50 and for women's 0.45, both highly significant ($p < 0.01$). Correlations for objective (photo) attractiveness was 0.38, and for self-perceived attractiveness was 0.31 (both $p < 0.01$).

Discussion

The results indicate that physical attractiveness, both as subjectively experienced and objectively measured, operates in accordance with exchange-market rules. Individuals with equal market value for physical attractiveness are more likely to associate in an intimate relationship such as premarital engagement than individuals with disparate values.

The fact that the comparison for the couples' respective perceptions of the partner failed to follow this rule is probably due to the fact, as the data reveal, that most subjects tend to overvalue their partner's physical attractiveness, and give him or her a higher rating than they give themselves. Thus the mean self-attractiveness ratings for men and women were both 3.4, while the men's average rating for women was 4.1 and that of women for men 3.9. This overestimation of the partner seems to result in a ceiling effect for attractiveness which destroys the possibility of differences being found between random and real couples. Also, many individuals' self-concepts for attractiveness are based in objective reality to some extent, the correlation between self-concept and photo attractiveness being 0.33 for men and 0.24 for women (both $p < 0.01$).

In sum, although the typical subject sees his partner as slightly above himself in physical attractiveness, he nevertheless perceives both himself and his partner as quite comparable in this respect. It is readily acknowledged that physical attractiveness is only one of many factors influencing marital choice; stimulus-value-role theory (Murstein, 1970) holds that value homogeneity and role compatibility (the last two stages of the theory) are also quite important. However, the fact that equality of physical attractiveness tends to influence marital choice even when other stimulus variables are not controlled, testifies to its ubiquitousness during the entire course of marital courtship.

Commentary

Aim and nature

The aim of the study is to test the 'similarity' hypothesis, namely that premarital couples will show greater than chance similarity with respect to physical attraction. This was done in two separate non-experimental (correlational), laboratory-based, studies, in which 99 engaged or steady couples, then a separate sample of 98, had to rate their own and their partner's physical attractiveness while judges rated their photos, without knowing who the couples were ('who belonged to whom'). There were clearly no manipulations: the couples were 'ready-made', real couples, and the data was collected through questionnaires which included 'critical' questions on the attractiveness of self and partner.

Background and context

What Murstein calls the 'similarity hypothesis' is often referred to elsewhere (e.g. Brown, 1986) as the 'matching hypothesis' and is derived from the Exchange Theory of Blau (1964), Homans (1961) and Thibaut and Kelley (1959), which Murstein briefly summarizes on page 82. The way in which the matching hypothesis was first tested was in the form of the computer-dance, early examples of which tended to contradict the hypothesis (Walster *et al.*, 1966; Brislin & Lewis, 1968; Byrne *et al.*, 1970; Walster, 1970; Tesser & Brodie, 1971). But in these studies, *Ss* were already sure of a date *before* interacting with their partners and expressed their preference *after* having dated. This, according to Berscheid *et al.* (1971), minimizes the possibility of social rejection as a result of one's choice: the date had already been *assigned* and so there was no risk of choosing a more attractive partner who would rebuff them, hence dampening the aspirations of the unattractive. This implies that a more realistic or valid test of the matching hypothesis is under conditions where one has to *attain* a relationship, to choose a dating partner. So later computer-dance studies have asked *Ss* to stipulate in advance what kind of partners they would like: here, people rated as high, low or of average attractiveness tended to ask for dates of a corresponding level of attractiveness, thus supporting the matching hypothesis (Dion & Berscheid, 1970; Walster & Walster, 1970; Berscheid *et al.*, 1971; Berscheid & Walster, 1974).

The implication is, then, that the kind of partner we would be satisfied with is one whom we feel will not reject us as much as one we positively desire. However, Roger Brown (1986) disagrees. He says the matching phenomenon results from a well-learned sense of what is 'fitting', rather than a fear of being rebuffed, i.e. we learn to adjust our expectations of rewards in line with what we believe we have to offer others. The computer-dance studies which do support the matching hypothesis also imply that how attractive we see ourselves quite accurately reflects how attractive others see us. *Ss* were rated by observers for attractiveness, and this attractiveness rating is what was correlated with the preferred level of attractiveness in the date: the significant positive correlation obtained implies a correspondence between the attractiveness rating and the *S*'s self-rating (though this wasn't actually elicited and is usually probably unconscious).

Despite the more recent support for the matching hypothesis, these studies still only test interpersonal attraction based on, at most, a few hours interaction, as Murstein points out. So what about real couples?

Berscheid and Walster (1974) claim that 'couples who have formed viable affectional relationships should appear to outside observers to be of approximately equal levels of physical attractiveness'. Some support for this comes from a study by Silverman (1971) of *'fait accompli'* matching (i.e. matching which has already occurred). Couples were observed in naturalistic dating settings: bars, social events, theatre lobbies. Two males and two females formed the observer team. The observed couples were predominantly 18 to 22 years and unmarried. Each observer independently rated the dating partner of the opposite sex, on a five-point scale. There was an extremely high degree of similarity between the attractiveness of the couple members. Also, the more similar their attractiveness, the happier they seemed to be with each other (as reflected by the degree of physical intimacy, e.g. holding hands): 60 per cent of highly similar, 46 per cent of moderately similar and 22 per cent of least similar.

However, the observers saw both dating partners *together*, so a 'halo' emanating from one dating partner might have influenced the observers' rating of the other partner (Berscheid & Walster, 1974); i.e. the expectation of similarity could have biased the observers' ratings towards a more similar rating of the one member based on the rating of the other. It has also been questioned (Udry, 1971) whether the degree of matching observed could have occurred by chance. Since 85 per cent of the couples were not separated by more than one scale point and no couple was disparate by more than 2.5 points, it is argued that the scale did not permit discriminations to be made between individuals because there were only five points on the scale!

Murstein's study, is, of course, also concerned with real couples. Price and Vandenberg (1979) went a step or two further by studying married couples, aged between 28 and 60. Allowing for age effects on attractiveness (e.g. young people tend to rate older people as less attractive, everything else being equal), they concluded that 'the matching phenomenon [of physical attraction levels between marriage partners] is stable within and across generations'.

Evaluation

1 Although like Silverman, Murstein used a five-point scale for rating attractiveness, he did, unlike Silverman, determine whether the degree of matching observed was significantly above what would have been expected by chance. In the first study, he did this by comparing the discrepancies between the mean ratings of the eight judges for each subject arranged into their actual pairs/couples, with the discrepancies between the mean ratings of the eight judges for each subject arranged into random pairs. The question then asked was: is the photo attractiveness of the real couples significantly less discrepant than those of the artificially-paired couples? He first took the most representative of five randomly-produced sets of 99 couples (trial 4) [the median value of frequency of discrepancies greater than 0.5 (50) for all five random groups]. A table of binomials showed that the probability of getting 50 or more cases with discrepancies greater than 0.5 is very low ($p<0.01$), where $n = 99$ and the probability of a discrepancy greater than 0.5 for the actual couples is 0.39. Murstein concluded from this that the photo attractiveness of real couples is significantly less discrepant than those of artificially-paired couples. [The binomial distribution applies to data with two mutually exclusive outcomes, e.g. heads/tails, and indicates the proportion of each ratio of scores which would be expected for each sample size. The actual proportions obtained can be compared with the expected proportions, to see if, in this case, the scores for actual couples really are less dissimilar than those of the random couples. With large samples, the binomial distribution becomes very similar to a normal distribution – Stratton & Hayes, 1988.]

2 The same procedure was used to test the discrepancy between each *S*'s perception of his/her partner and between the self-concepts for physical attractiveness of the couple (i.e. how each individual *S* rated his/her own attractiveness). The former was clearly non-significant, while the latter was significant at $p = 0.06$, i.e. in the predicted *direction* (but not significantly so, i.e. 0.05 or less). So physical attractiveness was being measured in three different ways: (*i*) judges' rating of photos; (*ii*) each partner's rating of the other; (*iii*) self-rating.

3 In study 2, using 98 different couples, essentially the same procedure was used, except that the photo attractiveness, which had been clearly significant in study 1, was omitted and only three sets of random couples – instead of five – were used. Again, discrepancy between partners' perception of each other's physical attractiveness was not significantly smaller for actual couples than random ones. But as far as self-concepts were concerned, the discrepancy was highly significant ($p<0.001$), thus supporting the hypothesis.

4 Another important difference between this and Silverman's *'fait accompli'* matching is that the judges in Murstein's study did not know the identity or pairing of the couples when seeing the photographs, thus preventing any chance of a halo effect. Presumably, the photos were of faces, since the questions about the partner's physical attractiveness included the words 'good-looking', 'looks', etc. But isn't the concept of 'physical attractiveness' wider than facial appearance, e.g. could the findings that physical attractiveness may be of even more importance to men than women in making their dating choices (Berscheid & Walster, 1974) be partly explained by the fact that different (or more) aspects of appearance are taken into account? (For example, a 'good figure' is more important to men than a 'good physique' is to women.) Clearly, if such differences do exist, they are symptomatic of the pervasive difference in gender roles in our society, in which, traditionally, a woman has been regarded as a man's property, whereby her beauty increases his status and respect in the eyes of others

(Sigall & Landy, 1973). But the reverse does not seem to apply; the attractiveness of a man does not seem to enhance a woman's standing among other women (Bar-Tal & Saxe, 1976).

5 Extending this theme, Murstein's study is limited in that it is heterosexist and ethnocentric: (*i*) would the matching hypothesis apply to homosexual/lesbian couples and (*ii*) do different cultures have different criteria of what constitutes physical beauty? There is some (anecdotal) evidence that chipped teeth, body scars, artificially elongated heads and bound feet have all been regarded as 'beautiful' (Garfield, 1982) and in Western culture definitions change over time (e.g. the 'ideal' figure for a woman). Research in both these areas would be of great interest.

Exercises

1 In study 2, where S's perception of his/her partner was compared with his/her perception of him/herself, correlations of 0.50 for men's perceptions and 0.45 for women's were found (both highly significant, $p < 0.01$). Correlations were 0.38 for objective (photo) attractiveness and 0.31 for self-perceived attractiveness (both $p < 0.01$). How is it possible for such relatively low correlation coefficients to be so highly significant?

2 Why was it important to have an equal number of male and female judges?

3 What scale of measurement was being used for judging the photos?

A. S. R. MANSTEAD AND CAROLINE MCCULLOCH (1981)

Sex-role stereotyping in British television advertisements

British Journal of Social Psychology, 20, pp. 171–80

The present study examined the portrayal of men and women in a sample of British television advertisements, with a view to establishing whether men and women were depicted differently, and if so, in what respects. 170 advertisements were analysed by classifying the following attributes of their adult central figures: sex, mode of presentation, relationship to products, role, location, arguments, rewards and product type. It was found that males and females were portrayed in markedly different ways, the most salient of which were that women were significantly more likely than men to be shown as product-users, in dependent roles, at home, to provide no arguments in favour of advertised products, and to appear in conjunction with domestic products. These findings are compared with those of a similar study of American television commercials, and are also considered in the context of other studies of sex-role stereotyping in the mass media. The implications of such findings for the development and maintenance of sex roles are discussed.

Television advertisements are a potentially rich source of data for the social scientist. On the one hand, the images they contain are drawn from society at large, and can therefore be seen as in some degree *reflecting* prevailing cultural values; on the other hand, given the importance of TV as an agent of socialization (cf. Murray *et al.*, 1972), TV advertisements are likely to play an active role in *shaping* these cultural values.

An advertisement is a highly condensed form of communication which has to be easily understood in order to be effective. Given these constraints, some degree of stereotyping in the portrayal of actors in advertisements is inevitable. As Millum (1975) has noted, 'the need to represent "typical" situations leads to the production of compromises or composites or of stereotypes'. So, because the actors and situations featured in advertisements must be readily identifiable by their audience, they have to be consonant with prevailing cultural values.

However, they cannot be seen simply as mirror images of society, for advertising is a selective process in which advertisers isolate and emphasize certain features of society for the purposes of promoting their products; as Millum (1975) puts it, 'the advertisements can be seen to reflect – selectively – and to mediate and reinforce certain *preferred* meanings taken from the overall cultural knowledge-to-hand'. It is therefore interesting and important to examine *which* aspects of society and cultural values are selected by advertisers for particular emphasis, with a view to establishing whether a consistent set of cultural values is being promoted through the advertising medium and, if so, to identify the nature of these values.

The present study focuses on sex-role stereotyping in British TV advertisements. Given the need to project 'typical' images of social relationship, advertisements should provide an insight into the present nature of sex roles in British society, which is of special interest in view of the developments of the last decade. Since 1970 the development of the women's movement has received some official recognition in the shape of legislation designed to reduce discrimination on the basis of sex, and through the establishment of the Equal Opportunities commission. TV advertisements as a socializing agency, with the capacity to facilitate or impede progress towards sexual equality, must be monitored through examination of the ways in which they portray males and females, to see whether these portrayals reflect the changes of the past decade and are consistent with the officially sanctioned aim of greater equality of women.

American research suggests that TV advertisements are not responsive to changes in sex roles in the USA since the late 1960s. Dominick and Rausch (1972) found that women were portrayed as housewife/mother in 56 per cent of their advertising roles, while men were cast as husband/father in only 14 per cent of theirs. Culley and Bennett (1976) replicated the study and also found a significant difference (45 and 15 per cent respectively). Courtney and Whipple (1974) reviewed four studies (including that of Dominick and Rausch) and concluded that women were overrepresented in domestic settings and underrepresented in out-of-home occupations; their findings 'support the claim' that the reality of the out-of-home working woman has not yet permeated TV advertising.

Similarly, McArthur and Resko (1975) noted that despite the fact that women constituted 37 per cent of the US labour force (in 1969) they were only 11 per cent of the central figures in the advertisements they studied in occupational settings. Marecek *et al.*, (1978) and O'Donnell and O'Donnell (1978) confirm this finding.

Women's roles as housewives/mothers also seem to define their apparent interests: they are shown predominantly in association with domestic products and products related to personal hygiene or appearance, while men are associated with a wide range of products, such as leisure, finance, motor-cars and even (according to Culley and Bennett, 1976) the family pet.

A third way in which American portrayals of men and women differ is regarding their authority and expertise, with males having a virtual monopoly, especially in connection with voice-overs, which 'typically imparts information to the viewers and, by implication, holds the role of the expert' (Maracek *et al.*, 1978). Courtney and Whipple (1974) found that men overwhelmingly outnumbered women as voice-overs, announcing or authority figures (87 to 89 per cent men) and O'Donnell and O'Donnell (1978) found an even higher figure (93 per cent men). McArthur and Resko (1975) found that only 14 per cent of women were 'experts' (on or off screen) compared to 70 per cent of men.

Courtney and Whipple (1974) concluded that 'there is little evidence in the world of TV commercials to show that the family structure may be changing or that women are capable of performing responsible tasks other than those associated with the family and home'.

The present study was intended to assess the situation in Britain. The procedure involved viewing all evening advertisements televised by one commercial TV company during a one-week period, and systematically classifying the attributes of male and female adults depicted in these advertisements. The coding scheme used for this classification was modelled closely on that used by McArthur and Resko (1975), so as to be able to make legitimate comparisons between the two studies.

Method

Sample of commercials

This was selected by video-recording all commercials transmitted by Granada Television between 6 and 11.30 p.m. during a seven-day period in July 1979, a total of 493 commercials. All repeat advertisements ($n = 309$) were excluded from the final sample, as were those in which only children or fantasy characters appeared, leaving 170 independent advertisements for coding.

Coding procedure

This was modelled very closely on the one used by McArthur and Resko (1975), and involved two investigators independently coding the following characteristics of each central figure depicted: mode of presentation, sex, credibility basis, role, location, arguments presented in favour of product, reward type and product type.

Central figures

Adults playing a central role, regardless of whether they were depicted visually, vocally or both, were classed as central figures. No more than two central figures were coded for any one commercial; if more than two were depicted, those featuring most prominently were selected for further coding.

Mode of presentation

Central figures were classified as *voice* where they simply appeared as disembodied voice-overs, and as *visual* when they were depicted visually (whether or not they had a speaking part).

Credibility basis

Central figures who were depicted primarily as users of the product were categorized as *user*, while those who were depicted primarily as sources of information concerning the products were categorized as *authority*. Central figures who fell into neither of these categories were categorized as *other*.

Role

Central figures were classified, according to their apparent role in everyday life, as one of the following: *spouse, parent, homemaker, worker, professional, celebrity, interviewer/narrator, boyfriend, girlfriend, sex object,* or *other*.

Location

The location of central figures was categorized as one of the following: *home, store, occupational setting,* or *other*.

Arguments

Central figures were classified according to the type of arguments they presented in favour of the product, either *scientific*, if they contained or claimed to contain factual evidence, or *non-scientific* if they simply consisted of opinions or testimonials in favour of the product. If no argument was offered, the central figure was classified as *none*.

Reward type

Eight categories of reward were coded: *opposite sex approval*; *family approval*; *friends' approval*; *self-enhancement* (improvement in health and/or appearance); *practical* (saving of time or effort, or relative cheapness of product); *social/career advancement* (assist progress in some social or occupational hierarchy); *other* (rewards suggested but could not be coded in any of the foregoing categories); and *none*.

Product type

Six types of product were coded: *body* (bodily health, hygiene, cleansing or clothing); *home* (home or housework); *food*; *auto* (cars, car accessories and related products); *sports*; *other*.

Coding reliability

Particular effort was made to achieve satisfactory reliability of coding by use of video-recordings of the sampled commercials, which allowed multiple replays and thereby placed less emphasis on coders' ability to process complex information rapidly. Each of the two coders independently made a total of 2152 codings, of which only 86 were discrepant, i.e. the overall extent of agreement was 96 per cent. As might be expected, the highest incidence of disagreement arose in codings which required a greater degree of interpretation, i.e. in determining whether or not a given argument was scientific (33/86 discrepancies) and what type of reward was involved (30/86); but even here, the agreement levels were 87.7 and 88.8 respectively.

Results

Central figures   In the final sample of 170 commercials, 269 central figures were coded. 66 per cent of these were male, 34 per cent were female ($\chi^2 = 26.86$, *d.f.* $= 1$, $p<0.001$). The main findings concerning the relationship between sex of central figure and the categories of each of the dependent variables are shown in table 8.1.

Table 8.1   Relationship between sex of central figure and principal categories of dependent variables (numbers represent absolute frequencies)

Variable	Category	Sex of central figure	
		Male ($n = 177$)	**Female** ($n = 92$)
Mode	Visual	58	85
	Voice-over	119	7
Credibility basis	Product user	38	69
	Product authority	132	12
Role	Autonomous (a)	151	22
	Dependent (b)	17	63
Location	Home	13	35
	Work	6	9
	Other (c)	148	48
Argument	Scientific	48	7
	Non-scientific	94	27
	None	35	58
Reward type	Social approval or self-enhancement	38	37
	None	8	10
	Other (d)	131	45
Product type	Domestic (e)	100	70
	Other	77	22

(a) Worker, Professional, celebrity and interviewer/narrator.
(b) Spouse, homemaker, boyfriend/girlfriend and sex object.
(c) Includes store locations.
(d) Includes practical rewards.
(e) Body, home and food products.

Mode   94 per cent of central figures who appeared as voice-overs were males, while 59 per cent depicted visually were females ($\chi^2 = 84.05$, *d.f.* $= 1$, $p<0.001$).

Credibility basis   251 central figures were coded either as product users or as authorities on the product. Females were much more likely to be product users than authorities compared with males ($\chi^2 = 88.56$,

$d.f. = 1, p<0.001$). A further analysis was performed of the association between sex of central figure and credibility basis, excluding all voice-over central figures (who were invariably product authorities). Of the visually presented product users, 65 per cent were female, and of the visually presented authorities, 70 per cent were male; the relationship between sex and credibility basis was again significant ($\chi^2 = 8.58$, $d.f. = 1$, $p<0.01$), indicating that this association is independent of that between sex and mode of presentation.

Role   Initial analysis of the full 2×11 contingency table relating sex to role category revealed a reliable association between these two variables ($\chi^2 = 135.3$, $d.f. = 10$, $p<0.001$). In a subsequent analysis, this table was collapsed into a 2×2 contingency table by pooling spouse, parent, home-maker, boyfriend, girlfriend and sex object into one role category ('dependent' roles), and worker, professional, celebrity and interviewer into another ('autonomous' roles). 253 central figures fell into one or other of these two pooled-role categories. Males were much more likely than females to be depicted in autonomous roles ($\chi^2 = 106.91$, $d.f. = 1$, $p<0.001$). Of the dependent roles, females were most highly represented (32 per cent of all female central figures) in the parent category, and of the autonomous roles, males were most highly represented (72 per cent of all male central figures) in the interviewer/narrator category. Since the role of inerviewer/narrator almost always entailed also being a product authority, it was necessary to reanalyse the data excluding the former (i.e. controlling for sex differences in credibility basis). This reduced the percentage of autonomous roles filled by males from 87 to 67 per cent but did not affect the significance of the sex difference in role depiction ($\chi^2 = 22.43$, $d.f. = 1, p<0.001$).

Location   Initial analysis of the 2×4 contingency table relating sex to location revealed a significant association ($\chi^2 = 41.53$, $d.f. = 3$, $p<0.001$). However, this could simply have been a reflection of the sex difference in mode of presentation, since all voice-overs were categorized as 'other'. When all voice-over central figures were removed and the data reanalysed, there was still a significant association ($\chi^2 = 11.00$, $d.f. = 3$, $p<0.02$). Further, 73 per cent of visually presented central figures shown at home were females, while only 53 per cent shown in all other locations were females ($\chi^2 = 7.49, d.f. = 1$, $p<0.01$); similarly, 64 per cent of those shown at work were males while only 36 per cent shown in all other locations were males ($\chi^2 = 6.91$, $d.f. = 1, p<0.01$).

Argument   Initial analysis of the 2×3 contingency table relating sex to type of argument revealed significant association ($\chi^2 = 51.65$, $d.f. = 2, p<0.001$). Males were more likely than females to provide both scientific ($\chi^2 = 11.26$, $d.f. = 1$, $p<0.001$) and non-scientific arguments ($\chi^2 = 7.59$, $d.f. = 1, p<0.01$). While females were 62 per cent of those who provided *no* argument at all, they were only 19 per cent of those who provided some form of argument or other. ($\chi^2 = 50.09$, $d.f. = 1, p<0.001$).

Reward type   This data was initially reduced from eight to five categories because some of the categories attracted relatively low scores. Analysis of the resulting 2×5 contingency table relating sex to reward type showed a significant association ($\chi^2 = 20.83$, $d.f. = 4$, $p < 0.001$) and females were significantly more likely than males to be shown suggesting social approval, self-enhancement or no rewards, rather than others ($\chi^2 = 16.84$, $d.f. = 1$, $p < 0.001$).

Product type This data was initially reduced from six categories to four (by combining auto and sports categories with 'other'), producing a significant association (2×4 contingency table) between sex and product type ($\chi^2 = 10.53$, $d.f. = 3$, $p < 0.02$).

Males comprised 78 per cent of the 'other' products category but only 59 per cent of the body, home and food products categories ($\chi^2 = 9.99$, $d.f. = 1$, $p < 0.01$). However, this underrepresentation of males in advertisements for 'domestic' products did not reduce the extent to which they were portrayed as *authorities* on such products: 94 per cent, 83 per cent and 89 per cent on body products, home products and food products respectively. It was also found that females were 88 per cent of all body-products users, compared with 57 per cent of all other products users ($\chi^2 = 7.87$, $d.f. = 1$, $p < 0.01$); similarly, males comprised only 24 per cent of all body, home and food products users but 63 per cent of all other products users ($\chi^2 = 14.53$, $d.f. = 1$, $p < 0.001$).

Discussion

The general picture that emerges is unambiguous: adult males and females in this sample of British TV advertisements were portrayed in markedly and systematically different ways, consistent with traditional sex roles. Males were typically shown as having expertise and authority, as being objective and knowledgeable about reasons for buying particular products, as occupying autonomous roles and as being concerned with the practical consequences of product purchase. By contrast, females were typically shown as consumers of products, unknowledgeable about the reasons for buying particular products, occupying dependent social roles and concerned with the social consequences of product purchase.

Compared with the findings reported by McArthur and Resko (1975), the present study found a greater tendency for males to predominate (57 and 66 per cent, respectively). However, McArthur and Resko also reported that males were 70 per cent of the central figures in advertisements broadcast between 8 and 10 p.m. and, since the sample in this study was drawn exclusively from 6 to 11.30 p.m. broadcasts, the tendency for males to outnumber females as central figures appears comparable across the two samples.

They found that 70 per cent of their male central figures were product authorities (78 per cent in the present study) and that 86 per cent of the females were product users (85 per cent in the present study). They also found a reliable tendency for females to be shown in dependent roles and at home proportionally more often than males, and for males to be shown in autonomous and in occupational settings proportionally more often than females, as did the present study.

One rather striking difference is to do with the use of arguments. McArthur and Resko reported that 30 per cent of females gave no argument at all (compared with 63 per cent in the present study). They also found no reliable association between sex and rewards, unlike the present study, which showed females to be significantly more likely than males to suggest social approval and self-enhancement rewards. Overall, the differences between the two studies suggest that adults are portrayed in a more sex-stereotyped way in British than in American commercials.

To what degree does this stereotyping in TV advertisements contribute to the learning of stereotyped perceptions and behaviours by children and to their maintenance in adults?

One way in which this learning might occur is through differential imitation of same-sex models. Both the social-learning (e.g. Mischel, 1970) and cognitive-developmental (Kohlberg, 1969) approaches to sex-role development attach considerable importance to the role of imitation of same-sex models. In two reviews of imitation studies, Maccoby and Jacklin (1974) and Barkley *et al.* (1977) concluded that there is little evidence to support the notion of differential imitation of same-sex models. However, Perry and Bussey (1979) raised methodological and conceptual objections to the research on which those reviews based their conclusions, and proposed a modified social learning account of how imitation contributes to sex-role development. They stress the importance of children's perceptions of the appropriateness of behaviours to each sex, preferring to imitate actions coded as same-sex-appropriate, and this coding of responses as male-or-female appropriate is based on 'having witnessed different proportions of available male and female models performing the responses'.

Clearly, the mass media in general, and TV programmes in particular, constitute potentiality powerful sources of information concerning the sex-appropriateness of a wide variety of behaviours. Magazine advertisements (Sexton and Haberman, 1974; Millum, 1975), and children's books (Weitzman *et al.*, 1972; Lobban, 1975) also portray males and females in sex-role stereotyped ways, so it seems very likely that any influence exerted by the mass media in this respect is an internally consistent one. Such consistency of stereotyping could be responsible not simply for the rapid acquisition of knowledge of sex-*trait* stereotypes between the ages of five and 11 (Best *et al.*, 1977), but is also a critical factor in the learning of stereotyped *behaviours*.

Until recently, there has been a serious shortage of hard evidence concerning the impact of stereotyping because of the difficulty of finding a control group which has never been exposed to stereotyped advertising but which in all other respects is comparable to an experimental group. However, Jennings *et al.* (1980) sought to overcome this problem by testing a contrast hypothesis. Rather than testing their theoretical hypothesis that stereotyped commercials depress women's self-confidence and independence of judgment, they tested the contrast hypothesis, that commercials which *break* sex-role stereotyping *raise* women's self-confidence and independence of judgement. Indeed, female college students exposed to reversed-role commercials were both more independent (deviated further from the false majority judgements) and more self-confident in their non-verbal behaviour while making an impromptu speech than women exposed to the stereotyped commercials. This was nothing to do with the *explicit* content of the advertisements, and subjects seemed to be unaware of their influence. Jennings *et al.* conclude that 'this research strongly implies that even if women do not buy the advertised products, they buy the implicit image of femininity conveyed by the commercials, whether they know it or not'.

The fact that there is, as yet, relatively little direct evidence of the influence of sex-stereotyped advertisements on sex-role perceptions and behaviour should not give advertisers any cause for complacency. In 1978, women constituted 41 per cent of all employees in the UK (Manley and Sawbridge, 1980), yet in the present sample of TV advertisements, women comprised a mere 13 per cent of central figures occupying autonomous roles. The sheer size of this discrepancy between reality and the fantasy world of TV advertisements suggests that advertisers should be encouraged to take more seriously this aspect of their social responsibilities.

Commentary

Aim and nature

The study is a *content analysis* of British TV commercials aimed at establishing whether men and women are depicted differently and, if so, in what respects. The study is also intended as a replication of an American study by McArthur and Resko (1975), so that a comparison is made between the two sets of results. A content analysis really represents a research method in its own right, but perhaps the traditional and more commonly-used method which it most resembles is observation. This is clearly the major way of collecting the data, although the categories by which the observed content is to be coded must be pre-determined (as in all focused observational studies). It is naturalistic observation in the sense that the TV commercials are the ones normally broadcast: they constitute the 'behaviour' being studied. Although in table 8.1 the variables (mode, credibility, basis, etc.) are referred to as dependent variables, there is no independent variable as such: essentially, the study aims to find whether or not there is a correlation or *association* between sex of central figure and the way he/she is portrayed in terms of six characteristics. This could be thought of in different terms as testing the hypothesis that sex will affect how central figures are portrayed (with sex being an un-manipulated independent variable).

Context and background

The general context is the study of the influence of the mass media on beliefs, attitude and behaviour; more specifically, their influence on sex-role stereotypes through their stereotyped portrayal of men and women, and, more specifically still, on the portrayal of men and women in TV commercials.

There has been an enormous number of studies of the behavioural effects of the media, particularly TV, during the 1970s and 1980s, along with a large number of reviews. The emphasis seems to have been on the harmful effects, especially the effects of violence and aggression, on children's behaviour, and the studies have been of four main kinds: laboratory experiments, field experiments, correlational studies and Panel Studies (in which people's viewing habits and behaviour patterns are followed over time). According to Gunter (1987), perhaps the two most fundamental problems in TV research are (*i*) inferring causality from correlational evidence (a general problem in psychology and social science) and (*ii*) generalizing to real life from the findings derived from artificial, contrived, laboratory settings (also a problem throughout psychology as a whole).

As far as sex-role stereotyping is concerned, there are fairly consistent findings regarding the differential portrayal of men and women in relation to how often they are shown, their age, the importance of their physical attractiveness, occupation and status and behaviour and settings (Durkin, 1986).

(*i*) Although in most populations women slightly outnumber men, the media present radically different ratios: in most areas of TV entertainment, men outnumber women by about 7 : 3, men are more likely to be shown as stars, men perform the vast majority of commercial voice-overs, men form a higher proportion of leading characters in films, male characters or masculine themes dominate children's literature, 81 per cent of newspaper photographs include men but only 30 per cent women, and men predominate on newspaper front pages, inside news sections, business and sports sections. Even psychology textbooks use more male than female examples and sources; (*ii*) women are generally shown up to the age of about 30 on TV, magazines and films, while the male age range is much greater, including older men enjoying prestige and attractiveness; (*iii*) not surprisingly, correlated with age is the general emphasis on female physical attractiveness and the use of beautiful young women to support images of powerful men in TV and film, and to add sexual decoration in magazine and newspaper advertisements (even though this is irrelevant to the product); (*iv*) men are more often shown in work settings outside the home and often in high-status or dynamic jobs, while women are cast in a narrow range of occupations, most commonly housewife, nurse, secretary and air stewardess. Quiz-show presenters, weather forecasters and radio DJs are also predominantly male; (*v*) men are usually more aggressive and autonomous, and more likely to be dominant over females than dominated by them. Women tend to have superior nurturant and empathetic abilities. In toy catalogues, boys and girls are usually playing with sex-stereotyped toys, and even the background music for TV toy advertisements varies dramatically according to the sex-typing of the product. The Manstead and McCulloch study is, in keeping with the vast majority of the research to date, concerned with content.

Evaluation

1 The nature of content analysis itself as a method imposes certain restrictions on the value of studies such as this. Although a popular and widely-used method for quantifying 'the manifest content of communication' (Berelson, 1952), Durkin (1985, 1986) believes it has serious limitations:

(a) The scoring process is very subjective. For instance, not everyone would agree on what constitutes an abusive racial or sexist comment, and even the same words may mean different things when uttered by different people (e.g. 'nigger' spoken by a white policeman or a black radical). However, this can be overcome, to some extent, by an explicit definition of scoring criteria and by having more than one judge (analyser of the content). The Manstead and McCulloch study would seem to have taken both precautions.

However, once the scorers have been trained in the application of a particular set of criteria, the investigator might be testing little more than the ability to enforce his/her theoretical biases. Durkin believes this is an especially delicate problem in the area of sex-role stereotypes in the media: many such studies have been conducted by researchers avowedly committed to feminist perspectives and so it is conceivable that when scoring something such as 'male dominance', feminists may be more inclined to identify such elements in human interaction than less socially-aware coders or they might interpret as symbols of male oppression incidents which others would interpret differently.

(b) A more fundamental problem is to do with the social *meaning* of the data and the gaps they leave. Content analysis concentrates primarily on the *counting* of instances of a given phenomenon as opposed to their *organization*; this means they reflect sex-role stereotypes in TV at the level of *traits* and relatively discrete behaviours. But they offer only gross characterizations of the *meaning* of the content, even within the terms of the individual programmes assessed. The significance of a particular behavioural act may be lost or misrepresented in this way because content analysis does not study the *interrelationship* of whole sequences of events; it ignores the unifying structure of those events. We lack an account of the scripts (surface and underlying) in which sex-role portrayals in TV are located, making description of the raw data being transmitted incomplete.

What this amounts to is the risk that content analysis may provide too simple a picture, leading to an even simpler dichotomy between male and female portrayal. This oversimplification may in turn lead to a minimization of attention to within-sex portrayals, and *interactions* between sex, race and class.

2 Durkin, more positively, believes that we should still take note of the results of such studies and consistent findings across different studies deserve to be taken seriously. Content analysis studies are currently the most prolific type of study in this field and they represent an inevitable starting point. However, no amount of content analysis can establish anything about the *effects* of sex-role stereotyping. He argues that the main contribution that psychologists can hope to make is to uncover the processes of *reception*, i.e. how people discern, encode and respond to the content of the media. A fundamental difficulty in this regard is that so many media are integrated into our lives in so many ways that any attempt to evaluate the functions of any one of them is confounded by the co-occurrence of the others. Also, because of the sheer diversity of the audience, it is naïve to think of the media as having the same effect on all of them. Indeed, overall there is no statistical relationship between consumption of a particular mass medium and an individual's traditional sex-role beliefs.

Does this mean that the media play no part or that we shall never have the research technology? Durkin says 'no' to both parts of the question but we do need to develop (a) more sophisticated theories and (b) more ingenious approaches.

(a) A starting point is to recognize that the process of media influence is *social* and not *unidirectional*, i.e. we need to ask what the media user him/herself brings to the media, and how this interacts with the media content. We are *not* passive recipients of media content. For example, there is already quite a lot of evidence that children impose their pre-existing beliefs about sex-roles on what they see, and in this way *use* the media to confirm or supplement their developing social knowledge. Adults probably do the same; we must place the media in their social context by studying how and where they are used. There is remarkably little investigation of reception and Durkin believes there is a pressing need for more experimental and field research.

(b) There is beginning to accumulate a body of experimental research in which subjects are shown counter-stereotyped media content to see if this produces any change in their beliefs and/or behaviour. Most have involved children, but many have found significant effects on beliefs and attitudes following exposure to non-traditional stories, films or TV programmes. A few studies of female undergraduates shown sex-role reversals in TV commercials (e.g. Geis *et al.*, 1984) have shown them to be more independent of judgement in conformity tests and measures of personal achievement orientation. But there is also evidence of resistance and wide individual differences. Durkin (1986) concludes by saying 'society is more than its media'.

Exercises

1 Why was it important to use the same coding (classification) system as McArthur and Resko (1975)?

2 Was the sample of advertisements adequate?

3 What kind of reliability was used to check the coding?

4 What statistical test is used to establish the degree of reliability?

5 The χ^2 (Chi-squared) test was used throughout to test for the significance of the male–female differences for the various codes. But in the case of the total number of central figures, χ^2 is being used in a special way. Can you draw the appropriate χ^2 table and say *how* the test is being used in a special way?

Cognitive consequences of forced compliance

Journal of Abnormal and Social Psychology, 58, pp. 203–10

What happens to a person's private opinion if he is forced to do or say something contrary to that opinion? Only recently has there been any experimental work related to this question; two studies by Janis and King (1954, 1956) clearly showed that, at least under certain conditions, the private opinion changes so as to bring it into closer correspondence with the overt behaviour the person was forced to perform. Specifically, they showed that if a person is forced to improvise a speech supporting a point of view with which he disagrees, his private opinion moves toward the position advocated in the speech. The observed opinion change is greater than for persons who only hear the speech, or who read a prepared speech with emphasis solely on elocution and manner of delivery. Janis and King explain the results by proposing that, through mental rehearsal and thinking up new arguments, the subject convinces himself. They present some not totally conclusive evidence to support this explanation which will be discussed later in this report.

Kelman (1953) reasoned that if the person is induced to make an overt statement contrary to his private opinion by the offer of some reward, then the greater the reward offered, the greater should be the subsequent opinion change. However, his data did not support this hypothesis; he found instead that a large reward produced less subsequent opinion change than a smaller reward. In fact, Kelman's finding is consistent with the theory outlined below, but not perfectly so; one reason is that not all subjects in the experiment actually complied, i.e. made an overt statement contrary to their private opinion in order to obtain the reward; another is that, as one might expect, the percentage of subjects who complied increased as the size of the reward increased.

Recently, Festinger (1957) proposed a theory of cognitive dissonance which makes certain predictions about opinion change following forced compliance. The reasoning is as follows:

Let us consider a person who privately holds opinion X but has, as a result of pressure brought to bear on him, publicly stated that he believes 'not X'.

1 This person has two cognitions which, psychologically, do not fit together: one of these is the knowledge that he believes X, the other the knowledge that he has publicly stated that he believes 'not X'. If no factors other than his private opinion are considered, it would follow, at least in our culture, that if he believes X he would publicly state X. Therefore, his cognition of his private belief is dissonant with this cognition concerning his actual public statement.

2 Similarly, the knowledge that he has said 'not X' is consonant with those cognitive elements corresponding to the reasons, pressures, promises of rewards and/or threats of punishment which induced him to say 'not X'.

3 In evaluating the total magnitude of dissonance, we must take into account both dissonances and consonances. If we think of the sum of all the dissonances involving some particular cognition as D, and the sum of all the consonances as C, then we might think of the total magnitude of dissonance as being a function of D divided by D plus C.

With everything else held constant, the total magnitude of dissonance experienced by the person who believes X but says 'not X' would decrease as the number and importance of the pressures which induced him to say 'not X' increased. From this point on, as the promised rewards or threatened punishments become larger, the magnitude of dissonance becomes smaller.

4 One way of reducing dissonance is for the person to change his private opinion so as to bring it into line with what he has said. One would therefore expect to observe such opinion change after a person has been forced or induced to say something contrary to his private opinion. Furthermore, since the pressure to reduce dissonance will be a function of the magnitude of the dissonance, the observed opinion change should be greatest when the pressure used to elicit the overt behaviour is just sufficient to do it.

The present experiment was designed to test this hypothesis under controlled, laboratory conditions. The amount of reward used to force subjects to make a statement contrary to their private views was varied; the prediction (from **3** and **4** above) is that the larger the reward given to the subject, the smaller will be the subsequent opinion change.

Procedure

71 male students in the introductory psychology course at Stanford University were used. In this course, students are required to spend a certain number of hours as subjects (*Ss*) in experiments; they choose among the available experiments by signing their names on a sheet posted on the bulletin board which states the nature of the experiment. The present experiment was listed as a two-hour experiment dealing with 'Measures of Performance'.

During the first week of the course, when the requirement of participating in experiments was announced and explained to the students, the instructor also told them about a study that the psychology department was conducting. He explained that, since they were required to serve in experiments, the department was conducting a study to evaluate these experiments in order to be able to improve them in the future. They were told that a sample of students would be interviewed after having served as *Ss* and they were urged to cooperate in these interviews by being completely frank and honest. This enabled us to measure the opinions of our *Ss* in a context not directly connected with our experiment and in which we could reasonably expect honest expressions of opinion.

When the *S* arrived for the experiment on 'Measures of Performance', he had to wait for a few minutes in the secretary's office. The experimenter (*E*) then came in, introduced himself to the *S*, and together they entered the laboratory room where *E* said:

> This experiment usually takes a little over an hour but, of course, we had to schedule it for two hours. Since we have that extra time, the introductory psychology people asked if they could interview some of our subjects. (*Offhand and conversationally*) Did they announce that in class? I gather that they're interviewing some people who have been in the experiments. I don't know much about it. Anyhow, they may want to interview you when you're through here.

With no further introduction or explanation, *S* was shown the first task, which involved putting 12 spools onto a tray, emptying the tray, refilling it with spools and so on. He was told to use one hand and to work at his own pace. He did this for half an hour. *E* then removed the tray and spools and placed before *S* a board containing 48 square pegs which he was to turn a quarter turn clockwise, then another quarter turn and so on. Again he was to use one hand and to work at his own pace; this took another half hour.

While *S* was working at these tasks, *E* sat, stop-watch in hand, busily making notes; this was to convince *S* that it was the tasks and *S*'s performance on them which comprised the total experiment. In reality, the experiment had hardly begun. The hour spent working on the repetitive, monotonous tasks were meant to provide for each *S* an experience about which he would have a rather negative opinion.

After the hour was over, *E* conspicuously set the stop-watch back to zero, put it away, pushed his chair back, lit a cigarette and said:

> OK. Well, that's all we have in the experiment itself. I'd like to explain what this has been all about, so you'll have some idea of why you were doing this. (*E pauses*) Well, the way the experiment is set up is this. There are actually two groups in the experiment. In one, the group you were in, we bring the subject in and give him essentially no introduction to the experiment. That is, all we tell him is what he needs to know in order to do the tasks, and he has no idea of what the experiment is all about, or what it's going to be like, or anything like that. But in the

other group, we have a student that we've hired that works for us regularly, and what I do is take him into the next room where the subject is waiting – the same room you were waiting in before – and I introduce him as if he had just finished being a subject in the experiment. That is, I say:

'This is so-and-so, who's just finished the experiment, and I've asked him to tell you a little of what it's about before you start'.

The fellow who works for us then, in conversation with the next subject, makes these points: (*E then produced a sheet headed 'For Group B' which had written on it: 'it was very enjoyable', 'I had a lot of fun', 'I enjoyed myself', 'it was very interesting', 'it was intriguing', 'it was exciting'. E showed this to S and then proceeded with his false explanation of the purpose of the experiment*). Now, of course, we have this student to do this, because if the experimenter does it, it doesn't look as realistic and what we're interested in doing is comparing how these two groups do on the experiment: the one with this previous expectation about the experiment, and the other, like yourself, with essentially none.

Up to this point, the procedure was identical for *S*s in all conditions but from this point on they diverged. There were three conditions, Control, $1 and $20, run as follows:

Control condition

E continued:

Is that fairly clear? (*Pause*). Look, that fellow (*looks at watch*) I was telling you about from the introductory psychology class said he would get here a couple of minutes from now. Would you mind waiting to see if he wants to talk to you? Fine. Why don't we go into the other room to wait? (*E left S in the secretary's office for four minutes. He then returned and said:*) OK. Let's check and see if he does want to talk to you.

$1 and $20 conditions

E continued:

Is that fairly clear how it is set up and what we're trying to do? (*Pause*) Now, I also have a sort of strange thing to ask you. The thing is this. (*Long pause, some confusion and uncertainty in the following, with a degree of embarrassment on E's part, which contrasted strongly with the preceding unhesitant and assured false explanation of the experiment. The point was to make it seem to S that this was the first time E had done this and that he felt unsure of himself.*) The fellow who normally does this for us couldn't do it today – he just phoned in, and something or other came up for him – so we've been looking around for someone that we could hire to do it for us. You see, we've got another subject waiting (looks at watch) who is supposed to be in that other condition. Now Professor ..., who is in charge of this experiment, suggested that perhaps we could take a chance on your doing it for us. I'll tell you what we had in mind; the thing is, if you could do it for us now, then of course you would know how to do it, and if something like this should ever come up again, that is, the regular fellow couldn't make it, and we had a subject scheduled, it would be very reassuring to us to know that we had somebody else we could call on who knew how to do it. So, if you would be willing to do this for us, we'd like to hire you to do it now and then be on call in the future, if something like this should ever happen again. We can pay you $1 ($20) for doing this for us, that is, for doing it now and then being on call. Do you think you could do that for us?

If S hesitated, E said things like, 'It will only take a few minutes; the regular person is pretty reliable; this is the first time he has missed' or 'if we needed you, we could phone you a day or two in advance; if you couldn't make it, of course we wouldn't expect you to come'. After S agreed to do it, E gave him the 'For Group B' sheet of paper and asked him to read it through again. E then paid the $1 or $20, and made out a hand-written receipt form for S to sign. He then said:

OK, the way we'll do it is this. As I said, the next subject should be here by now. I think the next one is a girl. I'll take you into the next room and introduce you to her, saying that you've just finished the experiment and that we've asked you to tell her a little about it. And what we want you to do is just sit down and get into a conversation with her and try to get across the points on that sheet of paper. I'll leave you alone and come back after a couple of minutes. OK?

E then took S into the secretary's office, where he had previously waited and where the next S was waiting. He introduced the girl and S to one another, saying that S had just finished the experiment and would tell her something about it. He then left, saying he would return in a couple of minutes. The girl, an undergraduate hired for this role, said little until S made some positive remarks about the experiment and then said she was surprised because a friend of hers had taken the experiment the week before, and had told her it was boring and that she ought to try to get out of it. Most Ss responded by saying something like, 'Oh, no, it's really very interesting. I'm sure you'll enjoy it'. After this, the girl listened quietly, accepting and agreeing to everything S told her. The discussion between S and the girl was recorded on a hidden tape recorder.

After two minutes, E returned, asked the girl to go into the experimental room, thanked S for talking to the girl, wrote down his phone number to continue the fiction about calling on him again in the future and then said, 'Look, could we check and see if that fellow from introductory psychology wants to talk to you?'

From this point on, the procedure for all three conditions was once more identical. As E and S started to walk to the office where the interviewer was, E said: 'Thanks very much for working on those tasks for us. I hope you did enjoy it. Most of our subjects tell us afterward that they found it quite interesting. You get a chance to see how you react to the tasks and so forth'. This short persuasive communication was made in all conditions in exactly the same way; theoretically, the reason for doing it was to make it easier for anyone who wanted to persuade himself that the tasks had, indeed, been enjoyable.

When they arrived at the office, *E* asked the interviewer if he wanted to talk to *S*, which, of course he did. *E* shook hands with *S*, said goodbye, and left. The interviewer was always unaware of which condition *S* was in. The interview comprised four questions, on each of which *S* was first encouraged to talk before rating his opinion on an 11-point scale. The questions were as follows:

1 Were the tasks interesting and enjoyable? In what way? In what way were they not? Would you rate how you feel about them on a scale from −5 to +5, where −5 means they were extremely dull and boring, +5 means they were extremely interesting and enjoyable, and zero means they were neutral, neither interesting nor uninteresting.
2 Did the experiment give you an opportunity to learn about your own ability to perform these tasks? In what way? In what way not? Would you rate how you feel about this on a scale from 0 to 10, where 0 means you learned nothing and 10 means you learned a great deal.
3 From what you know about the experiment and the tasks involved in it, would you say the experiment was measuring anything important? That is, do you think the results may have scientific value? In what way? In what way not? Would you rate your opinion on this matter on a scale from 0 to 10, where 0 means the results have no scientific value or importance and 10 means they have a great deal of value and importance.
4 Would you have any desire to participate in another similar experiment? Why? Why not? Would you rate your desire to participate in a similar experiment again on a scale from −5 to +5, where −5 means you would definitely dislike to participate, +5 means you would definitely like to participate and 0 means you have no particular feeling about it one way or another.

At the end of the interview, *S* was asked what he thought the experiment was about, and was then asked directly if he was suspicious of anything and, if so, what. *S* was then taken back to the experimental room, where *E* was waiting together with the girl who had posed as the waiting *S* (except in the control group). The true purpose of the experiment was then explained to *S* in detail and the *Ss* in the $1 and $20 conditions were asked to return the money; without exception, all *Ss* did this willingly.

The data for 11 of the 71 *Ss* had to be discarded for the following reasons:

1 Five *Ss* (three in the $1 and two in the $20 condition) indicated in the interview that they were suspicious that the true purpose of the experiment was to tell the girl that the experiment was fun.

2 Two *Ss* (both in the $1 condition) told the girl that they had been hired, that the experiment was really boring but they were supposed to say it was fun.
3 Three *Ss* (one in the $1 and two in the $20 condition) refused to take the money and be hired.
4 One *S* (in the $1 condition), immediately after having talked to the girl, demanded her phone number, saying he would call her and explain things, and also told *E* he wanted to wait until she was finished so he could tell her about it.

These 11 *Ss* were run through the total experiment anyway and the experiment was explained to them afterwards. However, their data are not included in the analysis, which consists of 20 *Ss* in each of the three conditions.

Results

The major results are summarized in table 9.1, which lists, separately for each of the three conditions, the average rating given by *Ss* to each question on the interview; each question was intended to measure different things. In all the comparisons, the control condition should be regarded as a baseline from which to evaluate the results in the other two conditions; it gives us, essentially, the reactions of *Ss* to the tasks and their opinions about the experiment as falsely explained to them, without the experimental introduction of dissonance.

Table 9.1   Average ratings on interview questions for each condition

	Experimental condition		
Questions on interview	**control** **n = 20**	**$1** **n = 20**	**$20** **n = 20**
How enjoyable tasks were (rated from −5 to +5)	−0.45	+1.35	−0.05
How much they learned (rated from 0 to 10)	3.08	2.80	3.15
Scientific importance (rated from 0 to 10)	5.60	6.45	5.18
Participate in similar experiment (rated from −5 to +5)	−0.62	+1.20	−0.25

How enjoyable the tasks were

This was the most important result to the experiment because they are the ones most directly relevant to the specific dissonance which was experimentally created. The control group results confirmed that the tasks were rather boring and monotonous (−0.45) but in the other two conditions, *Ss* told someone the tasks were interesting and enjoyable. The resulting dissonance could, of course, most directly be reduced by persuading themselves that they were, indeed, interesting and enjoyable. In the $1 condition, since the magnitude of dissonance was high, the pressure to reduce it would also be high; the average rating of $+1.35$ was significantly different from the control condition at the 0.02 level for a two-tailed test ($t = 2.48$).

In the \$20 condition, where less dissonance was experimentally created, there is correspondingly less evidence of dissonance reduction, the average rating of -0.05 is not significantly higher than the control condition. The difference between the \$1 and \$20 conditions is significant at the 0.03 level for a two-tailed test ($t = 2.22$). In short, when *Ss* were induced, by offer of reward, to say something contrary to their private opinions, this private opinion tended to change so as to correspond more closely with what they had said. The greater the reward offered (beyond what was necessary to elicit the behaviour), the smaller was the effect.

Desire to participate in a similar experiment

This was less directly related to the dissonance that was experimentally created, but the more interesting and enjoyable they felt the tasks were, the greater would be their desire to participate in a similar experiment. In fact, the results are in the same direction, and the size of the mean differences as large as on the first question. However, the difference between the \$1 condition ($+1.20$) and the control condition (-0.62) is significant only at the 0.08 level for a two-tailed test ($t = 1.78$), and the difference between the \$1 condition and the \$20 condition (-0.25) is only significant at the 0.15 level, for a two-tailed test ($t = 1.46$).

The scientific importance of the experiment

Another way in which the experimentally created dissonance could be reduced would be for *S* to magnify the importance of the cognition that it was necessary for the experiment that they should say what they did to the waiting girl. The more scientifically important they considered the experiment to be, the less was the total dissonance. The results are weakly in line with what one would expect if dissonance were partially reduced in this way. The difference between the \$1 and \$20 conditions reaches the 0.08 level of significance for a two-tailed test ($t = 1.79$), while that between the \$1 and control conditions is not significant ($t = 1.21$). The finding that the \$20 condition is actually lower than the control conditions is undoubtedly a matter of chance ($t = 0.58$).

How much they learned from the experiment

There are only negligible differences between the conditions, which confirms the expectation that the question had nothing to do with the dissonance and could not be used for dissonance reduction.

Discussion of a possible alternative explanation

Janis and King (1954, 1956) proposed an explanation for their own findings in terms of the self-convincing effect of mental rehearsal and thinking up new arguments by the person who had to improvise a speech. Kelman (1950), in attempting to explain the unexpected finding that the persons who complied in the moderate-reward condition changed their opinion more than in the high-reward condition, also proposed a similar explanation. Can this explanation serve as an alternative to the cognitive dissonance explanation being offered here?

It would mean that, for some reason, *Ss* in the $1 condition worked harder at telling the waiting girl that the tasks were fun and enjoyable, i.e. they may have rehearsed it more mentally, thought up more ways of saying it, may have said it more convincingly and so on. Wouldn't this have been more likely in the $20 condition, since they were paid more?

The conversations between each *S* and the girl were tape-recorded, transcribed and then rated, by two independent raters, on five dimensions (unaware of which condition each *S* was in). The inter-rate reliability ranged from 0.61 to 0.88, with an average of 0.71. The five ratings were:

1 The content of what *S* said *before* the girl remarked that her friend told her it was boring. The stronger *S*'s positive statements about the tasks and the more ways in which he said they were interesting and enjoyable, the higher the rating.
2 The content of what *S* said *after* the girl made the above-mentioned remark. This was rated in the same way as for the content before the remark.
3 A similar rating of the overall content of what *S* said.
4 A rating of how persuasive and convincing *S* was in what he said, and how he said it.
5 A rating of the amount of time *S* spent discussing the tasks as opposed to digressing.

The mean ratings for the $1 and $20 conditions (based on average ratings of the two raters) are shown in table 9.2. In all cases, the $20 condition is slightly higher and only in the case of 'amount of time'

Table 9.2 *Average ratings of discussion between subject and girl*

Dimension rated	Condition		
	$1	$20	*t*-value
Content before remark by girl (rated from 0 to 5)	2.26	2.62	1.08
Content after remark by girl (rated from 0 to 5)	1.63	1.75	0.11
Overall content (rated from 0 to 5)	1.89	2.19	1.08
Persuasiveness conviction (rated from 0 to 10)	4.79	5.50	0.99
Time spent on topic (rated from 0 to 10)	6.74	8.19	1.80

does the difference even approach significance. We are certainly justified in concluding that *Ss* in the $1 condition did not improvise more or act more convincingly. Hence, the alternative explanation can be ruled out.

Summary

Recently, Festinger (1957) has proposed a theory of cognitive dissonance. Two predictions from this theory are tested here:

1 If a person is induced to do or say something contrary to his private opinion, there will be a tendency for him to change his opinion so as to bring it into line with what was done or said.
2 The larger the pressure to elicit the overt behaviour (beyond the minimum needed to elicit it), the weaker will be the above-mentioned tendency.

A laboratory experiment was designed to test these hypotheses: subjects were subjected to a boring experience and then paid to tell someone that the experience had been interesting and enjoyable. The amount of money paid was varied. The private opinions of the *Ss* concerning the experiences were then assessed. The results strongly support the theory of cognitive dissonance.

Commentary

Aim and nature

The aim of the study is to test Festinger's (1957) cognitive dissonance theory through a controlled laboratory experiment. Specifically, the two related hypotheses being tested were:

1 A person induced to do or say something contrary to his private opinion will tend to change his opinion so as to bring it in line with what was done or said.
2 The larger the pressure to elicit the overt behaviour (beyond the minimum needed to elicit it), the weaker will be the above-mentioned tendency.

The experiment involves three groups/conditions: control, $1 and $20 (and is often referred to as the '$1–$20' experiment).

Background and context

Although it is clear how the hypotheses are derived from the theory, there is an unstated assumption which makes it even clearer, and which is a fundamental one as far as the theory is concerned. This is the principle of cognitive consistency, whereby human beings are seen as internally active information processors, who sort through and modify a large number of cognitive elements in order to achieve some kind of cognitive coherence. It is really a part of human nature, a basic human need, along with physiological ones, and so cognitive dissonance theory can be seen as not just a theory of attitude change, but a theory of human motivation too: people need cognitive consistency. Two other major theories of cognivitive consistency are

Osgood and Tannenbaum's (1955) congruity theory and Heider's (1958) balance theory.

Dissonance is a negative drive state, a state of 'psychological discomfort or tension', which motivates the individual to reduce it by achieving consonance; a major way of achieving this is through changing one of our cognitions, namely our attitude.

The theory has been tested under three main headings: (*i*) dissonance following a decision (e.g. having to choose between two equally attractive alternatives, with the prediction that we will devalue the alternative we have rejected); (*ii*) dissonance resulting from effort (e.g. deciding to put yourself through an embarrassing or stressful situation, only for it to turn out to be trivial and not warranting the embarrassment/stress, with the prediction that the situation will be judged as more important and worthwhile the greater the embarrassment, etc.), and (*iii*) engaging in counter-attitudinal behaviour, which is where the $1–$20 experiment fits in.

Evaluation

1 One of the strengths of dissonance theory is that the predictions it makes are counter-intuitive (i.e. contrary to what 'common sense' would predict): the 'common-sense' prediction based on the $1–$20 experiment is, surely, that the subjects offered the $20 would be more likely to change their attitude towards liking the task than the $1 group. The results, of course, go in the opposite direction. These findings have been confirmed by several studies in which children are given either a mild or severe threat not to play with an attractive toy (e.g. Aronson & Carlsmith, 1963; Freedman, 1965; Turner & Wright, 1965). If children obey a *mild* threat, they will experience *greater* dissonance because it is more difficult for them to justify their behaviour compared with children receiving a severe threat. Similarly, the *$1* group experience the *greater* dissonance. How can you *justify* lying about the boring task for a mere $1? The solution is to see the task as actually being interesting!

2 What is referred to here as the 'common-sense' view is, essentially, that proposed by Incentive Theory (based on the notion of reward). It seems that both theories can be shown to be true – but under different conditions – and a key variable is whether or not the counter-attitudinal behaviour is *volitional* (voluntary), i.e. when we feel we have acted of our own free will. If we believe we had no 'choice', there is no dissonance and, hence, no attitude change.

But the Festinger and Carlsmith study is called 'Cognitive consequences of *forced compliance*'; surely this implies *lack* of choice and, therefore, you would expect incentive theory (and *not* cognitive dissonance) to hold. The title is rather misleading, since lying to the waiting stooge was, in theory anyway, something the subject chose to do, albeit as a favour to *E*. This is shown by the fact that three *Ss* did, indeed, refuse to take the money and be hired. So the dilemma for the $1 subjects was 'I chose to lie for just $1! How can I justify that?'.

A study by Freedman (1963) brings out the difference between 'voluntary' and 'involuntary' behaviour very clearly. He asked subjects to perform a dull task after *first* informing them that either (*i*) the data would be definitely of *no* value to *E* since his experiment was already completed, or (*ii*) the data would be of *great* value to him. Dissonance theory would predict that group (i) would enjoy the task more because they would experience the greater dissonance (as a result of doing it *knowing* that the data would be of no value). The results supported the dissonance prediction. But in a parallel experiment, the information regarding the value of the data to *E* was withheld untol *after Ss* had completed the task, so here, the subjects had no choice and the results went in the direction predicted by incentive theory: group (ii) subjects enjoyed the task much more (rewarded with gratitude) while group (i) subjects could reason 'If I'd known, I wouldn't have done it', and so experienced no dissonance. The findings were supported by Linder *et al.* (1967).

3 Another variable which influences dissonance (and which interacts with voluntary/involuntary behaviour) is degree of *commitment*. Carlsmith *et al.* (1966) used a procedure similar to the $1–$20 study and confirmed Festinger and Carlsmith's findings. However, the dissonance effect was only found under conditions where subjects lied in a highly committing, face-to-face situation (they had to make an identifiable video recording); where they merely had to write an essay and were assured of complete anonymity, then an incentive effect occurred. This face-to-face variable was not manipulated in the original study.

4 A major critic of dissonance theory has been Bem. He claims that dissonance as such is neither a necessary nor sufficient explanation, and he rejects any reference to hypothetical, intervening variables. According to his Self-Perception theory (1965, 1967), any self-report of an attitude is an inference from observation of one's own behaviour and the situation in which it occurs. If the situation contains cues (e.g. offer of a large, $20, incentive) which imply that we might have behaved that way regardless of how we personally felt (we lie about the task being interesting even though it was boring), then we make no inference that our behaviour reflected our true attitudes. But in the absence of obvious situational pressures ($1 conditon), we assume that our attitudes are what our behaviour suggests they are. Put another way, the $20 subjects can easily make a *situational attribution* ('I did it for the money') whereas the $1 subjects had to make a *dispositional attribution* ('I did it because I really enjoyed it'). Bem's way of testing his theory is a form of experiment he callse *Interpersonal Simulation*, in which he presents so-called 'observer' subjects with a summary description of the procedure used in some well-known dissonance experiment (e.g. the $1–$20), telling them of the *Ss* agreement to perform the counter-attitudinal act requested by *E*, and then asking them to estimate the original *Ss* final attitudinal response. The 'observer's' estimate usually matches the original *Ss* responses quite closely, and shows the predicted effects of different levels of incentive; so when told that *Ss* were offered $20, they are less likely to assume a match between the *S*'s behaviour and their attitude. However, it has not fulfilled its promise as a general alternative to dissonance theory (Eiser & van der Pligt, 1988). Empirically, it is far from clear that Bem's *Ss* were using the *same* information as the original *Ss*; on the contrary, when *Ss* are given further details of the original procedures than contained in Bem's summaries, their estimates tend to be *more* discrepant from the original *S*'s responses (Jones *et al.*, 1968; Piliavin *et al.*, 1969).

Eiser and van der Pligt (1988) believe that, conceptually, it is very difficult to distinguish the hypothesis that people change their self-reports of attitudes so that these self-reports correspond more closely to what their behaviour would be taken to imply (self-perception), from the alternative hypothesis that they do so in order to feel they made the correct decision in terms of what they believed and wanted all the time (dissonance). Greenwald (1975) claims that there is no experimental procedure which could unambiguously choose between these two alternatives.

Perhaps, as with dissonance and incentive theories, both processes operate, but to different extents in different contexts. Fazio *et al.* (1977) argue, for example, that dissonance may apply when people behave contrary to their initial attitude, while self-perception may apply better where their behaviour and initial attitude are broadly consistent.

5 Another general issue is whether what matters is our *own* inferences about the way we behave, or the inferences we feel *others* might draw about us ('impression management theory'). Tedeschi *et al.* (1971) argue that the effects of many dissonance experiments might not reflect genuine cases of 'private' attitude change but rather an adoption of a public response that protects Ss against the possible accusation of insincerity (i.e. the need is to *appear* consistent rather than a drive to actually *be* consistent). So Ss might pretend they really believed the task was interesting so that it wouldn't appear as though they had let themselves be 'bribed'.

But how would this argument distinguish the $1 from the $20 Ss? Surely the $20 Ss would have *more* motivation for pretending and so should rate the task as much more interesting than the $1 Ss – the reverse of the actual findings! Again, S's final attitudinal responses were elicited by a separate E, unaware of their initial attitudes, actual behaviour or which condition they were in.

Impression-management theorists (e.g. Schlenker, 1982; Tedeschi & Rosenfeld, 1981) no longer tend to claim that changes in attitude responses are a mere pretence. Instead, much attitude change is seen as an attempt to avoid social anxiety and embarrassment, or to protect positive views of one's own identity. Accordingly, the roots of the 'tension' hypothesized by Festinger may be in peoples' *social* concerns with how others might evaluate them, and how they should evaluate themselves.

6 An objection that can be made to experiments like the $1–$20 study is that the reasoning involved is circular: (*i*) the only evidence for the greater dissonance of the $1 subjects is the fact that they rated the task as more interesting; (*ii*) the fact that they rated the task as more interesting is evidence of the greater dissonance. Is there any *independent* evidence for the existence of dissonance? What kind of evidence do we require/would we accept? What about physiological? Croyle and Cooper (1983) found evidence for more persistent increase in physiological arousal as measured by GSR (Galvanic Skin Response) in Ss who wrote a counter-attitudinal essay under high-choice as against low-choice instructions, or who wrote an essay consistent with their own opinion. However, feelings of unpleasant tension may also be produced by factors less directly related to the notion of dissonance, e.g. the belief that a decision they have made will have bad consequences (Cooper & Fazio, 1984). According to such an interpretation, attitude change in such experiments should depend both on the amount of arousal experienced by the S (from whatever sources) *and* on how the S interprets/explains this arousal.

Support for this notion comes from a study (Zanna & Cooper, 1974) in which Ss wrote a counter-attitudinal essay under instructions which implied either high or low freedom of choice: consistent with previous findings, the prediction that high-choice Ss change their opinions more than low-choice Ss was confirmed. The novel feature of the experiment was that Ss were also given a placebo pill, which they were either told would make them feel tense or relaxed or told nothing about it at all. The dissonance theory prediction was upheld when Ss were given no information, and even more strongly when they were told it would relax them. But when Ss were told the pill would make them feel tense, no difference between the high- and low-choice conditions was found.

These results unite themes from a variety of theoretical perspectives: (*i*) there is evidence for the existence of an internal state of arousal (Festinger's dissonance); (*ii*) there is also evidence of the dependence of attitude change on S's own interpretations of their feelings and behaviour (broadly compatible with Bem's self-perception theory) (see chapter 19).

7 It is arguable that the dissonance was produced *not* by having to lie to the stooge as such, but the extra time and effort involved. The prediction may be the same either way (i.e. that $1 *Ss* would experience more dissonance), but if *Ss* had been asked to tell the truth, might there still have been a dissonance effect (on the grounds that spending even more time talking about how boring it was is inconsistent with already having wasted time doing it)? A replication could involve two extra groups, each asked to tell the truth, one for $1 and the other for $20. Would you expect greater dissonance among the $1 group again?

8 Given that all the *Ss* were male and the stooge was female, could there be an interaction effect between (*i*) the size of the reward and (*ii*) the gender of the stooge? Perhaps lying to a female is seen (or was in 1957) as more acceptable – by males – than to a fellow male: but much less so for $1 than $20. And holding gender constant, would lying to an *attractive* female be more dissonant than lying to an unattractive one, and how would this interact with size of reward?

9 In addition to the customary deceit involved, the *S* (in the two experimental conditions) was being asked to lie (as a favour to *E* in the context of a psychological experiment), and this could be objected to on moral grounds, although debriefing did occur.

Exercises

1 What kind of experimental design was used?

2 What statistical test was used and is it the only one which could have been used?

3 Both hypotheses are referred to as two-tailed (see Summary). However, as it stands, could **2** be one-tailed? Give your reasons.

4 Why was it important that the interviewer did not know which conditions *Ss* were being tested under?

5 What were the independent and dependent variables?

6 What statistical test is used to measure the reliability of ratings between the two raters of *S*'s behaviour?

7 Were the *Ss* a biased sample? Give your reasons.

8 How do you explain the Zanna and Cooper (1974) findings?

Behavioural study of obedience

Journal of Abnormal and Social Psychology, Vol. 67, pp. 371–8

Obedience is as basic an element in the structure of social life as one can point to. Some system of authority is a requirement of all communal living, and it is only the man living in isolation who is not forced to respond, through defiance or submission, to the commands of others. Obedience, as a determinant of behaviour, is of particular relevance to our time. It has been reliably established that from 1939 to 1945 millions of innocent persons were slaughtered on command; gas chambers were built, deathcamps were guarded, daily quotas of corpses were produced with the same efficiency as the manufacture of appliances. These inhumane policies may have originated in the mind of a single person, but they could only be carried out on a massive scale if a very large number of persons obeyed orders.

Obedience is the psychological mechanism which links individual action to political purpose, the dispositional cement which binds men to systems of authority. Facts of recent history and observation in daily life suggest that, for many people, obedience may be a deeply ingrained behaviour tendency, indeed, a pre-potent impulse overriding training in ethics, sympathy and moral conduct. C. P. Snow (1961) points to its importance when he writes:

> When you think of the long and gloomy history of man, you will find more hideous crimes have been committed in the name of obedience than have ever been committed in the name of rebellion. If you doubt that, read William Shirer's 'Rise and Fall of the Third Reich'. The German Officer Corps were brought up in the most rigorous code of obedience ... in the name of obedience they were party to, and assisted in, the most wicked large-scale actions in the history of the world.

While the particular form of obedience involved in the present study has its antecedents in these episodes, it must not be thought that all obedience entails acts of aggression against others; it may also be ennobling and educative and refer to acts of charity and kindness, as well as to destruction.

General procedure

Milgram (1961) devised a procedure which consists of ordering a naïve subject to administer electric shocks to a victim. A simulated shock generator is used, with 30 clearly marked voltage levels ranging from 15 to 450 volts; the instrument bears verbal designations that range from 'slight shock' to 'danger: severe shock'. The responses of the victim, who is a trained confederate of the experimenter, are standardised. The orders to administer shocks are given to the naïve subject in the context of a 'learning experiment', ostensibly set up to study the effects of punishment on memory. As the experiment proceeds, the naïve subject is commanded to administer increasingly more intense shocks, even to the level marked 'danger: severe shock'. Internal resistances become stronger, and, at a certain point, the subject refuses to go on with the experiment; behaviour prior to this is considered 'obedience', in that the subject complies with the commands of the experimenter. A quantitative value is assigned to the subject's performance based on the maximum intensity shock he is willing to administer before he refuses to participate further. The crux of the study is to systematically vary the factors believed to alter the degree of obedience to the experimental commands.

The technique allows important variables to be manipulated at several points in the experiment, including aspects of the authority figure, content and form of command, instrumentalities for its execution, target object, general social setting, etc. So the problem is not one of designing increasingly numerous experimental conditions but of selecting those which best illuminate the *process* of obedience from the sociopsychological standpoint.

Related studies

The investigation bears an important relation to philosophical analyses of obedience and authority (Arendt, 1958; Friedrich, 1958, Weber, 1947), an early experimental study of obedience by Frank (1944), studies in 'authoritarianism' (Adorno, Frenkel-Brunswik, Levinson & Sanford, 1950; Rokeach, 1961), and a recent series of analytic and empirical studies in social power (Cartwright, 1959). It owes much to the long concern with *suggestion* in social psychology, both in its normal froms (e.g. Binet, 1900) and in its clinical manifestations (Charcot, 1881). But it derives primarily from direct observation of the ubiquitous and indispensable fact of social life that when people are commanded by a legitimate authority, they usually obey.

Method

Subjects

The subjects were 40 males aged 20 to 50, drawn from New Haven and the surrounding communities, obtained by a newspaper and

Table 10.1   Distribution of age and occupational types in the experiment

Occupations	20–29 years n	30–39 years n	40–50 years n	Percentage of total (occupation)
Workers skilled and unskilled	4	5	6	37.5
Sales, business and white collar	3	6	7	40.0
Professional	1	5	3	22.5
Percentage of total (age)	20	40	40	

Total *n* = 40

direct mail advertisement which asked for volunteers to participate in a study of memory and learning at Yale University. They represented a wide range of occupations, including postal clerks, high-school teachers, salesmen, engineers and labourers. Their education ranged from one who had not finished elementary school to those who had doctorates and other professional degrees. They were paid $4.50 for their participation in the experiment but there were told that payment was simply for coming to the laboratory, regardless of what happened after they arrived.

Personnel and locale

The experiment was conducted on the grounds of Yale University in the elegant interaction laboratory. (This detail is relevant to the perceived legitimacy of the experiment; in further variations the experiment was dissociated from the university, with consequences for performance.) The role of experimenter was played by a 31-year-old high-school biology teacher; his manner was impassive and his appearance somewhat stern throughout, and he was dressed in a grey technician's coat. The victim was played by a 47-year-old accountant, trained for the role, of Irish–American stock, whom most observers found mild-mannered and likeable.

Procedure

One naïve subject and one victim (an accomplice) performed in each experiment. A cover story was invented in order to justify the administration of electric shock by the naïve subject; after a general introduction on the presumed relation between punishment and learning, subjects were told:

> But actually, we know *very little* about the effect of punishment on learning, because almost no truly scientific studies have been made of it in human beings.
> For instance, we don't know how *much* punishment is best for learning, and we don't know how much difference it makes as to who is giving the punishment, whether an adult learns best from

a younger or an older person than himself, or many things of that sort.

So in this study we are bringing together a number of adults of different occupations and ages. And we're asking some of them to be teachers and some of them to be learners. We want to find out just what effect different people have on each other as teachers and learners, and also what effect *punishment* will have on learning in this situation.

Therefore, I'm going to ask one of you to be the teacher here tonight and the other one to be the learner.

Does either of you have a preference?

Subjects then drew slips of paper from a hat to determine who would be the teacher and who the learner; it was rigged so that the naïve subject was always the teacher and the accomplice always the learner (both slips contained the word 'teacher'). The teacher and learner were immediately taken to an adjacent room and the learner was strapped into an 'electric chair' apparatus. The experimenter explained that the straps were to prevent excessive movement while the learner was being shocked; the effect was to make it impossible for him to escape from the situation. An electrode was attached to the learner's wrist and electrode paste was applied 'to avoid blisters and burns'. Subjects were told that the electrode was attached to the shock generator in the adjoining room.

In order to improve credibility, the experimenter declared, in response to a question by the learner: 'Although the shocks can be extremely painful, they cause no permanent tissue damage'.

Learning task The lesson administered by the subject was a paired-associate learning task; the subject read a series of word pairs to the learner and then read the first word of the pair along with four terms. The learner had to indicate which of the four terms had originally been paired with the first word. He communicated his answer by pressing one of four switches in front of him, which in turn lit up one of four numbered quadrants in an answer box, located above the shock generator.

Shock generator The instrument panel consisted of 30 lever switches set in a horizontal line. Each switch is clearly labelled with a voltage designation ranging from 15 to 450 volts. There is a 15 volt increment between switches going from left to right. In addition, the following verbal designations are clearly indicated for groups of four switches: 'slight shock', 'moderate shock', 'strong shock', 'very strong shock', 'intense shock', 'extreme intensity shock', 'danger: severe shock'; (two switches after this are simply marked XXX).

When a switch is depressed, a pilot light corresponding to each switch is illuminated in bright red, an electric buzzing is heard, an electric blue light ('voltage energiser') flashes, the dial on the voltage meter swings to the right and various relay clicks are sounded. The upper left-hand corner of the generator is labelled 'Shock Generator, Type ZLB, Dyson Instrument Company, Waltham, Mass. Output 15 volts–450 volts'.

The generator was very authentic in appearance and no subject suspected it was merely simulated.

Sample shock   Each naïve subject is given a sample shock on the generator of 45 volts, applied by pressing the third switch; it has its source in a 45-volt battery wired into the generator. This further convinces the subject of the authenticity of the generator.

Shock instructions   The subject is told to administer a shock to the learner each time he gives a wrong answer. Moreover – and this is the key command – he is told to 'move one level higher on the shock generator each time the learner flashes a wrong answer'. Also, he must announce the voltage level before administering a shock, intended to continually remind subjects of the increasing intensity of shocks administered to the learner.

Preliminary and regular run   Pre-tests revealed that the procedure of reading words and administering shocks requires some practise before it can be handled smoothly. A preliminary series of ten words is therefore read to the learner, with seven producing incorrect answers and hence shock, the maximum shock being 105 volts (moderate shock). The regular run involves a second list, using the same procedure, except that the subject is told: 'When you get to the bottom of the list, repeat it over again and continue giving shocks, until the learner has learned all the pairs correctly; start from 15 volts and increase the shock level one step each time the learner gives a wrong answer'.

Feedback from the victim   In all conditions the learner gives a predetermined set of responses to the word-pair test, based on a schedule of approximately three wrong answers to one correct answer. In the present experimental condition no vocal response or other sign of protest is heard from the learner until shock level 300 is reached, when he pounds on the wall of the room and this can be heard by the subjects. From this point on, the learner's answers no longer appear on the panel, and subjects usually turn to the experimenter for guidance. He instructs the subject to treat the absence of a response as a wrong answer and to shock the learner according to the usual schedule, allowing five to ten seconds before considering no response as a wrong answer. The pounding on the wall is repeated after the 315-volt shock but subsequently he is not heard from, and answers do not reappear on the panel.

Experimenter feedback   At various points during the experiment the subject may turn to the experimenter for advice on whether he should continue administering shocks, or he may indicate that he does not wish to go on. The experimenter's responses were standardized in the form of a number of 'prods', using as many as necessary to bring the subject into line.

Prod 1: 'Please continue' or 'Please go on'
Prod 2: 'The experiment requires that you continue'
Prod 3: 'It is absolutely essential that you continue'
Prod 4: 'You have no other choice, you *must* go on'

The prods were always made in sequence: only if Prod 1 was unsuccessful could Prod 2 be used, etc. If the subject continued to disobey after Prod 4, the experiment was terminated. The experimenter's tone of voice was always firm, but not impolite. The sequence was begun anew each time the subject balked or showed reluctance to follow orders.

If the subject asked if the learner could suffer permanent physical injury, a special prod ('Although the shocks may be painful, there is no permanent tissue damage, so please go on') was used (followed by Prods 2, 3 and 4 if necessary). If the subject said that the learner did not want to go on, another special prod was used ('Whether the learner likes it or not, you must go on until he has learned all the word pairs correctly. So please go on'), followed by Prods 2, 3 and 4 if necessary.

Dependent measures The primary dependent measure for any subject is the maximum shock he administers before refusing to go any further. In principle this can vary from 0 to 450; a subject who breaks off at any point prior to the highest shock level is called a *defiant* subject, while one who obeys up to 450 volts is called an *obedient* subject.

Further records With few exceptions, experimental sessions were recorded on magnetic tape; occasional photographs were taken through one-way mirrors. Notes were kept on any unusual behaviour, sometimes by additional observers. The latency and duration of shocks were measured by accurate timing devices.

Interview and dehoax Following the experiment, subjects were interviewed; open-ended questions, projective measures and attitude scales were used. It was ensured that the subject would leave the laboratory in a state of well-being; a friendly reconciliation with the victim was arranged and an attempt was made to reduce any tensions that arose as a result of the experiment.

Results

Preliminary notions It is useful to consider how others predicted that the subjects would perform. 14 Yale psychology majors were asked to reflect carefully on the experimental situation and predicted that only an insignificant minority of '100 Americans of diverse occupations, and ranging in age from 20 to 50 years' would go through to 450 volts (the estimates ranging from 0 to 3 per cent, with a mean of 1.2 per cent). When the author's colleagues were asked informally, most said that few, if any, subjects, would go beyond 'very strong shock'.

Result of experiment 1

Subjects accept situation With few exceptions, subjects were convinced of the reality of the situation, that they were administering shocks to another person and the most potent shocks were extremely painful. In the post-experimental interview, subjects were asked: 'How painful to the learner were the last few shocks that you administered to him?'. On a printed 14-point scale ranging from 'not at all painful' to 'extremely painful', the modal response was 14 ('extremely painful'), with a mean of 13.42.

Signs of extreme tension Many subjects showed signs of nervousness and especially when giving the more powerful shocks. In many cases, the degree of tension reached extremes rarely seen in sociopsychological laboratory studies: subjects sweated, trembled, stuttered, bit their lips, groaned, dug fingernails into their flesh, and these were typical, not exceptional, responses. Quite a common sign of tension was nervous laughing fits (14 out of 40 subjects) which seemed entirely out of place, even bizarre. Full-blown, uncontrollable seizures were observed for three subjects. On one occasion, a subject had such a violently convulsive seizure that the experiment had to be halted; the 46-year-old encylcopaedia salesman was extremely embarrassed. Subjects took pains to point out that they were not sadistic types, and that the laughter did not mean they enjoyed shocking the victim.

Distribution of scores As can be seen from table 10.2, the obtained distribution of scores deviates radically from the prediction. No subject stopped before administering a shock level of 300 volts (at which point the victim kicks on the wall and no longer gives answers to the teacher's questions). Of the 40 subjects, five refused to obey beyond 300 volts, four more gave one further shock before refusing, two broke off at the 330-volts level and one each at 345, 360 and 375 volts. A total of 14 subjects, therefore, defied the experimenter. It is instructive to reproduce their remarks at the point of defiance as transcribed from the tape recordings:

subject no. [0124]   I think he's trying to communicate, he's knocking . . . Well it's not fair to shock the guy . . . these are terrific volts. I don't think this is very humane . . . Oh, I can't go on with this, no, this isn't right. It's a hell of an experiment. The guy is suffering in there. No, I don't want to go on. This is crazy. [Subject refused to administer more shocks.]

subject no. [0123]   He's banging in there. I'm gonna chicken out. I'd like to continue, but I can't do that to a man . . . I'm sorry I can't do that to a man. I'll hurt his heart. You take your check . . . No really, I couldn't do it.

These subjects were often highly agitated and even angry sometimes, verbal protest was sometimes at a minimum and the subject simply got up from his chair and indicated that he wished to leave the laboratory. Even the 26 subjects who obeyed right up to 450 volts often did so under extreme stress; some expressed reluctance to administer shocks beyond the 300-volt level, and displayed fears similar to those who defied the experimenter – yet they obeyed. After the maximum shock

Table 10.2   Distribution of break-off points

Verbal designation and voltage indication	Number of subjects for whom this was maximum shock
Slight shock	
15	0
30	0
45	0
60	0
Moderate shock	
75	0
90	0
105	0
120	0
Strong shock	
135	0
150	0
165	0
180	0
Very strong shock	
195	0
210	0
225	0
240	0
Intense shock	
255	0
270	0
285	0
300	5
Extreme intensity shock	
315	4
330	2
345	1
360	1
Danger: severe shock	
375	1
390	0
405	0
420	0
XXX	
435	0
450	26

had been delivered, and the experimenter called a halt to the proceedings, many obedient subjects heaved sighs of relief, mopped their brows, rubbed their fingers over their eyes or nervously fumbled cigarettes. Some shook their heads, apparently in regret; some had remained calm throughout the experiment and showed only minimal signs of tension from beginning to end.

Discussion

Two surprising findings were (*i*) the sheer strength of obedient tendencies shown. Despite having learned from childhood that it is a fundamental breach of moral conduct to hurt another person against his will, 26 subjects abandon this principle in following the instructions of an authority who has no special powers to enforce his commands; no punishment or material loss would result from disobedience. It is clear from the remarks and outward behaviour of many subjects that in punishing the victim they are often acting against their own values, despite their deep disapproval of shocking a man who objects and its denouncement by others as stupid and senseless, the majority complied with the experimenter's commands. The serious underestimation of obedience by the 14 Yale students can be explained by their remoteness from the actual situation, and the difficulty of conveying to them the concrete details of the experiment. But the results were also unexpected to people observing the experiment through one-way mirrors; they often expressed disbelief at what they were witnessing, despite being fully acquainted with the details of the situation; and (*ii*) the extraordinary tension and emotional strain generated by the procedure. One observer related:

> I observed a mature and initially poised businessman enter the laboratory smiling and confident. Within twenty minutes he was reduced to a twitching, stuttering wreck, who was rapidly approaching a point of nervous collapse. He constantly pulled on his earlobe, and twisted his hands. At one point he pushed his fist into his forehead and muttered: 'Oh God, let's stop it'. And yet he continued to respond to every word of the experimenter, and obeyed to the end.

Any understanding of the phenomenon of obedience must rest on an analysis of the particular conditions in which it occurs. The following features of the experiment go some way to explaining the high amount of obedience observed in the situation.

1 The experiment is sponsored by and takes place on the grounds of an institution of unimpeachable reputation, Yale University. It may be reasonably presumed that the personnel are competent and reputable. The importance of these factors is now being studied by conducting a series of experiments outside of New Haven, without any visible ties to the university.

2 The experiment is, on the face of it, designed to attain a worthy purpose: advancement of our knowledge about learning and memory. Obedience occurs not as an end in itself, but as an instrumental element in a situation which the subject construes as significant and meaningful; at least he may assume that the experimenter sees its full significance.

3 The subject perceives that the victim has voluntarily submitted to the authority system of the experimenter. He is not (at first) an unwilling captive but has taken the trouble to come to the labora-

tory, presumably to aid the experimental research. That he later becomes an involuntary subject does not alter the fact that, initially, he consented to participate without qualification and so has an obligation to the experimenter.

4 The subject has also entered the experiment voluntarily and perceives himself as having an obligation to the experimenter.

5 This sense of obligation to the experimenter is strengthened by the fact of being paid for coming to the laboratory. However, this is partly cancelled out by the experimenter's statement that: 'Of course, as in all experiments, the money is yours simply for coming to the laboratory. From this point on, no matter what happens, the money is yours' (43 undergraduates at Yale acted as subjects without payment and the results are very similar to those obtained with paid subjects).

6 From the subject's standpoint, the fact that he is the teacher and the other man the learner is a purely chance occurrence (determined by drawing lots), i.e. they both had equal chance of being assigned the learner role. So the learner cannot complain on this count.

7 There is, at best, ambiguity regarding the respective rights of a psychologist and his subjects; it is unclear what a psychologist may require of his subject and when he is overstepping the mark. Because the experiment occurs in a closed setting, the subject is unable to remove these ambiguities by discussion with others; there are few standards which seem directly applicable to this situation which is a novel one for most subjects.

8 Subjects are assured that the shocks are 'painful but not dangerous', and so assume that the victim's discomfort is momentary, while the scientific gains from the experiment are lasting.

9 The victim continues to provide answers on the signal box right up to 300 volts and subjects may construe this as a sign that the victim is still willing to 'play the game'.

These features help to explain the high amount of obedience and many of the arguments raised can be reduced to testable propositions.

The following features of the experiment concern the nature of the conflict faced by the subject.

1 The subject is placed in a position where he must respond to the competing demands of two people: the experimenter and the victim; satisfaction of their demands is mutually exclusive. Also, the resolution must take the form of a highly visible action, either continuing to shock or breaking off the experiment. The subject is forced, therefore, into a public conflict for which there is no completely satisfactory solution.

2 While the demands of the experimenter carry the weight of scientific authority, the demands of the victim spring from his personal experience of pain and suffering. The two claims need not be seen as equally pressing and legitimate, since the experimenter

seeks an abstract scientific datum, while the victim cries out for relief from physical suffering caused by the subject's actions.

3 The experimenter gives the subject little time for reflection: it is only minutes after the experiment begins that the victim begins his protests. Moreover, the first protests are heard after the subject has only gone through two thirds of the shock levels, implying that the conflict will be persistent and may well become more intense as increasingly powerful shocks are given. This may well be a source of tension to the subject.

4 More generally, the conflict stems from the opposition of two deeply ingrained behaviour dispositions: first, the tendency not to harm other people, and second, the tendency to obey those whom we perceive to be legitimate authorities.

Commentary

Aim and nature

The article describes an experimental study of obedience and has become one of the most famous (and indeed, infamous) in the whole of social psychology (indeed, psychology as a whole). Reactions to it have been quite emotional and Milgram has been severely criticized, both on ethical and methodological grounds (see below). The study should be understood in the context of a whole series of experiments, of which this was the original. It represents a kind of baseline situation, with subsequent experiments systematically varying different variables, intended to throw light on the findings of the original. The obedience rate in these later studies is always compared with the 65 per cent who went all the way up to 450 volts. But it should be stressed that this series was not planned; Milgram was as shocked as anybody by the original findings, which were totally unexpected, but which had to be explored further. Observation is also used as a technique for collecting data within the overall experimental design. Milgram states that tape-recorders and photographs were used to record unusual behaviour on the part of subjects (sometimes by additional observers via one-way mirrors). Later studies also made film records of the proceedings and all subjects were interviewed immediately after the experiment. All these techniques generate *qualitative* data which complement the *quantitative* data, which are the number of subjects continuing to shock up to different shock levels.

Context and background

In a very real sense, it is the horrific events of the Nazi concentration camps which form the background to the study. Milgram, originally, was attempting to test 'the Germans are different' hypothesis, used by historians to explain the systematic destruction of millions of Jews, Poles and others in the 1930s and 1940s. It maintains that (*i*) Hitler could not have put his evil plans into effect without the cooperation of thousands of others; and (*ii*) the Germans have a basic character defect, namely a readiness to obey without question, regardless of the acts demanded by the authority figure, and that it is this readiness to obey which provided Hitler with the cooperation he needed. It is really the second part of this hypothesis which Milgram was trying to test. He had originally planned to take the experiment to Germany and the New Haven experiment was really intended as a 'pilot', a dummy run. The results clearly made this unnecessary: the 'Germans are different' hypothesis had clearly been shown to be false.

Evaluation

1 The experiment (and, by implication, those in the series which followed it) have been condemned on ethical grounds and severely criticized also on methodological grounds. An appendix in Milgram's 'Obedience to Authority' (1974) is devoted to the ethical criticisms, and Milgram's defence and the following points are taken from that appendix.

2 Baumrind (1964), one of Milgram's harshest critics, expressed concern for the welfare of the subjects: were adequate measures taken to protect them from the undoubted stress and emotional conflict which they experienced? Milgram replies that this presupposes that the outcome of the experiment was expected; she (Baumrind) is confusing the (unanticipated) outcome with the basic experimental procedure. The production of stress was *not* an intended and deliberate effect of the manipulation; it was discussed with colleagues beforehand, and none anticipated the reactions that occurred. You cannot know your results in advance! He maintains that:

> 'Understanding grows because we examine situations in which the end is unknown. An investigator unwilling to accept this degree of risk must give up the idea of scientific inquiry.'

In addition, there was every reason to believe that subjects would refuse to obey beyond the point where the victim protested.

3 Milgram asks whether the criticism is based as much on the nature of the (unanticipated) findings as the procedure itself. Aronson (1988) asks if we would question the ethics if none of the *Ss* had given shocks beyond the 'moderate shock level'. Apparently not. It seems that individual's ratings of the 'harmfulness' of the procedure varies according to the type of outcome they believe to have happened. Could it be that underlying the criticism of Milgram is the shock and horror of the 'banality of evil' (the sub-title of Hannah Arendt's book on the Israeli trial of Adolf Eichmann, the Nazi war-criminal)? To believe that 'ordinary people' could do what Eichmann did – or what Milgram's subjects did – is far less acceptable than that Eichmann was an inhuman monster, or that experimental subjects were put under immorally high levels of stress by an inhuman psychologist!

4 A very thorough de-briefing ('de-hoax') was carefully carried out with all subjects during which (*i*) they were reunited with the unharmed actor–victim; (*ii*) they were assured that no shock had been delivered; (*iii*) Milgram and the subject had an extended discussion. Obedient subjects were assured that their behaviour was entirely normal and that their feelings of conflict and tension were shared by other subjects, while defiant subjects were supported in their decision to disobey the experimenter. All subjects were told they would receive (and did) a comprehensive report when all the experiments were over detailing the procedure and the results, and they were also sent a follow-up questionnaire regarding their participation. There was a 92 per cent response rate and the only difference between those who responded and those who did not was that younger people were overrepresented in the latter. Nearly 84 per cent said they were glad or very glad to have participated while less than 2 per cent said they were sorry or very sorry. 80 per cent felt that more experiments of this kind should be carried out and 74 per cent had learned something of personal importance.

Milgram points out that the de-briefing and assessment were carried out as a matter of course and *not* stimulated by the distress the subjects (unexpectedly) experienced.

5 One year following the completion of the experiments, an impartial psychiatrist interviewed 40 subjects, several of whom had experienced extreme stress; none showed any signs of having been psychologically harmed or having suffered any traumatic reactions.

6 In reply to Baumrind's criticism that the experimenter *made* the subject shock the victim, Milgram states that he started with the belief that every person who came to the laboratory was free to accept or reject the dictates of authority. Far from being a passive creature, subjects are active, choosing adults.

7 Criticism also comes in a play called 'The Dogs of Pavlov' by Dannie Abse (1971), in which the obedience experiment is a central theme. Kurt, the main character, repudiates the experimenter for treating him as a guinea-pig. In the play's introduction, Abse condemns the illusions used in the experiment but at the same time seems to admire its dramatic quality.

Milgram's reply is included in the foreword to the play. Just as illusion is necessary in theatre and is accepted by the audience, so it is in the experiment. Misinformation is used, 'illusion is used when necessary in order to set the stage for the revelation of certain difficult-to-get-at truths, and these procedures are justified for one reason only: they are in the end accepted and endorsed by those who are exposed to them . . .' (i.e. feedback in interviews with subjects).

> 'The central moral justification for allowing a procedure of the sort used in my experiment is that it is judged acceptable by those who have taken part in it. Moreover, it was the salience of this fact throughout that constituted the chief moral warrant for the continuation of the experiments.'

He goes on to say that any criticism of the experiment which does not take into account the tolerant reactions of the participants is hollow. 'Again, the participant, rather than the external critic, must be the ultimate source of judgement'.

8 This moral point relates to a central methodological dilemma faced by social psychologists in particular: how to make their experiments have maximum impact on subjects without sacrificing control over the situation (Aronson, 1988). Aronson and Carlsmith distinguished between two kinds of realism: (*i*) if an experiment has an impact on the subjects, forces them to take the situation seriously and involves them in the procedures, it has achieved *experimental realism*; (*ii*) the similarity of the laboratory experiment to the events which commonly happen to people in the real world is referred to as *mundane realism*. Aronson (1988) believes that a confusion between these is often responsible for the criticism that experiments are artificial and worthless, because they do not reflect the world. He claims that Milgram's experiments are high in (i) but lower in (ii). There is no doubt that it was taken very seriously by subjects, and Baumrind's criticism in fact testifies to this. But Milgram would say it has great (ii) also: he argues that the essential process involved in complying to the demands of an authority figure is the same, whether the setting is the contrived one of the laboratory or a naturally occurring one outside the laboratory. Is there any evidence to support the claim? The famous field study of nurses obeying doctors' instructions (Hofling *et al.*, 1966) would seem to support Milgram's argument that his experiments also have mundane realism.

9 On the positive side, Erikson (1968) praises Milgram for making 'a momentous and meaningful contribution to our knowledge of human behaviour . . . To engage in such studies as Milgram has requires strong men with strong scientific faith and a willingness to discover that to man himself, not to 'the devil' belongs the responsibility for, and the control of, his inhumane actions'. Etzioni (1968) believes the experiments are of major significance and that they combine 'meaningful, interesting humanistic study' with 'accurate, empirical, quantitative research'. Finally, Elms (1972) rates the experiment as 'some of the most morally significant research in modern psychology'.

Exercises

1 Which variables in the experimental situation were varied in subsequent experiments in order to determine precisely what accounts for such high levels of obedience? (Milgram mentions one himself).

2 Does the importance of the experiment outweigh the moral objections (assuming, of course, that you accept the moral criticisms)?

3 What kind of a sample were Milgram's subjects?

IRVING M. PILIAVIN, JUDITH RODIN AND JANE ALLYN PILIAVIN (1969)

Good Samaritanism; an underground phenomenon?

Journal of Personality and Social Psychology, Vol. 13, No. 4, pp. 289–99

A field experiment was performed to investigate the effect of several variables on helping behaviour, using the express trains of the New York 8th Avenue Independent subway as a laboratory on wheels. Four teams of students, each comprising a victim, model and two observers, staged standard collapses in which type of victim (drunk or ill), race of victim (black or white) and presence or absence of a model were varied. Data recorded by observers included number and race of observers, latency of the helping response and race of helper, number of helpers, movement out of the 'critical area', and spontaneous comments. Major findings were that (*i*) an apparently ill person is more likely to receive aid than one who is apparently drunk, (*ii*) race of victim has little effect on race of helper except when the victim is drunk, (*iii*) the longer the emergency continues without help being offered, the more likely it is that someone will leave the area of the emergency and (*iv*) the expected decrease in speed of responding as group size increases ('diffusion of responsibility' effect found by Darley and Latané) does not occur in this situation. Implications of this difference between laboratory and field results are discussed, and a brief model for the prediction of behaviour in emergency situations is presented.

Since the murder of Kitty Genovese in Queens [New York], a rapidly increasing number of social scientists have turned their attentions to the study of the Good Samaritan's act and an associated phenomenon, the evaluation of victims by bystanders and agents. Some of the findings of this research have been provocative and non-obvious. For example, there is evidence that agents, and even bystanders, will sometimes derogate the character of the victim's misfortune, instead of feeling compassion (Berscheid & Walster, 1967; Lerner & Simmons, 1966), and under certain circumstances, instead of 'safety in numbers', there is 'diffusion of responsibility'. Darley and Latané (1968) found that among bystanders hearing an epileptic seizure over earphones, those who believed other witnesses were present were less likely to seek assistance for the victim than were bystanders who believed they were alone. Latané and Rodin (1969) confirmed this finding for response to a victim of a fall, and also suggested that assistance from a group of bystanders was less likely if the group members were strangers than if they were prior acquaintances. Field experiments by Bryan and Test (1967) support the common sense expectation that one is more likely to be a Good Samaritan if one has just observed another individual performing a helpful act.

Much of the work on victimization to date has been performed in the laboratory, which gives greater control, while field studies are more realistic; the present study was designed to provide more information from the latter setting.

The primary focus of the study was on the effect of type of victim (drunk or ill) and race of victim (black or white) on speed of responding, frequency of responding and the race of the helper. Based on the large body of research on similarity and liking as well as that on race and social distance, it was assumed that an individual would be more inclined to help someone of the same than of a different race. As far as type of victim was concerned, the expectation was that help would be offered more often and more quickly to the apparently ill victim. Why? Firstly, it was assumed that people who are regarded as partly responsible for their plight [i.e. drunk] would receive less sympathy and, consequently, help than people seen as not responsible (Schopler & Matthews, 1965). Secondly, it was assumed that whatever sympathy individuals may experience when they observe a drunk collapse, their inclination to help will be dampened by the realisation that the victim may become digusting, embarrassing and/or violent. This realisation may not only constrain helping but also lead observers to leave the scene of the emergency.

The present study also sought to investigate the impact of modelling in emergency situations. Several investigators have found that an individual's actions in a given situation lead others in that situation to engage in similar actions and these situations include those involving Good Samaritanism (Bryan & Test, 1967). A final concern of the study was to examine the relationship between size of group and frequency and latency of helping, with a victim who was both seen and heard. In previous (laboratory) studies (Darley & Latané, 1968, Latané & Rodin, 1969), increases in group size led to decreases in frequency and increases in latency of responding. In these studies, however, the emergency was only heard, not seen; since visual cues are likely to make an emergency much more arousing for the observer, it is not clear that, given these cues, such considerations as crowd size will be relevant determinants of the observer's response to the emergency. Visual cues also provide clear information as to whether anyone has yet helped the victim or if he has been able to help himself. Thus, in the laboratory studies, observers lacking visual cues could rationalise not helping by assuming assistance was no longer needed when the victim ceased calling for help. Staging emergencies in full view of observers eliminates the possibility of such rationalisation.

To conduct a field investigation of the above questions under the desired conditions required a setting which would allow the repeated staging of emergencies in the midst of reasonably large groups which remained fairly similar in composition from incident to incident. It was also desirable that each group retain the same composition over the course of the incident and that a reasonable amount of time be available after the emergency occurred for Good Samaritans to act. To meet these requirements, the emergencies were staged during the approximately 7½ minute express run between the 59th Street and 125th Street stations of the 8th Avenue Independent (IND) branch of the New York subways.

Method

Subjects

About 4,450 men and women who travelled on the 8th Avenue IND in New York City, weekdays, between 11 a.m. and 3 p.m. during the period April 15th to June 26th, 1968, were the unsolicited participants. The racial composition of a typical train, which travels through Harlem to the Bronx, was about 45 per cent black and 55 per cent white. The mean number of people per compartment during these hours was 43 and the mean number of people in the 'critical area' where the incident was staged was 8.5.

Field situation The A and D trains were selected because they make no stops between 59th and 125th Streets; so, for about 7½ minutes there was a captive audience who, after the first 70 seconds of their journey, became bystanders to an emergency. A single trial was a non-stop, 7½-minute journey in either direction. Trials were run only on the old subway carriages since these had two-person seats (rather than extended seats), and the critical area was the end section of any compartment whose doors led to the next compartment. There are 13 seats and some standing room in this area on all trains (see figure 11.1).

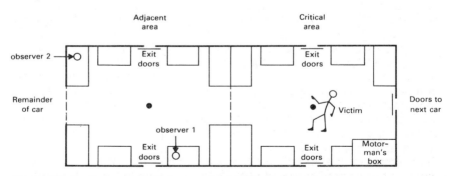

Figure 11.1   Layout of adjacent and critical areas of subway car.

Procedure

On each trial, a team of four Columbia General Studies students, two males and two females, boarded the train using different doors. Four different teams, whose members always worked together, collected data for 103 trials. Each team varied the location of the experimental compartment from trial to trial. The female confederates sat outside the critical area and recorded data as unobtrusively as possible during the journey, while the male model and victim remained standing. The victim always stood next to a pole in the centre of the critical area (see figure 11.1). As the train passed the first station (approximately 70 seconds after departing), the victim staggered forward and collapsed. Until receiving help, he remained supine on the floor, looking at the ceiling. If he received no help by the time the train slowed to a stop, the model helped him to his feet. At the stop, the team got off and waited separately until other passengers had left the station before proceeding to another platform to board a train going in the opposite direction for the next trial. Six to eight trials were run on any given day and all trials on a given day were in the same 'victim condition'.

Victim The four victims (one from each team) were males, aged between 26 and 35, three white, one black, all identically dressed in Eisenhower jackets, old slacks and no tie. On 38 trials the victims smelled of liquor and carried a liquor bottle wrapped tightly in a brown bag (drunk condition), while on the remaining 65 trials they appeared sober and carried a black cane (cane condition). In all other aspects, victims behaved identically in the two conditions, and each victim participated in drunk and cane trials. (Not only were there more cane than drunk trials but they were unevenly distributed across black and white victims. This is because Team 2 violated their instruction to alternate the conditions across days because they 'didn't like' playing the drunk!)

Model Four white males (aged 24 to 29) assumed the role of model in each team, all casually, but not identically, dressed. There were four different model conditions used across both drunk and cane victim conditions:

1 *Critical area – early:* model stood in critical area and waited until passing the fourth station before assisting the victim (approximately 70 seconds after the collapse).
2 *Critical area – late:* model stood in critical area and waited until passing the sixth station before assisting the victim (approximately 150 seconds after the collapse).
3 *Adjacent area – early:* model stood in middle of the compartment, adjacent to critical area and waited until passing the fourth station.
4 *Adjacent area – late:* model stood in adjacent area and waited until passing the sixth station. When the model provided assistance, he raised the victim to a sitting position and stayed with him for the remainder of the trial. An equal number of trials in the no-model condition and in each of the four model conditions were preprogrammed by a random number table.

Measures   On each trial one observer noted the race, sex and location of every passenger, seated or standing, in the critical area, together with the total number of passengers and the total number who came to the victim's assistance, plus their race, sex and location. A second observer coded the race, sex and location of all passengers in the adjacent area, plus the latency of the first helper's arrival after the victim had fallen and, on appropriate trials, the latency of the first helper's arrival after the model had intervened. Both observers recorded comments spontaneously made by nearby passengers and also tried to elicit comments from a passenger sitting next to them.

Results and discussion

Table 11.1   Percentage of trials in which help was given, by race and condition of victim, and total number of trials in each condition

Trials	White victims		Black victims	
	Cane	**Drunk**	**Cane**	**Drunk**
No model	100%	100%	100%	73%
Number of trials run	54	11	8	11
Model trials	100%	77%	—	67%
Number of trials run	3	13	0	3
Total number of trials	57	24	8	14

As can be seen from table 11.1, the frequency of help received by the victims was impressive, at least compared with earlier laboratory studies. The cane victim received spontaneous help (i.e. before the model acted) on 62 out of 65 trials, and even the drunk was helped spontaneously on 19 of 38 trials. The difference cannot be attributed to differences in the number of potential helpers in the compartments; mean number of passengers on cane trials was 45 compared with 40 on the drunk trials.

In all but three of the cane trials planned to be model trials, the victim received help before the model was scheduled to intervene; this was less likely to happen with the drunk victim, where, in many cases, the early model was able to intervene, and in a few even the delayed model could act.

A direct comparison between the latency of response in the drunk and cane conditions might be misleading, since on model trials one does not know how long it might have taken for a helper to arrive without the stimulus of the model. But omitting the model would drastically reduce the number of drunk trials. Consequently, the trials have been divided into those in which someone helped *before* 70 seconds (the time at which the early model was programmed to help) and those in which no one had helped by this time (including some trials in which people helped the model and a very few in which no one helped at all). (Comparing latencies between cane and drunk non-model trials only, the median latency for cane trials is five seconds and

109 seconds for drunk trials, a difference significant at $p<0.0001$ using the Mann–Whitney U test.)

It is quite clear from the first section of table 11.2 that there was more immediate, spontaneous helping of the cane victim than the drunk victim and the effect seems to be essentially the same for the black and white victims.

What of the total number of people who helped? On 60 per cent of the 81 trials on which the victim received help, he received it not from one Good Samaritan, but from two, three or even more. (This analysis only includes data from the non-model trials, since the model's role was to raise the victim to a sitting position and then appear to need assistance, while most real helpers managed to drag the victim to a seat or standing position on their own. Thus the model received rather more help than did real first helpers.) There are no significant differences between black and white victims, or between cane and drunk victims, in the number of helpers, who, subsequent to the first, came to his aid. It would seem, then, that the presence of the first helper has important implications which override whatever cognitive and emotional differences were initially engendered among observers by the victim's characteristics. Perhaps the victim's uniformly passive response to the individual trying to assist him reduced observers' fear about possible unpleasantness in the drunk condition. Another possi-

Table 11.2 Time and responses to the incident

Trials on which help was offered	Total number of trials		% of trials on which 1+ persons left critical area*		% of trials on which 1+ comments were recorded*		Mean number of comments	
	White victim	Black victim	White victim	Black victim	White victim	Black victim	White victim	Black victim
Before 70 seconds								
Cane	52	7	4%	14%	21%	0%	0.27	0.00
Drunk	5	4	20%	0%	80%	50%	1.00	0.50
Total	57	11	5%	9%	26%	18%	0.33	0.18
After 70 seconds								
Cane	5	1	40%	—	60%	—	0.80	—
Drunk	19	10	42%	60%	100%	70%	2.00	0.90
Total	24	11	42%	64%	96%	64%	1.75	0.82
χ^2	36.83	(a)	χ^2 time = 23.19 $p<0.001$ χ^2 cane–drunk = 11.71 $p<0.001$		χ^2 time = 31.45 $p<0.001$ χ^2 cane–drunk = 37.95 $p<0.001$			
p	0.001	0.03						

(a) Fisher's exact test, estimate of two-tailed probability.
* Black and white victims are combined for the analysis of these data.

bility is that second and third helpers were primarily going to the aid of the first helper rather than to the victims.

Characteristics of spontaneous first helpers

On average, 60 per cent of the people in the critical area were males, yet, of the 81 spontaneous first helpers, 90 per cent were males. In this situation, then, men are considerably more likely to help than are women ($\chi^2 = 30.63$, $p < 0.001$).

Of the first 81 helpers, 64 per cent were white, a figure which does not differ significantly from the expected 55 per cent based on racial distribution in the compartments. On the 65 trials on which spontaneous help was offered to the white victims, 68 per cent of the helpers were white which is significantly different ($\chi^2 = 4.23$, $p < 0.05$) from the expected 55 per cent. On the 16 trials on which spontaneous help was offered to the black victim, 50 per cent of the first helpers were white, which represents a slight (non-significant) tendency toward 'same race' helping.

However, when race of helper is analysed separately for cane and drunk conditions, an interesting, though non-significant, trend emerges (see table 11.3). With both black and white cane victims, the proportion of helpers of each race was consistent with the expected 55 per cent–45 per cent split. But with the drunk, it was mainly members of his own race who came to his aid. Why should this occur? In the case of an innocent victim (i.e. the cane victim), sympathy and trust are relatively uncomplicated by other emotions, and so assistance can readily cut across group lines. But in the case of the drunk (and potentially dangerous) victim, blame, fear and disgust are likely to complicate emotions, especially when the victim is not a member of one's own group; consequently, help is less likely to be offered. Black and Reiss's (1967) study of the behaviour of white police officers towards apprehended persons tends to support this suggestion: observers noted very little prejudice towards sober individuals, whether white or black, but there was a large increase in prejudice towards drunks, especially if they were black.

Table 11.3 Spontaneous helping of cane and drunk by race of helper and race of victim

Race of helper	White victims			Black victims			All victims		
	Cane	Drunk	Total	Cane	Drunk	Total	Cane	Drunk	Total
Same as victim	34	10	44	2	6	8	36	16	52
Different from victim	20	1	21	6	2	8	26	3	29
Total	54	11	65	8	8	16	62	19	81

White victims: $\chi^2 = 2.11$, $p = 0.16$; black victims, $p = 0.16$ (two-tailed estimate from Fisher's exact probabilities test); all victims $= 3.26$, $p = 0.08$

Modelling effects

There were too few cases of programmed model to allow an analysis. However, while the area variable (critical or adjacent) had no effect on help received, the early model (70 seconds) elicited significantly more help than the late model (150 seconds).

Other responses to the incident

No one left the compartment on any of the trials, but on 21 of the 103 trials, a total of 34 people did leave the critical area. These results are shown in the second section of table 11.2: people left the area on a higher proportion of trials with the drunk than with the cane victim, and were also far more likely to leave on trials on which help was not offered by 70 seconds than when help was received before that time. The frequencies are too small to make comparisons with each of the variables held constant.

As far as comments of passengers is concerned, content analysis revealed little of interest in the comments themselves. However, far more comments were obtained on drunk than cane trials and most of these were obtained when no one helped until after 70 seconds; this could be due to the discomfort passengers felt in sitting inactive in the presence of the victim, perhaps hoping that others would confirm that inaction was appropriate. Many women, for example, made comments such as 'It's for men to help him' or 'I wish I could help him – I'm not strong enough', 'I never saw this kind of thing before – I don't know where to look', 'You feel so bad that you don't know what to do'.

A test of the diffusion of responsibility hypothesis

In the Darley and Latané experiment it was predicted and found that as the number of bystanders increased, the likelihood that any individual would help decreased and the latency of response increased. Their study involved bystanders who could see neither each other nor the victim. In the Latané and Rodin study, the effect was again found, with bystanders who were face-to-face but with the victim still only heard. In the present study, bystanders saw both the victim and each other. Did diffusion of responsibility still occur? Two analyses were performed to check this hypothesis. First, all non-model trials were separated into three groups according to the number of males in the critical area (the assumed reference group for spontaneous first helpers). Mean and median latencies of response were then calculated for each group, separately by type and race of victim. No evidence was found for diffusion of responsibility; in fact, response times using either measure were consistently faster for the seven or more groups compared to the one to three groups.

Second, based on an analysis used by Darley and Latané, latencies actually obtained for each size group were compared with a base line of hypothetical groups of the same size made up by combining smaller groups. (As Darley and Latané pointed out, different-size real groups cannot be meaningfully compared to one another, since, as group size increases, the likelihood that one or more people will help also increases.) To ensure maximum control, the analysis was confined to cane trials with white victims and male first helpers coming from the critical area. Within this set of trials, the most frequently occurring natural groups (of males in the critical area) were three ($n = 6$) and seven ($n = 5$). Hypothetical groups of three ($n = 4$) and seven ($n = 25$) were composed of all combinations of smaller sized groups. For example, to obtain the hypothetical latencies for groups of seven, combinations were made of (i) all real-size six groups with all real-size one groups, plus (ii) all real-size five groups with all real-size two groups etc. The latency assigned to each of these hypothetical groups was that recorded for the faster of the two real groups of which it was composed. Cumulative response curves for real and hypothetical groups of three and seven are shown in figure 11.2.

As can be seen, members of real groups responded more quickly than would be expected on the basis of the faster of the two scores obtained from the combined smaller groups, and these findings do not follow the pattern of findings obtained by Darley and Latané who tentatively conclude that 'a victim may be more likely to receive help ... the fewer people there are to take action' (Latané and Darley, 1968). How can we explain this discrepancy? (i) As indicated earlier, the fact that observers could see the victim may not only have constrained their ability to conclude there was no emergency but may also have overwhelmed with other considerations any tendency to diffuse responsibility. (ii) Even if diffusion of responsibility *is* experi-

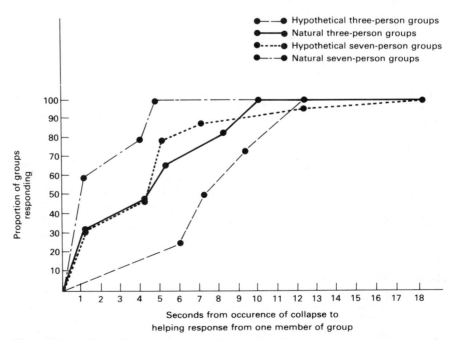

Figure 11.2   Cumulative proportion of groups producing a helper over time (cane trials, white victims, male helpers from inside critical area).

enced by people who can actually see an emergency, when groups are larger than two, the increment in deterrence to action resulting from increasing the number of observers may be less than the increase in probability that within a given time interval at least one of the observers will take action to help the victim. Clearly, more work is needed in both natural and laboratory settings before we understand the conditions under which diffusion of responsibility will or will not occur.

Conclusions

In this field study, a personal emergency occurred in a public, face-to-face situation, from which it was virtually impossible for the bystander to escape, thus making it different from previous laboratory studies. Some of the major conclusions are:

1 An individual who appears to be ill is more likely to receive help than one who appears to be drunk, even when the immediate help needed is of the same kind.
2 Given mixed groups of men and women, and a male victim, men are more likely to help than are women.
3 Given mixed racial groups, there is some tendency for same-race helping to be more frequent, especially when the victim appears drunk rather than ill.
4 No diffusion of responsibility was found, i.e. help is not less frequent or slower in coming from larger as compared to smaller groups of bystanders; if anything, the effect is in the opposite direction.
5 The longer the emergency continues without help being offered (i) the less impact a model has on the helping behaviour of observers, (ii) the more likely it is that individuals will leave the immediate area in order to avoid the situation, and (iii) the more likely it is that observers will discuss the incident and its implications for their behaviour.

A model of response to emergency situations is briefly presented here as a possible heuristic device, and includes the following assumptions: observation of any emergency creates an emotional arousal state in the bystander, and will be interpreted differently in different situations (Schachter, 1964) as fear, disgust, sympathy, etc. and possibly a combination of these. This arousal state is higher (i) the more one can empathize with the victim, i.e. see oneself in his situation (Stotland, 1966), (ii) the closer one is to the emergency and (iii) the longer the emergency continues without intervention of a helper. It can be reduced by a number of possible responses: (i) helping directly, (ii) going to get help, (iii) leaving the scene of the emergency and (iv) rejecting the victim as undeserving of help (Lerner & Simmons, 1966). The response that is chosen is a function of the cost–reward matrix that includes costs associated with helping (i.e. effort, embarrassment, possible disgusting or distasteful experiences, possible physical harm, etc.), costs associated with not helping (mainly self-blame and perceived censure from others), rewards associated with helping (mainly self-praise and priase from victim and others), and rewards associated with not helping (mainly those stemming from continuation of other activities). Note that the model implies that the major source of motivation is to selfishly rid oneself of an unpleasant emotional state rather than a positive, altruistic, desire to help. In terms of this model, the following after-the-fact interpretations can be offered:

1 The drunk is helped less because costs for helping are higher (greater disgust) and costs for not helping are lower (less self-blame and censure because he is partly responsible for his own victimization).

2 Women help less because costs for helping are higher (effort mainly), and costs for not helping are lower (less censure from others; it is not her role).

3 Same-race helping, particularly of the drunk, can be explained by differential costs for not helping (less censure if one is of opposite race) and, with the drunk, differential costs for helping (more fear of opposite race).

4 Diffusion of responsibility is not found on cane trials because costs of helping in general are low, and costs of not helping are high (more self-blame because of possible severity of problem). This suggestion that diffusion of responsibility will increase as costs of helping increase and costs of not helping decrease is consistent with real-life public incidents, in which possible bodily harm to a helper is almost always involved, and with previous research in which either (i) it was easy to assume someone had already helped, and thus costs of not helping were reduced (Darley & Latané), or (ii) it was possible to think the emergency was minor, which also reduces the costs of not helping (Latané & Rodin).

5 All of the effects of time are also consistent with the model. The longer the emergency continues, the more likely observers are to be aroused and so will have chosen among the possible responses. Thus, (i) a late model will elicit less helping since people have already reduced their arousal by one or other method; (ii) unless arousal is reduced by other methods, people will leave more as time goes by, because arousal is still increasing; (iii) observers will discuss the incident in an attempt to reduce self-blame and arrive at the fourth resolution, namely a justification for not helping based on rejection of the victim.

Commentary

Aim and nature

This is a field experiment which set out to test certain aspects of helping behaviour or bystander intervention in the natural setting of a tube train. The main focus was the effect of type of victim (drunk or ill) and race of victim (black or white) on speed of helping, frequency of helping and race of helper. It also sought to study the impact of modelling in emergency situations, i.e. the effect on others of seeing someone go to the help of the victim. A final aim was to examine the relationship between size of the group and frequency and latency of helping, with a victim who was both seen and heard. Up until 1969, most of the studies of altruism had been laboratory experiments so the tube train (New York subway) experiment represents a major landmark in this research area. Although the main method used is that of an experiment (manipulation of an independent variable) there was also observation involved (over and above that used in *all* empirical research).

Background and context

Like the emergency staged in the New York subway, the real-life, New York murder of Kitty (real name Catherine) Genovese which inspired the 'unresponsive bystander' research, was both seen and heard. It is ironic that Piliavin *et al.* wanted to take the research out of the laboratory (where the victim was only heard and only other subjects were seen) and into the real world, where it had all begun. And not only was Kitty Genovese heard but she and her murderer were seen too. 'For more than half an hour, 38 respectable, law-abiding citizens in Queens watched a killer stalk and stab a woman' and did not call the police. After she was stabbed the first time she screamed, 'Oh, my God, he stabbed me! Please help me! Please help me!'. After the murderer had first grabbed her, lights went on in the ten-storey apartment block and windows were opened. From one of the upper windows in the apartment house, a man called down: 'Let that girl alone'. He walked off a little way up the street; lights went out. He returned to stab her a second time. 'I'm dying'', she shrieked, 'I'm dying'. Windows were opened again, lights went on in many apartments. The assailant got into his car and drove off. He returned to stab her a third time, this time fatally. It was all over by about 3.30 a.m., but the first call to the police was recorded at 3.50 a.m. Witnesses had watched from behind their curtains: one couple pulled up chairs to the window and turned the light out to see better. The caller was a man who did not want to 'get involved'.

This information, from the *New York Times* (March 27th, 1964) suggests that there was no doubt that people knew a serious crime was taking place (defining the situation). And the repeated stabbings must have conveyed to any witness that no one else had gone for help, i.e. the rationalisation about others having already helped which is often used to explain diffusion of responsibility is difficult to bring into play here. This leaves the variable relating to 'the cost of intervention': the actual caller's not wanting to get involved suggests this might be the key variable. Other reasons given by witnesses for their inaction included: 'We thought it was a lovers' quarrel', 'Frankly we were afraid' and 'I was tired'. It would seem that 'apathy' is too simple a label to attach to the inaction of the 38 witnesses.

In March, 1984, a Catherine Genovese Memorial Conference on Bad Samaritanism was held in which experts could share what they had learned in the 20 years since the tragic event. The *New York Times* again reported the conference. 'It's held the imagination because, looking at those 38 people, we were really looking at ourselves. We might not have done anything either. That's the ugly side of human nature' (O'Connor, law professor). 'The case touched on a fundamental issue of the human condition, our primordial nightmare. If we need help, will those around us stand around and let us be destroyed or will they come to our aid? Are those other creatures out there to help us sustain our life and values or are we individual flecks of dust just floating around in a vacuum?' (Milgram, psychology professor).

Evaluation

1 It is useful to look at the major conclusions of the Piliavin *et al.* study in relation to

the three variables referred to above: (*i*) defining the situation as an emergency; (*ii*) diffusion of responsibility; (*iii*) cost of intervention.

a An individual who appears to be ill is more likely to receive help than one who appears to be drunk, even when the immediate help needed is of the same kind. Why? The costs of helping the drunk are higher (greater disgust) and costs of not helping are lower (less self-blame and censure since he is partly responsible for his own victimization).

b Given mixed groups of men and women, and a male victim, men are more likely to help than are women. Why? Costs of helping are higher for women (effort mainly), and costs of not helping are lower (less censure from others: it is not her role). So what might have been predicted if the victim were female? There is good reason (according to Eagly, 1987) to believe the results would not have been very different. She suggests that helping behaviour is at least as much determined by conforming to gender roles as the demands of the particular situation. The social psychological studies of helping, whether laboratory or field, are confined to short-term encounters with strangers and this seems to increase the chances that men will be the helpers rather than women because such encounters are more consistent with the traditional male gender-role, namely, men are 'heroes' who perform altruistic acts of saving others from harm with some risk to themselves. This sort of behaviour may be encouraged by having an 'audience'. Related to this is the notion of chivalry, i.e. going to the aid of 'helpless females' (the 'damsel-in-distress syndrome'). So male helping is often directed towards strangers and women and, in addition, men are expected to be dominant (compared to the submissive female) and assertive, making helping an assertive act of intervention.

Women, by contrast, are expected to place the needs of others (especially family members) before their own. Their orientation is towards caring, kindness, compassion and devotion to others and are generally more empathic and sympathetic. This *communal* (concern for the welfare of others) focus of the female role is expressed most readily in the context of long-term relationships and contrasts with the male's *agentic* focus (i.e. agent of assertiveness and control). This, combined with the female role encouraging avoidance of strangers (particularly men), means that the sexes should differ in their perception of whether providing aid is likely to lead to danger to themselves as helpers. Especially in situations with an element of risk, men should be more likely to help. Where there is also an audience to witness the helping act and other potential helpers available, this tendency will be even greater.

According to Eagly, the literature (including the Piliavin *et al.* study) by and large confirms these predictions: (*i*) men are more likely to help than women; (*ii*) men are more likely to help women than other men; (*iii*) women help men and other women to an approximately equal extent. But because of the kind of help required in most of the helping research (including the present study), we cannot draw any general conclusions about sex differences in helping behaviours: role theory predicts that in other kinds of situations, women will be the greater helpers.

c Given mixed racial groups, there is some tendency for same-race helping to be more frequent, especially when the victim appears drunk. Why? The costs of not helping are lower (less censure if one is of the opposite race – at least in a racist society! – and see (a) above). But the costs of not helping include the threat to one's self-concept as a fair, non-prejudiced individual etc., which might explain why there were no significant differences between black and white cane victims and only a trend ($p = 0.08$) in the drunk condition. Sympathy and trust for the innocent victim are relatively uncomplicated by other emotions, and so assistance can readily cut across race lines. But with the potentially dangerous drunk, blame, fear and disgust do come into play, especially if he is of a different racial group to oneself.

d No diffusion of responsibility was found, i.e. help was not less frequent or slower in coming from larger groups compared with smaller groups of bystanders; if anything the effect is in the opposite direction. Why? In the case of the cane victims, the costs of helping are low and those of not helping are high (more self-blame because of possible severity of the problem). It was clearly an emergency, and it was obvious whether help had already been offered; it happened in full view of the bystanders (i.e. no rationalization to the effect that 'someone must have already helped' was possible). Also, helping is more likely when people share a sense of common fate, a sense of interdependence which can so easily be disregarded in our society, as in Kitty's case ('I didn't want to get involved') (Aronson, 1988).

e The longer the emergency continued without help being offered, (*i*) the less impact a model has on the helping behaviour of bystanders; (*ii*) the more likely individuals are to leave the critical area in order to avoid the situation; (*iii*) the more likely observers are to discuss the incident and its implications for their behaviour. Why? The longer it continues, the more likely observers are to be aroused and so will have chosen among the possible responses: (1) a late model will elicit less helping since people have already reduced their arousal one way or other; (2) unless arousal is reduced by other methods, people will leave as time goes by: arousal is still increasing; (3) observers will discuss the incident in an attempt to reduce self-blame and rationalize their inaction 'by blaming the victim' (cf. Cognitive–Dissonance theory).

2 Whatever the advantages of a field experiment like this may be (compared with laboratory studies), an unavoidable feature is that all the subjects are unsolicited, i.e. they don't know they *are* subjects in an experiment because they don't know there *is* an experiment taking place. Nor is it possible to debrief them for obvious, practical, reasons. So this raises the ethical problem as to how to justify, putting 'innocent' (non-volunteer) subjects through what, for some, might be a distressing episode (whether they help or not) when it is not possible to explain to them its false nature and its purpose!

Exercises

1 What are the independent and dependent variables in the study?

2 Name *two* advantages and disadvantages of the field experiment compared with laboratory experiments.

3 Name two other kinds of experiment.

4 Why is the Chi-squared (χ^2) test used?

5 What is Fisher's exact probability test?

JOHN GARCIA, FRANK R. ERVIN AND ROBERT KOELLING (1966)

Learning with prolonged delay of reinforcement

Psychonomic Science, Vol. 5 (3), pp. 121–2

Gustatory aversions, induced in rats by conditionally pairing a distinctive flavour with a noxious drug, were readily established, even when injections were delayed an hour or more. The optimal interstimulus interval and effectiveness of cues for learning appear to be a function of the specific effects of the reinforcer on the organism.

It is considered axiomatic in theory and practice that no learning will occur without immediate reinforcement. For example, a hungry rat will not learn to press a lever for food unless the response is immediately followed by food (primary reinforcement) or by a signal which has been associated with food in the past (secondary reinforcement). Food can be described as rewarding, but the same general rule has also been applied to punishing agents. Delays of three to 45 seconds have a harmful effect upon learning in a wide variety of experimental situations. The significance of these findings for reinforcement theory was discussed by Spence (1947), and a review by Renner (1964) shows that there has been no major modification of the temporal contiguity aspect. However, our data indicates that immediate reinforcement is not a general requirement of all learning.

Method

Young adult male rats (Sprague–Dawley, 300 to 400 g) were maintained in individual cages with *Purina Laboratory Chow* ad lib. Drinking was restricted to a ten-minute period each day. After one week of habituation to this schedule, treatment began.

In Experiment A, five groups (*n* = 8 each) were treated. One experimental group (Sac–Apo : inj) was given a gustatory cue in its drinking water (1 g saccharine per litre) and, after a delay, was injected with a drug which produced gastric disturbances (7 mg/kg apomorphine hydrochloride I.P.). The animals were injected in serial order at one-minute intervals, with the first animal injected at 5 minutes and the last one at 12 minutes after the saccharine water bottle was removed from the home cage. One control group (Sac–Sal : inj) drank saccharine water and was injected with saline, while another control (Wat–Apo : inj) drank water and was injected with apomorphine. An additional experimental group (Sac–Apo : inj) received delayed injections in serial order from 15 to 22 minutes post-drinking. Other rats (Sac–Shock), immediately after drinking saccharine-water, were taken from their cages and placed in a box with an electric grid floor and three shocks (lasting 0.5 seconds each) were delivered within one minute to the paws. All groups received four treatments, one every third day, and then three extinction tests (i.e. no injections or shock) on the same schedule. Between treatment days, the animals were given water for ten minutes.

In Experiment B, five experimental groups ($n = 6$ each) drank saccharine-water and received apomorphine injections (15 mg/kg I.P.) with delays of 30, 45, 75, 120 and 180 minutes. Five treatments were given, one every third day. One control group drank saccharine-water but received no injections.

Results and discussion

The apomorphine-injected animals (Sac–Apo : inj) showed a progressive decrease in intake of saccharine-water, indicating that the pairing of this distinctly flavoured fluid with the drug effects produced a gustatory aversion (see figure 12.1). The difference in saccharine-water intake between the apomorphine-injected group and their saline-injected controls (Sac–Sal : inj) was statistically significant after two injections ($p < 0.01$ by ranks test). The decrement increased

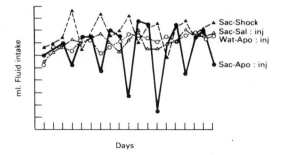

Figure 12.1 Experiment A: daily mean fluid intake during a ten-minute period on acquisition days (A), extinction days (E), and water intake on days between treatments. Only the group receiving Saccharine followed by an apomorphine injection (Sac-Apo : inj) learned to reduce saccharine-water intake. Neither apomorphine (Wat-Apo : inj) nor saccharine alone (Sac-Sal : inj) had an appreciable effect, while Saccharine followed by shock (Sac-Shock) had a converse effect.

following each drug administration and then was reversed during the extinction trials. Apomorphine injections had no effect on those animals (Wat–Apo : inj) which drank water every day, showing that differential reinforcement of the gustatory cue is necessary to produce the fluid intake decrement (figure 12.1).

The size of the decrement in saccharine intake produced by four doses of apomorphine (Sac–Apo : inj) was independent of the delay of the reinforcing injection ($r = 0$) from 5 to 22 minutes. Furthermore, Experiment B indicated that five apomorphine injections could produce a significant effect at delays up to 75 minutes (see figure 12.2).

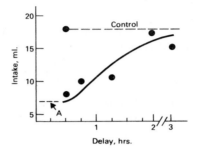

Figure 12.2   Experiment B: mean fluid intake of saccharine-flavoured water on the first extinction day, following five conditional pairings of saccharine and apomorphine for groups differing in delay of injection. Results of Experiment A are also indicated.

Apomorphine causes nausea and emesis in humans, but in rats emesis is blocked by the cardiac sphincter. Our doses caused the animals to stop eating for 30 minutes and caused visible signs of illness within several minutes in most animals.

The rats receiving electrocutaneous shock (Sac–Shock) showed a significant increase in saccharine-water intake after the first shock (figure 12.1); this may be due to the activating effects of shock rather than to associative learning. However, there was also a marked difference between shock rats and drug rats in their responses to handling and treatment: the drug and control rats progressively habituated to handling and injection but the shock rats made strong attempts to escape after the first shock trial. This observation supports a previous study indicating that the avoidance reactions induced by electrocutaneous shock were readily transferred to auditory and visual signals but not to gustatory ones. Conversely, the avoidance reactions induced by X-ray or toxin were readily transferred to gustatory cues, but not to auditory and visual ones (Garcia et al., 1966).

Two other, non-laboratory, sources indicate similar learning with prolonged delays of reinforcement. Aversions have been produced with a discrimination learning paradigm where one gustatory cue is paired with ionizing radiation and an alternative cue is not so paired (Garcia et al., 1961). Yet, this effect of radiation is not manifested until over an hour post-exposure (Smith et al., 1965). Aversions have been established for unflavoured water and for merely sniffing a distinctive odour during exposure, indicating that the phenomenon is not dependent upon lingering traces of a strongly flavoured solution (Garcia & Koelling, 1965).

Rats using olfaction and gustation also learn to avoid poisons with slow cumulative effects, such as dicoumarin which gradually reduces the clotting power of the blood and eventually causes internal bleeding. These bait-shy responses often do not develop until hours after eating the bait (Barnett, 1963).

These data indicate again that the mammalian learning mechanisms do not operate randomly, associating stimuli and reinforcers only as a function of recency, frequency and intensity. The omnivorous rat displays a bias, probably established by natural selection, to associate gustatory and olfactory cues with internal malaise, even when these stimuli are separated by long time periods. Auditory, visual and tactual stimuli are not so readily associated with malaise, though they also are discriminable and informative, i.e. supra-threshold and differentially reinforced. On the other hand, the latter cues are more readily associated with peripheral pain; here, both cue and reinforce are localized in external space by the rat and, under 'natural' conditions, escape movements are particularly adaptive. This bias has a practical diagnostic value for drug research: since the gustatory aversion is sensitive to toxicity yet insensitive to peripheral pain, it can be conveniently used in conjunction with injection and surgical procedures.

Commentary

Aim and nature

This is a laboratory experiment, using rat subjects, which attempted to produce conditioned aversions to saccharine-flavoured water by pairing it with a drug (apomorphine hydrochloride) which induces nausea. What makes the experiment of special interest is that there is a definite time interval between the tasting of the saccharine-water and the onset of the drug-induced nausea. In fact, the precise time lapse was varied in two separate experiments: (A) 5, 6, 7, 8, 9, 10, 11 and 12 minutes, and 15, 16, 17, 18, 19, 20, 21 and 22 minutes (Sac–Apo : inj) [There were three control groups: (Sac–Sal : inj), (Wat–Apo : inj) and (Sac–Shock).] and (B) five experimental groups (Sac–Apo : inj) at 30, 45, 75, 120 and 180 minutes. [There was one control group which just drank saccharine-water, but received neither injection nor shock.] The experiments involve the use of classical (Pavlovian/respondent) conditioning whereby a stimulus (UCS) (in this case the apomorphine hydrochloride) which naturally produces a response (UCR) (nausea) is associated with a second, neutral stimulus (CS) (in this case the saccharine solution), which comes to elicit the response on its own (the CS now produces a conditioned response or CR). In essence, an 'old' response comes to be produced by a 'new' stimulus.

Context and background

According to Walker (1984), the fact that many experiments involving a variety of species can all be described as classical conditioning does *not* in itself mean that there is only one mechanism involved or that only one explanation applies, equally, to all species and all cases. Although conditionability seems to be an almost universal property of nervous systems, many psychologists, such as Seligman (1970), have argued that there can be no general laws of learning. But what might such laws be?

One candidate is the law of *contiguity*: events (or stimuli) which occur close together in time and space are likely to become associated with each other. Most laboratory demonstrations of conditioning (and probably the vast majority of real-life examples) do appear to 'obey' the law of contiguity. This is a tenet of traditional theories of conditioning, both classical (Pavlov) and operant (Skinner). For example, (*i*) Pavlov's original work with dogs involved presenting a stimulus (e.g. ringing a bell) about half a second before the food was presented; (*ii*) in the case of Little Albert (see chapter 22) the hammer was brought down on the steel bar just as Albert reached out to touch the rat, and (*iii*) if you learn to fear the sound of the dentist's drill, then in classical conditioning terms it is because the sound of the drill has accompanied the drill hitting your nerve. But are there exceptions to this general rule which serve to disprove it?

Evaluation

1 The present study, together with others by the same researchers (Garcia *et al.*, 1966) and others (Riley & Baril, 1976) do represent important exceptions to the so-called 'law' of contiguity; although it may be important, it seems that it is neither necessary nor sufficient for conditioning to take place.

2 Just as noteworthy is the speed with which such conditioned taste aversions are acquired: in experiment A, the rats received just four treatments (one every third day, followed by three extinction tests (no injections or shock)), and in B five treatments were given (one every third day). In some replications, just a single trial has been needed.

3 Garcia's work shows that the use of slow-acting rat poisons are really a waste of time and effort because the interval between food consumption and illness can be several *hours* without abolishing the aversions. However, as Mackintosh (1984) has pointed out, the interval does have some effect: everything else being equal, 30 minutes will show a more marked aversion than 300 minutes (see figure 12.2), although there will still be some learning in the latter. The control conditions suggest that the aversion to the saccharine solution is a genuinely conditioned response as a result of association with the apomorphine (the illness is 'attributed' to the solution) as opposed to neophobia, i.e. the tendency to avoid any novel substance made stronger by the experience of illness.

4 Is there any evidence that contiguity is not necessary in experimental situations other than conditioned taste aversion? Mackintosh (1984) cites a study by Bow Tong Lett in which rats were removed from a maze immediately after choosing on each trial, regardless of whether they were right or wrong, and only several minutes later were they returned to receive food in the maze if they had chosen correctly. They learned successfully with delays of at least five minutes. 'The association span of the rat, it appears, is capable of bridging quite long intervals' (Mackintosh, 1984). But clearly this is not always so. Why not?

Mackintosh (1984) argues that if we assume that the function of conditioning is to enable organisms to find out what produces or signals certain important events, i.e. to attribute the occurrence of, say, food or danger to their most probable antecedent causes, it makes no sense for an animal to associate the occurrence of food with any or every event that has happened in the preceding hour. The mechanisms of conditioning are nicely designed, he says, to help an animal distinguish between the probable causal relations and occasional chance conjunctions of events. Conditioning, therefore, makes some functional sense.

While it is true that successful conditioning can occur to a stimulus even though there is a substantial interval between it (CS) and the reinforcer (the UCS), such conditioning will be prevented if there is some other event which predicts the occurrence of the reinforcer more accurately. As Mackintosh (1984) says, 'Conditioning occurs selectively, to good predictors of reinforcement at the expense of poorer predictors'. He cites a study by Williams in which pigeons learnt to peck at a disc briefly illuminated with a red light despite a ten-second delay between such pecks and the delivery of food. However, this was effectively abolished if some other stimulus (e.g. a brief green light) occurred in the interval between the peck on the red disc and food. It is as if they attribute food to the more recent event (green light) as opposed to the earlier red light.

Again, rats will learn an aversion to saccharine (if followed by a lithium injection) even though they actually receive the injection on only 50 per cent of the occasions on which they drink it (Mackintosh, 1984). If, in addition, rats drink a saline solution on days when the lithium is to be injected, they attribute the illness to the saline as opposed to the saccharine solution and show no serious aversion to the latter (Luongo, cited by Mackintosh).

These findings suggest that whether or not a particular event is associated with a particular reinforcer does not depend solely on the relation holding between the two (as the traditional learning theories would have it), but also on whether other intervening events are more easily associated with that reinforcer. This explains why even short intervals between stimulus and reinforcer can prevent conditioning. It also explains why conditioning can still occur despite the often long intervals in the taste-aversion experiments: the animal is denied access to food or drink other than the saccharine-solution or whatever the CS happens to be.

5 Apart from these important theoretical implications of the Garcia *et al.* experiment, there are clearly questions about the moral acceptability of injecting animals with a drug known to induce nausea (and the use of electric shock). We need to ask how much the rat is likely to be suffering and whether this can be justified on moral grounds.

According to Gray (1987), rats are the most commonly used experimental subjects in psychology, with food deprivation and electric shock being the most commonly objected-to treatments. As far as the former is concerned, he claims it is *not* a source of suffering: they are either fed once per day when the day's experimentation is over, or they are maintained at 85 per cent of their free-feeding (ad lib) body weight; both are actually healthier than allowing them to eat ad lib. Regarding shock, this may cause *some* pain but not *extreme* pain (based on observation of their behaviour). The level permitted is controlled by Home Office inspectors: the average level used in the UK is 0.68 mA, for an average of 0.57 seconds at a time (Garcia *et al.* used 0.5 seconds, but we're not told the intensity). This usually produces an unpleasant tickling sensation in humans. But how can even slight pain be justified?

Usually, the two justifications made are in terms of (*i*) the pursuit of scientific knowledge or (*ii*) the advancement of medicine. In either case, for the argument to be valid, we must be able to rule out the fact that the experimenter is deriving pleasure from the animal's suffering (i.e. that this is the major reason it is done!). There can be little doubt that taste aversion studies do add to our knowledge about the conditioning process and there seems no reason to believe that the nausea is induced gratuitously. (Regarding their medical relevance, see Exercises below.)

Exercises

1 Do Garcia *et al.* provide their own 'medical relevance' justificiation for their inducement of taste aversion?

2 Can you think of an application of classical conditioning with human beings which involves the use of apomorphine (or other emetic drugs)?

3 We are told that the difference in saccharine intake between (Sac–Apo : inj) and (Sac–Sal : inj) was statistically significant, using a rank's test.
(*i*) What test was it?
(*ii*) Could a parametric test have been used?

4 The size of the decrement in saccharine intake produced by four doses of apomorphine (Sac–Apo : inj) was independent of the delay of the reinforcing injection: 5 to 22 minutes ($r = 0$).
What does '$r = 0$' mean and what is another way of expressing this finding?

JAMIE BENNETT-LEVY AND THERESA MARTEAU (1984)

Fear of animals: what is prepared?

British Journal of Psychology, 75, pp. 37–42

The present study examines one aspect of the concept of preparedness: what characteristics of animals humans are prepared to fear. Group I subjects (n = 64) rated how fearful they were of 29 small, harmless, animals. Group II subjects (n = 49) made ratings of the perceptual characteristics of these same animals. Fear ratings were found to be significantly correlated with animal characteristics ratings. It was suggested that preparedness to fear certain animals (e.g. snakes) is not a function of the animals *per se*, but of their fear-evoking perceptual properties and their discrepancy from the human form.

Both Gray (1971) and Seligman (1971) have proposed that humans are in some way biologically predisposed or 'prepared' to fear certain animals (e.g. snakes). The assumption rests upon three main classes of evidence:

(i) the distribution of animal phobias is non-random (Marks, 1969);
(ii) there does not appear to be an equivalent distribution of traumatic experience with these animals (Marks, 1969; Murray & Foote, 1979; but see Ost & Hugdahl, 1981);
(iii) age of onset of animal problems is non-randomly distributed, reaching a peak around age of four years (Gray, 1971).

Seligman postulated that fears which are 'prepared' involve stimuli which are of biological significance to the survival of the species. However, he did not specify how such a mechanism might operate. The present study represents a first attempt to shed light on this problem.

It has also been suggested that animals' fears of other dangerous animals are innate (e.g. Hebb, 1946; Tinbergen, 1951). Hebb noted that a realistically painted snake elicited a stronger reaction in chimpanzees than all but one of the other test objects, but his chimps were a mixture of wild and laboratory-reared animals which may have been previously exposed to snakes. Mineka *et al.* (1980) found that, while most wild-reared monkeys showed considerable fear of real, toy and model snakes, most of the laboratory-reared monkeys showed only very mild responses, and concluded that 'snake fear does not appear to be very common or pronounced in laboratory-reared monkeys'. But they neglected another very interesting result, namely that where the laboratory-reared monkeys did show marked fear, the 'real' snake showed a significant amount of movement. So Mineka *et al.* (1980) have clearly demonstrated that chimps (and, presumably, humans), do not have a 'prepared template' of snakes (a fear of snakes *per se*), but they may have a prepared fear of snake-like movements. Schneirla (1965) also noted that certain stimulus configurations typically elicit withdrawal responses; these stimuli are generally abrupt, irregular in timing and of high magnitude, and are effective in the visual, auditory and tactile or proprioceptive modalities, so large animals which move unpredictably and very quickly (towards the observer) should elicit maximal withdrawal (fear) responses.

Hinde (1974) has proposed another class of stimuli which may produce fear in animals, namely marked novelty and strangeness, and similar dimensions seem to affect human infants' responsiveness to irregular face-like stimuli (Fantz & Nevis, 1967) as well as, perhaps, adult reaction to alien creatures in films. Hinde suggested that a large discrepancy between the stimulus and the organism's model of the world is the basis for this response.

When patients with specific phobias of animals describe what it is they fear about them, it is invariably the animal's perceptual characteristics; in Britain these feared animals are almost all small and harmless, and, although the patient may 'know' this, they nevertheless remain terrified by the sight, feel and thought of it.

The present study investigates the hypothesis that human beings, like animals, are prepared to fear certain stimulus configurations, such as rapid or abrupt movement, and stimuli which are discrepant from the human form. The hypothesis predicts that the perceptual characteristics of small, harmless, animals should be meaningfully related to the distribution of ratings of fear and avoidance of these animals. The corollary of the hypothesis is that such a relationship might help to explain why the distribution of animal phobias is non-random, and why certain small, harmless creatures, but not others, become the subject of fear.

Method

Subjects

Subjects ($n = 113$) attending a local health centre were asked to fill in one of two questionnaires, distributed in random order.

Group I subjects ($n = 64$, F 34, M 30) completed Questionnaire 1 (see *Materials*). Their mean age was 35.5 years, $S.D. = 16.9$.

Group II subjects ($n = 49$, F 25, M 24) completed Questionnaire 2. Their mean age was 35.1 years, $S.D. = 16.4$.

Materials

Questionnaire 1: this was designed to measure the self-reported fear and avoidance of a number of small, harmless animals and insects. The rationale for inclusion of 'harmless' animals was dictated by the stimulus configuration hypothesis, which suggests that certain perceptual characteristics of animals should be meaningfully related to aversion and fear ratings, even among harmless animals of no biological significance to the survival of the species! 29 animals and insects were listed on the questionnaire. Where the animals might have been thought of as harmful (e.g. grass snake and jellyfish), the instruction '*not* harmful' was included and subjects were asked to rate them as harmless. Subjects rated these animals on two scales:

1 *Fear scale:* subjects were asked to rate how afraid they were of the animals, using a three-point scale (1 = not afraid; 2 = quite afraid; 3 = very afraid).
2 A *five-point rating scale of nearness:* subjects were asked how near they would go to the animals. The rating scales consisted of the following points: 1 = enjoy picking it up; 2 = would pick it up, but unpleasant; 3 = touch it or go to within six inches; 4 = stand one to six feet away; 5 = move further than six feet away.

Subjects were instructed that 'as some animals and insects are difficult to pick up in the wild, imagine that they have been injured in some way. For instance, the birds have a broken wing, or the squirrel a broken foot etc . . .'.

This scale was included because it was thought that subjects would be only 'quite afraid' or 'very afraid' of a small percentage of the animals.

Behavioural and physiological dimensions of fear were not assessed in the current study, for reasons of expediancy. Given the individual desynchrony between different indices of fear (Lang, 1968), it cannot necessarily be assumed that the four stimulus dimensions will affect behavioural and physiological measures of fear in a similar fashion.

Questionnaire 2: this was designed to measure subjects' ratings of the same 29 animals and insects as in Questionnaire 1, along four perceptual dimensions. The following instructions were given: 'We would like you to consider how UGLY, SLIMY and SPEEDY the animals are, and how SUDDENLY they appear to MOVE'. A three-point rating scale (1 = not; 2 = quite; 3 = very) was used.

Results

Table 13.1 shows the mean scores for the 29 animals on the four dimensions rated by Group II subjects (ugly, slimy, speedy, suddenness of movement), and the fear and nearness ratings of Group I. The mean ratings show that subjects were disproportionately more fearful of rats than of the other animals. Informal questioning revealed that this was almost certainly because rats were perceived as potentially harmful, unlike the other animals. Clearly, the attempt to remove the effects of perceived harmfulness from the questionnaire failed in this specific instance.

Table 13.1   Mean ratings of animal characteristics, fear and nearness ratings

	Ugly	Slimy	Speedy	Moves Suddenly	Fear	Nearness
Rat	2.24	1.10	2.35	2.53	2.08	3.90
Cockroach	2.53	1.20	1.96	2.04	1.58	3.25
Jellyfish (*not* harmful)	2.00	2.47	1.39	1.51	1.81	2.95
Spider	2.43	1.06	2.25	2.52	1.64	2.88
Slug	2.63	2.90	1.04	1.02	1.19	2.84
Grass snake (*not* harmful)	1.80	1.78	2.12	2.42	1.55	2.78
Beetle	2.10	1.18	1.55	1.57	1.33	2.50
Lizard	1.88	1.54	2.53	2.78	1.25	2.45
Worm	2.18	2.45	1.14	1.20	1.16	2.37
Frog	1.88	2.24	1.80	2.31	1.17	2.28
Moth	1.53	1.09	2.04	2.32	1.25	2.27
Ant	1.86	1.04	2.04	2.14	1.14	2.22
Crow	1.67	1.02	2.02	2.08	1.22	2.14
Mouse	1.35	1.02	2.35	2.56	1.27	2.13
Grasshopper	1.76	1.12	2.48	2.77	1.16	2.06
Squirrel	1.02	1.02	2.44	2.71	1.11	2.03
Caterpillar	1.65	1.24	1.14	1.12	1.05	1.84
Baby seal	1.06	1.42	1.50	1.48	1.03	1.63
Blackbird	1.10	1.00	2.04	2.20	1.08	1.59
Hamster	1.02	1.00	1.98	2.23	1.00	1.50
Baby chimpanzee	1.33	1.00	1.63	1.73	1.09	1.48
Butterfly	1.06	1.02	2.08	2.36	1.00	1.33
Spaniel (dog)	1.08	1.02	2.06	1.84	1.08	1.31
Tortoise	1.41	1.08	1.08	1.06	1.00	1.31
Robin	1.02	1.00	2.10	2.29	1.00	1.31
Lamb	1.02	1.00	1.61	1.90	1.00	1.16
Cat	1.02	1.00	2.17	2.31	1.03	1.14
Ladybird	1.10	1.00	1.71	1.99	1.02	1.14
Rabbit	1.04	1.00	2.35	2.65	1.02	1.13

An analysis of sex differences in ratings of nearness showed that females rated themselves as significantly less willing to approach or pick up ten of the animals than males. These were in descending order: jellyfish, cockroach, ant and moth ($F = 7.08$; $p < 0.01$); and crow, worm, beetle, slug, mouse and spider ($F = 4.00$; $p < 0.05$). Similar sex differences were found on the fear rating. In contrast, there were no sex differences in ratings of ugliness, sliminess, speediness and suddenness of movement. Although Group I men generally rated themselves as less fearful than women, as found in other studies (e.g. Geer, 1965), both sexes were evidently responsive to the same characteristics of the animals. The rank-order correlation between nearness ratings of animals in men and women was $r = 0.96$ ($p < 0.001$).

Table 13.2 shows the Spearman intercorrelations between the measures listed in table 13.1. Ratings of ugliness and sliminess were significantly correlated with nearness and fear measures. Ratings of speediness and suddenness of movement were highly correlated with

Table 13.2 Correlation matrix of animal characteristics, fear and nearness measures

	Ugly	Slimy	Speedy	Moves suddenly	Fear	Nearness
Ugly						
Slimy	0.75*					
Speedy	−0.20	−0.29				
Moves Suddenly	−0.16	−0.21	0.95*			
Fear	0.82*	0.61*	0.17	0.20		
Nearness	0.87*	0.77*	−0.02	0.05	0.90*	

* $p < 0.001$

each other, but, initially, not with fear and nearness measures; however, when ugliness was partialled out, suddeness of movement was significantly correlated with nearness ($r = 0.61$, $p < 0.001$), and when sliminess was partialled out, the correlations with these measures were 0.33 (not significant) and 0.48 ($p < 0.01$).

Similar partial correlations were found between speediness and the fear and nearness measures. Thus, fear and nearness ratings are related to quality of movement as well as to the qualities of sliminess and ugliness.

To summarize: each of the four ratings of perceptual characteristics is significantly related to both fear and nearness ratings, as predicted. Ugliness and sliminess seem to be the most important but when their effects are partialled out, speediness and suddenness of movement are both seen to exert a significant influence. The hypothesis is clearly supported.

Discussion

The results suggest that the perceptual characteristics of animals are important in determining their positive or negative appraisal by humans: animals rated as ugly, slimy, speedy or sudden-moving are experienced as less approachable and more fear-provoking than those without these qualities. Also, the attempt to remove harmfulness as a factor in the ratings suggests that this may be a major influence in the genesis of phobias, and this was most clearly seen in the case of rats, rated as the most feared animal, almost certainly because they were perceived as potentially harmful.

However, many phobias are of common animals which can do little harm (if any), and this is acknowledged by the phboic person; the term 'phobia' is used to denote the apparent irrational, as well as the intense, nature of the fear response. The present study focused on small, harmless animals to determine why some become the object of phobias, while others do not.

One problem in interpreting the results is: to what extent are these perceptual characteristics implicated in the genesis of clinical phobias? Subjects showed little fear on the fear scale for the vast majority of the animals, but ratings may have been higher if, for example, they had been asked to imagine specific situations. Although there was more variation on the nearness scale, the population as a whole is clearly non-phobic. It may be concluded that the rank orderings of animal characteristics and ratings of aversion (if not fear) are highly related in a normal population.

To study actual clinical patients would be a more direct test of the importance of perceptual characteristics in the genesis of phobias, but there are inherent problems of bias and selectivity: they already have one or more specific animal phobias and their fear ratings will, therefore, be systematically biased by their feared animal(s) and their ratings of that animal's characteristics may be exaggerated and distorted (Landau, 1980). Data from clinical patients would provide interesting insights into their perceptions (e.g. do they perceive feared animals as uglier or more sudden-moving than non-phobics?), but would not answer the questions about aetiology and non-random distribution of phobias (which can only be gained from studying the normal population). However, if the clinical referral of phobias of different animals were correlated with ratings of the perceptual characteristics of those animals, a very similar outcome to the present study would be expected.

Both Gray (1971) and Seligman (1971) proposed that humans have innate tendencies to fear certain animals, and the present study is aimed at specifying the mechanism underlying these prepared fears. To do this, two concepts have been borrowed from the animal behaviour literature; firstly, the discrepancy principle (Hinde, 1974), which may plausibly account for the very strong relationship between ratings of ugliness and sliminess and the fear and nearness ratings, and, secondly, that of aversive stimulus configurations (Schneirla, 1965). Although ratings of ugliness are essentially subjective, there was no sex difference here (unlike the fear measures), which suggests there was a shared construct of ugliness across the sexes. Subjects reported that their judgements of ugliness incorporated elements of sliminess, hairiness, colour of animal, perceived dirtiness, number of limbs and antennae projecting from the body, compactness of body and relation of eyes to the head; all these characteristics relate to how far the animal departs from the human, mammalian form.

In terms of the range of animals included in the questionnaire, the aversive stimulus configurations of speed and suddenness of movement were not as strongly related to the fear and nearness ratings as ratings of ugliness and sliminess (cf. slugs). But once the effect of these latter variables was partialled out, both the former became significantly correlated with fear ratings. Subjects referred to tactile and auditory, as well as visual, cues as an integral part of their perceptions of the movement of these animals, e.g. a number said that the feel of spiders was particularly unpleasant ('spiders can run very fast and I couldn't stand the thought of one running up my leg'; 'they have long hairy legs that can grab you'), and others drew attention to auditory properties ('cockroaches, the noise they make and their quick, unpredictable actions'; 'the hissing of snakes, the darting movements of their tongue . . .').

These findings suggest a model in which the fear response of animal phobic patients should be desensitized to specific perceptual characteristics; e.g. in the case of fear of slimy creatures, treatment might start with the presentation of wet soap or porridge before proceeding to the gradual presentation of the animal (either in imagination or *in vivo*).

In conclusion, the present study represents a first attempt to investigate the claim that certain fears of animals are innate and prepared, and that this in part accounts for the non-random distribution of animal phobias (Gray, 1971; Seligman, 1971). A template theory of specific animal fears was discussed and rejected in favour of a 'perceptual characteristics' hypothesis. The results suggest that humans are probably not prepared specifically to fear animals of biological significance to the species! Rather, the degree to which humans are prepared to approach or fear an animal depends not only on its objective harmfulness, but also on the presence of certain fear-evoking perceptual properties, and its discrepancy from the human form.

Commentary

Aim and nature

The article describes a correlational study of the concept of preparedness, in which the two variables of fear (of 29 small, harmless animals) and animal characteristics are being measured. It is the relationship between the two variables that is being investigated: because it is a correlational study, there is no independent variable being manipulated. The hypothesis being investigated is that human beings, like animals, are prepared to fear certain stimulus configurations, such as rapid or abrupt movement and stimuli which are discrepant from the human form. More specifically, the hypothesis predicts that the perceptual characteristics of small, harmless animals should be meaningfully related to the distribution of ratings of fear and avoidance of these animals (i.e. that the more rapid or abrupt the movements of these animals are, and the more they depart from the human form, the greater will be the fear ratings of these animals).

The corollary of the hypothesis is that such a relationship might help to explain why the distribution of animal phobias is non-random and why certain small, harmless creatures, but not others, become the subject of fear.

Context and background

The central concept being explored in the study, that of preparedness, relates to the more general topic of learning and, in particular, to the process of conditioning. An important – and controversial – question is whether conditioning works in the same way for all species or, put another way, whether there are any general 'laws' of learning.

According to Walker (1984), the fact that many experiments involving a variety of species can all be described as classical conditioning (since in all cases a response comes to be elicited by a new stimulus) does *not* in itself mean that there is only one mechanism involved, or only one explanation which applies, equally, to all species and all cases.

One possible 'law' is the law of *contiguity*: events (or stimuli) which occur close together in time or space are likely to become associated with each other. But a famous and important exception are the *taste aversion* studies of Garcia *et al.* (1966) and Garcia and Koelling (1966) (see chapter 12).

What Garcia's work shows is that there are definite biological limitations on the ability of animals to develop a conditioned aversion. This has led Bolles (1980) and others to conclude that we cannot regard the basic principle of learning as applying equally to all species in all situations: we must take into account the evolutionary history of the species as well as the individual organism's learning history.

Seligman's (1970) concept of *preparedness* is meant to emphasize the fact that animals are biologically prepared to learn actions which are closely related to the survival of their species (e.g. learned food/water aversions) and these prepared behaviours are learned with very little training. By the same token, there are also 'contra-prepared' behaviours which are contrary to an animal's natural tendencies, and so are learned with great difficulty, if at all. Seligman believes that most of the behaviour studied in the laboratory falls somewhere between these two extremes.

Applied to human phobias of animals, the concept of preparedness suggests that we are in some way biologically predisposed to fear certain animals (rather than others) and that these fears have somehow helped the species to survive. The Bennett-Levy and Marteau study is intended to find empirical support for the concept of preparedness by studying animal phobias in people.

Evaluation

1 If indeed we are prepared to fear certain animals and if these fears have helped us to survive as a species, it would seem to follow that the most common fears would be of those animals which are actually life-threatening (i.e. the fear would be rational, at least in terms of our evolutionary history). But Bennett-Levy and Marteau provide evidence which suggests that, in the main, it is certain perceptual qualities of animals which make them more likely to be feared, namely, how much they differ from the human form and *not* their objective threat; this finding fits the irrational nature of phobias much better.

2 However, there are still a number of questions left unanswered by their findings:
(a) Unless difference from the human form is highly correlated with dangerousness (which it does not seem to be, e.g. most spiders are *not* poisonous), what is the biological function (either now or in our evolutionary past) of showing fear towards animals which look very unlike human beings?
(b) If we are prepared, biologically, to fear certain animals because they are slimy, etc., how can we account for individual differences, both within and between the sexes? Why do some men, and some women, develop phobias and not others? If, as the present study shows, both sexes were evidently responsive to the same characteristics of the animals, i.e. ugliness, sliminess, speediness and suddenness of movement, why is it females rate themselves as significantly less willing to approach or pick up ten of the animals than men (jellyfish, cockroach, ant, moth, crow, worm, beetle, slug, mouse and spider)? And why is it that similar sex differences were found on the fear ratings (as also found by Geer, 1965)? Is the stereotypically female fear of spiders and mice, for example, supported by these findings? If so, how do we account for it, or is it *just* part of our female stereotype? Presumably, any biological predisposition such as Seligman proposes, applies equally to males and females. Does it make sense to say that some people are 'more prepared' than others? Even if we accept the importance of the concept of preparedness, it cannot be a *sufficient* explanation of the development of

phobias, since on its own it cannot account for individual difference. And what about cultural differences? Would we expect similar results to be found in different cultures regarding ugliness, sliminess, etc., or are these themselves culturally determined ways of perceiving and evaluating animals? This, in turn, leads on to the more fundamental question as to whether the human form is conceptualized in the same way in different cultures.

(c) Laboratory studies, in which fears have been artificially induced in non-phobic subjects, do not always support the concept of preparedness. McNally and Reiss (1982) reviewed a number of such studies, as well as reporting the results of one of their own. Ohman *et al.* (1976) used snakes and flowers as conditioned stimuli and, according to preparedness, a fear of snakes should (*i*) have been acquired more rapidly; (*ii*) be more resistant to extinction; (*iii*) be more resistant to cognitive influences. Ohman *et al.* found support for (ii) as have several other studies (Hugdahl, 1978; Hugdahl & Ohman, 1977; Ohman *et al.*, 1975a,b). These provide the most important experimental evidence in support of the theory. There has been less support for (iii), but most studies have failed to find any support for (i) (except Hugdahl *et al.*, 1977).

However, even regarding (ii), things are less than clear-cut. For instance, McNally and Reiss (1982) point out that the resistance-to-extinction hypothesis seems inconsistent with clinical observations that snake phobias are amenable to treatment (e.g. Bootzin & Max, 1982). Also, they point out that it is possible that slow extinction effects found in previous experiments may have been caused by subjects having been afraid of snakes *prior* to conditioning. For example, Hugdahl *et al.* (1977) and Ohman *et al.* (1975a) found that subjects showed significantly higher electrodermal responses (or GSRs) to a fear-relevant conditioned stimulus than a fear-irrelevant CS on habituation trials *before* conditioning trials began. This means it is not *necessary* to assume a biologically determined tendency to condition strongly to certain stimuli, as the preparedness concept requires.

McNally and Reiss (1982) were interested in the concept of preparedness as it relates to safety-signalling conditioning, whereby the CS signals an imminent period of *absence* from an aversive UCS. Fear-relevant stimuli (e.g. snakes) should be *contraprepared* for this kind of conditioning, and they tested this hypothesis by comparing pictures of a snake and flowers for how easily these CSs could be established as conditioned safety-signals. Contrary to the preparedness hypothesis, a pictorial snake was easily established as a conditioned safety signal.

3 Finally, the preparedness concept assumes that phobias result from classical conditioning (with fear-relevant, i.e. prepared, CSs being much more easily conditioned than fear-irrelevant CSs). Recent evidence has motivated a reconsideration and reformulation of the conditioning model (Eysenck, 1976), and Rachman (1977, 1978) has gone as far as to suggest that direct conditioning of any kind accounts for relatively few phobias. Instead, he claims that many fears are acquired on the basis of information transmitted through observation and instruction. Some support for Rachman comes from a study by Murray and Foote (1979) who conclude by saying that although preparedness for direct conditioning does not seem to be relevant, a preparedness for observational and instructional learning is possible.

Exercises

1 Is the (main) hypothesis one- or two-tailed?
   And if it is one-tailed, is it predicting a positive or a negative correlation?

2 The *F*-test was used to test for sex differences in ratings of nearness/fear. What is the *F*-test?

3 The design is correlational, in which it is predicted that two variables (fear of animals and animal characteristics, both measured by questionnaires) are significantly correlated. They were measured separately for two different groups of subjects. Is there anything unusual about this?

4 Could the *same* subjects have been given *both* questionnaires? If so, what precautions would need to be taken?

5 The subjects were people attending a local health centre:
(*i*) How should they have been selected?
(*ii*) They were chosen, as against phobic patients, for their 'normality'. Is this condition actually fulfilled (i.e. why might they themselves have been a biased sample)?

6 Given that they were not seeking help for phobias (as far as we know), was it right that they should be asked about their fear of animals?

R. A. GARDNER AND B. T. GARDNER (1969)

Teaching sign language to a chimpanzee

Science, Vol. 165, no. 3894, pp. 664–72

The extent to which another species might be able to use human language is a classical problem in comparative psychology. One approach to this problem is to consider the nature of language, the processes of learning, the neural mechanisms of learning and of language, their genetic basis and so on; another is to try to teach a form of human language to an animal. We chose the latter alternative and, in June, 1966, began training an infant female chimpanzee, named Washoe, to use the gestural language of the deaf. Within the first 32 months of training it became evident that we had been correct in at least one major aspect of method, the use of a gestural language; additional aspects of method have evolved in the course of the project. In this article we discuss the considerations which led us to use the chimp as a subject and American Sign Language (the language used by the deaf in North America) as a medium of communication, describe the general methods of training as they were initially conceived and as they later developed during the project, and summarize those results which could be reported with some degree of confidence by the end of the first phase of the project.

Preliminary considerations

The chimpanzee as a subject

Whether or not the chimp is the most intelligent animal after man can be disputed; the gorilla, orangutan and even the dolphin all have their supporters in this debate. Nevertheless, it is generally agreed that chimps are highly intelligent and, perhaps more importantly, that they are sociable and capable of forming strong attachments to human beings.

However, as affectionate as they are, chimps are still wild animals, in contrast with the animals which have been chosen, and sometimes bred, for docility and adaptability to laboratory procedures. They are also very strong animals: a full-grown chimp is likely to weigh more than 120 pounds, and is estimated to be three to five times as strong as a man, pound-for-pound. This great strength presents serious difficulties for a procedure which requires interaction at close quarters with a free-living animal.

A more serious disadvantage is that human speech sounds are unsuitable as a medium of communication for the chimp. The vocal apparatus of chimps is very different from that of man (Bryan, 1963) and, more importantly, their vocal behaviour is very different. Although they do make many different sounds, generally vocalization occurs in situations of high excitement and tends to be specific to the exciting situations. Undisturbed, they are usually silent. Thus it is unlikely that a chimp could be trained to make refined use of its vocalizations. The intensive work of Hayes and Hayes (1951) with Viki indicates that a vocal language is not appropriate for chimps; they used modern, sophisticated, psychological methods, and yet in six years, Viki learned only four sounds that approximated English words.

Use of the hands, however, is a prominent feature of chimp behaviour; manipulatory, mechanical problems are their forte and, more to the point, even caged, laboratory chimps develop begging and similar gestures spontaneously (Yerkes, 1943). Chimps which have had extensive contact with people have displayed an even wider variety of communicative gestures (Hayes & Hayes, 1951; Kellogg & Kellogg, 1967; Kellogg, 1968). This behavioural evidence that sign language is appropriate to chimps was more influential than the anatomical evidence of similarity between the hands of chimps and humans; although chimps can use tools and mechanical devices made to fit the human hand very skilfully, they seem unable to adapt their vocalizations to approximate human speech. It was reasoned that gestures for chimps should be analogous to bar-pressing for rats, key-pecking for pigeons and babbling for humans, i.e. to instrumentally condition an animal, you must choose responses which are suited to members of that species.

American Sign Language

Sign language consists of a set of manual configurations and gestures which correspond to particular words or concepts. Unlike fingerspelling, which is the direct encoding of a spoken language, sign languages have their own rules of usage.

American Sign Language (ASL), with certain regional variations, is used by the deaf in North America. It can be compared to pictograph writing in which some symbols are quite arbitrary and some are quite representational or iconic, but all are arbitrary to some degree. For example, in ASL the sign for 'always' is made by holding the hand in a fist, index finger extended (the pointing hand), while rotating the arm at the elbow; this is clearly an arbitrary representation of the concept 'always'. However, the sign for 'flower' is highly iconic: it is made by holding the fingers of one hand extended, all five fingertips touching (the tapered hand), and touching the fingertips first to one nostril, then to the other, as if sniffing a flower. While this is an iconic sign for 'flower', it is only one of several conventions by which the concept 'flower' could be iconically represented and so is arbitrary to some degree. Undoubtedly, many ASL signs which seem quite arbitrary today had an iconic origin that was lost through years of stylized usage. Thus, the signs of ASL are neither uniformly arbitrary nor uniformly iconic but vary in their degree of abstraction. The literate deaf typically use a combination of ASL and finger spelling. This research avoided finger spelling as much as possible. A great range of expression is possible within the limits of ASL; technical terms and proper names are a problem when first introduced but it is quite easy for a community of signers to agree on some convention. For example, we render 'psychologist' as 'think doctor' and 'psychology' as 'think science'.

The fact that ASL is in current use by human beings is an additional advantage. The early linguistic environment of the deaf children of deaf parents is in some respects similar to what could be provided for an experimental subject and this should permit some comparative evaluation of Washoe's eventual level of competence. For example, in discussing Washoe's early performance with deaf parents, it seems that many of her variants of standard signs are similar to the baby-talk variants commonly observed when human children sign.

Washoe

While there may be a critical early age for the acquisition of this type of behaviour, newborn chimps tend to be quite helpless and vegetative and are considerably less hardy than older infants. Nevertheless, we reasoned that the dangers of starting too late were much greater than the dangers of starting too early, so we sought the youngest infant we could find. Newborn laboratory chimps are very scarce, and it seemed perferable to obtain a wild-caught infant, even though it would be at least eight to ten months old before it was available for research.

Washoe was named after Washoe County, the home of the University of Nevada. Her age was estimated to be between eight and 14 months at the end of June, 1966, when she first arrived at the laboratory. They are normally completely dependent until the age of two and semi-dependent until four, full adult growth being reached between 12 and 16 (Goodall, 1965; Riopelle & Rogers, 1965).

Washoe was very young when she arrived; she did not have her first canines or molars, had only rudimentary hand–eye coordination, was only beginning to crawl, and slept a great deal. Apart from making friends with her and adapting her to the daily routine, very little could be done during the first few months.

Laboratory conditions

At the outset we were quite sure that Washoe could learn to make various signs in order to obtain food, drink, etc. But we wanted Washoe not only to ask for objects but to answer questions about them and also to ask us questions, i.e. to develop behaviour which could be described as conversation. With this in mind, confinement was to be about the same as a human infant, her human companions were to be friends and playmates as well as providers and protectors, and they were to introduce a great many games and activities which would maximize interaction with Washoe.

In practice, such an environment is readily achieved with a chimp. A number of human companions have been enlisted to participate in the project and relieve each other at intervals, so that at least one person would be with her during all her waking hours. Washoe adapted very well to this procedure: apparently, it is possible to provide an infant chimp with affection on a shift basis. All her companions have had to master ASL and use it extensively in her presence, in conjunction with interesting activities and also in a general way, as one chatters at a human infant. Occasional finger spelling has been allowed and, of course, there are lapses into spoken English, as when medical personnel examine her.

However, the environment described here is not a silent one. The humans can vocalize in many ways, laughing, making sounds of pleasure and displeasure, whistles and drums are sounded in a variety of imitation games, and hands are clapped for attention. The rule is that all meaningful sounds, whether vocalized or not, must be sounds that a chimp can imitate.

Training methods

Imitation

The imitativeness of apes is proverbial, and rightly so:

> Chim and Panzee would imitate many of my acts, but never have I heard them imitate a sound, and rarely make a sound peculiarly their own in response to mine. As previously stated, their imitative tendency is as remarkable for its specialization and limitations as for its strength. It seems to be controlled chiefly by visual stimuli. Things which are seen tend to be imitated or reproduced. What is heard is not reproduced. Obviously an animal which lacks the tendency to reinstate auditory stimuli – in other words to imitate sounds – cannot reasonably be expected to talk. The human infant exhibits this tendency to a remarkable degree. So also does the parrot. If the imitative tendency of the parrot could be coupled with the quality of intelligence of the chimpanzee, the latter undoubtedly could speak. (Yerkes & Learned, 1925)

The Hayes' (1952) devised a game with Viki in which she would imitate various actions on hearing the command 'Do this'; once established, this was an effective means of training Viki to perform actions that could be visually guided and the same method should be admirably suited to training a chimp to use sign language. Getting Washoe to imitate us was not difficult, for she did so quite spontaneously, but getting her to imitate on command has been another matter: not until she was 16 months did we achieve any degree of control over her imitation of gestures. Eventually, we reached a point where she would imitate a simple gesture, such as pulling at her ears, or a series of gestures, for the reward of being tickled. However, imitation of this sort had not been an important method for introducing new signs into Washoe's vocabulary.

As a method of prompting, imitation has been used extensively to increase the frequency and refine the form of signs. Washoe sometimes fails to use a new sign in an appropriate situation, or uses another, incorrect sign; at such times we can make the correct sign to Washoe, repeating the performance until she makes the sign herself. (With more stable signs, more indirect forms of prompting can be used, e.g. pointing at or touching Washoe's hand or a part of her body that should be involved in the sign, making the sign for 'sign', or asking a question in signs, such as 'What do you want?' or 'What is it?'.) Her 'diction' (with both new and old signs) has often been improved by simply repeating, in exaggeratedly correct form, the sign she has just made until she repeats it herself in more correct form. But there are limits to the use of prompting with a wild animal; pressed too hard, Washoe can become completely diverted from her original object, may ask for something entirely different, run away, throw a tantrum or even bite her tutor.

Chimps also imitate, after some delay. A typical example is to do with her bath and the dolly she always had to play with (from her second month with us). One day, during the tenth month of the project, she bathed one of her dolls in the way we usually bathed her. She filled her little bathtub with water, dunked the doll in the tub, then took it out and dried it with a towel. She has repeated the entire performance, or parts of it, many times since, sometimes also soaping the doll.

This is a type of imitation which may be very important in the acquisition of language by children. Routine activities – feeding, dressing, bathing etc. – have been highly ritualized, with appropriate signs figuring prominently in the rituals. Many games have been invented which can be accompanied by appropriate signs; objects and activities have been named as often as possible, especially when Washoe seemed to be paying particular attention to them. New objects and new examples of familiar objects, including pictures, have been continually brought to her attention, together with the appropriate signs. All of this has been done in the hope that she would come to associate the signs with their referents and later make the signs herself. We have reason to believe that she has come to understand a large vocabulary of signs.

Some of Washoe's signs seem to have been originally acquired by delayed imitation. A good example is the sign for 'toothbrush'. A part of the daily routine has been to brush her teeth after every meal; at first, she resisted but gradually came to make less and less fuss until after several months she would even help sometimes to brush her teeth herself. Usually, having finished her meal, Washoe would try to leave her highchair; we would restrain her, signing 'first, toothbrushing, then you can go'. One day, in the tenth month of the project, she was visiting the Gardner home and found her way into the bathroom, she looked at the mug full of toothbrushes and signed 'toothbrush'. At the time, we believed she understood this sign but we had not seen her use it. It is unlikely that she was asking for the toothbrushes, since she could easily reach them or that she was asking to have her teeth brushed. This was the first and one of the clearest examples of Washoe apparently naming an object or event for no obvious motive other than communication.

Babbling

Because the Hayes' were trying to teach Viki to speak English, they were interested in babbling. After early encouragement at the number and variety of spontaneous vocalizations she made, these became fewer and fewer to the point where the Hayes' felt that there was almost no vocal babbling from which to shape speech. As far as manual 'babbling' is concerned, the reverse happened: it has increased as the project has progressed. We have been particularly encouraged by the increase in movements which involve touching parts of the head and body, since these are important components of many signs. Also, more and more often, when Washoe has been unable to get something she wants, she has burst into a flurry of random flourishes and arm-waving.

We have encouraged Washoe's babbling by clapping, smiling and repeating the gestures (just as you might repeat 'goo goo' to a baby). If the babbled gesture has resembled a sign in ASL, we have made the correct form of the sign and tried to engage in some appropriate activity.

Closely related to babbling are certain gestures which seem to have appeared independently of any deliberate training on our part and which resemble signs so closely that they could be incorporated into Washoe's repertoire with little or no modification. Almost from the first she had a bagging gesture: an extension of her open hand, palm up, toward one of us. She made this gesture in situations in which she wanted aid or in which we were holding something she wanted. The ASL signs for 'give me' and 'come' are very similar to this, except that they involve a prominent beckoning movement; gradually Washoe incorporated a beckoning wrist movement into her use of the sign ('come–gimme' in table 14.1).

Instrumental conditioning

It seems intuitively unreasonable that the acquisition of language by human beings could be strictly a matter of repeated instrumental conditioning; that a child acquires language in a similar way to a rat which is conditioned, first to press a lever for food in the presence of a stimulus, then to turn a wheel in the presence of another stimulus, and so on until a large repertoire of discriminatory responses is acquired. Nevertheless, the so-called 'trick vocabulary' of early childhood is probably acquired in this way, and this may be a critical stage in childrens' language acquisition. Besides, a main objective of the project was to teach Washoe as many signs as possible, by whatever methods we could enlist, including conventional procedures of instrumental conditioning.

There is no doubt that tickling is the most effective reward that we have used with Washoe. In the early months, when we paused in our tickling Washoe placed her hands against her ribs or around her neck, indicating unmistakably that she wanted more tickling. It was decided to shape an arbitrary response which she could use for requesting more tickling; we noticed that, when being tickled, she tended to bring her arms together to cover the place being tickled. The result was a very crude approximation of the ASL sign for 'more' (see table 14.1), so we would stop tickling and then pull Washoe's arms away from her body. When we released her arms and threatened to resume tickling, she tended to bring her hands together again, in which case we would tickle her again. Occasionally, we would stop tickling and wait for her to put her hands together by herself. At first, any approximation to the 'more' sign, however crude, was rewarded; later, closer approximations were required, and imitative prompting was introduced. Soon, a very good version of the 'more' sign could be obtained but it was quite specific to the tickling situation.

In the sixth month of the project, Washoe signed 'more' for a new game which consisted of pushing Washoe across the floor in a laundry basket; imitative prompting was used from the start. It then began to appear as a request for more swinging (by the arms), again after first being elicited by imitative prompting. From this point on, Washoe transferred the 'more' sign to all activities including feeding, usually spontaneously, when there was some pause in a desired activity or when some object was removed. Often we ourselves were not sure that Washoe wanted 'more' until she signed to us.

Results

Vocabulary

Early on we were able to keep fairly complete records of Washoe's daily signing behaviour, but as the amount of signing behaviour and number of signs increased, trying to keep exhaustive records became too cumbersome. So, during the sixteenth month, we settled on the following procedure. When a new sign appeared, we waited for it to be reported by three different observers as having occurred in an appropriate context and spontaneously (i.e. with no prompting other than a question such as 'What is it?' or 'What do you want?'). The sign was then added to a checklist in which its occurrence, form, context, and the kind of prompting needed were recorded. Two such checklists were filled out each day, one for each half of the day. A reported frequency of at least one appropriate and spontaneous occurrence each day over a period of 15 consecutive days was taken as the criterion of acquisition. Table 14.1 shows 30 signs which met this criterion by the end of the 22nd month of the project. Four others have been listed ('dog', 'smell', 'me' and 'clean') which were judged to be stable, despite the fact that they had not met the stringent criterion by the end of 22 months; however, they had been reported to occur appropriately and spontaneously on more than half of the days in a period of 30 consecutive days.

During the 22nd month, 28 of the 34 signs were reported on at least 20 days and the smallest number of different signs reported for a single day was 23, with a median of 29. Four new signs appeared during the first seven months, nine during the next seven and 21 during the next seven. Clearly, if Washoe's rate of acquisition continues to accelerate, we will have to assess her vocabulary on the basis of sampling procedures.

Differentiation

Column 1 of table 14.1 lists English equivalents for each of Washoe's signs. However, this equivalence is only approximate, since (*i*) equivalence between ASL and English, as between any two human languages, is only approximate and (*ii*) Washoe's usage differs from that of standard ASL. Although to some extent her usage is indicated in the 'Context' column of table 14.1, the definition of any given sign must always depend upon her own vocabulary which has been continually changing. For example, when she had very few signs for specific things, Washoe used 'more' for a wide class of requests, but this declined as she acquired signs for specific requests until she was using the sign mainly to ask for repetition of some action that she could not name, such as a somersault. (Perhaps 'do it again' is the best English equivalent of her current use of the sign.)

Differentiation of the signs for 'flower' and 'smell' is further illustration of usage depending on size of vocabulary. As the 'flower' sign became more frequent, it occurred in several inappropriate contexts which all seemed to include odours; for example, opening a tobacco pouch or entering a kitchen with cooking smells. Gradually, through passive shaping and imitative prompting, she came to make the appropriate distinction, although 'flower' (in the single-nostril form: see table 14.1) continues to occur as a common error in 'smell' contexts.

Transfer

In general, when introducing new signs we have used a very specific referent for the initial training: a particular door for 'open', a particular hat for 'hat'. But Washoe has always been able to transfer her signs spontaneously to new members of each class of referents (see the examples of 'more' above). The sign for 'flower' is a particularly good example of transfer, because flowers occur in so many varieties indoors, outdoors and in pictures, and she uses the same sign for all. She also transferred the 'dog' sign to the sound of barking of an unknown dog.

To improve her manual dexterity, Washoe was allowed to practise with padlock keys which opened many cupboards and doors in her quarters. Once she mastered this skill, it transferred to all kinds of locks and keys, including ignition keys. At about the same time, we taught her the 'key' sign using the original padlock keys as a referent. She came to use this sign both to name keys presented to her and to

Table 14.1   Signs used reliably by Chimpanzee Washoe within 22 months of the beginning of training (The signs are listed in the order of their original appearance in her repertoire; see text for the criterion of reliability and for the method of assigning the date of original appearance)

Signs	Description	Context
Come–gimme	Beckoning motion with wrist or knuckles as pivot.	Sign made to person or animals, also for objects out of reach. Often combined: 'come tickle', 'gimme sweet', etc.
More	Fingertips are brought together, usually overhead. (Correct ASL form: tips of the tapered hand touch repeatedly.)	When asking for continuation or repetition of activities such as swinging or tickling, for second helpings of food etc. Also used to ask for repetition of some performance, such as a somersault.
Up	Arm extends upward and index finger may also point up.	Wants a lift to reach objects such as grapes on vine, or leaves, or wants to be placed on someone's shoulders or wants to leave potty-chair.
Sweet	Index or index and second fingers touch tip of wagging tongue. (Correct ASL form: index and second fingers extended side by side.)	For dessert, used spontaneously at end of meal. Also when asking for candy.
Open	Flat hands are placed side by side, palms down, then drawn apart while rotated to palms up.	At door of house, room, car, refrigerator, or cupboard, or containers such as jars, and on faucets.
Tickle	The index finger of one hand is drawn across the back of the other hand. (Related to ASL touch.)	For tickling or for chasing games.
Go	Opposite of come–gimme.	While walking hand-in-hand or riding on someone's shoulders. Washoe usually indicates the direction desired.
Out	Curved hand grasps tapered hand; then tapered hand is withdrawn upward.	When passing through doorways, until recently used for both 'in' and 'out'. Also when asking to be taken outdoors.
Hurry	Open hand is shaken at the wrist. (Correct ASL form: index and second fingers extended side by side.)	Often follows signs such as 'come–gimme', 'out', 'open' and 'go', particularly if there is a delay before Washoe obeyed. Also used while watching her meal being prepared.
Hear–listen	Index finger touches ear.	For loud or strange sounds: bells, car horns, sonic booms, etc. Also for asking someone to hold a watch to her ear.

Signs	Description	Context
Toothbrush	Index finger is used as brush, to rub front teeth.	When Washoe has finished her meal, or at other times when shown a toothbrush.
Drink	Thumb is extended from fisted hand and touches mouth.	For water formula, soda pop, etc. For soda pop often combined with 'sweet'.
Hurt	Extended index fingers jabbed toward each other. Can be used to indicate location of pain.	To indicate cuts and bruises on herself or on others. Can be elicited by red stains on a person's skin or by tears in clothing.
Sorry	Fisted hand clasps at shoulder. (Correct ASL form: fisted hand is rubbed over heart with circular motion.)	After biting someone, or when someone has been hurt in another way (not necessarily by Washoe), when told to apologise for mischief.
Funny	Tip of index finger presses nose, and Washoe snorts. (Correct ASL form: index and second fingers used, no snort.)	When soliciting interaction play, and during games. Occasionally when being pursued after mischief.
Please	Open hand is drawn across chest. (Correct ASL form: fingertips used and circular motion.)	When asking for objects and activities. Frequently combined 'please go', 'out please', 'please drink'.
Food–eat	Several fingers of one hand are placed in mouth. (Correct ASL form: fingertips of tapered hand touch mouth repeatedly.)	During meals and preparation of meals.
Flower	Tip of index finger touches one or both nostrils. (Correct ASL form: tip of tapered hand touch first one nostril, then the other.)	For flowers.
Cover–blanket	Draws one hand toward self over the back of the other.	At bedtime or naptime and on cold days when Washoe wants to be taken out.
Dog	Repeated slapping on thigh.	For dogs and for barking.
You	Index finger points at a person's chest.	Indicates successive turns in games. Also used in response to questions such as 'Who tickle?', 'Who brush?'.
Napkin–bib	Fingertips wipe the mouth region.	For bib, for washcloth, and for Kleenex.
In	Opposite of 'out'.	Wants to go indoors or wants someone to join her outdoors.
Brush	The fisted hand rubs the back of the open hand several times. (Adapted from the ASL 'polish'.)	For hairbrush, and when asking for brushing.

Signs	Description	Context
Hat	Palm pats top of head.	For hats and caps.
I–me	Index finger points at or touches chest.	Indicates Washoe's turn when she and a companion share food, drink, etc. Also used in phrases such as 'I drink' and in reply to questions such as 'Who tickle?' (Washoe: 'you'), 'Who I tickle?' (Washoe: 'Me').
Shoes	The fisted hands are held side by side and strike down on shoes or floor. (Correct ASL form: the sides of the fisted hands strike against each other.)	For shoes and boots.
Smell	Palm is held before nose and moved slightly upward several times.	For scented objects: tobacco, perfume, sage, etc.
Pants	Palms of the flat hand are drawn up against the body towards waist.	For diapers, rubber pants, trousers.
Clothes	Fingertips brush down the chest.	For Washoe's jacket, nightgown, and shirts, also for our clothing.
Cat	Thumb and index finger grasp cheek hair near side of mouth and are drawn outward (representing cat's whiskers).	For cats.
Key	Palm of one hand is repeatedly touched with the index finger of the other. (Correct ASL form: crooked index finger is rotated against palm.)	Used for keys and locks and to ask us to unlock a door.
Baby	One forearm is placed in the crook of the other.	For dolls, including animals, such as a toy horse and duck.
Clean	The open palm of one hand is passed over the open palm of the other.	Used when Washoe is washing, or being washed, or when a companion is washing hands or some other object. Also used for 'soap'.

ask for the key to various locks when no one was in sight. She readily transfered the sign to all varieties of keys and locks.

Combinations

No deliberate attempts were made to elicit combinations or phrases, although we may have responded more readily to strings of two or more signs than to single ones. As far as we can judge, Washoe's early use of strings was spontaneous. Almost as soon as she had eight to ten signs in her vocabulary, she began to use two or three of them at a time, and this tendency has increased in line with her vocabulary, so that it is now a common mode of signing. We, of course, usually signed to her in combinations but if Washoe's use of combinations has been imitative, then it must be a generalized sort of imitation, since she has invented several combinations, e.g. 'gimme tickle' (before we had even asked her to tickle us) and 'open food drink' (for the fridge, which we have always called the 'cold box'). Four signs ('please', 'come–gimme', 'hurry' and 'more') used with one or more other signs account for the largest share of Washoe's early combinations; they function mainly as emphasizers, as in 'please open hurry' and 'gimme drink please'. Five others ('go', 'out', 'in', 'open' and 'hear–listen') accounted for most of the remaining combinations until recently. Typical examples include 'go in'/'go out' (when at some distance from a door), 'go sweet' (for being carried to a raspberry bush), 'open flower' (to be let through the gate to a flower garden), 'open key' (for a locked door), 'listen eat' (at the sound of an alarm clock signalling mealtime) and 'listen dog' (at the sound of the barking of an unseen dog). All but the first and last of these six examples were Washoe's inventions.

More recently, Washoe learnt 'I–me' and 'you' so that combinations which resemble short sentences have begun to appear.

Concluding observations

It is very difficult to answer questions such as 'Do you think that Washoe has language?' or 'At what point will you be able to say that Washoe has language?', because they imply a distinction between one class of communicative behaviour that can be called language and another class that cannot. This in turn implies a well established theory that could provide the distinction; if the objectives of our research had required such a theory, we would certainly not have been able to begin it as early as we did.

We have been able to verify the hypothesis that sign language is an appropriate medium of two-way communication for the chimp. Washoe's intellectual immaturity, the continuing acceleration of her progress, the fact that her signs do not remain specific to their original referents but are transferred spontaneously to new referents and the emergence of rudimentary combinations, all suggest that significantly more can be achieved by Washoe. Subsequent problems will be to do with the technical business of measurement; we are now developing a procedure for testing Washoe's ability to name objects in which an object or picture of an object is placed in a box with a window. An observer, who does not know what is in the box, asks Washoe what she sees through the window; however, this method is currently limited to items which can fit in the box. The ability to combine and recombine signs must be tested; our hope is that Washoe will eventually be able to describe events and situations to an observer who has no other source of information.

Washoe's achievements will probably be exceeded by another chimp, because it is unlikely that the training conditions have been optimal in this first attempt. Theories of language that depend upon the identification of aspects of language that are exclusively human must remain tentative until a considerably larger body of intensive research with other species becomes available.

Commentary

Aim and nature

The study was intended to help answer the question (a classical problem in comparative psychology): to what extent might another species be able to use human language? One way to approach the problem is to try to teach a form of human language to an animal. The report describes the first phase of a training project, involving an infant female chimp called Washoe. It is a kind of case study of a single subject, in which detailed records were kept of Washoe's progress over an extended period of time (32 months). Unlike most case studies (see chapter 24), there was no problem the subject had for which (s)he was receiving help; instead this was a deliberate attempt to change the subject's behaviour in a particular way in order to test a scientific hypothesis. This raises ethical issues not faced by most case studies (see below). To the extent that a deliberate attempt was made to change Washoe's behaviour in a particular way, it can be thought of as an experiment, with the training programme the independent variable and Washoe's actual use of signs the dependent variable. But unlike most dependent variables, operationalizing them doesn't seem to be sufficient to be able to determine whether the independent variable has actually had an effect: it is the *interpretation* of the dependent variable which is crucial, i.e. does Washoe's use of signs *constitute* language?

Context and background

For many psychologists, philosophers and linguists, language is the characteristic which makes humans unique amongst animals; it is what makes us the intelligent species we are. Chomsky (1957, 1965), for example, believes that language is unique to humans (is species-specific) and so cannot be acquired by other species; language learning can only occur in organisms possessing various innate linguistic mechanisms, and only humans possess such mechanisms (Language Acquisition Device).

Early attempts to teach chimps to speak were almost totally unsuccessful (Kellogg & Kellogg, 1933; Hayes & Hayes, 1951); it became obvious that a chimp's vocal apparatus is unsuited to making speech sounds. But this does not rule out the possibility that they are capable of learning language in some non-spoken form, and it was the Gardners who first attempted to do this using ASL.

Major subsequent studies have been (*i*) Premack (1971), involving a female chimp called Sarah, taught to use small plastic symbols of various shapes and colours, each standing for a word and arranged on a special magnetized board; (*ii*) Rumbaugh (1977); Savage-Rumbaugh *et al.* (1980), involving another female chimp, Lana, taught to use a special typewriter (controlled by a computer), with 50 keys, each displaying a geometric pattern representing a word in a specially devised language ('Yerkish') which, when typed, appeared on a screen in front of her; (*iii*) Patterson (1978, 1980), involving a female gorilla, Koko, taught, like Washoe, ASL; (*iv*) Terrace (1979), involving a male chimp, Nim (Neam) Chimpsky, also taught ASL.

Whatever the particular method used, the debate, as indicated above, has always been about how to evaluate the findings. To be able to judge a chimp's signing as language clearly depends on what we mean by language. The starting point for making such a judgement is Hockett's (1960) criteria for language, which reflect the Discontinuity theory of language, i.e. the view that there are *qualitative* (and not just quantitative) differences between human and animal language.

Based on Hockett, Aitchison (1983) proposes that ten should be sufficient (not all mentioned by Hockett), namely:

(a) use of the Vocal–Auditory Channel
(b) arbitrariness (use of neutral symbols (words) to denote objects, etc.)
(c) semanticity (the use of symbols to *mean* or refer to objects/actions)
(d) cultural transmission (handing down the language from generation to generation)
(e) spontaneous usage (freely initiating speech, etc.)
(f) turn-taking (conversation is a two-way process)
(g) duality (organization into basic sounds plus combinations or sequences of these)
(h) displacement (reference to things not present in time or space)
(i) structure-dependence (the patterned nature of language and use of 'structured chunks' e.g. word order)
(j) creativity (what Brown (1973) calls productivity: the ability to produce and understand an indefinite number of novel utterances).

By analyzing human and animal language in terms of all ten criteria, Aitchison concludes that four are unique to humans: semanticity, displacement, structure-dependence and creativity (productivity), and it is in terms of *these* that studies like the Gardners' should be evaluated.

Evaluation

1 It seems almost indisputable that Washoe had *Semanticity*: after four years of intensive training (based on reports subsequent to the 1969 paper), she had acquired 132 signs. She was also able to generalize from one situation to another (e.g. 'open', 'more') and sometimes over-generalized too (e.g. 'hurt'). There is also some limited evidence of *displacement*, as when she asked for absent objects or people (e.g. 'all gone cup'/'more milk'). Once she had learned eight to ten signs, she spontaneously began to combine them (showing *creativity*), e.g. 'gimme tickle' (come and tickle me), 'Go sweet' (take me to the raspberry bushes), 'listen eat' (listen to the dinner gong), 'listen dog', 'Roger come', 'Open food drink' (open the fridge), 'Hurry gimme toothbrush' and 'Roger Washoe tickle'.

However, as regards structure-dependence, although she combined some signs in a consistent order (e.g. 'baby mine' rather than 'mine baby'/'tickle me' rather than 'me tickle'), she did not always seem to care about sign order, e.g. she was as likely to sign 'go sweet' as 'sweet go'. Why?

Aitchison (1983) suggests four reasons; (*i*) the Gardners' overeagerness may have led them to reward her every time she signed correctly (regardless of order) so that the idea that order was important may never have been learnt; (*ii*) it may be easier with words to preserve order than with signs, e.g. deaf adults are also inconsistent in their word order; (*iii*) this may have been a temporary, intermediate stage before she eventually learnt to keep to a fixed order. The Gardners claim (1971, 1975, 1978, 1980) she did so; (*iv*) she did not and could not understand the essentially patterned nature of language.

2 So where does this leave us in deciding whether Washoe did, or did not, acquire language? There are clearly certain respects in which she displayed language (semanticity, displacement and creativity) but others in which she did not (structure-dependence). And this pattern is more or less confirmed by the other studies. As far as sign-order is concerned, both Sarah and Lana were trained to use a fixed order (were not rewarded if they deviated from this). However, Sarah could obey instructions and answer simple questions, while Lana could distinguish between 'Lana groom Tim' and 'Tim groom Lana'. Koko does not seem to have kept to any particular sign order, while Nim Chimpsky showed a statistical preference for putting certain words in a certain order but no evidence of understanding any *rules*.

3 It is worth looking at Nim more closely because the data was analyzed more carefully than in any other study (Aitchison, 1983), and is the most 'scientific' of all the studies (Eysenck, 1984). Approximately half Nim's 20,000 recorded signs were two-sign combinations and 1378 were different. They seemed to be structured; e.g. of the two-sign utterances including 'more', 789 had 'more' at the beginning, and of those involving a transitive verb (one taking an object), 83 per cent had the verb before the object. But he simply had a statistical preference for putting words in certain places, while there was no such preference for other words, e.g. 'more' at the beginning, 'Nim' at the end and any foods at the beginning too. Many other words had a random distribution (e.g. 'eat', regardless of length of sequence).

Petitto and Seidenberg (1979) conclude that 'repetitive, inconsistently structured strings are in fact characteristic of ape signing'. Nim's longest recorded utterance is: Eat drink, eat drink, eat Nim, eat Nim, drink eat, drink eat, Nim eat, Nim eat, me eat, me eat.

4 Even semanticity, which seems to be the one criterion of language which can be agreed upon, is problematical. Is the correct use of signs to refer to things a sufficient definition of semanticity? The toothbrush example (Washoe) seems to be the use of a sign in order simply to *name* something. But not only is this a very isolated example, when compared with semanticity as it is displayed by young children, major doubts arise; Savage-Rumbaugh *et al.* (1980) seriously doubt whether any of the apes (including their own, Lana) used the individual elements in their vocabularies as words. Terrace (1987) suggests that a strong case can be made for the hypothesis that the deceptively simple ability to use a symbol as a name required a cognitive advance in the evolution of human intelligence at least as significant as the advances that led to grammatical competence.

The function of much of a child's initial vocabulary of names is to inform another person (usually the adult) that (s)he has noticed something (MacNamara, 1982); often, the child refers to the object spontaneously, showing obvious delight from the sheer act of naming. And it is precisely this aspect of uttering a name which has *not* been observed in apes. Could any amount of training produce an ape with such ability? MacNamara thinks not, for the simple reason that the act of referring is not learnt but is a 'primitive of cognitive psychology' (and is a necessary precursor of naming). By contrast, chimps usually try to 'acquire' objects (approach it, explore it, etc.), and show no signs of trying to communicate the fact that it has noticed an object as an end in itself (Terrace, 1987).

5 Three other important differences between children's and Nim's language led Brown (1986) to the conclusion that young children have a syntactic capacity which young apes lack, i.e. roughly 'the ability to put symbols into construction so as to express compositionally meanings that are other than the sum of the meanings of the individual symbols', a paradigm example being 'dog chase cat' and 'cat chase dog', where word order changes the meaning, but is only one of a large number of syntactic devices for expressing meaning by composition.

(*i*) Children initially produce utterances containing an average of 1½ words (Mean Length of Utterance (MLU) = 1½) but this quickly rises to MLU = 4. By contrast, Nim's MLU did not rise at all but held steady at 1.1 to 1.6 signs. The steady rise in children probably results from both brain maturation and the accumulation of linguistic information. A failure to increase suggests that the symbol combinations being produced are *not* constructions but merely strings of single (unrelated) signs. Young children's longest construction is, for many years, around the mean but Nim's longest unbroken string (see above) is unrelated to MLU and far exceeds it. This suggests that MLU does not reflect complexity, and so reinforces the impression that Nim's strings are *only* strings ('Give orange me give eat orange me eat orange give me eat orange give me you'). Clearly the information transmitted does not increase with increase in MLU.

(*ii*) In many languages, word order (symbol-sequencing) has syntactic significance and children learn to follow the ordering rules as soon as they begin combining words. It is probably the first syntactic device children can use and it's largely because they use it that the constructions of child speech are roughly intelligible from the start (Brown, 1970, 1973). But chimps tend to produce their multisign combinations in *all* possible orders [although there are some *statistical* preferences: see above] which suggest the absence of syntax (Brown, 1970; Terrace, 1979).

(*iii*) A frame-by-frame analysis of videotapes revealed that Nim seldom signed spontaneously (about 10 per cent of the time) on his own initiative, but almost always required human prompting to sign at all, and when he signed with a teacher his signs were very often complete or partial imitations of those produced by the teacher (about 40 per cent of all utterances). By contrast, in children just beginning to talk, under 20 per cent of their utterances are imitations of parents' speech and approximately 30 per cent are spontaneous (Eysenck, 1984), and this proportion quickly approaches zero (i.e. nearly all spontaneous). In fact, Nim's rate of imitations actually increased as he got older (Aitchison, 1983). Brown concludes that 'in so far as prompted imitation accounts for multisign combinations, there is, of course, no reason to invoke creative syntax' (Brown, 1986).

Eysenck (1984) also notes that over 70 per cent of Nim's utterances began while his teacher was still signing, so Nim interrupted his teacher much more often than children typically interrupt their parents. This suggests he was not interested in having a genuine conversation.

6 Terrace's use of videotapes, allowing the leisurely and analytic study of the data, together with his circulation of progress reports comprising large samples to experts (who could analyze them for themselves), plus his calculation of MLU (standard in child language research) made his study different from all previous ones (Brown, 1986). However, he is not without his critics. Nim had instruction from 60 different signers ('babysitters') and much of it was done in a classroom (not 'home'). Despite the fact that several trainers were with him for long periods, especially Petitto, to whom he became attached, (as well as to Terrace himself, plus a couple of others), the Gardners (1980), Patterson and Fouts see Nim as an underprivileged chimp, subject to routine drills, not reared like a child at all (which they all did), and for these reasons his ASL performance was below that of Washoe and the others. The Gardners go so far as to claim that he was highly disturbed, insecure and maladjusted, and a computer analysis of chimp utterances which takes no account of the actual context is bound to give odd results.

Terrace (1987) replies by claiming that neither the Gardners nor Patterson have revealed enough of their own procedure to allow evaluation of the significance of their criticisms.

7 The very status of ASL as language is itself questionable. Eysenck (1984) points out, for example, that signs in ASL are defined in terms of four parameters – hand configurations, movement, orientation and location – but the Gardners consistently focused on just one, i.e. hand configuration. Brown (1986) states that it is not related to spoken English and is very unlike English in grammatical structure; however, it is capable of expressing any meaning whatsoever – it is language in a manual–visual (as opposed to vocal–auditory) modality. However, while when used by humans ASL is undoubtedly a language, we cannot just assume that it is so when used by chimps.

> What must be shown, if chimps are to be credited with a given linguistic capacity, is that they are able to use the signs of ASL in just those ways that would convince us that a human had the capacity in question. (Brown, 1986)

There is the danger of anthropomorphizing here, but we must also beware of excluding signing as language just because it is chimps and not humans moving their hands (Brown, 1986).

8 While Patterson (1978) claims that 'language is no longer the exclusive domain of man' and Rumbaugh (1977) argues that 'neither tool using skills nor language serve qualitatively to separate man and beast any more', Chomsky (1980) believes that the higher apes 'apparently lack the capacity to develop even the rudiments of the computational structure of human language', and Aitchison (1983) agrees by saying 'the apparent ease with which humans acquire language, compared with apes, supports the suggestion that they are innately programmed to do so'.

Eysenck (1984) concludes that 'as of now ... language in its complete form is unique to man'. And Carroll (1986) agrees: '... although these chimps have grasped some of the rudiments of human language, what they have learned and the speed at which they learn it ... is qualitatively different from those of human beings'.

Exercises

1 What does 'anthropomorphise' mean?

2 Throughout the commentary, comparisons have been made between children and chimps. Can you identify some important *differences* between Washoe and children acquiring language under normal circumstances?

3 Can you think of a more valid comparison group for the 'experimental group chimps' than 'normal children'?

4 Does it matter that different studies have used different training methods involving different kinds of language?

5 How reliable are the reports of Washoe's acquisition of new signs? Are the criteria strict enough?

6 Is there anything ethically wrong with the way Washoe was 'acquired' for the study? And what do you think about the very attempt to teach them what is 'unnatural'?

W. SLUCKIN AND E. A. SALZEN (1961)

Imprinting and perceptual learning

Quarterly Journal of Experimental Psychology, Vol. 13, 2, pp. 65–77

Filial responses are first considered by reference to the initial stimulus situations. Findings on variability in responsiveness of chicks are reported and discussed. Facilitated responsiveness subsequent to visual stimulation is reported. The concept of critical period is examined in the light of others' and our own findings; it is concluded that imprinting ends as a result of its own actions rather than through the effects of fear. Following responses are further considered by reference to the influences of early experiences and the act of following upon the occurrence and strength of subsequent responses. The degree of attachment to a moving object tends to be proportional to the amount of experience. Individual chicks were allowed to spend several hours following a box in a runway, and their ability to discriminate between familiar and unfamiliar moving objects and static environments was studied. Strong evidence for imprintability to environment has been found. Imprinting phenomena are discussed in terms of perceptual learning.

Introduction

Following responses of newly-hatched nidifugous birds have been used by many workers to investigate imprinting, especially since Thorpe's (1956) review. In one kind of study (e.g. Fabricius, 1951; Ramsay & Hess, 1954; Jaynes, 1956, 1958b; Hess. 1957; Guiton, 1959), the birds were required to discriminate between objects by approaching and following one object rather than another. In the second type (e.g. Jaynes, 1957, 1958a; Moltz and Rosenblum, 1958a), they were required to respond repeatedly to a single object, and the degree of attachment to that object, i.e. imprinting, was taken to be indicated by the occurrence, latency and strength of the following response. As originally stated by Lorenz (1937), imprinting involves the discrimination of species characteristics, which implies the production of different response patterns to different patterns of movement, form, colour and sound. Strictly, then, studies of the second type were not studies of imprinting but simply studies of the development and establishment of the approach and following responses, and discrimination experiments were needed to determine whether these responses had become attached to a specific object. However, the following response is clearly important in imprinting studies, since this is the response required in the discrimination tests. Salzen and Sluckin (1959) tried to investigate the incidence and duration of following responses in domestic chicks without reference to imprinting; the present paper contains observations and experiments on both the following response and imprinting.

I The original stimulus situation

The work of Fabricius and Boyd (1954) and Hinde, Thorpe and Vince (1956) shows that a wide variety of moving objects may elicit the following response in birds. Smith (1960) found that movement in one plane in the form of a distant rotating black-and-white disc is a sufficient stimulus to cause chicks to approach and give contentment calls, as is a flashing light (James, 1959; Smith, 1960), certain repetitive sounds with low-frequency components (Collins, 1952), short, repeated calls, in ducks (Fabricius, 1951; Weidmann, 1958) and a moving box (Salzen & Sluckin, 1959). We have found that knocking, tapping, rustling of paper and clucking will make some chicks approach. It seems likely, therefore, that a wide variety of moderately intense visual or auditory disturbances of the environment that are brief and repetitive are capable of eliciting filial responses in chicks and ducklings.

II Variability in responsiveness

There is some evidence of constitutional differences in sensitivity to a moving object even within one breed of domestic chicks. Hess (1957) claims that imprintability, which may be related to this responsiveness, is inherited in domestic fowl and can be bred into or out of a strain, and that it is probably sex-linked in Cochin Bantams. Klopfer (1956) has also suggested a genetic explanation of reported differences in sensitive periods and imprintability. Guiton (1959) found that visually isolated chicks followed better than socially reared ones, and that a few hours of social experience preceding a period of isolation resulted in greater responsiveness to a moving object than did complete isolation. These findings were largely confirmed by Salzen and Sluckin (1959).

The influence of some social experience upon later responsiveness may account for the apparent rise in 'imprintability' found by Jaynes (1957) for the first half of the critical period, since his birds had been kept in groups before testing. The same may apply to Hess's similar results with mallards (1957) and chicks (1959a), since, though they were reared in darkness, they could hear one another, and sound was used in both the imprinting and the testing situations.

III Loss of sensitivity: the critical period

The work of Fabricius (1951), Ramsay and Hess (1954), Weidmann (1956), Hess (1957) and Jaynes (1957) has shown that ducklings and chicks will not follow a moving object if exposure is delayed for two to three days. This early period has been called the 'sensitive', or 'critical', period, and in general it is clear that ducklings and chicks are most easily imprinted during the first day or so after hatching. Salzen and Sluckin (1959) noted that in individual cases chicks remained responsive for up to five days. Guiton (1958) has shown that isolated chicks remain responsive to a moving object after three days, by which time most socially reared chicks failed to respond. In a later study, Guiton (1959) concluded that socially reared chicks become imprinted on one another and that when subsequently exposed to a moving object they show 'searching' behaviour and 'distress' rather than strong and fearful avoidance of the moving object itself. The Salzen and Sluckin (1959) study showed that 24 hours of social life was sufficient experience to significantly reduce responsiveness to a moving box compared with isolates, and it was only isolated birds which remained responsive after five days; in another case, three birds isolated for six days responded vigorously within three minutes of exposure. There is support, therefore, for Guiton's contention that the end of the critical period results from the increasing selectivity of responsiveness with experience, i.e., imprinting brings about its own end.

Hinde *et al.* (1956) originally proposed the alternative explanation that the loss of responsiveness was due to the development of fear, and it was supported by Hess (1957). Hess (1959a) has claimed that all his chicks showed fear, i.e. distress notes and avoidance by 33 to 36 hours and that this corresponds with the loss of the following response. Jaynes (1957) has recorded that weak flight begins to appear at 30 to 36 hours and strong flight at 54 to 60 hours, and he suggests that fear of strange, moving objects in socially-reared chicks may reach a maximum in the first week of life and decrease thereafter. Guiton (1959) states that fear is sufficiently developed to interfere with following at four days, whereas most socially reared birds are imprinted by three days. It is possible, therefore, that fear responses – at least in the form of avoidance – are the ones which imprinted birds make to strange objects, i.e. on ones to which they are not imprinted.

Fabricius (1951), Weidmann (1958), Jaynes (1957) and Guiton (1959) amongst others have all observed that birds may show fear and avoidance of a moving box at first, yet may subsequently come to follow it strongly. Salzen and Sluckin (1959) have also observed this: on three occasions a chick was selected which showed extreme avoidance of a moving box, isolated and then exposed to the box for three minutes every day. These chicks finally began to follow, and in this way chicks were responding for the first time when over two weeks old. On another occasion a similar procedure was used with three chicks that had 'frozen' and three which had shown active avoidance of the box, selected from a batch of chicks first tested when one day old. The former three followed well after a few days but the latter three had not begun to follow when the experiment ended after 12 days. It is possible that further treatment would have induced these birds to follow as in the previous experiment. Similarly, some chicks have been isolated for two to three days before exposing them to a moving box; at first, some showed avoidance and fear of the box but in all (six) cases, prolonged exposure resulted in following, usually within the first hour. Similar findings have been reported by Jaynes (1957) with five- to six-day-old chicks reared socially.

It seems, then, that habituation to the strange object may cause the avoidance response to disappear and the following response – and presumably imprinting – to occur. Hess (1959) has claimed that birds induced to follow objects in this way do not in fact become imprinted on these objects. Following similarly takes place under the influence of a tranquillizing drug, chlorpromazine (but not meprobomate) (Hess, 1957), and in this particular case, it seems that imprinting did occur.

Guiton (1959) maintains that, although avoidance is most marked in isolated birds, experience of the moving object usually reduces fear and results in following. In socially reared birds, avoidance or crouching also disappears due to habituation, but usually does not result in following; instead they show 'searching' behaviour with distress calls, and the model is ignored, i.e. true habituation has taken place. The evidence, therefore, seems to be against fear being the cause of the end of the sensitive period and suggests that imprinting can end only as a result of its own action in increasing the selectivity of the animal's responses.

IV The effect of experience

The development of filial responsiveness (as indicated by the following response) is shown both by the bird's immediate response to a moving object and by its performance after a time interval, i.e. by the amount of retention of responsiveness. Jaynes (1958a) has shown that, under his particular experimental conditions, ten minutes' experience of a moving box was sufficient to induce following in some day-old chicks, but that 40 minutes was required before all his chicks responded. This experience was effective whether given on the first day or spread over the first four days, and the greater the amount of experience, the greater was the probability of a response 30 and 70 days later. In a similar study, Salzen and Sluckin (1959) found that the percentage of chicks which followed a moving box on the first day after hatching was approximately proportional to the amount of experience of that box, so that after ten movements of the box, 50 per cent of the chicks had begun to follow and after 50 movements, 80 per cent were following. There was a significant difference between the chicks which had received these two amounts of experience which approximated to two and eight minutes exposure. However, considerable variability of responsiveness, within and between batches, suggested that further data was desirable.

Table 15.1 shows the results of an experiment carried out by us in

Table 15.1   Effects of a moving box on socially reared chicks

Amount of experience of a moving box	Three minutes	30 minutes	
Distribution of this experience	One session of three minutes on the first day	Three sessions of ten minutes on the first day	One session of six minutes on each of the first five days
Proportions of birds that responded to the moving box in a three-minute test on sixth day after hatching	3/16 (19%)	6/14 (43%)	6/11 (55%)

which chicks from a Brown Leghorn X Light Sussex cross were exposed to one of three treatments: three- or 30-minutes experience of a moving box at one day of age, or six-minutes experience on each of the first five days after hatching. Chicks which failed to respond within the first three minutes were rejected. All the chicks were tested for three minutes in the same situation on the sixth day. The results confirm Jaynes' claim that, within these conditions, the degree of imprinting is proportional to the amount of experience of the moving object. The detection of the effect of ten movements of a box on subsequent responsiveness (Salzen & Sluckin, 1959) suggests that the mechanism is extremely sensitive but needs strengthening by repetition.

Table 15.1 shows the effects on socially-reared chicks of the amount and distribution of experience of a moving box on subsequent responsiveness to this stimulus. The probability that the difference between the first and third columns was a chance occurrence is $p = 0.032$, as determined by Fisher's exact probability test.

V The effect of effort

The experiment described in the previous section did not separate the effects of visual experience of the moving object from the effects of the act of following. Hess (1957) tried to do this by running ducks at different speeds for the same length of time and found that the longer distance resulted in better imprinting as judged by responsiveness in discrimination tests. But could it be that the faster-moving object is a more potent stimulus? Salzen and Sluckin (1959) found no support for this relationship. However, Hess' (1957) results with drugs appeared to support his claim and he suggested that meprobamate, being a muscle relaxant, prevented imprinting by interfering with the 'muscular tension or other afferent consequences' of following. Yet at the same time he stated that this drug did not interfere with mobility or coordination either in the training or test sessions. It is difficult to see how these two claims can be reconciled. While Hess found that chlorpromazine gave good imprinting, Ryall (1958) and Taeschler and Carletti (1959) found that it simultaneously reduces emotional behaviour and motor activity in rats and mice. Hess (1958) found that obstructions in the runway resulted in stronger imprinting (greater effort required in following) and this is perhaps the strongest evidence for the effect of effort. Hess (1959a) showed that chicks' ability to run improved over the first 16 hours during which time 'imprintability' showed a corresponding improvement, but a correlation like this does not prove the causal effect of effort on imprinting.

Jaynes (1957) also found that although the percentage of chicks responding decreased throughout the critical period, the strength of imprinting, judged by retention tests, tended to increase during the first day, i.e. as locomotory ability increased. Poor locomotory ability does not necessarily mean poor locomotory effort, but in both Jaynes' and Hess' experimental conditions it may well have resulted in the chick spending very little training time near the box and so having little experience of it. Salzen and Sluckin (1959) ensured that the box was never more than 12 to 18 inches from the chicks and found that very good runners often failed to respond later on, while some non-runners performed very well later on. But they all had social experience between the tests (unlike Hess' chicks), and this may have affected their responsiveness in the second test. Baer and Gray (1960) allowed chicks to see but not to follow or contact a white or black guinea-pig during one of the first four days after hatching; at seven days they spent significantly more time near the familiar guinea-pig, when given a choice, than the unfamiliar one and this effect was strongest when the exposure to the guinea-pig had been on the second day after hatching. It seems, therefore, that some imprinting can occur without the act of following and the evidence regarding the role of effort is not yet convincing.

VI Later stimulus situation

As imprinting progresses, so the bird becomes less likely to respond to stimuli other than the experienced one(s); the extent to which a bird will generalize is, therefore, an inverse measure of the degree of imprinting. As we have already seen, the first effect of experience seems to be to facilitate responsiveness to stimulation, while further experience restricts this responsiveness to an increasingly well-defined stimulus pattern, as suggested by the individual recognition of two humans by chicks (Gray & Howard, 1957). In Guiton's (1959) study, after two to three days of social life, chicks had become imprinted specificially to chicks: they would not follow other objects which they could discriminate from chicks.

Repeated presentation of the imprinted stimulus may lead to an apparent loss of the following response, e.g. Moltz and Rosenblum (1958a), using a moving box with Peking ducks. We observed that when chicks were exposed singly to an intermittently moving box (in a mechanized version of our standard imprinting runway with a suspended white cylindrical box which travelled up and down the centre of the ten-foot alley in alternating 30 seconds periods of rest and movement), they all began to follow within the first half hour and stopped following after several hours. Food and water were situated to one side of the alley and the chicks spent progressively more time in their vicinity. While in the Moltz and Rosenblum study the chicks had become habituated to the stimulus, in ours they had become at least temporarily satiated with it; if the experimenter started waving his arms and shouting, clapping and stamping his feet, very strong and close following was produced, showing that the box had not ceased to be a stimulus for the chicks. When left undisturbed again, they would gradually cease following the box once more.

Moltz and Rosenblum (1958b) found that if ducks are first habituated to the testing enclosure, they are less responsive to a moving box than ducks not so treated, while Moltz *et al.* (1959) have shown that electric shocks given inside the enclosure increased the level of ducks' responsiveness, supposedly through the effect of anxiety.

We have found that, following 'satiation', the response can be restored by either (*i*) introducing a second moving object (a red duster) or (*ii*) quietly and surreptitiously introducing strange static objects into the alley. Filial responses can therefore be restored by making some change in the environment; birds come to discriminate by approach and avoidance responses both between familiar and unfamiliar moving objects and between familiar and strange environments. According to Thorpe (1956), an exclusive attachment to an environment may be a form of imprinting, so both processes may be imprinting.

VII Reversibility

Thorpe (1956) has quoted several observations suggesting that imprinting is reversible. We have already seen that attachments can be induced after the end of the so-called critical period, provided the bird has not been previously exposed to moving objects. Guiton (1959) found that socially-reared birds become imprinted to one another, in that they will not respond to a moving box; if such birds are isolated for a time they may subsequently respond to other objects. Table 15.2 shows our own results for experiments of this kind; it can be seen that day-old socially-reared chicks did not respond to a moving box until they had been isolated for three hours (batch E), and that chicks reared socially for two days would not respond after three hours of isolation but would so after 24 hours (batch F).

Table 15.2 shows the effect of a period of isolation on the responsiveness of socially-reared chicks to three-minute experience of a moving box. It also indicates that the length of the isolation period necessary to produce this effect may be related to the amount of social experience. The probabilities recorded were determined by the Fisher exact probability test.

If the strength of social attachment is proportional to the amount of experience, then it might be expected that reversibility could be similarly effected, so that the longer the social experience, the longer

Table 15.2   Effect of isolation on the responses of socially-reared chicks to a moving box

Batch of chicks	Pre-test treatment of newly-hatched chicks	Proportions of birds that responded to the three-minute experience of a moving box by following
E	21 hours of social life followed by 3 hours of isolation	7/8
		Probability of this difference being a chance occurrence is
	24 hours of social life	0/6 $p = 0.0023$
F	48 hours of social life followed by 3 hours of isolation	0/8
		Probability of this difference being a chance occurrence is
	48 hours of social life followed by 24 hours of isolation	2/3 $p = 0.054$

the isolation required before responses to strange objects will occur. Goodwin's (1948) birds responded sexually to the species with whom they were reared and not to their parent species with whom they had spent only the first week or so of their lives; Lorenz's (1937) Muscovy ducklings were reared for nearly seven weeks with Greylag geese before being removed, and it is therefore not impossible that one of them should subsequently still prefer geese. It may be that reversibility of imprinting involves the acquisition of new objects but not necessarily the loss of old ones, and several studies suggest that birds may become attached to several objects (Fabricius, 1951; Hinde *et al.*, 1956; Jaynes, 1957; Guiton, 1959). If the bird's preference for objects is related to the relative amounts of previous experience of these objects, then Lorenz's observation is still a remarkable one.

VIII Imprinting and perceptual learning

As implied in the introduction, it is probably best to restrict the term 'imprinting' to those experimental situations in which the 'imprinted' bird is required to discriminate between patterns of movement, form, colour, sound, etc., and not simply to repeat earlier responses to the same stimulus pattern or object. The development of the imprinting process, or attachment to a class of stimuli, consists of a sharpening of discrimination between this and other classes. This view seems to conform to the criterion of perceptual learning put forward by Wohlwill (1958).

The development of attachment to environmental stimuli (imprinting) also seems to fit Gibson's (1959) account of the progress of perceptual learning. He distinguishes between the environment (e.g. in the case of vision, surfaces) and the social or animal environment (e.g. movement and deformation of surfaces), and these are the kinds of information which the organism receives and has to differentiate. Similarly, the process of which imprinting is a part may be considered in terms of perception of the inanimate and the animate environment, and development of social responses is part of the latter. Chicks first have to discriminate moving surfaces from the static and this may be revealed by their contentment calls and their approach and following responses. As their perceptions of the stimulus situation become further differentiated with respect to movement, form, colour and sound, so discrimination in the form of choice of object-following will occur: this is the process of imprinting as originally conceived.

If 'imprinting' is extended to cover development of the tendency to orientate social responses to moving or changing stimulus patterns (e.g. flashing light, intermittent sounds, moving object), then the concept becomes identical with that of the development of perception of the animate or social environment; if it also covers development of perception of the inanimate environment, then Thorpe's (1956) discussion of cases of attachment to environments, and our own observations of the effect of changes in the static environment on chicks' following responses become relevant. The imprinting process, then, could be regarded as part of a process of developing perception resulting from repeated stimulation.

Commentary

Aim and nature

This is essentially a review article in which a large number of studies of imprinting are summarized and evaluated, including some experiments by the authors themselves. Part of what they are trying to do is to clarify the concept of imprinting itself (i.e. just what the process involves), and this is done by examining a number of independent variables which have been shown (or claimed) to affect the following response, in particular (*i*) the original stimulus situation (i.e. what stimuli will elicit the following response in the first place); (*ii*) variability in responsiveness (i.e. constitutional differences in sensitivity to moving stimuli both within and between different species of birds, plus the effect of early experience); (*iii*) the 'sensitive' or critical period for imprinting (i.e. the optimum time for exposure to stimuli), including discussion of what it is that brings the period to an end: fear or increased selectivity of the animal's responses; (*iv*) the effect of experience (i.e. how much exposure to the stimulus and how that exposure is distributed); (*v*) the effect of effort (i.e. how much physical activity is involved in the actual act of following; (*vi*) later stimulus situations (i.e. exposure to the imprinted stimulus plus non-imprinted objects following imprinting); (*vii*) reversibility (i.e. can later exposure 'undo' the effects of early exposure so that imprinting is not permanent); (*viii*) perceptual learning (i.e. what kind of phenomenon is imprinting: a form of perceptual learning or simply a learning to follow?). This last point is much more to do with interpreting the findings concerning the first seven variables in order to arrive at a theoretical or conceptual conclusion. We should also note that almost all the studies cited are laboratory experiments.

Context and background

It was Konrad Lorenz's (1935/37) famous studies of imprinting (for which he won the Nobel prize in 1973) that really helped to popularize ethology in Britain and USA, where the laboratory experiments of animal learning (especially rats and pigeons) had held sway since the early days of psychology itself. Lorenz and Tinbergen, two of the key European founders of this branch of zoology, were trying to put the study of behaviour back into its natural context (i.e. the 'field'), and at the same time to use evolutionary theory to understand it (see chapter 16).

As biologists, the ethologists believe that behaviour can be studied in the same way as any other aspect of life; just as different species have different skeletons, so they have different behaviour, and if species with similar skeletons also display similar behaviour, this is strong evidence in favour of the view that the behaviour is *inherited* or *instinctive.*

Although the concept of instinct plays a crucial role in ethology, this does not mean that learning is excluded from the explanation of behaviour. Indeed, imprinting is a good example of a kind of behaviour which is a blend of both influences; put simply, the tendency to become imprinted (*imprintability*) is genetically determined (and species-specific), but what the young bird becomes imprinted *on* is a matter of learning and experience. It has to *learn* to recognize its parents so that it can stay close to them, and in that way be assured of food and protection. As members of a *precocial* species, nidifugous (ground-nesting) birds are mobile at birth, and so could easily wander off. So the learning has to happen pretty quickly (this was in fact one of the characteristics of imprinting as Lorenz originally described it). Clearly, then, imprinting is more complex than a simple instinct. When precocial birds live in groups, both parents and young are faced with the problem of recognizing each other; there is a selective pressure on parents to care only for their own young which then creates a selective pressure on the offspring to approach only their own parents. While much of the interaction between parents and young can be left to instinct alone (e.g. we can imagine a genetically determined mechanism to ensure that herring-gull chicks will peck at red, contoured, objects: Tinbergen & Perdeck, 1950), it is less obvious how the genes could tell a gosling which of several geese mothers it should follow. What nature seems to give the gosling is 'knowledge' that it will have a mother and should respond to her by following, but it does not tell it what she will look like; i.e. 'instinct gives the chick a concept of mother, but the environment has to supply the details' (Lea, 1984). (Interestingly, Lea compares this instinctive 'knowledge' with the Jungian archetype, which may represent some kind of residues of these imprinting-like processes which were involved in our ancestors' social behaviour.)

Again, although ethologists are primarily zoologists, they believe in the importance of carrying out laboratory experiments, but only as a way of identifying the critical variables which operate in the natural habitat (which requires the kind of experimental control which only a laboratory can provide). So findings from laboratory studies are always 'put back' into into the animal's natural context of behaviour.

Evaluation

1 The speed with which imprinting seems to (and needs to) take place is, of course, related to the concept of a critical period, a term borrowed by Lorenz from embryology, implying that there are periods in development during which the individual is especially vulnerable, i.e. when particular experiences exert a profound and lasting influence on later behaviour. This means that unless imprinting occurs during a particular period after hatching, it will *never* occur, and that once it has occurred, it cannot be 'unlearnt', i.e. it is irreversible. The critical period concept implies that imprintability is genetically 'switched on' and then 'switched off' again at the end of the period (in the case of mallard ducklings from between five to 24 hours after hatching, with a peak between 13 and 16 hours, according to Ramsay and Hess (1954). The precise timing of the critical period differs for different species).

However, many studies (including some cited by Sluckin and Salzen) have shown that the period during which imprintability can still be demonstrated can be extended beyond the end of the normal critical period by artificially changing the animal's environment, e.g. keeping ducklings isolated (Sluckin & Salzen, 1961; Bateson, 1964), keeping chicks or ducklings in an unstimulating environment (especially if it is visually unstimulating) (Guiton, 1958; Moltz & Stettner, 1961). It was Sluckin (1965) who originally proposed that the term 'sensitive' period should be used instead of 'critical'. A sensitive period is 'a time during an organism's development when particular influence is most likely to have an effect' (Hinde, 1966). This suggests that it is more useful to think in terms of the *probability* that imprinting will occur rather than 'whether-or-not it will occur' (Gross, 1987).

2 According to Suomi (1982), since the early 1970s there has been a substantial change in how ethologists and developmental psychologists have come to view imprinting. As originally defined by Lorenz, imprinting did not seem to be a very widespread phenomenon, but was confined to a few species of precocial birds. Now it is considered to be a very common phenomenon in many species (including many breeds of fish, insects, sheep, deer, buffalo, dogs, goats, higher primates and human beings). For example, a human infant will respond selectively to its own mother's breast-pads by three days after birth (MacFarlane, 1975) and to her voice by 30 days at the latest (Mehler *et al.*, 1978, both cited in Lea, 1984). Lea (1984) suggests that imprinting-like processes may be involved in this rapid learning (and may be examples of the instinctive 'concept' which requires specific experience to 'flesh it out'). However, imprinting is no longer seen as confined to attachment-behaviours, but can apply to choice of habitat, preferences for specific foods, learning communications, signals, choice of sexual partner and control of aggression (Suomi, 1982). 'As such, the existence of sensitive phases most likely represents a general psychobiological principle of development' (Suomi, 1982).

3 So what are the developmental mechanisms responsible for these sensitive periods? Suomi (1982) believes that these are generally unknown. Butr he cites some highly suggestive evidence for at least one case of imprinting, namely 'sexual imprinting' in zebra finches. The sensitive phase usually lasts between days 15 to 45 after hatching and their choice of mate will last the rest of its life. Studies of sexual imprinting (Immelman & Wolff, 1981) have tried to identify possible changes in the structure of the birds' brain which might coincide or overlap with the sensitive period.

Roughly on day 21, there begins a massive cell death in the hyperstriatum and this is followed by a period of secondary growth and synapse formation by the remaining neurons in the hyperstriatum which is largely completed by day 45. Of course, the evidence is only 'circumstantial' (correlation): we cannot rule out the possibility that imprinting is 'marked' in other parts of the brain or that the emergence and establishment of imprinting preference is not completely limited to the sensitive period. However, the best current evidence suggests *something* is going on in the zebra finch hyperstriatum at the very same time that the bird establishes a life-partner preference. And the same brain area does *not* change substantially at any time once the sensitive phase has passed.

Suomi (1982) is tempted to speculate that the zebra finch case represents a specific case of a far more general developmental principle, namely that:

> For any developing brain region, during that period when the greatest neuronal cell death occurs and the most secondary synaptic connections are sub-sequently found, stimuli that impinge on that brain area will become 'imprinted' in the pattern of emerging synapses. The organism will be especially sensitive to

such stimuli during this period, and thereafter it will be able to 'remember' such stimuli as long as the synapses involved remain functional. (Suomi, 1982)

Of course, different brain regions develop at different rates in different species, so you would expect major differences in the sensitive period from region to region and species to species. Where cell death and secondary neuronal growth occur during a short and well-defined period, the sensitive period will correspondingly be short and well defined and the behaviours/preferences established largely permanent (as in filial imprinting in ducks and geese and sexual imprinting in zebra finches). But this would not apply to attachment to the mother in monkeys, apes and humans (Bowlby, 1969). Here the sensitive period is much more drawn out, and the resulting behavioural tendencies more easily altered in later life. Again, where secondary synapses continue to be formed throughout life, there is no sensitive period as such; the organism will continue to absorb new information and establish new behavioural tendencies well into maturity (e.g. some association areas of the human brain/'wisdom' in Erikson's psychosocial theory). Finally, although the specific mechanisms underlying phenomena based on sensitive periods no doubt differ from case to case and species to species (Immelman & Suomi, 1981), a general rule seems to be that the *timing* of the sensitive period is nearly always in the genes: the timing of cell migration, orientation, growth, interconnection etc. in any particular brain region is largely genetically determined. However, *which* nerve cells survive is largely a product of environmental stimulation, i.e. the information which actually gets 'imprinted' in the subject's brain depends entirely on what stimuli it is exposed to during the sensitive phase. It is determined by the subject's environment: it is impossible to separate the two sets of factors. Development is a product of both in interaction with each other (Suomi, 1982).

Exercises

1 In tables 15.1 and 15.2:
   (*i*) What scale of measurement is being used?
   (*ii*) What is the Fisher's exact test?

2 Why should psychologists be interested in a biological approach to the study of behaviour (i.e. an ethological one)?

3 *Precocial* species are usually contrasted with what?

4 Name two examples of human behaviour where it has been suggested that critical/sensitive periods are involved.

RICHARD RAWLINS (1979)

Forty years of rhesus research

New Scientist, Vol. 82, no. 1150, pp. 108–10

The rhesus monkey is, perhaps, the best known of all primates. It was fundamental in the dicovery of blood types and was the first primate to be rocketed into the stratosphere. We have detailed information on its anatomy and physiology, and a very good idea of its behaviour, and we have had this information for many years. But little of this wealth of knowledge comes from the forests of south-east Asia where the rhesus normally lives; instead, because the rhesus is hardy and easy to breed, we have studied it in the laboratory, rather than in the field.

The island of Cayo Santiago provides a laboratory in the field, where we have gained a great deal of understanding of the organisation of rhesus society and the way the society develops from the growth and evolution of the animals that make it up. The colony on Cayo Santiago is now 40 years old and this seems a good time to look back on the birth and development, not of the monkeys, but of the oldest continuously maintained primate colony in the world.

Cayo Santiago is a 15.5 hectare island, lying about one kilometre off the coast of Puerto Rico in the Caribbean. It was founded in the late 1930s when, through the work of men like Robert Yerkes, Solly Zuckerman and Otto Kohler, modern primatology was emerging as a discipline. C. R. Carpenter was a student of Yerkes and was one of the first behaviourists to go out and watch primates in the field, both in Panama and Asia. He was frustrated by the difficulties of field work and the growing demand for monkeys as laboratory animals, and so decided to set up a 'wild' population that would supply animals for biomedical work and allow long-term observations of behaviour. His initial plan was for a mixed group of rhesus monkeys and gibbons.

At the time, the Indian government periodically banned the export of monkeys; freighted ones suffered terribly and often died from rampant tuberculosis or diarrhoea. Carpenter got together with G. W. Bachman, Director of the Columbia University School of Tropical Medicine in San Juan, Puerto Rico, and staff from the Columbia University College of Physicians and Surgeons in New York and obtained a grant to begin a research and breeding programme on Cayo Santiago; it was to be the first of a series of facilities that would ensure a controlled and regular supply of monkeys for institutions on the mainland.

Bachman hired M. I. Tomlin, a primatologist from the Philadelphia Zoological Park, to manage Cayo. Carpenter, meanwhile, went back to Indo-China, Thailand and Malaya in 1938 to collect Lar gibbons and to India to trap rhesus monkeys. During December 1938 and January 1939, 450 rhesus monkeys and 14 gibbons were released on Cayo Santiago, having first been screened for tuberculosis and marked with an identifying tattoo.

The rhesus organized themselves in the 18 months after they were introduced to the island. There was a lot of fighting and many monkeys died, but when the dust settled there were six social groups. The gibbons were not so lucky; they competed with the rhesus for food and living space, attacked monkeys and people, and were recaptured, caged and eventually sold. Once the gibbons were out of the way, the work on rhesus took priority and no more animals were added.

Carpenter and Tomlin watched the population into the 1940s recording who made up the groups, how they behaved socially and sexually, what kind of dominance hierarchy existed and how the troop moved around the island. At the same time scientists from the School of Tropical Medicine studied sexual behaviour and menstrual cycling, intestinal parasites and haematology. The Second World War made it difficult to get supplies out to Cayo and 490 animals were shipped to the mainland for research on disease. By 1944 there were only about 200 animals left, and behaviour studies had ended. The colony was poorly managed, food supplies were extremely irregular and the monkeys took to eating any vegetation there was. The colony and island went into general decline.

But somehow the colony survived. Then the island was designated the behavioural branch of the Laboratory of Perinatal Physiology (sponsored by the National Institute of Neurological Disease and Blindness); the animals were used in the laboratory to study medicine and physiology. However, for students of behaviour, a crucial event was the 1956 arrival of Stuart Altmann. He reintroduced the regular census of the population, marked all the individuals and worked on the monkeys for two years, eventually producing a masterly study of rhesus behaviour and social organisation which set the stage for all the subsequent studies. Kaufmann, Koford, Varley and Sade continued Altmann's pioneering work, and through their efforts, the records of the Cayo monkeys are probably the most complete for any monkey troops anywhere.

The Perinatal Laboratory was disbanded in 1970, and Cayo became part of the Caribbean Primate Research Centre, a new facility sponsored by the National Institute of Health (NIH) and the University of Puerto Rico's School of Medicine. Before, the primary purpose of Cayo was to supply monkeys for medical research, and behavioural studies were not allowed to interfere with this function. Individuals were selected for 'export' haphazardly, with no regard to their social group, age or sex, with the result that many of the groups were extremely unbalanced and artificial. One could not even guess what the effects of these unthinking removals were on the patterns of behaviour. Donald Sade was appointed scientist in charge in 1970, and he saw to it that the policies were changed; all but the intact social groups were taken off the island and the four remaining troops were not disturbed again. Sporadic capture and manipulation were stopped in an attempt to set up the naturalistic conditions that would be best for long-term studies. Sade's foresight, and the support of the Animal Resources Branch of NIH, allowed Cayo to emerge as a unique site for developmental studies of free-ranging rhesus monkeys, a pre-eminence it retains today.

The island is easy to get around and the animals are generally clearly visible; we have accurate estimates of the population age structure and detailed long-term histories of the social and physical development of all the animals. All this is in sharp contrast to field studies, where unknown animals are invisible most of the time. But the monkeys are given provisions, so that there are some aspects of their feeding ecology which we cannot study. However, this disadvantage is more than offset by the special opportunities to follow the behavioural development and population dynamics of a species over many generations.

In 1956 there were 150 animals, in two groups, alive on the island. There are now 610, all descendants of the stock released 40 years ago. Apart from six solitary males, who seem to dislike company, the animals are in six social groups, ranging in number from 53 to 139. We know the age, sex and maternal geneology (neither we nor the monkeys can be certain of the paternal side of things) of every individual and have a detailed biography too. Each year the monkeys are trapped once – to tattoo the youngsters born that year and draw blood samples for the continuing genetic work – but otherwise there are no other interventions.

We especially encourage people to study the rhesus over a long time period because the monkeys have a distinct annual cycle. The way they divide their time between different activities depends on the time of year: broadly speaking, the year can be divided into the mating season (July to December) and the birth season (January to June).

Daily activity also shows a clear rhythm. The animals look for food and eat in the cool of first light and spend the heat of the day resting and grooming one another on the ground or in the trees. As the afternoon wears on, they begin to feed and play again, finally going back up into the trees at sunset to sleep. Much of the day is spent in grooming, which is partly sanitary, because it helps to eliminate crud and parasites from the skin and fur, and partly social, because it establishes and cements the bonds between members of the group. Indeed, grooming tells us an enormous amount about the group's social structure; such things as who grooms him, who he grooms, how often and for how long, provide excellent measures of each monkey's social status relative to the others.

Each social group is composed of a number of adult males and two to four matrilines; each matriline, in turn, consists of an adult female, her adult daughters and all their juvenile offspring. Juvenile males leave the troop they were born into when they become mature (about three to four years) but the females remain in the natal troop, so that the maternal genealogies form a stable nucleus around which the day's activity is centred. The adult males in a troop, unlike the females, were born into another troop and will, occasionally, move from one troop to another, though they never return to their natal troop. So, as in many vertebrates, it is the males who, by their movements, stir the genetic pot, but we do not know what controls the males' movements.

Within each troop there is a social order, with separate hierarchies for males and females (and their offspring). The hierarchy controls access to desirable objects, including food and grooming partners, and limits the amount of aggression in the group. Rhesus, like all primates and several other species, have a well-developed code system for signalling dominance and threat, defeat and subordinance, so there is not too much overt fighting, and aggressive encounters rarely end in death. But it is still necessary to control aggression as wounds sustained in a fight can go septic, and are a major cause of death. Rank is established by fighting but, thereafter, the hierarchy minimizes conflict. Each monkey can recognize the others and predict the most likely outcome of an interaction with any individual; the strong gain access to priority items and the weak avoid being further weakened. There is little time-wasting for all members of the troop who can get on with other tasks.

In general, adult males hold the highest rank, above juvenile males and all females, though there have been occasional exceptions. Each matriline has a rank too, established by fighting among the females at the time the group was formed, and all members of one matriline outrank all members of a subordinate one. Within a matriline, as juvenile females reach puberty they rise in rank over their older sisters, but not their mothers, so that the most dominant female is the mother, followed by her youngest daughter and any of her offspring, then the next daughter and her offspring, and so on. Young males benefit from their mother's rank until they become adolescent, but when they disperse to a new group they have to establish themselves slowly and carefully, which often means a few years at the bottom of the troop hierarchy.

Despite what has been described, we still do not know what causes these monkeys to behave this way. General social structure is consistent across the six groups on the island but, despite this and the ecological uniformity of the island, there are still significant differences in the amounts of friendship and fighting from troop to troop. The monkeys of Cayo provide an ideal set-up to check out some theoretical ideas based on evolutionary biology; for instance, group splitting (see figure 16.1) allowed Chepko-Sade to ask whether the monkeys are aware of their relations, and she found that they were (New Scientist, Vol. 82).

We are looking at microevolution by checking on blood groups and enzymes on a regular basis, and relating male rank to reproductive success using the same blood groups; we can definitely exclude certain animals from certain matings and can often be reasonably sure who was the father of which infant. We are also looking for evidence of changes in female reproductive strategies; these should change with age, as the loss of future offspring becomes less important.

As we pass our 40th anniversary, the need for primate colonies has become, if anything, more pressing; habitats are still being destroyed

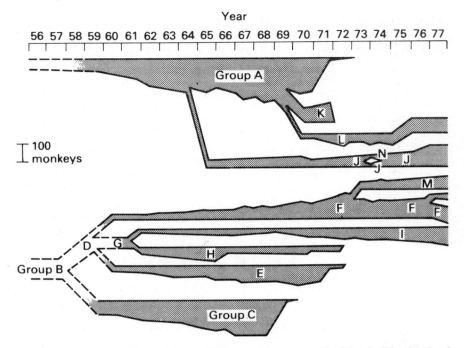

Figure 16.1　A summary history of the social groups on the island. The depth of the shaded areas represents the number of animals in the groups, which split when they become too large.

and species are still under threat. Biological stations such as Cayo Santiago can relieve the pressure imposed by medical research on wild populations, and can also enhance our understanding of the nature and development of primate behaviour, and provide a valuable yardstick against which to measure laboratory studies and observations on wild animals.

Commentary

Aim and nature

The article really has a two-fold purpose: (*i*) to provide a brief history of Cayo Santiago, almost literally a laboratory in the field (or 'open air laboratory'), the oldest continuously maintained primate colony in the world; (*ii*) to report some of the major findings from the 40 years of research which has taken place. The article is (probably) unique because of its focus on the 'laboratory' itself, but that is because the laboratory is unique and raises some fundamental questions about methodology (see below). There are also some important ethical issues raised by the existence of such an animal colony.

Context and background

Animals have traditionally played a prominent part in psychology, especially the rat and pigeon subjects in the behaviourists' laboratory studies of learning. But they have entered psychology via another door, namely that of Ethology, which stresses the importance of studying animals in their natural habitat, and which tends to see instinct as being a critical source of behaviour and tries to use as wide a range of species as possible.

Ironically, it was Darwin's theory of evolution which helped shape behaviourism; if more complex species have evolved from less complex ones (so that the differences between them are merely quantitative), it made sense to study the simpler ones (e.g. rats) in order to enhance our understanding of the more complex ones (e.g. humans). This could conveniently be carried out in laboratories, and so the natural world of Darwinian theory became virtually forgotten, or at least irrelevant (Gross, 1987). The ethologists try to redress the balance by putting behaviour back into its natural context and bringing evolutionary theory back into the centre of the attempt to understand that behaviour.

Two of the critical questions they ask are (*i*) what is the behaviour for (*function*)? and (*ii*) how has it evolved within the species (phylogeny)? (Hinde, 1982). These are clearly derived from evolutionary theory; a basic assumption is that behaviour which has no purpose will disappear and that behaviour shared by all members of a species (or all the males/females) has been retained because, ultimately, it has helped the species survive. Precisely how it evolved can partly be investigated by comparing species known to be related morphologically (i.e. structurally). This, together with the fact that ethologists are zoologists (and not psychologists) who study behaviour as a biological entity, means that, unlike comparative (animal) psychologists, they are interested in the behaviour of a species for its own sake and not necessarily because of the light it can shed on human behaviour. However, a way of finding out about human nature is to study the behaviour of our close zoological relatives. By studying other primates we can, for example, begin to understand how the social bond may have originated (Chance, 1959). [It is worth noting two names which are mentioned on the first page of the article: that of Yerkes and Kohler, as founders of primatology in the late 1930s. Yerkes is the Yerkes of the Yerkes–Dodson law and the same Yerkes who had a language named after him: the artificial language of Yerkish taught to Lana, the chimp subject of Rumbaugh *et al.* (see chapter 14). [Kohler is not to be confused with Köhler, one of the founders of Gestalt psychology who also carried out famous experiments on 'insight learning' with chimps.]

Rhesus monkeys, like humans, are highly social animals, i.e. they live in groups. In trying to explain this species characteristic ethologists start off by assuming that there must be sound evolutionary reasons for it; it must in some way contribute to the survival of individuals who can then reproduce offspring, i.e. to their fitness (Ferry, 1984). According to Clutton-Brock (1974) there are three broad kinds of explanation as to the advantages of living in groups: (*i*) defence and avoidance of predators; (*ii*) finding and handling food; (*iii*) reproduction.

In the case of Cayo Santiago, there are no predators, although this may still have contributed to the evolution of their 'social groupings'; in terms of the 40-year history of the island, it is (*ii*) and (*iii*) which are of immediate interest.

Evaluation

1 Rhesus monkeys are not, of course, our closest relatives: the great apes are, i.e. chimps, gorillas and orang-utans. There are fewer differences between some of the

biochemicals of chimps and gorillas on the one hand and man on the other than exist between other 'sibling' species, such as goats/sheep, horses/zebras (Harcourt & Stewart, 1977). Some taxonomists want to put chimps and gorillas in the same genus (*Pan*), others prefer to classify them separately (*Pan* and *Gorilla*). But what is really interesting for the ethologists is that they *behave* very differently from each other, especially in their social and sexual behaviour (Harcourt & Stewart, 1977).

Chimps live in 'loose' communities, where, for much of the time, equal numbers of males and females move around separately. Today, they live scattered in a belt across central Africa in environments varying from dense woodland to relatively open grassland. Males travel over the whole community territory, sometimes alone, sometimes with others, which they defend communally against males from other communities. Not only do they threaten and attack trespassers, but even go on boundary patrols to check incursions.

A distinctive phenomenon is the fate of maturing males: unlike the young males of most mammals (including rhesus monkeys) adolescent male chimps do *not* leave the natal group and spend their reproductive lives with unrelated females. This means that the males within groups are more closely related to each other than they are to males in other communities. But adolescent females do usually leave the home troop to join a neighbouring one. Generally, much less is known about female social behaviour. They live in overlapping home ranges about half the size of males; many are mothers with young who spend much of their time wandering with their offspring and travelling with other mother–offspring pairs.

Gorillas live in stable groups which forage through dense undergrowth or scattered trees of their leafy home ranges (also in central Africa); neighbouring home ranges may overlap. Each group comprises at least one silverback (fully mature male), one or several adult females (some of whom will have been with the silverback for years) plus their offspring. Here, as with chimps, adolescent females leave the natal group to join other groups. The silverback tolerates one or two young males – probably his sons – who will take over leadership of the group when he dies. Other young males leave the group and wander till they find mates.

As far as their sexual behaviour and structure is concerned, there are three interesting and striking differences:

(a) Male chimps are bigger than females (but not dramatically so), are of the same colour and general build. But male gorillas are twice as heavy as females (so there is much greater sexual dimorphism in gorillas). Why might this be? Some adult male gorillas have several females in their 'harem', others wander alone and so, unless they acquire females from neighbouring groups and manage to hold onto their females, they will have no chance of producing offspring. So not surprisingly, males compete quite openly for females (by chest beating/ground thumping/foliage slapping), but usually no one gets hurt. However, sometimes fierce fighting can lead to blood spilling, and the winner is likely to be the larger animal. So a large body size is an advantage. He also fights off predators to protect females and offspring, so it is to the female's advantage to choose a larger male.

Male chimps do not fight over females as often or as fiercely, although they often try to prevent others from mating. Why not? One answer is that while fighting they could lose an oestrous female to other potential partners who might 'sneak in'. But aggression is sometimes used. Also, since males within a community are related to each other, as far as inclusive reproductive fitness is concerned, it is not a good idea to fight your relatives who share some of your genes. Gorilla males do not have such inhibitions, since they are usually unrelated.

(b) A female chimp's sexual swellings are enormous while a gorilla's are so small that it is almost imperceptible. The former's last about ten days, the latter's one to two days. The whole point of swellings is to attract the male. Though an individual female probably knows most of her potential mates individually, she might not know them too well, or does not associate with them on a permanent basis. Swellings, therefore, are (*i*) a way of signalling to males that she is ready to mate; (*ii*) a method by which she can compare males and select the one she prefers: they collect around her and she does not have to compare them one by one. By contrast the female gorilla has already shown her preference; she transferred to the group led by her mate. She has no special need to exhibit herself, so her swellings are minute compared to a chimp's.

(c) The male chimps energetically and flamboyantly display themselves to the female, erecting their hair and penis and waving branches around. The male gorilla has hardly any courtship display. Related to this are anatomical and behavioural differences. The male chimp, under pressure from other males, can mount, thrust, ejaculate and dismount in seven seconds while the gorilla takes a much more leisurely 1½ to 15 minutes. Also, despite being three times the size of a chimp, the gorilla has testes only ⅛ the size of the chimp's. It has been suggested that this could have resulted from selection for production of large amounts of sperm: the more the chimp produces, the greater the chance that one of *his* sperm will bring about fertilization. The silverback, by contrast, is the only gorilla likely to inject his sperm (Short, cited in Harcourt & Stewart, 1977). The chimp has been selected for his ability to mate, the gorilla for his ability to fight.

Harcourt & Stewart (1977) conclude that we need to take great care in making comparisons between animals and men. If chimps and gorillas, who are closely related, can show such contrasting mating systems and social organization, we must not try to make any direct comparison between only *one* of them and man. It is through comparative studies of *many* non-human species that we may work out the principles governing their behavioural and morphological traits and these principles are the key to understanding the biological bases and evolution of human behaviour.

2 Rhesus monkeys can add to this comparative study even though they are less closely related to man than are chimps and gorillas. But the study of rhesus on Cayo Santiago has a distinct methodological advantage over that of the chimps and gorillas, i.e. the island is a self-contained, open-air laboratory, easy to get around. The animals are generally clearly visible, it is possible to get accurate estimates of the population age structure and detailed long-term histories of the social and physical development of all the animals. Certain animals can definitely be excluded from certain matings and one can often be reasonably sure who fathered a particular infant. All this is, of course, vital information to have: the same degree of confidence about family relationships, etc. is impossible in field studies where unknown animals are invisible most of the time.

3 But what is the price that has to be paid? How does the interference which any 'laboratory' study involves detract from the naturalness of field studies? The monkeys are given provisions, so some aspects of their feeding ecology cannot be studied. But Rawlins feels this disadvantage is more than offset by the special opportunities to follow the behaviour/development and population dynamics of a species over many generations. Each year the monkeys are trapped – to tattoo the youngsters born that year and to take blood samples – but these are the only interventions. And without this, the age, sex and maternal geneology of every individual – plus a detailed biography – would not be known.

4 These methodological issues in turn raise ethical ones. Prior to 1970 the primary purpose of Cayo was to supply monkeys for medical research (having already taken them away from their natural habitats), and behavioural studies were not allowed to interfere with this function. Since 1970, no animal is captured and the developmental study of the free-ranging monkeys is at least as important as the medical research (which still continues). But what if there were, say, an outbreak of some infectious disease which threatened the colony: the dilemma would be between practical considerations and moral ones. Interference to save the monkeys could be defended *and* attacked on moral grounds (the scientists' moral duty is to save them if they have the power to do so, but they are also bound to retain and preserve the naturalness of Cayo, i.e. should they be free to die?). This dilemma seems to underline the dual nature of Cayo as both natural and man-made, both 'field' and laboratory.

Exercises

1 Name *two* advantages and disadvantages of Cayo compared with (*i*) Field Studies and (*ii*) Laboratory studies.

2 Just how useful/valuable are comparisons between human and non-human species?

3 What constitutes the 'natural' environment or habitat of human beings?

4 In what ways could the study of other species be to the (long-term) advantage of the animals themselves?

R. W. SPERRY (1968)

Hemisphere deconnection and unity in conscious awareness

American Psychologist, 23, pp. 723–33

The following article is a result of studies my colleagues and I have been conducting with some neurosurgical patients; all advanced epileptics, in whom an extensive midline section of the cerebral commissures had been carried out in an effort to contain severe epileptic convulsions, not controlled by medication. In all these patients the surgical sections included division of the entire corpus collosum, plus division of the smaller anterior and hippocampal commissures, plus in some cases the massa intermedia. So far as I know, this is the most radical disconnection of the cerebral hemispheres attempted to date in human surgery. All the sections were performed in a single operation.

No major collapse of mentality or personality was anticipated as a result of this extreme surgery: earlier clinical observations on surgical section of the corpus callosum in man, as well as the results from dozens of monkeys on which I had performed exactly the same surgery, suggested that the functional deficits might very well be less damaging than some of the more common forms of cerebral surgery, such as frontal lobotomy, or even some of the unilateral lobotomies performed more routinely for epilepsy.

The first patient on whom this surgery was tried had been having seizures for over ten years with generalized convulsions that continued to worsen despite treatment. At the time of surgery, he had been averaging two major attacks per week, each leaving him debilitated for another day or so. Episodes of *status epilepticus* (recurring seizures which fail to stop, and represent a medical emergency with a fairly high mortality risk) had also begun to occur at two to three-month intervals. Since leaving the hospital following his surgery over 5½ years ago, this man has not had a single generalized convulsion (according to latest reports). His level of medication has been reduced and his overall behaviour and well-being have improved (see Bogen & Vogel, 1962).

The second patient, a housewife and mother in her 30s has also been seizure-free since recovering from her surgery, more than four years ago (Bogen *et al.*, 1965). Even her EEG has regained a normal pattern. The excellent outcome in the initial, apparently hopeless, last resort cases led to further application of the surgery to some nine more individuals to date, most of whom are too recent for therapeutic evaluation. Although two patients are still having seizures (but much less severe and frequent, and largely confined to one side), the results overall continue to be predominantly beneficial and the outlook remains promising for selected severe cases.

Our own work has been confined entirely to an examination of the functional outcome, i.e. the behavioural, neurological and psychological effects of this surgical disruption of all cross-talk between the hemispheres. Initially, we were concerned as to whether we would be able to find in these patients any of the numerous symptoms of hemisphere deconnection shown in the so-called 'split-brain' animal studies of the 1950s (Myers, 1961; Sperry, 1967a, b). The historic Akelaitis (1944) studies had set the prevailing doctrine of the 1940s and 1950s, namely that no important functional symptoms are found in man following even complete surgical section of the corpus callosum and anterior commissure, provided that other brain damage is excluded.

These observations have been confirmed to the extent that the most remarkable effect of sectioning the neocortical commissures is the apparent lack of effect on ordinary behaviour. However, in contradiction of the earlier Akelaitis doctrine, we know today that with appropriate tests it is possible to demonstrate a large number of behavioural symptoms which correlate directly with the loss of the neocortical commissures in man and in animals (Gazzaniga, 1967; Sperry, 1967a,b; Sperry *et al.*, 1968). Collectively, these symptoms may be referred to as the syndrome of the neocortical commissures/ forebrain commissures, or, less specifically, of hemisphere deconnection.

One of the more general and also more interesting and striking features of this syndrome may be summarized as an apparent doubling in most realms of conscious awareness. Instead of the normally unified single stream of consciousness, these patients behave in many ways as if they have two independent streams of conscious awareness, one in each hemisphere, each cut off from, and out of contact with, the mental experiences of the other, i.e. each hemisphere seems to have its own separate and private sensations, perceptions, concepts and impulses to act, with related volitional, cognitive and learning experiences. Following surgery, each hemisphere also has its own chain of memories which become inaccessible to the recall processes of the other.

This presence of two minds in one body, as it were, is manifested in a large number and variety of test responses which I will try to review here very briefly, and in a rather simplified way.

Most of the main symptoms can be described for convenience by referring to a single testing set-up (shown in figure 17.1). Principally, it allows for the lateralized testing of the right and left halves of the visual field, separately or together, and the right and left hands and legs with vision excluded. The tests can be arranged in different

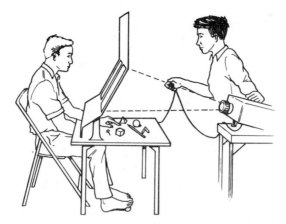

Figure 17.1 Apparatus for studying lateralization of visual, tactual, lingual and associated functions in the surgically separated hemispheres.

combinations, and in association with visual, auditory and other input, while eliminating unwanted stimuli. In testing vision, the subject with one eye covered centres his gaze on a designated fixation point on the upright translucent screen. The visual stimuli on 35 mm transparencies are arranged in a standard projector equipped with a shutter and are then back-projected at 1/10 of a second or less, too fast for eye movements to get the stimulus into the wrong half of the visual field. Figure 17.2 shows that everything seen to the left of the vertical meridian through either eye is projected to the right hemisphere and vice versa, without significant gap or overlap (Sperry, 1968).

When the visual perception of these patients is tested under these conditions, they seem to have two separate visual inner worlds, one serving the right visual field and the other serving the left, each, of course, in its respective hemisphere. This doubling in the visual sphere shows up in many ways; e.g. after a projected picture of an object has been identified and responded to in one half-field, it is recognized again only if it reappears in the same half of the visual field; if it reappears in the opposite half, the subject responds as if he had no recollection of the previous exposure. Each half of the visual field in commissurotomized patients has its own train of visual images and memories.

Another example relates to speech and writing, the cortical mechanisms for which are centred in the dominant hemisphere. Visual material projected to the right half of the field – and hence to the hemisphere system of the typical right-handed patient – can be described in speech and writing in an essentially normal way. However, when the same material is projected into the left half of the field, and hence to the right hemisphere, the subject consistently insists that he did not see anything, or that there was only a flash of light on the left side. The subject acts as if blind or agnostic for the left half of the visual field. If, however, instead of asking the subject to tell you what he saw, you instruct him to use his left hand to point to a

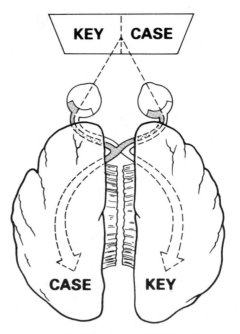

Figure 17.2   Things seen to the left of a central fixation point with either eye are projected to the right hemisphre and vice versa.

matching picture or object presented among a collection of other pictures or objects, he has no trouble, usually, in pointing out consistently the very item he has just insisted he did not see. Everything indicates that the hemisphere which is talking to the tester genuinely did not see the left-field stimulus, and so had no recollection of it. But the non-lingual right hemisphere did see it, and can recognize it, as indicated by pointing out selectively the matching item; like a deaf mute or some aphasics, this hemisphere cannot talk about the perceived object and, worse still, cannot write about it either.

If two different figures are flashed simultaneously to both visual fields, (e.g. a dollar sign on the left and a question mark on the right) and the subject is asked to draw what he saw using the left hand out of sight, he regularly reproduces the figure seen on the left half of the field, i.e. the dollar sign. If we now ask him what he has just drawn, he tells us without hesitation that what he drew was the question mark (or whatever it was presented to the right half of the field); i.e. one hemisphere does not know what the other hemisphere has been doing.

When words are flashed partly in the left field and partly in the right, the letters on each side of the midline are perceived and responded to separately. In the 'key case' example in figure 17.2, the subject might first reach for and select with the left hand a key from among a collection of objects, indicating perception through the minor (right) hemisphere. With the right hand he might then spell out the words 'case', or he might speak the word if asked to give a verbal response. When asked what kind of 'case' he was thinking of, the answer coming from the left hemisphere might be something like 'in *case* of fire', or 'the *case* of the missing corpse', or 'a *case* of beer', etc., depending on the particular mental set of the left hemisphere at the time. Any reference to 'key case' under these conditions would be purely fortuitous, assuming that visual, auditory and other cues have been properly controlled.

In tests of stereognostic or other somaesthetic discriminations, objects put in the right hand for identification by touch are readily described or named in speech or writing, whereas if the same objects are placed in the left hand, the subject can only make wild guesses and may often seem unaware that anything at all is present. But again, if one of these objects is taken from the left hand and placed in a grab bag or scrambled among a dozen other test items, the subject is then able to search out and retrieve the initial object even after a delay of several minutes. However, unlike normal subjects, these people are obliged to retrieve the object with the same hand with which it was initially identified; they fail at cross-retrieval, i.e. they cannot recognize with one hand something identified only moments before with the other hand. Again, the second hemisphere does not know what the first hemisphere has been doing.

When the subjects are first asked to use the left hand for these stereognostic tests, they commonly complain that they cannot 'work with that hand', that 'the hand is numb', that they 'just can't feel anything or can't do anything with it' or 'don't get the message from that hand'. If they successfully retrieve a series of objects which previously they claimed they could not feel, and if this contradiction is then pointed out to them, they say things like 'Well, I was just guessing' or 'Well, I must have done it unconsciously'.

If two objects are placed simultaneously, one in each hand, and then are removed and hidden for retrieval in a scrambled pile of test items, each hand will hunt through the pile and search out selectively its own object. In the process, each hand may explore, identify and reject the item for which the other hand is searching. It is like two separate individuals working with no cooperation between them; indeed the interpretation of this, and many similar findings, is less confusing if we try to think of the commissurotomy patient not as a single individual but in terms of the mental faculties and performance capacities of the two hemispheres separately. Mostly it is the dominant, i.e. left, hemisphere which is in control, but in some tasks, particularly when these are forced in testing procedures, the minor hemisphere seems able to take over temporarily.

When you split the brain in half anatomically, you do not divide in half its functional properties. In some respects cerebral functions may be doubled as much as halved because of the extensive bilateral redundancy in brain organization, whereby, particularly in subhuman species, most functions are separately and rather fully organized on both sides. Probably neither of the separated visual systems senses or perceives itself to be cut in half or even incomplete, just as the hemianopic patient who, following accidental destruction of an entire visual cortex of one hemisphere may not even notice the loss of the entire half sphere of vision until it is pointed out to him in specific optometric tests. Commissurotomy patients continue to watch T.V. and to read with no complaints about peculiarities in the perceptual appearance of the visual field.

Although intelligence, as measured by IQ, is not much affected and personality is little changed, commissurotomy patients do seem to be intellectually handicapped in ways that are probably not revealed in the ordinary tests. They all have marked short-term memory deficits, especially during the first year, have orientation problems and fatigue more quickly in reading and other tasks requiring concentration. Studied comparisons of the upper limits of performance before and after surgery are still needed.

Much of the foregoing is summarized in figure 17.3. The left hemisphere in the right-handed patient is equipped with the expressive mechanisms for speech and writing, and with the main centres for the comprehension and organization of language. It can communicate about the visual experiences of the right visual field and about the somaesthetic and volitional experiences of the right hand and leg, and right half of the body generally. Also, but not shown in figure 17.3, it communicates, of course, about all the more general, less lateralized, cerebral activity that is bilaterally represented and common to both hemispheres. On the right side we have the mute aphasic and agraphic hemisphere, which cannot express itself verbally but which shows

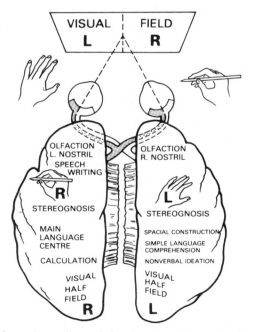

Figure 17.3 Schematic outline of the functional lateralization evident in behavioural tests of patients with forebrain commissurotomy.

non-verbally that it is not agnostic; mental processes are indeed present and centred around the left visual field, hand, leg and half of the body.

To try to find out what goes on in that speechless agraphic minor hemisphere has always been one of the main challenges in our research. Does it really possess a true stream of conscious awareness, or is it just an agnostic automaton carried along in a reflex or trancelike state? This is related to many problems to do with lateral dominance and specialization in the human brain, the functional roles of the neocortical commissures and similar aspects of cerebral organization.

Clearly, the minor hemisphere can perform inter-modal or cross-modal transfer of perceptual and mnemonic information at a characteristically human level. For example, after a picture of some object, such as a cigarette, has been flashed to the minor hemisphere via the left visual field, the subject can retrieve the item pictured from a collection of objects using blind touch with the left hand, which is mediated through the right hemisphere. However, unlike the normal person, the commissurotomy patient is obliged to use the corresponding hand (i.e. the left, in this case) for retrieval, and fails when asked to search out the same item with the right hand (see figure 17.4). Using the right hand, the subject recognizes and can call off the names of each object that he comes to, but the right hand or its hemisphere does not know what it is looking for, and the hemisphere that can recognize the correct answer gets no feedback from the right hand. Hence, the two never get together, and the performance fails. Speech and other auditory cues must be controlled.

It also works the other way round, i.e., if the subject is holding an object in the left hand, he can then point out a picture of this object or the printed name of the object when these appear in a series presented visually. But again, these latter must be seen through the correspond-

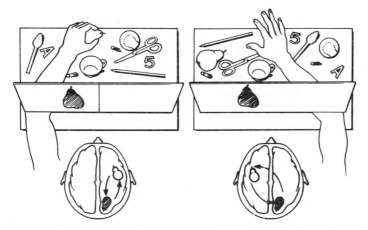

Figure 17.4 Visuo-tactile associations succeed between each half of the visual field and the corresponding hand. They fail with crossed combinations in which visual and tactual stimuli are projected into opposite hemispheres.

ing half of the visual field; an object identified by the left hand is not recognized when seen in the right half of the visual field. Intermodal associations of this kind have been demonstrated between vision, hearing and touch and, more recently, smell, in various combinations within either hemisphere but not across from one hemisphere to the other. This transfer is of special theoretical interest, since it is extremely difficult or impossible for the monkey brain, i.e. the right hemisphere may be animal-like in not being able to talk or write, but in other respects it shows mental capacities which are definitely human.

Other responses suggest the presence of ideas and a capacity for mental associations, and at least some simple logic and reasoning. In the same visuo-tactual test described above, the minor hemisphere, instead of selecting objects which match exactly the pictured item, seems able to select related items or ones which 'go with' the particular visual stimulus. For example, if we flash a picture of a wall clock and the nearest item that can be found tactually by the left hand is a toy wrist-watch, this is chosen. It is as if the minor hemisphere has an idea of a timepiece and is not just matching sensory outlines. Again, if the picture is of a hammer, the subject may choose a nail or a spike after checking out and rejecting all other items.

The minor hemisphere can also perform simple arithmetical problems. After a correct left-hand response has been made by pointing or by writing the number, the major hemisphere can then report the same answer verbally, but only after the left-hand response. If an error is made with the left hand, the verbal report contains the same error. If two different pairs of numbers are flashed to right and left fields simultaneously, the correct sum or product may be signalled separately by both hands. But when verbal confirmation of correct left-hand signals is required, the speaking hemisphere can only guess, showing again that the answer must have been obtained from the minor hemisphere.

In contradiction to the traditional belief that the disconnected minor hemisphere becomes 'word blind', 'word deaf' and 'tactually alexic', we found in commissurotomy patients that it is able to understand both written and spoken words to some extent, although it cannot express the understanding verbally (Gazzaniga & Sperry, 1967; Sperry, 1966; Sperry & Gazzaniga, 1967). If a word such as 'eraser' is flashed to the left visual field, the subject is able to search out an eraser from among a collection of objects using only touch with the left hand. But if he is asked what the item is after correct selection has been made, his answers show that he does not know what he is holding in his left hand, as is the general rule for left-hand stereognosis. This means, of course, that the *talking* hemisphere does not know the correct answer so the minor hemisphere must, in this situation, have read and understood the test word.

Again, if asked to find a 'piece of silverware', the subject may explore the array of test items and pick up a fork; if asked what it is he has chosen, he is just as likely to reply 'spoon' or 'knife' as fork. Both hemispheres have heard and understood the word 'silverware', but only the minor hemisphere knows what the left hand has actually found and picked up. Other tests show that the minor hemisphere can understand fairly complex spoken definitions like 'shaving instrument' (razor), 'dirt remover' (soap) and 'inserted in slot machines' (quarter).

It can also sort objects into groups by touch on the basis of shape, size and texture, and is superior to the major in tasks which involve drawing spatial relationships and performing block design tests.

The minor hemisphere demonstrates appropriate emotional reactions, as, for example, when a pin-up of a nude is interjected unexpectedly among a series of geometric shapes flashed to the right and left fields at random. The subject typically denies seeing anything, but a sneaky grin and perhaps blushing and giggling on the next couple of trials or so belies the verbal answer of the speaking hemisphere; apparently, only the emotional effect gets across, as if the cognitive component cannot be articulated through the brainstem. Similarly, Gordon and Sperry (1968) find that when odours are presented through the right nostril to the minor hemisphere, the subject cannot name it but can often indicate whether it is pleasant or unpleasant, whether verbally or by exclaiming (like 'phew!'). The specific information which fails to reach the major hemisphere is implied by the subject's correct selection, through left-hand stereognosis, of corresponding objects associated with the given smell. The minor hemisphere also expresses genuine annoyance at the errors made by its 'better', speaking, half in ordinary testing situations, when it knows the correct answer but cannot say it.

It seems, then, that in the right hemisphere we deal with a second conscious entity which is characteristically human and runs along in parallel with the more dominant stream of consciousness in the major hemisphere (Sperry, 1966). The quality of mental awareness in the minor hemisphere is perhaps comparable to that which survives in some types of aphasic patients following damage to the motor and main language centres. The dominant hemisphere may, under most ordinary conditions, be unaware of the presence of the minor one.

The more we see of these patients and the more of them we see, the more impressed we become with their individual differences and with the consequent qualifications that must be made to the general picture of the deconnection symptoms described.

Commentary

Aim and nature

The study is one of a series published by the psychologist Sperry and his colleagues (e.g. Gazzaniga) in which they report their findings concerning the 'functional outcome' of commissurotomy, i.e. the behavioural, neurological and psychological effects of having the two cerebral hemispheres disconnected through the surgical operation of dividing the entire corpus callosum (plus the smaller anterior and hippocompal commissures, and in some cases the massa intermedia). It is important to point out (although it should be clear enough from the article) that in no way was this surgery performed *as part of* psychological research: Sperry's subjects were patients suffering from severe epilepsy which could not be controlled in any less drastic way (e.g. drugs). He then took the opportunity to study these 'split-brain' patients; what better way to study the functioning of the two cerebral hemispheres than to present tasks to each hemisphere separately in subjects whose hemispheres cannot 'communicate' with each other? In this way, Sperry's investigations are a kind of 'natural experiment' whereby the experimental manipulation is either done literally by nature (e.g. identical twins raised in different environments) or in the 'natural' course of the subject's life (i.e. epileptics undergoing surgery for their epilepsy which disconnects the two halves of their brain). This also means that the studies are clinical studies (as are studies of brain-damaged patients and memory, for example). The tasks are presented to subjects under carefully controlled laboratory conditions. Sperry's work began in 1961 and he was awarded a Nobel Prize in 1981.

Context and background

According to Ornstein (1986), the cerebral cortex appeared in our ancestors quite recently, about 50 million years ago. It performs the functions which have greatly increased our adaptability as a species. A feature of all primate brains is its division into hemispheres, *but* only with the human brain are they specialized for different functions (i.e. lateral specialization or functional lateralization). This represents the most recent development in human evolution, less than four million years old and is uniquely human.

According to Bogen (1969) (see Ornstein, 1986), scientists have been trying to characterize the nature of the left and right hemispheres for well over 100 years, and Sperry's work has made a tremendous contribution to our understanding of functional lateralization. The great physiologist Hughlings Jackson (1864) distinguished between the expressive nature of the left (i.e. its use of language as propositional) and the perceptual nature of the right. Zangwill (1961) proposed that the left is predominantly symbolic while the right is predominantly visuospatial. Similarly, Bogen and Gazzaniga (1965) regarded the left as verbal and the right as visuo-spatial. Again, Levy-Agresti and Sperry (1968), concluded that the '... mute, minor hemisphere is specialized for Gestalt perception, being primarily a synthesist in dealing with information input. The speaking, major hemisphere, in contrast, seems to operate in a more logical, analytic, computer-like fashion ...'.

Ornstein (1986) summarizes the differences like this: (*i*) the left is specialized for analytic and logical thinking (i.e. breaking things down into their component parts), especially in verbal and mathematical functions, processes information sequentially (one item at a time) and its mode of operation is primarily linear (straight-line); (*ii*) the right is specialized for synthetic thinking, (bringing different things together to form a whole), particularly in the area of spatial tasks, artistic activities, crafts, body image and face recognition, processes information more diffusely (several items at once) and its mode of operation is much less linear (more holistic).

Evaluation

1 One of the difficulties associated with generalizations in psychology (even with something as 'biological' as cerebral function) is the existence of individual differences. Some people seem to have much more lateralized brains than others; others have language more or less equally represented on both sides (bilateral representation) (Beaumont, 1988). As far as the left hemisphere being dominant for language, this seems to be true for 95 per cent of right-handed patients, while only five per cent had their right hemisphere dominant. But with left-handers, things are much

less clear-cut: 75 per cent had their left hemisphere dominant, none has the right dominant but 25 per cent showed bilateral representation (based on a review by Satz (1979) of all studies between 1935 and 1975, cited in Beaumont, 1988). Over and above this left–right handed difference, is the finding that women show less lateralization than men; for example, damage to one side will, on average, affect a woman's brain less than a man's. Similarly, damage to the right hemisphere will interfere with a man's spatial abilities more than a woman's. So, the left–right specialization is most prevalent in right-handed men (and not 'all people'!) (Ornstein, 1986).

Ornstein (1986) refers to the work of De Lacoste and her colleagues in which they are beginning to be able to identify the male and female corpus callosum by sight alone. They are, it seems, as 'dimorphic' as are male and female arms; women's are larger overall and larger towards the back of the brain.

But Bogen (1969) believes that we must not let the 'rich diversity of natural phenomena obscure our recognition of the common and representative types', i.e. the similarities still outweigh the differences.

2 Another difficulty raised by Bogen (1969) is the question as to exactly what *is* a function, i.e. isn't it a rather arbitrary decision to call what the left hemisphere is good at 'verbal' and what the right is good at 'non-verbal'? He makes the important point that lateralization is a *relative* matter (not either/or), for example, as Sperry shows, the right does have some language ability. Ornstein (1986) points out that some recent studies have shown that the primary factor in hemisphere lateralization is *not* the type of information (words or pictures versus sounds or shapes) which is processed, but *how* it is processed. For example, subjects were given a technical passage and two folk tales. There was no change in the level of activity in the left hemisphere, but the right was more activated while the subject was reading the stories than while reading the technical material.

3 Much of what we know about normal brain function in general (and lateralization in particular) is based upon the study of those who have suffered brain damage or, in the case of split-brain patients, undergone drastic surgery for epilepsy. In the case of the former, we assume that the damaged area has stopped working correctly but that the rest of the brain carries on more or less as normal. This may or may not be a reasonable assumption (Beaumont, 1988). In the case of the latter, longstanding pre-surgical pathology might have caused an abnormal reorganization of their brains so that generalizing to normal brains may be invalid (Cohen, 1975). She cites a study by Kinsbourne in which the left hemisphere of aphasic patients (unable to produce or understand speech) was anaesthetized but they continued to speak fluently, but unintelligibly, suggesting that the abnormal speech is produced by the right hemisphere. This, according to split-brain studies, has some language understanding but is supposed to be *mute*.

But Ornstein (1986) and others cite many studies of 'normal' brains which seem to support the lateralization findings from split-brain studies (e.g. Kimura 1961, 1964b). Cohen is also critical of these, since she believes the two hemispheres do not function in isolation but form a highly integrated system. Most everyday tasks involve a mixture of 'left' and 'right' skills, e.g. in listening to speech we analyze both the words *and* the pattern of intonation; in reading, analysis of visual shapes and linguistic knowledge are both required. Far from 'doing their own thing', the two hemispheres work very much together (Cohen, 1975).

4 This leads on to what is perhaps both the most interesting and the most controversial of all the issues relating to lateralization and, in particular, split-brain

patients; that is, do the two halves of the brain represent two kinds of consciousness, i.e. two minds?

Ornstein (1986) refers to reports of an entire hemisphere being removed for the treatment of certain kinds of epilepsy, after which the 'person' remained, no matter which hemisphere was removed. So if possession of a 'mind' requires only one hemisphere, does having two hemispheres make possible the possession of two minds? Indeed, do split-brain patients have two minds, two separate, distinct modes of consciousness? Ornstein and Sperry certainly think so. Does this mean that the normal role of the corpus callosum is to keep the two hemispheres in exact synchrony, so that we normally have one, unified, mind? Ornstein asks if cerebral commissurotomy produces a splitting or doubling of the mind, or is it more correctly considered a manoeuvre which helps to manifest the duality there all the time? He believes each of us has two minds in one person. But this seems to conflict with our subjective experience of unity.

Sperry (1966) described split-brain patients as having 'two free wills in one cranial vault'. According to Mackay (1987) there is no reason in principle to object to the science fiction speculation that if a human nervous system could be *completely* bifurcated and each half left in working order, that the resulting structure might embody two distinct persons (as in Siamese Twins). However, in the real world of split-brain patients, he doubts whether any of the evidence to date requires or justifies such a drastic interpretation of their condition.

The most significant implication of talk of 'two minds' or 'two persons' is the possibility, in principle, of a dialogue between them (in which each comes to know the other as 'thou': Buber, 1937). (This is also related to the role of the therapist treating patients with multiple personality, attempting to put various personalities 'in touch' with each other: see chapter 31.)

Mackay (1978) and Mackay and Mackay (1982) spent several months, courtesy of Sperry and Gazzaniga, in New York and Passadena, testing a variety of split-brain patients in an attempt to do this! The most ambitious tests were performed on a cooperative and intelligent patient, J.W., aged 27.

Each hemisphere was in turn trained to participate in a guessing game of the '20 Questions' type in dialogue with one experimenter.

(*i*) *E* first assumed the role of 'guesser' attempting to name a 'mystery number' written by the other *E* on a piece of paper in full view of J.W. *E* invited J.W. to use his left hand to point to the appropriate answers on a card also in full view, with 'go up', 'go down', 'OK', printed on it. The left hand proved immediately capable of providing reliable feedback in this mode.

(*ii*) *E* invited J.W. to 'guess a number from nought to nine which I've been shown'. In response to each guess, *E* pointed mutely to one of three messages on the card. He quickly learned to adapt his vocal guesses so as to home in on the correct answer under this mute feedback from *E*.

(*iii*) Single digits from nought to nine were flashed to J.W.'s left and distractor letters to the right. *E* proposed that J.W. play both roles, using his mouth (controlled by the left hemisphere) to make guesses and the left hand (controlled by the right hemisphere) to offer feedback by way of a card so as to guide the guessing process. He had no apparent difficulty doing this, though all his guesses were addressed to *E* who invariably had to prompt him to use his left hand to answer. He proved well able to 'talk himself down' onto the correct target each time, often showing satisfaction by a smile when the target was finally named.

These results show that a form of low-level dialogue, exchanging information by question and answer, could be sustained between the two hemispheres (Mackay,

1987). But they did nothing to answer the question as to whether the two half-participants had the kind of 'independence of will' possessed by two normal human players on opposite sides of a guessing game. How *could* it be answered? What about the capacity to *bargain*? An attempt to do this with J.W. led Mackay (1987) to conclude that all the existing evidence (including his) is insufficient to justify claims that the two hemispheres *do* embody 'two free wills'.

> . . . it would seem more parsimonious to describe a split-brain patient not as 'two people' or 'two free wills' but as one person who is liable in certain circumstances to show a peculiarly elaborate form of absent-mindedness

and again

> It is only if the neural equipment for self-supervisory normative activity were known to be completely duplicated (in *each* hemisphere), at cortical levels normally linked by the corpus callosum that we could plausibly regard split-brain patients as two people. (Mackay, 1987)

Parfit (1987) agrees that, while the split-brain patient does have two streams of consciousness, we should not regard them as constituting two persons, because, in a sense, there is *none*. He distinguishes the ego theory (of what persons are) from the bundle theory, which explains the unity of consciousness by claiming that ordinary people are, at any time, aware of having several different experiences. This can easily be extended to cover split-brain cases: at any time, there is not one state of awareness of several different experiences, but two such states (*not* two separately existing egos). Split-brain cases have great theoretical importance because they 'challenge some of our deepest assumptions about ourselves' (Parfit, 1987).

Exercises

1 Referring to the *Evaluation* section in the Commentary, why should there be a difference between the two hemispheres in their respective responses to the technical passage and the stories?

2 Ornstein (1986) reports an experiment in which brain activity was recorded while subjects mentally rotated objects in space. They were then asked to count the number of boxes. Which hemisphere would be mainly involved in each case?

3 In what way could split-brain patients be considered unrepresentative of adult subjects in general?

4 Why can split-brain experiments not be considered *true* experiments?

Positive reinforcement produced by electrical stimulation of septal area and other regions of rat brain

Journal of Comparative and Physiological Psychology, 47, pp. 419–27

Stimuli have eliciting and reinforcing functions. In studying the former, one concentrates on the responses which come after the stimulus; in studying the latter, one looks mainly at the responses which precede it. In its reinforcing capacity, a stimulus increases, decreases, or leaves unchanged the frequency of preceding responses, and accordingly it is called a reward, punishment or neutral stimulus (see Skinner, 1938).

Previous studies using chronic implantation of electrodes have tended to focus on the eliciting functions of electrical stimuli delivered to the brain (Delgado, 1952; Delgado & Anand, 1953; Dell, 1952; Gastant, 1952; Hunter & Jasper 1949; MacLean & Delgado, 1953; Rosvold & Delgado, 1953). But the present study has been concerned with the reinforcing function of the electrical stimulation.

Method

General

Stimulation was carried out by means of chronically implanted electrodes which did not interfere with the health or free behaviour of *Ss* to any appreciable extent. They were 15 male hooded rats, weighing approximately 250 g at the start of the experiment. Each was tested in a Skinner box which delivered alternating current to the brain so long as a lever was pressed. The current was delivered through a loose lead, suspended from the ceiling, which connected the stimulator to the rat's electrode. *Ss* were given a total of six to 12 hours of acquisition testing and one to two hours of extinction testing. During acquisition, the stimulator was turned on, so that a response produced electrical stimulation; during extinction, the stimulator was turned off so that a response produced no electrical stimulation. Each

S was given a percentage score denoting the proportion of his total acquisition time given to responding which could be compared with the animal's extinction score to determine whether the stimulation had a positive, negative or neutral reinforcing effect. After testing, the animal was sacrificed. Its brain was frozen, sectioned, stained and examined microscopically to determine which structure of the brain had been stimulated. This allowed correlation of acquisition scores with anatomical structures.

Electrode implantation

Electrodes are constructed by cementing a pair of enamelled silver wires of 0.010 inch diameter into a Lucite block. The parts of the wires which penetrate the brain are cemented together to form a needle, and this is cut to the correct length to reach the desired structure in the brain. The exposed cross section of the wire is the only part of the needle not insulated from the brain by enamel: so stimulation only occurs at the tip.

The operation of implantation is performed with the rat under Nembutal anaesthesia (0.88 cc/kg) and held in a Johnson–Krieg stereotaxic instrument (Krieg, 1946). A mid-line incision is made in the scalp and the skin held out of the way by muscle retractors. A small hole is drilled in the skull with a dental burr at the point indicated by the stereotaxic instrument for the structure it is desired to stimulate. The electrode, which is clamped into the needle carrier of the instrument, is lowered until the flange of the Lucite block rests

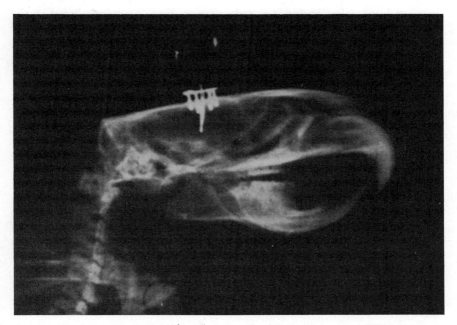

Figure 18.1   X-ray showing electrode in place in intact animal. There are two wires insulated completely from each other, stimulating the brain with their tips.

firmly on the skull. Four screw holes are then drilled in the skull through four fixing holes in the flange, and the electrode, still clamped firmly in the instrument, is fastened to the skull with jeweller's screws. The electrode is then released from the clamp and the scalp wound closed with silk sutures. The skin is pulled tightly around the base of the Lucite block and kept well away from the contact plates. A recovery period of three days is allowed before testing. Figure 18.1 is an X-ray picture of an electrode in place.

Testing

The testing apparatus consisted of a large-levered Skinner box 11 inches long, five inches wide and 12 inches high. The top was open to allow passage for the stimulating lead. The lever activated a micro-switch in the stimulating circuit, so that when it was pressed, the rat received electrical stimulation, which continued as long as the lever was pressed, though for some tests a time-delay switch was incorporated, which cut the current off after a predetermined interval if the rat continued to hold the lever down. Responses were recorded automatically on paper strip.

On the fourth day after the operation rats were given a pretesting session of about an hour in the boxes. Each was placed in the box and on the lever by E with the stimulus set at 0.5V. During the hour, stimulation voltage was varied to determine the threshold of a 'just noticeable' effect on the rat's behaviour. If the S did not respond regularly from the start, it was placed on the lever periodically (at about five-minute intervals). Data collected on the first day were not used in later calculations. On subsequent days, Ss were placed in the box for about $3\frac{1}{2}$ hours a day (three hours of acquisition and half an hour of extinction). During the former, the rats were allowed to stimulate themselves with a voltage just high enough to produce some noticeable response in the resting animal. As this threshold voltage fluctuated over time, E made a determination of it every half hour, unless S was responding regularly. At the beginning of each acquisition period, and after each voltage test, S was placed on the lever once by E. During extinction periods, conditions were precisely the same except that a bar press produced no electrical stimulation.

At first, rats were tested in this way for four days, but as there seemed to be little difference between the results on different days, this period was reduced to three and then two days for subsequent animals. Thus, the first rats had about 12 hours of acquisition after pretesting, while later rats had about six hours. However, when calculating the scores, we have used only the first six hours of acquisition for all animals, so the scores are strictly comparable. In behavioural curves, we have shown the full 12 hours on the earlier animals so as to illustrate the stability of the behaviour over time.

At no time during the experiment were the rats deprived of food or water, and no reinforcement was used except the electrical stimulation.

Rats were scored on the percentage of time they spent bar pressing regularly during acquisition. In order to find how much time the rat would spend in the absence of reward or punishment, a similar score was calculated for extinction periods. This extinction score provided a base line: when the acquisition score is above the extinction score we have reward, when it is below, we have punishment. In order to determine percentage scores, periods when the rat was responding regularly (at least one response every 30 seconds) were counted as periods of responding, i.e. *intervals of 30 seconds or longer without a response were counted as periods of no responding.* The percentage scores were calculated as the proportion of total acquisition or extinction time given to periods of responding.

Determination of locus

On completion of testing, rats were perfused with physiological saline, followed by 10 per cent formalin. The brains were removed, and after further fixation in formalin for about a week, frozen sections 40 microns thick were cut through the region of the electrode track. These were stained and the position of the electrode tip determined (see figure 18.2).

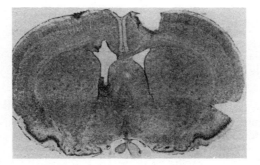

Figure 18.2 Photomicrograph showing the electrode track in a cresyl-violet-stained brain section. The section is 1 mm in front of the anterior commissure. The electrode protruded through the lateral ventricle, and its stimulating tip was in the septal area.

Results

Locus

In table 18.1, acquisition and extinction scores are correlated with electrode placements

Figure 18.3 presents the acquisition scores again, this time on three cross-sectional maps of the rat brain, one at the forebrain level, one at the thalamic level, and one at the mid-brain level. The position of a score on the map indicates the electrode placement from which this acquisition score was obtained.

Table 18.1　Acquisition and extinction scores for all animals, together with electrode placements and threshold voltages used during acquisition tests

Animal's number	Locus of electrode	Stimulation voltage r.m.s.	Percentage of acquisition time spent responding	Percentage of extinction time spent responding
32	septal	2.2–2.8	75	18
34	septal	1.4	92	6
M-1	septal	1.7–4.8	85	21
M-4	septal	2.3–4.8	88	13
40	c.c.	0.7–1.1	6	3
41	caudate	0.9–1.2	4	4
31	cingulate	1.8	37	9
82	cingulate	0.5–1.8	36	10
36	hip.	0.8–2.8	1	14
3	m.l.	0.5	0	4
A-5	m.t.	1.4	71	9
6	m.g.	0.5	0	31
11	m.g.	0.5	0	21
17	teg.	0.7	2	1
9	teg.	0.5	77	81

Key　　*c.c.* corpus callosum　　　　　　　*hip.* hippocampus
　　　　m.l. medial lemniscus　　　　　　 *m.t.* mammillothalamic tract
　　　　m.g. medial geniculate　　　　　　*teg.* tegmentum

The highest scores are found together in the central portion of the forebrain. Beneath the corpus callosum and between the two lateral ventricles in section I of figure 18.3, we find four acquisition scores ranging from 75 per cent to 92 per cent. This is the septal area, and is the focus of the first four *Ss* in table 18.1. They all spent less than 22 per cent of their extinction time responding. Thus electrical stimulation of the septal area has an effect which is apparently equivalent to that of a conventional primary reward as far as the maintenance of a lever-pressing response is concerned.

If we move outside the septal area, either towards the caudate nucleus (across the lateral ventricle) or towards the corpus callosum, acquisition scores drop abruptly to levels from four per cent to six per cent. This definitely indicates neutral effects. However, above the corpus callosum in the cingulate cortex, we find an acquisition score of 37 per cent and, as the extinction score was nine per cent, we may say that stimulation was rewarding.

At the thalamic level (section II of figure 18.3) we find a 36 per cent acquisition score produced by an electrode placed again in the cingulate cortex, 11 per cent in the hippocompus, 71 per cent in the mammillothalamic tract, and 0 per cent in the medial lemniscus.

At the mid-brain level (section III of figure 18.3) there are two zeros in the posterior portion of the medial geniculate bodies, with corresponding extinction scores of 31 per cent and 21 per cent, two per cent in the medial, posterior tegmentum (extinction score one per cent) and, finally, 77 per cent for an electrode which was actually 1½ mm

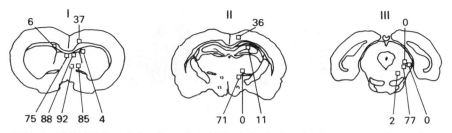

Figure 18.3 Maps of three sections, (I) through the forebrain, (II) through the thalamus and (IV) through the mid-brain of the rat. Boxed numbers give acquisition percentage scores produced by animals with electrodes stimulating at these points. On section I the acquisition scores 75, 88, 92 and 85 fall in the septal forebrain area. On the same section there is a score of 4 in the caudate nucleus, a score of 6 in the white matter below the cortex, and a score of 37 in the medial (cingulate) cortex. On section II, the acquisition score of 36 is in the medial (cingulate) cortex, 11 is in the hippocampus, 71 is in the mammillothalmic tract, and 0 is in the medial lemniscus. On section III, the two zeroes are in the medial geniculate, 2 is in the tegmental reticular substance, 77 falls 2 mm anterior to the section shown; it is between the posterior commissure and the red nucleus.

anterior to the point where it is shown (between the red nucleus and the posterior commissure). The extinction score of 81 per cent makes this difficult to interpret.

Behaviour

The lowest-scoring septal area rat (no. 32) gave a total of slightly over 3000 responses in 12 hours of acquisition. When the current was turned on, the rat responded at the rate of 285 responses an hour, when it was turned off, the rate fell close to zero.

The highest-scoring septal area rat (no. 34) stimulated itself over 7500 times in 12 hours. Its average response rate during acquisition was 742 responses an hour; during extinction, practically zero.

Figure 18.4 represents an unsmoothed cumulative response curve of one day of responding for rat no. A-5. This shows in detail the degree of control exercised by the electrical reward stimulus. While this rat was actually bar pressing, it did so at 1920 responses per hour, i.e. about one response for every two seconds. Durring the first period of the day it responded regularly while on acquisition, extinguished very rapidly when the current was turned off, and reconditioned readily when it was turned on again. At reconditioning points, *E* gave *S* one stimulus to show that the current was back on, but *E* did not place *S* on the lever. During longer periods of acquisitions, *S* occasionally stopped responding for short periods, but in the long run spent almost 75 per cent of its acquisition time responding. During the long period of extinction at the end of the day, there was very little responding, but *S* could be brought back to the lever quite quickly if a stimulus was delivered to show that the current had been turned on again.

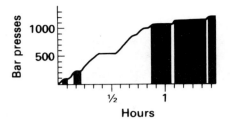

Figure 18.4 Unsmoothed cumulative response curve showing about ¾ hour acquisition and ¾ hour extinction for rat no. A-5. Shading indicates extinction.

Discussion

Clearly electrical stimulation in certain parts of the brain, particularly the septal area, produces acquisition and extinction curves which compare favourably with those produced by a conventional primary reward. With other electrode placements, the stimulation seems to be neutral or punishing.

Because the rewarding effect has been most pronounced in the septal area (but also, to a lesser degree, in the mammillothalamic tract and cingulate cortex), there may be a system of structures which provides the locus for the reward phenomenon; we shall call these structures 'reinforcing structures', since localization studies are still in progress. How can the phenomenon provide a methodological basis for study of physiological mechanisms of reward?

The possibility that the implantation produces some painful 'drive stimulus' which is alleviated by electrical stimulation of reinforcing structures does not accord with our findings. If there were some such painful drive state, it would be shown by emotional signs in the rat's daily behaviour, but our *Ss*, from the first day after the operation, are normally quiet, non-aggressive, eat and sleep regularly and gain weight. Also, septal rats which have lived healthy and normal lives for months after the operation have given excellent response rates.

There does not appear, therefore, to be any explicitly manipulated drive to be reduced by electrical stimulation. We have evidence for a primary rewarding effect, not associated with the reduction of any primary drive state, and the *E*'s 'clinical impression' is that the phenomenon represents strong pursuit of a positive stimulus rather than escape from some negative condition. If we are correct, we have perhaps located a system within the brain whose peculiar function is to produce a rewarding effect on behaviour. This enables us to collect evidence which may help us choose between conflicting theories of reward; e.g. the reinforcing structures might act selectively on sensory or motor areas of the cortex, which would be relevant to the current S-S versus S-R controversies (Hebb, 1949; Hull, 1943; Olds, 1954; Skinner, 1938).

Similarly, extirpation studies may show whether reinforcing structures have primarily a quieting or an activating effect on behaviour;

this would be relevant to activation versus negative feedback theories of reward (Deutsch, 1953; Olds, 1954; Seward, 1952; Wiener, 1949). Brady and Nanta (1953) suggest that the septal area is a quieting system, since its surgical removal produced an extremely active animal.

We believe that such examples suggest that the methodology reported here should have important consequences for physiological studies of mechanisms of reward.

Summary

A preliminary study was made of rewarding effects produced by electrical stimulation of certain areas of the brain. Rats were stimulated with voltages ranging from ½ V to 5 V. Bipolar needle electrodes were permanently implanted at various points in the brain. Rats were tested in Skinner boxes where they could stimulate themselves by pressing a lever. They received no other reward during the experiments. The primary findings were: (*i*) there are numerous lower brain centres where electrical stimulation is rewarding, in that the experimental *S* will stimulate itself in these places frequently and regularly for long periods of time if allowed to do so; (*ii*) these results can be obtained from as far back as the tegmentum, as far forward as the septal area, and as far up as the cingulate gyrus of the cortex; (*iii*) there are also sites in the lower centres where the animals do nothing to obtain or to avoid stimulation; (*iv*) the reward results are obtained more dependably with electrodes placed in some areas than others, especially the septal area; (*v*) in the septal area, the control exercised over the rats' behaviour is extreme, possibly exceeding that for any other reward previously used in animal experimentation.

Commentary

Aim and nature

The aim of this laboratory experiment using rat subjects was to study the reinforcing properties of the implantation of electrodes, which deliver electric shock to the rat's brain. While previous studies had focused on the eliciting functions of electrical brain-stimulation (i.e. studying the responses produced by the stimulation: i.e. respondent or classical conditioning), the present study focuses on the responses which precede it and are instrumental in producing it (i.e. operant conditioning). Does this mean that direct brain stimulation can be used to reinforce behaviour, specifically, lever pressing in a Skinner box, in the same way that food can? And if so, are there particular brain sites where such stimulation will be effective and others where it will not?

Context and background

In the rat brain (as in the human brain), the three main structural areas are (*i*) the forebrain (cerebral hemispheres, thalamus, hypothalomus, basal ganglia and limbic system); (*ii*) midbrain (Reticular Activating System or RAS); and (*iii*) the hindbrain (cerebellum, pons and medulla). The structures or areas which were stimulated in the Olds and Milner study are:

(a) the corpus callosum: a dense mass of commissurial ('joining') fibres connecting the two cerebral hemispheres;

(b) the medial geniculate body: a part of the thalamus which processes auditory information;

(c) the cingulate gyrus: a part of the limbic system (which also includes the thalamus, hypothalamus, hippocampus, amygdala, and septal area/septum pellucidum) which, as a whole, is closely involved with behaviours which satisfy certain motivational and emotional needs, such as feeding, fighting, escape and mating. It also represents a meeting place between the cortex (or 'neocortex') and older parts of the brain such as the hypothalamus;

(d) the septal area: part of the limbic system (see (c) above);

(e) hippocampus: as seen above, part of the limbic system (in humans, anyway, it plays an important part in memory);

(f) the caudate nucleus: part of the corpus striatum which, in turn, comprises part of the basal ganglia. These are embedded within each cerebral hemisphere, are closely linked to the thalamus, and play a part in muscle tone and posture;

(g) mammillothalamic tract: connects the mamillary body (part of the limbic system) to the thalamus (the limbic system is often referred to as the 'old mammillian brain');

(h) the medial lemniscus: a large bundle of sensory nerve fibres taking messages from the lower brain stem into the thalamus;

(i) the tegmentum: a part of the midbrain which extends into the region below the thalamus.

It was Walter Hess who developed the technique of implanting electrodes in animal brains while investigating the RAS of the rat's brain (Roediger *et al.*, 1984). He accidentally implanted an electrode in an area near the hypothalamus known to be involved in sleep and arousal. The rat repeatedly returned to the place where it had been stimulated; further stimulation at the same cage location resulted in the animal spending most of its time there. It was Olds (1956) who is credited with discovering the so-called 'pleasure centre'.

Evaluation

1 One of the important *theoretical* implications of Olds and Milner's work is that it challenges the homeostatic drive-reduction theory (Hull, 1943), which maintains that animals (and by implication, people) *always* learn through primary drive-reduction, and *never* learn if drive-reduction does not occur (an example of a primary drive is the drive for food/the hunger drive). Clearly drives *can* occur in the absence of any obvious physiological need, electrical self-stimulation of the brain (ESB) being one such non-homeostatic drive (in animals).

Further, it appears to be a very powerful drive. In this experiment, the lowest-scoring septal area rat gave a total of just over 3000 responses in 12 hours, and the highest over 7500 responses in 12 hours. Olds (1956) reported that one rat stimulated itself more than 2000 times per hour for 24 hours consecutively, and in 1958 found that rats which normally press a lever 25 times per hour for a food reward will press 100 times per *minute* for a reward of ESB.

An even more dramatic demonstration of its power is the finding that a male rat with an electrode in its lateral hypothalamus (LH) will self-stimulate in preference to eating if hungry, drinking if thirsty or having access to a sexually receptive female. This effect has also been found in cats, monkeys and pigeons.

2 According to Green (1980) and Beaumont (1988), the main reward site for ESB is the median forebrain bundle (MFB), a fibre tract running from the brain stem up to the forebrain through the LH, and the effects seem to depend on the presence of the synaptic transmitters dopamine and noradrenaline (the catecholamines). These neurotransmitters have been shown to be released from limbic structures during rewarding brain stimulation, and drugs which interfere with the operation of these pathways reduce the effect of ESB (Beaumont, 1988). These reward or 'pleasure' centres are generally thought of as the neural substrate of 'pleasure', so that any behaviour defined as pleasurable involves their activation; ESB is a 'short cut' to pleasure, 'eliminating the need for natural drives and reinforcers' (Green, 1980).

3 However, two important qualifications need to be made:
(*i*) Rather lower down in the hypothalamus, ESB produces pain and rats will go to great lengths to avoid it; often one press of the lever will be sufficient for the rat to avoid the lever thereafter. Other sites seem to yield both reward and punishment. For example Bower and Miller (1958) trained rats to press one lever for ESB and then another to turn it off, and it seems that prolonged brain stimulation might be aversive (Roediger *et al.*, 1984). Beyond a certain point, stimulation becomes less effective, and may become negative if sufficiently intense; brief stimulation is more reinforcing than prolonged, so an intermediate level of stimulation seems to be pleasurable, but not if it is extreme (Hilgard *et al.*, 1979).
(*ii*) The actual region in the hypothalamus which will produce self-stimulation is considerably more diffuse than those involved in other hypothalamic drive centres (such as hunger and thirst), and other parts of the limbic system can also produce pleasure responses (Rose, 1976).

4 Are there any important differences between the effects of ESB and (other) primary reinforcers? According to LeFrancois (1983) there are four:
(*i*) Animals eventually become satiated following repeated reinforcement with food or water, but not with ESB (see **1** above).
(*ii*) ESB seems to take precedence over other types of reinforcement: rats would rather die of hunger or thirst than go without ESB (e.g. Routtenberg & Lindy, 1965; Spies, 1965), are prepared to cross an electric grid floor (Olds & Sinclair, 1957), and females will abandon their squealing new born pups (Sonderegger, 1970).
(*iii*) When ESB is discontinued, extinction is remarkably more rapid than when food or water are used (but this seems to be contrary to what Olds and Milner claim in the *Locus* section). Pressing stops very abruptly, but reappears very rapidly when given just one or two shocks.
(*iv*) Partial reinforcement has much less of an effect (relative to a continuous schedule) compared with food/water, and it is usually impossible to train maze-running in rats using ESB alone.

5 According to Rose (1976), although rats seem to enjoy ESB, their observed behaviour does not correspond to any obvious or easily identifiable behavioural state (e.g. rage, fear or sexual arousal). Is there a human equivalent?

During the mid 1960s and 1970s, reports came from the US of implantations of electrodes into the pleasure centre of human beings (generally inmates of psychiatric hospitals, particularly schizophrenics and people with low IQ's). They are prepared to give themselves several 100 shocks per hour, and give vague descriptions of subjective experiences of 'feeling good'. It does not seem to be a sexual feeling, but is sometimes described as feeling like orgasm or the relaxed feeling which follows orgasm (Olds, 1958, 1962).

According to Campbell (1973), psychotics, epileptics and cancer patients have all reported relief from pain and anxiety, feeling 'wonderful', 'happy' or 'drunk' following stimulation of certain areas of the limbic system. Those who have received 1000+ stimulations per hour are content to do nothing else for six hours (the maximum period allowed). Rose asks how such experiments could be construed as 'treatment', and wonders if they can be compared with Nazi concentration camp 'experiments'? He believes that the idea of implanting electrodes into a person's brain (regardless of who does the stimulating) raises possibilities which are almost universally regarded as repugnant (such as mood and thought control).

6 A little more banal, perhaps, are the ethical issues raised by the Olds and Milner experiment itself. They point out that the implanted electrode did not interfere with the health or free behaviour of the rats to any appreciable extent, the operation to implant them was carried out with the rat under anaesthetic, and a recovery period of three days was allowed before testing. At no time during the experiment were they deprived of food or water. Quite apart from the fact that the animals were finally 'sacrificed' (a euphemism for 'killed'), can this surgery be justified? The arguments here are essentially those raised by the Garcia and Koelling study (chapter 12).

Exercises

1 What is meant by (*i*) 'acquisition' and (*ii*) 'extinction'?

2 How were 'reward' and 'punishment' operationally defined in terms of the baseline provided by the extinction score?

3 How was 'responding' operationalized?

STANLEY SCHACHTER AND JEROME E. SINGER (1962)

Cognitive, social and physiological determinants of emotional state

Psychological Review, 69, 5, pp. 379–99

The problem of which cues, internal or external, permit a person to label and identify his own emotional state has been with us since James (1890) first proposed that 'the bodily changes follow directly the perception of the exciting fact, and that our feeling of the same changes as they occur *is* the emotion'. Since we are aware of a variety of emotional states, it should follow from James' proposition that the various emotions will be accompanied by a variety of distinguishable bodily states. James stimulated a formidable number of studies which searched for such bodily states, but almost all the early studies were negative; all the emotional states experimentally manipulated were characterized by a general pattern of excitation of the sympathetic nervous system, but there seemed to be no clear-cut physiological discriminators of the various emotions. Cannon (1929) concluded, by way of criticism of the James–Lange theory, that 'the same visceral changes occur in very different emotional states and in non-emotional states'.

More recent work, however, has suggested that there may be differentiators. Ax (1953) and Schachter (1957) found that fear and anger were both characterised by a high level of autonomic activation but also differed on several measures. Wolf and Wolf (1947) distinguished two patterns in the physiological responses of the stomach wall in a subject with a gastric fistula.

Whether or not there are physiological distinctions among the various emotional states must be considered an open question. Any differences which do exist are at best rather subtle, and the variety of emotion, mood and feeling states do not appear to be matched by an equal variety of visceral patterns.

This rather ambiguous situation has led Ruckmick (1936), Hunt *et al.* (1958), Schachter (1959) and others to suggest that cognitive factors may be major determinants of emotional states. It is suggested that one labels, interprets and identifies this general pattern of sympathetic excitation in terms of the characteristics of the precipitating situation; an emotional state may be considered a function of a state of physiological arousal and of a cognition appropriate to this state of arousal. The cognition, in a sense, exerts a steering function. Cognitions arising from the immediate situation as interpreted by past experience provide the framework within which one understands and labels his feelings; it is the cognition which determines whether the state of physiological arousal will be labelled 'anger', 'joy', 'fear', etc.

How would the two elements, physiological arousal and cognitive factors, interact? In most emotion-inducing situations, of course, both are completely interrelated. Imagine a man walking alone down a dark alley, a figure with a gun suddenly appears. The perception-cognition 'figure with a gun' in some way initiates a state of physiological arousal: this arousal is interpreted in terms of knowledge about dark alleys and guns, and the state of arousal is labelled 'fear'.

Sometimes, however, the two elements are, to some extent, independent. Marañon (1924) injected 210 of his patients with the sympathomimetic agent adrenalin, and then simply asked them to introspect. 71 per cent simply reported their physical symptoms with no emotional overtones, 29 per cent responded in an apparently emotional way, most of them describing their feelings in a way which Marañon described as 'cold' or 'as if' emotions (e.g. 'I feel *as if* I were afraid'). A very few cases apparently reported a genuine emotional experience, but even here, subjects had to be provided with an appropriate cognition, e.g. by speaking to the patients, while the injection was taking effect, of their sick children or dead parents. His results suggest that physiological arousal alone is insufficient to induce an emotion and have been replicated by Cantril and Hunt (1932) and Landis and Hunt (1932).

Marañon's subjects knew they were receiving an injection and probably knew that it was adrenalin and what its effects are. Consequently, they had a completely appropriate cognition or explanation as to why they underwent the physiological changes they did. This, we suggest, is why so few of Marañon's subjects reported any emotional experience.

Consider now a person in a state of physiological arousal for which no immediately explanatory or appropriate cognitions are available, e.g. they had been covertly injected with adrenalin or 'fed' a sympathomimetic drug, such as ephedrine. The person would be aware of palpitations, tremor, face flushing and most of the other symptoms associated with stimulation of the sympathetic nervous system (SNS), but, in contrast to Marañon's subjects, would be utterly unaware of why he felt this way. What would be the result of such a state?

Schachter (1959) suggests that 'evaluative needs' (Festinger, 1954) would be aroused, i.e. the need to understand and label his feelings, and he will do so in terms of his knowledge of the immediate situation. Should he at the time be with a beautiful woman, he might decide that he was madly in love or sexually excited, while should he be arguing with his wife, he might explode in fury and hatred. Again, should the situation be completely inappropriate, he could decide he was excited about something which had recently happened to him, or simply, that he was sick. In any case, it is our basic assumption that emotional states are a function of the interaction of such cognitive factors with a state of physiological arousal.

This line of thought leads to the following propositions:

(*i*) Given a state of physiological arousal for which an individual has no immediate explanation, he will 'label' this state and describe it in terms of the cognitions available to him. Thus precisely the same state of arousal could be labelled 'joy', or 'fury', or 'jealousy' or any of a great diversity of emotional labels depending on the cognitive aspects of the situation.

(*ii*) Given a state of physiological arousal for which an individual has a completely appropriate explanation (e.g. 'I feel this way because I have just received an injection of adrenalin'), no evaluative needs will arise and the individual is unlikely to label his feelings in terms of the alternative cognitions available.

Now consider a person who is aware that he is in great danger (emotion-inducing cognitions) but for some reason (drug or surgical) remains physiologically calm. Does he experience the emotion 'fear'? We believe that he would not, which leads to:

(*iii*) Given the same circumstances, the individual will react emotionally or describe his feelings as emotions, only to the extent that he experiences a state of physiological arousal.

Procedure

The experimental test of these propositions requires (i) the experimental manipulation of a state of physiological arousal, (ii) the manipulation of the extent to which the subject has an appropriate explanation of his bodily state, and (iii) the creation of situations from which explanatory cognitions may be derived.

In order to satisfy (i) and (ii), the experiment was presented as a study of the effects of vitamin supplements on vision. As soon as a S arrived, he was taken to a private room and told by E:

> In this experiment we would like to make various tests of your vision. We are particularly interested in how certain vitamin compounds and vitamin supplements affect the visual skills. In particular, we want to find out how the vitamin compound called 'Suproxin' affects your vision. What we would like you to do, then, if we can get your permission, is to give you a small injection of Suproxin. The injection itself is mild and harmless; however, since some people do object to being injected we don't want to talk you into anything. Would you mind receiving a Suproxin injection?

If the S agrees to the injection (and 184 out of 195 did), E continues with instructions (see below), then leaves the room. After a few minutes, a doctor enters the room, briefly repeats E's instructions, takes S's pulse and then injects him with Suproxin.

Depending upon conditions, S receives one of two forms of Suproxin: epinephrine or placebo.

Epinephrine (adrenalin) is a sympathomimetic drug whose effects are almost always a perfect mimicry of stimulation of the SNS; shortly after injection, systolic blood pressure increases markedly, heart rate increases somewhat, cutaneous blood flow decreases, muscle and cerebral blood flow increase, blood sugar and lactic acid concentrations increase, and respiration rate increases slighty. The major subjective symptoms are palpitation, tremor and sometimes a feeling of flushing and accelerated breathing. Such effects usually begin within three to five minutes of injection and last anywhere from 10 to 60 minutes; for most *Ss*, these effects have subsided within 15 to 20 minutes after injection.

Ss in the *placebo* condition received the same quantity (½ cubic centimetre) of saline solution, which has no side-effects at all.

Manipulating an appropriate explanation

By 'appropriate', we mean the extent to which the subject has an authoritative, unequivocal explanation of his bodily condition, i.e. a *S* who had been told that, as a direct consequence of the injection, he would feel palpitations, tremor, etc. A *S* who was told only that the injection would have no side-effects would have no appropriate explanation of his state.

Immediately after the *S* had agreed to the injection and before the doctor entered the room, *E* gave *S* one of three sets of information, depending on which condition the *S* had been assigned to:

(*i*) *Epinephrine Informed (Epi Inf)*: the *S* was told the actual side-effects of the injection, and that they would last for about 15 to 20 minutes. This information was reinforced by the doctor while she was actually giving the injection. So *Ss* here have a completely appropriate explanation of their bodily state: they know precisely what they will feel and why.

(*ii*) *Epinephrine Ignorant (Epi Ign)*: *E* said nothing about side-effects and simply left the room. The doctor told the *S* that the injection was mild and harmless and would have no side-effects, so *Ss* have no experimentally provided explanation for his bodily state.

(*iii*) *Epinephrine Misinformed (Epi Mis)*: *E* tells *S* that some subjects have experienced side-effects from Suproxin which last for about 15 to 20 minutes and involve the feet feeling numb, an itching sensation over parts of the body and a slight headache. Again, the doctor confirmed these symptoms. Of course, none of these is a symptom of epinephrine, and so *S* was being provided with a completely inappropriate explanation of his bodily condition. This represented a kind of control condition; if *Ss* in the *Epi Inf* became introspective, perhaps slightly troubled, then any differences between them and *Epi Ign Ss* on the dependent variable could be due to those factors rather than to differences in appropriateness.

Ss in all the above conditions were injected with epinephrine. There was also a placebo condition in which *Ss* were injected with a saline solution and treated exactly the same as the *Epi Ign* condition.

Producing an emotion-inducing condition

It was decided to manipulate emotional states which can be considered quite different: euphoria and anger. Schachter (1959) and Wrights-man (1960) have shown that people evaluate their own feelings by comparing themselves with others around them, and this is how emotional state is manipulated in this experiment.

Euphoria

Immediately after the S's injection, the doctor left the room and E returned with a stooge, whom he introduced as another S and stated that both had had the Suproxin shot and that they had to wait for 20 minutes while the Suproxin was absorbed into the bloodstream, after which they would both be given the same tests of vision.

The room had been deliberately put into a state of mild disarray and, as E was leaving, he apologetically added that, if they needed any rough paper, rubber bands or pencils, they should help themselves. As soon as E had left, the stooge introduced himself again, made a series of standard icebreaker comments and began his routine. This was broken into a series of standard units, marked by a change in activity or a standard comment: (1) he starts doodling a fish on the rough paper; (2) crumples the paper and attempts to throw it into a wastebasket but misses and this leads to a 'basketball game'; gets up and does a jump shot; (3) if S has not joined in, he throws a paper ball to S saying, 'Here, you try it'; (4) continues his game; (5) continues but then gives up and decides to make paper airplanes instead; (6) fires plane, gets up and retrieves it, and fires again; (7) throws plane at S; (8) continues to fly plane; (9) tears off part of plane, screws up the paper and uses rubber band as sling and starts to shoot the paper; (10) continues shooting; (11) builds a tower of manilla folders and then shoots at it; (12) misses several times, finally hits and cheers as the tower falls; (13) while picking up the folders notices a pair of hula hoops and tries one; (14) twirls hoop wildly on arm, saying 'Hey, look at this – this is great'; (15) replaces hula hoop and sits down with feet on table. E returns shortly afterwards.

This routine was completely standard, and the only variations were those forced by the subject (e.g. introducing some nonsense of his own, asking the stooge to join in, making comments, etc.). Ss in all four conditions experienced this set-up; the stooge never knew which condition any particular S was in.

Anger

This began as the Euphoria condition did, but the S and stooge were asked to spend the 20 minutes waiting time answering questionnaires. Before looking at the questionnaires, stooge told S that he thought it unfair to be given injections, and that they should have been told when they were first called.

The five-page questionnaire started innocently enough, but then grew increasingly personal and insulting. The stooge, sitting opposite the S, paces his own answers so that at all times they are both working on the same question. At regular points, the stooge makes a series of standardized comments about the questions, starting off innocently enough, but growing increasingly querulous and finally he ends up in a rage; e.g. question 17 asks 'What is your father's average annual income?', and the stooge says, 'This really irritates me. It's none of their business what my father makes. I'm leaving that blank'. Question 28 reads: 'How many times each week do you have sexual intercourse?', to which the stooge responds, 'The hell with it! I don't have to tell them all this'. He rips up his questionnaire, crumples the pieces and hurls them to the floor, saying, 'I'm not wasting any more time. I'm getting my books and leaving', and he stamps out of the room.

Ss in the *Epi Ign*, *Epi Inf*, and *Placebo* conditions experienced this set-up, and the stooge never knew which condition any particular subject was in. The *Epi Mis* condition was not run in the Anger sequence because it was originally conceived as a control condition and it was felt that its inclusion in the Euphoria sequence above would suffice as a means of evaluating the possible artifactual effects of the *Epi Inf* instructions.

Measurement

Emotional state was measured in two ways; (i) standardized observation through a one-way mirror to assess *Ss*' behaviour, and (ii) self-report on a number of scales.

Observation

Euphoria   For each of the first 14 units on the stooge's standardized routine an observer kept a running record of what the *S* said and did; for each unit the observer coded *S*'s behaviour in one or more of the following categories:

Category 1: Joins in activity (e.g. made or flew airplanes, hula-hooped);
Category 2: Initiates new activity (e.g. threw open window and, laughing, hurled paper basketballs at passers-by);
Categories 3 and 4: Ignores or watches stooge.

Two observers independently coded two experimental sessions and they agreed completely on 88 per cent of the units.

Anger   For each of the units of stooge behaviour, an observer recorded *S*'s responses and coded them according to the following category scheme:

Category 1: Agrees (e.g. 'I don't like that kind of personal question either') (Score of +2);
Category 2: Disagrees (e.g. 'Take it easy, they probably have a good reason for wanting the information') (Score of −2);
Category 3: Neutral (noncommittal or irrelevant response to the stooge's remarks) (Score of 0);
Category 4: Initiates agreement or disagreement (e.g. 'Boy, I hate this kind of thing' or 'I'm enjoying this') (Score of +2 or−2);
Category 5: Watches (Score of 0);
Category 6: Ignores (Score of −1).

Two observers independently coded three experimental sessions; they agreed completely on 71 per cent of the units and their scores differed by a value of 1 or less for 88 per cent of the units (but always in the same direction).

Self report of mood and physical condition

When *S*'s session with the stooge was completed, *E* returned, took pulses, and told them that there are many things besides Suproxin which affect performance on the vision tests, such as hunger, tiredness and mood at the time. The only way this information can be obtained is through questionnaires. He handed out a questionnaire which contained a number of mock questions about all these aspects of mental and physical state. To measure mood or emotional state, the following were the crucial questions:

1 How irritated, angry or annoyed would you say you feel at present?

I don't feel at all irritated or angry	I feel a little irritated and angry	I feel quite irritated and angry	I feel very irritated and angry	I feel extremely irritated and angry
(0)	(1)	(2)	(3)	(4)

2 How good or happy would you say you feel at present?

I don't feel at all happy or good	I feel a little happy and good	I feel quite happy and good	I feel very happy and good	I feel extremely happy and good
(0)	(1)	(2)	(3)	(4)

There were questions about the physical effects of epinephrine: (*i*) Have you experienced any palpitation (consciousness of your own heart beat)? and (*ii*) Did you feel any tremor (involuntary shaking of the hands, arms or legs)? To measure possible effects of the instructions in the *Epi Mis* condition, *Ss* were asked (*i*) Did you feel any numbness in your feet? (*ii*) Did you feel any itching sensation? (*iii*) Did you experience any feeling of headache? Answers to all these questions were given on a four-point scale (from 'Not at all' to 'An intense amount'). *Ss* were also asked two open-ended questions about other physical or emotional sensations. Pulse rate was taken immediately before the injections and immediately after the session with the stooge.

When *Ss* had completed these questionnaires, *E* announced that the experiment was over, explained the deception in detail, answered any questions and swore the *Ss* to secrecy. Finally, *Ss* answered a brief questionnaire about their experiences, if any, with adrenalin and their suspicion about the experimental set-up. None knew anything about the experiment beforehand, but 11 were so extremely suspicious of some crucial aspect of the experiment that their data were automatically discarded.

Subjects

They were all male college students taking classes in introductory psychology at Minnesota University. 90 per cent of all such students volunteer for a subject pool for which they receive two extra points on their final exam for every hour they serve as subjects.

Evaluation of the experimental design

The disguised injection of Suproxin was far from ideal as a way of manipulating the absence of an immediate explanation of bodily state: some *Ss* would inevitably attribute their feelings to the injection regardless of what *E* told them. The effect of this would be to reduce differences between the several appropriateness conditions.

Although epinephrine unquestionably produces a state of physiological arousal, there is no question that a placebo does not prevent it. To the extent that the experimental situation produces sympathetic arousal, differences between epinephrine and placebo conditions will be reduced.

Results

Effects of the injections on bodily state

Does the injection of epinephrine produce symptoms of sympathetic arousal compared with the placebo injection? On all items, *Ss* in the epinephrine conditions showed considerably more evidence of sympathetic arousal than those in placebo conditions, as measured by pulse rate and self-ratings on palpitation, tremor, numbness, itching and headache. (All comparisons showed a significant difference in excess of $p < 0.001$.) These results include data for five subjects who showed no relevant symptoms to the epinephrine, and these were automatically excluded from further calculation. *Ss* in the *Epi Mis* condition did not differ on numbness, itching and headache from *Ss* in any of the other experimental conditions.

Effects of the manipulations on emotional state

Euphoria   Self report: the scores in table 19.1 are derived, for each *S*, by subtracting the value of the point he checks on the irritation scale from the value of the point he checks on the happiness scale, i.e. the higher the positive value, the happier the *S* reports himself as feeling.

Table 19.1   Self report of emotional state in the euphoria conditions

Condition	n	Self-report scales	Comparison	p
Epi Inf	25	0.98	Epi Inf vs. Epi Mis	<0.01
Epi Ign	25	1.78	Epi Inf vs. Epi Ign	0.02
Epi Mis	25	1.90	Placebo vs. Epi Mis,	
Placebo	26	1.61	Ign or Inf	ns

All *p* values reported throughout paper are two-tailed

Comparison of *Epi Mis* and *Epi Inf* makes it immediately clear that the experimental differences are not due to artefacts resulting from the instructions; in both conditions, *S* was warned to expect a variety of symptoms as a result of the injection, but in *Epi Mis*, self-report score is almost twice that in *Epi Inf* where the symptoms were completely appropriate to *S*'s bodily state.

Consistent with expectations, *Ss* were more susceptible to the stooge's mood, and consequently more euphoric, when they had no explanation of their own bodily states than when they did: the means of both *Epi Ign* and *Epi Mis* are considerably greater than the mean of *Epi Inf*.

Comparing placebo *Ss* to the epinephrine conditions, we note a recurring pattern, i.e. placebo *Ss* are less euphoric than either *Epi Mis* or *Epi Ign Ss* but rather more so that *Epi Inf Ss*. None of these differences is statistically significant.

Behaviour   To the extent that his mood has been affected, *S* should join in the stooge's manic activity and initiate similar activities of his own. The relevant data are shown in table 19.2.

Table 19.2   Behavioural indications of emotional state in the euphoria conditions

Condition	*n*	Activity index	Mean number of acts initiated
Epi Inf	25	12.72	0.20
Epi Ign	25	18.28	0.56
Epi Mis	25	22.56	0.84
Placebo	26	16.00	0.54
		p value	
Comparison		Activity index	Initiates*
Epi Inf vs. Epi Mis		0.05	0.03
Epi Inf vs. Epi Ign		ns	0.08
Placebo vs. Epi Mis, Ign or Inf		ns	ns

* Tested by comparison of the proportion of *Ss* in each condition initiating new acts.

The activity index takes into account the degree of euphoria involved in different acts and the amount of time spent in each activity. On both behavioural measures (activity index and initiated acts), we find precisely the same pattern of relationships as those obtained with self reports: *Epi Mis Ss* behave somewhat more euphorically than *Epi Ign Ss*, who in turn behave more euphorically than do *Epi Inf Ss*. On all measures, then, there is consistent evidence that a *S* will take over the stooge's euphoric mood to the extent that he has no other explanation of his bodily state.

Anger   Self report: anger, if manifested, is most likely to be directed at *E* and his annoyingly personal questionnaire. But *Ss* were afraid of endangering the extra points on their final exam by admitting their irritation to E's face or spoiling the questionnaire. Though they were willing to express anger when alone with the stooge, they hesitated to do so on the mood self-rating and questionnaire which E might see, and only after the purposes of the experiment had been revealed were many of these Ss willing to admit to E that they had been annoyed. This pretty much forces us to rely on the behavioural measures derived from observation of S's presumably private interaction with the stooge.

Behaviour To calculate an 'Anger index', the numerical value assigned to a S's responses to the stooge is summed together for the various units of stooge behaviour. A positive index value indicates that S agrees with the stooge's comment and is growing angry; a negative value indicates that S either disagrees with the stooge or ignores him. The stooge's routine has been divided into two phases: the first two 'neutral' units and the following 'angry' ones, the latter being the crucial ones as far as the prediction that $Epi\,Ign\,Ss$ will be angrier than $Epi\,Inf\,Ss$. This is indeed the case (see table 19.3).

Table 19.3 Behavioural indications of emotional state in the anger conditions

Condition	n	Neutral units	Anger units
Epi Inf	22	+0.07	−0.18
Epi Ign	23	+0.30	+2.29
Placebo	22	−0.09	+0.79

Comparison for anger units	p
Epi Inf vs. Epi Ign	<0.01
Epi Ign vs. Placebo	<0.05
Placebo vs. Epi Inf	ns

Conformation of data to theoretical expectations

In both the euphoria and anger conditions, the emotional level in Epi Mis and $Epi\,Ign$ conditions is considerably greater than that in the Epi Inf condition, as predicted. However, the results for the $Placebo$ condition are ambiguous because they consistently fall between the $Epi\,Ign$ and $Epi\,Inf\,Ss$. This is troublesome because it makes it impossible to evaluate unambiguously the effects of the state of physiological arousal. It is possible to account for the emotional restraint of the $Epi\,Ign$ and $Epi\,Mis\,Ss$, namely, their attribution of their bodily state to the injection, thus making the stooge less of an influence. Some were clearly 'self-informed' (e.g. 'the shot gave me the shivers') and were not angry or euphoric at all. If these Ss are removed, the difference between the $Epi\,Ign$ and the $Placebo\,Ss$ becomes significant for anger $(p = 0.01)$, and for euphoria, the difference between $Epi\,Mis$, $Epi\,Ign$ and $Placebo\,Ss$ is significant $(p = 0.03)$.

How can we account for the consistent finding that $Placebo\,Ss$ attain a higher emotional level (both reported and behavioural) than

Epi Inf Ss? The assumption that there is no sympathetic arousal in the *Placebo* condition is completely unrealistic, for the injection is quite a dramatic situation and physiological arousal was produced. In both the anger and euphoria conditions, *Placebo Ss* who show signs of sympathetic arousal (pulse-rate increase or maintenance as opposed to decrease) show considerably more anger than *Ss* who show no such signs. Consistent with expectations, therefore, sympathetic arousal accompanies an increase in emotional level. Also, the emotional level of *Placebo Ss* showing no signs of arousal are very similar to that of *Epi Inf Ss*, implying that both factors (sympathetic arousal and appropriate cognition) are essential to an emotional state.

Discussion

Although the pattern of data falls neatly in line with theoretical expectations, the fact that we had to some extent to rely on internal analyses to partial out the effects of experimental artifacts makes our conclusions rather tentative. Consequently, a series of additional experiments, published elsewhere, was designed. In the first of these, Schachter and Wheeler (1962) used three experimental groups: epinephrine, placebo and chlorpromazine, a sympatholytic agent. Laughter at a slapstick movie was the dependent variable, and the evidence is good that amusement is a direct function of manipulated sympathetic arousal.

Two experiments with rats (Singer, 1961; Latané & Schachter, 1962) showed clearly that, when the self-informing tendency is eliminated, epinephrine, compared with a placebo, causes sympathetic arousal.

What are the implications of these findings, then, for the studies reviewed in the introduction, which have largely failed to differentiate between various emotional states? Perhaps they should be taken at face value, i.e. emotional states may, indeed, be generally characterised by a high level of sympathetic activation with few, if any, physiological distinguishers among the many emotional states. Although this study does *not* rule out the possibility of physiological differences, we have, through cognitive manipulation, produced in *Ss* the very disparate states of euphoria and anger, despite the same state of epinephrine-induced arousal. It may indeed be the case that cognitive factors are major determinants of the emotional labels we apply to a common state of sympathetic arousal.

'Activation theory' (Lindsley, 1951; Woodworth & Schlosberg, 1958) which sees emotional states as at one end of a continuum of activation defined by degree of autonomic arousal and EEG patterns, is clearly inadequate; this experiment shows that it is possible to have very high degrees of activation without a *S* either appearing to be, or describing himself as, 'emotional'. Cognitive factors seem to be indispensable elements in any theory of emotion.

Summary

If emotional states are a function of a state of physiological arousal and of a cognition appropriate to this state of arousal, three propositions follow:

1 Given a state of physiological arousal for which an individual has no immediate explanation, he will label this state and describe his feelings in terms of the cognitions available to him. To the extent that cognitive factors are potent determinants of emotional states, it is predicted that precisely the same state of physiological arousal could be labelled 'joy' or 'fury' or 'jealousy' or any of a great diversity of emotional labels depending on the cognitive aspects of the situation.
2 Given a state of physiological arousal for which an individual has a completely appropriate explanation, no evaluative needs will arise, and he is unlikely to label his feelings in terms of the alternative cognitions available.
3 Given the same cognitive circumstances, the individual will react emotionally or describe his feelings as emotions only to the extent that he experiences a state of physiological arousal.

An experiment is described which, together with the results of other studies, supports these propositions.

Commentary

Aim and nature

The aim of the study is to test, experimentally, three propositions regarding the interaction between physiological and cognitive factors in the experience of emotion:

1 If an individual experiences a state of physiological arousal for which (s)he has no immediate explanation, (s)he will 'label' this state and describe it in terms of the cognitions available. So precisely the same state of arousal could receive different labels (e.g. 'joy'/'anger'), depending on the cognitive aspects of the situation.
2 If an individual experiences a state of physiological arousal for which they have a completely appropriate explanation (e.g. 'I've just been given an injection of adrenalin'), (s)he will 'label' this state accordingly.
3 Given the same circumstances, an individual will react emotionally, or describe his/her feelings as emotions, only to the extent that (s)he experiences a state of physiological arousal.

These three propositions constitute the basic hypotheses being tested, by manipulating, separately, (*i*) physiological arousal (epinephrine or placebo); (*ii*) the extent to which *S* has an appropriate explanation of his/her bodily state (*Epi Inf/Epi Ign/Epi Mis*) and (*iii*) situations from which explanatory cognitions may be derived (angry or euphoric stooge). So subjects in all four conditions (*Epi Inf/Epi Ign/Epi Mis/Placebo*) encountered either a euphoric or an angry stooge. The design, therefore, was independent subjects. The dependent variable was the subject's emotional state, measured as (*i*) standardized observation of *Ss* through one-way mirror (during the experiment in company of stooge) and (*ii*) scores on a number of self-report scales (following the experiment but before the de-briefing).

Context and background

Just what emotion is and just how it can be explained has been a matter of controversy during most of psychology's history. It is useful to think of every emotion as comprising (a) a subjective experience (happiness, anger, etc.); (b) a set of physiological changes involving the nervous system and the endocrine system, over which we have little, if any, conscious control (although we may become aware of some of their effects, e.g. 'butterflies' in the stomach, sweating, etc.); (c) the behaviour associated with a particular emotion, e.g. crying, running away, screaming etc.

Again, research interest has focused on four broad classes of emotional variable (Parkinson, 1987), namely, (*i*) cognitive appraisal of the situation (individuals react emotionally to stimulus events to the extent that they are perceived as relevant to their current goals/interests); (*ii*) the body's internal reaction (as in (b) above); (*iii*) overt behaviour (as in (c) above); (*iv*) facial expressions (which can be thought of as a sub-set of (iii).

Although all the above are characteristic features of 'emotion', as understood by both psychologists and lay people, none is a necessary condition of emotional experience, so their presence cannot provide the material for a classical or logically exclusive definition (Parkinson, 1987). For example, Zajonc (1980) argues that emotion is possible without cognitive appraisal, Valins (1966) believes it is possible without physiological arousal and Leventhal (1980) argues that it is possible without facial expression. But Schachter and Singer would take the view that both physiological arousal *and* cognitive interpretation are necessary (and sufficient), but neither on its own is sufficient. (This corresponds to the three propositions regarding the interaction of physiological and cognitive factors.) What evidence is there to support Schachter and Singer?

(*i*) If physiological arousal were sufficient for emotions, in order to be able to subjectively distinguish one emotion from another, there would have to be a distinct set of physiological changes corresponding to each different emotion. This is implied by the James-Lange theory, and has been criticized by Cannon and Schachter and Singer (among others).

(*ii*) Marañon's (1924) findings also support the view that physiological arousal is not sufficient: most subjects injected with adrenalin reported 'as if' emotions. The vital ingredient missing, according to Schachter and Singer, was the perception of an emotion-producing situation through which to interpret their arousal. They could explain their arousal in terms of the injection, and so did not have reason to label it as emotion. Hohmann's (1966) spinal-cord injured patients (paraplegics and quadriplegics) also reported 'as if' emotions, but this time because their injuries disrupted visceral responses and interfered with their emotional physiology. They described appropriate reactions to emotion-inducing situations, but didn't feel aroused: 'It's as if they're labelling a situation, not describing a feeling'. This strongly suggests that physiological arousal is necessary though not sufficient. 'Obviously, this contrasting set of introspections is precisely what should be anticipated from a formulation of emotion as a joint function of cognitive and physiological factors' (Schachter, 1964).

(*iii*) Studies by Valins (1966) and Laird (1974) suggest that not only is physiological arousal not sufficient, it may not even be necessary. Valins (1966) provided male subjects with feedback of their supposed heart rate while watching slides of semi-nude 'Playboy' females. The heart rate was pre-recorded and programmed to increase in apparent response to presentation of half the slides, so that subjects believed they were reacting to these pictures. These slides were rated as more attractive than those supposedly associated with unchanged heart rate. If people are prepared to *infer* emotion on the basis of information about their reactions to stimuli (Parkinson, 1987), this suggests physiological arousal is not necessary and that cognitive factors may be sufficient. Similarly, Laird (1974) told subjects that the activity of facial muscles was being measured by electrodes and that they should relax and contract certain muscles to allow accurate recording. In this way, he was able to induce smiles and frowns in the subjects covertly. Subjects evaluated slides according to their facial expression at the time: those seen while 'smiling' were rated more positively (even though there was no corresponding physiological arousal).

(*iv*) According to Schachter (1964), Cannon was wrong in thinking that bodily changes and the experience of emotion are independent, and the James-Lange theory was mistaken in claiming that physiological changes cause the feeling of emotion. However, he shares the James-Lange belief that physiological changes *precede* the experience of emotion, but for different reasons, i.e. the latter depends on *both* physiological change *and* the interpretation of those changes; we have to *decide* which particular emotion we are feeling and which label we attach to our arousal depends on to what we *attribute* that arousal. This is the 'two factor theory of emotion' (or cognitive labelling theory).

Evaluation

1 According to Parkinson (1987), the predominant influence in the study of emotion since Schachter has been a cognitive one. The focus of Schachter's model is an atypical state of affairs where the subject is unsure about the cause of arousal (*Epi Ign/Mis*). But Schachter (1964) admitted that usually we *are* aware of a precipitating situation prior to the onset of arousal (which usually takes one to two seconds to reach consciousness) and so it is normally perfectly obvious to the person what aspects of the situation have initiated the emotion. However, even here the meaning of the emotion-inducing circumstances requires some cognitive analysis before the emotion can be labelled. Schachter claims that, although the quantitative aspect of emotion can arise without cognitive mediation ('am I in a state of emotional arousal?'), the qualitative aspect requires prior cognition ('what emotion is it I am experiencing?'). According to Zajonc (1980), 'this view that affect is post cognitive is now probably the most popular attitude among emotion theorists'.

2 Related to this point about the role of cognition is the question as to whether environmental cues really are as easily accepted as the basis for inferences about our own feelings as Schachter claims (Fiske & Taylor, 1984). Using the original Schachter–Singer paradigm, several studies (e.g. Maslach, 1979; Marshall & Zimbardo, 1979; Plutchik & Ax, 1967) have concluded that subjects' efforts to understand an unexplained state of arousal is more extensive than a quick examination of salient cues in the surrounding environment. They also found that such arousal is more likely to be interpreted negatively (e.g. as unease or nervousness), suggesting that emotional lability is not as great as Schachter maintains. (Mandler, 1984, has called Schachter and Singers' theory the 'jukebox' theory: arousal is like the coin which gets the machine going and cognition is the button we push to select the emotional tune.)

3 One of the ways in which Schachter's work has influenced the cognitive approach to emotion is in the form of an *attributional theory* of emotion, i.e. the nature and/or intensity of an emotion seems to depend largely on the causes to which the individual attributes his/her physiological changes. For example, Abramson and Martin (1981) grafted attribution principles onto Seligman's (1975) theory of learned helplessness in order to try to explain clinical depression. Clearly, the experience of the inability to control the outcome of one particular situation (helplessness) does not inevitably lead to clinical depression in most people. So what other factors are involved? Abramson and Martin (1981) believe that depression only occurs when subjects make certain attributions about their helplessness, specifically, when they believe it is caused by (*i*) *internal* factors (as opposed to environmental) which are perceived as (*ii*) stable (as opposed to variable), and when they are believed to reflect (*iii*) a global deficiency (as opposed to one particular to the kind of bad experiences which have happened). So people get depressed when they conclude that helplessness is likely to pervade all aspects of their future lives. Schachter's theory implies that emotional reactions induced by a threatening experience can be reattributed to a neutral or less threatening source. For example, if you blame some external stimulus rather than your own inadequacies, you may calm down sufficiently to break the vicious circle. A number of experiments using this kind of intervention have found support for the re-attribution approach (Fiske & Taylor, 1984).

In turn, this is related to stress. Cox (1978) argues that the experience of stress is usually described in ways associated with emotions: anger, anxiety, depression, fear, grief, guilt, jealousy and shame; the experience of stress is indeed an emotional one. Lazarus (1976) refers to these as the 'stress emotions'. Agreeing with Schachter, Kagan (1975) believes that it is how an individual cognitively appraises the situation which shapes basic feelings into a specific emotion. This of course raises again the question of just how flexible/labile emotional experience is, and implies the crucial question as to how much stress can be reduced (or prevented) by changing people's cognitive appraisal of the situation.

A famous study by Speisman *et al.* (1964) involved showing subjects a film on anthropology ('Subincision in the Arunta'), in which the penises of aboriginal boys are seen being cut with a jagged flint knife as part of a puberty rite. This normally causes high levels of stress. However, the sound track was manipulated, so that (*i*) the pain, jaggedness of the knife, etc. were emphasized ('trauma'), or (*ii*) the boys' anticipation of entering manhood was stressed ('denial'), or (*iii*) the emotional elements were ignored and the traditions of the tribe were stressed ('intellectualization'), or (*iv*) there was no commentary at all ('silent' control). As predicted, arousal (measured by GSR) was highest in (*i*), next highest in (*iv*) and lowest in (*ii*) and (*iii*). What we tell ourselves about external situations influences the level of arousal we experience. But we should also ask if the converse is true: does the level of arousal influence how we appraise the situation? Several studies have failed to replicate the Schachter and Singer findings, including Rogers and Deckner (1975), Marshall (1976), Marshall and Zimbardo (1979) and Maslach (1979). They all suggest that emotion is rather less malleable than Schachter believed: (*i*) if the dosage is high enough, adrenalin seems to produce an unpleasant mood, even in the *Epi Mis* condition and in the presence of the euphoric 'stooge'; (*ii*) the *Epi Ign/Mis* were more likely to interpret the unexplained arousal negatively, regardless of the mood of the stooge.

4 Finally, Hilgard *et al.* (1979) make some important criticisms: (*i*) epinephrine does not affect everyone in the same way and Schachter and Singer in fact eliminated from their analysis five subjects who later reported they experienced no physiological symptoms; (*ii*) no assessment was made of subjects' mood *before* the injections; presumably, a subject in a better mood to begin with might respond more positively to a playful stooge; (*iii*) how comparable are arousal states created by drugs and manipulated in the laboratory to naturally-occurring, real-life emotions?

Exercises

1 What scale of measurement is being used on the euphoria and anger scales (*Self report of mood and physical conditon*)?

2 In table 19.1, what statistical test is likely to have been used?

3 In table 19.2, the *Epi Mis* subjects were somewhat (but not significantly) more euphoric than the *Epi Ign* subjects. How could you account for this?

4 The subjects were all male, as were the stooges. Can you think of any reasons why these results would not generalize to females? And what would be the effect of having an opposite-sex stooge?

5 All the tests used are two-tailed. What does this mean, and could one-tailed tests have been used?

6 Is it ethically acceptable to mislead subjects about the side-effects of the injection (either *Epi Mis* or *Epi Ign*)?

The relation of eye movements during sleep to dream activity: an objective method for the study of dreaming

Journal of Experimental Psychology, 53, no. 5, pp. 339–46

The study of dream activity and its relation to physiological variables during sleep requires a reliable method of determining precisely when dreaming occurs. Ultimately, this knowledge always depends upon the subjective report of the dreamer, but becomes relatively objective if such reports can be significantly related to some physiological phenomena which in turn can be measured by physical techniques.

Such a relationship was reported by Aserinsky and Kleitman (1955), who observed periods of rapid, connected eye movements during sleep and found a high incidence of dream recall in *Ss* awakened during these periods and a low incidence when awakened at other times. The occurrence of these characteristic eye movements and their relation to dreaming were confirmed in both normal *Ss* and schizophrenics (Dement, 1955), and they were shown to appear at regular intervals in relation to a cyclic change in the depth of sleep during the night, as measured by the EEG (Dement & Kleitman, 1955).

This paper presents the results of a rigorous testing of the relation between eye movements and dreaming. Three approaches were used: (*i*) dream recall during rapid eye-movement or quiescent periods was elicited without direct contact between *E* and *S*, thus eliminating the possibility of unintentional cueing by *E*; (*ii*) the subjective estimate of the duration of dreams was compared with the length of eye-movement periods before awakening, reasoning that there should be a positive correlation if dreaming and eye movements were concurrent; (*iii*) the pattern of the eye movements was related to the dream content to test whether they represented a specific expression of the visual experience of dreaming or merely a random motor discharge of a more active central nervous system.

Method

The *Ss* for the experiments were seven adult males and two adult females. Five were studied intensively while data from the other four were minimal, the main intent being to confirm the results of the first five.

In a typical experiment, *S* reported to the laboratory a little before his usual bedtime. He was instructed to eat normally but to abstain from alcoholic or caffeine-containing drinks on the day of the experiment. Two or more electrodes were attached near the eyes for registering changes in the corneoretinal potential fields as the eyes moved, two or three were attached to the scalp for recording brain waves as a criterion of depth of sleep. *S* then went to bed in a quiet, dark room. All electrode lead wires were further attached to the top of the head and from there to the lead box at the head of the bed in a single cord to minimize the possibility of entanglement and allow *S* a free range of movement. The potentials were amplified by a Model III Grass Electroencephalograph in an adjoining room; it was run continuously throughout the sleep period at a paper speed of 3 or 6 mm per second which allowed easy recognition of eye-movement potentials. A faster speed (3 cm/sec) was used for detailed examination of the brain waves, although the slower speed permitted at least an approximate estimation of the gross pattern.

At various times during the night *Ss* were awakened to test their dream recall. It usually took less than five minutes to return to sleep after such awakening. Table 20.1 summarizes the experiments, showing the number of nights each *S* slept, and the number of awakenings. In all, 21 per cent of the awakenings fell in the first two hours of sleep, 29 per cent in the second two, 28 per cent in the third two, and 22 per cent in the fourth two.

Table 20.1 Summary of experiments

Ss	Nights slept	Awakenings	Average nightly awakenings	Average sleeping time
DN	6	50	8.3	7:50
IR	12	65	5.4	4:20
KC	17	74	4.4	6:00
WD	11	77	7.0	6:30
PM	9	55	6.1	6:20
KK	2	10	5.0	6:00
SM	1	6	6.0	6:40
DM	1	4	4.0	7:00
MG	2	10	5.0	6:10
Totals	61	351	5.7	6:00

Results

The occurrence of rapid eye movements (REM)   Discrete periods during which their eyes showed rapid movements were observed in all nine *Ss* every night they slept, and were characterised by a low-voltage, relatively fast EEG pattern. In between the REM periods, EEG patterns indicating deeper sleep were either predominantly high-voltage, slow activity, or frequent, well-defined sleep spindles with a low-voltage background. No REMs were ever observed during the initial onset of sleep, although the EEG always passed through a stage similar to that accompanying the REM periods occurring later in the night. These findings were identical with previous observations on uninterrupted sleep (Dement & Kleitman, 1955).

REM periods which were not terminated by awakening varied between three and 50 minutes with a mean of about 20 minutes, and they tended to increase the later in the night they occurred. The eyes were not constantly in motion during such periods; rather, the activity occurred in bursts of one or two, up to 50 or 100 movements. A single movement generally took 0.1 to 0.2 seconds and was followed by a fixational pause of varying duration. The amount, pattern and size of the movement varied irregularly from period to period.

The REM periods occurred at fairly regular intervals throughout the night. The frequency of occurrence seemed to be relatively constant and characteristic for the individual: DM and WD averaged one eye-movement period every 70 minutes and 75 minutes respectively, KC 104 minutes; the other *Ss* fell between these extremes. The average for the whole group was one REM period every 92 minutes.

Despite the considerable disturbance of being awakened a number of times, the frequency and regularity with which REM periods occurred was almost exactly comparable to that found in an earlier study of uninterrupted sleep (Dement & Kleitman, 1955). If the awakening occurred during a period of no rapid eye movements (NREM), the return to sleep was never associated with REMs, nor was the time of onset of the next REM period markedly changed from what would have been expected in the absence of awakening. An awakening during an REM period generally terminated the REMs until the next period, and the sequence of EEG changes (excluding the brief period of wakefulness) was the same as that following an REM period which ended spontaneously. Exceptions did occur when *S* was awakened during an REM period in the final hours of sleep, when it was likely to be quite long if uninterrupted; the REMs sometimes started up again when *S* fell asleep. It seemed as though a period of heightened CNS activity had not run its normal course and, although *S* was able to fall asleep, he continued to dream.

Eye-movement periods and dream recall   The arousing stimulus was the ringing of an ordinary doorbell placed near the bed and sufficiently loud to ensure immediate awakening in all levels of sleep. *Ss* then spoke into a recording device near the bed. They were instructed to first state whether or not they had been dreaming and then, if they could, to relate the content of the dream. When *S* had finished speaking, *E*, who could hear their voices, occasionally entered the room to question them further on some detail of the dream. There was no communication between *S* and *E* until *S* had definitely committed himself, and was considered to have been dreaming only if he could relate a coherent, fairly detailed description of dream content; assertions that he had dreamed without recall of content, or vague fragmentary impressions of content, did not count.

The awakenings were done either during REM periods or at varying intervals of time after the cessation of eye movements during the interspersed periods of NREMs. *Ss*, of course, were never told when awakened whether or not their eyes had been moving.

Table 20.2 shows the results of the attempts to recall dreams after the various awakenings. The REM and NREM awakenings for PM and KC were chosen according to a random numbers table to eliminate any possibility of intentional pattern. For DN, a pattern was followed, namely, three REM awakenings followed by three NREM awakenings, and so on. WD was told he would be awakened *only* when the recordings indicated he was dreaming, but REM and NREM awakenings were interspersed randomly. IR was awakened at the *E*'s whim.

Table 20.2   Instances of dream recall after awakenings during periods of REMs or periods of NREMs

S	Rapid eye movements		No rapid eye movements	
	Dream recall	No recall	Dream recall	No recall
DN	17	9	3	21
IR	26	8	2	29
KC	36	4	3	31
WD	37	5	1	34
PM	24	6	2	23
KK	4	1	0	5
SM	2	2	0	2
DM	2	1	0	1
MG	4	3	0	3
Totals	152	39	11	149

Ss uniformly showed a high incidence of dream recall following REM awakenings and a very low incidence following NREM awakenings, regardless of how the awakenings were chosen. DN was no more accurate than the others although there was a pattern he might have learned, and WD was no less accurate for being deliberately misled to expect to have been dreaming every time he was awakened. Over a narrow range, some *Ss* seemed better able to recall dreams than others.

Table 20.3 compares the results of the first half of the series of REM awakenings with the last half; practise was certainly not a significant factor as only one *S* showed any degree of improvement on later nights compared with early ones.

Table 20.3   Comparison of first half of series of REM awakening with second half

S	First half		Second half	
	Dream recall	**No recall**	**Dream recall**	**No recall**
DN	12	1	5	8
IR	12	5	14	3
KC	18	2	18	2
WD	19	2	18	3
PM	12	3	12	3
Total	73	13	67	19

The incidence of dream recall dropped dramatically almost immediately upon cessation of REMs. In 17 NREM awakenings done within eight minutes of the end of an REM period, five dreams were recalled; although small, this was a much higher incidence than occurred when the NREM awakenings followed the end of REM periods by *more* than eight minutes (six dreams recalled in 132 awakenings).

In general, *Ss* were best able to make an emphatic statement that they had not been dreaming when the NREM awakenings were done during an intermediate stage of sleep, as indicated by a brain-wave pattern of spindling with a low-voltage background. When aroused during a deep stage of sleep characterised by high-voltage, slow waves, *Ss* often awoke rather bewildered, and often felt that they must have been dreaming although they could not remember the dream. They often described feelings of pleasantness, anxiety, detachment, etc. but could not relate them to any specific dream content.

When *Ss* failed to recall following REM awakenings, this was usually early on in the night. 19 out of 39 such instances occurred during the first two hours, 11 during the second two hours, five in the third and four in the last.

Length of REM periods and subjective dream – duration estimates   At first, *Ss* were awakened at various intervals of time after the REMs had begun and were asked to estimate to the nearest minute the amount of time they had been dreaming. This proved too difficult,

Table 20.4   Results of dream duration estimates after five or 15 minutes of REMs

S	Five minutes		15 minutes	
	Right	**Wrong**	**Right**	**Wrong**
DN	8	2	5	5
IR	11	1	7	3
KC	7	0	12	1
WD	13	1	15	1
PM	6	2	8	3
Totals	45	6	47	13

and a series was then done in which *Ss* were awakened either five or 15 minutes after the onset of REMs and were required on the basis of their recall of the dream to decide which was the correct duration. The two durations were chosen on the basis of a random series. Table 20.4 shows the results: all *Ss* were able to choose the correct dream duration very accurately except DN who could only recall the latter part of the dream and so underestimated its length.

In addition to the actual dream length, the lengths of the dream narratives were influenced by factors such as *Ss* talkativeness. However, the narrative length still showed a significant relationship to the duration of REM periods before awakening. Table 20.5 shows the correlation between minutes of REMs and lengths of dream narratives for each *S*. Length was measured by the number of words. Narratives for dreams recalled after 30 to 50 minutes of REMs were not a great deal longer than those after 15 minutes, although *Ss* had the impression of having been dreaming for an unusually long time. This was perhaps due to inability to remember all the details of very long dreams.

Table 20.5   Correlation between duration of REM periods in minutes and number of words in dream narratives

S	Number of Dreams	r	p
DN	15	0.60	<0.02
IR	25	0.68	<0.001
KC	31	0.40	<0.05
WD	35	0.71	<0.001
PM	20	0.53	<0.02

Specific eye-movement patterns and visual imagery of the dream-

The quality and quantity of the REMs themselves showed endless variation. Although the movements occurred in bursts of activity separated by periods of relative inactivity, the brain-wave pattern during the whole period remained the same, whether there was much or little movement at any given moment of the period.

It was hypothesized that the movements represented the visual imagery of the dream, i.e. they corresponded to where and at what the dreamer was looking. It was impossible for *Ss* to state chronologically in what direction he had gazed during the dream. Instead, *Ss* were awakened as soon as one of four predominant patterns of movement had persisted for at least one minute, and were asked to describe in detail the dream content just before awakening. The four patterns were: (*i*) mainly vertical eye movements, (*ii*) mainly horizontal; (*iii*) both vertical and horizontal; (*iv*) very little or no movement.

Altogether, 35 awakenings were collected from the nine *Ss*. Periods of either pure vertical or horizontal movements were extremely rare but three such periods of vertical movements were seen. One *S* dreamed of standing at the bottom of a tall cliff operating some sort of hoist and looking up at climbers at various levels, and down at the hoist machinery. Another dreamed of climbing up a series of ladders looking up and down as he climbed. The third *S* dreamt of throwing basketballs at a net, first shooting and looking up at the net, and then looking down to pick another ball off the floor. In the only instance of pure horizontal movement, the dreamer was watching two people throwing tomatoes at each other. On ten occasions, *Ss* were awakened after one minute of little or no eye movement, and in all cases the dreams involved the dreamer watching something at a distance or just staring fixedly at some object. In two of these cases, about one minute of ocular inactivity was followed by several large movements to the left just a second or two before the awakening. The corresponding dream content was almost identical for both *Ss*: in one dream, *S* was driving a car, staring at the road ahead and as he approached an intersection was startled by the sudden appearance of a car speeding at him from the left; in the other, the dreamer was also driving a car, staring at the road ahead, when he saw a man on the left side of the road, and hailed him as he drove past.

In the 21 awakenings after a mixture of movements, *Ss* were always looking at people or objects close to them, e.g. talking to a group of people, looking for something, fighting with someone. There was no recall of distant or vertical activity.

In order to confirm the meaningfulness of these relationships, 20 naïve *Ss* as well as five of the experimental *Ss* were asked to observe distant and close-up activity while awake. Eye-movement potentials, as measured by electrodes, were in all cases comparable to those occurring during dreaming, both in amplitude and pattern. Further more, there was virtually no movement when viewing distant activity but much while viewing close-up activity.

Discussion

The results of these experiments indicate that dreaming accompanied by REMs and a low-voltage EEG occurred periodically in discrete episodes during the course of a night's sleep. The lack of dream recall, plus the fact that the brain waves were at the lightest level of sleep only during REM periods and at deeper levels at all other times, suggests that dream activity does not occur at other times. The few instances of dream recall during NREM periods are best explained by assuming that the memory of the preceding dream persisted for an unusually long time; most such instances did, in fact, occur very soon (within eight minutes) after the end of REM periods.

Other workers have tried to relate dreaming to physiological phenomena during sleep. Wada (1922) believed that dreaming and gastric contractions occurred simultaneously, but this conclusion was based on only seven awakenings in two *Ss*, one of whom could not recall dream content. Scantlebury *et al.* (1942) also studied gastric activity, but did not draw any firm conclusions. McGlade (1942) suggested that dreaming occurs during a series of foot twitches immediately after the onset of sleep but the dreams were recalled on the morning after the experiments, and only three out of 25 *Ss* actually exhibited foot twitches.

Incidental observations have been made on the occurrence of dreaming by investigators studying brain waves during sleep (Blake *et al.*, 1939; Davis *et al.*, 1938; Henry, 1941; Knott *et al.*, 1939; Loomis *et al.*, 1937). All stages of brain waves were related to dreaming in these five papers, but no mention was made of whether or not actual dream content was recalled, and the number of reports by sleepers was generally very small.

In other studies of dreaming, excellently reviewed by Ramsey (1953), attempts were made to localise dream activity by simply awakening *Ss* at various times during the night. In general, it was found that dreams might be recalled at any time during the night, but that most were recalled in the later hours of sleep. This would correspond to the statistical incidence of REMs as previously reported by Aserinsky and Kleitman (1955) and Dement (1955) and is also consistent with the finding here that, even when the awakenings occurred during REM periods, recall was still more difficult earlier in the night.

We found that all *Ss* showed periods of REMs *every* night they slept, and so did Dement and Kleitman (1955), involving 16 *Ss* over 43 nights. It appears that periods of REMs and dreaming and the regularity of their occurrence are an intrinsic part of normal sleep. So why did Aserinsky and Kleitman (1955) and Dement (1955) find occasional subjects without REMs? One explanation could be that the recording was done by sampling rather than continuously, so that shorter-than-usual REM periods could have occurred between the samples, thus escaping observation. Alternatively, a lower amplification of the REM potentials was used which failed to record very small movements. A third possibility is that these *Ss'* dreams happened to be of the kind (e.g. watching distant activity) in which eye movements were at a minimum.

Rather than occurring instantaneously or with great rapidity, it seems that dreams progress at a rate comparable to a real experience of the same sort. An increase in the length of REM periods was almost always associated with a proportional increase in the length of the dream.

It seems reasonable to conclude that an objective measurement of dreaming may be achieved by recording REMs during sleep. This contrasts sharply with the forgetting, distortion and other factors involved in the reliance on the subjective recall of dreams. It thus becomes possible to objectively study the effect on dreaming of environmental changes, psychological stress, drugs, and a variety of other influences.

Summary

Regularly occurring periods of REMs were observed during every night of experimental sleep in nine adult *Ss*. A high incidence of dream recall was obtained from *Ss* when awakened during REM periods, and a very low incidence when awakened at other times. A series of awakenings was done either five or 15 minutes after the

REMs (dreaming) had begun, and *Ss* judged the correct dream duration very accurately. The pattern of the REMs was related to the visual imagery of the dream, and the eye movements recorded in analagous situations while awake corresponded closely in amplitude and pattern to those observed during dreaming.

Commentary

Aim and nature

The study reports the results of a rigorous testing of the relationship between eye movements and dreaming. Three main hypotheses were being tested: (*i*) there is a significant association between REM/NREM sleep and dreaming, such that (based on previous research) REM sleep is associated with dreaming and NREM is not; (*ii*) there is a significant positive correlation between the subjective estimate of the duration of dreams and the length of eye-movement period prior to awakening; (*iii*) there is a significant association between the pattern of eye movement and the context of the dream, such that the former actually reflects the visual experience of the dream. Subjects were studied under controlled laboratory conditions, whereby they spent a night in the laboratory, being woken at various intervals during the night and during which physiological recordings were made of (*i*) changes in corneoretinal potential fields as the eyes moved and (*ii*) brain waves. This was done by (*i*) attaching two/more electrodes near the eyes and (*ii*) by attaching two or three electrodes to the scalp. Why the study is so important is that it represents a way of objectively measuring physiological indicators of dreaming, although as Dement and Kleitman say, ultimately the only 'proof' that dreaming has occurred is that the dreamer reports having dreamt.

Context and background

Dreaming has always fascinated human beings, although it is only very recently that it (and its relationship to sleep) has been studied scientifically. Although theories of sleep and theories of dreaming have been proposed separately, it is difficult to discuss one without the other; sleep deprivation is a common way of studying the normal function of sleep, and the findings are often expressed in terms of how the dreaming process is disrupted. Similarly, as in the Dement and Kleitman study, dreaming is often studied using objective, physiological correlates or indicators (eye movements and EEG patterns in particular).

Starting with sleep, it is true that all mammals, reptiles, amphibians and fish have periods of sleep (or sleeplike periods), and different species also have different cycles of sleep and wakefulness; the human cycle is monophasic (one period of sleep/waking per 24 hour cycle), while, e.g. rats, rabbits and other rodents are polyphasic. Human infants are also polyphasic to begin with but they gradually adopt the monophasic pattern. Sleeping, therefore, is part of our circadian rhythm (*circa dies* = about one day), a daily cyclical change in body temperature, blood pressure, blood-plasma volume, hormone secretions, etc. (Moor-Ede & Czeisler, 1984, cited in Smith *et al.*, 1986). We normally sleep during the low point of the temperature cycle.

What are the effects of disrupting the circadian rhythm? One common type of study involves shift workers. For example, Colligan *et al.* (1978) (cited in Smith *et al.*, 1986) found that workers who rotated from shift to shift had more accidents than others doing the same job, consumed more alcohol and sleeping pills, reported more digestive problems, menstrual disorders, colds, anxiety, fatigue and less satisfactory social relationships.

When the sleep–wake cycle is abruptly disrupted (as in the case of the workers above who did not have a chance to adapt to their shift before it changed again), the temperature cycle may continue to adhere to old rhythms for a while and this can (at least partly) account for why psychological functioning and general well-being are adversely affected, i.e. it is not lack of sleep but disruption of the circadian rhythm which is the critical variable. This applies also to explanations of jet lag. For example, Klein *et al.* (1972: cited in Roediger *et al.*, 1984) flew eight students from the US to Germany, where they stayed for 18 days. Psychological tests were conducted three days prior to departure, continued up to 13 days after arrival in Germany and for 13 days after returning home. Peak performance on a number of tests did not reappear for as long as 12 days after the flight; even some easier tasks required six days before they performed at top capacity. Body temperature did not readjust to the new cycle for about 14 days after the initial flight.

So what about studies of people actually being deprived of sleep (without a disruption of the circadian rhythm)?

Webb and Bonnet (1979; cited in Lahey, 1983) limited subjects to two hours sleep on one particular night. They suffered no ill effects the following day but that night they fell asleep more quickly and slept longer than usual. Longer periods of sleep deprivation may result in some unpleasant psychological effects, but people are remarkably able to do without sleep. Webb and Bonnet gradually reduced the length of sleep in a group of volunteers from eight to four hours per night over a two-month period with no detectable effects.

However, when sleep is *abruptly* reduced (as, say, in the case of hospital doctors who may be on duty for up to 72 hours at a stretch), the effects are rather more serious: irritability, intellectual inefficiency, and an intense fatigue and need for sleep. And interestingly, these are more or less the same effects as are produced by depriving subjects of approximately two hours of REM sleep (but otherwise allowing them to sleep normally); the following night, there is an increase in REM sleep (so as to compensate for the previous night's loss). (This is called the 'REM rebound': Webb and Bonnet, 1979.) When volunteers are able to get by on greatly (but gradually) reduced amounts of sleep, it is apparently because they pack their two hours of REM tightly into the sleeping time they do have (thus reducing the amount of NREM sleep in between their dreams). When sleep is *abruptly* reduced, there is no time to adopt this additional dreaming–sleep pattern.

So we seem to have found a crucial link between sleep and dreams: deprivation of REM sleep seems to be much more damaging (at least in the short-term) than loss of NREM, and this would seem to be because of the loss of dream time associated with REM sleep.

Evaluation

1 There has been a good deal of support for the REM rebound phenomenon. For example, Dement (1960) woke subjects from their REM sleep on five successive nights (while a control group was only woken during their NREM sleep). The former became nervous, grumpy, irritable, unable to concentrate and some even began to hallucinate. When allowed to sleep normally (without interruption), they did 60 per cent more dreaming until they had made up their lost REM time; for as many as five nights following their REM deprivation, they spent more time in REM than usual, and on some nights doubled their REM time.

Many drugs, including alcohol and various sleeping pills, suppress REM sleep without affecting NREM sleep.

2 But is it possible that the difference between REM and NREM sleep regarding the dreaming which goes on is actually an artifact of the ability to *recall* dreams following the 'rude awakening'? Beaumont (1988) argues that being woken from NREM (or S-sleep) may lead to the dream being forgotten before *S* is sufficiently awake to report it (this is a deeper kind of sleep in which the brain is much less active, and shows EEGs very different from the waking state), while being woken from REM (or D-sleep) may allow the ongoing dream to be remembered and then reported (here the brain is much more active and EEGs are much like those of the waking state).

Clearly, if this is so, then we have stumbled upon a major confounding variable which challenges the very basis of the sleep/dream research of Dement and Kleitman. Herman *et al.* (1978) (cited in Smith *et al.*, 1986) claim that an appreciable amount of mental activity occurs during NREM sleep, and there are no completely consistent differences between dream reports obtained when subjects are woken from either kind of sleep. But the evidence regarding REM rebound, together with that concerning the actual eye-movements in REM and how these are related to the dream's content, would seem to represent support for the view of REM sleep as dream-state sleep independently of the sleeper's report of having dreamed (or not).

3 So why are dreams so important? Ornstein (1986) believes that REM sleep and dreaming may be involved in the re-organization of our schemas (mental structures) so as to accommodate new information. People placed in a 'disturbing and perplexing' atmosphere for four hours just before sleep (asked to perform difficult tasks with no explanation) will spend longer in REM sleep than normal. And REM time also increases after people have had to learn complex tasks. This may explain why REM decreases with age: newborns spend half their 18 hours of sleep in REM sleep, while adults usually spend only a quarter of their eight in REM sleep. It has been suggested (consistent with Ornstein's suggestion) that babies' brains need to process and assimilate the flood of new stimuli pouring in from the outside world and this is (partly) achieved through REM sleep.

4 An influential and fairly recent theory of dreaming is the Activation-Synthesis Model (McCarley, 1983). REM sleep is characterized by neuronal 'spikes' (produced by the brain stem), a blocking of signals to the muscles and stimulation of the vestibular system. The model sees the brain as being *activated* in REM sleep, and dreams are a conscious interpretation or synthesis of the information in consciousness during dreams. When we are awake, the mental operating system organizes sensory information into the simplest meaningful interpretation. Supposing that the same system is at work during dreams, mental processes attempt to organize diverse material, e.g. the sensation of falling (from vestibular activity), experience of paralysis (from blocking of motor output) and specific events of the day all need to be made sense of; a dream is therefore the simplest way of interpreting these diverse experiences by combining them into some meaningful whole. Many dreams do involve vigorous physical activity, e.g. running, jumping, struggling (see *Specific eye-movement patterns and visual imagery of the dream* in the article). Recordings show that the motor cortex is quite active at these times, even though our bodies are temporarily paralyzed.

Again, many common dream experiences do seem to reflect the brain's and body's state (and so can be thought of as an *interpretation* of those physical states), e.g. being chased, locked up or frozen with fear, may well reflect the blocked motor commands to our muscles during REM. Floating, flying and falling experiences may reflect vestibular activation. The sexual content of dreams may reflect vaginal engorgement and penile erection (Ornstein, 1986).

Perhaps there is also a sense in which we dream instead of acting (maybe suggesting the need for rest/restoration of the body); neural mechanisms in the brain stem block nerve impulses from the brain to the skeletal muscles ('paralysis'). Cats with brain stem injury act out their dreams by, for example, chasing the mouse of their dream, while ignoring a real mouse in their cage (Morrison, 1983, cited by Smith *et al.*, 1986). Dreams are often incoherent and even bizarre. Abrupt shifts in imagery may simply be the brain's 'making the best of a bad job in producing partially coherent dream imagery from the relatively noisy signals sent up ... from the brain stem' (Ornstein 1986).

But does the truth of the activation synthesis model *exclude* other theories of dreams? Not necessarily. Like other *neural* theories of dreaming (e.g. Rose, 1976), McCarley's model may account for 'where dreams come from' but not 'what dreams are for' (Gross, 1987). Psychological theories of dreaming focus on the synthesis component of the model (rather than the activation component), and try to explain its significance for the dreamer. Freud's is probably the best known (and the most controversial) and, like Jung, he saw symbolism as of central importance, and took the view that dreams can put the dreamer in touch with parts of the self usually inaccessible during waking life. According to Calvin S. Hall (1966), dreams are 'a personal document, a letter to oneself' and, like Jung, he advocated the study of dream *series* rather than single, isolated, dreams.

Exercises

1 Does it matter that seven of the nine subjects were males and only two were females?

2 Why were subjects asked to abstain from alcoholic or caffeine-containing drinks on the day of the experiment?

3 REM periods not terminated by awakening varied from 3 to 50 minutes, the mean being about 20 minutes. Would an alternative measure of central tendency be justified?

4 Why was it important that subjects were never told, after wakening, whether their eyes had been moving or not?

5 Different subjects were woken according to a variety of schedules: (*i*) random number tables (×2); (*ii*) three REM, three NREM etc. (×1); (*iii*) told only woken from REM but actually woken from REM and NREM randomly (×1); (*iv*) at *E*'s whim. Why was this done? Why weren't random number tables used for all subjects?

6 What statistical test would be used *re* tables 20.2, 20.3 and 20.4? Why?

7 In table 20.5, (*i*) what test of correlation was used and (*ii*) were there any correlation coefficients that were not significant (at or below the five per cent level)?

MARTIN T. ORNE (1966)

Hypnosis, motivation and compliance

American Journal of Psychiatry, 122, pp. 721–6

Recent research findings have indicated the need to reconsider what had appeared to be reasonable assumptions about the nature of hypnosis. At first sight, the implications of these studies seem to be at variance with clinical experience and common sense, but careful consideration actually allows us to reconcile clinical and experimental findings in a more satisfactory way than has been possible in the past.

It has been widely held that hypnosis alters the relationship between subject and hypnotist by changing the subject's motivation; one of the more extreme versions of this view was proposed by Orne (1954, 1959) based on White (1941). It was assumed that the hypnotic state increases the subject's motivation to please the hypnotist, i.e. it makes him unusually compliant. This assumption seems soundly based on the behaviour of hypnotized individuals who certainly *appear* to do things that they would not normally do. Nevertheless, a careful evaluation has failed to uncover any evidence for increased compliance in hypnosis, which is how the hypnotic state has usually been defined. To reconcile this finding with the effectiveness of hypnosis in clinical practice, it has been necessary to clarify the definition of hypnosis itself.

The alternative view of hypnosis is that, rather than it representing a change in the degree of compliance, it is a change in the subjective experience of hypnotized individuals. This latter definition can encompass adequately the kinds of phenomena usually subsumed under the concept of hypnosis, and suggests that the observed compliance of hypnotized subjects, and especially their responsiveness to therapeutic suggestions, may not be an intrinsic part of hypnosis itself.

The motivational view of hypnosis seems compelling because hypnotized subjects are quick to comply with the hypnotist's requests even when unusual or bizarre behaviour is requested. However, the source of the subject's motivation in such cases need not be the hypnotic state itself. In lecturing to college students about hypnosis, I often illustrate this point with a simple demonstration: I ask a number of students to perform certain actions, e.g. one to take off his right shoe, another to exchange his tie with his neighbour, another to give me his wallet and so on. After these things have been done, I point out that if the same behaviour had occurred after a hypnotic induction, it would have seemed that the students were under hypnotic control, i.e. while all the behaviours were admissible requests in a hypnosis situation, it is unusual for lecturers to make such 'unreasonable' requests and, therefore, it is tempting to assume – incorrectly – that only hypnotized persons would comply with them.

An experimental demonstration of this point is provided by Orne and Evans (1965), replicating studies by Rowland (1939) and Young (1952), which appeared to prove that subjects can be compelled to carry out antisocial and self-destructive acts under hypnosis. The earlier studies had shown that deeply hypnotized subjects can be compelled to pick up a rattlesnake, lift a penny out of fuming nitric acid and throw the acid at an assistant. Orne and Evans confirmed these findings but also found that this behaviour could be obtained equally well from non-hypnotized individuals in the waking state. The waking subjects were fully aware that the behaviour they were being asked to perform would normally be highly self-destructive, antisocial and dangerous but, in a post-experimental interview, they revealed that they were convinced (correctly) that appropriate safeguards would be taken to protect them and the assistant from any real harm.

So far it has not been possible to find any behaviour which subjects will perform under hypnosis which they will not perform in the waking state. This does not necessarily mean that hypnosis may not increase the range of behaviours that people are willing to perform, but it shows that subjects tend to do anything that might conceivably be required of them in an experimental setting. Any behaviour which subjects might *not* carry out is well beyond the range that an experimenter could afford to request, a point underlined by Milgram's (1963) studies in which subjects continued to give what seemed to be extremely high and dangerous levels of electric shock to another person in the context of a learning experiment.

Effect on performance of difficult tasks

Rather than examining the range of tasks that subjects will perform, one can study the effect of hypnosis on performance quantitatively by using difficult, fatiguing tasks. If the subject is used as his own control, he may indeed perform much better in hypnosis than when awake; however, experimental subjects are extremely compliant, even without being hypnotized. If they think that the experimenter is trying to prove that hypnosis increases performance, they may easily provide him with supporting data; not necessarily by *increasing* their hypnotic performance, but by *decreasing* their waking performance (Evans & Orne, 1965; Orne, 1959). Moreover, Orne (1954, 1959), Barber and Calverley (1964) and Levitt and Brady (1964) have shown that with proper motivation, waking subjects can surpass their own hypnosis performance. In these studies, however, no attempt was made to equate instructions in the two conditions, so that subjects were motivated very differently during waking and hypnosis. Consequently, they shed no light on whether hypnosis alone increases the subjects' motivation to comply with the hypnotist's requests.

To answer this question, *identical instructions* would have to be given in both conditions, e.g. asking a subject to hold a kilogram weight at arm's length as long as possible; performance would be a measure of the degree of compliance induced by identical instructions in different states. A serious methodological problem involved in such experiments is the difficulty, if not the impossibility, of giving instructions to a hypnotized subject in the same way as to a waking subject. While the 'lyrics' may remain constant, the 'melody' is usually drastically altered, and therefore the total communication is quite different, so any differences in performance (which are to be expected) could be due either to how the instructions are given or the presence of hypnosis.

An ingenious experimental design by London and Fuhrer (1961) gets around this difficulty. A large number of subjects are given an initial test of susceptibility to hypnosis and from them, the extreme responders and nonresponders are selected. They are all told that they are sufficiently deeply hypnotizable for the purposes of the experiment. In the main part of the experiment, a very neutral, relaxing form of trance induction is used and subjects are tested on a motor task. A comparison is then made between performance of good and poor hypnotic subjects; if hypnosis makes subjects more compliant, the performance of the former should be superior to that of the latter. But in several studies, London and Fuhrer (1961) and Rosenhan and London (1963a, b) found that, if anything, it was the poor hypnotic subjects who performed better under hypnotic conditions. In a detailed replication, Evans and Orne (1965) found *no* difference between good and poor subjects. It certainly seems as though hypnotizable subjects are not more motivated to comply with the wishes of the hypnotist than the others.

Evans and Orne have carried out a great deal of experimental work involving not only excellent hypnotic subjects, but also essentially unhypnotizable ones used as controls. Retrospectively, it occurred to us that the number of cancelled appointments and actual drop-outs in the highly hypnotizable group was greater than in the non-hypnotizable group, so we began to record subjects' time of arrival for experimental sessions and correlated their punctuality with their hypnotic performance. We found a modest but significant *negative* relationship: the good subjects tended to arrive late for the experiments while the poor subjects tended to arrive early. Whatever the explanation for these findings, they are not what would be expected if good hypnotic subjects are especially motivated to please the hypnotist.

Similarly, Shor (1964) asked subjects to choose the highest level of shock they would be willing to tolerate, prior to an experiment involving electric shock; the poor hypnotic subjects chose significantly higher shock levels than the good ones.

All these findings argue against the hypothesis that being susceptible to hypnosis leads to a generalized tendency to comply with requests from the hypnotist. No such tendency appears when the requests are not directly relevant to the hypnotic situation, i.e. a subject who carries out hypnotic suggestions may not necessarily be more likely to carry out other requests.

Criteria for hypnosis

In order to understand these results, it is necessary to examine the definition of hypnosis itself. What criteria do we have in mind when we say that someone is hypnotized? Observers watching a subject respond to suggestions usually agree on whether he is hypnotized, and how deeply. The most widely used objective scale of hypnotic depth is probably the Stanford Hypnotic Susceptibility Scale, Form C (Weitzenhoffer & Hilgard, 1962), and is used in most of the empirical work done today. Scale scores agree very well with the judgements of trained observers.

But what criteria do observers actually use? What must a subject do to achieve a high score on the scale? Clearly, the critical variable is the subject's ability to respond to suggestions, but hypnotic suggestions are not all of the same kind. They can be classified into four groups: (*i*) ideomotor; (*ii*) challenge; (*iii*) hallucinations and memory distortions (of which amnesia is a special example) and (*iv*) post-hypnotic behaviour. Such a classification has received empirical support from the factor analytic results of Evans (1965).

In a classic ideomotor suggestion, such as the sway test, the subject is told that he is falling backwards, and is told what to experience: 'You are falling backward . . . you feel yourself falling further and further backward'. The response is defined as positive by the extent to which the subject actually falls but it is implicitly assumed that he falls *because he feels himself drawn backward* rather than because of the conscious volitional decision: 'I will fall backward', which would not count as an ideomotor response. The experimenter is not trying to measure behavioural compliance as such, but rather the behavioural manifestations of a subjective experience. If one were measuring only behavioural compliance, one would use the simple instruction, 'Fall backward now'; in an experimental context, anyway, compliance would be almost total.

The challenge suggestion (e.g. 'Your eyes are tightly glued together; you cannot open them. Try to open them. You cannot') is also scored behaviourally, on the basis of the subject's failure to open them. Here too it is hoped that this behaviour accurately reflects a subjective inability to open the eyes, rather than mere compliance with the hypnotist's wish. While these two possibilities are difficult to distinguish operationally, the response measures 'depth of hypnosis' only in so far as it reflects an *experienced* inability on the part of the subjects to open his eyes, i.e. the extent to which a subject *cannot* comply even when he is challenged to do so.

Suggestions dealing with hallucination, amnesia or other memory distortions are also designed to produce responses which reflect a presumed change in the subject's experience; a subject is genuinely hypnotized not because he is willing to report certain things, but because his report really describes his personal subjective experience.

Post-hypnotic phenomenon

This is most difficult to deal with in this context, because the usual criterion is purely behavioural: does the subject carry out the suggestion? Nevertheless, the response is subjectively quite different from simple compliance, for it is presumed that subjects experience a *compulsion* to carry out the suggested behaviour, regardless of whether they actually recall the suggestion. Evans (1965) has tried to measure separately the compulsion and recall elements of typical post-hypnotic suggestions, and found them to be only moderately correlated. Orne (1965) summarized data on post-hypnotic behaviour and concluded that, despite this subjective compulsion, a post-hypnotic suggestion is likely to be less effective than a simple request to carry out the behaviour. These quantitative and qualitative differences provide convincing evidence that post-hypnotic suggestion is not merely a matter of behavioural compliance.

So the criteria for determining whether a subject is hypnotized do not focus primarily on whether he does what he is told, but are attempts to measure the extent to which distortions in his perception or memory can be induced by appropriate cues. If a wide range of distortions can easily be induced, the subject is said to be deeply hypnotized. Thus the essence of hypnosis is not so much a way of manipulating a person's behaviour (as it is often protrayed in popular literature and patients' fantasy) as of creating distortions of perception and memory; this explains why it does not necessarily increase compliance or obedience as such, especially in experimental contexts which already predispose subjects to a very high degree of compliance.

If we take this experiential definition of hypnosis, a simple motivational theory cannot be sustained and has been repeatedly contradicted by experimental findings. Tasks which could, in principle, be carried out by non-hypnotized individuals are not carried out better under hypnosis; the hypothetical 'increased motivation to please the hypnotist' which ought to manifest itself in performance on such tasks, apparently does not occur.

In a clinical context, the therapist is often more interested in changing the patient's behaviour than in studying his experience. So-called 'hypnotic' therapy has been found useful in changing habit patterns and in suppressing a wide range of neurotic symptoms. Therapists have often decided that a patient was successfully hypnotized whenever his behaviour was changed by the therapist's suggestion, and a suggestion is 'hypnotic' if it follows a trance-induction procedure and has successful results, even without any evaluation of depth of hypnosis by the usual means. This definition is clearly different from the subjective criterion discussed above. It is quite possible that patients fail to enter hypnosis in the experiential sense, and yet respond to a therapeutic suggestion; conversely, other patients may be *deeply hypnotized and fail to respond to such a suggestion*. The clinical procedure which defines 'hypnosis' *post hoc* would, by its nature, fail to recognize such a situation.

It is highly probable that hypnotizability in our sense does not correlate highly with response to therapeutic suggestion, as indicated by the puzzling phenomenon of 'light hypnotic trance', which may be sufficient to produce therapeutically marked changes in behaviour. Two recent patients were totally unable to manifest hypnotic phenomena, and did nothing more than close their eyes in response to a request to do so. By any of the usual criteria they were not hypnotized at all, yet therapeutic suggestions produced dramatic positive responses.

It is possible that a hypnotic trance-induction procedure may fail to induce hypnosis itself, and yet make the patient more responsive to therapeutic suggestions. We should separate two aspects of the therapeutic situation using trance induction: (*i*) the effect of suggestions made during a situation defined by doctor and patient as 'hypnosis' and (*ii*) the classic state of hypnosis in which the patient responds to suggestions from the hypnotist by distorting reality. Susceptability to (ii) may be different from susceptibility to (i), which often involves no cognitive distortion.

The necessary and sufficient conditions for the classic subjective phenomena of hypnosis are as yet unclear, but the hypothesis that it is essentially a matter of compliance seems untenable. Even the more plausible hypothesis that it depends on an increased motivation to carry out any tasks requested by the hypnotist must be rejected, or at least restricted to apply only to tasks involving cognitive distortions. If so, how can we understand the clinical effectiveness of the hypnotic induction procedure? This procedure does seem to change the existing transference relationship, and 'hypnotic' suggestions do often change symptoms which resisted other forms of suggestion.

Effect on role relationship

Such therapeutic effects may not be primarily a function of hypnosis itself, but may result from the changed relationship which exists when a therapist assumes the role of 'hypnotist', and shares with the patient the expectation that hypnosis involves unlimited compliance. This is certainly a different role relationship from the usual therapeutic one: not only are magical powers ascribed to the therapist by the patient, but the therapist's behaviour tends to reinforce these fantasies. Also, therapists encourage regressive behaviour, and allow an intense closeness which they might otherwise be unwilling to tolerate. These changes in the doctor–patient relationship may be among the sufficient conditions for evoking a real hypnotic state.

Perhaps the increased response to suggestions usually attributed to hypnosis relates more to these relationship changes than to the hypnotic potentiality for distorted perceptions. Even in individuals for whom this relationship fails to evoke hypnosis, the relationship as such may still alter the patient's motivation, and dramatically affect his reponse to certain types of suggestion. If this were true, it would help to explain many of the apparent contradictions about hypnosis, including the vastly differing reports by different hypnotists about the percentage of hypnotizable individuals in the population, and the lack of correlation between hypnotizability and compliance.

Commentary

Aim and nature

This is primarily a review article in which Orne attempts to reconcile what seems to be the contradictory findings from (i) experimental studies of hypnosis and (ii) clinical experience (i.e. the use of hypnosis with patients in a therapeutic setting). While presenting data from his own studies, he is also discussing the findings of several other researchers and clinicians, and so no one study is looked at in any great detail. He suggests two alternative ways of looking at hypnosis: (i) it involves a change in the subject's motivation to please the hypnotist, i.e. makes him/her unusually compliant; (ii) it involves a change in the subject's subjective experience. As far as (i) is concerned, he cites a number of studies (including his own) which argue against the hypothesis that 'being susceptible to hypnosis leads to a generalized tendency to comply with requests from the hypnotist'. Regarding (ii), the criteria used by trained observers for establishing that a subject is actually hypnotized all focus on the critical variable of the subject's ability to respond to suggestions (ideomotor/challenge/hallucinations and memory distortions/post-hypnotic behaviour). Although this suggestibility refers at one level to overt behaviour, more importantly, at another level, it refers to an assumed change in the subject's experience: 'a subject is genuinely hypnotized not because he is willing to report certain things, but because his report really describes his personal subjective experience', (e.g. a *compulsion* to carry out the post-hypnotic suggestion regardless of whether (s)he actually recalls it). Further, the wider the range of distortions in his/her perception or memory, which can be induced by appropriate cues, the more deeply the subject is said to be hypnotized.

Context and background

This distinction between (a) the motivational theory of hypnosis and (b) the subjective experience theory of hypnosis corresponds, respectively, to (i) the 'non-state'/social psychological view and (ii) the 'state'/'special process' view (Wagstaff, 1987). (The following sections are based on Wagstaff's excellent review.)

According to Wagstaff (1987), this controversy as to the nature of hypnosis has raged since the late 18th century. Although it was once thought that hypnosis is a special sort of sleep (the Greek 'hypnos' = sleep), not all modern state theorists subscribe to this view. However, they continue to see hypnosis as an altered state of consciousness with various depths, the assumption being made that the deeper the hypnotic state, the more likely it is that the subject will manifest hypnotic phenomena (Hilgard, 1978; Bowers, 1983). The state of hypnotic trance (supposedly qualitatively different from a normal waking state) may occur spontaneously, but is usually brought about through induction procedures (e.g. eye-fixation and vocal suggestions for sleep and relaxation).

In order to measure/quantify hypnotic susceptibility and depth, a number of standardized scales have been developed, including the Stanford Hypnotic Suscepti-bility Scale, Form C (referred to by Orne) (plus forms A and B), and the Harvard Group Scale of Hypnotic Susceptibility. These typically suggest to the subject that 'your hand is heavy and falling' (hand lowering), 'you cannot bend your arm' (arm rigidity) or 'you will find it difficult to remember' (amnesia) and sometimes 'there is a fly buzzing round your head' (hallucination). What they imply is that the response is automatic, that subjects experience their responses as 'happening to them' (Bowers, 1983). The special state view also claims that subjects will be able to do things whilst under hypnosis of which they would be incapable in the waking state (or at least their performance is superior), including the ability to control pain (Hilgard & Hilgard, 1984), and distinctive abilities in displays of amnesia and hallucinations (Orne, 1979; Kihlstrom, 1980; Bowers, 1983). However, most academic state theorists do *not* accept the claims that 'hypnotized' people can actually be regressed back to before their birth and former lives in Roman Britain or Medieval York. Again, less sensational claims (including losing warts, phobias, becoming deaf or blind, surviving ice-cold water or a surgeon's knife without flinching) cannot just be dismissed, since many seem to have considerable empirical support. But is there an alternative explanation for all these phenomena?

This, of course, is where the non-state theorists enter the debate. They comprise mainly social and cognitive psychologists (including Wagstaff himself), who see the hypnotic situation as a social–psychological interaction, i.e. the hypnotist and subject act out social roles: the subject's role is to act according to previous expectations and to cues provided by the hypnotist and to try very hard to act *as if* 'hypnotized'. (This does *not* mean that the subject is faking or shamming, but this may happen.) Wagstaff (1983) proposes three stages that may be involved in hypnotic responding:

(*i*) the subject figures out what is expected, based on previous experience and instructions;
(*ii*) (s)he uses imaginative or other deliberate strategies to try to produce the suggested effects;
(*iii*) if the strategies fail or are judged inappropriate, the subject either gives up or reverts to behavioural compliance or shamming.

Wagstaff asks if it is ridiculous to believe that the subject might start acting out the role and then, sometimes, actually fake effects? He answers by saying there is an impressive literature indicating that subjects who enter experiments etc. have a strong desire to please the experimenter and to 'look good': (*i*) Milgram (1974) (see chapter 10) claims that the desire not to commit a social impropriety and not to ruin an experiment can be extremely powerful (more than we realize); (*ii*) Sheridan and King (1972) found that 72 per cent of ordinary people were prepared to give high levels of *real* shock to a *real* innocent, puppy; (*iii*) Orne (1962) himself found that subjects will agree to ridiculous requests if the context is appropriate, e.g. he asked subjects to perform additions on sheets filled with random numbers (224 additions per sheet × 2,000 sheets) and told them to continue working while he was away, but that he would return eventually. 5½ hours later it was Orne who had to give up! The subjects were quite willing to go on for hour after hour rather than let the experimenter down.

Similar pressures apply in the hypnotic situation. In addition, the subject may be genuinely curious and wish to experience hypnosis. Having started, it may be difficult to back out; having finished, it may be difficult to understand why they did it.

Evaluation

1 Are these two views – the state and non-state – mutually exclusive; i.e. can only one be true and the other false? State theorists do not reject social psychological factors; indeed Orne (1959, 1966, 1970, 1979) is actually a state theorist who has been a major experimentalist trying to tease out the effects of simple compliance or sham behaviour to see what is left. However, non-state theorists argue that it is unnecessary to propose any unique/special hypnotic process over and above compliance, imagination, relaxation and other 'normal' processes.

2 Most experiments have compared groups of hypnotic subjects (those given a hypnotic induction procedure) with various control groups, set up to test alternative, non-state explanations. One commonly used control group is the *simulating group* (Orne, 1959, 1979) in which subjects are told to fake hypnosis *but* they are not told how to do it. Other control groups include 'task-motivated' groups, instructed, for example, to try hard to imagine and experience suggestions (but they are not given a formal hypnotic induction procedure (Barber, 1969). The rationale here is that if hypnotic subjects respond no differently from non-hypnotic controls, then there is no need to postulate a special state to explain the behaviour of the former. Conversely, if controls *cannot* reproduce the behaviours of hypnotic subjects, then it seems that hypnosis *does* involve an additional, unique, element.

3 Do hypnotized subjects show physiological changes not shown by control subjects? Many measures have been used, including EEG, blood pressure, blood-clotting time, breathing rate, skin temperature and oral temperature. None of these consistently differentiates between hypnotic subjects and controls. Although these responses may *change* when a person is given hypnotic induction, equivalent changes are shown when a person is asked to, e.g. close their eyes, relax or imagine various effects. Nor are hypnotic physiological changes equivalent to people when asleep or sleepwalking (e.g. Wagstaff, 1981a; Spanos, 1982).

4 Are hypnotized subjects capable of extraordinary feats of which controls are incapable? Not only do many state theorists deny that hypnotic subjects can transcend normal human capacities, but there is no conclusive evidence that they are superior on a whole variety of tasks (see *Context and background* above), assuming that the controls are motivated to try hard and take the task seriously (e.g. Wagstaff, 1981a, 1982b,c, 1984). Indeed, some studies have shown that simulators may overplay their role and actually outperform the hypnotic subjects (e.g. picking up a poisonous snake, throwing acid at the *E* (both tricks!), peddling heroin, mutilating the Bible and committing slanders (Wagstaff, 1981a, 1982b). Hypnosis does *not* increase memory for the details of crimes any more than instructing people to relax or vividly imagine events (Wagstaff, 1984) and simulators are just as able as hypnotized subjects to give the impression that painful stimuli do not hurt (Hilgard *et al.*, 1978).

5 But are there any more subtle measures of hypnotic responding? Wagstaff believes that probably the most significant demonstration of the differences between hypnotic and simulating behaviour is what Orne (1959, 1979) calls 'Trance-Logic'. For example, if it is suggested to hypnotized subjects that they cannot see an object actually in front of them (e.g. a chair), though some subjects will claim they cannot see it, they will still walk around it rather than bump into it. By contrast, simulators tend to bump into it whilst claiming they cannot see it. Again, if shown a chair and asked to hallucinate a man sitting in it, hypnotized subjects will tend to report the image is transparent (i.e. they can still see the chair through the man!). But simulators tend to report it as opaque (not transparent) and so cannot see the chair through the man.

According to the state view, hypnotized subjects have little need for logical consistency and can tolerate illogical responses: this is 'Trance-Logic'.

Is there a non-state explanation for these findings? In the case of hallucinations, simulators, in order to be excellent subjects, feel they have to report complete, opaque hallucinations. But when Johnson *et al.* (1972) instructed non-hypnotized subjects to *imagine* an object, they tended to report the same transparent images (just like hypnotized ones). So it could be that 'Trance-Logic' hypnotic subjects are really imagining an object (Wagstaff, 1981a, 1986).

6 The most popular contemporary state theory is the Neo-Dissociation Theory (Hilgard, 1974, 1977, 1978, 1979; Bowers, 1983). Basically this maintains that we have multiple systems of control, not all conscious at the same time but which can be brought into consciousness 'under hypnosis'. This is best illustrated by Hilgard's demonstration of the 'Hidden Observer' phenomenon. The subject is hypnotized and then given the following instruction:

> When I place my hand on your shoulder, I shall be able to talk to a hidden part of you that knows things are going on in your body, things that are unknown to the part of you to which I am now talking. The part to which I am now talking will not know what you are telling me or even that you are talking ... You will remember that there is a part of you that knows many things that are going on that may be hidden from either your normal consciousness or the hypnotized part of you. (Knox, Morgan & Hilgard 1974, quoted in Wagstaff, 1987)

By doing this, you can contact another system of control or 'part' of you, which will then speak, unaware of the normal 'waking part' or 'hypnotized part'. Trance-Logic can now be explained in terms of dissociated 'parts', e.g. the 'part' which does not see the chair is dissociated from the 'part' which knows it is there and walks round it. Also, the 'part' which sees the man in the chair is dissociated from that which does not. So both the man *and* the back of the chair are reported at the same time. These 'parts' are unaware of each other because they are separated by 'amensia barriers', but they can break through simultaneously, so that subjects report incongruities and logical inconsistencies. One of the appeals of the theory is its ability to re-interpret some results which otherwise would seem to support the non-state view, e.g. some hypnotic subjects instructed to go deaf, when asked 'Can you hear me?', will answer 'No, I can't hear you' (Barber *et al.*, 1974). Instead of falling for a simple trick (non-state view), the 'part' which answers is dissociated from the 'part' which cannot hear (neo-dissociation theory). (Although, as Wagstaff says, it would make more sense if the 'hidden part' said, 'Yes, I *can* hear you'!) Wagstaff concludes that, ultimately, it's a question of parsimony as to which is the 'true' explanation: is it *necessary* to postulate dissociative processes and amnesic barriers when more 'normal' factors will do?

7 Finally, the *pièce de résistance* of hypnosis (state theory) is hypnotic analgesia (i.e. the control/elimination of surgical and non-surgical pain through hypnosis). It seems undeniable that hypnotic techniques can be useful in this way (e.g. Hilgard & Hilgard, 1984). But this in itself does not prove conclusively that it is a special state which is responsible; non-state theorists are not arguing that all hypnotic phenomena are faked, but pain relief could occur for a variety of reasons other than the inducement of a special state (e.g. relaxation and distraction). Wagstaff points out that pain is a complex psychological experience in which anxiety plays a major part. Also, many surgical procedures are less painful than might be commonly predicted, e.g. many internal organs are insensitive to pain: it's not true that the deeper you cut into the body the more it hurts, but pulling and stretching of damaged tissue is painful. Also there are important individual differences in pain thresholds.

8 Is there a particular kind of person more likely to respond to hypnotic suggestions? Both 'camps' agree that the degree to which a subject is willing to become absorbed in imaginings is important. Wilson and Barber (1983) believe there may be a 'fantasy-prone personality' who is particularly susceptible to both hypnotic *and* non-hypnotic suggestions. Finally, there is some evidence that the more negative the subjects' attitudes and expectations regarding hypnosis, the less susceptible they are (Spanos, 1982).

> The onus now must surely be on the state theorists to show that non-state explanations are inadequate, rather than vice versa. (Wagstaff, 1987)

Exercises

1 In the *Criteria for hypnosis* section, referring to the Stanford Hypnosis Susceptibility Scale, Orne writes 'Scale scores agree very well with the judgement of trained observers'.

(*i*) What's another word for 'agree' and (*ii*) how would this agreement be measured statistically?

2 Orne refers to Form C of the above Scale. Wagstaff refers to Forms A and B. What is the purpose/advantage of having different forms of the same test? What are they used for?

3 Wagstaff's reference to Orne's (1962) findings (*re* 5½ hours of adding up numbers etc.) can be explained in terms of what Orne calls 'demand characteristics'. What does this mean, and what is its importance for human psychological experiments in general?

4 Whereas the clinical use of hypnosis may be morally quite as acceptable as any other therapeutic procedure, do you find anything wrong with the experimental use of hypnosis (e.g. when people may be asked to 'make fools of themselves')?

JOHN B. WATSON AND ROSALIE RAYNER (1920)

Conditioned emotional reactions

Journal of Experimental Psychology, 3(1), pp. 1–14

In recent literature there have been various speculations regarding the possibility of conditioning various types of emotional response, but direct experimental evidence has been lacking. If the theory advanced by Watson and Morgan (1917) is true, i.e., that in infancy the original emotional reaction patterns are few, consisting of fear, rage and love, then there must be some simple method by which the range of stimuli which can elicit these emotions and their compounds is greatly increased. Otherwise, complexity in adult response could not be accounted for. Watson and Morgan proposed that this range was increased by means of conditioned reflex factors, and that the early home life of the child provides a laboratory situation for establishing conditioned emotional responses (CERs). The present authors have recently put the whole matter to an experimental test.

Experimental work so far has been done on only one child, Albert B, reared almost from birth in a hospital environment: his mother was a wet nurse in the Harriet Lane Home for Invalid Children. His life was normal: he was healthy from birth and one of the best developed youngsters ever brought to the hospital, weighing 21 pounds at nine months of age. He was, on the whole, stolid and unemotional; his stability was one of the major reasons for using him as a subject. We felt that we could do him relatively little harm by carrying out such experiments as described below.

At approximately nine months of age, we ran him through the emotional tests that have become part of our routine for determining whether fear reactions can be elicited by other stimuli than sharp noises and the sudden removal of support. Briefly, the infant was confronted suddenly, and for the first time, successively with a white rat, a rabbit, a dog, a monkey, masks with and without hair, cotton wool, burning newspapers, etc. Manipulation was the most usual reaction produced. *At no time did this infant ever show fear in any situation.* These experimental records were confirmed by the casual observations of his mother and hospital attendants; no one had ever seen him in a state of fear and rage, and he practically never cried.

Up to approximately nine months, we had not tested him with loud sounds. When he was eight months, 26 days old, a sound was made by striking a hammer upon a suspended steel bar four feet in length and

¾ inch in diameter. The laboratory notes are as follows:

> One of the two experimenters caused the child to turn its head and fixate her moving hand; the other, stationed back of the child, struck the steel bar a sharp blow. The child started violently, his breathing was checked and the arms were raised in a characteristic manner. On the second stimulation the same thing occurred, and in addition the lips began to pucker and tremble. On the third stimulation the child broke into a sudden crying fit. This is the first time an emotional situation in the laboratory has produced any fear or even crying in Albert.

We had expected exactly these results on account of our work with other infants brought up under similar conditions. However, dropping and jerking the blanket on which Albert was lying was done exhaustively without producing the fear response. This loss of support does effectively produce fear in younger infants but at what age such stimuli lose their potency is not known. Nor is it known whether less placid children ever lose their fear of them; it probably depends on the training the child gets and are quite common in adults.

The sound stimulus, therefore, at nine months, gives us the means of testing several important factors: (*i*) Can we condition fear of an animal, e.g. a white rat, by visually presenting it and simultaneously striking a steel bar? (*ii*) If such a CER can be established, will there by a transfer to other animals or other objects? (*iii*) What is the effect of time on such conditioned emotional responses? (*iv*) If, after a reasonable period, such CER's have not died out, what laboratory methods can be devised for their removal?

1 At first there was considerable hesitation on our part in making the attempt to set up fear responses experimentally. A certain responsibility attaches to such procedure. We decided finally to go ahead, comforting ourselves by the reflection that such responsibilities would arise anyway as soon as the child left the sheltered environment of the nursery for the rough and tumble of the home. We did not begin this work until Albert was 11 months, three days old. As before, we put him through all the regular emotional tests. *Not the slightest sign of a fear response was obtained in any situation.* The steps taken to condition emotional responses are shown in our laboratory notes.

11 months, three days

(*i*) White rat suddenly taken from the basket and presented to Albert. He began to reach for rat with left hand. Just as his hand touched the animal the bar was struck immediately behind his head. He jumped violently and fell forward, burying his face in the mattress. But he did not cry.
(*ii*) Just as the right hand touched the rat, the bar was struck again. Again Albert jumped violently, fell forward and began to whimper.
In order not to disturb him too seriously, no further tests were given for one week.

11 months, ten days

(*i*) Rat presented suddenly without sound. There was steady fixation but no tendency at first to reach for it. It was then placed nearer, whereupon Albert began to reach, tentatively, with right hand. When the rat nosed his left hand, he immediately withdrew it. He started to reach for the rat's head with forefinger of left hand, but withdrew it suddenly before contact. Thus the two-joint stimulations given the previous week were not without effect. He was tested with his blocks immediately afterwards to see if they shared in the process of conditioning. He began immediately to pick them up, dropping them, pounding them, etc. In the rest of the tests the blocks were given often to quieten him and to test his general emotional state. They were always removed from sight when the process of conditioning was under way.

(*ii*) Joint stimulation with rat and sound. Started, then fell over immediately to right side. No crying.

(*iii*) Joint stimulation. Fell to right side and rested on hands, with head turned away from rat. No crying.

(*iv*) Joint stimulation. Same reaction.

(*v*) Rat suddenly presented alone. Puckered face, whimpered and withdrew body sharply to the left.

(*vi*) Joint stimulation. Fell over immediately to right side and began to whimper.

(*vii*) Joint stimulation. Started violently and cried, but did not fall over.

(*viii*) Rat alone. *The instant the rat was shown, the baby began to cry. Almost instantly he turned sharply to the left, fell over on left side, raised himself on all fours and began to crawl away so rapidly that he was caught with difficulty before reaching the edge of the table.*

This was as convincing a case of a completely conditioned fear response as could have been theoretically pictured. In all, seven joint stimulations were given to produce the complete reaction. If the sound had been of greater intensity, or of a more complex clang character, the number of joint stimulations might have been materially reduced.

2 When a CER has been established for one object, is there a transfer? Five days later, Albert was again brought back into the laboratory and tested as follows:

11 months, 15 days

(*i*) Tested first with blocks. He reached steadily for them, playing with them as usual. This shows that there has been no general transfer to the room, table, blocks, etc.

(*ii*) Rat alone. Whimpered immediately, withdrew right hand, turned head and trunk away.

(*iii*) Blocks again offered. Played readily with them, smiling and gurgling.

(*iv*) Rat alone. Leaned over to left side as far away from rat as possible, then fell over, getting up on all fours and scurrying away as rapidly as possible.

(*v*) Blocks again offered. Reached immediately for them, smiling and laughing as before.

This shows that the CER had carried over completely for the five days in which no tests were given. The question of transfer was next taken up.

(*vi*) Rabbit alone. The rabbit was suddenly placed on the mattress in front of him. The negative reaction was pronounced. He leaned as far away from it as possible, whimpered, then burst into tears. When it was placed in contact with him he buried his face in the mattress, then got up on all fours and crawled away, crying as he went. This was a most convincing test.

(*vii*) The blocks were next given to him, after an interval. He played with them as before. Four people observed that he played far more energetically with them than ever before.

(*viii*) Dog alone. The dog did not produce as violent a reaction as the rabbit. The moment fixation occurred, Albert shrank back and, as it approached, he tried to get on all fours, but did not cry at first. As soon as the dog passed out of his range of vision he became quiet. The dog was then made to approach Albert's head (who was lying down); he straightened up immediately, fell over to the opposite side and turned his head away. He then began to cry.

(*ix*) The blocks were again presented and he began to play with them immediately.

(*x*) Fur coat (seal). Withdrew immediately to left side and began to fret. Coat put close to him on the left side, he turned immediately, began to cry and tried to crawl away on all fours.

(*xi*) Cotton wool. Presented in paper package. At the end, the cotton wool was not covered by the paper. Placed first on his feet. He kicked it away, but did not touch it with his hands. When his hand was placed on it he immediately withdrew it but did not show the shock produced by the animals or fur coat. He then began to play with the paper, avoiding contact with the wool itself. He eventually began to lose some of his negativism.

(*xii*) Just in play, Watson put his head down to see if Albert would play with his hair. Albert was completely negative. Two other observers did the same thing but he began to play immediately with their hair. A Santa Claus mask was then presented to Albert, and again he was markedly negative.

11 months, 20 days

(*i*) Blocks alone. Played with them as usual.

(*ii*) Rat alone. Withdrawal of whole body, bending over to left side, no crying. Fixation and following with eyes. The response much less marked than on first presentation the previous week. It was decided to freshen up the reaction by another joint stimulation.

(*iii*) Just as the rat was placed on Albert's hand, the rod was struck. Violent reaction.

(*iv*) Rat alone. Fell over at once to left side. Reaction practically as strong as on former occasion but no crying.

(*v*) Rat alone. Fell over to left side, got up on all fours and started to crawl away. No crying, but as he moved away, he began to gurgle and coo, even while trying to avoid rat.

(*vi*) Rabbit alone. Leaned over to left side as far as possible. Did not fall over. Began to whimper but reaction not as violent as on previous occasions.

(*vii*) Blocks again offered. Albert reached for them immediately and began to play.

So far, all the tests had been performed on a table with a mattress in a small, well-lit dark-room. What would happen if the situation were markedly changed? Before testing this, we freshened up the reaction to both the rabbit and the Dog by joint stimulation; this was the first time such joint stimulation had taken place.

(*viii*) The rabbit at first was given alone. The reaction was exactly as in (vi) above. When the rabbit was left on Albert's knees for a long time, he began tentatively to reach out and manipulate its fur with forefingers. While doing this, the steel rod was struck, causing a violent reaction.

(*ix*) Rabbit alone. Reaction the same as on trial (vi) above.

(*x*) Rabbit alone. Started immediately to whimper, holding hands far up, but no crying. Conflicting tendency to manipulate very evident.

(*xi*) Dog alone. Began to whimper, shaking head from side to side, holding hands as far away from the dog as possible.

(*xii*) Dog and sound. A violent, negative reaction caused. Began to whimper, turned to one side, fell over and started to get up on all fours.

(*xiii*) Blocks. Played with them immediately and readily.

Immediately after the above experiment, Albert was taken into the large, well-lit lecture room belonging to the laboratory. He was placed on a table in the centre of the room immediately under the skylight. Four people were present. The situation was thus very different from the small dark-room.

(*i*) Rat alone. No sudden fear reaction at first. But the hands were held up and away, and no positive manipulatory reactions appeared.

(*ii*) Rabbit alone. Fear reaction slight. Turned to left and kept face away, but reaction never pronounced.

(*iii*) Dog alone. Turned away, but did not fall over. Cried. Moved hands as far away as possible, and whimpered as long as the dog present.

(*iv*) Rat alone. Slight negative reaction.

(*v*) Rat and sound. Albert jumped violently, but did not cry.

(*vi*) Rat alone. No negative reaction at first, but when rat placed nearer, he began to draw back his body, raising hands, whimpering, etc.

(*vii*) Blocks. Played with them immediately.

(*viii*) Rat alone. Pronounced withdrawal of body and whimpering.

(*ix*) Blocks. Played with them as before.

(*x*) Rabbit alone. Pronounced reaction. Whimpered, fell over backwards and had to be caught.

(*xi*) Dog alone. At first no pronounced reaction; hands held high over head, breathing checked, but no crying. Just at this moment, the previously quiet dog barked loudly, three times, just six inches away from Albert's face. He immediately fell over and started wailing, stopping only when the dog was removed.

The above results suggest that emotional transfers do take place, and that the number of transfers from an experimentally produced CER may be very large.

3 We have already shown that the CER will continue for a week and, because of Albert's imminent departure from the hospital, it was impossible to make the interval longer than one month. Accordingly, no further experimentation was undertaken for 31 days after the above test. During the month, however, Albert was brought weekly to the laboratory for tests on right–left handedness, imitation and general development.

One year, 21 days

(*i*) Santa Claus mask. Withdrawal, gurgling, then slapped at it without touching. When his hand was forced to touch it, he whimpered and cried. This happened on two further occasions. He finally cried at the mere sight of the mask.

(*ii*) Fur coat. Wrinkled his nose and withdrew both hands, drew back whole body and began to whimper as coat brought nearer. Reached tentatively with left hand, but drew back before making contact. He accidentally touched it while moving to one side and immediately began to cry, nodding his head in a very peculiar way (not seen before). Withdrew both hands as far as possible from the coat. When laid on his lap, he continued nodding and whimpering, withdrawing his body as far as he could, pushing it with his feet, but never touching it with his hands.

(*iii*) Fur coat. Removed from sight and presented again after a minute. He immediately began to fret, withdrawing body and nodding as before.

(*iv*) Blocks: began to play with them as usual.

(*v*) The rat. He allowed it to crawl towards him without withdrawing. He sat very still and fixated it intently. Rat touched his hand, Albert withdrew it immediately, leaned back as far as possible, but did not cry. When rat placed on his arm, he withdrew body and began to fret, nodding head. Rat then allowed to crawl against his chest. He first began to fret, then covered his eyes with both hands.

(*vi*) Blocks. Reaction normal.

(*vii*) Rabbit. Placed directly in front of him. Albert showed no avoidance at first. After a few seconds he puckered up his face, began to nod and then to push rabbit away with feet, withdrawing body at same time. As it came nearer he began pulling his feet away, nodding and wailing 'da da'. After about a minute, he reached out tentatively and touched rabbit's ear with right hand, finally manipulating it. Again he began to fret and withdrew hands. Reached out tentatively with left hand and touched it, shuddered and withdrew whole body. Left hand placed on rabbit. Albert immediately withdrew hand and began to suck thumb. Rabbit put in his lap. He began to cry, covering face with both hands.

(*viii*) Dog. It was very active. Albert fixated it intently for a few seconds, sitting very still. He began to cry but did not fall over backwards as on last contact with dog. When dog pushed closer, he first sat motionless, then began to cry, covering face with both hands.

These experiments would seem to show conclusively that directly conditioned emotional responses, as well as those conditioned by transfer, persist, although with a certain loss of intensity, for over one month. Our view is that they persist and modify personality throughout life. Albert was extremely phlegmatic. Had he been emotionally unstable, both kinds of CERs would probably have persisted through the month unchanged in form.

4 Unfortunately, Albert was taken from the hospital the day the above tests were made. Hence the opportunity of developing an experimental technique for removing the CERs was denied us. We believe that these responses in the home environment are likely to persist indefinitely, unless an accidental method for removing them is hit upon. Had the opportunity existed, we should have tried several methods: (*i*) constantly confronting the child with those stimuli which produced the responses, in the hope that habituation would occur corresponding to 'fatigue' of reflex when differential reactions are to be set up; (*ii*) trying to 'recondition' by showing objects producing fear responses (visual) while simultaneously stimulating the erogenous zones (tactual), first the lips, then the nipples, and, as a last resort, the sex organs; (*iii*) trying to 'recondition' by feeding him candy or other food just as the animal is shown; (*iv*) building up 'constructive' activities around the object by imitation and putting the hand through the motions of manipulation.

Incidental observations

Whenever Albert was emotionally upset, he would continually thrust his thumb into his mouth which instantly made him impervious to the stimuli producing fear. This method of blocking noxious and emotional stimuli (fear and rage) through erogenous stimulation seems to persist from birth onwards, throughout adolescent and adult life. Freud's conception of the stimulation of erogenous zones as being the expression of an original 'pleasure' seeking principle may be turned about and possibly better described as a compensatory (and often conditioned) device for the blockage of noxious and fear and rage producing stimuli.

While in general our results do not conflict with Freudian concepts, we would dispute the Freudian belief that sex (or in our terms, love) is the principal emotion in which CERs arise, which later limit and distort personality. We see fear as much a primal factor as love in influencing personality; it does not gather its potency from love, but belongs to the original and inherited nature of man.

Freudians, 20 years from now, if they come to analyse Albert at that age, will probably tease from him the recital of a dream which will be interpreted as showing that Albert, at three years old, tried to play with his mother's pubic hair and was scolded violently for it. Albert may be fully convinced of the truth of this interpretation of his fear if the analyst has the authority and personality to put it over convincingly.

It is probable that many of the phobias in psychopathology are true CERs either of the direct or transferred type. These may persist only in people who are constitutionally inferior. Emotional disturbance in adults cannot be traced back to sex alone. They must be retraced along at least three parallel lines; to conditioned and transferred responses set up in infancy and early youth in all three of the fundamental human emotions.

Commentary

Aim and nature

The aim of the study is to provide an empirical demonstration of the claim that various kinds of emotional responses can be conditioned. The study is a laboratory experiment involving a single subject, Albert B (more commonly known in the literature as 'Little Albert'). In some situations, considerations of economy (both of time and effort) lead to the use of just one subject in an experiment (Robson, 1973). Albert was certainly a desirable subject, because his mother was a wet-nurse in the hospital (Harriet Lane Home for Invalid Children) where Watson and Rayner happened to be working. Far from being an invalid, he was strong, healthy and was not easily upset, and this made him an especially suitable subject. The single-subject design has a long history in psychology, perhaps the most famours example being the pioneering work of Ebbinghaus in the study of memory – the psychologist acting as his own (single) subject – in the 1880s.

The study also represents a diary study, the detailed record of the behaviour of one child over a period of approximately 1½ months (though not on each day during that period), but unlike the diary studies of Darwin and, to some extent, Piaget, it was very specific behaviour which was being observed, i.e. his fear response (or otherwise) to certain specific animals and objects.

Context and background

Watson was the founder of Behaviourism, the school of thought which claims that behaviour – the overt, observable and measurable aspects of human activity – is the only appropriate subject matter for the scientific discipline of psychology. Watson was reacting against the attempts of the early psychologists, such as Wundt, to study the conscious human mind through introspection (inspection of one's own mind) as a way of trying to establish general laws of human thought. Watson saw this as a futile pursuit since only the individual has access to his/her mind and so no one else can inspect it in order to check the accuracy of what the introspections reveal; the mind is 'private', while behaviour is 'public', i.e. accessible to other observers, and this is a basic requirement of all science.

If behaviour is a valid subject matter for psychology, we have to have some way of defining it and analyzing it, and Watson found the key in the concept of the conditioned reflex (or conditioned response). All behaviour can be broken down into a number of such conditioned responses; however complex it may appear to be, it is composed of these simple units, all of which, in turn, are based on the three inborn human emotions, namely, rage, fear and love (sex).

The conditioned reflex had been discovered by Pavlov, the Russian physiologist, in his study of the digestive system of dogs. Through associating a stimulus (UCS) which naturally produces a particular response (UCR) with a neutral stimulus which does not (CS), the latter eventually comes to produce the response on its own; when it does, it is referred to as a conditioned response (CR). Watson was the first psychologist to apply this process of classical (or respondent/Pavlovian) conditioning to human behaviour, with Little Albert destined to become (along with Little Hans: see chapter 24) one of the most famous children in the whole of the psychological literature.

Evaluation

1 Little Albert is often cited as an example of 'classic research', being reported in every textbook of psychology from generation to generation. But, ironically (according to Cornwell & Hobbs, 1976), its 'classic' reputation has resulted in the details of the experiment being obscured, making psychologists less (rather than more) cautious, producing a false impression of familiarity with the details and a 'painting out the warts'.

In *The Strange Saga of Little Albert*, Cornwell and Hobbs argue that the experiment is a classic example of how a piece of research can become misreported/ misrepresented until it assumes 'mythical' proportions. In 1917, Watson was awarded a grant to do research into the development of reflexes and instincts in infants. As we have seen, he believed that there is a limited number of inborn emotional reactions which are the starting point for building, through the process of conditioning, the complex emotions of adulthood. He began his experiments with Little Albert in 1919, attempting to show how conditioned emotional responses (CERs) come about and how they can be removed, with the results being published in 1920.

Watson and Rayner stressed the limited nature of their evidence. They may have planned to study other children, but were unable to continue their research at the John Hopkins University (Baltimore); in 1920, in a sensationally publicised case, Watson was divorced by his wife, and immediately married Rosalie Rayner. He was forced to resign from his job.

In 1921, Watson and Rosalie Rayner Watson published a second account of Little Albert (*Scientific Monthly*); in it, they stated that Albert *did* show fear in response to a loss of support (i.e. if held and then let go), the opposite of the original paper. Also Watson subsequently referred to this 1921 paper as the original, although the 1920 paper is the one more often cited. A third account was given in some lectures by Watson which were eventually incorporated into his book *Behaviourism* (1924). It is also recounted in other books and articles. Each of these accounts is, at least once, referred to as 'the original'.

In a survey of 76 'general psychology' books at Glasgow University, Cornwell and Hobbs found at least one distortion in 60 per cent of the 30 different reports of the experiment. They ask if all the mistakes are just the result of carelessness. There is no doubt that several accounts seemed to put the experiment in a more favourable light, both methodologically and ethically. For example: (*i*) the implication is made that Albert was one of a series of infants studied, i.e. a larger sample; (*ii*) on the assumption that a child will instinctively show fear of rats, the rat is often reported as a 'rabbit', making Albert's initial *lack* of fear seem more plausible, and his conditioned fear more striking; (*iii*) many accounts claim that the conditioned fear was removed before he left the hospital: indeed, Watson and Rayner knew a month in advance that he would be leaving. Eysenck, for example, gives details of a fictitious extinction involving pieces of chocolate! This last 'myth' raises two major issues: (a) did Watson and Rayner in fact intend to remove the CER (and even if they did, does this let them off the hook morally)? and (b) how might they have done it?

(a) At the beginning of their paper, they state 'a certain responsibility attaches to such a procedure' (i.e. inducing the CER experimentally), and they were very hesitant about doing so. They eventually decided to go ahead, since '... such responsibilities would arise anyway as soon as the child left the sheltered environment of the nursery for the rough and tumble of the home'. They seem to mean 'risk' when they say 'responsibility', thus giving a false impression of having grappled long and hard with the moral issues involved. But what sort of justification is it to say Albert would have acquired the CERs anyway? Is he likely to have encountered rats at all, and is he likely to have encountered any of the other stimuli while his ears were assaulted by the sound of a full-grown man striking a hammer upon a large steel bar immediately behind his head? The fact that he was stolid and unemotional, and the belief that the experiment could do him relatively little harm, cannot be used in their defence either; some stimulus had to be able to frighten him, otherwise the experiment could not proceed, and so Watson and Rayner were knowingly deciding to cause him distress.
(b) They state that they would have tried several methods in an attempt to remove the CER ('had the opportunity existed'): (i) constantly confronting Albert with the feared object sounds like flooding, a form of forced reality testing from which there is no escape; (ii) and (iii) sound like systematic desensitization, whereby the fear is gradually extinguished by exposing the patient to increasingly frightening situations, (iv) sounds like modelling (e.g. Bandura), whereby the patient observes a model encountering the feared object, but without showing any fear.

Not so long after the Little Albert experiment, Watson supervised the treatment of Little Peter, a two-year-old living in a charitable institution, and who had an extreme fear of rats, rabbits, fur coats, feathers, cotton wool, frogs and fish. Mary Cover-Jones (1924b) used the method of direct (un)-conditioning, whereby the feared object is associated with something pleasurable, and exposure to it is gradually increased. The rabbit was put in a wire cage in front of Peter while he ate his lunch; 40 sessions later, he ate his lunch with one hand and stroked the rabbit (now on his lap) with the other. By a series of 17 steps the caged rabbit was moved a little closer each day, then let free in the room and eventually sat on Peter's tray. This is generally regarded as the first reported use of (what is now known as) systematic desensitization, a commonly used method for the removal of phobias.

2 Watson believed that the child's unconditioned responses (fear, rage and love) to simple stimuli are only the starting points in 'building up those complicated habit patterns we later call our emotions' (Watson, 1931). For example, the emotion of jealousy is not innate or inevitable, but rather is '... a bit of behaviour whose stimulus is a (conditioned) love stimulus, the response to which is rage', (e.g. stiffening of whole body, reddening of face, pronounced breathing, verbal recrimination and possibly shouting).

This is a good illustration of the *reductionist* nature of Watson's behaviourism (and of behaviourism in general), i.e. complex human emotions are broken down into (reduced to) simple CERs, a whole broken down into its constituent parts.

Along with this reductionist approach to the explanation of emotional development, Watson was proposing a *quantitative* view of development, i.e. as the child grows up, its behaviour becomes more complex, but is basically the same kind of behaviour as it was earlier (i.e. a series of CERs which become added and re-combined). The same basic principles are involved at all ages (those of classical conditioning). By contrast, a qualitative view (e.g. Freud, Piaget) sees development as passing through a series of distinct stages, with different kinds of behaviour involved at each stage.

3 The case of Little Albert seems to support the general belief that (even) babies are not indifferent to their experiences, and that nasty experiences, especially, may have peculiar after-effects (Walker, 1984). Here, Watson and Freud seem to be in agreement. However,

In my view, it would be foolish to claim that experiences as extreme as those suffered by Albert are not likely to have some carry-over effects in infants, but even more ridiculous to assume that conditioning is a sufficient explanation for all adult emotions. (Walker, 1984)

Exercises

1 How does the single-subject design relate to other kinds of experimental design?

2 According to Cornwell and Hobbs (1976), figure 22.1 below contains over 20 mistakes. How many can you spot?

Figure 22.1

The myth of little Albert

In the 1920s, J. B. Watson did a series of experiments with children showing how emotional responses can be conditioned and deconditioned. Watson's first subject was an eight month old orphan, Albert B, who happened to be fond of rabbits, rats, mice and other furry animals. He appeared to be a healthy, emotionally stable infant, afraid of nothing except loud sounds, which made him cry.

To establish a conditioned fear response in Albert, Watson selected a toy rabbit as a conditioned stimulus. Initially this rabbit evoked no fear in the child. Then the rabbit was displayed to Albert and, half a second or so later, Watson made a sudden loud noise (the unconditioned stimulus) by crashing metal plates together right beside Albert's head. This noise alarmed the infant and he began to cry. Thereafter the sight of the formerly friendly rabbit alone, without the loud noise, was sufficient to elicit crying – a conditioned fear response.

This fear response to the toy rabbit did not die away after a day or two, but continued. Moreover, it spread to other stimuli that bore a resemblance to the rabbit, such as a glove, a towel, a man's beard, a toy and a ball of wool.

Watson did not leave Albert with his conditioned fear. In the second part of the experiment, Alfred's fear response was deconditioned by pairing the rabbit with stimuli that had pleasant associations (such as mother, favourite dessert and so on). By presenting the rabbit at mealtimes, at a distance which Albert could tolerate without whimpering, it was possible to gradually move the animal closer without any open signs of fear in the child.

Eventually Albert was once more able to stretch out his hand to feel the rabbit, and the two were happily re-united.

---

3 What's another word for 'transfer' (of the CR to other, similar, stimuli)?

4 The CER did not transfer to Albert's building blocks. What feature of conditioning does this illustrate?

5 What are the other two basic phenomena involved in conditioning (in addition to your answers to 3 and 4 above)?

JILL HODGES AND BARBARA TIZARD (1989)

Social and family relationships of ex-institutional adolescents

Journal of Child Psychology and Psychiatry, Vol. 30 (1), pp. 77–97

[This is in fact one of two articles, by the above authors, which appeared in the same volume, reporting on different aspects of the same study. The Introduction section of the summary that follows contains some material from the companion article.]

A group of children raised in institutions and experiencing multiple-changing caregivers until at least two years of age, then adopted or restored to a biological parent, have been followed longitudinally into mid-adolescence. Such maternal deprivation did not necessarily prevent them forming strong and lasting attachments to parents once placed in families; but whether such attachments developed, depended on the family environment, being much more common in adopted children than in those restored to a biological parent. Both groups were, however, more oriented towards adult attention and had more difficulties with peers and fewer close relationships than matched comparison adolescents, indicating some long-term effects of their early institutional experiences.

Introduction

The classic studies of the effects of early institutionalization saw the ability to make deep relationships as particularly endangered. Bowlby (1951) and Goldfarb (1945) focused on maternal deprivation as the salient aspect of institutional care responsible for this effect. Goldfarb (1943a) found that children with early institutional experience were more emotionally withdrawn in early adolescence, even after years in a foster family, than children who had been in families throughout. He related their incapacity for deep human relationships to their early years when 'strong anchors to specific adults were not established'.

A follow-up study of institutional children has allowed a detailed look at some of these questions.

Earlier studies by Tizard and co-workers (Tizard & Joseph, 1970; Tizard & Tizard, 1971; Tizard and Rees, 1974; Tizard, 1977; Tizard & Hodges, 1978) followed a group of children who had experienced institutional care for the first years of their lives, most of whom were then adopted, fostered, or restored to their biological parents. The children received good physical care in the institutions, which also appeared to provide adequately for their cognitive development: by $4\frac{1}{2}$ years, the mean WPPSI [Wechsler Pre-School Primary Scale of Intelligence] score of the institution children was 105, and earlier signs of some language retardation were no longer evident. However, staff turnover, and an explicit policy against allowing too strong an attachment to develop between children and the nurses who looked after them, had given the children little opportunity to form close, continuous relationships with an adult. By the age of two, an average of 24 different caregivers had looked after them for at least a week; by age four, the average was 50. This seems to fit Bowlby's (1951) description of maternal deprivation as 'not uncommonly almost complete in institutions . . . where the child often has no one person who cares for him in a personal way and with whom he feels secure'. As a result, the children's attachment behaviour was very unusual. At two, they seemed to be attached to a large number of adults, i.e., they would run to be picked up when anyone familiar entered the room and cry when they left. At the same time, they were more fearful of strangers than a home-reared comparison group (Tizard & Tizard, 1971). By four, 70 per cent of these still in institutions were said by the staff 'not to care deeply about anyone' (Tizard & Rees, 1975). It seems likely that generally the children's first opportunity for a close, reciprocal, long-term attachment came when they left the institutions, and were placed in families, at ages ranging from two to seven years.

Although most formed attachments to their parents, the ex-institution children showed a number of atypical features in social development. At four, they were no longer shy of strangers. About a third were markedly attention-seeking and over-friendly to strangers, and a few were indiscriminately affectionate to all adults. Although these traits were shown only by a minority of the children they did set the ex-institution children off as a group from comparison, non-institution children.

The study is a form of natural experiment, with a fundamental change in the children's environment; usually children from a poor early environment have a poor later one too. This fundamental change allows us to see whether the early environment had a persisting influence, despite very different later experience, and also whether different types of later experience lead to different outcomes. These issues are clearly relevant to questions of child-care policy, especially which kind of placements seem to have the best outcome for the child, and whether adoption is a satisfactory placement option for children past infancy. According to BAAF (British Agencies for Adoption and Fostering) (1984), while the overall number of adoptions by people unrelated to the child has dropped considerably, the proportion of older children adopted has risen (37 per cent over three in 1983, 14 per cent in 1970). However, Bacon and Rowe (1978) found that adoption was still relatively rare for older children in residential care, and Hapgood (1984) suggests there is an unmet need for older child placement.

By eight, the majority of adopted children and some of the restored children had formed close attachments to their parents, despite their lack of early attachments in the institutions. The adoptive parents very much wanted a child, and put much time and energy into building up a relationship. The biological parents, by contrast, were more likely to be ambivalent about having the child back, and to have other children, plus material difficulties, competing for their attention. According to their parents, the ex-institutional children did not present more problems than a comparison group who had never been in care; but according to their teachers, more of them showed problems, notably attention-seeking behaviour, especially from adults, restlessness, disobedience and poor peer relationships; they were quarrelsome and unpopular (as they had been at four). Their earlier over-friendliness also persisted (Tizard & Hodges, 1978). These difficulties are very similar to those reported by Goldfarb (1943, 1945), but whereas he found many other problems in his ex-institutional group, including poorer cognitive and language skills, this was not the case with the present sample, presumably because the care offered in institutions has improved considerably since the 1940s.

So the present study indicated that, on the one hand, early institutional care and the lack of close attachments had not had the drastically damaging effects predicted by Bowlby (1951), but on the other hand there were indications that, despite more adequate institutional care, and despite in many cases the formation of deep and lasting attachments to parents once the children entered families, some of the children still showed lasting effects of their earlier institutional rearing. This raises two major questions:

1 How enduring are these effects of early experience? Could they be reversed after the age of eight? Given the degree to which ex-institutional children had 'normalized' within their families, it seemed possible that further time in the family would reduce still further the remaining effects of early institutional care. At age eight, the children had spent an approximate minimum of 25 per cent of their lives in institutions, reducing to 12 or 13 per cent by age 16. Do the remaining effects of early institutionalisation reduce similarly, or do they remain?

2 How satisfactory is the outcome for adopted children and families, especially compared with possible alternative placements? At age eight, the adoptive children were doing better in virtually every way than restored children, although still showing more difficulties than children who had never been in care (especially at school). Do adopted children continue to do relatively well? The National Child Development Study (Lambert & Streather, 1980) found that at 11, when their better home circumstances were taken into account, adopted children, as well as illegitimate children were less well-adjusted than legitimate children in similar home circumstances, and that the adjustment of the adopted group had apparently deteriorated relative to that of other

children between seven and 11. Further, adolescence is generally thought to be a time of particular potential stress for adopted children and adoptive families (Mackie, 1982), whether the adoption is seen as causing difficulties in itself (Schechter, 1960) or as complicating pre-existing difficulties and normal developmental tasks (Chess, 1953). This in itself would suggest that difficulties might increase rather than decrease during adolescence. To some extent, the same may apply to the small group of restored children, as many had become members of step-families, recognised as a source of difficulty for family members (Robinson, 1980).

However, other studies of adopted children placed in infancy suggests that their earlier difficulties might decrease with age. Bohman and Sigvardsson (1985) found this to be true up to 18, while restored and fostered children showed markedly more difficulties than the adopted group. Raynor (1981) supports the picture of a decrease in problems as adoptees grew older. During adolescence, peer group relationships become more important, and family relationships change as adolescents begin to move towards eventual independence from parents. Because of the ex-institution group's earlier difficulties with peers, it seemed important to look at how they were negotiating this adolescent task, and how far they had become able to form close relationships with peers, as well as deep attachments to parents.

For all these reasons it was decided to trace all the children who had been followed up until the age of eight and reassess them at age 16.

Attrition in the sample

Considerable difficulty was experienced in locating the children after eight years without contact, but eventually all were found. However, of the 51 children studied at age eight, nine were not available for study at age 16. These nine, added to the 14 unavailable after age four, mean that the losses over the 12 years (four to 16) amount to 35 per cent. (The NCD study similarly lost approximately one third of its sample by age 11.)

Whereabouts of adopted children

Of the 28 adopted children seen at age eight, 26 were still in their adoptive homes at age 16. A further child who had been adopted shortly before her tenth birthday was added to the group. Two placements had broken down between eight and 16 (one with new foster parents, one in local authority residential care), and neither of these children was included in the groups analysed for this article. A third adopted adolescent was seen in a residential psychiatric unit, but spent some weekends at home and was included in the adopted group.

The adopted group included three boys who were fostered when seen at age eight in what were intended as permanent placements, and were still in these families at 16. Since there was no possibility of the biological parent reclaiming the child, it was felt that psychologically, if not legally, they should be counted as adoptions.

Whereabouts of restored children

Twelve out of the 13 restored children seen at age eight were still with their parents at 16; the remaining one was currently in a secure unit for disturbed and delinquent adolescents but was included in the restored group. Three others had either spent time in residential units for young people with emotional/behavioural problems, or lived with friends after running away from home. But all three were back with their families.

Whereabouts of children in residential or foster care

Only one child had remained in residential care throughout until 16. The rest of those who had been in residential or temporary foster care at age eight had experienced many changes, but five were back in residential care at 16.

Numbers seen at 16

Altogether, 17 adopted boys and six adopted girls, six restored boys and five restored girls, three boys and two girls in institutional care were interviewed.

Stability of different types of placement between two and 16

A total of 33 children were placed in adoptive families after age two; information is provided about the stability of the placement for 24 of them. A total of 25 children were restored to biological parents after age two; information is provided about 16 of these. As many placements had broken down, at least temporarily, as had not; a much higher proportion than in the case of the adoptive placements. But the greatest amount of instability occurred in the institutional group.

Effects of attrition and changes in placement groups upon characteristics of sample

The adopted children unavailable for study at age eight had shown somewhat fewer problems of adjustment at age four, and the restored children somewhat more, than the average of their respective groups. The data do not suggest a systematic loss of children who, as eight year olds, presented fewer or more problems at home than those who remained and were studied at 16.

Comparison groups

A new, matched comparison group was formed to replace the one used in earlier stages of the study. This previous comparison group of 30

London working-class children was set up when the study children were in institutions at age two, and no longer seemed appropriate either for the primarily middle-class adopted group, or for the restored group who often lived in primarily disadvantaged homes. In addition, the majority of ex-institutional children were boys, while the former comparison group had been half boys and half girls.

A comparison 16 year old was found for each of the adopted and restored adolescents, matched on sex, one- or two-parent family, Registrar General's occupational classification of main breadwinner, and position in family. Any adolescent with a mental or physical handicap, or chronic illness, or who had spent longer than a few weeks away from their family in residential care or hospital at any age, was excluded from the comparison group. For logistical reasons, all the matched comparisons were drawn from the London area, while the study adolescents were scattered throughout the British Isles.

The matched comparisons were obtained via General Practitioner medical practices.

Fifty-three practices were approached: eight refused, 22 failed to respond. The final comparison group was obtained from 16 different practices; all families of 16 year olds in these practices were approached via a letter from the GP asking for cooperation in a study of adolescents and their families. About 30 per cent indicated that they did not wish to be contacted, and the final comparison group was selected from the remainder. A possible source of bias is that the 30 per cent included families with severe difficulties in childrearing.

An additional comparison group was used to assess information obtained from the schools; this comprised study children's same-sex classmate, nearest in age.

Assessment procedure

The study adolescents and their mothers (fathers too were occasionally present) or careworkers were interviewed by J. Hodges, and their matched comparisons by one of four other researchers, all experienced interviewers. It was not possible, practically, for the authors to interview all the study families themselves, so different groups of subjects were studied by different interviewers. However, this disadvantage is offset by the advantage of having the study families assessed by an interviewer already known to them: some families probably would have refused to be interviewed by a stranger.

Interviews were tape recorded with the permission of the adolescent or adult being interviewed. Each visit to the house or institution lasted several hours, and occasionally a second visit was needed to complete the assessment. The parent or careworker was interviewed, and also completed the 'A' scale questionnaire (Rutter, Tizard & Whitmore, 1970) on the adolescent's behaviour; the adolescent was interviewed and completed the 'Questionnaire on Social Difficulty' (Lindsay & Lindsay, 1982).

Permission was obtained from both the parents and adolescent to contact the school via a postal questionnaire, comprising the 'B' scale

(Rutter, 1967; Rutter *et al.*, 1970), used for comparison with the previous stage of the study, and a questionnaire, devised for the study, focusing on relationships with teachers and peers. Teachers were asked to complete one set for the study adolescent and one for the same-sex classmate next in age (forming the school comparison group).

Results

Relationships within the family

Attachments to parents   Figure 23.1 shows the proportion of adopted, restored and comparison children said by the mother to be attached to her at ages eight and 16, and also the proportion of those institutional children said to have a close attachment to an adult.

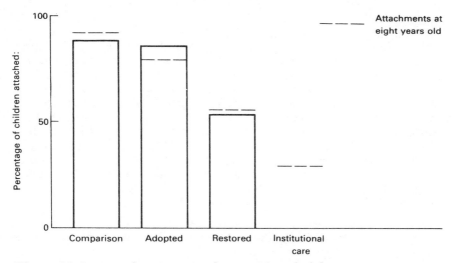

Figure 23.1   attachment to mother at 16 and eight years.

As at eight, the vast majority (17 out of 21) of the adoptive mothers felt that their child was deeply attached to them, and this was true for all their comparisons. Of the four mothers who felt that their child was not closely attached to them, at 16, one had taken the same view when the child was eight; at 16, the relationship seemed mutually rejecting and hostile. The other three had described their eight year old as closely attached but now doubted the strength of their attachment.

By contrast, only five out of nine restored children were described as deeply attached to their mother (the figure for age eight was six out of 13).

When asked if the child was easy to love, and whether the mother found any of her children easier to love than others, one out of seven of the mothers of restored adolescents who also had other children felt she loved each child equally (compared with six out of eight comparisons); five of the other six restored mothers preferred a sibling to the restored child. Nine out of 14 adoptive parents and 13 out of 16 of their comparisons felt they loved their children equally.

Adopted adolescents were more often said by their mothers to be attached to their father at 16 than the restored group ($p < 0.01$), who, in turn, differed similarly from their comparisons. No adopted or comparison adolescents were said to have become less attached to their father as they grew older, but two out of five restored adolescents were.

Relations with siblings   The comparison adolescents reported fewer marked problems with siblings than the ex-institution group as a whole ($p = 0.03$), and the mothers confirmed this ($p = 0.02$). The restored group got on particularly badly with their siblings, as they had at age eight.

Showing affection   At age eight, the adopted children and those still in institutional care were found to be the most affectionate and cuddly, with restored children strikingly the least cuddly. At 16, mothers were asked how easy it was to be affectionate to them, e.g. giving them a kiss or cuddle. As they grew older, ten out of 22 adopted children had become less demonstrative; as a group, they were not significantly more demonstratively affectionate at 16 then their matched comparisons. However, the restored group were still strikingly less affectionate; less than the adopted group ($p < 0.01$), and less than their own matched comparsions ($p < 0.01$). There was also a clear (but not significant) tendency for adoptive parents to find it easier to show affection to their adolescents than parents of restored adolescents. The difference was especially marked regarding the father (as perceived by the mothers); fathers of restored adolescents also showed affection less readily than their matched controls, and this, apparently, had also been true at eight.

Confiding and support   A majority of all the groups of mothers believed they knew when their son or daughter was upset, and the adolescents felt the same (see table 23.1).

Table 23.1   Issues relating to closeness with parents, confiding and support

	Adopted	Their comparisons	Restored	Their comparisons
Mother believes adolescent would confide over at least some anxieties	17 (85%)	19 (91%)	8 (80%)	8 (80%)
Mother feels she would realise if adolescent upset	16 (84%)	16 (76%)	5 (56%)	8 (80%)
Adolescent feels parent would realise if upset, at least sometimes	13 (65%)	15 (71%)	8 (80%)	6 (60%)
Parent feels adolescent would ask for support	13 (72%)	14 (67%)	7 (78%)	7 (70%)
Adolescent feels (s)he could ask for support	11 (58%)	12 (57%)	5 (51%)	6 (64%)

Though restored mothers were less certain than others, their children indicated no such doubts. Around 70 per cent of the adolescents would ask the mothers for support or advice over some – but not all – problems (according to the mothers), and over 50 per cent of the adolescents felt they would do so.

The adopted and restored groups did not differ greatly from their comparison groups in the proportion who would turn to a parent if they felt depressed or miserable. A higher proportion of adopted and restored adolescents than their comparisons would not confide in anyone, and fewer, at least of the adoptees, would confide in a peer.

Table 23.2 Adolescents' views: who would they confide in? (Based on a range of nine questions)

Confide in	Adopted	Their comparisons	Restored	Their comparisons
Nobody	28%	17%	23%	22%
Parent	44%	39%	43%	35%
Other family member	2%	5%	4%	1%
Outside adult	6%	5%	8%	6%
Peer	16%	30%	17%	33%
N/A (not worried)	3%	4%	5%	3%
(Total number of responses)	(177)	(191)	(96)	(89)

Table 23.2 shows answers to questions about who, if anyone, they would confide in if worried about a range of concerns, namely: (*i*) if they felt very miserable; (*ii*) if anxious about their appearance; (*iii*) if worried that something was wrong with them; (*iv*) if worried about not being liked by the opposite sex; (*v*) if they felt something was wrong with their body; (*vi*) if they were in severe financial difficulty; (*vii*) if they were unhappy over their boy/girlfriend; (*viii*) if they needed to know about contraception; (*ix*) if they became pregnant, or made someone pregnant, without wishing to. They tended to confide in different people depending on the particular anxiety, e.g. 75 to 80 per cent in all groups would turn to a parent over financial difficulty, but only one ex-institution and two comparison adolescents would do so if worried about not being liked by the opposite sex; instead, they would either keep it to themselves, deny it or share it with a peer. Table 23.2 shows a composite score based on pooled responses to all nine kinds of question.

The adopted and restored adolescents were at least as likely to turn to parents as comparisons were, who had always lived in their families, but were less likely to turn to their peers.

Disagreement over control and discipline   Both the adolescents and their mothers believed that disagreements over style of dress or hairstyle were very rare in all groups; disagreements over staying out late, doing homework, helping round the house and pocket money was significantly less frequent in adoptive families than in their comparisons, according to the parents ($p < 0.01$). However, comparison adolescents themselves reported fewer rows than ex-institution adolescents, especially in the case of the restored group ($p < 0.02$). Significantly more of the restored adolescents felt their parents were too strict, compared with their own comparisons ($p = 0.05$).

Peer relationships

Overall ratings Based on the mothers' answers to five open-ended exploratory questions, plus questions about specific difficulties, a rating was made of the adolescents' peer relationships over the last year. Another rating was made based on the interview with the 16 year olds who also completed a 46 item self-report questionnaire on social difficulty (Lindsay & Lindsay, 1982). The questionnaire sent to teachers also asked them to rate how popular the adolescents were with peers, compared with classmates.

Specific difficulties with peer relations Overall, the ex-institutional adolescents had poorer peer relationships than their comparisons. Six out of 30 of the former were definitely said to be 'friendly with anyone who's friendly towards him/her' as opposed to 'choosing his/her friends', another seven parents were uncertain if this was so. There were no differences regarding the number of contacts with same- or opposite-sex friends, or whether the 16 year old currently had a boy/girlfriend (with parents and the adolescents more or less agreeing on this). Ex-institution adolescents reported themselves less often than their matched comparisons as belonging to a 'crowd' of young people who generally went around together ($p < 0.02$), and this difference was significant between the adopted group and their matched comparisons ($p < 0.01$).

Teachers rated the ex-institution group as more often quarrelsome, less often liked by other children and as bullying other children more than the comparison group.

Special friends According to the mothers, the ex-institution adolescents were much less likely to have a definite special friend than their comparisons ($p < 0.002$) (11/31 compared with 24/31), but there was no difference between adopted and restored. Interviews with the adolescents showed a similar, but not significant, pattern.

Table 23.2 shows that fewer ex-institution adolescents said they would confide in peers on a range of issues; significant differences (compared with comparisons) were found for feeling miserable or unhappy (13 per cent vs. 43 per cent, $p < 0.01$), being worried something was wrong with them (3 per cent vs. 19 per cent, $p < 0.05$), and being concerned about contraception (14 per cent vs. 39 per cent, $p < 0.04$). These differences remained even allowing for the finding that the comparison groups were more likely to have a special friend.

Relationship between attachment and peer relations

Overall ratings of the adolescents' peer relationships were not related to attachment to the mother at 16. However, the ex-institution children, who at eight were described as closely attached to their mothers, had better peer relationships at 16 than those who were not attached at eight. Also, 16 year olds who were closely attached to the mother at 16 were less likely to be seen as 'friendly towards anyone who's friendly towards him/her' by peers.

Overfriendly behaviour Some institutional children at four, had been indiscriminately friendly towards adults; although this had become much less apparent by eight, it was still present in some children. Of the 11 16 year olds seen as 'overfriendly' at eight, two were still seen as exceptionally friendly, and keen to get attention from an adult (as were two not seen as 'overfriendly' at eight). However, their behaviour was socially acceptable, and did not worry the parent as it usually had done at eight.

Although there was no overall relationship between being 'overfriendly' at eight and friendliness towards strangers at 16, there was a clear tendency for 'overfriendliness' at eight to be associated with parents' rating at 16 that the adolescent was friendly with any peer who was friendly towards them, rather than choosing their friends.

Relationships to teachers

As eight year olds, the ex-institution children were seen by their teachers as trying more than most to get attention from teachers and from a stranger entering the room. Teachers saw these 16 year olds as still 'trying to get a lot of attention from adults', more often than the school comparison group ($p < 0.05$), but not significantly more than their matched comparisons. The restored 16 year olds were more often aggressive than the adopted ($p < 0.03$) and their matched ($p < 0.01$) and school comparisons ($p < 0.04$).

Discussion

There is an interesting asymmetry about the findings; while the whole ex-institutional group differs from the comparison adolescents in their peer relationships and with adults outside the family, only the restored group differs from comparisons in their family relationships.

The family relationships of most of the adopted 16 year olds seemed satisfactory, both for them and their parents, and differed little from non-adopted comparisons who had never been in care. In contrast, the restored group still suffered difficulties and poor family relationships much more often than either the adoptees or their own comparison group. They and their parents were less often attached to each other, and, where there were siblings, their mothers tended to prefer them to the restored child. Restored 16 year olds showed less affection to their parents than did any other groups (as they had when eight), and their parents, equally, found it difficult showing affection to them; they seemed to identify less with their parents and wanted less involvement in family discussions. Restored adolescents also had more difficulty with siblings than did adoptees, probably because the former had entered their families to find younger siblings already there; the problems remained at mid-adolescence.

Although good relationships were not universal in the adoptive families, these families differed very little from their comparison group, but contrasted greatly with the restored group. Early institutional care had not necessarily led to a later inability to form a close attachment to parents and to become as much a part of the family as any other child. Where the parent wanted the child, and put a lot into the relationship, attachments were encouraged to develop and the adoption was successful; where this was lacking, the adoption situation broke down. This also seems to account for the difference between the adopted and restored groups, and there is no evidence that differences in the children before family placement account for the adopted/restored differences (Tizard, 1977). The adoptive parents differed as a group from the restored parents; they had very much wanted a child, put a lot of time and energy into building a relationship with the child, were often ready to accept very dependent behaviour initially, while the restored parents tended to have fewer resources, more other children and had been more ambivalent about the child living with them, and often expected great independence from their young child (Tizard & Hodges, 1978).

In contrast, the two ex-institution groups showed very similar relationships to peers and adults outside the family. Although the indiscriminate 'overfriendliness' of some eight year olds no longer seemed a problem at 16, the ex-institution group was still more often oriented towards adult attention and approval than comparison adolescents; they were also more likely to have difficulties in peer relations, less likely to have a special friend or to see peers as a source of emotional support, and more likely to be friendly to any peer, rather than choosing their friends. Taking all these five characteristics together, ex-institution adolescents are very much more likely to show four to five of them than comparison adolescents. This suggests an ex-institution 'syndrome' which does not seem to be merely a reflection of general behavioural and emotional disturbance. However, it only occurs in half the group, and the behaviour characteristics are *differences* from the comparison group, not necessarily *difficulties*.

The pattern of differences resembled the picture when the children were eight. So is the 'syndrome' permanent and, if so, how will the adolescents be able to make close emotional attachments and sustain love relationships and marriage as they enter adulthood? How can we explain the findings?

(*i*) Could there be a class-related difference in the child-rearing practices of the families of the adopted and restored adolescents compared with their comparison groups? This seems unlikely, since the difference between the adopted and restored parents in their attitudes and child-rearing patterns was more striking than how the two ex-institution groups differed from their comparison groups. For example, adoptive parents spent more time playing with their children, involved in 'educative' pursuits with them, and involved them more in joint household activities than a middle-class comparison group, while the restored parents spent *less* time doing these things than a working class comparison group.

(*ii*) Lambert and Streather (1980) suggest that the relatively poorer adjustment of adoptees at 11, compared to non-adopted children, may have been based on the adoptive parents' uncertainty about their own reactions, which had communicated itself to the children and made relationships harder for them. If this applies to the present study, how could the uncertainty have operated to produce the differences found? (*iii*) Clarke and Clarke (1979) have suggested a transactional explanation. While the adoptive parents made great efforts to foster close attachments in their children, they did not put the same sort of effort into helping them get on with peers or teachers, so the difficulties remained in these areas. Furthermore, unlike the highly motivated parents, there was no reason for the ex-institution children's peers, or teachers and other non-family adults, to tolerate or make special efforts towards children who could not already relate reasonably well, or who were attention-seeking; such difficulties would thus be likely to be self-perpetuating.

(*iv*) Another possible transactional hypothesis puts more emphasis on the long-lasting impact of the early institutional experience on development, i.e. what the child has become able to elicit from the environment (rather than what it has to offer). The early insecurity of their relationships with the nurses (assessed at two by running to be picked up when staff entered the room and crying when they left) mirrored the rapid change of nurses who looked after them.

These findings seem to parallel those of La Fremiere and Sroufe (1985) and Waters *et al.* (1979), who view social relationships with peers as an aspect of development particularly vulnerable to difficulties in early attachment. Children who as infants had been seen as having secure attachments to their mother (assessed by Ainsworth's (1978) Strange Situation), managed peer relationships better at $3\frac{1}{2}$ and five than those who had not been securely attached. However, others (e.g. Kagan, 1984; Campos *et al.*, 1983) have proposed alternative interpretations of the link between strange situation behaviour and other behaviour, such as the effect of underlying temperamental variables and cultural influences on socialisation.

(*v*) A related hypothesis, which also stresses the direct impact of early experience on the child's development, invokes the concept of developmental delay. Anna Freud (1966) outlines a detailed 'developmental line', a sequence in which adequate development of the child's relation to parents forms a precondition for normal, later peer relationships and others outside the family. The ex-institution children had their first opportunity to develop these close, exclusive attachments at around an age when most children, in their families at birth, have already done so. They may continue to lag somewhat behind these children in the broadening of their social horizons beyond the family and the increase in the emotional importance of peers relative to parents. Some support for this comes in the findings that (a) close attachment to a parent at eight was related to good peer relationships at 16, while attachment at 16 was not so related; (b) close attachment at eight was more strongly linked than attachment at 16 to selectivity in choosing friends; (c) children described as 'solitary through choice' at eight, suggesting less peer involvement (and possibly more with parents) than is usual at that age, seemed to have the most satisfactory peer relationships at 16.

There is insufficient data to be able to choose between these theories; indeed, more than one may be needed to account for the findings.

In conclusion, the study suggests that children who are deprived of close and lasting attachments to adults in their first years of life can make such attachments later. But these do not arise automatically if the child is placed in a family, but depend on the adults concerned and how much they nurture such attachments. Yet despite these attachments, certain differences and difficulties in social relationships are found over 12 years after the child joined a family; these are not related to the kind of family, but seem to originate in the children's early institutional experience. Since they affect relationships with peers, as well as adults outside the family, they may have implications for the future adult relationships of these 16 year olds. Whether these differences are now permanent, or further modifiable, we do not know.

Commentary

Aim and nature

The article represents the latest in a series of reports on the development of a number of ex-institutional children who subsequently grew up in family situations, and who had been studied since the time they were still in institutions. This 'progress report' is characteristic (though not an inevitable feature) of longitudinal studies, in which the same group of subjects is followed up over a period of time, usually years (as opposed to a cross-sectional study, in which subjects of various ages are all studied at (approximately) the same point in time).

Like cross-cultural studies (see chapter 3), longitudinal (and cross-sectional) studies represent an overall approach. They are exclusively found in the area of developmental psychology, because they are ways of studying *change over time*. The actual collection of data is done, in the present case, through interviews, questionnaires, both with the subjects (adolescents) themselves and their parents and teachers. The authors also refer to it as a 'form of natural experiment', i.e. some change is, in the natural course of events, brought about (here the child's environment) (the independent variable) which can be studied for its effect on some aspect of the child's development (here, social relationships) (the dependent variable). Those children whose environment is changed are compared with (matched) controls whose environments have not changed, so this represents an independent-groups design. The independent variable has two main 'values' (adoption and restoration), and this allows the two ex-institution groups to be compared with each other (as well as with the comparison groups).

Just as importantly, since it is a longitudinal study, the children are being compared with themselves, i.e. how were the adolescents behaving at four and eight?

Context and background

The general context is that of the effect of early experience on later behaviour and development; more specifically, the effect of institutional upbringing on later attachments (both to adults and peers, within and outside the family).

Related to this are several questions, all interrelated, namely:

(*i*) If the later environment continues to be deprived, you would expect a continuation of deprived behaviour. But if the change in environment is sufficiently great, is there a corresponding change in behaviour?

(*ii*) Can early deprivation effects be reversed or at least modified?

(*iii*) Are some aspects of development (e.g. social/linguistic) more vulnerable than others?

(*iv*) Are there critical or sensitive periods for the development of behaviour?

According to Rutter (1989), over the last 30 years there have been major changes in how the developmental process has been conceptualized:

(*i*) During the 1950s, the dominant view was the consistency of personality and the lack of major changes after the first few years of life. Longitudinal studies (like those of Goldfarb, Spitz, etc) sought to chart this early stabilization of personality, and urged that maternal deprivation in infancy caused permanent and irreversible damage (Bowlby, 1951).

(*ii*) But longitudinal studies failed to show high stability over time, and the claims regarding maternal deprivation were severely criticized (e.g. Yarrow, 1961). It became clear that people changed a good deal over the course of development, and that the outcome of early adversities were quite diverse, with long-term affects heavily dependent on the nature of subsequent life experiences (Clarke & Clarke, 1976). Even markedly adverse experiences in infancy carry few risks for later development if the subsequent rearing environment is good (Rutter, 1981).

(*iii*) It was then argued that there is little consistency in psychological development; what there was depended on people's interpretation of their experiences (Kagan, 1984). Mischel (1968, 1969) challenged the very notion of personality traits, claiming that most behaviour is situation-specific.

(*iv*) In recent years, there has been a limited swing back to a rather complex mix of continuities and discontinuities. (Rutter, 1987a).

He then goes on to identify and discuss a number of principles and concepts of development directly related to (*iv*) above, including:

(*i*) A life-span perspective is necessary because homo sapiens is a social animal, and social development occurs relative to a person's interactions and transactions with the social environment (Erikson, 1963; Bronfenbrenner, 1979; Hinde, 1987; Hinde & Stevenson-Hinde, 1988). Key social experiences, such as marriage and childbearing, tend to happen after childhood, so social development needs to be studied into adult life.

(*ii*) The *timing*, as well as the nature, of experiences is likely to influence their impact. For example, very young infants are protected from separation experiences, because they are yet to develop strong attachments; older children are protected because they have learned to maintain relationships over time and space; toddlers are most at risk because attachments are just becoming established at that age, and therefore they lack the cognitive skills required to maintain a relationship during an absence (Rutter, 1981, 1987a). Again, experiences may be felt differently, and/or produce different societal responses if they arise at non-normative times, e.g. teenage pregnancy and difficulties in parenting (Hayes, 1987), early marriage and the increased risk of divorce (Otto, 1979), differences in effects between redundancy in middle life and retirement in old age (Warr, 1987) and the psychological consequences of unusually early puberty (Graham & Rutter, 1985).

(*iii*) Both continuities and discontinuities are to be expected (Hinde, 1988; Rutter, 1987a). The process of development is concerned with change, and it is not reasonable to suppose that the pattern will be set in early life. Physiological changes (e.g. puberty) and new experiences will both serve to shape psychological functioning. But also continuities will occur, because children carry with them the results of earlier learning and of earlier structural and functional change.

A major source of data regarding the whole continuity – discontinuity debate (especially in the context of adverse early experience) are studies of children who have (not through any intervention by the psychologist) experienced major changes (for the better) in their environments. The Hodges and Tizard longitudinal study is a major study of this kind.

Even more dramatic are studies of children who are discovered after having suffered severe and prolonged privation, the most famous cases including Anna (Davis, 1940, 1947), Isabelle (Mason, 1942), the Czech Twins (Koluchova, 1972, 1976), Genie (Curtiss, 1977), and Mary and Louise (Skuse, 1984). The first four cases are quite well known, the most recent (Skuse, 1984) much less so (e.g. see Clarke & Clarke 1976; Gross, 1987). In 1977, Mary, almost nine, was referred to the Children's Department at a large post-graduate teaching hospital. During the previous year she had shown increasingly disruptive behaviour in the small children's hospital where she had lived the previous six years with her sister Louise (14 months older). Their early lives were spent in a remarkably deprived environment, with a mentally-retarded and microcephalic mother, who may have also been schizophrenic. Upon their discovery by the Social Services, they were described as '. . . very strange creatures indeed'.

Aged $3\frac{1}{2}$ and $2\frac{1}{3}$ respectively, they took no notice of anything or anyone, except to scamper up and sniff strangers, grunting and snuffling like animals. Both still sucked dummies, and no attempt had been made to toilet train them (so they were still in nappies). Neither had any constructive play, but picked up objects, handled, smelt and felt them. Mary had no speech at all, and made no hearing responses; she made just a few high-pitched sounds. It later came to light that they had been tied on leashes to the bed, partly as a way their mother could ensure the flat stayed spotless, and partly to ensure they would not fall off the balcony. If they became too noisy or active, they were put onto a mattress and covered with a blanket. They were subsequently taken into care.

Louise made rapid progress in the children's home. With the help of regular speech therapy, her previous unintelligible speech began to resemble natural language. She began half time at local primary school when five years two months, then full time. She was disruptive at first, was easily frustrated and upset. But she was inquisitive, and soon settled in, growing to love school and soon making one special friend. At $5\frac{3}{4}$, her social skills were nine to 15 months below her age level, and she seemed pleasant, cooperative and friendly to all who had dealings with her. Over the next few years, her social and academic development proceeded in most respects far more rapidly than Mary's. She won the affection of the woman in charge of the children's home. Her cognitive functioning was at borderline level, and she was educated throughout at a normal school.

By contrast, Mary remained distant and aloof, lacking social responses, failing to initiate interactions with children and adults and having little to do with Louise. She barely responded to verbal/gestural commands; after a trial period she was judged unsuitable for speech therapy. Despite gradual progress in toilet training, she seemed unsuitable, at $4\frac{1}{2}$, for normal school. A year after entering care, she made her first spontaneous attempt to communicate and she started smiling socially. She showed excellent motor coordination, but often crawled instead of walking. At five years, two months, she joined the local ESN (M) school, where her main problem remained language: still no spontaneous speech at $5\frac{3}{4}$. At seven, she could no longer be tolerated by a local youth group or Brownies, and she was transferred to an Autistic Unit at seven years, five months. A year later she was speaking rather like a deaf child. She showed some remarkable abilities, e.g. jigsaw puzzles, and concentrated well during IQ testing. She seemed to understand all spoken instructions, was amicable, affectionate and made good eye-contact. But following a visit from Uncle Rupert (her father?) and an occasional home overnight visit, she regressed; her concentration faded, she became enuretic, showed rage for no obvious reason and became very aggressive, even violent, to others, property and herself. She ran away, and was moved to a unit for mentally retarded children within a psychiatric hospital.

What the cases of Louise and the others mentioned above demonstrate is that theories which stress the overriding importance of early experience for later growth (i.e. critical periods) are inadequate (Clarke, 1972). Adverse early life experiences may, but not necessarily, have serious lasting effects on development in some circumstances (Rutter, 1981). Individuals show much resilience to such events and circumstances, and there is no straightforward connection between cause and effect in most cases. Further, according to Skuse (1984), there is an increasing tendency to see the child as part of a social system in which they are in a mutually modifying relationship (Berger, 1973), with the mother no longer playing such a pivotal role. Materal deprivation is too general and heterogeneous, and its effects too varied to be of continuing value (Rutter, 1981).

> There is now a need to focus instead on the particularities of specific early experience in order to understand better the various mechanisms by which they operate.
>
> Not only must variation in outcome relate to the specific deprivations and distortions of early experience, but the vulnerability of the individual to such adversity will itself vary. (Skuse, 1984)

Skuse (1984) asks if there is a characteristic clinical picture of the victim of such deprivation upon discovery? And do certain aspects of development seem more vulnerable than others? Yes, there is a pattern: motor retardation, absent or very rudimentary vocal and symbolic language, grossly retarded perceptuomotor skills, poor emotional expression, lack of attachment behaviour and social withdrawal. (This combination is unlikely to be found in any other condition, except, perhaps, profound mental retardation and childhood autism.)

Language is undoubtedly the most vulnerable cognitive faculty; it was profoundly retarded at first in all cases (even where other features of mental development are apparently unaffected). By contrast, perceptuomotor skills are relatively resilient to lack of stimulation, as is gross motor development. The early combination of profound language deficit and apathy/withdrawal from social contact leads to special difficulties in developing a normal range and quality of relationships later on (as in Mary's case).

The evidence suggests that, if recovery of normal ability in a particular faculty is going to occur, rapid progress is the rule.

However, Mary's case suggests that further progress may be made several years after discovery, even in cases where the obstacles to success were thought to be genetic/congenital; she, (and Louise) received speech therapy soon after discovery, but this was abandoned with Mary due to poor progress. Her relative lack of social communication and language at age nine were reminiscent of autism. But four years later, a remarkable transformation had occurred; she had made tremendous progress in both areas and such autistic features vanished. Despite having been placed in a variety of children's homes over that period, she did receive some consistent, intensive speech therapy (Skuse, 1984). Most human characteristics (with the possible exception of language) are strongly 'canalized' (Scarr-Salapatek, 1976), and thus virtually resistant to obliteration by even the most dire early environments (Skuse, 1984).

Fortunately the evidence reviewed suggests that, in the absence of genetic or congenital abnormalities or a history of gross malnourishment, victims of such deprivation have an excellent prognosis. Some subtle deficits in social adjustment may persist. (Skuse, 1984)

What about long-term personality and social adjustment? As yet, there is little evidence on the adult status of such cases. But what there is is encouraging, e.g. Skeels (1966). Koluchova (1976) reported that at 14 (seven years after their discovery) the Czech twins had no psychopathological symptoms or eccentricities. In a personal communication to Clarke (Skuse, 1984), she reported that by 20, they had completed quite a demanding apprenticeship (in the maintenance of office machinery), were above average in intelligence, still had very good relationships with their foster mother and her relatives and their adopted sisters, and they had developed normal heterosexual relationships, both recently experiencing their first love affairs.

Evaluation

1 The Hodges and Tizard study is clearly an important contribution to this body of evidence, although the subjects are still only adolescents. If their major relationship difficulties are with peers, would we expect this to apply to heterosexual relationships as much as to same-sex friendships? We need to know whether the ex-institution adolescents will be able to form stable, long-term relationships (Erikson's intimacy vs. despair) and, in turn, be able to nurture children of their own (Generativity vs. Stagnation). Ideally, follow-up for another 20 to 30 years would need to be carried out.

2 The results strongly support the view that Bowlby greatly oversimplified the effects of early (de)privation by emphasizing the mother's role in a much wider-ranging and more complicated set of relationships and influences. A critical period for development (except arguably for language, but even here it seems doubtful, e.g. Mary) seems *not* to exist, though arguably a sensitive one does; the fact that even the adopted children were not 'unscathed' supports the view that the first $1\frac{1}{2}$ to two years is still the optimum time for the development of attachments (but not the *only* time).

3 Hodges and Tizard refer to their study as a kind of natural experiment. This inevitably raises the question as to how it was decided which children would be adopted and which restored to their biological parents. If it was because of certain characteristics of the children themselves (e.g. the adopted were seen as more socially responsive), wouldn't this spoil the logic of the 'experiment'? Hodges and Tizard in fact deny this (see *Discussion*).

4 One of the major problems associated with longitudinal studies is discussed in the study, namely attrition. Of the 51 ex-institution children studied at eight, nine were unavailable: two families of restored adolescents refused contact, as did four adoptive families (all these adolescents were still with their families). The remaining three consisted of one girl who had been in a foster family at eight, but disappeared in between being traced and interviewed, and another two who had left care after eight, one to parents abroad and one to adoptive parents who did not reply to the original letter. How representative of the original institution sample was the sample of 16 year olds? How much additional attrition could the researchers afford over, say, a further 20- to 30-year period? (Would this be within the researchers lifetime? We've discovered another problem with longitudinal studies!)

5 The data was collected mainly through interviews and questionnaires, and so can only be as reliable and/or valid as those methods are. Was there any independent way of checking the accuracy of the answers given? How objective can we be about our own children and parents and, indeed, ourselves? How objective could the teachers be, given that they knew which pupils were ex-institution children?

6 Reference is made to the Strange Situation. This is a way of studying attachments, devised by Ainsworth *et al.* (1971/78), which comprises a sequence of eight episodes in which the mother (and/or father) and a stranger come and go from the room, each episode lasting about three minutes. Trained observers record the child's attachment behaviour in the mother's presence, when she leaves and returns, how the child responds to the stranger, and how its play is affected throughout.

Exercises

1 Briefly describe three advantages and disadvantages of the longitudinal, compared with the cross-sectional, approach (*not* including the attrition of the sample in longitudinal studies).

2 Briefly describe two ways in which a natural experiment differs from a laboratory experiment.

3 Why was it thought necessary to form a new, matched comparison group for the study of the ex-institution adolescents, and who were they?

4 Why was it necessary at all to have a comparison group?

Analysis of a phobia in a five-year-old boy

Pelican Freud Library, Vol. 8, Case Histories 1 (1977)

[This, in fact, appears in three parts: Introduction, Case History and Analysis, and Discussion. The summary that follows is based on the Discussion, but includes material from the Case History and Analysis also.]

Part 1

My impression is that the picture of a child's sexual life presented in this observation of Little Hans agrees very well with the account I gave of it (basing my views upon psychonalaytic examinations of adults) in my *Three essays [on the Theory of Sexuality, 1905d]*. But before going into the details of this agreement, I must deal with two objections which will be raised against my making use of the present analysis for this purpose. The first objection is to the effect that Hans was not a normal child, but (as events – the illness itself, in fact – showed) had a predisposition to neurosis, and was a young 'degenerate'; it would be illegitimate, therefore, to apply to other normal children conclusions which might perhaps be true of him. I shall postpone consideration of this objection. According to the second, and more uncompromising, objection, an analysis of a child conducted by his father, who went to work instilled my *my* theoretical views and infected with *my* prejudices, must be entirely devoid of any objective worth. A child, it will be said, is necessarily highly suggestible, and in regard to no one, perhaps, more than to his own father; he will allow anything to be forced upon him, out of gratitude to his father for taking so much notice of him.

I do not share the view, which is at present fashionable, that assertions made by children are invariably arbitrary and untrustworthy. The arbitrary has no existence in mental life. The untrustworthiness of the assertions of grown-up people is due to the predominance of their prejudice. For the rest, even children do not lie without a reason. If we reject Little Han's statement root and branch, we should certainly be doing him a grave injustice. On the contrary, we can quite clearly distinguish from one another the occasions on which he was falsifying the facts or keeping them back under the compelling force of a resistance, the occasions on which, being undecided himself, he agreed with his father (so that what he said must not be taken as evidence), and the occasions on which, freed from every pressure, he burst into a flood of information about what was really going on inside him and about things which, until then, no one but himself had known. Statements made by adults offer no greater certainty. It is a regrettable fact that no account of a psychoanalysis can reproduce the impressions received by the analyst as he conducts it, and that a final sense of conviction can never be obtained from reading about it, but only from directly experiencing it. But this disability attaches in an equal degree to analyses of adults.

Little Hans is described by his parents as a cheerful, straightforward child, and so he should have been, considering the education given him by his parents, which consisted essentially in the omission of our usual educational sins. It was with the outbreak of illness and during the analysis that discrepancies began to make their appearance between what he said and what he thought; this was partly because unconscious material, which he was unable to master all at once, was forcing itself upon him, and partly because the content of his thoughts provoked reservations on account of his relation to his parents. It is my unbiased opinion that these difficulties, too, turned out no greater than in many analyses of adults.

It is true that, during the analysis, Hans had to be told many things that he could not say himself, that he had to be presented with thoughts which he had so far shown no signs of possessing, and that his attention had to be turned in the direction from which his father was expecting something to come. This detracts from the evidential value of the analysis, but the procedure is the same in every case. For a psychoanalysis is not an impartial scientific investigation, but a therapeutic measure. Its essence is not to prove anything, but merely to alter something. In a psychoanalysis, the physician always gives his patient the conscious anticipatory ideas by the help of which he is put in a position to recognise and to grasp the unconscious material. It is true that a child, on account of the small development of his intellectual systems, requires especially energetic assistance. And yet, even during the analysis, the small patient gives evidence of enough independence to acquit him upon the charge of 'suggestion'.

The first trait in Little Hans which can be regarded as part of his sexual life was a quite peculiarly lively interest in his 'widdler': an organ deriving its name from that one of its two functions which, scarcely the less important of the two, is not to be eluded in the nursery. This interest aroused in him the spirit of enquiry, and he thus discovered that the presence or absence of a widdler made it possible to differentiate between animate and inanimate objects. He assumed that all animate objects were like himself, and possessed this important bodily organ; he observed that it was present in the larger animals, suspected that this was so too in both his parents, and was not detered by the evidence of his own eyes from authenticating the fact in his new-born sister:

> A little later, Hans was watching his seven-day-old sister being given a bath. 'But her widdler's still quite small', he remarked; and then added, as though by way of consolation, 'When she grows up, it'll get bigger all right'.

One might also say that it would have been too shattering a blow to his *'Weltanschauung'* if he had had to make up his mind to forgo the presence of this organ in a being similar to him; it would have been as though it were being torn away from himself. It was probably on this account that a threat of his mother's which was concerned precisely with the loss of his widdler, was hastily dismissed from his thoughts, and only succeeded in making its effects apparent at a later period.

> When he was $3\frac{1}{2}$, his mother found him with his hand on his penis. She threatened him in these words: 'If you do that, I shall send for Dr. A. to cut off your widdler. And then what'll you widdle with?'
>
> Hans: 'With my bottom.'

The reason for his mother's intervention had been that he used to like giving himself feelings of pleasure by touching his member: the little boy had begun to practise the commonest – and most normal – form of auto-erotic sexual activity.

The pleasure which a person takes in his own sexual organ may become associated with scopophilia (or sexual pleasure in looking) in its active and passive forms, in a manner which has been very aptly described by Alfred Adler (1908) as 'confluence of instincts'. So Little Hans began to try to get a sight of other people's widdlers; his sexual curiosity developed, and at the same time he liked to exhibit his own widdler. One of his dreams, dating from the beginning of his period of repression, expressed a wish that one of his little girl friends should assist him in widdling, that is, that she should share the spectacle. The dream shows, therefore, that up until then, this wish had subsisted unrepressed, and later in formation confirmed the fact that he had been in the habit of gratifying it. The active side of his sexual scopophilia soon became associated in him with a definite theme. He repeatedly expressed both to his father and his mother his regret that he had never yet seen their widdlers, and it was probably the *need for making a comparison* which impelled him to do this. The ego is always the standard by which one measures the external world; one learns to understand it by means of a constant comparison with oneself. Hans had observed that large animals had widdlers that were correspondingly larger than his; he consequently suspected that the same was true of his parents, and was anxious to make sure of this. His mother, he thought, must certainly have a widdler 'like a horse'. He was then prepared with the comforting reflection that his widdler would grow with him. It was as though the child's wish to be bigger had been concentrated on his genitals.

Thus, in Little Hans' sexual constitution, the genital zone was from the outset the one among his erotogenic zones which afforded him the most intense pleasure. The only other similar pleasure of which he gave evidence was excretory pleasure, the pleasure attached to the orifices through which micturition and evacuation of the bowels are affected. In his final phantasy of bliss, with which his illness was overcome, he imagined he had children, whom he took to the WC, whom he made to widdle, whose behinds he wiped; for whom, in short, he did 'everything one can do with children'. It therefore seems impossible to avoid the assumption that, during the period when he himself had been looked after as an infant, these same performances had been the source of pleasurable sensations for him.

At this juncture, it is as well to emphasize at once the fact that, during his phobia, there was an unmistakable repression of these two, well-developed components of his sexual activity. He was ashamed of micturiting before other people, accused himself of putting his finger to his widdler, made efforts to give up masturbating, and showed disgust at 'lumf' and 'widdle', and everything that reminded him of them. In his fantasy of looking after his children, he undid this latter repression.

In his attitude towards his father and mother, Hans really was a little Oedipus who wanted to have his father 'out of the way', to get rid of him, so that he might be alone with his beautiful mother and sleep with her. This wish had originated during his summer holidays, when the alternating presence and absence of his father had drawn Hans' attention to the condition upon which depended the intimacy with his mother which he longed for. At that time the form taken by the wish had been merely that his father should 'go away', and at a later stage it became possible for his fear of being bitten by a white horse to attach itself directly into this form of the wish. But subsequently (probably not until they had moved back to Vienna, where his father's absences were no longer to be reckoned on), the wish had taken the form that his father should be *permanently* away, that he should be 'dead'. The fear which sprang from this death-wish against his father, and which may thus be said to have had a normal motive, formed the chief obstacle to the analysis.

The most important influence upon the course of Hans' psychosexual development was the birth of a baby sister when he was $3\frac{1}{2}$ years old. That event accentuated his relations to his parents, and gave him some insoluble problems to think about; and later, as he watched the way in which the infant was looked after, the memory traces of his own earliest experiences of pleasure were revived in him.

At five in the morning, labour began, and Hans' bed was moved into the next room. He woke up there at seven and, hearing his mother groaning, asked, 'Why's Mummy coughing?'. Then, after a pause, 'The stork's coming today for certain'. Naturally he has often been told during the last few days that the stork is going to bring a little girl or a little boy, and he quite rightly connected the unusual sounds of groaning with the stork's arrival.

He was then called into the bedroom. He did not look at his mother, however, but at the basins and other vessels, filled with blood and water, that were still standing about the room.

Pointing to the blood-stained bedpan, he observed in a surprised voice, 'But blood doesn't come out of *my* widdler'. Everything he says shows that he connects what is strange in the situation with the arrival of the stork. He meets everything he sees with a very suspicious and intent look, and *there can be no question that his first doubts about the stork have taken root.*

Hans is very jealous of the new arrival, and whenever anyone praises her, says she is a lovely baby and so on, he at once declares scornfully: 'But she's not got any teeth yet'. During the first few days, he was naturally put very much in the background. He was suddenly taken ill with a sore throat. In his fever he was heard saying: 'But I don't *want* a baby sister!'

Affection for his sister might come later, but his first attitude was hostility. From that time forward, fear that yet another baby might arrive found a place among his conscious thoughts. In the neurosis, his hostility, already suppressed, was represented by a special fear, a fear of the bath.

I asked him whether he was afraid and if so, of what.

Hans: Because of falling in.
I: But why were you never afraid when you had your bath in the little bath?
Hans: Why, I sat in that one. I couldn't lie down in it, it was too small.
I: When you went in a boat at Gmunden, weren't you afraid of falling into the water?
Hans: No, because I held on, so I couldn't fall in. It's only in the big bath that I'm afraid of falling in.
I: But Mummy baths you in it. Are you afraid of Mummy dropping you in the water?
Hans: I'm afraid of her letting go and my head going in.
I: But you know Mummy's fond of you and won't let go of you.
Hans: I only just thought it.
I: Why?
Hans: I don't know at all.
I: Perhaps it was because you'd been naughty and thought she didn't love you any more?
Hans: Yes.
I: When you were watching Mummy giving Hanna her bath, perhaps you wished she would let go of her so that Hanna should fall in?
Hans: Yes.

In the analysis he gave undisguised expression to his death-wish against his sister. His inner conscience did not consider this wish so wicked as the analagous one against his father, but it is clear that in his unconscious he treated both persons in the same way, because they both took his mummy away from him, and interfered with his being alone with her.

Part 2

One day, while Hans was in the street, he was seized with an attack of anxiety. He could not yet say what it was he was afraid of, but at the very beginning of this anxiety state, he betrayed to his father his motive for being ill; the gain from illness. He wanted to stay with his mother and to coax with her; his recollection that he had also been separated from her at the time of the baby's birth may also, as his father suggests, have contributed to his longing. It soon became evident that his anxiety was no longer reconvertible into longing; he was afraid even when his mother went with him. In the meantime, indications appeared of what it was to which his libido (now changed into anxiety) had become attached. He gave expression to the quite specific fear that a white horse would bite him.

In the early days of his illness, when the anxiety was at its highest pitch, he expressed a fear that 'the horse'll come into the room', and it was this that helped me so much towards understanding his condition.

The first thing we learn is that the outbreak of the anxiety state was by no means so sudden as appeared at first sight. A few days earlier the child had woken from an anxiety dream to the effect that his mother had gone away, and that now he had no mother to coax with.

But the beginnings of this psychological situation go back further still. During the preceding summer Hans had had similar moods of mingled longing and apprehension, in which he had said similar things, and at that time they had secured him the advantage of being taken by his mother into her bed. We may assume that since then Hans had been in a state of intensified sexual excitement, the object of which was his mother. The intensity of this excitement was shown by his two attempts at seducing his mother (the second of which occurred just before the outbreak of his anxiety).

Hans, $4\frac{1}{4}$. This morning Hans was given his usual daily bath by his mother, and afterwards dried and powdered. As his mother was powdering round his penis and taking care not to touch it, Hans said: 'Why don't you put your finger there?'

Mother: Because that would be priggish.
Hans: What's that? Priggish? Why?
Mother: Because it's not proper.
Hans (laughing): But it's great fun.

and he found an incidental channel of discharge for it by masturbating every evening, and in that way obtaining gratification.

We have already described the child's behaviour at the beginning of his anxiety, as well as the first content which he assigned to it, namely, that a *horse* would bit him. It was at this point that the first piece of therapy was interposed. His parents represented to him that his anxiety was the result of masturbation, and encouraged him to break himself of the habit. I took care that, when they spoke to him, great stress was laid upon his affection for his mother, for that was what he was trying to replace by his fear of horses. This first intervention brought a slight improvement, but the ground was soon lost again during a period of physical illness. Hans' condition remained unchanged. Soon afterwards, he traced back his fear of being bitten by a horse to an impression he had received at Gmunden. A father had addressed his child on her departure with these words of warning: 'Don't put your finger to the white horse or it'll bite you'. The words 'don't put your finger to', which Hans used in reporting this warning, resembled the form of words in which the warning against masturbation had been formed. It seemed at first, therefore, as though Hans' parents were right in supposing that what he was frightened of was his own masturbatory indulgence. But the whole nexus remained loose, and it seemed to be merely by chance that horses had become his bugbear.

I had expressed a suspicion that Hans' repressed wish might now be that he wanted at all costs to see his mother's widdler. As his behaviour to a new maid fitted in with this hypothesis, his father gave him his first piece of enlightenment, namely, that women have no widdlers. He reacted to this first effort at helping him by producing a fantasy that he had seen his mother showing her widdler. This fantasy, and a remark made by him in conversation to the effect that his widdler was 'fixed in, of course', allow us our first glimpse into the patient's unconscious mental processes. The fact was that the threat of castration made to him by his mother some 15 months earlier was now having a deferred effect upon him. For his fantasy that his mother was doing the same as he had done was intended to serve as a piece of self-justification; it was a protective or defensive fantasy.

Having partly mastered his castration complex, he was now able to communicate his wishes in regard to his mother. He did so, in what was still a distorted form, by means of the fantasy of the two giraffes.

Hans:	In the night there was a big giraffe in the room and a crumpled one, and the big one called out because I took the crumpled one away from it. Then it stopped calling out, and then I sat down on top of the crumpled one.
I (puzzled):	What? A crumpled giraffe? How was that?
Hans:	Yes. (*He quickly fetched a piece of paper, crumpled it up and said*:) It was crumpled like that.
I:	And you sat down on top of the crumpled giraffe? How? (*He again showed me by sitting down on the ground.*)
I:	Why did you come into our room?
Hans:	I don't know myself.
I:	Were you afraid?
Hans:	No, of course not.
I:	Did you dream about the giraffe?
Hans:	No, I didn't dream. I thought it. I thought it all. I'd woken up earlier.
I:	What can it mean: a crumpled giraffe? You know you can't squash a giraffe together like a piece of paper.

Hans:	Of course I know. I just thought it; of course there aren't any really and truly. The crumpled one was all lying on the floor, and I took it away – took hold of it with my hands.
I:	What? Can you take hold of a big giraffe like that with your hands?
Hans:	I took hold of the crumpled one with my hand.
I:	Where was the big one meanwhile?
Hans:	The big one just stood further off.
I:	What did you do with the crumpled one?
Hans:	I held it in my hand for a bit, till the big one had stopped calling out. And when the big one had stopped calling out, I sat down on top of it.
I:	Why did the big one call out?
Hans:	Because I'd taken away the little one from it.

His father recognised the fantasy as a reproduction of the bedroom scene which used to take place in the morning between the boy and his parents; and he quickly stripped the underlying wish of the disguise which it still wore. The boy's father and mother were the two giraffes.

The giraffe fantasy strengthened a conviction which had already begun to form in my mind when Hans expressed his fear that 'the horse'll come into the room', and I thought the right moment had now arrived for informing him that he was afraid of his father because he himself nourished jealous and hostile wishes against him. In telling him this, I had partly interpreted his fear of horses for him – the horse must be his father – whom he had good internal reasons for fearing. Certain details of which Hans had shown he was afraid, the black on horses' mouths and the things in front of their eyes (the moustaches and eyeglasses which are the privilege of a grown-up man), seemed to me to have been directly transposed from his father onto the horses.

By enlightening Hans on this subject, I had cleared away his most powerful resistance against allowing his unconscious thoughts to be made conscious, for his father was himself acting as his physician. The worst of the attack was now over, there was a plentiful flow of material; the little patient summoned up courage to describe the details of his phobia, and soon began to take an active share in the conduct of the analysis.

It was only then that we learnt what the objects and impressions were of which Hans was afraid. He was not only afraid of horses biting him – he was soon silent upon that point – but also of carts, of furniture vans, and of buses (their common quality being, as presently became clear, that they were all heavily loaded), of horses that started moving, of horses that looked big and heavy, and of horses that drove quickly. The meaning of these specifications was explained by Hans himself: he was afraid of horses *falling down*, and consequently incorporated in his phobia everything that seemed likely to facilitate their falling down.

It was at this stage of the analysis that he recalled the event, insignificant in itself, which immediately preceded the outbreak of the illness, and may no doubt be regarded as the precipitating cause of its outbreak. He went for a walk with his mother, and saw a bus horse fall down and kick about with its feet. This made a great impression on him. He was terrified, and thought the horse was dead; and from that time on he thought that all horses would fall down. His father pointed out to him that when he saw the horse fall down he must have thought of him, his father, and have wished that he might fall down in the same way and be dead. Hans did not dispute this interpretation, and a little while later he played a game consisting of biting his father, and so showed that he accepted the theory of his having identified his father with the horse he was afraid of. From that time forward, his behaviour to his father was unconstrained and fearless, and in fact a trifle overbearing. Nevertheless, his fear of horses persisted; nor was it yet clear through what chain of association the horse's falling down had stirred up his unconscious wishes.

Quite unexpectedly, and certainly without any prompting from his father, Hans now began to be occupied with the 'lumf' complex and to show disgust at things that reminded him of evacuating his bowels.

We learn that, formerly, Hans had been in the habit of insisting upon accompanying his mother to the WC, and that he had revived this custom with his friend Berta, at a time when she was filling his mother's place, until the fact became known and he was forbidden to do so. In the end, his father went into the lumf symbolism, and recognised that there was an analogy between a heavily loaded cart and a body loaded with faeces, between the way a cart drives out through a gateway and the way in which faeces leave the body, and so on.

Without any warning, as it were, Hans produced a new fantasy.

Later on, he began: 'Daddy, I thought something: *I was in the bath, and then the plumber came and unscrewed it. Then he took a big borer and stuck it into my stomach*'.

Henceforward, the material brought up in the analysis far outstripped our powers of understanding it. It was not until later that it was possible to guess that this was a remoulding of a *fantasy of procreation*, distorted by anxiety. The big bath of water, in which Hans imagined himself, was his mother's womb, the 'borer' which his father had, from the first, recognized as a penis, owed its mention to its connection with 'being born'. The interpretation that we are obliged to give to the fantasy will of course, sound very curious: 'With your big penis you "bored" me (i.e. "gave birth to me") and put me in my mother's womb'. For the moment, however, the fantasy eluded interpretation, and merely served Hans as a starting point from which to continue giving information.

Hans showed fear of being given a bath in the big bath, and this fear was once more a composite one. One part of it escaped us as yet, but the other part could at once be elucidated in connection with his baby sister having her bath. Hans confessed to having wished that his mother might drop the child while she was being given her bath, so that she should die. His own anxiety while he was having his bath was a fear of retribution for this evil wish, and of being punished by the same thing happening to him. Hans now left the subject of lumf, and passed on directly to that of his baby sister. We may well imagine what this juxtaposition signified – nothing less, in fact, than that little Hanna was a lumf herself – that all babies were lumfs, and were born like lumfs. We can now recognise that all furniture vans, drays and buses were only stork-box carts, and were only of interest to Hans as being symbolic representations of pregnancy, and that when a heavy or heavily loaded horse fell down, he can have seen in it only one thing: a childbirth, a delivery. Thus, the falling horse was not only his dying father, but also his mother in childbirth.

And at this point Hans gave us a surprise. He had noticed his mother's pregnancy and had, at any rate after the confinement, pieced the facts of the case together; without telling anyone, it is true, and perhaps without being able to tell anyone. All that could be seen at the time was that, immediately after the delivery, he had taken up an extremely sceptical attitude towards everything that might be supposed to point to the presence of the stork. *But that – in complete contradiction to his official speeches – he knew in his unconscious where the baby came from and where it had been before*, is proved beyond a show of doubt by the present analysis; indeed, this is perhaps its most unassailable feature.

The most cogent evidence of this is furnished by the fantasy of how Hanna had been with them at Gmunden the summer before her birth, of how she had travelled there with them, and of how she had been able to do far more then than she had a year later, after she had been born. All of this was intended as a revenge upon his father, against whom he harboured a grudge for having misled him with the stork fable. It was just as though he had meant to say: 'If you really thought I was as stupid as all that, and expected me to believe that the stork brought Hanna, then in return I expect *you* to accept *my* inventions as the truth'.

There are not many more mysteries ahead of us now. What remains are just such confirmations on Hans' part of analytical conclusions which our interpretations had already established. Another symptomatic act, happening as though by accident, involved a confession that he had wished his father dead, for, just at the moment his father was talking of this death-wish, Hans let a horse that he was playing with fall down; knocked it over in fact. Furthermore, he confirmed in so many words the hypothesis that heavily loaded carts represented his mother's pregnancy to him, and the horse's falling down was like having a baby.

We have already considered Hans' two concluding fantasies, with which his recovery was rounded off. One of them:

> *The plumber came, and first he took away my behind with a pair of pincers, and then gave me another, and then the same with my widdler.* He said: 'Let me see your behind!' and I had to turn round, and he took it away; and then he said: 'Let me see your widdler!'

Hans' father grasped the nature of this wishful fantasy, and did not hesitate a moment as to the only interpretation it could bear.

I: He gave you a *bigger* widdler and a *bigger* behind.
Hans: Yes.

I: Like Daddy's; because you'd like to be Daddy.
Hans: Yes, and I'd like to have a moustache like yours and hairs like yours (*he pointed to the hairs on my chest*).

This was not merely a repetition of the earlier fantasy concerning the plumber and the bath. The new one was a triumphant, wishful, fantasy, and with it, he overcame his fear of castration. His other fantasy:

April 30th. Seeing Hans playing with his imaginary children again. 'Hallo', I said to him, 'are your children still alive? You know quite well a boy can't have any children'.

Hans: I know. I was their Mummy before, *now I'm their Daddy*.
I: And who's the children's Mummy?
Hans: Why Mummy, and you're their *Grandaddy*.
I: So then you'd like to be as big as me and be married to Mummy, and then you'd like her to have children.
Hans: Yes, that's what I'd like, and then my Lainz Grandmummy, (my mother) will be their Grannie.

This did not merely exhaust the content of the unconscious complexes which had been stirred up by the sight of the falling horse and which had generated his anxiety. It also corrected that portion of those thoughts which was entirely unacceptable; for, instead of killing his father, it made him innocuous by promoting him to a marriage with Hans' grandmother. With this fantasy, both the illness and the analysis came to an appropriate end.

Commentary

Aim and nature

The study reports the findings of the psychoanalytic treatment of a five-year-old boy. In fact, the actual account of the analysis comprises the middle section of the report as a whole, the others being Introduction, in which a great deal of background information is provided, and Discussion. The preceding summary incorporates elements of all three sections. The kind of study being reported is a *case study*, sometimes referred to, misleadingly, I think, as a *case history*. The latter is really just the collection of background information as a necessary preliminary to the primary aim of the study, which is to understand and/or treat the 'subject' of the study. Most case studies take place in a *clinical* context, i.e. they are reports on attempts by doctors, psychiatrists, psychologists and others to help a patient who may have suffered some brain damage/injury, mental illness, etc. (This is not to be confused with the *clinical interview* as used by, for example, Piaget.) Interesting as it may be in itself, the case study is usually intended to throw light on the form of illness under investigation (in this case, phobia as a form of neurosis) or, in the case of brain-damaged patients, certain aspects of normal psychological functioning, (e.g. how memory works). The actual collection of data can take place in many ways, e.g. psychological testing, observation, experimentation, etc. In Freud's case (as in most case studies), there is no real distinction to be made between the case study as a form of helping and as a piece of scientific research. However, there is a major difference which Freud's critics have stressed, namely, the 'fact' that it is not possible to be 'objective' about the patient one is psychoanalyzing. We'll return to this theme in the *Evaluation* section.

Context and Background

Freud's work represents many things (often just referred to as 'psychoanalysis'). It is a theory of personality, personality development (hence, a theory of child development, including moral), a theory of motivation and dreams, as well as being an approach to the treatment of (certain kinds of) mental illness. It is useful to refer to all the theoretical aspects of his work as 'psychoanalytic theory', and to the form of psychotherapy which he created as 'psychoanalysis'.

The case of Little Hans is important, because of the claims Freud made for it, i.e. it confirms the Oedipal theory already set out in *Three Essays on the Theory of Sexuality* (1905). It also demonstrates Freud's explanation of the origin of phobias (in contrast with, say, the learning theory explanation) (see chapters 22 and 28).

Little Hans is also the only child patient which Freud reported on, and this assumes particular significance in the light of a standard criticism of Freud's theorizing, namely, that he built up a whole theory of *child development* around his almost exclusive treatment of *adult* patients.

Evaluation

1 Freud is aware of the methodological objections which could be raised to the fact that Hans was being analyzed by his father, who was a follower of Freud, and whose mother had been treated by Freud before her marriage to Hans' father, i.e. how could the father be objective in his observations and psychoanalyze someone with whom he was so emotionally involved? Also the child will be susceptible to his father's suggestions. Doesn't this immediately invalidate the case study as an *independent* confirmation of Freud's Oedipal theory? Freud himself seems to agree with this criticism by saying that Hans' father did have to put into words things Hans could not himself say, be presented with thoughts which he had not previously shown signs of possessing, etc. *But* (and this is perhaps the critical point), although this 'detracts from the evidential value of the analysis', the 'procedure is the same in every case' (i.e. with adult patients too). 'For a psychoanalysis is not an impartial scientific investigation, but a therapeutic measure. Its essence is not to prove anything but merely to alter something'.

This may meet the immediate criticism outlined above, but doesn't it at the same time condemn the whole of Freud's work to the realm of 'non-science', because his theories are all constructed on the basis of his work with neurotic patients? Isn't the consulting room his 'laboratory', his patients his 'subjects', what the patient says about him/herself (especially their childhood) the data?

2 This point is answered by Storr (1987), a leading popularizer of psychoanalytic theory and himself a trained psychoanalyst. He claims that, although some of the hypotheses of psychoanalytic theory can be tested scientifically (i.e. are refutable), this applies only to a minority; the majority are based on observations made in the course of psychoanalytic treatment, which cannot be regarded as a scientific procedure. Such observations are inevitably contaminated by the subjective experience and prejudice of the observer, however detached (s)he tries to be, and so cannot be regarded in the same light as observations made during, say, a chemistry or physics experiment. It is certainly possible, he goes on, to study human beings as if they were objects merely responding to the stimuli impinging on them (i.e. experimental psychology). But it is *not* possible to conduct psychoanalysis (or any form of psychotherapy) in this way.

So do we have to accept Storr's conclusion that psychoanalytic theory can never be thought of as scientific? One defence of Freud may be that to study people as objects responding to stimuli is not truly scientific, because that is not what people are actually like, and so to study them in this way is not only immoral but inaccurate. Perhaps Freud is much closer to treating people *as* people and, to that extent, perhaps more of a scientist than most experimental psychologists!

3 One of the most serious problems faced by much of Freud's theory in general, and Little Hans in particular, is that of *alternative explanations*. Is Freud's interpretation of Hans' phobia the only reasonable, feasible one?

Amongst those who offer alternative interpretations are two very eminent psychoanalysts, Erich Fromm and John Bowlby.

(a) According to Fromm (1970), Freud wanted to find support for the theory of sexuality based on adults by directly reviewing material drawn from a child. But are Hans' parents as positive in their behaviour towards Hans as Freud claims? Freud says that:

> His parents were both among my closest adherents, and they had agreed that, in bringing up their first child, they would use no more coercion than might be absolutely necessary for maintaining good behaviour. And, as the child developed into a cheerful, good natured and lively little boy, the experiment of letting him grow up and express himself without being intimidated went on satisfactorily.

He adds:

> Considering the education given by his parents, which consisted essentially in the omission of our usual educational sins, [undoubtedly they] were determined from the very beginning that he was neither to be laughed at nor bullied.

But what about the threat of castration from the mother, her threats not to come back, the lies they told (e.g. about the stork, and the mother telling Hans she too has a penis, which was confirmed by the father)?

According to Fromm, Freud has a 'blind spot'; he was a liberal, rather than a radical, critic of bourgeois society. He wanted to reduce and soften the degree of severity in educational methods, but he did not go so far as to criticize the basis of bourgeois society, namely the principle of force and threat. His original belief that his adult patients had all been victims of incest as children ('Seduction Theory') was later changed (to become the 'Oedipus and Electra Complexes') in line with this same, non-radical attitude, according to Fromm. Emphasizing the child's incestuous desires is a way of defending the parents, who are thereby absolved of their incestuous fantasies and the actions known to occur (e.g. weren't there cases of his mother actively seducing him?).

While Freud claims that the dread of castration came from 'very slight allusions', Fromm believes that there were clear, strong threats made by the mother!

Nor does the dream about the plumber necessarily suggest the fear of castration is focused on the father, nor even that it expresses fear of castration at all. It is at least as probable that the dream manifests Hans' desire to have a penis as large as his father's and to be able to exchange his small one for a larger one, i.e. the wish to be grown up (as opposed to a fear of castration). [But this seems to be the interpretation which

Hans' father actually provides!] Freud's extreme patriarchical attitude prevented him from conceiving that the woman *could* be the main cause of fear. Indeed:

> ... clinical observation amply proves that the most intense and pathogenic fears are indeed related to the mother; by comparison, the dread of the father is relatively insignificant. (Fromm, 1970)

It would seem that Hans needed his father to protect him from a menacing mother. Fromm believes that the successful outcome of the therapy was due not so much to the interpretations made of Hans' fear, as the protective role of the father and the 'super-father' (Freud). He believes the fear of horses has two origins; (*i*) fear of the mother (due to her castration threat) and (*ii*) fear of death (he had witnessed the funeral at Gmunden, and then later the fallen horse which he thought dead). To avoid both fears, he developed a fear of being bitten, which protects him both from horses and from experiencing both types of anxiety.

According to Freud, the boy's incestuous desire for the mother is 'endogenous', i.e. *not* the result of maternal seduction. But is it as intense, exclusive and spontaneous as Freud believed? Fromm points out that Hans' mother liked to have him in bed with her, and to take him with her to the bathroom. But Hans wanted to sleep with Mariedl*, and once said he prefers her company to his mother's.

Finally, Fromm suggests that, rather than being directed towards his father (as the Oedipus theory states), Hans' hostility is aimed at his mother (based on her castration threats, her 'treason' at giving birth to Hanna and his desire to be free from fixation on her).

Referring to a fantasy about a horse he took out of the stable:

Father: You took it out of the stables?
Hans: I took it out because I wanted to whip it.
Father: Which would you really like to beat? Mummy, Hanna or me?
Hans: Mummy.
Father: Why?
Hans: I should just like to beat her.
Father: When did you ever see someone beating their Mummy?
Hans: I've never seen anyone do it, never in all my life.
Father: And yet you'd just like to do it?
Hans: With a carpet-beater. (*His mother often threatened to beat him with it.*)

Fromm believes that Hans' yearning to take his father's place was *not* necessarily an expression of hate, or desire for the father's death, but of the universal tendency to want to be grown up and no longer subject to adult power. Indeed, there is much evidence of great warmth and friendship in their relationship.

Fromm concludes this way:

> Finally, this was a slight phobia, such as occurs in many children, and it would probably have disappeared by itself without any treatment, and without the father's support and interest.

(b) Bowlby's (1973) re-interpretation of Little Hans is, as you might expect, in terms of attachment theory. He asks whether Hans' anxiety about the availability of attachment figures played a larger part than Freud realized. Agreeing with Fromm, Bowlby argues that most of Hans' anxiety arose from threats by the mother to desert the family. The

---

* Mariedl was their landlord's 13-year-old daughter.

main evidence comes from (*i*) the sequence in which the symptoms developed and statements made by Hans himself; and (*ii*) evidence in the father's account that the mother was in the habit of using threats of an alarming kind to discipline Hans, including the threat to abandon him.

The symptoms did not come out of the blue; Hans had been upset throughout the preceding week. They began when Hans had woken up one morning in tears. Asked why he was crying he said to his mother:

> When I was asleep I thought you were gone, and I had no Mummy to coax with. ('coax' = cuddle)

Some days later, his nursemaid had taken him to a local park, as usual. But he started crying in the street, and asked to be taken home, so he could 'coax' with his mother. During that evening, he became very frightened and cried, demanding to stay with his mother. The next day, his mother, eager to find out what was wrong, took him to Schönbrunn, when the horse phobia was first noticed. But the week preceding the onset of the phobia was *not* the first time Hans had expressed fear his mother might disappear. Six months earlier, he made remarks such as:

> Suppose I was to have no Mummy. Suppose you were to go away.

When Hanna was born, Hans was kept away from his mother. The father states that Hans' 'present anxiety, which prevents him leaving the neighbourhood of the house, is in reality the longing for [his mother] which he felt then'.

Freud endorses this by describing Hans' 'enormously intensified affect' for his mother as 'the fundamental phenomenon in his condition'.

> Thus, both the sequence of events leading up to the phobia and Hans' own statements make it clear that, distinct from and preceding any fear of horses, Hans was afraid that his mother might go away and leave him. (Bowlby, 1973)

Did she actually threaten, implicitly or explicitly, to leave the family? She certainly does use rather alarming threats:

(*i*) To cut off his widdler.

(*ii*) A year later, when the phobia was first reported, she was still trying to break him of the habit (of masturbating). She 'warned him' not to touch his penis, but no details are given of the warning.

(*iii*) Three months later, Hans came into his father's bed one morning and told him:

> Hans: When you're away, I'm afraid you're not coming home.
> Father: And have I ever threatened you that I shan't come home?
> Hans: Not you, but Mummy. Mummy's told me she won't come back.
> Father: She said that because you were naughty.
> Hans: Yes.

(*iv*) Even the fear of being bitten by a horse is consistent with the view that fear of the mother's departure is the main source of anxiety. During the summer holiday of the previous year, Lizzi, a little girl staying in a neighbouring house, had gone away. The luggage was taken to the station in a cart pulled by a white horse. Lizzi's father was there and had warned her:

> Don't put your finger to the white horse or it'll bite you.

So, fear of being bitten was closely linked in Hans' mind to someone's departure. Table 24.1 summarizes the different interpretation of Freud and Bowlby.

4 There is a fascinating postscript to the case study (Freud, 1922), which tends to

Table 24.1 Differences of interpretation between Freud and Bowlby

Item	Freud	Bowlby
Hans' insistent desire to remain with mother	Expression of genitally sexual love for mother, having reached extreme 'pitch of intensity'	Anxious attachment ('separation anxiety')
Dreams that she had gone away and left him	Expression of fear of punishment for his incestuous wishes	Expression of fear that she'd carry out threat to desert the family
White horse will bite	Wish that father would go away	Fear of her desertion
Mother's displays of affection and allowing him to come into her bed	Action which might have encouraged Hans' oedipal wishes	Natural and comforting expression of motherly feeling

support various aspects of both Fromm and Bowlby's interpretation. He lost touch with Hans after 1911.

> The publication of this first analysis of a child had caused a great stir and even greater indignation, and a most evil future had been foretold for the poor little boy, because he had been 'robbed of his innocence' at such a tender age and had been made the victim of psychoanalysis.
>
> But none of these apprehensions had come true. Little Hans was now a strapping youth of 19. He declared that he was perfectly well, and suffered from no troubles or inhibitions. Not only had he come through his puberty without any damage, but his emotional life had successfully undergone one of the severest of ordeals. His parents had been divorced, and each of them had married again. In consequence of this, he lived by himself, but he was on good terms with both of his parents, and only regretted that, as a result of the breaking-up of the family, he had been separated from the younger sister he was so fond of.

It seemed that he had gone with his father, when the parents first split up. When he heard his case history, he failed to recognize himself; he could remember nothing. The analysis had not preserved the events from amnesia, but had been overtaken by amnesia itself.

Exercises

1 Why is the case study considered to be the least scientific of all empirical methods used by psychologists?

2 Quite apart from any of your answers to **1**, is there anything about the case of Little Hans which makes it less scientific than it might otherwise have been?

3 The kind of data Freud presents is *qualitative*. What is the difference between this and *quantitative* data?

4 Is it possible – or necessary – to choose between Freud's, Fromm's and Bowlby's interpretations? Can they all be (partially) true?

JUDITH SAMUEL AND PETER BRYANT (1984)

Asking only one question in the conservation experiment

Journal of Child Psychology and Psychiatry, Vol. 25, No. 2, pp. 315–18

Introduction

It is often claimed that young children do not understand the principle of the invariance of quantity. This conclusion is based on the results of the well-known conservation experiments by Piaget and Szeminska (1952), which apparently show that children below seven or eight often wrongly treat a perceptual change as a real one, e.g. simply lengthening a row of counters or squashing balls of plasticine seems to change the child's judgements about their number or volume respectively.

However, one cannot be certain about this conclusion. As Donaldson (1978, 1982) has pointed out, the experimenter might unwittingly force children to produce wrong answers against their better judgement. One of the most powerful empirical demonstrations of the justice of Donaldson's criticism was provided by Rose and Blank (1974). They varied the traditional number conservation experiment slightly by asking one question rather than two. The usual procedure is first to show the child two identical rows of counters side-by-side, and ask him/her whether they are the same number (pre-transformation question) (the answer almost invariably is 'yes'), and then to lengthen or shorten one of the rows and ask the same question once again (post-transformation question). Rose and Blank's variation was to drop the pre-transformation question and to only ask the child to compare the rows after the transformation, a manoeuvre which had a significant effect: children who failed the traditional task often succeeded when one question only was asked.

The result suggests that young children often fail the traditional task for a reason which is quite different to the one suggested by Piaget. Instead, the child may think that the experimenter asks the question the second time because he wants another answer. If this is so, the child's error in the conservation task has nothing to do with the transformation (and, therefore, with the principle of invariance), but is simply a misinterpretation of what the experimenter wants to hear.

Thus the experiment is an extremely important one, but it is also limited: it deals only with number, and involves only one age-group, six-year-old children. We badly need to know whether younger and older children are affected in the same way by being asked one question only, and also whether other versions of the conservation task will produce the same pattern of results.

Method

Subjects

In all, 252 boys and girls between the ages of five and $8\frac{1}{2}$ took part in this experiment. They were all in schools and playgroups in and around Crediton, Devon. They were divided into four age groups of 63 children, whose mean ages were five years three months, six years three months, seven years three months and eight years three months. Each group was divided into three subgroups, which were closely matched in age.

Design and procedure

Subgroups and conditions The groups were divided into three subgroups of equal mean age, and each subgroup underwent a different condition. The three conditions were:

(*i*) standard: the traditional two question conservation task;
(*ii*) one judgement: the conservation task with only one question asked, the post-transformation;
(*iii*) fixed-array control: the child saw no transformation being made but only saw the post-transformation display. The purpose of this third condition was to check that children who answered the post-transformation correctly in the other two conditions did so by bringing over information from the pre-transformation display.

Material Three kinds of material were used in different trials. These were:

(a) *Mass*, in which condition (i) and (ii) children were first shown two equal and identical Playdoh cylinders or two similar but unequal cylinder shapes, one longer than the other; the transformation was to squash one of these into a sausage or a pancake. After this, the children were asked to compare the cylinder and the pancake (or the cylinder and the sausage). The condition (iii) children also made this comparison without seeing the first display or the transformation.
(b) *Number*, in which the children in conditions (i) and (ii) were shown two rows of counters of equal length arranged side-by-side in one-to-one correspondence. The rows contained either six and six counters or six and five counters. Then one row was spread out or bunched up. The condition (iii) saw only the post-transformation displays.
(c) *Volume*, in which the children in conditions (i) and (ii), were first shown two identical glasses, either with the same or with different

amounts of liquid. Then the liquid from one glass was poured into a narrower one or a shallow wider one.

Trials Each child was given four trials with each kind of material, two with equal and two with unequal quantities. The order of these trials, and the order in which the three types of material were introduced, were systematically varied between children.

Results

No systematic difference between equal and unequal quantity trials was found, so the results were pooled for the two types of trial.

The results are presented in tables 25.1 and 25.2. They show the reliability and generality of Rose and Blank's experimental results. The one-judgement task (Rose and Blank's task) was typically easier than the standard conservation task and the fixed-array control. This seems to be generally true of all three types of material and of all four levels. Table 25.1 shows that there are few exceptions to this general pattern, and the statistics suggest that these are chance variations.

A mixed-design analysis of variance was used, in which the main terms were age groups (five, six, seven and eight year olds), conditions (standard, one judgement, fixed array), and material (mass, number, volume); the last variable was a repeated measure. This analysis produced significant age differences $(d.f.3,240, F = 44.53, p < 0.001)$; conditions differences $(d.f.2,240, F = 8.64, p < 0.001)$ and materials differences $(d.f.2,480, F = 25.35, p < 0.001)$. There were no significant interactions.

Subsequent Newman-Keuls tests showed the following facts about these differences:

(i) age: there was a significant difference between every age group,

Table 25.1 Mean errors (out of four) in the three conditions and with the three types of material

Age (Yr.)	Material	Standard	One judgement	Fixed array
	Mass	2.762 (1.109)*	2.095 (1.444)	2.524 (0.906)
5	Number	2.524 (1.622)	2.095 (1.540)	2.619 (1.463)
	Volume	3.238 (1.191)	3.048 (1.290)	3.286 (0.825)
	Mass	1.571 (1.247)	1.286 (1.350)	2.143 (1.082)
6	Number	1.809 (1.468)	1.381 (1.759)	1.476 (1.367)
	Volume	2.286 (1.694)	1.667 (1.522)	2.762 (1.230)
	Mass	0.952 (1.430)	1.000 (1.414)	1.286 (0.983)
7	Number	1.143 (1.424)	0.381 (0.844)	1.429 (1.620)
	Volume	1.143 (1.582)	1.000 (1.414)	2.238 (1.151)
	Mass	0.667 (1.321)	0.381 (0.844)	0.905 (0.868)
8	Number	0.429 (0.791)	0.238 (0.610)	0.619 (0.844)
	Volume	0.571 (1.218)	0.667 (1.321)	1.714 (1.314)

* Figures in brackets are standard deviations

Table 25.2 *Mean errors summed across materials (A) and age (B)*

	Standard	One judgement	Fixed array
(A) The three conditions and four age groups summed across materials (mean errors out of 12)			
5 yr	8.524 (2.805)*	7.333 (3.427)	8.571 (2.083)
6 yr	5.714 (3.6214)	4.333 (4.075)	6.381 (2.149)
7 yr	3.238 (3.766)	2.571 (3.646)	4.857 (2.965)
8 yr	1.667 (2.494)	1.333 (1.755)	3.333 (2.055)
(B) The three conditions and mass, number and volume summed across age (mean errors out of four)			
Mass	1.512 (1.516)	1.190 (1.427)	1.714 (1.160)
Number	1.476 (1.570)	1.024 (1.488)	1.536 (1.531)
Volume	1.810 (1.769)	1.595 (1.663)	2.500 (1.286)

* Figures in brackets are standard deviations.

and the ordering was quite regular, the older groups doing consistently better than the younger.

(*ii*) conditions: the one-judgement task was significantly easier than the other two tasks (Rose and Blank's result). The standard task was also significantly easier than the fixed-array task.

(*iii*) materials: the number task was significantly easier than the mass and the volume tasks. Thus, despite overall differences in the skills of the four groups and in the difficulty posed by the three types of material, Rose and Blank's result held good. Children who failed the traditional conservation task nevertheless succeeded more often when only one question was asked.

Discussion

The consistent superiority of the one-question condition leads inexorably to one conclusion; children who fail the traditional conservation task often do understand the principle of invariance, and make their mistakes for a quite extraneous reason, this being that the experimenter's repetition of the same question about the same material makes them think that they must change their answer the second time.

Any other explanation seems far fetched. The children must have been using their knowledge of invariance when they solved the one-judgement task, because they carried over information from the pre-transformation display, and to do so, they must have realised that nothing had changed. How do we know they carried over this information? Because they did much better than the fixed-array children who never saw the first display. All in all, it does seem that the repetitive questioning of the traditional conservation experiment actively misleads the child.

Once again, as in many other cognitive experiments (Bryant, 1982a,b), we must conclude that the important question is not whether a child possesses an intellectual skill, but how and when he decides to apply that skill. Young children, it seems, often do use the principles of invariance, unless experimenters unwittingly persuade them not to.

Summary

Rose and Blank have shown that six-year-old children do a great deal better in a conservation-of-number task if they are only asked to make a comparison after the transformation, rather than both before and after seeing the quantity transformed. The present experiment shows that this important result also applies to other materials (mass and volume), and to a wide age range (five to eight years).

Commentary

Aim and nature

The study is a partial replication of an earlier study by Rose and Blank, in which only the post-transformation question in Piaget's conservation experiment was asked. While Rose and Blank used only six year olds to study number conservation, Samuel and Bryant used five, six, seven and eight year olds to study conservation of mass (or substance) and volume, as well as number. So the latter is on a much larger scale and far more wide ranging than the former. It also represents quite a complex experimental design; as well as the manipulation of the form of the task (standard (Piaget) or one-judgement), (*i*) there is a control condition (fixed-array); (*ii*) age is an additional independent variable (though not a manipulated one); and (*iii*) there is a mixed design, such that the four age groups, of course, constitute independent samples, with each being randomly split into three (corresponding to (i) and (ii) above), and within each of these conditions, subjects are tested on all three types of conservation (i.e. repeated measures). To the extent that age is an independent variable that is selected for, rather than actually manipulated, that part of the study is not a true experiment, but a quasi-experiment.

Background and context

The ability to conserve represents one of the major landmarks within Piaget's theory of cognitive development; it marks the end of pre-operational and the beginning of operational thought (at about seven), a major qualitative shift from non-logical to logical thought, albeit still tied to actual, concrete situations.

Piaget's conservation experiments are probably his most famous, and have been replicated many times with important modifications, like that of Rose and Blank (1974). Significantly, when their six year olds were re-tested on the standard form of the task a week later, they made fewer errors (than the controls who had been tested originally on the standard form).

Another alternative to Piaget's method was the famous 'Naughty Teddy' experiment (McGarrigle & Donaldson, 1974). It procedes in the normal way up to the point where the child agrees that there is an equal number of counters in the two rows. Then 'Naughty Teddy' emerges from a hiding place and sweeps over one of the rows and disarranges it, so that the one-to-one correspondence is disrupted. The child is invited to put Teddy back in his box and the questioning resumes: 'Now, where were we? Ah, yes, is the number in this row the same as the number in that row?' and so on.

Fifty out of 80 four to six year olds conserved, compared with 13 out of 80 tested using the standard form. According to Piaget, it should not matter *who* re-arranges the counters (or *how* this happens), but it seems to be relevant to the child.

However, Light *et al.* (1979) criticized 'Naughty Teddy' on the grounds that the children were, non-verbally and unwittingly, being instructed to 'ignore the rearrangement', so in a sense the task itself may be 'lost', i.e. they may have been so intent on Naughty Teddy's antics and putting him back in his box etc. that they did not actually notice the perceptual transformation.

A way of testing this hypothesis was designed by Moore and Frye (1986). They distinguished between an *irrelevant* perceptual change (which is what the traditional conservation procedure involves, i.e. nothing is added/subtracted) and a relevant one (something is actually added/subtracted). They predicted that if Naughty Teddy is, in fact, distracting, then children should do worse when a relevant change occurs, and better when an irrelevant change occurs. This is, indeed, what they found, thus supporting the criticism of Light *et al.* and so, indirectly, supporting Piaget.

The present experiment represents one in a long line of studies which challenge Piaget's conclusions regarding conservation through criticizing his *methods*; the common feature of these studies seems to be to look at the conditions under which children will display their ability to conserve, rather than whether or not they can conserve at all!

Evaluation

1 As indicated earlier, the study represents a great advance on the Rose and Blank study, because it involves four age-groups (five, six, seven and eight year olds), three conditions of testing (standard, one judgement and fixed array) and three kinds of conservation task (mass, number and volume). Thus there were three independent variables with age being selected for (rather than manipulated), with the dependent variable being success on the conservation task. Where there is more than one independent variable, the design is referred to as a *factorial* design $(4 \times 3 \times 3 =$ four age-groups $\times$ three conditions $\times$ three conservation tasks), and the appropriate test is the *Analysis of Variance* (ANOVA) test. This is one of the must useful and versatile of all statistics used in psychology today (Solso & Johnson, 1989). It is a parametric test which calculates from the scores, the proportion of total variance due to each of the independent variables and the interactions between them, plus the proportion due to all other variables (error variance). These are known as F ratios ($F =$ the ANOVA statistic symbol). This produced significant age, condition and materials differences, but no significant interaction. Note that the experimental design was mixed with age and conditions, constituting an independent-groups (unrelated) design), and the materials constituting a repeated-measures (related) design; just like the parametric *t*-test, there are ANOVAs for related and unrelated designs.

What about the Newman-Keuls tests which were used after the ANOVAs? It is probably the most commonly used post-ANOVA test, a necessary next step used to test for significant differences between the items of each main term, e.g. not only did age contribute significantly to the overall variance in the scores (along with conditions and materials), but eight year olds did significantly better than seven year olds, who did significantly better than six year olds and so on. This analysis found the one-judgement task to be significantly easier than the other two tasks (confirming Rose and Blank's results), and the number conservation to be significantly easier than the mass and volume tasks. This last finding is interesting, because it seems to support Piaget's concept of horizontal décalage; conservation does not appear all in one go during the concrete operational stage, but in an invariant order during the stage (e.g. number and liquid quantity: six to seven years; substance (or mass) and length: seven to eight years; weight: eight to ten years; volume: 11 to 12 years). (Note that what Samuel and Bryant call volume is more accurately called liquid/continuous quantity: volume was tested by Piaget through *displacement* of liquid.)

2 A more recent, partial replication of the Samuel and Bryant experiment was carried out by Porpodas (1987). Using six- and seven-year-old Greek children, he used the three same conditions as Samuel and Bryant, plus volume and number conservation, and the results by and large confirmed those of both Samuel and Bryant and Rose and Blank.

But Porpodas was also interested in testing the *explanation* given by those investigators, namely the 'extraneous reason hypothesis' (i.e. the traditional two-question task may unwittingly force the child to give the wrong answer by essentially asking the same question twice). The superior performance of subjects in the one-question condition compared with the fixed-array children seems to indicate that they carry over information from the pre-transformation display, i.e. they use their working or short-term memory (STM) to help them realize nothing changes when the transformation is made. This suggests that in the traditional Piagetian task, the child's failure may be due to interference in its STM due to the experimenter talking to the child when (s)he asks the first (pre-transformation) questions. If this hypothesis is correct, then children's difficulty in carrying over information from the pre-transformational display should be observed, even in the one-question condition, if something interferes with the child's STM.

Accordingly, Porpodas tested a different sample of 186 boys and girls, six and seven year olds, who were tested under one of three conditions: (*i*) traditional; (*ii*) one question and (*iii*) one question with interference, again using number and volume conservation. In the latter, *E* started a short discussion with the child (irrelevant to the task), during which *E* performed the transformation in full view of the child, but without referring to it in any way. Children of both age groups under this condition did worse than children under both (i) and (ii) for both number and volume, but significantly more so for the six year olds on volume and seven year olds with number.

Porpodas concludes from his findings that asking one question does not guarantee the child will reveal its understanding of the principle of invariance (so that it will conserve). What is mainly needed is the uninterrupted functioning of the child's STM (which the traditional form of the task prevents!). So this explanation is an *additional* one to the 'extraneous reason' explanation for failure in the Piagetian task, not an alternative to it.

Exercises

1 In relation to the order in which each child was tested with the three types of material, Samuel and Bryant say that these were 'systematically varied' between children.

(*i*) What's another term for 'systematically varied?'
(*ii*) Why was this necessary?
(*iii*) How might this have been done?

2 Why was the fixed-array condition used?

W. DEWI REES (1971)

The Hallucinations of Widowhood

British Medical Journal, 4, pp. 37–41

227 widows and 66 widowers were interviewed to determine the extent to which they had hallucinatory experiences of their dead spouse. The people interviewed formed 80.7 per cent of all widowed people resident within a defined area in mid-Wales, and 94.2 per cent of those suitable through the absence of incapacitating illness, for interview.

Almost half the people interviewed had hallucinations or illusions of the dead spouse. The proportion of men and women who had these experiences was similar. The hallucinations often lasted many years, but were most common during the first ten years of widowhood. Social isolation did not affect the incidence of hallucination, nor was it related to the incidence of known, depressive illness. There was no variation within cultural groups, or with place of residence, whether this was within town, country or village, or within England and Wales.

Young people were less likely to hallucinate than those widowed after the age of 40. The incidence of hallucination increased with length of marriage, and was particularly associated with a happy marriage and parenthood. Members of the 'professional and managerial' group were particularly likely to hallucinate, while widows of 'non-manual and sales workers' were the ones least likely. The incidence was greater with hysteroid than obsessoid people. It was unusual for the hallucinations to have been disclosed, even to close friends or relatives.

These hallucinations are considered to be normal and helpful accompaniments of widowhood.

Introduction

The extent to which widowed people experience hallucinations and illusions of their dead spouse had not been previously investigated, so it seemed worthwhile to determine its incidence.

Method

The intention was to interview all widowed people resident within a defined area in mid-Wales, centred on Llanidloes, where, with few exceptions, all residents are patients of one group practice. It has about 7,500 patients, and of these about 5,200 live in the survey area. The age and sex distribution of this survey group has been reported by Rees and Lutkins (1967).

The identity of most widowed people in the area was already known, but a further check was made with the aid of the practice secretaries who had lived in the area for many years, district nurses and local clergy. It was found that 363 widowed people resided in the area. Because of serious physical or mental defects, 52 were considered unfit for interview and were excluded from the sample. The age and sex distribution of those excluded from and included in the sample is given in table 26.1, while the reasons for exclusion are given in table 26.2. Most of the people excluded were aged 80 or over, and 25 per cent of those excluded died during the course of the survey.

Out of 311 people considered fit for interview, 18 were not interviewed and the reasons for this are shown in table 26.3. Two women refused to be interviewed, and this refusal rate of 0.64 per cent is much lower than usual in studies on bereavement, where refusal

Table 26.1 Age and sex distribution when interviewed of widowed people resident in area

Age in years	Men		Women		Total	%
	Included in sample	Excluded from sample	Included in sample	Excluded from sample		
20–29	–	–	2	–	2	0.55
30–39	1	–	2	–	3	0.83
40–49	1	–	9	–	10	2.75
50–59	8	–	38	1	47	12.95
60–69	18	–	69	1	88	24.24
70–79	30	4	77	11	122	33.61
80–89	12	12	41	14	79	21.76
90–99	–	2	3	6	11	3.03
≥100	–	–	–	1	1	0.28
Total	70	18	241	34	363	100.00

Table 26.2 Reasons for exclusion

	Male	Female	Total	%
Deaf	8	11	19	36.5
Speech barrier	1	1	2	3.9
Low IQ	–	1	1	1.9
Carcinomatosis	–	1	–	1.9
Cardiac failure	4	6	10	19.2
Confused	1	8	9	17.3
Subdural haematoma and personality change	1	–	1	1.9
Parkinson's disease	1	1	2	3.9
Bedridden for other reasons	2	5	7	13.5
Total	18	34	52	100.0

Table 26.3 Reasons for no interview

	Male	Female	Total	%
Refused interview	–	2	2	0.6
Sudden death precluded interview	1	3	4	1.1
Not contacted	3	9	12	3.3
Excluded because of illness	18	34	52	14.3
Interviewed	66	227	293	80.7
Total	88	275	363	100.0

rates of 16 to 41 per cent are the norm. A total of 80.7 per cent of all widowed people resident in the area were interviewed, and 94.2 per cent of those considered fit for interview.

Interview

Each person was interviewed separately and, with four exceptions, no other person was present during the interviews, which were conducted in a semi-rigid manner. Each person was encouraged to talk freely about the deceased spouse, but enough direction was given to ensure that all items listed on a standardised form were covered. In particular, the interview was used to determine whether the widowed person had experience of hallucinations (visual, auditory or tactile) or illusions (sense of presence) of the deceased.

Particular care was taken in assessing the statements of those who reported hallucinatory experiences. Only those who did not rationalise the experience, e.g. by saying that they had seen the deceased in 'their mind's eye', were listed as hallucinating. If there was any doubt about the reality of the experience, a nil response was recorded. Experiences occurring in bed at night, other than those occurring immediately after retirement, were discounted and recorded as dreams.

Hysteroid–obsessoid questionnaire

The interviewees were asked to complete the hysteroid–obsessoid questionnaire devised by Caine and Hope (1967). The purpose was to determine whether a relation exists between post-bereavement hallucinations and personality type. Though most were willing, and often eager, to talk during the interview, some of the older people were unable or unwilling to complete the questionnaire. Results were obtained from 54 men and 199 women; of these, 39 men and 149 women were obsessoid, 15 men and 50 women hysteroid. No data were obtained from 12 men and 28 women, all aged 50 or over, 30 of them being over the age of 70.

Results

For simplification, and except where otherwise specifically stated, the word 'hallucination' is used to include all hallucinations and illusions. Of the 193 people interviewed, 137 (46.7%) had post-bereavement hallucinations, which often lasted many years, and at the time of interview, 106 people (36.1%) still had hallucinations. The proportions of hallucinating men and women were similar, 33 men (50%) and 104 women (45.8%).

The most common type of hallucination is the illusion of feeling the presence of the dead spouse. The incidence of various illusions is shown in table 26.4. Auditory hallucinations (13.3%) are slightly less common than visual ones (14%), and more than one person in 10 has spoken to the dead spouse. The least common hallucination is the feeling of being touched by the dead spouse (2.7%).

Table 26.4 Incidence of various hallucinations

	All widowed people		
	Male	**Female**	**Total**
Feels presence of deceased	29 (43.9%)	86 (37.9%)	115 (39.2%)
Sees deceased	11 (16.7%)	30 (13.2%)	41 (14.0%)
Hears deceased	7 (10.6%)	32 (14.1%)	39 (13.3%)
Speaks to deceased	13 (19.7%)	21 (9.3%)	34 (11.6%)
Touched by deceased	1 (1.5%)	7 (3.1%)	8 (2.7%)

(Some people experienced more than one type of hallucination)

Though the total incidence of hallucination is similar for men and women, variations occur in the incidence of certain hallucinations. Widows are more likely to have auditory hallucinations than widowers ($p < 0.001$), 32 (14.1%) and 7 (10.6%) respectively. In contrast, widowers (13, 19.7%) are more likely to have spoken to the dead spouse ($p < 0.05$) than widows (21, 9.3%).

Age when widowed

Most people were in the older age groups when widowed. Altogether, 38 (57.6%) men and 96 (42.3%) women were 60 or over when widowed, while three (4.5%) men and 31 (13.7%) women were below the age of 40. Table 26.5 shows that people widowed below 40 are the ones least likely to hallucinate ($p < 0.05$).

Table 26.5 Age when widowed

Age (years)	less than 29	less than 39	less than 49	less than 59	less than 69	less than 79	less than 89
No. widowed	16	18	57	68	86	41	7
% hallucinated	20.7	22.2	54.4	44.1	52.3	48.8	0

Variation also occur with the age when widowed and certain types of hallucinations. A total of 11 (7.7%) of the 159 people widowed below the age of 60 conversed with the dead, compared with 23 (17.2%) or the 134 widowed at an older age. Of those aged below 60 when widowed, 15 (10.6%) visually hallucinated compared with 26 (19.4%) of those widowed at an older age. So people under 60 when widowed have a lower incidence of conversing with the dead ($p < 0.01$) and of visual hallucinations ($p < 0.05$) than those widowed at an older age.

Duration of widowhood

As association exists between the duration since bereavement and the incidence of hallucination, as shown in table 26.6. A significantly higher proportion of people widowed for less than ten years hallucinated compared with those widowed for a longer period ($p < 0.05$).

Table 26.6 Duration of widowhood

Duration (years)	less than 10	less than 20	less than 30	less than 40
No. widowed	158	68	45	22
% hallucinated	52.6	42.7	40.0	31.8

Significant variations occur also with duration of bereavement and type of hallucination. Nine men (13.6%) and 58 women (25.6%) were widowed for over 20 years, while 25 (37.8%) men and 68 (30.8%) women were widowed for under five years. Of the former, three (4.5%) visually hallucinated compared with 38 (16.8%) of those widowed for less than 20 years. Similarly, of those widowed for over 20 years 2 (3.0%) conversed with the dead spouse compared with 15 (16.1%) of those widowed for under five years. Both these differences were significant ($p < 0.05$).

Place of death

Rees and Lutkins (1967) found that the mortality associated with bereavement varied with the site of death of the first spouse. In general, no such variation occurs with the place of death and incidence of hallucination. No difference occurs in the total proportion of hallucinated people whose spouse died at home (161) compared with hospital (109) or at some other place (23).

However, a sex-linked difference is present in the case of hospital deaths: of the 26 widowers whose wives died in hospital, nine (34.6%) hallucinated compared with 24 (60.8%) widowers whose wives died outside hospital ($p < 0.05$). Conversely, of the 83 (36.8%) widows whose husbands died in hospital, 46 (55.4%) hallucinated, compared with 37 (25.7%) widows whose husbands died elsewhere ($p < 0.05$).

Marital harmony

Surviving spouses of unhappy marriages are unlikely to hallucinate

($p<0.01$). 11 widows stated that their marriage was unhappy, and none reported post-bereavement hallucinations.

Remarriage

Those who hallucinated were more likely to decline an opportunity to remarry than those who didn't ($p<0.05$). 11 of the 21 widowed people who remarried hallucinated. The four who rejected subsequent remarriage all hallucinated. They gave as their reason the feeling that the dead spouse was opposed to it, and one widow broke off a subsequent engagement for this reason.

People widowed twice

11 people were widowed twice. Two were men, both in their 70s and neither hallucinated. One 71-year-old widow had illusions of the presence of both dead spouses. A 58-year-old widow reported having had visual hallucinations on two occasions of her first husband, but none of her second. An 80-year-old widow had visual hallucinations of a son who died in early adulthood, but none of her two husbands, of one of whom she was very fond while the other she disliked intensely.

Childless marriages

Widowed spouses of childless marriages hallucinated less frequently than those who had had children ($p<0.05$). Out of 137 hallucinating people, 20 (14.6%) were childless compared with 37 (23.7%) of the 156 non-hallucinating people.

Husband's occupation

In order to obtain reasonably sized figures, the occupation only of the husband was taken, and these were grouped into the seven categories shown in table 26.7. The high incidence of hallucination among the professional and managerial group compared with other groups is significant ($p<0.01$). Widows of men engaged in non-manual and sales work were the ones least likely to hallucinate ($p<0.05$).

Table 26.7 Occupation and incidence of hallucination

	Professional and managerial	Self-employed, industry and commerce	Farmers	Supervisors and skilled manual workers	Non-manual and sales workers	Agricultural and forestry	Labourers
No. widowed	25	47	62	68	40	25	26
% hallucinated	72.0	39.0	47.6	44.1	32.5	40.0	50.0

Factors not affecting incidence of hallucination

Table 26.8 lists some of the factors which did not affect the incidence of hallucination. This shows in particular that social isolation, certain cultural factors and residence when bereaved were not associated with the incidence of hallucination.

Table 26.8 Factors which do not affect incidence of hallucination: (Percentages of people involved are given in brackets)

Sex	
Age when interviewed	
Factors associated with death	Sudden (39.6%) Inquest (7.5%) Necropsy (11.9%)Relatives present (55.3%)Relatives expected death (46.7%)
Cultural background	Ability to speak Welsh (44.4%) Sectarian allegiance with Christian faith* Regularity of church attendance* Wales outside Llanidloes area (9.9%) Outside Wales (8.2%)
Change of residence after bereavement	(43.7%)
Social isolation	Feeling lonely (41.3%)Living alone (42.6%)Relatives nearby (76.6%)Regular job (30.7%)
Depression requiring treatment	Before bereavement (2.7%) After bereavement (17.7%)

* No figures available

In addition, the expected and observed frequencies of hallucination with geographical area were looked at. Table 26.9 shows that, rather surprisingly, these tally exactly, suggesting strongly that the figures obtained in Llanidloes are generally applicable for England and Wales.

Table 26.9 Expected and observed frequency of hallucinations

	Within Llanidloes area	Wales (outside Llanidloes)	Outside Wales	Total
Total residents	240	29	24	293
Expected number hallucinated	112	14	11	137
Observed number hallucinated	112	14	11	137

Altogether, 17.7 per cent of all widowed people had received treatment for depression by either electro-convulsive therapy or anti-depressant drugs, sometimes after widowhood. The proportion who were depressed before the bereavement was small (2.7%), but everyone in this group also suffered from depression after bereavement. The proportion of widowers (7.6%) receiving treatment for post-bereavement depression was significantly smaller ($p < 0.05$) than for widows (20.7%). The incidence of depression was similar for the hallucinated (17.5%) and non-hallucinated (18.0%) groups.

Hysteroid–obsessoid questionnaire

The questionnaire was used to determine whether a relation exists between basic personality type and post-bereavement hallucinations. Of the 253 people who completed it, 39 men and 149 women were obsessoid, while 15 men and 50 women were hysteroid.

As the hysteroid type is more imaginative than the obsessoid, more of the former would be expected to hallucinate than the latter which was confirmed (see table 26.10). A total of 40 (61.5%) hysteroid people hallucinated, compared with 85 (45.2%) obsessoid people ($p < 0.05$). People scoring in the lower range of hysteroid scores were particularly likely to hallucinate.

Table 26.10 Percentage of hallucinated people scoring at the various levels of the Hysteroid–Obsessoid questionnaire

	Obsessoid					Hysteroid				
Score	−16	−18	−20	−22	−23	−24	−26	−28	−30	31+
No. widowed	30	38	51	42	27	15	19	21	4	6
% hallucinated	46.7	36.8	43.1	50.0	51.0	66.2	63.2	57.1	50.0	50.0

Previous disclosure of hallucinations

Most widowed people do not disclose their hallucinations ($p < 0.01$), and only 38 (27.7%) had done so. 20 (14.6%) had made the disclosure to more than one person. The 34 (32.7%) widows who had previously disclosed was a significantly larger proportion than the 4 (12.1%) widowers ($p < 0.05$). The most commonly given reason for not previously mentioning their hallucinations was fear of ridicule. Others included that it was too personal, no previous inquiry, people would not be interested, would upset relatives if they knew, unlucky to talk about it. Social isolation did not affect the frequency of previous disclosure.

Help from hallucinations

Most were helped by their hallucinations: 32 (78.0%) of those who visually hallucinated, 26 (66.7%) of those who auditorily hallucinated, 84 (73.0%) with illusions of the deceased's presence and 28 (82.4%) of those who spoke to the deceased. The proportions are all significantly greater than for those who were not helped ($p < 0.01$). 6 (75.0%) of those with tactile hallucinations found them helpful, but this figure was not significant. While 94 (68.6%) were helped, 8 (5.9%) found the hallucinations unpleasant and 35 (25.5%) found them neither helpful nor unpleasant.

Time of occurrence of hallucinations

99 (72.3%) hallucinating people experienced them at variable times throughout the day. 15 (10.9%) continually hallucinated and felt the dead spouse was always with them.

Duration of marriage

It was predicted that the incidence of hallucinations would be greater for those who had been happily married for many years, and that the period of living together would be directly related to the occurrence of hallucinations. Data was obtained from 104 widows and 23 widowers, and was subsidiary to the main survey which had elapsed some considerable time previously. During that period, seven widows and ten widowers had died, so that 46.0 per cent of the remaining 276 people were included in this additional test.

The figures for frequency of hallucinations with relation to duration of marriage are shown in table 26.11. The x^2 value for the 2×6 contingency table is 5.1, and is not significant.

Table 26.11 Relation between duration of marriage and occurrence of hallucinations in widows and widowers

	Duration of marriage in years					
Non-hallucinating	13 (72)	9 (56)	18 (51)	9 (41)	3 (43)	70 (55)
Hallucinating (including 'sense of presence')	5 (28)	7 (44)	11 (38)	17 (49)	4 (57)	57 (45)
Total	18	16	29	35	22	7	127

However, regression analysis takes into account the time sequence, and so uses more information, and this yields a result significant at five per cent (and almost at one per cent). The linear regression curve in figure 26.1 shows the continual trend of hallucinations with duration

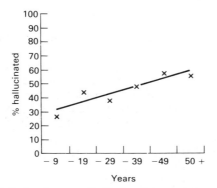

Figure 26.1 Relation between hallucinations and duration of marriage.

of marriage, so the predicted increase in hallucinations with increased duration of marriage does occur.

Discussion

It is generally thought that the Celtic character is highly imaginative and perceptive, which might suggest that post-bereavement hallucinations will be more common in mid-Wales than elsewhere in the British Isles. There are four reasons for believing this is not so: (*i*) No variation was found with incidence of hallucination and residence when bereaved; (*ii*) no variation occurred within the cultural groups studied; (*iii*) the proportion of hysteroid people (25.7%) studied was considerably smaller than the proportion of less imaginative, obsessoid people (74.3%); (*iv*) Marris (1958) interviewed 72 young widows in south-east London, and though his main interest was socioeconomic, he found that 50% had experienced hallucinations or illusions of the dead spouse. Although Marris interviewed only 69% of his original sample, the reported incidence of hallucinations in London is very similar to the 45.8% found in mid-Wales.

It remains possible that, between countries with very different cultural traditions, the incidence of post-bereavement hallucinations may vary considerably. Yamamoto *et al.* (1969), wishing 'to examine the process of mourning in a culture whose religions sanction the implied presence of the deceased through ancestor worship', interviewed 20 widows living in Tokyo, Japan. (The original sample was 55, but for various reasons most could not be interviewed.) Of the 20 interviewed, 18 (90%) reported feeling the presence of the dead spouse, though none reported cultivation of the idea of the presence of the deceased.

None of the Tokyo widows worried about their sanity because they felt the husband's presence. Yamamoto *et al.* (1969) believed that religion helped this aspect of grieving, for in their religious beliefs, the husband was present as an ancestor. This may be so.

It seems reasonable to conclude from the mid-Wales study that hallucinations are normal experiences after widowhood, providing helpful psychological phenomena to those experiencing them. Evidence supporting this statement is as follows: they are common experiences after widowhood, occur regardless of sex, race, creed or domicile, do not affect overt behaviour, tend to disappear with time, are not associated with any illness or abnormality, are more common in people whose marriages were happy and who became parents, and they can be integrated by people and keep them a secret. Most people feel they are helped by their hallucinations and, significantly, among those least likely to hallucinate are those widowed below the age of 40, the very group which is particularly likely to die soon after widowhood (Kraus and Lilienfeld, 1959).

Commentary

Aim and nature

This is a survey in which a large number (363) of widows and widowers, all living within a defined area of mid-Wales, Llanidloes, and all attending the same group practice, were interviewed about their hallucinatory experiences of their dead spouse. This is something which had not been previously investigated, and so Rees thought it worthwhile to determine the incidence of these hallucinatory experiences.

Each person was interviewed (in 359 cases with no one else present) in what Rees calls a 'semi-rigid' manner, i.e. each person was encouraged to talk freely about the deceased spouse 'but enough direction was given to ensure that all items listed on a standardized form were covered', in particular, whether the widowed person had experience of hallucinations (visual, auditory or tactile). [This has some similarities to Piaget's clinical interview, in which the investigator's questions are as much determined by the child's previous answer as by the specific information (s)he is trying to elicit.]

During the course of the interview, widow(er)s were also asked to complete the hysteroid–obsessoid questionnaire (Caine & Hope, 1967).

Rees wanted to find out if there is an association between incidence of hallucinations and (*i*) age when widowed; (*ii*) duration of widowhood; (*iii*) place of death; (*iv*) marital harmony; (*v*) remarriage; (*vi*) being widowed twice; (*vii*) childless marriages; (*viii*) husband's occupation; (*ix*) personality (hysteroid–obsessoid); (*x*) previous disclosure of hallucinations; (*xi*) the helpfulness of hallucinations; (*xii*) time of occurrence of hallucinations; (*xiii*) duration of marriage. [These all turned out to be significantly related.] He also considered a number of variables (which turned out to be non-significantly associated): sex, age when interviewed, factors associated with death, cultural background, residence when bereaved, change of residence after bereavement, social isolation and depression requiring treatment.

Context and background

Death of a spouse is at the top of the list of Life Events in the Holmes–Rahé (1967) Social Readjustment Rating Scale, the most commonly used stress questionnaire. It is a major life change which many elderly people will experience, especially if they are female. Most married women will outlive their husbands (Hendricks & Hendricks, 1977) so there are many more widows than widowers around. More than half the married women in the USA are widowed by their early 60s, and 80 per cent by their early 70s. Among people over 65, widows outnumber widowers by 4:1. By 65, 50 per cent of women have lost their husbands and by 75, 66 per cent (Botwinick, 1984).

As well as putting a severe financial strain on the survivor (especially women), the loss of a spouse can also shatter the person's social world and lead to social isolation: 75 per cent of widowed adults also live alone, and so experience physical as well as social isolation. Significantly, Gubrium (1973) found that people who had remained single all their lives felt more satisfied in late adulthood than widows or widowers of the same age.

Similarly, Barnett (1978), who studied over 400 people over 62, found that widowers felt more lonely, had a harder time with routine household chores and were generally less happy with their lives than widows. Widowers were more likely to be emotionally dependent on their spouse and for the running of the house, etc. Not surprisingly, widowers are considerably more likely to remarry (and do so sooner) than widows.

Bromley (1988) believes it is useful to distinguish between isolation and desolation in old age. The elderly may be isolated from their contemporaries by physical incapacity or disengagement from younger adults by cultural change and social mobility, all of this making social contact less frequent than it was before (isolation). Far more serious is desolation, which is to be left alone, neglected, forsaken by the person one deeply wants to be with, a kind of emotional deprivation, having no one to confide in or trust. Desolation may be the result of the loss of someone to whom one was deeply attached, in particular a spouse.

Yet bereavement usually produces strong supportive and sympathetic reactions from friends and relatives, and this can help reduce the severity of the loss. But people react very differently to loss of a spouse, and physical incapacity or lack of mobility will probably hinder recovery. Partly because of their greater life expectancy, more elderly women than men become socially isolated – and desolated – and more are infirm (Bromley, 1988). According to Rowland (1977), widows have a greater chance of developing either physical or mental illness, and are more likely to die within the first six to 12 months of their husband's death, compared with non-widows of the same age. They are especially at risk when the death was sudden (the 'broken heart' syndrome).

Evaluation

1 As the major source of stress (according to Holmes & Rahé, 1967), loss of a spouse is associated with physical and mental ill health and an increased risk of death. As far as hallucinations are concerned, these are perception-like experiences which are subjectively indistinguishable from veridical or real perceptions, i.e. those involving stimulation of the sense organs. If these are not known to have been caused by drugs, then they are usually taken as 'first rank' symptoms of mental illness, especially schizophrenia (e.g. Schneider, 1959). Although these do not usually appear in isolation, they are sometimes used as the sole basis for the diagnosis of schizophrenia (see chapter 29), because they illustrate a fundamental split between fantasy and reality which is seen as the essence of psychotic illness.

But there is no suggestion that any of Rees's interviewees were psychotically disturbed just *because* they had hallucinations of their dead spouse (almost half did). Indeed, Rees concludes that hallucinations would seem to be normal experiences after widowhood which provide helpful psychological phenomena to those experiencing them; they are common, occur regardless of sex, race, creed or place of residence, do not affect overt behaviour, tend to disappear with time, are not associated with any illness or abnormality, are more common in people whose marriages were happy and who became parents, and can be integrated by people and kept a secret. Most of the interviewees who experienced them felt their hallucinations to be helpful and, significantly, among those least likely to hallucinate are those widowed below the age of 40: the very group which is particularly likely to die soon after widowhood.

It is also noteworthy that auditory hallucinations (hearing the voice of the deceased) were slightly less common than visual (seeing the deceased), though both are more common than tactile (feelings of being touched by the deceased). In the case of schizophrenia, auditory hallucinations are the most common and tend to take the form of 'alien' voices talking about oneself, not the voice of a known (and usually loved) person who has died. (Patients with organic – as opposed to functional – psychoses have predominantly visual hallucinations.)

2 Rees found that most widowed people do not reveal their hallucinations to others, but widows are significantly more likely to do so than widowers. The most commonly

given reason was fear of ridicule; others included it was too personal, no one had asked, people would not be interested, it would upset relatives and it was unlucky to talk about it. This suggests that attitudes to death and grief in general, and hallucinations in particular, as perceived by the bereaved spouse, will influence their own attitude towards these experiences: are they 'normal', 'acceptable' or are they something to be kept quiet about, because they might be seen as symptoms of mental illness? It is interesting to note that none of the Tokyo widows interviewed by Yamamoto *et al.* (1969) worried about their sanity, because they felt their husband's presence; the researchers believed religion helped this aspect of grieving, for in their religious beliefs the husband was present as an ancestor.

3 In western culture, funerals reflect religion's beliefs about death and fulfil the *sacred* function of providing rite of passage from the living to the dead (Schulz, 1978). They also fulfil a *secular* function, whereby they provide a socially acceptable and healthy means of dealing with the body.

They also provide psychological support; they serve as a kind of final symbol of the fact that the deceased has lived, and also help to reaffirm the group identity of the survivors so they can continue to function after the death. So funerals can help the mourners to begin working through their grief immediately after the death (Hayslip & Panek, 1989).

However, grief is a very complex and essentially private process; it may take years to be fully resolved (if ever). It is very difficult, therefore, to judge grief reactions as being 'abnormal', even grief which extends over a long period of time. The bereaved are often avoided or treated as if they were sick (Kalish, 1985a, cited in Hayslip & Panek, 1989). Widowed people will need the support of others, but also will want to spend some time alone in order to come to terms with their feelings. However, self-imposed isolation over an extended period of time, out of a desire to deny the loss, may indicate a difficulty in coping (Hayslip & Panek, 1989). According to Lindemann (1944), it is not the quantity (length of time) of grieving that determines whether we judge it as abnormal or not, but the quality (harmful, self-destructive, unrealistic behaviour). There was no indication in Rees's sample of widows and widowers that their hallucinations were part of an abnormal pattern of grieving.

Exercises

1 How might it have been a disadvantage to have made the interview more rigid?

2 How were 'hallucinations' operationalized?

3 What was the target population, and how was the sample selected?

4 In tables 26.4 and 26.5, which statistical test would be used?

5 In table 26.11, how many degrees of freedom are there?

6 What is meant by 'Regression Analysis' or the 'Linear Regression Curve' (see figure 26.1)?

THOMAS J. BOUCHARD Jr AND MATTHEW McGUE (1981)

Familial studies of intelligence: a review

Science, 212, pp. 1055–9

A summary of 111 studies identified in a survey of the world literature on familial resemblances in measured intelligence reveals a profile of average correlations consistent with a polygenic mode of inheritance. There is, however, a marked degree of heterogeneity of the correlations within familial groupings, which is not moderated by sex of familial pairing or by type of intelligence test used.

In 1963, Erlenmeyer-Kimling and Jarvik published a summary of the world literature on IQ correlations between relatives. Their finding that the pattern of correlations averaged over independent studies was consistent with the pattern predicted by a polygenic theory of inheritance has been widely cited as strong evidence for some genetic determination of IQ (Matarazzo, 1972). Although the accumulation of a great many new studies, as well as the discrediting of Burt's important study on monozygotic (MZ) twins reared apart (Hernshaw, 1979; Dorfman, 1978), has outdated that review, the authors' summary or slightly modified versions of it (Jarvik & Erlenmeyer-Kimling, 1967) continue to be widely reproduced (Vernon, 1979). Plomin and DeFries (1980) have recently reported a comparison of those summary data with the results of several large, recent familial studies of IQ. They conclude that, in general, the recent studies show less resemblance between relatives than the Erlenmeyer-Kimling and Jarvik data. However, the summary is not comprehensive and it does not identify the factors which distinguish the two bodies of data. Roubertoux and Carlier (1978) have also published a recent review, but it contains only 37 per cent of the studies cited here.

The purpose of this report is to provide a comprehensive summary of the world literature on the IQ correlations between relatives. We have updated the 1963 summary, adding recent data and deleting several studies included in the earlier review which do not meet our methodological criteria for inclusion. Although the pattern of averages reported here and in earlier reviews is remarkably consistent with polygenic theory, the individual data points are quite heterogeneous. Therefore, we have also assessed the extent to which the reported correlations are heterogeneous, and have attempted to identify some factors contributing to this.

In our survey of the literature, we found 140 relevant studies. These were reduced to 111 by the application of explicit selection criteria. The 111 studies, which include 59 reported in the 17 years since the Erlenmeyer-Kimling and Jarvik summary, yielded 526 familial correlations based upon 113,942 pairings. Figure 27.1 shows correlation between relatives, biological and adoptive, in the 111 studies. The median correlation in each distribution is indicated by a vertical bar, and the small arrow indicates the correlation that would be predicted by a genetic model with no dominance, no assortative mating, and no environmental effects. Although researchers do not

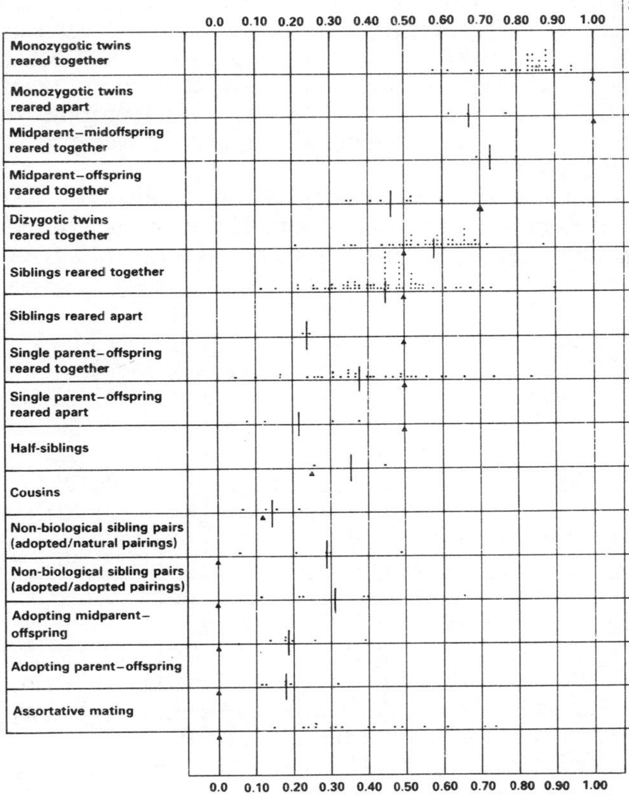

	No. of correlations	No. of pairings	Median correlation	Weighted average	χ^2 (d.f.)	$\chi^2 \div$ d.f.
Monozygotic twins reared together	34	4672	.85	.86	81.29 (33)	2.46
Monozygotic twins reared apart	3	65	.67	.72	0.92 (2)	0.46
Midparent–midoffspring reared together	3	410	.73	.72	2.66 (2)	1.33
Midparent–offspring reared together	8	992	.475	.50	8.11 (7)	1.16
Dizygotic twins reared together	41	5546	.58	.60	94.5 (40)	2.36
Siblings reared together	69	26,473	.45	.47	403.6 (64)	6.31
Siblings reared apart	2	203	.24	.24	.02 (1)	.02
Single parent–offspring reared together	32	8433	.385	.42	211.0 (31)	6.81
Single parent–offspring reared apart	4	814	.22	.22	9.61 (3)	3.20
Half-siblings	2	200	.35	.31	1.55 (1)	1.55
Cousins	4	1.176	.145	.15	1.02 (2)	0.51
Non-biological sibling pairs (adopted/natural pairings)	5	345	.29	.29	1.93 (4)	0.48
Non-biological sibling pairs (adopted/adopted pairings)	6	369	.31	.34	10.5 (5)	2.10
Adopting midparent–offspring	6	758	.19	.24	6.8 (5)	1.36
Adopting parent–offspring	6	1397	.18	.19	6.64 (5)	1.33
Assortative mating	16	3817	.365	.33	96.1 (15)	6.41

Figure 27.1   Familial correlations for IQ. The vertical bar in each distribution indicates the median correlation; the arrow, the correlation predicted by a simple polygenic model.

subscribe to such a simple model, it provides a noncontroversial pattern against which to compare the results of various familial groupings. Different investigators will no doubt fit different models to the data.

In general, the pattern of average correlations in figure 27.1 is consistent with the pattern of correlations predicted on the basis of polygenic inheritance, i.e. the higher the proportion of genes two family members have in common, the higher the average correlation between their IQs.

The data set contains considerable heterogeneity, as indicated by the χ^2 statistics. In an attempt to identify the factors contributing to the heterogeneity, we subdivided the familial groupings into opposite-sex and same-sex pairings (figure 27.2) and male and female pairings (figure 27.3). Among dizygotic (DZ) twins, the IQs of same-sex twins are more similar than those of opposite-sex twins. This may reflect a social-environmental effect (parents may treat same-sex twins more similarly than opposite-sex twins). The difference between non-twin same-sex and opposite-sex siblings and between same-sex and opposite-sex parent–offspring pairings is negligible. The male–female comparison does not yield consistent trends. For example, the average correlations are larger in male than female twins, but the reverse is true for other siblings. The absence of any demonstrable sex effect is consistent with a polygenic theory of inheritance, which does not posit the existence of sex linkage. Environmental theories which emphasize the importance of sex-role effects on general cognitive development are not supported by these results.

Another possible source of heterogeneity is the intelligence test used. We found great diversity in test selection. For example, the 34 correlations for MZ twins reared together were based on results from

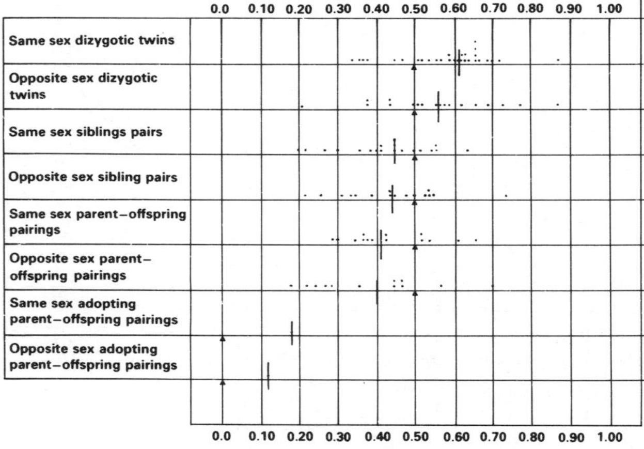

	0.0 0.10 0.20 0.30 0.40 0.50 0.60 0.70 0.80 0.90 1.00	No. of correlations	No. of pairings	Median correlation	Weighted average	$\chi^2(d.f.)$	$\frac{\chi^2}{d.f.}$
Same sex dizygotic twins		29	3670	.61	.62	68.14 (28)	2.43
Opposite sex dizygotic twins		18	1592	.565	.57	58.6 (17)	3.45
Same sex siblings pairs		19	6098	.45	.48	84.65 (17)	4.98
Opposite sex sibling pairs		16	5127	.445	.49	70.4 (14)	5.03
Same sex parent–offspring pairings		14	4648	.41	.40	55.4 (13)	4.26
Opposite sex parent–offspring pairings		12	4476	.40	.39	70.1 (11)	6.37
Same sex adopting parent–offspring pairings		1	460	.18	.18		
Opposite sex adopting parent–offspring pairings		1	461	.12	.12		

0.0 0.10 0.20 0.30 0.40 0.50 0.60 0.70 0.80 0.90 1.00

Figure 27.2   Familial correlations for IQ organized by opposite-sex and same-sex pairings.

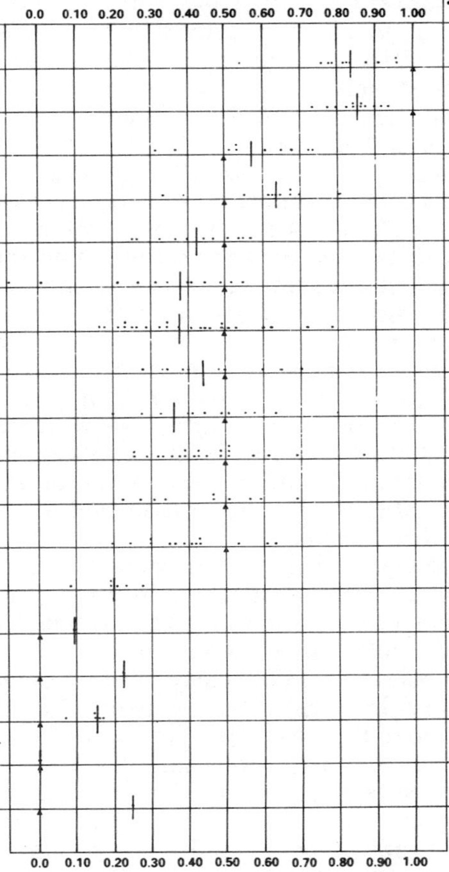

	No. of correlations	No. of pairings	Median correlation	Weighted average	χ^2 (d.f.)	$\frac{\chi^2}{d.f.}$
Female mz twin pairs	10	869	.835	.86	26.35 (8)	3.29
Male mz twin pairs	12	1,013	.86	.86	24.4 (10)	2.44
Female dz twin pairs	10	730	.58	.61	14.73 (8)	1.84
Male dz twin pairs	11	964	.64	.65	20.32 (9)	2.26
Female sibling pairs	11	1,986	.42	.50	28.34 (9)	3.15
Male sibling pairs	12	2,321	.38	.47	54.69 (10)	5.47
Mother–offspring reared together	25	5,660	.38	.41	119.02 (24)	4.96
Mother–daughter reared together	10	1,804	.44	.43	36.80 (9)	4.09
Mother–son reared together	12	2,802	.37	.39	38.52 (11)	3.50
Father–offspring reared together	22	5,497	.43	.41	141.17 (21)	6.72
Father–daughter reared together	10	1,658	.46	.39	33.08 (9)	3.68
Father–son reared together	14	2,843	.40	.38	36.86 (13)	2.84
Adopting mother–offspring	6	1,393	.195	.20	4.28 (5)	0.86
Adopting mother–daughter	1	212	.10	.10		
Adopting mother–son	1	247	.22	.22		
Adopting father–offspring	6	1,279	.155	.18	10.1 (5)	2.02
Adopting father–daughter	1	214	.00	.00		
Adopting father–son	1	248	.25	.25		

0.0 0.10 0.20 0.30 0.40 0.50 0.60 0.70 0.80 0.90 1.00

Figure 27.3 Familial correlations for IQ organized by male and female pairings.

22 different tests, the 41 DZ twin correlations upon results from 25. We do not have sufficient data to determine whether the size of the familial correlation is moderated by the specific test used. We did investigate whether individually administered tests and group-administered tests produced different correlations: (*i*) for the MZ twins reared together, the 24 correlations calculated on group tests produced a weighted average of 0.86, and the ten calculated on individual tests a weighted average of 0.84; (*ii*) for the DZ twins reared together, the weighted average of 32 correlations based on group tests is 0.60, and of nine correlations based on individual tests it is 0.61. In neither case was the difference significant.

The 34 correlations reported on 4,672 MZ twin pairs reared together produce a weighted average correlation of 0.86, which is very close to those reported in earlier reviews, and is approximately the same for male and female pairs. Although the test of homogeneity yields a significant χ^2 value ($p < 0.02$), the degree of heterogeneity is not extreme, and from a few rather low correlations. The two most extreme values are the 0.58 reported by Blewett (1954) and the 0.62 reported by Nichols (1970); in both cases, the sample sizes are small (26 and 36 pairs respectively). The observation that 79 per cent of the reported correlations lie above 0.80 convincingly demonstrates the remarkable similarity of MZ twins.

After deleting the Burt data, we are left with results on just 65 pairs of MZ twins reared apart, as reported in three separate studies. The weighted average of 0.72 is much less than that for the MZ twins reared together, the difference suggesting the importance of between-family environmental differences. At the same time, the size of the correlation would be difficult to explain on the basis of any strictly environmental hypothesis.

Three studies give mid-parent–midoffspring correlations, the weighted average being 0.72. In this case, the genetic expectation would depend upon the number of offspring which define midoffspring value, and is thus indeterminate. The correlation between midparent and individual offspring does have a determinate simple genetic expectation of 0.707. The observed weighted average is only 0.50, a discrepancy discussed below.

The weighted average of the 41 correlations in DZ twin pairs is 0.60, considerably larger than for non-twin siblings, and same-sex DZ pairs show somewhat greater similarity than opposite-sex DZ pairs (0.62 vs. 0.57), with males being slightly more similar than females (0.65 vs. 0.61). As with the MZ twins, the test of homogeneity is significant ($p < 0.01$), although 75 per cent of the correlations fall within the narrow range 0.50 to 0.70. The two extreme values were reported in old studies on rather small samples, the lowest being the 0.21 reported by Wingfield (1928) on 26 pairs, the highest the 0.87 reported by Merriman (1924) on 51 pairs. The greater similarity of DZ twins is usually interpreted as reflecting greater environmental similarity, but it is also likely that bias in the recruitment of DZ twins is in the direction of increasing psychological similarity (Lykken *et al.*, 1978).

The weighted average for siblings reared together is 0.47 which, although close to the simple expectation of 0.50, is based upon 69 values, with a range of correlations from 0.13 to 0.90. Opposite-sex and same-sex siblings yield almost identical weighted averages (0.49 vs. 0.48), as do female and male siblings (0.50 vs. 0.47). The sibling correlations are based on over 25,000 pairs: one large representative study by Record *et al.* (1969) showed a correlation of 0.55 for over 5,000 pairs.

While there is a wealth of data on siblings reared together, there is a dearth of information on siblings reared apart. Only 203 such pairs have been studied, in two investigations, yielding a weighted average of 0.24, much less than the expected value for such pairs and the average value for siblings reared together.

The weighted average correlation between individual parent and individual offspring is 0.42, based upon 32 correlations. There is a marked degree of heterogeneity, as evidenced not only by a significant χ^2 value ($p < 0.01$), but also by the broad range of the correlations. This cannot be attributed to a sex effect, since opposite-sex and same-sex pairings yield equivalent averages, or to a maternal effect, the average correlation of mother and offspring being the same as that of father and offspring. Although the large discrepancies between expected and observed correlations for parent and offspring reared in the parental home (reared together) may be easily interpreted as a result of a generational (social-environmental) effect, we cannot discount the role of biological factors: characteristics which are affected very little by the social environment, such as height and total fingerprint ridge count, show similar generational differences.

Similarly, correlations for parent and separated offspring are quite heterogeneous; the weighted average is 0.22, much less than the simple expectation of 0.50. McAskie and Clarke (1976) suggest that one possible explanation could be that parents and offspring are given different tests. In fact, roughly half our intergenerational correlations were based upon data from cases in which this did happen.

Two pairings which are rarely studied are half-siblings and cousins. Two half-sibling correlations, both reported by Nichols (1970) produce a weighted average of 0.31. The four reported correlations for cousins are quite homogeneous, the average being 0.15, very similar to the simple genetic expectation.

A number of recent adoption studies have added considerable knowledge, and enough studies are available to permit comparison of adopted/natural sibling pairs and adopted/adopted sibling pairs. The adopted/natural correlation should be higher, since it would contain a component for the covariance of genotype and environment (Plomin *et al.*, 1977). The present review in fact finds the reverse (see figure 27.1).

The weighted average correlation of adoptive midparent and offspring is 0.24, and that of adoptive parent and offspring is 0.19. Genetic theory requires the biological midparent–offspring correlation to exceed the biological single parent–offspring correlation, and it does, although not by much (0.50 vs. 0.42). Some environmental theories predict the same effect (McAskie & Clarke, 1976); the failure to find any difference in the adoptive case must be considered surprising from an environmental point of view.

Unlike natural families, adopted offspring are rather more similar to the same-sex adoptive parent than to the opposite-sex adoptive parent (see figure 27.2). However, this conclusion is based on a single study (Horn *et al.*, 1979). Overall, adoptive mothers are no more like their adopted children than adoptive fathers are.

The weighted average of 0.33 for correlations between mates is much smaller than the 0.50 sometimes reported (e.g. Jensen, 1978). The marked heterogeneity of the distribution indicates the sample-specific nature of these measures.

As in the earlier review, the pattern of averaged correlations is remarkably consistent with polygenic theory. This is not to discount the importance of environmental factors; MZ twins reared apart are far from perfectly correlated, DZ twins are more similar than other biological siblings, and adoptive parents' IQs show a consistent relation with the IQs of their adoptive offspring. However, we found no evidence for two factors: sex-role and maternal effects, sometimes thought to be important. It is indisputable that the data support the inference of partial genetic determination of IQ, but it is doubtful whether they tell us about the precise strength of this effect. Certainly the large amount of unexplained variability within degrees of relationship suggests that any models used to explain the data should be used cautiously.

Commentary

Aim and nature /

The article reports the findings of a comprehensive survey of the world literature on familial resemblance and measured intelligence, i.e. IQ correlations between relatives. It is an update of an earlier and much cited review by Erlenmeyer-Kimling and Jarvik (1963). A number of new studies have been reported since that review (59 in all), as well as the notorious exposure of the invalidity of Burt's twins-study data (through his falsification and fabrication of his results), so the latter is excluded from the present review and the former are included. (The whole debate about Burt's results has been re-opened by Joynson, 1989.) Altogether, 140 relevant studies were found, but the application of explicit selection criteria (see *Evaluation* section below) reduced these to 111. The median correlation for each degree of blood-tie was found, and overall the results are consistent with those of Erlenmeyer-Kimling and Jarvik (1963). Although not explicitly intended to support the 'genetic theory' of intelligence (i.e. the view that the largest proportion of the variance between individuals' IQ scores – and, by implication, between that of different racial and other groups – derives from genetic differences), it is implicitly so; explicitly, it is an update of the earlier review, which is certainly used more to support the genetic theory than oppose it. However, overall, the results of both surveys would seem to be equally supportive of both the genetic *and* the environmentalist views, with the important exception of studies of separated MZs and adoption studies.

Context and background

Along with gender differences, the debate about the source of differences in intelligence must be the most controversial and divisive in the whole of psychology (Gross, 1987). Much of the debate about the heredity–environment/nature–nurture issue in relation to intelligence seems to go on, based on the assumption that IQ tests are reliable and valid measures of this elusive human characteristic.

However, there are good reasons for being cautious in making this assumption:

(*i*) It is possible for two IQ tests, A and B, to have different standard deviations (a measure of dispersion of scores around an average or central value – the mean – and the usual way in which IQ scores are expressed today), and therefore for the same individual to score differently on the two tests. For example, if Test A has an SD of 10 and Test B an SD of 20, in both cases, 68 per cent of children would be expected to have scores one SD below or above the mean (i.e. between 90 and 110 in Test A and between 80 and 120 in Test B). So a particular child might have a score of 110 on Test A and 120 on Test B, and yet the scores would be telling us the same thing (Fontana, 1982). This suggests that while intelligence is a psychological concept, that of IQ is purely statistical, i.e. it is possible for the same characteristic of a person (their intelligence) to be assigned different values according to which test is used to measure it. So perhaps instead of asking 'How intelligent is this individual?', we should ask 'How intelligent is this individual as measured by this particular test?' (Gross, 1987). This is not normally a problem when measuring physical characteristics such as height or weight, but would apply to measuring other psychological characteristics. (Bouchard and McGue point out the diversity of tests used in their 111 studies overall, e.g. 22 in the case of MZs reared together and 25 for DZs.) We cannot just take the scales to be equivalent, which makes the procedure of finding the median correlation for different studies far from straightforward.

(*ii*) This leads straight onto a second problem: because intelligence is expressed as a number, the impression is created that IQ tells us in some absolute way about an individual's intellectual ability (in the same way as feet and inches tell us about their height). However, whereas height is measured on a ratio scale (and by implication an interval scale too), many psychologists believe that intelligence can only be measured on an ordinal scale, i.e. IQ can tell us only how intelligent we are relative to others, i.e. higher or lower, but we cannot say anything more precise about the size of those differences (Ryan, 1972).

(*iii*) Whereas we are usually prepared to accept an operational definition of, say, height (as the number of feet and inches using a tape measure), an equivalent definition of intelligence is not satisfactory, precisely because there is such a variety of definitions: IQ is an unwarranted reduction of a very diverse and complex characteristic to a single number (Gross, 1987).

Leaving these issues largely to one side, the debate has raged on for most of psychology's history about how to account for the differences revealed by the tests; 'IQ' and 'intelligence' are equated in much of the research which provides the data for the nature–nurture/heredity–environment issue.

Evaluation

1 The idea that intelligence is hereditary (i.e. *differences* in IQ are inherited) is deeply built into the theory of IQ testing itself, because of its commitment to the measurement of something intrinsic and unchangeable. From the very beginning of the American and British mental testing movement, it was assumed that IQ was biologically heritable (Rose *et al.*, 1984). The same authors point out what they consider to be certain mistaken senses of 'heritable' used by psychometricians, which are mixed up with the geneticist's technical meaning of the term, and which contribute to false conclusions about the consequences of heritability: (*i*) genes do not determine intelligence; there is no 1:1 correspondence between the genes inherited from one's parents and even physical characteristics. What we inherit is the *genotype*, the genes which are involved in the development of a particular trait, while the *phenotype* is the actual trait itself as it manifests itself in the organism. While the former is fixed, the latter develops and changes constantly. The first principle of developmental genetics is that every organism is a unique product of the interaction between genes and environment at every stage of life; (*ii*) even allowing that genes alone do not determine the phenotype, it is claimed that they determine the effective limits of the phentotype, i.e. genes determine capacity or potential. But, as Ryan (1972) points out, it is impossible to measure potential separately from actual behaviour/performance, i.e.

some of the skills which an individual has developed during his/her lifetime must be used when they do an IQ test: 'there is nothing extra "behind" the behaviour corresponding to potential that could be observed independently of the behaviour itself' (Ryan, 1972). She concludes that the notion of 'innate potential' itself does not make sense.

2 In general, heritability is estimated from the correlation of a trait between relatives (Rose *et al.*, 1984). Unfortunately, as we noted earlier, most of the results of studies of family resemblance (or concordance studies) can be interpreted as either supporting the genetic *or* the environmentalist theory; this is because relatives resemble each other not only in terms of their genes, but also in terms of their environments, and the greater the degree of blood (genetic) relationship, the greater the likelihood that they will share the same environment. This is why psychologists and geneticists take advantage of the 'natural experiments' of twin studies (particularly the separation of MZs) and adoption studies. Here is the opportunity to study the relative influence of the two (normally inseparable) variables: heredity and environment.

3 With Burt's twin studies no longer included in the survey, the three remaining studies of separated MZs are (presumably): (*i*) Newman *et al.* (1937); (*ii*) Shields (1962); and (*iii*) Juel-Nielsen (1965). One of the criteria for selection used by Bouchard and McGue (in 'notes') was that 'the procedure for zygosity determination was both objective and valid. Use of a validated questionnaire was considered an acceptable procedure', i.e. it should be possible to establish objectively whether or not any of the volunteers are MZs or DZs. But this was clearly not so in the case of the Newman *et al.* study (see, e.g. Kamin, 1977); in 1937 there was no reliable/valid medical test for zygosity which, surely, is the only kind of test that *should* be used! Perhaps, more seriously, the whole rationale of these studies is that MZs are reared separately, i.e. in truly different (un-correlated) environments. But this requirement is blatantly not fulfilled in both the Shields and the small Juel-Nielsen study, where several pairs were reared in related branches of the same biological family, went to school with each other, lived next door to each other, etc. This and the several other problems with twin studies are discussed in detail by Kamin (1977).

The most recent study, the Minnesota Twin Study (Bouchard, 1984) involves 34 pairs of separated MZs who, even though separated in infancy and raised in different environments, have shown remarkable similarity over a very diverse range of physical and psychological traits, including intelligence. But there were also some differences which were as surprising as some of the similarities. 'Further study of the similarities *and* the differences between the twin pairs may shed more light on the direct and indirect way in which nature and nurture interact to influence our behaviour' (Smith *et al.*, 1986).

4 As far as adoption studies are concerned, the problem with early studies (e.g. Burks, 1928; Leahy, 1935) was that adoptive families differ, as a group, in a variety of ways from the 'matched control group' of ordinary biological families with which the former are compared (see Kamin, 1977). The obvious improvement on this 'classical' design is to study adoptive parents who also have a biological child of their own. Here, the two children will have been reared in the same environment by the same parents, although they will be genetically unrelated to each other, and, of course, the adopted children will be genetically unrelated to the adoptive parents. Two recent studies, Scarr and Weinberg (1977, 1983) and Horn *et al.* (1979), used this new design, the former involving transracial adoptions, i.e. in almost all cases the mother and her biological child were white, while the adopted child was black.

In both studies there was no significant difference between (*i*) the correlation of the mother's IQ and her biological child's IQ; and (*ii*) the correlation of her IQ with that of her adopted child's IQ, although Horn *et al.* found a slightly greater correlation between the mother and the *adopted* child, while for Scarr and Weinberg it was slightly greater with the *natural* child. 'The child's race, like its adoptive status, had no effect on the degree of parent–child resemblance in IQ. These results appear to inflict fatal damage to the notion that IQ is highly heritable ... children reared by the same mother resemble her in IQ to the same degree, whether or not they share her genes' (Rose *et al.*, 1984).

5 The heritability estimate for intelligence (i.e. the amount of variance between the IQ scores of individuals attributable to genetic factors) has been variously taken to be 80 per cent (Eysenck, 1973 and Jensen, 1969), 30 to 70 per cent (Henderson, 1984) and 50 to 80 per cent (Herrnstein, 1982). What is important to note is that it is *not* a fixed value, but a relative index referring to a particular population at a particular time. If everybody's environment were to become very similar, the higher the heritability estimate would become. This is another way of regarding heredity and environment as interacting variables, and it may be much more fruitful to try to understand *how and in what ways* they act to produce the phenotype intelligence, rather than to measure *how much* each affects it.

Exercises

1 What is meant by a *polygenic* theory of intelligence?

2 What is meant by genetic *'dominance'*?

3 What is meant by assortative mating?

4 Why would the median be chosen as the 'average'?

5 In the tables, what does each of the column headings mean:
   (*i*) weighted average
   (*ii*) χ^2 (d.f.)
   (*iii*) $\chi^2 \div d.f.$.

6 What is the difference between Individual and Group tests of intelligence? Give at least one example of each.

The effects of psychotherapy: an evaluation

Journal of Consulting Psychology, 16, pp. 319–24

The recommendation of the committee on Training in Clinical Psychology of the American Psychological Association regarding the training of clinical psychologists in the field of psychotherapy has been criticised by this author in a series of papers (1949, 1950). The most cogent argument presented in favour of the Committee's policy is perhaps that which refers to the social need for the skills possessed by the psychotherapist. In view of the importance of the issues involved, it seemed worthwhile to examine the evidence regarding the actual effects of psychotherapy.

Baseline and unit of measurement

In the only other previous attempt to carry out such an evaluation, Landis (1938) has pointed out that 'before any sort of measurement can be made, it is necessary to establish a baseline and a common unit of measure. The only unit of measure available is the report made by the physician, stating that the patient has recovered, is much improved, is improved or unimproved. This unit is probably as satisfactory as any type of human subjective judgement, partaking of both the good and bad points of such judgements'. For a unit, Landis suggests 'that of expressing therapeutic results in terms of the number of patients recovered or improved per 100 cases admitted to the hospital'. As an alternative, he suggests 'the statement of therapeutic outcome for some given group of patients during some stated interval of time'.

Landis realised quite clearly that, in order to evaluate the effectiveness of any form of therapy, data from a control group of non-treated patients is necessary in order to compare the effects of therapy with the spontaneous remission rate. In the absence of anything better, he used the improvement rate in state mental hospitals for patients diagnosed under the heading of 'neuroses'. He points out the objections to using such patients as a control group.

The fact that psychoneurotic cases are not usually committed to state hospitals unless in a very bad condition; the relatively small number of voluntary patients in the group; the fact that such patients do get some degree of psychotherapy, especially in the reception hospitals; and the probably quite different economic, educational and social status of the State Hospital group compared to the patients reported from each of the other hospitals; all argue against the acceptance of [this] figure ... as a truly satisfactory baseline, but in the absence of any other better figure, this must serve.

Actually, the various figures quoted by Landis agree very well. The percentage of neurotic patients discharged annually as recovered or improved from New York state hospitals is 70 (for the period 1925 to 1934); for the USA as a whole, it is 68 (1926 to 1933). The percentage discharged as recovered or improved within one year of admission is 66 for the USA (1933) and 68 for New York (1914). The consolidated improvement rate of New York state hospitals (1917 to 1934) is 72 per cent, and this is the one chosen by Landis and which is accepted here. So, by and large, we may say that, of severe neurotics receiving mainly custodial care, and very little of any psychotherapy, over two-thirds recovered or improved to a considerable extent. 'Although this is not, strictly speaking, a basic figure for "spontaneous recovery", still any therapeutic method must show an appreciably greater size than this to be seriously considered' (Landis, 1938).

Another estimate of the required 'baseline' is provided by Denker (1946):

500 consecutive disability claims due to psychoneurosis, treated by general practitioners throughout the country, and not by accredited specialists or sanatoria, were reviewed. All types of neurosis were included, and no attempt made to differentiate the neurosthenic, anxiety, compulsive, hysteric, or other states, but the greatest care was taken to eliminate the true psychotic or organic lesions, which in the early stages of illness so often simulate neurosis. These cases were taken consecutively from the files of the Equitable Life Assurance Society of the United States, were from all parts of the country, and all had been ill of a neurosis for at least three months before claims were submitted. They, therefore, could be fairly called 'severe', since they had been totally disabled for at least a three-month period, and rendered unable to carry on with any 'occupation for remuneration or profit' for at least that time.

These patients were regularly seen and treated by their own doctors with sedatives, tonics, suggestion, and reassurance, but in no case was any attempt made at anything but this most superficial type of 'psychotherapy', which has always been the stock-in-trade of the GP.

Repeated statements, every three months or so, by their doctors, as well as independent investigations by the insurance company, confirmed the fact that these people were not actually engaged in productive work during the period of their illness, when they received disability benefits. Denker points out that this fact of receiving benefit may have actually prolonged the total period of disability, and acted as a disincentive to recovery. Therefore, the therapeutic results would not be expected to be as favourable in such a group as in other groups, where there was a financial incentive for the patient to adjust to his neurotic illness. The cases were all followed up for a least a five-year period, and often up to ten years, after the period of disability had begun. The criteria of 'recovery' used by Denker were as follows: (*i*) return to work, and ability to carry on well in economic adjustments for at least five years; (*ii*) complaint of no further or very slight difficulties; (*iii*) making successful social adjustments. Using these criteria, which are very similar to those normally used by psychiatrists, Denker found that 45 per cent of the patients recovered after one year, another 27 per cent after two years, making 72 per cent in all. Another ten, five and four per cent recovered during the third, fourth and fifth years, respectively, making a total of 90 per cent recoveries after five years.

This sample contrasts in many ways with that used by Landis. The former cases were probably not quite as severe, they were all voluntary, non-hospitalised patients and came from a much higher socio-economic background, mostly clerical workers, executives, teachers and professionals. In spite of these differences, the recovery figures for the two samples are almost identical. The most suitable figure to choose for Denker's sample is probably that for the two-year recovery rate, since follow-up would overestimate the efficiency of this 'baseline' procedure. The figure of 72 per cent for two-year recovery rate agrees exactly with that given by Landis. We may, therefore, conclude with some confidence that our estimate of two-thirds of severe neurotics showing recovery or considerable improvement without the benefit of systematic psychotherapy is not likely to be very far out.

Effects of psychotherapy

The results of 19 studies, covering over 7000 cases, and dealing with both psychoanalytic and eclectic types of treatment, are shown in table 28.1. An attempt has been made to report results under four headings: (*i*) cured, or much improved; (*ii*) improved; (*iii*) slightly improved; (*iv*) not improved, died, discontinued treatment, etc. It was usually easy to reduce additional categories given by some writers to these basic four; some gave only two or three, and in those cases it was, of course, impossible to subdivide further, and the figures for combined categories are given. (In one or two cases, where patients who improved or improved slightly were combined by the original author, the total figure has been divided equally between the two categories.) A slight degree of subjectivity inevitably enters into this procedure, but it is unlikely to have caused much distortion. Rather more subjectivity is probably implied in the writers' judgement as to which disorders and diagnoses should be categorised as 'neurosis'. Schizophrenic, manic-depressive and paranoid states have been excluded,

Table 28.1 Summary of reports of the results of psychotherapy

	n	Cured; much improved	Improved	Slightly improved	Not improved; died; left treatment	% cured; much improved; improved
(A) Psychoanalytic						
1 Fenichel (1920–1930)	484	104	84	99	179	39
2 Kessel & Hyman (1933)	34	16	5	4	9	62
3 Jones (1926–1936)	59	20	8	28	3	47
4 Alexander (1932–1937)	141	28	42	23	48	50
5 Knight (1941)	42	8	20	7	7	67
All Cases	760	335		425		44
(B) Eclectic						
1 Huddleson (1927)	200	19	74	80	27	46
2 Matz (1929)	775	10	310	310	145	41
3 Maudsley Hospital Report (1931)	1721	288	900	533		69
4 Maudsley Hospital Report (1935)	1711	371	765	575		64
5 Neustatter (1935)	46	9	14	8	15	50
6 Luff & Garrod (1935)	500	140	135	26	199	55
7 Luff & Garrod (1935)	210	38	84	54	34	68
8 Ross (1936)	1089	547	306	236		77
9 Yaskin (1936)	100	29	29	42		58
10 Curran (1937)	83	51		32		61
11 Masserman & Carmichael (1938)	50	7	20	5	18	54
12 Carmichael & Masserman (1939)	77	16	25	14	22	53
13 Schilder (1939)	35	11	11	6	7	63
14 Hamilton & Wall (1941)	100	32	34	17	17	66
15 Hamilton et al. (1942)	100	48	5	17	32	51
16 Landis (1938)	119	40	47	32		73
17 Institute Med. Psychol. (quoted Neustatter)	270	58	132	55	25	70
18 Wilder (1945)	54	3	24	16	11	50
19 Miles et al. (1951)	53	13	18	13	9	58
All Cases	7293	4661		2632		64

while organ neuroses, psychopathic states and character disturbances have been included. The number of cases where there was genuine doubt is probably too small to make much difference to the final figures, however they are allocated.

A number of studies have been excluded because of such factors as excessive inadequacy of follow-up, partial duplication of cases with others included in the table, failure to indicate types of treatment used, and other reasons which made the results useless for our purposes. Their inclusion would not have altered our conclusions to any considerable degree, although, as Miles *et al.* (1951) points out: 'When the various studies are compared in terms of thoroughness, careful planning, strictness of criteria and objectivity, there is often an inverse correlation between these factors and the percentage of successful results reported'.

Certain difficulties have arisen from the inability of some writers to make their column figures agree with their totals, or to calculate percentages accurately. Again, the writer has used his judgement as to which figures to accept. In certain cases, writers have given figures of cases where there was a recurrence of the disorder after apparent cure or improvement, without indicating how many patients were affected in these two groups respectively; all recurrences of this kind have been subtracted from the 'cured' and 'improved' totals, taking half from each. The total number of cases involved in all these adjustments is quite small.

We may now turn to the figures as presented. Patients treated by means of psychoanalysis improve to the extent of 44 per cent; patients treated eclectically improve to the extent of 64 per cent; patients treated only custodially or by GPs improve to the extent of 72 per cent. Thus there appears to be an inverse correlation between recovery and psychotherapy: the more psychotherapy, the smaller the recovery rate. This conclusion requires certain qualifications.

In the psychoanalytic results, we have classed those who stopped treatment as 'not improved'. It seems reasonable to regard someone who fails to finish treatment as a therapeutic failure, and the same rule has been followed with the data summarised under 'eclectic' treatment, except when the patient was definitely classified as 'improved' by the therapist. However, in view of the peculiarities of Freudian procedures it could be argued that it is more just to class those cases separately, and deal only with the percentage of successful completed treatments. Approximately one-third of the psychoanalytic patients listed broke off treatment, so that the percentage of successful treatments who finished treatment is approximately 66 per cent, approximately the same as under eclectic treatment and slightly worse than under a GP or custodial treatment.

Two further points require clarification: (*i*) are patients in our 'control' groups (Landis & Denker, 1948) as seriously ill as those in our 'experimental' groups? and (*ii*) are standards of recovery perhaps less stringent in our 'control' than in our 'experimental' groups? Although it is difficult to answer these questions definitely, from a close scrutiny of the literature it seems that the 'control' patients were probably at least as seriously ill as the 'experimental' patients, and possibly more so. As regards standards of recovery, those in Denker's study are as stringent as most of those used by psychoanalysts and eclectic psychiatrists, but those used by the State Hospitals in the Landis study are very probably more lenient.

What general conclusions can be drawn from these data? They fail to prove that psychotherapy, Freudian or otherwise, facilitates the recovery of neurotic patients; roughly two-thirds of a group of neurotic patients will recover or improve to a marked extent within about two years of the onset of their illness, whether they receive psychotherapy or not. This figure seems to be remarkably stable from one study to another, regardless of type of patient treated, standard of recovery used, or method of therapy used. From the point of view of the neurotic, these figures are encouraging; from the psychotherapist's point of view, they can hardly be called very favourable to his claims.

The results do not necessarily disprove the possibility of therapeutic effectiveness. There are obvious shortcomings in any actuarial comparison, and these are particularly serious when there is so little agreement among psychiatrists regarding even the most fundamental concepts and definitions. Definite proof would require a special investigation, carefully planned and methodologically more adequate than these *ad hoc* comparisons. But even so, the results should make us seriously question the justification of giving an important place in the training of clinical psychologists to a skill whose existence and effectiveness is still unsupported by any scientifically acceptable evidence.

These results and conclusions will no doubt contradict the strong feeling of usefulness and therapeutic success which many psychiatrists and clinical psychologists have. In the absence of agreement between fact and belief, there is urgent need for a decrease in the strength of belief and an increase in the number of facts available. Until such facts as may be discovered in a rigorous analysis support the prevalent belief in therapeutic effectiveness of psychological treatment, it seems premature to insist on the inclusion of training in such treatment in the curriculum of the clinical psychologist.

Summary

A survey was made of reports on the improvement of neurotic patients after psychotherapy, and the results compared with the best available estimates of recovery without benefit of such therapy. The figures fail to support the hypothesis that psychotherapy facilitates recovery from neurotic disorder. In view of the many difficulties associated with such actuarial comparisons, no further conclusions could be drawn from the data, whose shortcomings highlight the necessity of properly planned and executed experimental studies of this important field.

Commentary

Aim and nature

The study is a survey of a large number of studies dealing with the improvement of neurotic patients following psychotherapy (either psychoanalytic or eclectic). It is intended to test the hypothesis that 'psychotherapy facilitates recovery from neurotic disorder', i.e. increases the chances of recovery. Eysenck does this by comparing those patients who have received psychotherapy (the 'experimental' group) with a 'control' group of patients who had been hospitalized for 'neurosis' in state mental hospitals

(Landis, 1938) or had been treated only by their GPs with sedatives, tonics, suggestion and reassurance (Denker, 1946). These control groups provided a 'baseline' of spontaneous recovery ('remission') against which to compare the patients who received psychotherapy, and 66 per cent was the 'figure to beat'. (Eclectic means 'mixed', a combination of different therapeutic techniques, not based on one particular school, such as Freudian psychoanalysis.) Eysenck's article is largely responsible for the explosion of research into the effects of psychotherapy (and other forms of treatment) (Oatley, 1984).

Context and background

All forms of psychotherapy originate from Freud's psychoanalytic therapy, and Eysenck has always been one of Freud's most outspoken critics, both of his theory of personality and techniques of psychotherapy, which are intimately connected. Eysenck is a leading advocate of methods of treatment based on classical learning theory (i.e. conditioning), in particular those methods based on classical (Pavlovian) conditioning, known as behaviour therapy. From this perspective (*i*) all behaviour, whether adaptive or maladaptive, is acquired by the same principles of classical conditioning; (*ii*) according to Eysenck and Rachman (1965), the case of Little Albert (see chapter 22) exemplifies how *all* normal fears are acquired (i.e. through classical conditioning), although they have both modified their views since then (see chapter 13); (*iii*) the medical model is completely rejected, including any distinction between 'symptoms' and underlying pathology; according to Eysenck (1960), if you 'get rid of the symptoms ... you have eliminated the neurosis', i.e. what you see is what there is. However, MacKay (1975) observes that some behaviour therapists do use the formal diagnostic categories ('syndromes'), and try to discover which techniques are most effective with particular diagnostic groups; key figures in this nomothetic approach are Eysenck, Rachman and Marks ('*behavioural technology*'); (*iv*) the emphasis is on *current* behaviour and environmental influences; psychological problems are behavioural problems which need to be *operationalized* in terms of observable behaviours before any attempt can be made to change them.

(*i*) To some degree, Freud agrees with Eysenck regarding the same principles being involved in the development of normal/abnormal behaviour, except, of course, the principles are rather different. So, for example, neurotic symptoms and dreams (which have much in common 'structurally') and defence mechanisms are all compromises between the opposing demands, made on the ego by the id and superego-neuroses are maladaptive solutions to the individual's problems, but involve essentially the same compromises (especially defence mechanisms) involved in adaptive behaviour (e.g. phobias involve repression, as do all neuroses; displacement and projection, see chapter 24; (*ii*) Freud also rejected the medical model; although he did distinguish between 'symptoms' and 'underlying pathology', the latter is conceived in psychological (not genetic or biochemical) terms, and he was concerned with the individual and not the disorder. For example, a phobia is only the conscious, overt, manifestation of an internal, unconscious conflict. The phobic object has become symbolically associated with the underlying source of conflict and anxiety. Although he used diagnostic labels, he did so as linguistic conveniences rather than as an integral part of his theories, and he focused on understanding the patient's problems in their life context rather than on clinical labelling (Mackey, 1975); (*iii*) Freud's emphasis is very much on past events, particularly early childhood ones of a sexual nature and on unconscious (and other internal) factors; the latter, at best, can only be inferred from the patient's recollections etc., and are essentially based on hypothetical constructs.

Evaluation

1 Where Freud and Eysenck disagree, they seem to do so fundamentally. And this is most clearly seen when we ask how to assess the effectiveness of psychotherapy, the crux of Eysenck's famous 1952 paper. The criteria Eysenck refers to in the article (used by Denker) are (*i*) return to work and ability to carry on well in economic adjustments for at least five years; (*ii*) complaint of no further or very slight difficulties; (*iii*) making successful social adjustments. These are all fairly tangible indicators of improvement, and even more so are the behaviour therapists' criteria that cure is achieved when patients no longer manifest the original maladaptive behaviour (e.g. the fear of spiders is eliminated). If these more stringent (or more easily measured) criteria of actual behaviour change are required before the therapist can be viewed as successful, then behaviour therapists *do* seem to be more effective than psychoanalysts or humanistic therapists (with cognitive approaches in between) (Rachman & Wilson, 1980; Shapiro & Shapiro, 1982).

But are those kinds of criteria necessarily appropriate to assessing 'cure' or improvement as applied to psychoanalysis?

According to Jacobs (1984), the goals of therapy are limited by what the client consciously wants to achieve and is capable of achieving, together with his/her motivation, ego strength, capacity for insight, ability to tolerate the frustration of gradual change, financial cost and so on. These factors, in turn, determine how cure is defined and assessed.

In practice, psychonalysis ranges from 'psychoanalytical first aid' (Guntrip, 1968) or symptom relief to different levels of more intense work. However, Storr (1966) believes that a quick, complete 'cure' is very much the exception rather than the rule, and most people who undergo psychoanalysis cannot expect their symptoms to easily disappear or – even if this should happen – that they will be freed of emotional problems. This is because of what we have already noted about neurotic symptoms being merely the outward and visible signs of an inner, less visible conflict; exploration and analysis of the symptoms inevitably lead to an analysis of the whole person, his/her development, temperament and character structure. Symptom analysis, therefore, is usually just the *beginning* of the analytic process, and most patients do not have clear cut symptoms anyway! (Storr, 1966).

Again, psychoanalytic therapists may answer the question 'Does therapy work?' by saying it is a misleading question, like asking whether friendship 'works'. It is an activity that people take part in, which is important to them, affects, moves, even transforms them (Oatley, 1984). But for Eysenck, if it cannot be empirically demonstrated that it has well-defined beneficial effects, then it is worthless. Because he is interested in comparing recovery rates (measured statistically), his assessment of the effects of therapy is purely *quantitative*, while psychoanalysts and those from other non-behavioural approaches (e.g. Rogers' client-centred therapy) are likely to be much more concerned with the *qualitative* aspects of therapy: *how* does it work, what is the nature of the therapeutic process, the role of the relationship between client and therapist, important qualities of the therapist, etc. The point here is that there are different *kinds* of questions one can ask by way of trying to assess the effects of psychotherapy.

2 In Eysenck's own terms, there are important limitations to his study which are acknowledged in the article itself:

(*i*) If the many patients who drop out of psychoanalysis are not counted as 'failures' or 'not cured', the figure for those who do not benefit rises from 44 per cent to 66 per cent.

(*ii*) Landis (1938) points out a number of differences between psychotherapy patients and those state hospital patients he used as a control group to provide the baseline. He concludes by saying that these differences 'all argue against the acceptance of [this] figure ... as a truly satisfactory baseline, but in the absence of any other better figure this must serve'.

(*iii*) Bergin (1971) reviewed some of the papers included in Eysenck's review, and concluded that, by choosing different criteria of 'improvement', the success rate of psychoanalysis could be raised to 83 per cent, and cites certain studies (not included in Eysenck's review) which showed a 30 per cent remission rate.

(*iv*) Bergin and Lambert (1978) reviewed 17 studies of untreated 'neurotics', and found a median spontaneous remission rate of 43 per cent. They also found that the rate of spontaneous remission varies a great deal depending on the disorder, e.g. generalized anxiety and depression are much more likely to 'cure themselves' than phobias or obsessive-compulsive disorders.

3 Smith and Glass (1977) reviewed 400 studies of a wide variety of therapies (including psychodynamic, Gestalt, client-centred therapy, Transactional Analysis, Systematic Desensitization and eclectic) and concluded that all were more effective than no treatment, e.g. the 'average' client who had received therapy scored more favourably on the outcome measures than 75 per cent of those in the untreated control groups. Furthermore, there seemed to be no significant differences between behavioural and non-behavioural therapies. Luborsky *et al.* (1975) also found all forms of therapy to be equally effective. Smith *et al.* (1980) extended the earlier study to include 475 studies (an estimated 75 per cent of the published literature). Strict criteria for admission into their 'meta-analysis' included the comparison between a treated group (given a specified form of therapy) with a second group (drawn from the same population) given either no therapy, put on a waiting list or given some alternative form of therapy. Again, therapy was shown to have a significant effect: the average client was better off than 80 per cent of the control groups on the outcome measures. They confirmed their earlier finding that, overall, neither behaviour therapy nor psychoanalytic therapy was superior, but different treatments did seem to be more effective with different kinds of mental/behavioural disorder.

Consistent with these findings, Bergin (1971) has stated that to ask 'Is therapy effective?' is unanswerable; we have to ask about a particular treatment, given by particular therapists to some particular homogeneous group of clients if we're to have any hope of answering it.

4 Finally, Smith *et al.* (1980) say about psychotherapy that it:

> may not educate as well as schools; it may not produce goods and services as well as management science; it may not cure illnesses as well as medicine; but it reaches a part of life that nothing else touches as well. (cited in Oatley, 1984)

Exercises

1 Name three of the differences (or possible differences) between the patients receiving psychotherapy and the control groups Landis used to establish a baseline. Which of the two control groups (Landis and Denker) is more reliable?

2 Why was it necessary to establish a baseline at all?

3 What are the three basic techniques used in psychoanalysis?

4 Briefly describe the differences between Systematic Desensitization, Implosion and Flooding as forms of behaviour therapy.

5 What is meant by 'symptom substitution'?

D.L. ROSENHAN (1973)

On being sane in insane places

Science, 179, pp. 250–8

If sanity and insanity exist, how shall we know them?

The question is neither capricious nor itself insane. However much we may be personally convinced that we can tell the normal from the abnormal, the evidence is simply not compelling. It is commonplace, for example, to read about murder trials in which eminent psychiatrists for the defence are contradicted by equally eminent psychiatrists for the prosecution regarding the defendant's sanity. More generally, there are a great deal of conflicting data on the reliability, utility, and meaning of such terms as 'sanity', 'insanity', 'mental illness' and 'schizophrenia' (Ash, 1949; Beck, 1962; Boisen, 1939; Kreitman, 1961; Kreitman *et al.*, 1961; Schmitt & Fonda, 1956; Seeman, 1953). As early as 1934, Benedict suggested that normality and abnormality are not universal; what is viewed as normal in one culture may be seen as quite aberrant in another. Thus, notions of normality and abnormality may not be quite as accurate as people believe they are.

To raise questions about normality and abnormality is in no way to question the fact that some behaviours are deviant or odd. Murder and hallucinations are deviant. Nor does raising such questions deny the personal anguish often associated with 'mental illness'; anxiety, depression and psychological suffering exist. But normality and abnormality, sanity and insanity, and the diagnoses which flow from them may be less substantive than many believe them to be.

At its heart, the question of whether the sane can be distinguished from the insane (and whether degrees of insanity can be distinguished from each other) is a simple one: do the salient characteristics that lead to diagnosis reside in the patients themselves or in the environments and contexts in which observers find them? From Bleuler, through Kretschmer, through the recently revised *Diagnostic and Statistical Manual* of the American Psychiatric Association, there has been a strong belief that patients present symptoms which can be categorized and, implicitly, that the sane are distinguishable from the insane. But more recently, based on theoretical, anthropological, philosophical, legal and therapeutic considerations, the view has grown that psychological categorization of mental illness is, at best, useless and, at worst, harmful, misleading and pejorative. Psychiatric diagnoses are seen as being in the minds of the observers, and are not valid summaries of characteristics displayed by the observed (Becker, 1963; Braginsky *et al.*, 1969; Crocetti & Lemkau, 1965; Goffman, 1961, 1964; Laing, 1960; Phillips, 1963; Sarbin, 1972; Scheff, 1966; Schur, 1969; Szasz, 1963).

A way of deciding between these views is to get normal people (i.e. people who do not have, and have never suffered, symptoms of serious psychiatric disorders) admitted to psychiatric hospitals, and then determining whether they were discovered to be sane and, if so, how. If the sanity of such pseudo-patients were always detected, there would be prima-facie evidence that a sane individual can be distinguished from the insane context in which he is found, since it is carried within the person. But if the pseudopatients' sanity were never detected, serious difficulties would arise for those who support traditional modes of psychiatric diagnoses. Assuming that the hospital staff were not incompetent, that the pseudopatient had been behaving as sanely as he had been outside the hospital, and that it had never been previously suggested that he belonged in a psychiatric hospital, such an unlikely outcome would support the view that psychiatric diagnosis betrays little about the patient, but much about the environment in which he is observed.

This article describes such an experiment. Eight sane people gained secret admission to 12 different hospitals. (Data from a ninth pseudopatient are not included because, although his sanity went undetected, he falsified aspects of his personal history, and so his experimental behaviours were not identical to those of the others.) Too few psychiatrists and psychologists, including those who have worked in psychiatric institutions, know what the experience is like of being a patient, and while there have been occasional reports of researchers submitting themselves to psychiatric hospitalization (Barry, 1971; Belkaug, 1956; Candill *et al.*, 1952; Goldman *et al.*, 1970), these researchers have commonly stayed in the hospitals for short periods of time, often with the knowledge of the hospital staff. How much were they treated like patients and how much like research colleagues? Their reports about the inside of the psychiatric hospital have been valuable. This article extends those efforts.

Pseudopatients and their settings

The eight pseudopatients comprised a psychology graduate student in his 20s, three psychologists, a paediatrician, a psychiatrist, a painter and a housewife (three women, five men). All used pseudonyms, in case their alleged diagnoses embarrass them later. Those in the mental health professions claimed other occupations in order to avoid the special attentions which might be accorded by staff, as a matter of courtesy, or caution, to ailing colleagues. Apart from myself (I was the first pseudopatient, and my presence was known to the hospital administrator and chief psychologist and, as far as I can tell, to them alone), the presence of pseudopatients and the nature of the research program were unknown to the hospital staffs.

In order to generalise the findings, admission into a variety of hospitals was sought. The 12 hospitals in the sample were located in five different states on the East and West coasts. Some were old and shabby, some quite new, some were research orientated, others not, some had good staff–patient ratios, others were quite understaffed. Except for one private hospital, all were state or federal funded or, in one case, university funded.

After calling the hospital for an appointment, the pseudopatient arrived at the admissions office complaining that he had been hearing voices. Asked what the voices said, he replied that they were often unclear, but as far as he could tell they said 'empty', 'hollow', and 'thud'. The voices were unfamiliar and were of the same sex as the pseudopatient. These symptoms were chosen partly because of their apparent similarity to existential symptoms, which are alleged to arise from painful concerns about the perceived meaningfulness of one's life ('my life is empty and hollow'), and partly because of the *absence* of a single report of existential psychoses in the literature.

Beyond alleging the symptoms and falsifying name, vocation and employment, no further alterations of person, history or circumstances were made. The significant events of life history, relationships with parents and siblings, spouse and children, work colleagues and people at school (consistent with the above-mentioned exceptions) were described as they were or had been. Frustrations and upsets were described along with joys and satisfactions. If anything, these facts should have strongly biased the subsequent results in favour of detecting sanity, since none of their histories or current behaviours was seriously pathological in any way.

Immediately upon admission to the psychiatric ward, the pseudopatient stopped simulating *any* symptoms of abnormality. In some cases, there was a brief period of mild nervousness, since none really believed that they would be admitted so easily; indeed, their shared fear was that they would be immediately exposed as frauds and greatly embarrassed. Many had never visited a psychiatric ward before. So their nervousness was quite appropriate to the novelty of the hospital setting and abated rapidly.

Apart from this short-lived nervousness, the pseudopatients behaved 'normally' on the ward, speaking to patients and staff as they might ordinarily. Because there is uncommonly little to do on a psychiatric ward, they tried to engage others in conversation. When asked by staff how they were feeling, they indicated that they were fine and no longer experienced symptoms. They responded to instructions from attendants, to calls for medication (which was not swallowed), and to dining hall instructions. Beyond the activities that were available on the admissions ward, they spent their time writing down their observations about the ward, its patients and staff. Initially this was done 'secretly', but it soon became clear that no one much cared, so it was subsequently done quite openly, in such public places as the dayroom.

The pseudopatient, very much as a true psychiatric patient, entered hospital with no foreknowledge of when he would be discharged. Each was told that he would have to get out by his own devices, essentially by convincing the staff that he was sane. The psychological stresses associated with hospitalisation were considerable, and all but one of the pseudopatients wished to be discharged almost immediately after admission. They were, therefore, motivated not only to behave sanely, but to be paragons of cooperation. Nursing reports, obtained for most of them, all indicate that they were 'friendly', 'cooperative' and 'exhibited no abnormal indications'.

The normal are not detectably sane

Despite their public 'show' of sanity, the pseudopatients were never detected. Except in one case, they were admitted with a diagnosis of schizophrenia, and discharged with a diagnosis of schizophrenia 'in remission'. The label 'in remission' in no way indicates that the pseudopatient had been suspected of simulating mental illness; indeed the evidence is rather strong that, once labelled schizophrenic, the label stuck, so that if he was to be discharged, he must naturally be 'in remission', not sane, nor, in the institution's view, had he ever been sane.

Although there were considerable variations between the hospitals, several are considered excellent. Length of hospitalisation ranged from seven to 52 days (average 19 days), so there was plenty of opportunity for them to be carefully observed, although, in fact, they were not.

Pseudopatients' daily visitors could detect no serious behavioural consequences of hospitalisation, nor could other patients; indeed, it was quite common for the patients to 'detect' their sanity. During the first three hospitalisations, when accurate accounts were kept, 35 out of 118 patients on the admissions ward voiced their suspicions, some vigorously: 'You're not crazy. You're a journalist, or a professor [referring to the continual note-taking]. You're checking up on the hospital'. While most of the patients were reassured by the pseudopatients' insistence that he had been sick before he came in, but was fine now, some continued to believe that he was sane throughout the hospitalisation. So are patients better at detecting normality than psychiatrists?

Perhaps doctors are strongly biased towards Type-two errors (Scheff, 1966), i.e. they are more inclined to call a healthy person sick (a false positive) than a sick person healthy (a false negative, Type-one error). It is clearly more dangerous to mis-diagnose illness than health, so it is better to err on the side of caution. However, what holds for medicine does not hold equally well for psychiatry. Medical illnesses, while unfortunate, are not usually pejorative, but psychiatric diagnoses carry with them personal, legal and social stigmas (Cumming & Cumming, 1965; Farina & King, 1965; Freeman & Simmons, 1963; Johannsen, 1969; Linsky, 1970). It was therefore important to see whether the tendency toward diagnosing the sane insane could be reversed. An experiment was arranged at a research and teaching hospital whose staff had heard these findings, but doubted that such an error could occur in their hospital. They were informed that at some time during the next three months, one or more pseudopatients would attempt to be admitted into the hospital. Each staff member was asked to rate on a ten-point scale each patient who presented himself at admissions or on the ward as to the likelihood that he was a pseudopatient.

Judgements were obtained on 193 patients submitted for psychiatric treatment. All staff who had had sustained contact with, or primary responsibility for, the patient – attendants, nurses, psychiatrists, doctors and psychologists – were asked to make judgements. 41 patients were confidently judged to be pseudopatients by at least one staff member, 23 were suspected by at least one psychiatrist, and 19 were suspected by one psychiatrist *and* one other staff member. In fact, all patients during this period were genuine.

The experiment indicates that the tendency to designate sane people as insane can be reversed when the stakes are high (prestige and diagnostic acumen). But were the 19 people suspected of being 'sane' by one psychiatrist and another staff member truly 'sane', or was it that, in trying to avoid the Type-two error, the staff tended to make more Type-one errors? There is no way of knowing, but one thing is certain: any diagnostic process which lends itself so readily to massive errors of this sort cannot be a very reliable one.

The stickiness of psychodiagnostic labels

Beyond the tendency to call the healthy sick – a tendency which accounts better for diagnostic behaviour on admission than after a lengthy period of exposure – the data indicate the massive role of labelling in psychiatric assessment. Having been labelled schizophrenic, there is nothing the pseudopatient can do to remove it, and it profoundly colours others' perceptions of him and his behaviour.

These findings are consistent with Gestalt psychology's emphasis on the meaning given to elements by the context in which they occur, and with Asch's (1946) findings that there are powerful 'central' personality traits (e.g. 'warm' vs. 'cold') which markedly colour the meaning of other information when forming an impression of another person. 'Insane', 'schizophrenic' 'manic-depressive' and 'crazy' are probably some of the most powerful of such central traits; indeed, many of the pseudopatients' normal behaviours were entirely overlooked or profoundly misinterpreted. As far as I can determine, diagnoses were in no way affected by the relative health of the circumstances of a pseudopatient's life. Rather, the reverse occurred: the perception of his circumstances was shaped entirely by the diagnosis. For example, one pseudopatient had had a close relationship with his mother, but was rather remote from his father during early childhood. But during adolescence and beyond, his father became a close friend, while his relationship with his mother cooled. His present relationship with his wife was close and warm; apart from occasional angry exchanges, friction was minimal. The children had rarely been spanked. Surely there is nothing especially pathological about such a history; but observe how it was translated in the psychopathological context (the case summary prepared after the patient's discharge):

> This white 39-year-old male ... manifests a long history of considerable ambivalence in close relationships, which begins in early childhood. A warm relationship with his mother cools during his adolescence. A distant relationship to his father is described as becoming very intense. Affective stability is absent. His attempts to control emotionality with his wife and children are punctuated by angry outbursts and, in the case of the children, spankings. And while he says that he has several good friends, one senses considerable ambivalence embedded in these relationships also ...

The facts of the case were unintentionally distorted by the staff to achieve consistency with a popular theory of the dynamics of a schizophrenic reaction. If there were any ambivalence in his relationships, it was probably no greater than is found in all human relationships. Clearly, the meaning given to his verbalisations (i.e. ambivalence, affective instability) was determined by the diagnosis of schizophrenia. An entirely different meaning would have been attached if it were known that the man was 'normal'.

All pseudopatients took extensive notes, publicly, and this raised questions in the patients' minds, as you would expect. Indeed, it seemed so certain that the notes would arouse suspicion, that elaborate precautions were taken to remove them from the ward each day. However, the closest any staff member came to questioning these notes occurred when one pseudopatient asked about his medication, and began to write down the response; 'You needn't write it', he was told gently by the doctor. 'If you have trouble remembering, just ask me again'.

Nursing records for three pseudopatients indicate that the writing was seen as an aspect of their pathological behaviour. 'Patient engages in writing behaviour' was the daily nursing comment on one of the pseudopatients who was never questioned about his writing. Given that the patient is in hospital, he must be psychologically disturbed, and given that he is disturbed, continuous writing must be a behavioural manifestation of that disturbance, perhaps a subset of the compulsive behaviours sometimes correlated with schizophrenia.

Pseudopatients' notes are full of patient behaviours which were misinterpreted by well-intentioned staff as stemming from within the patient, rather than the complex of environmental stimuli surrounding him. For example, one kindly nurse found a pseudopatient pacing the long hospital corridors. 'Nervous, Mr X?', she asked. 'No, bored', he said. Again, not uncommonly, a patient would go 'beserk', because he had, wittingly or unwittingly, been mistreated by, say, an attendant. A nurse coming upon the scene would rarely inquire even cursorily into the possible environmental causes, but assumed that his upset stemmed from his pathology. Occasionally, a relative who had recently visited, or another patient might be suspected of triggering the outburst, but never a member of staff or the structure of the hospital. And a psychiatrist described a group of patients sitting outside the cafeteria half an hour before lunchtime as displaying the oral-acquisitive nature of the syndrome.

Just as Zigler and Phillips (1961) have shown that there is enormous overlap in the symptoms presented by patients with various diagnoses, so there is enormous overlap in the behaviours of the sane and the insane. We all lose our tempers 'for no good reason', feel depressed or anxious occasionally, again for no good reason, and find it difficult to get on with some other person. Conversely, the pseudopatients felt that the bizarre behaviour upon which patients' diagnoses were allegedly based constituted only a small fraction of their total behaviour. If it makes no sense to label ourselves as permanently depressed on the basis of occasional depression, then it takes better evidence than is currently available to label all patients insane or schizophrenic based on bizarre behaviours or cognitions. It seems more useful, as Mischel (1968) has suggested, to discuss *behaviours*, the stimuli which provoke them, and their correlates.

The experience of psychiatric hospitalization

'Mental illness' is a recent term, and was coined by people who, for humanitarian reasons, wanted to change the status of the psychologically disturbed from that of witches and 'crazies' to one akin to the physically ill. But while their treatment has improved, they are still not seen in the same way as the physically ill; for example, mental illness supposedly lasts forever, and public attitudes are characterised by fear, hostility, aloofness, suspicion and dread (Sarbin & Mancuso, 1970; Sarbin, 1967; Nunnally, 1961). The mentally ill are society's lepers.

More disconcerting is the observation that these attitudes affect mental health professionals, who, while insisting that they are sympathetic to the mentally ill, probably experience an exquisite ambivalence towards psychiatric patients which includes negative attitudes. These attitudes are the natural offspring of the labels patients wear, and the places in which they are found. In the typical psychiatric hospital, staff and patients are strictly segregated, having their own dining facilities, bathrooms and assembly places. Staff emerge from the glassed quarters (which the pseudopatients came to call the 'cage') mainly for caretaking purposes: to give medication, conduct a therapy or group meeting, instruct or reprimand a patient. Otherwise, staff keep to themselves, almost as if the disorder which afflicts their charges is somehow catching.

Doctors, especially psychiatrists, were even less available than nurses and attendants. They were rarely seen on the wards. Often they would be seen only when they arrived and departed, with the remaining time being spent in their offices or in the cage. Stanton and Schwartz (1954) have commented on the hierarchical organisation of the psychiatric hospital, but its hidden meaning is worth noting again. Those with the most power have least to do with patients, and those with the least power have most to do with them, i.e. the attendants.

However, in so far as they learn from their superiors' behaviour, they still spend as little time with the patients as they can, being seen mainly in the cage, which is were the models, the action and the power are.

In four hospitals, the pseudopatient approached a staff member with a request which took the following form: 'Pardon me, Mr [or Dr or Mrs] X, could you tell me when I will be presented at the staff meeting?' (or '. . . when am I likely to be discharged?'). While the content of the question varied according to the appropriateness of the target and the pseudopatient's (apparent) current needs, the form was always a courteous and relevant request for information. Care was taken never to approach a particular staff member more than once a day (so as not to arouse their suspicions or irritate them), and the behaviour was neither bizarre nor disruptive. The data from these experiments are shown in table 29.1. Small differences between the four institutions were overshadowed by the degree to which staff avoided continuing contacts which patients had initiated. By far their most common response was either a brief reply to the question while they were 'on the move' and with head averted, or no response at all. Often the reply was 'Good morning [Dave]. How are you today?' (moves off without waiting for an answer).

Table 29.1 also includes data recently obtained from Stanford University, where a young lady approached individual faculty mem-

Table 29.1 Self-initiated contact by pseudopatients with psychiatrists, nurses and attendants compared to contact with other groups

Contact	Psychiatric hospitals		University campus (non-medical)	University medical centre physicians		
	(1) Psychiatrists	(2) Nurses & attendants	(3) Faculty	(4) 'Looking for a psychiatrist'	(5) 'Looking for an internist'	(6) No additional comments
Responses						
Moves on, head averted (%)	71	88	0	0	0	0
Makes eye contact (%)	23	10	0	11	0	0
Pauses and chats (%)	2	2	0	11	0	10
Stops and talks (%)	4	0.5	100	78	100	90
Mean number of questions answered (out of six)	*	*	6	3.8	4.8	4.5
Respondents (No.)	13	47	14	18	15	10
Attempts (No.)	185	1283	14	18	15	10

* not applicable

bers who seemed to be walking purposefully to a meeting or teaching engagement, and asked them six questions, including how to get to various parts of the campus. Without exception, all the questions were answered, no matter how rushed they were, all the respondents maintained eye contact and stopped to talk. Similar results were found in the University medical centre; except that when the young lady indicated that she was looking for a psychiatrist, she received less cooperation than when she indicated that she was looking for an internist.

Powerlessness and depersonalisation

Absence of eye contact and verbal contact reflect avoidance and depersonalisation. I have records of patients who were beaten by staff just for having initiated verbal contact, as well as other kinds of punishment which seemed psychiatrically totally unjustifiable, but which seemed to go unquestioned. But neither anecdotal nor 'hard' data can convey the overwhelming sense of powerlessness which invades the individual as he is continually exposed to the depersonalisation of the psychiatric hospital, whether this is public or private.

Powerlessness was evident everywhere. The patient is deprived of many of his legal rights by virtue of his psychiatric commitment (Wexler & Scoville, 1971), his freedom of movement is restricted, he cannot initiate contact with staff, but only respond to their overtures, personal privacy is minimal, his personal history is available to any staff member (including volunteers) who chooses to read his file, and water closets may have no doors. Sometimes pseudopatients felt that they were invisible, as when the initial examination was taken in a semi-public room, where staff members went about their business as if we were not there. On the ward, attendants gave out verbal and occasionally serious physical abuse to patients in the presence of other observing patients, some of whom (the pseudopatients) were writing it all down, but it stopped quite abruptly when other staff members were known to be coming. Staff are credible witnesses, patients are not.

The sources of depersonalization

The ambivalent attitude, which was discussed above, leads to avoidance, while the hierarchical structure of the psychiatric hospital facilitates depersonalization. There is also genuine underfunding, which means staff shortages, and it is usually patient contact that is sacrificed. But the addition of more staff would not necessarily improve patient care in this respect, since, even during hard times, staff meetings and record keeping are given higher priority than patient contact. The heavy reliance on psychotropic drugs tacitly contributes to depersonalization by convincing staff that treatment is indeed being conducted and that further patient contact may not be necessary. And why is there such a reliance on drugs in the first place?

The consequences of labelling and depersonalization

Rather than confessing that we don't know, or are just embarking on understanding, we continue to label patients 'schizophrenic' etc., as if in those words we had captured the essence of understanding. But we have known for a long time that diagnoses are often not useful or reliable, and that we cannot distinguish insanity from sanity. How many people have been needlessly stripped of their privileges of citizenship, right to vote and drive and handle their own accounts? How many have feigned insanity in order to avoid the criminal consequences of their behaviour and, conversely, how many would rather stand trial than live interminably in a psychiatric hospital, but are wrongly thought to be mentally ill? A 'Type-two error in psychiatric diagnosis does not have the same consequences it does in medical diagnosis: a mis-diagnosed cancer is a cause for celebration, but psychiatric diagnoses are rarely found to be in error because the label sticks, a mark of inadequacy forever.

Finally, how many patients might be 'sane' outside the psychiatric hospital, but seem insane in it; not because craziness resides in them, but because they're responding to a bizarre setting. Goffman (1961) calls the process of socialisation to such institutions 'mortification', which includes depersonalization.

Summary and conclusions

It is clear that we cannot distinguish the sane from the insane in psychiatric hospitals, which themselves impose a special environment in which the meanings of behaviour can easily be distorted. Patients suffer powerlessness, depersonalization, segregation, moritification and self-labelling, all undoubtedly counter-therapeutic.

However, some promise seems to come from two sources; (*i*) the proliferation of community mental health facilities, crisis intervention centres, the human potential movement and behaviour therapies which avoid psychiatric labels, focus on specific problems and behaviours, and retain the individual in a relatively non-pejorative environment; (*ii*) the need to increase the sensitivity of mental health workers and researchers to the catch-22 position of psychiatric patients.

Our overwhelming impression of the staff was of people who really cared, were committed and were uncommonly intelligent. Where they failed, as they sometimes did painfully, it would be more accurate to attribute those failures to the environment in which they, too, found themselves than to personal callousness. In a more benign environment, one less attached to global diagnosis, their behaviours and judgements might have been more benign and effective.

Commentary

Aim and nature

The study is an experimental test of the hypothesis that psychiatrists cannot reliably tell the difference between people who are sane and those who are insane. The implication is that the classification system being used to make such a diagnosis cannot, therefore, be valid (since reliably differentiating the sane from the insane is a minimum requirement of a particular diagnostic label, e.g. schizophrenia, actually describing the mental illness the person is suffering from).

This was tested in two different ways: (*i*) the major experiment (what most of the article is devoted to describing and discussing, and the one usually cited by others) involved pseudopatients complaining of auditory hallucinations, and trying to get admitted to various hospitals in different parts of the US. So the manipulation involved this pretence (though this was dropped once admission had been gained), and the dependent variable was the psychiatrists' admission of the pseudopatient on the strength of a particular diagnostic label (in 11 out of 12 cases this was schizophrenia, the other being manic-depressive); (*ii*) a secondary experiment involved telling various members of staff at a research and teaching hospital, falsely, that they could expect one or more pseudopatients to try to gain admission during the next three months (based on accurate information concerning the first experiment). So this false information was the manipulated independent variable, and the dependent variable was the number of patients which staff subsequently suspected of being pseudopatients (remember, all patients were genuine).

The study also involves a large measure of participant observation, since, once admitted, the pseudopatients kept written records of how the ward as a whole operated, as well as how they personally were treated. One of the ironies of the findings is that it was (other) patients, if anybody, who suspected them, not the staff. Although they did not disclose their true identity (they did not 'blow their cover'), they did begin to behave as normally as possible (including saying they did not hear the voices any longer) and, to this extent, they were not 'fully participant'. However, the very nature of the findings meant that, at least as far as the *staff* were concerned, they were treated identically to other patients, which meant they could experience the ward from the patient's perspective while also maintaining the degree of objectivity required in a scientific investigation.

Context and background

The whole attempt to classify mental illness is, of course, an integral part of the *medical model* of mental illness. This is the view of mental disorder on which traditional psychiatry is based. Psychiatrists, as medical doctors, are trained to regard mental illness as comparable to other kinds of (physical) illness, but the symptoms are behavioural and cognitive rather than physical. (However, any hard-and-fast distinction between these two broad categories soon begins to break down: many symptoms of anxiety, for example, take a physical form, e.g. vomiting, sweating, goose-flesh, headaches and, conversely, physical illness will usually make us feel tired, depressed, lower our self-esteem, cause us anxiety, etc.)

The vocabulary used by psychologists and other non-psychiatrists, as well as the lay person, to refer to mental disorder is borrowed from medical terminology: deviant behaviour is referred to as *psychopathology*, is classified on the basis of *symptoms*, the classification being called a *diagnosis*, the methods used to try to change the behaviour are called *treatments* or *therapies* and these are often carried out in psychiatric *hospitals*. If the deviant behaviour ceases, the *patient* is said to be *cured* (Maher, 1966). It is the use of such vocabulary which reflects the pervasiveness of a 'sickness' model of psychological abnormality (together with terms such as 'syndrome', 'prognosis' and 'in remission'), i.e. we do tend to think about abnormal behaviour *as if* it were indicative of some underlying *illness*.

All systems of classification stem from the work of Emil Kraepelin (1913), who claimed that certain groups of signs and symptoms occur together sufficiently often to merit the designation 'disease' or syndrome; he then described the diagnostic indicators associated with each syndrome.

Kraepelin's classification is embodied in the 1959 Mental Health Act, and it is this that forms the basis of psychiatric classification in the UK, together with ICD-9: the Mental Disorders Section (9th Revision) of the International Classification of Diseases. Briefly, this identifies three main categories of mental disorder: mentall illness, personality disorder and subnormality/retardation. Mental illness in turn is subdivided into Neurosis and Psychosis, each with its own sub-divisions. As far as psychosis is concerned, a distinction is made between organic and functional, and schizophrenia is classified as a functional psychosis (i.e. there are as yet no known, identifiable, organic, causes).

In the USA, the American Psychiatric Association's official classification system is the Diagnostic and Statistical Manual of Mental Disorder (DSM), originally published in 1952, revised in 1968 (DSM-II) and revised again in 1980 (DSM-III), with a minor revision in 1987 (DSM-III-R). A major change between II and III (and so a major difference compared with the UK system) is that the distinction between neurosis and psychosis has been dropped: the category of 'neurosis' disappears, but there are categories for 'schizophrenic disorders' and 'psychotic disorders not elsewhere classified'.

Evaluation

1 The medical model, including the classification of mental disorders/abnormality, has been fiercely attacked and defended during the past 25 years or so, and there grew up in the 1960s what became known as the 'anti-psychiatry' movement, a group of psychiatrists and psychotherapists, among them R.D. Laing, Aaron Esterson, David Cooper and Thomas Szasz. Schizophrenia became the focus for their debate. Perhaps one of the best known and most controversial challenges to the medical model is that of Szasz (1972), who argues that the distinction between organic and functional disorder is really one between 'disease of the brain' (*not* the mind), or neurophysiological disorder, and 'problems in living'. Bailey (1979) makes a similar distinction, namely that between *physical* illness and *disorders of psychosocial* or *interpersonal functioning*. This way, the concept of *mental* illness is, effectively, got rid of.

2 The debate has taken place at many different levels, often less 'fundamental' than challenging the very concept of mental illness itself. In defence of classification, Kendell (1983) (cited in Miller & Morley, 1986), claims that every psychiatric patient has attributes at three levels: (A) those shared with *all* other psychiatric patients; (B) those shared with *some* other psychiatric patients; (C) those that are unique to them. Classification is feasible providing there are attributes at level (B) (the shared attributes are what constitutes one category as distinct from another). The value of classification depends on the relative size in importance of the attributes at (B) compared with (A) and (C). According to Miller and Morley (1986), 'It is certainly the conventional view of most psychologists and psychiatrists that there are important attributes at level B'.

3 But just how reliable is psychiatric classification? This question really lies at the heart of Rosenhan's experiment, since he was trying to show that psychiatrists cannot be 'trusted' to correctly identify people as genuine psychiatric patients as distinct from pseudopatients. Reliability is usually investigated by measuring the diagnostic agreement between two or more psychiatrists who have examined the *same* patients. Generally, agreement is quite high when discriminating between organic and functional disorders but can be very poor for specific diagnoses. For example, Kreitman (1961) found 75 per cent agreement for organic disorder, 61 per cent for functional psychoses, but only 28 per cent for neurotic disorders.

However, according to Cooper (1983) (cited in Miller & Morley, 1986), little attempt was made in any of these reliability studies to ensure that the different psychiatrists used agreed criteria, so there is scope for improving reliability even within the bounds of the present system. When attempts are made to construct special instruments or interview procedures for reaching a diagnosis based on operational criteria, and psychiatrists etc. are trained to use them, then fairly impressive levels of reliability are achieved, especially for schizophrenia and psychotic depression. Such instruments include the Present State Examination (Wing *et al.*, 1979), the Feighner Criteria (Feighner *et al.*, 1972), Research Diagnostic Criteria (Spitzer *et al.*, 1978), and Schedule for Affective Disorders and Schizophrenia (SADS) (Endicott & Spitzer, 1978).

4 DSM-III in the USA addressed itself largely to the whole problem of unreliability, especially unclear criteria. It covers a broader range of disorders, gives more specific categories, and uses more precise language than earlier versions; the use of check lists has helped to increase reliability, whereby the patient must show a specified number of observable symptoms before being given a particular diagnosis. Significantly, it was DSM-II which was in use at the time of Rosenhan's study; it seems much less likely that psychiatrists could be misled by pseudopatients using DSM-III, since a characteristic hallucination must be repeated on several occasions, whereas Rosenhan's colleagues basically made one such report! (Sarbin & Mancuso, 1980).

5 In defence of those psychiatrists, Kety (1974) poses the following (rather unsettling) scenario (cited in Sarbin & Mancuso, 1980):

> If I were to drink a quart of blood and, concealing what I had done, had come to the emergency room of any hospital vomiting blood, the behaviour of the staff would be quite predictable. If they labelled and treated me as having a bleeding peptic ulcer, I doubt that I could argue convincingly that medical science does not know how to diagnose that condition.

But as Sarbin & Mancuso (1980) say, Kety does not go on to ask what the doctors would say when no bleeding was observed the next day, and all the tests proved negative. Would they discharge the patient with a diagnosis of 'Bleeding peptic ulcer, in remission'? This, of course, is meant to parallel the situation Rosenhan's pseudopatients were in once they had been admitted.

One of Rosenhan's fiercest critics, Spitzer (1976), notes that the diagnosis 'Schizophrenia in remission' is extremely rare: in addition to his own New York hospital, he examined the records of discharged schizophrenic patients for 12 other US hospitals, and found that in 11 cases 'in remission' was either never used or used for only a handful of patients each year. Spitzer concluded from this that Rosenhan's pseudopatients were given a discharge diagnosis which is rarely given to *real* patients with an admission diagnosis of schizophrenia, and that, therefore, the diagnoses were a *function* of the pseudopatients' behaviours and *not* of the setting (psychiatric hospital) in which the diagnoses were made (as Rosenhan claims).

6 This, in turn, relates to the point about labelling which Rosenhan discusses at great length. Not only do psychiatric labels stick in a way that (other) medical labels do not, but, more seriously, *everything* the patient says and does is interpreted in accordance with the diagnostic label once it has been applied (e.g. the 'writing behaviour' of the pseudopatients). Rosenhan is arguing that mental illness is a purely social phenomenon, the consequence of a labelling process. A very relevant study here is one by Lindsay (1982). He obtained videotape recordings of subjects alleged to have schizophrenia and of normal controls. He showed them to a sample of ordinary people (patients in a general hospital), who acted as raters. One group was told nothing about the people in the video being rated, but two other groups were told either correctly or incorrectly, which were the schizophrenics and which were not. What would Rosenhan have predicted?

(*i*) Where information about the person's psychiatric status was withheld, ratings should not differ according to whether (s)he was actually a patient or not (especially as the tapes were carefully collected in order not to contain certain expressions of overt symptoms); (*ii*) for the other two groups, ratings should emerge as more abnormal for the people identified as schizophrenic, *regardless* of whether this attribution was correct.

What Lindsay found was that, although there was a small effect attributable to labelling, the overwhelming thrust of the results was that the schizophrenic patients were rated as more abnormal regardless of whether any information was provided or its accuracy. These results 'strongly indicate that the label is far from wholly an empty one, and that there is a reality of some kind behind it' (Miller & Morley, 1986).

Miller & Morley (1986) also point out that the patients taped by Lindsay were all fairly new cases, and so had not had long to adapt to the label and change their behaviour accordingly, as an extreme supporter of labelling would argue. They believe that to argue for 'labelling' as against the 'medical model' is a false dichotomy.

7 Finally, Spitzer (1976) points out that Rosenhan, as a professor of law and psychology, should know that the terms 'sane'/'insane' are *legal*, not psychiatric, concepts, and no psychiatrist makes a diagnosis of 'sanity'/'insanity'. This is ironic in view of Rosenhan's condemnation of the use of psychiatric labelling.

Exercises

1 Why was it important to use a range of hospitals, and in what respects did they differ?

2 Psychiatrists (and other doctors) are more likely to make Type-two errors. What does this mean here, and how does it differ from how Type-one and Type-two errors are usually defined in relation to hypothesis testing in psychology?

3 If Rosenhan had used control groups in the two experiments, what might have they have been?

4 Is there anything morally unacceptable about the concealment of the true identity of the pseudopatients and the inevitable deception involved?

SANDRA L. BEM (1974)

The measurement of psychological androgyny

Journal of Consulting and Clinical Psychology, Vol. 42, No. 2, pp. 155–62

This article describes the development of a new sex-role inventory that treats masculinity and femininity as two independent dimensions, thereby making it possible to characterize a person as masculine, feminine, or 'androgynous' as a function of the difference between his or her endorsement of masculine and feminine personality characteristics. Normative data are presented, as well as the results of various psychometric analyses. The major findings of conceptual interest are: (*i*) the dimensions of masculinity and femininity are empirically, as well as logically independent; (*ii*) the concept of psychological androgyny is a reliable one; (*iii*) highly sex-typed scores do not reflect a general tendency to respond in a socially desirable direction, but rather a specific tendency to describe oneself in accordance with sex-typed standards of desirable behaviour for men and women.

Both in psychology and society at large, masculinity and femininity have long been conceptualised as bipolar ends of a single continuum, such that a person has had to be either masculine or feminine, but not both. This sex-role dichotomy has served to obscure two very plausible hypotheses; (*i*) that many individuals might be 'androgynous', i.e. they might be *both* masculine *and* feminine, *both* assertive *and* yielding, instrumental *and* expressive (depending on the situational appropriateness of these various behaviours); conversely, (*ii*) that strongly sex-typed individuals might be seriously limited in the range of behaviours available to them as they move from situation to situation. Both Kagan (1964) and Kohlberg (1966) believe that the highly sex-typed individual is motivated to keep his/her behaviour consistent with an internalized sex-role standard, presumably by suppressing any behaviour thought to be sex-inappropriate or undesirable. Thus, a narrowly masculine self-concept might inhibit behaviours which are stereotyped as feminine (and similarly for a narrowly feminine self-concept and masculine behaviours), whereas a mixed, or androgynous, self-concept might allow an individual to freely engage in both kinds of behaviour.

Before the current research could begin, it was first necessary to develop a new type of sex-role inventory which would not automatically build in an inverse relationship between masculinity and femininity, and this article describes such an inventory.

The Bem-Sex Role Inventory (BSRI) contains a number of features which distinguish it from other, commonly used, masculinity–femininity scales, e.g. the Masculinity–Femininity scale of the California Psychological Inventory (Gough, 1957): (*i*) it includes both a Masculinity scale and a Femininity scale, each of which contains 20 personality characteristics (see table 30.1, below); (*ii*) because the BSRI was founded on a conception of the sex-typed person as someone who has internalized society's sex-typed standards of desirable behaviour for men and women, these personality characteristics were selected as masculine or feminine on the basis of sex-typed social desirability, and not on the basis of differential endorsement by males and females as most other inventories have done; i.e. a characteristic qualified as masculine if it was judged to be more desirable in American society for a man than for a woman, and, similarly, feminine if judged to be more desirable for a woman than a man; (*iii*)

Table 30.1 Items on the Masculinity, Femininity and Social Desirability scales of the BRSI

Masculine items	Feminine items	Neutral items
49 Acts as a leader	11 Affectionate	51 Adaptable
46 Aggressive	5 Cheerful	36 Concerted
58 Ambitious	50 Childlike	9 Conscientious
22 Analytical	32 Compassionate	60 Conventional
13 Assertive	53 Does not use harsh language	45 Friendly
10 Athletic	25 Eager to soothe hurt feelings	15 Happy
55 Competitive	20 Feminine	3 Helpful
4 Defends own beliefs	14 Flatterable	48 Inefficient
37 Dominant	59 Gentle	24 Jealous
19 Forceful	47 Gullible	39 Likeable
25 Has leadership abilities	56 Loves children	6 Moody
7 Independent	17 Loyal	21 Reliable
52 Individualistic	26 Sensitive to the needs of others	30 Secretive
31 Makes decisions easily	8 Shy	38 Sincere
40 Masculine	38 Soft spoken	42 Solemn
1 Self-reliant	23 Sympathetic	57 Tactful
34 Self-sufficient	44 Tender	12 Theatrical
16 Strong personality	29 Understanding	27 Truthful
43 Willing to take a stand	41 Warm	18 Unpredictable
28 Willing to take risks	2 Yielding	54 Unsystematic

Note: The number before each item refers to the position of each adjective as it actually appears on the inventory the BSRI characterizes a person as masculine, feminine or androgynous as a function of the difference between his/her endorsement of masculine and feminine personality characteristics. So a person is sex-typed, whether masculine or feminine, to the extent that this difference score is high, and androgynous to the extent that it is low; (*iv*) the BSRI also includes a Social Desirability scale which is completely neutral with respect to sex; it was used during the development of the BSRI to insure that the inventory was not simply tapping a general tendency to endorse socially desirable traits (see table 30.1).

Item selection

Both historically and cross-culturally, masculinity and femininity seem to have represented two complementary domains of *positive* traits and behaviours (Barry, Bacon & Child, 1957; Erikson, 1964; Parsons & Bales, 1955). In general, masculinity has been associated with an instrumental orientation, a cognitive focus on 'getting the job done', while femininity has been associated with an expressive orientation, an affective concern for the welfare of others.

Accordingly, as a preliminary to item selection for the Masculinity and Femininity scales, a list was compiled of approximately 200 personality characteristics that seemed to the author and several students to be both positive in value and either masculine or feminine in tone; this list served as the pool from which the masculine and feminine items were ultimately chosen. Similarly, an additional list of 200 characteristics was compiled which seemed to be neither masculine nor feminine in tone, half positive and half negative in value, from which the Social Desirability scale was chosen.

Because the BSRI was designed to measure how much a person divorces himself from those characteristics that might be considered more 'appropriate' for the opposite sex, the final items were selected if they were judged to be more desirable in American society for one sex than for the other. Specifically, judges used a seven-point scale, ranging from 1 ('Not at all desirable') to 7 ('Extremely desirable'), to rate the desirability of each of the approximately-400 personality characteristics mentioned above. (For example, 'In American society, how desirable is it for a man [woman] to be truthful [sincere]?'.) Each judge rated the desirability of all 400 characteristics either 'for a man' or 'for a woman'; no judge rated both. The judges were 40 Stanford undergraduates, who completed the questionnaires during the winter of 1972, and an additional 60 who did so the following summer in both samples; half were male and half were female.

A personality characteristic qualified as masculine if it was independently judged by both males and females in both samples to be significantly more desirable for a man than for a woman ($p < 0.05$, for a two-tailed t-test); similarly, for feminine personality characteristics. Of those characteristics which met these criteria, 20 were chosen for the Masculinity scale and 20 for the Femininity scale (see table 30.1). A neutral personality characteristic was one which (*i*) was independently judged by both males and females to be no more desirable for one sex than for the other ($t < 1.2, p > 0.2$), and (*ii*) did not produce significantly different desirability judgements by male and female judges ($t < 1.2, p > 0.2$). Ten positive and ten negative characteristics met these criteria, and were chosen for the Social Desirability scale in accordance with Edwards' (1964) finding that an item must be quite positive or quite negative in tone if it is to evoke a social desirability response set.

Once all the individual items had been selected, mean desirability scores were computed for the masculine, feminine and neutral items for each of the 100 judges. As table 30.2 shows, for both males and females, the mean desirability of the 60 masculine and feminine items was significantly higher for the 'appropriate' sex, whereas the mean desirability of the neutral items was no higher for one sex than the other. These results are, of course, a direct consequence of the criteria used for item selection.

Table 30.3 separates out the desirability ratings of the masculine and feminine items for male and female judges rating their *own* sex; this seems to best represent the desirability of these items as perceived by men and women when asked to describe *themselves* on the BSRI. Not only are 'sex-appropriate' characteristics more desirable for both sexes than 'sex-inappropriate' characteristics, but men and women are nearly equal in their perceptions of the desirability of sex-appropriate and sex-inappropriate characteristics and the differences between them ($t < 1$ in all three comparisons).

Table 30.2 Mean social desirability ratings of the masculine, feminine and neutral items

Item	Male judges			Female judges		
	Masculine item	Feminine item	Neutral item	Masculine item	Feminine item	Neutral item
For a man	5.59	3.63	4.00	5.83	3.74	3.94
For a woman	2.90	5.61	4.08	3.46	5.55	3.98
Difference	2.69	1.98	0.08	2.37	1.81	0.04
t	14.41★	12.13★	0.17	10.22★	8.28★	0.09

★ $p < 0.001$

Table 30.3 Mean social desirability ratings of the masculine and feminine items for one's own sex

Item	Male judges for a man	Female judges for a woman
Masculine	5.59	3.46
Feminine	3.63	5.55
Difference	1.96	2.09
t	11.94★	8.88★

★ $p < 0.001$

Scoring

The BSRI asks a person to indicate on a seven-point scale how well each of the masculine, feminine and neutral personality characteristics describes him/herself. The scale ranges from 1 ('Never or almost never true') to 7 ('Always or almost always true') and is labelled at each point. Each person receives a Masculinity score, a Femininity score and, most important, an Androgyny score; in addition, a Social Desirability score can also be calculated.

The Masculinity and Femininity scores indicate how much a person endorses masculine and feminine personality characteristics as self-descriptive. Masculinity equals the mean self-rating for all endorsed masculine items and Femininity equals the mean self-rating for all endorsed feminine items; both can range from 1 to 7 and the two scores, remember, are logically independent.

The Androgyny score reflects the relative amounts of masculinity and femininity that the person includes in his or her self description and, as such, it best characterizes the nature of the person's total sex role. Specifically, the Androgyny score is defined as students' t-ratio for the difference between a person's masculine and feminine self-endorsement; i.e. the difference between masculinity and femininity normalised with respect to the standard deviations of his or her masculinity and femininity scores. The use of a t-ratio (instead of a simple difference score) has two conceptual advantages; (i) it allows us to ask whether a person's endorsement of masculine characteristics differs significantly from his or her endorsement of feminine ones and, if it does ($|t| \geqslant 2.025$, $d.f. = 38$, $p < 0.05$), to classify that person as significantly sex-typed; (ii) it allows us to compare different populations in terms of the percentage of significantly sex-typed individuals present within each. (In the absence of computer facilities, one can use the simple Androgyny difference score, Femininity–Masculinity, as the index of androgyny. Empirically, the two indices are virtually identical ($r = 0.98$), and one can approximate the t-ratio value by multiplying the Androgyny difference score by 2.322: this conversion factor was derived empirically from the combined normative sample of 917 students at two different colleges.)

The greater the absolute value of the Androgyny score, the more the person is sex-typed or sex reversed, with high positive scores indicating femininity and high negative scores indicating masculinity. A 'masculine' sex role thus represents not only the endorsement of masculine characteristics, but the simultaneous rejection of feminine ones; similarly, with a 'feminine' sex role. By contrast, the closer the Androgyny score is to zero, the more the person is androgynous; an 'androgynous' sex role thus represents the equal endorsement of both masculine and feminine characteristics.

The Social Desirability score indicates how much a person describes him/herself in a socially desirable way on items which are neutral with respect to sex; it can range from 1 to 7, with 1 indicating a strong tendency to describe oneself in a socially undesirable direction and 7 indicating a strong tendency to describe oneself in a socially desirable direction.

Psychometric analyses

The BSRI was administered to 444 male and 279 female introductory psychology students at Stanford University, and to 117 male and 77 female paid volunteers at Foothill Junior College. Their data represent the normative data for the BSRI and serve as the basis for all of the analyses which follow.

Internal consistency

In order to estimate the internal consistency of the BSRI, coefficient alpha was calculated separately for the Masculinity, Femininity and Social Desirability scores of the subjects in both normative samples (Nunnally, 1967). The results showed all three scores to be highly reliable, both in the Stanford sample (Masculinity $\alpha = 0.86$; Femininity $\alpha = 0.80$; Social Desirability $\alpha = 0.75$), and in the Foothill sample (0.86, 0.82 and 0.70 respectively). Because the reliability of the Androgyny t-ratio could not be calculated directly, coefficient alpha was computed for the highly correlated Androgyny difference score (Femininity–Masculinity), and was found to be 0.85 for the Stanford sample and 0.86 for the Foothill sample.

Relationship between masculinity and femininity

These are logically independent scores, and the results of the two normative samples show them to be empirically independent as well (Stanford male $r = 0.11$, female $r = -0.14$; Foothill male $r = -0.02$, female $r = -0.07$).

Social desirability response set

Because the masculine and feminine items are all relatively desirable, even for the 'inappropriate' sex, it is important to verify that the Androgyny score is not simply tapping a social desirability response set. Accordingly, product-moment correlations were calculated between the Social Desirability score and the Masculinity, Femininity and Androgyny scores for the two samples separately. They were also calculated between the Social Desirability score and the absolute value of the Androgyny score. The correlations are shown in table 30.4. As

Table 30.4 Correlation of Masculinity, Femininity, and Androgyny with Social Desirability

Sample	Masculinity with social desirability		Femininity with social desirability		Androgyny with social desirability		Androgyny with social desirability	
Stanford	0.42	0.19	0.28	0.26	0.12	0.03	0.08	−0.10
Foothill	0.23	0.19	0.15	0.15	−0.07	0.06	−0.12	−0.09
Stanford and Foothill combined	0.38	0.19	0.28	0.22	0.08	0.04	0.03	−0.10

expected, both Masculinity and Femininity scores were correlated with Social Desirability, while near-zero correlations between Androgyny and Social Desirability confirm that the Androgyny score is not measuring a general tendency to respond in a socially desirable direction. Rather, it is measuring a very specific tendency to describe oneself in accordance with sex-typed standards of desirable behaviour for men and women.

Test-retest reliability

The BSRI was administered for a second time to 28 males and 28 females from the Stanford normative sample, approximately four weeks after the first. Subjects were told we were interested in how their responses on the test might vary over time, and more explicitly instructed not to try to remember how they had responded originally. Product-moment correlations were calculated between the first and second administrations for all four scores which all proved to be highly reliable (Masculinity, $r = 0.90$; Femininity, $r = 0.90$; Androgyny, $r = 0.93$; Social Desirability, $r = 0.89$).

Correlations with other measures of Masculinity–Femininity

During the second administration of the BSRI, subjects were also asked to complete the Masculinity–Femininity scales of the California Psychological Inventory and the Guilford-Zimmerman Temperament Survey, both of which have been used quite often in previous research on sex roles. As can be seen from table 30.5, the Guilford-Zimmerman scale is not at all correlated with any of the Masculinity, Femininity and Androgyny scales of the BSRI, whereas the California Psychological Inventory is moderately correlated with all three. The reason for this difference is not clear, but the fact that none of the correlations is particularly high indicates that the BSRI is measuring an aspect of sex roles which is not directly tapped by either of these other two scales.

Table 30.5 Correlation of the Masculinity–Femininity scales of the California Psychological Inventory (CPI) and Guilford-Zimmerman scale with the Masculinity, Femininity and Androgyny scales of the BSRI

Scale	CPI		Guilford-Zimmerman	
	Males	Females	Males	Females
BSRI Masculinity	−0.42	−0.25	0.11	0.01
BSRI Femininity	0.27	0.25	0.04	−0.06
BSRI Androgyny	0.50	−0.04	0.04	−0.06

Norms

Table 30.6 presents the mean Masculinity, Femininity and Social Desirability scores separately by sex for both normative samples, together with means for both the Androgyny *t*-ratio and the Androgyny difference score. As can be seen, males scored significantly

Table 30.6 Sex differences on the BSRI

Scale score	Stanford University			Foothill Junior College		
	Males ($n = 444$)	Females ($n = 279$)	t	Males ($n = 117$)	Females ($n = 77$)	t
Masculinity						
M	4.97	4.57		4.96	4.55	
SD	0.67	0.69	7.62*	0.71	0.75	3.86*
Femininity						
M	4.44	5.01		4.62	5.08	
SD						
Social Desirability						
M	4.91	5.08		4.88	4.89	
SD	0.50	0.50	4.40*	0.50	0.53	ns
Androgyny *t*-ratio						
M	−1.28	1.10		−0.80	1.23	
SD	1.99	2.29	14.33*	2.23	2.42	5.98*
Androgyny Difference Score						
M	−0.53	0.43		−0.34	0.53	
SD	0.82	0.93	14.28*	0.97	0.97	6.08*

*$p < 0.001$

higher than females on the Masculinity scale, and females scored significantly higher than males on the Femininity scale, in both samples. On the two measures of Androgyny, males scored on the masculine side of zero, and females on the feminine side; this difference is significant in both samples and for both measures. On the Social Desirability scale, females scored higher than males at Stanford, but not at Foothill; however, this sex difference is quite small, even at Stanford.

Table 30.7 shows the percentage of subjects within each normative sample who qualified as masculine, feminine or androgynous as a

Table 30.7 Percentage of subjects in the normative samples classified as masculine, feminine and androgynous

Item	Stanford University		Foothill Junior College	
	Males ($n = 444$)	Females ($n = 279$)	Males ($n = 117$)	Females ($n = 77$)
% Feminine ($t \geqslant 2.025$)	6	34	9	40
% near Feminine ($1 < t < 2.025$)	5	20	9	8
% androgynous ($-1 \leqslant t \leqslant +1$)	34	27	4	38
% near masculine ($-2.205 < t < -1$)	19	12	17	7
% masculine ($t \leqslant -2.205$)	36	8	22	8

function of the Androgyny *t*-ratio. Subjects are classified as sex-typed (whether masculine or feminine) if the Androgyny *t*-ratio reaches statistical significance ($|t| \geq 2.025$, $d.f. = 38$, $p < 0.05$), and as androgynous if the absolute value of the *t*-ratio is ≤ 1.00. Table 30.7 also shows the percentage of subjects who fall between these various cut-off points.

Concluding comment

Hopefully, the development of the BSRI will encourage investigators in the area of sex differences and sex roles to question the traditional assumption that it is the sex-typed individual who typified mental health, and to begin focusing on the behavioural and societal consequences of more flexible sex-role self-concepts. In a society where rigid sex-role differentiation has already outlived its usefulness, perhaps the androgynous person will come to define a more human standard of psychological health.

Commentary

Aim and nature

The article describes the development of a new sex-role inventory, the Bem Sex-Role Inventory (BSRI), a questionnaire designed to measure a person's degree of masculinity, femininity or androgyny. The study describes how the questionnaire items were selected, how it is scored, psychometric analyses of the internal consistency, test–retest reliability, correlations with other measures of masculinity and femininity, data for normative samples (standardization), as well as the problem of social desirability response set.

Background and context

According to Roger Brown (1986), masculinity and femininity have traditionally been conceived of as opposite poles on a single dimension, and many widely used psychological tests had this conception built into them. Because of the way they were designed and scored, it was impossible for an individual to register as both highly masculine and highly feminine; they were seen as mutually exclusive, in the sense that the nearer the masculine end of the scale you scored, the further away from the feminine end you were. So it was impossible to find any androgynous people. ('Mutually exclusive' usually implies 'either–or', i.e. one category or another. But here we're not using 'masculine' or 'feminine' in the sense of two categories or types, but as two ends of a single dimension. The point is that *high* scores in one implies *low* scores in the other.)

To 'discover' androgyny, it was necessary to see them as not mutually exclusive, but rather as two independent dimensions, and to incorporate this into a new sort of test which would produce two logically independent scores.

This traditional, 'lay' conception of masculinity/femininity was built into the tests developed between the 1930s and 1960s. For example, Terman and Miles' (1936) scale saw masculinity–femininity as a single bipolar dimension, the core of personality rooted somehow in sexual anatomy/physiology and relatively fixed. They selected items which would best differentiate between male and female. It was impossible for the same individual to obtain high scores on both, or low scores on both, masculinity and femininity.

Other tests, including those of Gough (1952), Guilford and Guilford (1936), Hathaway and McKinley, (1943) and Strong (1943) all shared this bipolar view. When scores on the tests were factor analyzed (i.e. tested for intercorrelations between different parts of the test), the same temperamental factors kept emerging: (*i*) independent, assertive, dominant and instrumental, (masculine) and (*ii*) interpersonal sensitivity, compassion and warmth (feminine). These corresponded closely with sociological (Parsons & Bales, 1955) and anthropological (Barry, Bacon & Child, 1957) ideas of what might be universal masculinity and femininity, and until the early 1970s, defined the dimensions most worth measuring (Brown, 1986).

Evaluation

1 The BSRI made it possible, logically and empirically, to measure androgyny by logically and empirically separating scores on masculinity and femininity, by having two separate scales. For large samples (male and female), the mean score on masculinity is higher for males and the mean score for femininity is higher for females (the scales really do differentiate the sexes). Where all subjects are either male or female, individual masculinity and femininity scales are uncorrelated, which means the two dimensions are empirically/factually – and not just logically – independent (Brown, 1986).

2 The BSRI is the most widely-used measure of sex-role stereotyping in adults (Hargreaves, 1986), but is not the only fairly recent test of androgyny. Quite independently of Bem, Spence, Helmreich and Stapp (1975) devised the 'Personal Attributes Questionnaire' (PAQ), which comprises instrumental (masculine) and expressive (feminine) trait terms (largely derived from the stereotypes described by Broverman *et al.*, 1972), which produces two essentially independent scores.

3 However, the PAQ did not assess androgyny in the same way as the BSRI, and this underlined a major problem with the BSRI, to do with the very concept of androgyny itself. By defining androgyny as the student *t*-ratio for the difference between a person's masculinity and femininity scores, Bem (unwittingly, of course) allowed for the same androgyny score (*t*-ratio of near zero) to be obtained in two very *different* ways: either by an individual who scores *high* on both scales or *low* on both. But surely two such individuals are likely to be very different kinds of persons, in which case what do their same androgyny scores mean? (Please note that what Bem calls the *t*-ratio is what is more commonly referred to as, simply, the *t*-test statistic.)

By contrast, PAQ allowed for four categories of persons: (*i*) the highly sex-typed male: *high* masculinity, low femininity; (*ii*) the highly sex-typed female: low masculinity, *high* femininity; (*iii*) the androgynous person: *high* masculine *and high* feminine; (*iv*) the 'undifferentiated' person: *low* masculine *and low* feminine. The crucial difference is that Bem did not distinguish between (iii) and (iv); she confounded them. Consequently, she compared her original (1974) results with those of Spence *et al.* and concluded that the four categories (2 × 2) was superior; androgyny was now defined as only high in both masculinity and femininity (not low in both too). Her revised, and shortened, version of the BSRI (1977) is considered to be equivalent to PAQ (Lubinski *et al*, 1983).

4 But Hargreaves *et al.* (1981) believe this four-way classification produces its own difficulties (e.g. the loss of information when subjects are divided into groups on the basis of median splits), and they proposed that androgyny is most parsimoniously (economically) assessed as the *product* of a subject's masculinity and femininity scores, i.e. they are conceptually distinct but *interacting* variables (Hargreaves, 1986).

5 Does the empirical research support the predictions made on the basis of the BSRI? Essentially, there are two: (*i*) scores on the BSRI will predict certain kinds of behaviour preference, and (*ii*) androgyny is a good predictor of psychological well-being/mental health.

(*i*) Bem's research strategy is to assess sex-typing by means of the BSRI, then to relate this to behaviour in real-life situations. For example, Bem and Lenney (1976) asked subjects to indicate which of a series of paired activities they would prefer to perform, for payment, while being photographed. 20 activities were stereotypically masculine (e.g. nail two boards together), 20 were stereotypically feminine (e.g. iron cloth napkins) and 20 were neutral (e.g. play with a yo-yo). Sex-typed subjects expressed a clear preference for sex-appropriate as opposed to sex-inappropriate activities, even though such choices paid less money than cross sex-typed activities.

(*ii*) Bem (1975) found that androgynous subjects show sex-role adaptability across situations, i.e. they will behave as the situation requires, even though this means behaving in a sex-inappropriate way. Lubinski *et al.* (1981) reported that they express greater subjective feelings of emotional well-being, and Spence *et al.* (1975) found that they show higher levels of self-esteem. However, the results are by no means clear that androgyny is a good predictor of psychological well-being; indeed, a review by Taylor and Hall (1982) suggests that masculinity in both males *and* females may be a *better* predictor than certain measures of androgyny, and Taylor (1986) makes the point that traditional sex roles are, on the whole, advantageous for men but disadvantageous for women. This asymmetry between males and females is expressed by Hefner *et al.* (1975) like this:

> ... both men and women are trapped in the prisons of gender ... but the situation is far from symmetrical; men are the oppressors and women are the oppressed. (quoted in Taylor, 1986)

Psychological well-being (measured by, for example, self-esteem, adjustment, relative absence of anxiety, depression, psychosomatic symptoms) is generally more strongly related to masculinity than femininity on the BSRI, and seems not to distinguish reliably between sex-typed and androgynous individuals (Taylor, 1986).

6 The BSRI does distinguish between male and female test-takers (Bem, 1974, 1977), as does the PAQ (Spence & Helmreich, 1978; Storms, 1979); although the differences in means are usually small, they are significant. As might be predicted, samples of gays (at the University of Texas), when compared with unselected male students, were found to be significantly lower on masculinity and higher on femininity, and the reverse pattern was found for lesbians, using PAQ (Spence & Helmreich, 1978). Larson (1981) found similar results using the BSRI.

However, Pedhazur and Tetenbaum (1979), after carrying out a large-scale factor analysis of BSRI scores, found that masculinity and femininity emerged as a distinct factor, independent of instrumentality and expressiveness. It seems that the relationship between these two temperaments and the popular understanding of masculinity and femininity is slight (Brown, 1986), and, as a result of the study, Bem dropped the latter from her revised, shorter BSRI (1977). PAQ had never included them.

7 So what do PAQ and the BSRI really measure? According to Spence (1983), they primarily measure instrumentality and expressiveness, and can no longer legitimately be characterized by the all-encompassing 'masculinity' and 'femininity'. It follows that androgyny is also inappropriate, and any attempt to link mental health with androgyny should be much more cautious/conservative, linking socially desirable instrumentality/ expressiveness with, mainly, high self-esteem.

By contrast, Bem (1984) has reformulated her ideas as *Gender Schema* theory. She believes that the BSRI and PAQ *are* adequate measures of sex-typing and androgyny. Sex-typing essentially involves spontaneously thinking of things in sex-typed terms, whereas androgyny is a disposition to process information in accordance with relevant non-sex principles. In deciding whether a particular attribute on the BSRI is(not) self-descriptive, the sex-typed person does not reflect on individual behaviour, but quickly 'looks up' the attribute in his/her gender schemas, and responds accordingly. The essential difference btween these two kinds of people is one of *cognitive* style. It no longer seems reasonable to expect androgynous *behaviour* in a sex-typed culture to be a mode of mental health, but Bem still believes that information-processing freed of the tyranny of sex-typing (androgyny) is desirable (Brown, 1986).

8 Perhaps another important qualification that should be made of the concept of androgyny is related to the variable of age. Hyde & Phillis (1979) gave the BSRI to 13 to 85 year olds, and Sinnot (1982) tested a large sample of 60 to 90 year olds (comparing them with Bem's (1974) younger subjects). Both studies found some evidence of reduced sex-typing in older men; they were likely to be more androgynous, less masculine and more feminine than younger men. But in older women, sex-typing was stronger. Sinnott also found that androgyny was generally associated with better physical and mental health (based mainly on self-reports) compared with highly sex-typed females and undifferentiated subjects. Allowing for income differences, masculinity scores were also overall associated with good mental health (Taylor, 1986).

9 Finally, what would be the consequences of Bem's goal of an androgynous society? If a society were to give meaning to behaviour in a way which ignored the actor's gender, the very notions of masculinity and femininity would cease to have significance. To the extent that we are currently able to specify the limits of masculinity and femininity, then we are able to measure androgyny. As Bem says:

> When androgyny becomes a reality, the *concept* of androgyny will have been transcended. (Bem, 1979)

But Archer and Lloyd (1985), amongst others, are very sceptical of the probability of an androgynous society; it will not be realized, they say, because some form of group differentiation seems essential to human social organization. They argue that it is difficult to imagine a completely androgynous society. Awareness of one's gender develops very early, and is essential to the development of self; it is difficult to imagine an individual functioning adequately in society as we understand it without a firm sense of self. Thus early gender awareness aids the child in organizing the social world, and reflects the child's understanding of it. Gender awareness arises not only from the infant's experience of his/her own body, but through interaction with adults in his/her society who are themselves moulded by their membership of gender groups. Nurture becomes second nature, and gender identity becomes an important schema in mental life (Constantinople, 1979; Liben & Signorella, 1980).

While advocating the retention of gender roles, Archer and Lloyd express the hope that change in their *content* (and that of gender stereotypes) will continue as they have over the last 50 years. But they firmly expect gender categories to continue to exist in some form.

Exercises

1 Why was it important to have an equal number of male and female judges when deciding on items for the BSRI?

2 What level of measurement is used by the BSRI?

3 What is meant by the 'internal consistency' of a psychological test? What is it a measure of?

4 In the assessment of test–retest reliability, why was it important that subjects didn't remember their answers on the original test?

5 The Pearson product-moment correlation was used to measure the degree of test–retest reliability:
   (*i*) is it parametric or non-parametric?
   (*ii*) what is the other most commonly used test of correlation?

6 When the BSRI scores are correlated with scores on the CPI and Guilford-Zimmerman Temperament Survey, the validity of the BSRI is being assessed.
   (*i*) What kind of validity is it?
   (*ii*) Name the other main kinds.

7 Can you name a famous test of personality which has a Social Desirability Scale built into it?

8 Explain why it is important to have a set of normative data for any psychological test, as in table 30.6.

A case of multiple personality

Journal of Abnormal and Social Psychology, 49, pp. 135–51

The psychiatric manifestation called multiple personality has been extensively discussed. So too have the unicorn and the centaur. Nevertheless, like the unicorn and centaur in some respects, *multiple*, or *dual personality*, despite vivid appearances in popularized books on psychology (Allen, 1937), is not commonly encountered in the full reality of life (Alexander, 1930; McDougall, 1926; Morgan, 1932). Nearly all those perplexing reports of two or more people in one body, so to speak, are reports of observations made in a relatively distant past. The most significant manifestations of this sort discussed in the current literature occurred in patients studied half a century or more ago (William James, 1890, Morton Prince, 1906). It is scarcely surprising that psychiatrists today, never having directly observed such things as Morton Prince found in Miss Beauchamp, might be rather sceptical, especially as, in Prince's case, he used hypnosis, which may have '. . . moulded the course of its development to a degree that cannot be determined . . .' (McDougall, 1926).

Significantly, the studies of Prince and others on multiple personality are not even mentioned in some leading textbooks of psychiatry used in medical schools today (Muncie, 1948; Strecker *et al.*, 1951); if mentioned at all, the subject is usually dismissed with a few words (Henderson & Gillespie, 1947; Noyes, 1948). Freud apparently showed no appreciable interest in the disorder, Erickson and Kubie (1939) could find only one brief reference to the problem (in 'Collected Papers', 1946).

Our direct experience with a patient has forced us to review the subject of multiple personality. It has also provoked in us the reaction of wonder, sometimes of awe.

One of us had, for several months, been treating a 25-year-old married woman referred because of 'severe and blinding headaches'. At the first interview, she also mentioned 'blackouts' following the headache. Her family was not aware of anything that would suggest a real loss of consciousness or serious mental confusion. During a series of irregular interviews (the patient had to travel from some distance), several important emotional difficulties were revealed and discussed. Although encouraging symptomatic improvement occurred, it was clear that her major problems had not been resolved. Eve White (as we

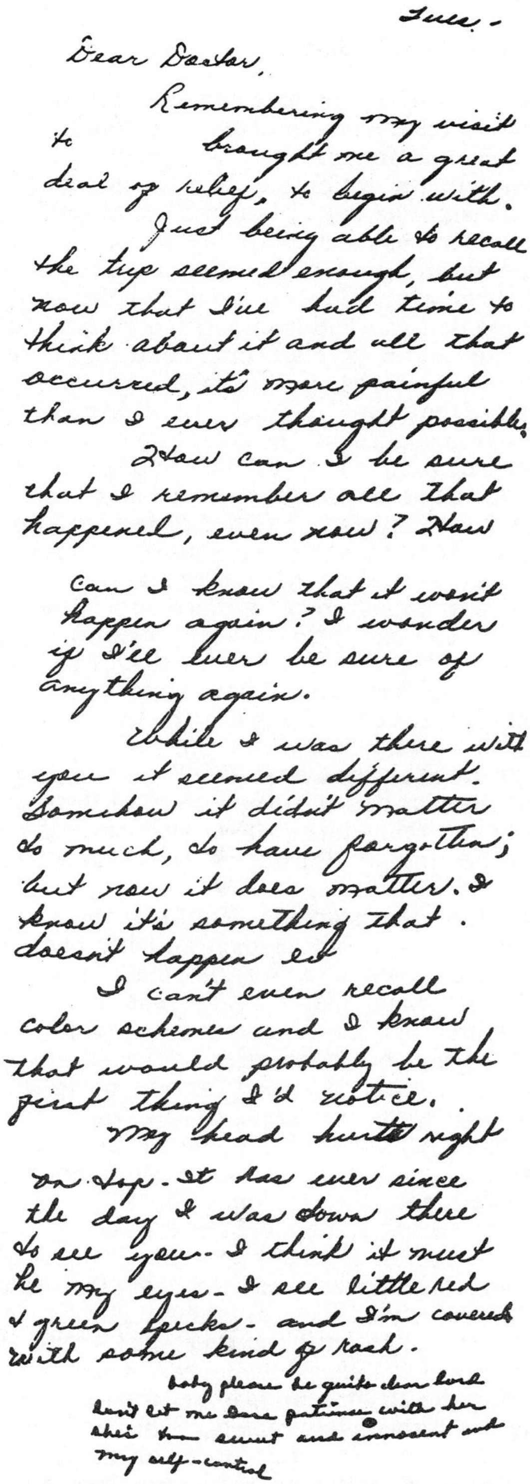

Tues.

Dear Doctor,

Remembering my visit to ____ brought me a great deal of relief, to begin with.

Jus' being able to recall the trip seemed enough, but now that I've had time to think about it and all that occurred, it's more painful than I ever thought possible.

How can I be sure that I remember all that happened, even now? How can I know that it won't happen again? I wonder if I'll ever be sure of anything again.

While I was there with you it seemed different. Somehow it didn't matter so much, to have forgotten; but now it does matter. I know it's something that doesn't happen ev

I can't even recall color schemes and I know that would probably be the first thing I'd notice.

My head hurts right on top. It has ever since the day I was down there to see you. I think it must be my eyes - I see little red & green specks - and I'm covered with some kind of rash.

baby please be quite dear lord don't let me done patience with her she's too sweet and innocent and my self-control

Figure 31.1 This letter in retrospect was the first intimation that our patient was unusual. The dramatic and unexpected revelation of the second personality shortly followed.

shall call her) seemed to be an ordinary case with commonplace symptoms and a relatively complex, but familiar, set of marital conflicts and personal frustrations. We are puzzled during therapy about a recent trip for which she had no memory. Hypnosis was induced, and the amnesia quickly cleared up. Several days after a visit to the office, a letter was received (figure 31.1).

What was the meaning of such a letter? Though unsigned, the postmark, the content, and the familiar penship in most of the message revealed that this had been written by Eve White. However, it raised puzzling questions. Had some child found the uncompleted page, scribbled those words, and, perhaps as a whim, mailed it in an already addressed envelope? Perhaps. The handwriting of the last paragraph certainly suggested the work of a child. Could Eve White herself, as a puerile prank, have decided to disguise her characteristic handwriting and added this inconsequential note? And if so, why? She seemed to be a circumspect, matter-of-fact person, meticulously truthful and consistently sober and serious about her grave troubles. It was rather difficult to imagine her becoming playful, or being moved by an impulse to tease, even on a more appropriate occasion. The 'blackouts' which she had rather casually mentioned, but which did not seem to disturb her very much, suggested, of course, that somnabulism or brief fugue might have occurred.

On her next visit, she denied sending the letter, though she recalled having begun one which she never finished; she thought she had destroyed it. During this interview, Eve White, usually an excessively self-controlled woman, began to show signs of distress and agitation. Apprehensively and reluctantly, she at last asked: did the occasional impression of hearing an imaginary voice indicate that she was 'insane'?

This information was startling. Nothing about Eve White suggested even an early schizoid change, and her own attitude toward what she now reported was in no way like that of patients experiencing 'ordinary' auditory hallucinations. Yet she insisted, with painful embarrassment, that she had, on several occasions over the last few months, heard briefly, but distinctly, a voice addressing her. Before the therapist could reply, an abstruse and inexplicable expression came over her face, apparently involuntarily. As if seized by pain, she put both hands to her head. After a tense moment of silence, her hands dropped. There was a quick, reckless smile and, in a bright voice that sparkled, she said, 'Hi there, Doc!'.

Instead of the retiring and conventional figure of Eve White, there was in this newcomer a childishly daredevil air, an erotically mischievous glance, a face marvellously free from the usual signs of care, seriousness and underlying distress, so long familiar in her predecessor. This new, and apparently carefree, girl spoke casually of Eve White and her problems always using *she* or *her* in every reference, always respecting the strict bounds of separate identity. When asked her own name she immediately replied, 'Oh, I'm Eve Black'.

A thousand minute alterations of manner, gesture, expression, posture, of nuances in reflex or instinctive reaction, of glance, of eyebrow tilting and eye movement, all argued that this could only be another woman. It is impossible to say just what all these differences were.

Over a period of 14 months, during a series of interviews totalling approximately 100 hours, extensive material was obtained about the behaviour and inner life of Eve White and Eve Black. How can the different personalities be called out? After the original spontaneous appearance of Eve Black, Eve White at first had to be hypnotised in order for us to talk with Eve Black. How Eve Black could 'pop out' of her own accord at unpredictable times, and yet could not come out on request, we do not know. After a few hypnotic sessions, we merely had to request Eve White to let us speak to Eve Black. Then we called Eve Black's name, and Eve Black would come out. The reverse was true when Eve Black was out, and we wished to speak to Eve White. Hypnosis was no longer necessary for obtaining the changes. This made things simpler for us, but complicated Eve White's life considerably, because Eve Black found herself able to 'take over' more easily than before.

Eve Black, so far as we can tell, has enjoyed an independent life since Eve's early childhood. She is not a product of disruptive, emotional stresses suffered during recent years. Eve White had no knowledge or suspicion of the other's existence until some time after she appeared unbidden before the surprised therapist. Though Eve White has learned that there is an Eve Black during the course of therapy, she does not have access to the latter's awareness. When Eve Black is 'out', Eve White remains functionally in abeyance, quite oblivious of what the coinhabitant of her body does, and apparently unconscious. However, Eve Black preserves awareness while absent, able to follow the actions and thoughts of her spiritually antithetical twin, but clearly not participating in them. For example, Eve Black regards Eve White's genuine and natural distress about her failing marriage as silly, and her warm, genuine, consistent and impressive love and concern for her four-year-old daughter as trite, bothersome, insignificant and 'something pretty corny'.

Eve White and her husband are temporarily separated, and the four-year-old child is living with her grandparents in a village, while Eve works and lives in a city about 100 miles away. She endures the loneliness, frustration and grief of separation from her warmly loved daughter, and she fears that, as the years pass, she will become little more than a cooly accepted stranger. But the vulnerable and delicately feminine Eve typically preserves a quiet dignity about personal sorrow. Under hypnosis, her unhappiness became clearer, but even then there is no frantic weeping or outbursts of self-pity; her quiet voice remains level as she discusses matters which leave her cheeks at last wet from silent tears.

Eve Black has little or no real compassion for her. Nor does she seem in any important sense actively, or purposefully, cruel. She seems to be immune to major affective events in human relations, equally free of mercy and hatefulness.

Eve Black freely tells of episodes in childhood when she emerged, usually to engage in acts of mischief or disobedience, but she lies glibly and without compunction, so her account alone can never be taken as reliable evidence. Although Eve White has no access to her 'twin's' awareness or memory, her own memory has afforded considerable indirect evidence of Eve Black's stories through confirmation of reports of punishments she received and accusations made against her for deeds unknown to her, but described to us by Eve Black. Some stories have been substantiated by the patient's parents and her husband, who have all been interviewed.

Eve Black's adult behaviour is characterized by irresponsibility and a shallowly hedonistic desire for excitement and pleasure. She succeeded in concealing her identity not only from the other Eve, but also from her parents and husband. She herself denies marriage to this man, whom she despises, and any relation to Eve White's little girl, except that of an unconcerned bystander. Though she had often 'come out' in the presence of all these people, she went unrecognized until she agreed to reveal herself to them in the therapist's office. They had accounted for her ill will, harshness and occasional violence in terms of unaccountable fits of temper in a woman habitually gentle and considerate.

During her longer periods 'out', she avoids her family and close friends, and seeks the company of strangers or those insufficiently acquainted with her alternate to evaluate accurately the stupendous transformation. It seemed to us at first scarcely possible that she could for so long have concealed her separate identity from others. But who is likely to reach a conclusion which is inconceivable? Her parents and husband observed the same changes that we have observed, but, unlike ourselves, they have not had the hypothesis of multiple personality. Eve Black meant to remain unrecognized: when it suits her, she deliberately and skilfully acts so as to pass herself off as Eve White, imitating her usual tone of voice, gestures and attitudes.

Psychometric and projective tests were conducted on the two Eves by a well-qualified expert.

Psychological consultation report

The patient is the oldest of three siblings, having twin sisters. She quit school two months before graduation from high school. She worked as a telephone operator. She has been married six years and has a four-year-old girl. She reports that she did things recently she cannot remember having done, and expresses serious concern about this condition. The following psychological tests were administered to both the predominant personality, Mrs White and the secondary personality, Miss Black: Wechsler-Bellevue Intelligence Scale, Wechsler Memory Scale, Drawings of Human Figures and Rorschach.

Test behaviour Patient was neat, friendly and cooperative. However, while Mrs White was more serious, conscientious and anxious, Miss Black seemed rather less anxious, and gave more superficial responses. Still the basic behaviour pattern was very similar in both personalities. Speech was coherent, and there were no distortions in ideations or behaviour according to the assumed personality. No psychotic deviations were observed.

Test results Mrs White obtained an IQ of 110 and Miss Black 104 on the Wechsler-Bellevue Intelligence Scale. Both scores are lowered by anxiety and tenseness, and superficiality and slight indifference to success, respectively. Miss Black's memory funtion is on the same level as her IQ, while Mrs White's is far above her IQ, although she complained of a disturbance in memory. The only difficulty experienced by both is on recall of digits, an ability on which telephone operators usually excel! The Rorschach record of Miss Black is by far healthier than that of Mrs White. Miss Black has a hysterical tendency, while Mrs White's shows anxiety, obsessive-compulsive traits, rigidity and an inability to deal with her hostility.

Personality dynamics The projective tests indicate repression in Mrs White and regression in Miss Black. The dual personality appears to be the result of a strong desire to regress to an early period of life, namely the one before marriage. Miss Black is actually the maiden name of Mrs White. Therefore, these are not two different personalities with completely dissimilar ideation, but rather one personality at two stages of her life. As is characteristic for this type of case, the predominant personality is amnesic for the existence, activities or behaviour of the secondary one, while the latter is aware and critical of the predominant personality's activities and attitudes.

Mrs White admits difficulty in her relation with her mother, and her performance on the Rorschach and drawings indicate conflict and resulting anxiety in her roles of wife and mother. Only with strong conscious effort can she compel herself to subject herself to these roles, which in turn increases the hostility. But she cannot accept this hostility, and regresses so as to avoid guilt feelings. By playing the role of Miss Black, she is able to discharge some of her hostility towards Mrs White. Miss Black has regained her previous freedom from marital and maternal conflicts, and so has escaped from the insoluble situation Mrs White found herself in through her marriage; she can also avert the – in her conviction – inevitable spiritual loss of her child. Not surprisingly, she shows contempt for Mrs White, who allowed herself to get into such a situation, because of lack of foresight and lack of courage to forcefully solve the dilemma.

Actually, the problem started much earlier in life, with a strong feeling of rejection by her parents, especially after the birth of her twin sisters; Mrs White loves them dearly, Miss Black despises them. Miss Black relates an episode in which she (i.e. Mrs White), having quit school to help support the family, sent home money to buy overcoats for her twin sisters, denying herself a badly wanted wristwatch. When the money was spent on two wristwatches instead, she reacted with strong, but repressed, hostility. Significantly, she removed her wristwatch while examined as Mrs White, stating that she doesn't like jewellery. There are several examples of her strong sense of rejection as well as sibling rivalry in her records.

Miss Black once recklessly bought several expensive and unneeded new dresses and two luxurious coats. On discovering this, Eve White's husband lost his temper and abused his wife for wantonly plunging him into debt. Her innocent denials could not reduce his anger, but her wholehearted agreement that it would be disastrous for them to run up such a bill, and her promptness in returning all the garments to the store did. Although Eve Black does not apparently regularly go out of her way to make trouble between them, her typical behaviour often adds to the genuine difficulties they already have. 'When I go out and get drunk', Eve Black with an easy wink once said to us, '*she* wakes up with the hangover. She wonder's what in the hell's made her so sick'.

In contrast with the case reported by Erickson and Kubie (1939), Eve Black has shown anything but a regular desire to help the other with her problems; often she has, by ingenious lies, misled the therapist into believing she was cooperating, when in fact her behaviour was particularly detrimental to Eve White's progress. However, one valuable means of influencing her is in the therapist's hands. Although Eve Black has apparently been able, since childhood, to disappear at will, the ability to displace Eve White's consciousness, and emerge to take control has always been limited: sometimes she could 'get out', sometimes not. Once Eve White, during treatment, learned of the other's existence, it has become clear that her willingness to step aside and 'release the imp' plays an important part in the alternate's ability to appear and express herself directly. Eve White cannot keep her suppressed permanently, but together with the therapist, Eve Black can be persuaded to avoid the more serious forms of misconduct by being allowed more time 'out'.

Even when invisible and inaccessible, she, apparently, has means of disturbing Eve White. She tells us she caues those severe headaches that brought the latter to us as a patient; her unsuccessful struggle to get out often produces this symptom in the other plus the (quasi-) hallucinatory voice which Eve White heard before the other Eve disclosed herself to us as her deliberate work.

From the two Eves during many interviews, and from her husband and parents, we obtained a great deal of information about the patient, and concluded that we had a reasonably complete and accurate history of her life since early childhood. So we were astonished by the report of a distant relative, who insisted that, a few years before she met her present husband, a previous marriage had taken place. Eve White denied this, and has never yet shown any knowledge of it, but Eve Black also maintained that we had been misinformed; however, under the persistent pressure of evidence, the latter admitted that she, and only she, had been the bride. No record of a legal union has been obtained, but there is considerable evidence that she did co-habit with such a man as she describes; she insists some sort of 'ceremony' was performed, saying that it was not formally recorded, and may have been a ruse. Eve Black was predominantly in control during this period, almost constantly present.

She claimed she had no desire for sex, but often enjoyed frustrating her supposed husband by denying herself to him. In turn, he beat her savagely, but she avoided most of the pain by 'going in', and leaving Eve White to feel the blows. But if this were the case, why did Eve White not remember them? Eve Black contends that she can, through great effort, 'pick out' or erase from Eve White's reach certain items of memory, and she did this with memory of the beatings. Several experiments by the therapist indicated that this claim is correct.

After approximately eight months of treatment, Eve White seemed to have made encouraging progress. For a long time she had not had headaches or 'blackouts', the imaginary voice had not been heard since the other Eve revealed herself to the therapist. Mrs White worked well at her job, and had progressed financially; she was hopeful of eventually reaching some acceptable solution to her marital problems, seemed to find some comfort in her successful efforts to provide for her daughter, and had made friends, with whom she occasionally enjoyed simple recreations.

Meanwhile, Eve Black had generally been causing less trouble. She seldom 'came out' to make errors to indulge in pranks while Eve White was at work, but in leisure hours she often mixed with bad company, picked up dates and flirted.

At this point, the situation changed for the worse. The headaches returned, grew worse and more frequent, and so did the 'blackouts'. Eve Black denied all responsibility. She did not experience the headaches but, surprisingly, seemed now to participate in the blackouts and could give no account of what happened during them. Two or three times the patient was found lying unconscious on the floor by her room-mate, something which had not occurred during the previous blackout episodes. It became difficult for her to work effectively, she became less accessible during interviews and increasingly distressed.

Under hypnosis, Eve White occasionally re-experienced considerable emotion in recalling events from childhood, but we have never been able to hypnotize Eve Black. Some time after the return of headaches and blackouts, with Eve White's maladjustment gradually getting worse, a very early recollection was being discussed, concerning a painful injury she had sustained when scalded by water from a wash basin. As she spoke her eyes shut sleepily, her words soon stopped, her head dropped back on the chair. After two minutes, her eyes opened, blankly staring about the room, trying to orient herself. When her eyes finally met those of the therapist, slowly, with an unknown husky voice and immeasurable poise, she said, 'Who are you?'.

It was immediately and vidily apparent that this was neither Eve White nor Eve Black. We have gradually established that this third personality lacks Eve Black's obvious faults and inadequacies, is far more mature, vivid, boldly capable and interesting than Eve White. She calls herself Jane and only superficially can she be described as a compromise between the others.

Some weeks after Jane emerged, all three personalities were given Electroencephalogram tests:

Report of Electroencephalogram: summary

All three personalities show alternate periods of alpha rhythm and low voltage fast activity, presumably due to alternate periods of mental relaxation and tenseness. The greatest amount of tenseness is shown by Eve Black, Eve White next, and Jane least. Eve Black shows a basic alpha rate of 12½ cycles per second, as compared with 11 cycles per second from Eve White and Jane. This places Eve Black's tracing on the borderline between normal and slightly fast (FI). Slightly fast records are sometimes (but not consistently) associated with psychopathic personality. Eve Black's record also shows evidence of restlessness and muscle tension, her EEG is definitely distinguished from the others, and could be classified as borderline normal. Eve White's and Jane's EEG cannot be distinguished: both are clearly normal.

For several months now there have been three patients to work with. Jane has awareness of what both Eves do and think, but incomplete access to their stores of knowledge and memories prior to her appearance on the scene. Through her, the therapist can determine when Eve Black has been lying. Jane feels free from Eve White's responsibilities and attachments, but is capable of compassion and, probably, of devotion and genuine love. She has cooperated with sincerity, and with judgement and originality beyond that of the others. She has learnt to take over many of Eve White's tasks at work and home in efforts to relieve and help her. She shows great wisdom and compassion towards Eve White's little girl. As time passes, she 'stays out' more and more. She emerges only through Eve White, and has not yet found a way to displace Eve Black, or to communicate through her. Could Jane remain in full possession of that integrated human functioning called personality, we believe our patient would probably regain full health, adjust satisfactorily and find her way to a happy life.

Discussion

What is the meaning of the events we have observed and reported? Some, no doubt, will conclude that we have been thoroughly hoodwinked by a skilful actress. But we think it is unlikely that someone consciously acting could, over a period of months, avoid even one telling error or imperfection. But it is not impossible.

Have we been taken in by what is no more than superficial hysterical tomfoolery? There does seem to be something more, and something different from ordinary hysterical conversions and dissociations. Could it be due to a process of disintegration as in schizophrenia? None of the three personalities shows any signs of schizophrenia. Are we justified in claiming that our three performers have become split off from a once unified whole? Or is is possible that the functional elements composing each have never in the past been really or completely unified?

Obviously, the differing manifestations we have observed in one woman's physical organism do not, in all senses of the term, indicate three quite separate people. So what do we mean by the term *multiple personality*? This, of course, begs the question of what we mean by *personality*. For all these questions, there is no simple or single answer.

Whatever progress may or may not have been made by psychology and psychiatry during the last half century, we suggest that further direct study of multiple personality and careful reappraisal of Morton Prince's generally neglected studies may provide some promising clues which may eventually yield insight we need but lack today.

Commentary

Aim and nature

The article is an account of the psychotherapeutic treatment of a 25-year-old woman referred to the authors (who are psychiatrists, i.e. medically qualified professionals concerned with helping those with psychological problems), because of 'severe and blinding headaches'. It soon became clear that Eve White was experiencing marital problems and personal frustrations (probably the cause of her headaches), but the receipt of the letter marked the beginning of what the article is really about, namely, a case of multiple personality. Eve Black could at first only be 'contacted' through hypnosis, but this then became no longer necessary. The major method of treatment seemed to be simply talking to one or other Eve (there is no reference to drug therapy, for example), especially trying to encourage them to talk about childhood memories and events. The case study includes the report by an independent expert who gave the two Eves four psychological tests: the Wechsler-Bellevue Intelligence Scale (now known as the Wechsler Adult Intelligence Scale: WAIS), the Wechsler Memory Scale, Drawings of Human Figures and the Rorschach ('Ink Blot') test, in which the testee has to say what a series of ambiguous drawings (ink blots) represent; it is a projective test, the idea being that the interpretation involves the projection of unconscious feelings and wishes etc. After eight months of treatment, Eve White suffered a major setback: her original symptoms returned, but were more intense and frequent, and this was the prelude to the appearance of a third personality, Jane, (hence 'The three faces of Eve'). An independent expert this time was asked to run EEG tests on all three personalities, with the outcome showing Eve White and Jane to be indistinguishable and normal, but Eve Black to be borderline normal/psychopathic personality.

Context and background

As far as the 1959 Mental Health Act and the 9th Revision of the International Classification of Diseases (ICD-9), Mental Disorders Section are concerned, multiple personality is a form of hysterical neurosis of the dissociative type. This is the classification used in the UK, which makes the broad distinction between two kinds of mental illness, neurosis and psychosis (based on Kraepelin's original 1913 claim that certain groups of signs and symptoms occur together sufficiently often to merit the designation 'disease' or syndrome; he then described the diagnostic indicators associated with each syndrome).

In the USA, the American Psychiatric Association's official classification system is the Diagnostic and Statistical Manual of Mental Disorder (DSM); originally published in 1952, it was first revised in 1968 (DSM-II) and most recently in 1980 (DSM-III) (a minor revision was made in 1987; DSM-III-R). According to DSM-III, the category 'neurosis' is dropped and neurotic disorders are dispersed among several categories, e.g. anxiety disorders, dissociative disorders and somatoform disorders. The distinction between 'neurotic' and 'psychotic' has also been dropped.

The somatoform disorders include the other major kind of hysterical neurosis recognized by the UK system (i.e. additional to the dissociative kind), namely the conversion type. (This was the 'model' of neurosis on which Freud based his psychoanalytic theory; most of his patients were 'suffering' from anxiety, which became 'converted' into apparent bodily or somatic symptoms.)

DSM-III has dissociative disorders (hysterical neurosis: dissociative type) as one of its categories, and specific disorders included within that category are precisely those normally included under the heading 'hysterical neurosis: dissociative type' in the UK system, namely somnambulism, amnesia, fugue and multiple personality. So despite some major differences between the two systems of classification, they do agree on how to classify multiple personality.

Dissociative neurosis involves psychological rather than physical dysfunction (although Eve White did suffer also from terrible headaches), and takes the form of a separation, or dissociation, of one part of the self from the other parts. (This has led to the common confusion between multiple personality and schizophrenia, in which a splitting occurs, but of a different kind from that involved in multiple personality. In terms of classification, DSM-III has a category 'schizophrenic disorders', and in the UK it is a major kind of functional psychosis.)

Multiple personality involves two or more integrated personalities residing within the same body, each dominating at different times. The 'original' personality (Eve White) is usually not aware of the other(s) (Eve Black, Jane), though these may be aware of the first. Often, the other personalities embody parts of the first personality which have become repressed, and so have remained unexpressed. Multiple personality is often accompanied by fugue. Fugue means 'flight', and is a kind of extension of amnesia, in which the patient flees from home and self by wandering off on a journey, not knowing how (s)he got there and unable to recall his/her true identity. The person assumes a new identity but, unlike many amnesic patients, does not experience confusion or disorientation. It is usually a brief episode, lasting hours or days rather than weeks. In the case of the multiple personality, the fugue will usually be a period of time during which one of the alternate personalities was in control, leaving the 'original' personality unable to account for his/her actions (e.g. the spending spree which made Eve White's husband so angry!).

The 'original' case was the fictional 'Dr Jekyll and Mr Hyde' by Robert Louis Stevenson. A more recent, real-life case, even more dramatic and remarkable than the present one, is that of Sybil (Schreiber, 1973), who had 16 separate personalities!

Evaluation

1 Traditionally, reported cases of multiple personality have been considered to be extremely rare, with Morton Prince's (1906) Miss Beauchamp, the present case of Eve and Sybil (Schreiber, 1973) being the most commonly cited. However, Allison (1977) (cited by Altrocchi, 1980) claims to have dealt with 31 such patients in a four-year period and he reports communications with other therapists who have seen numerous cases themselves. One reason for the generally very low reported frequency of such

cases is that often the existence of other personalities is discovered, initially, only through hypnosis, which no more than ten per cent of psychotherapists use. (This was not the case with Eve, where Eve Black made her first appearance quite spontaneously; but for a good while following this, she could only be 'summoned' hypnotically (Altrocchi, 1980)).

Altrocchi (1980) also points out that 85 per cent of Allison's patients were female, as were the three famous cases cited above. This preponderance of females is consistent, he claims, with the repressive lifestyle still experienced by women in western culture.

2 During several months of therapy following Jane's appearance, Eve White (real name Chris) learnt about the other two. A crucial moment was when Eve White was able to recall and deal with her feelings about a traumatic incident at age six, when her aunt forced her to kiss her dead grandmother. By then, Eve and her first husband had divorced, and Jane had married Don Sizemore, her (Chris's) present husband. During a crisis in Jane's life, a fourth personality appeared, Evelyn. She had all the memories of the other three, accepted responsibility for their actions, and seemed to be a much more mature and complete person than any one of them.

For almost 20 years, except for the movie 'The three faces of Eve', the public knew nothing more about the case. Then, on January 9th, 1975, Mrs Chris Sizemore of Fairfax, Virginia, revealed that she had been not only both Eves, Jane and Evelyn (all fictitious names), but many others besides, both before and after 1954, at least nine before Eve Black and approximately 22 altogether. Chris had had role models for denial, repression and dissociation while growing up. For example, her grandmother often refused to recognise something that displeased her, and tended to faint at times of stress, such as funerals. Chris also fainted at times of distress, and repressed memory of such events as her grandfather's funeral. And one of her personalities was blind, suggesting that a conversion reaction process was part of her make-up. (Remember this is usually contrasted with dissociative hysterical neurosis.)

Chris believes she began to develop separate personalities as a safety valve mechanism as young as two. By then she had seen a man drown, and another cut into three pieces by a saw at the lumber mill. (Her personalities tended to exist in groups of three!) In a personal communication to Altrocchi, she describes the time she witnessed her mother cut her arm badly; Chris could not handle this, and thought she was going to die; she ran to bed, stuck her head under the pillow, and felt herself receding into space, watching 'the other little girl' go get her father: 'It wasn't me, I was watching'.

She was always unusually sensitive, and unable to deal effectively with her kaleidoscopic emotions (Altrocchi, 1980). Chris Sizemore and her cousin, Elen Pittillo, together wrote 'I'm Eve' (Sizemore & Pittillo, 1977), and they say this:

> Paradoxically, to survive intact, she splintered; she created other selves to endure what she could not absorb, to view what she could not comprehend, to do what she had been forbidden, to have what she had been denied. (Sizemore & Pittillo, 1977)

When the pain became unbearable, Chris disappeared, and someone else took her place. But this produced the fugues and amnesias which made her even more inhibited and withdrawn, and did not help her to develop a coherent and acceptable self-concept.

She decided to reveal herself as the famous Eve as part of her therapy with Dr Tsitos, whose major strategy was to deal only with Chris, and to make it difficult for the others to come out. Over the years, as a personality died, she assimilated aspects of it.

With the support of family, friends, and the public, she has successfully withstood her father's death, the tensions of public-speaking engagements and national TV interviews.

3 Some mental health workers are sceptical about multiple personalities. Thigpen and Cleckley themselves ask if they have been hoodwinked by a skilful actress, and others have suggested that the behaviour is a combination of hypnotic suggestions and deliberate role playing. Is there any evidence independent of the case study itself for the separate existence of multiple personality as a form of mental illness?

(*i*) Osgood and Luria (1957) found different psychological test patterns for Eve White, Black and Jane, without knowing anything about the identity of the testees;
(*ii*) Condon *et al.* (1969) analyzed a film made by Thigpen, and discovered that Eve Black showed a different pattern of involuntary eye movements from the other two;
(*iii*) Cornelia Wilbur (Sybil's therapist) presented a detailed psychiatric, psychological, psychophysiological and neurophysiological analysis of a new case (Ludwig *et al.*, 1972). They reported 'defusion' into four personalities, and claimed that it could not be accounted for by hypnosis, and they showed distinctive and consistent patterns of psychological test results which could not easily be accounted for by deliberate role playing.
(*iv*) Allison (1974, 1977) proposes four key indicators of multiple personality: (a) periodic severe, unexplained headaches over a period of years; (b) documented periods of amnesia; (c) periodic hearing of voices without evidence of 'psychotic' disintegration or breakdown; (d) observations by relatives and others of strikingly different, integrated, behaviour patterns at different times.

The key therapeutic goal is the fusion of the several personalities into one, which integrates whatever repressed or dissociated feelings or motives the other personalities expressed (Allison, 1974, 1977; Schreiber, 1973).

4 Finally, how does a diagnosis of multiple personality stand as a legal defence of criminals? Altrocchi (1980) cites the case of Arthur D. Wayne Bicknall, who was acquitted by a Californian judge, in 1976, of drunk driving after his psychiatrist, Allison, testified that one of the accused's other personalities – 'Johnnie' – was the true criminal. Allison actually summoned, under hypnosis, two of Bicknell's other personalities as character witnesses!

Similarly, a Californian jury, in 1978, acquitted Ester Minor of forgery after three psychiatrists (including Allison) and two psychologists had testified that it was 'Raynell Potts' who had actually carried out the crimes without Ester's knowledge. The whole status of expert witnesses is problematical, and in the US, anyway, different States will have different legal and judicial systems. But what is interesting is that such cases put into sharp focus the whole notion of 'moral responsibility'; at the very least, one has to be performing the criminal act *knowingly* and in the case of multiple personality, this 'one' means the original personality. But couldn't we all plead 'not guilty' if we went out and got drunk, and committed a crime 'under the influence'? The two cases are very different if we focus on the getting drunk, because, presumably, *this* was done *knowingly*. By contrast, the multiple personality cannot knowingly switch personalities in order to escape responsibility. This, of course, presupposes that role playing, acting, hypnotic suggestion, etc. have been ruled out!

Exercises

1 Do you think that psychologists and psychiatrists should be used as expert witnesses in criminal cases?

2 Do you believe that, if the testimony of an expert witness is accepted as showing the defendant to be a multiple personality, that this should, necessarily, lead to a verdict of 'not guilty'?

3 Are there any advantages which the Thigpen and Cleckley case study has over Freud's way of working with his patients (e.g. Little Hans, see chapter 24)?

4 Name two important differences between multiple personality and schizophrenia.

Answers to exercises

Chapter 1 (Miller, 1969)

1 It seems impossible to live among people and to not try to understand (explain), predict and control their behaviour to some degree (as well as trying to understand our own!). In Interpersonal Perception, for example, the Attribution Process refers to the ways the lay person attributes causes to others' (and his/her own) behaviour, and stereotypes are one kind of 'implicit personality theory'. (Also, see Kelly's (1955) personal construct theory, in which a central notion is 'man the scientist'.)

2 According to Orne (1962), social situations involve mutual expectations by the participants, and this includes psychology experiments. On the subject's side, (s)he is trying to ascertain the true purpose of the experiment, and to respond in a way which will support the hypothesis being tested. In this context, any *cues* which convey an experimental hypothesis to the subject become important determinants of the subject's behaviour: 'demand characteristics' are the sum total of these cues.

   The central point is that the subject is not a passive responder but actively tries to work out what is going on and how to perform. The situation is very different from that in which a humen experimenter investigates some part of the physical world; people are *not* inanimate objects but animate, conscious, thinking beings.

3 Legge (1975) and others distinguish between *formal* and *informal* psychology; our common-sense, intuitive or 'natural' understanding is unsystematic, and does not constitute a body of knowledge. Part of the aim of formal psychology is to provide such a systematic body of knowledge. While he believes that most psychological research should be aimed at demonstrations of 'what we already know' (common sense), it should aim to go one step further: only the methods of science can provide us with the public communicable body of knowledge we need.

4 I will let you struggle with this one yourself!

Chapter 2 (McGinnies, 1949)

1 Related *t*-test.

2 There may be sex differences in response to taboo words. So if, for example, women, on average, respond more slowly to taboo words, and sex was not controlled for, and if there were more female subjects, sex could represent a confounding variable.

3 In order to get the subject used to the apparatus, allow the level of resistance to stabilize, and thus establish a baseline against which to

compare changes in response to neutral and emotive words.

4 The order was determined randomly and, in this form, was the same for all subjects. Order effects are always a potential problem in a repeated measures design. Counterbalancing is the alternative way of trying to reduce the effects of practice, fatigue etc.

5 (*i*) Length (they were, in fact, all five-letter words).
(*ii*) Familiarity (see *Evaluation*, point 2).

6 (*i*) 3 d.f. (Formula = (Rows − 1) × (Columns − 1) = (4 − 1) × (2 − 1) = 3 × 1 = 3).
(*ii*) Expected frequencies.

7 It was important that the second experimenter did not know which words were on the screen at any one time; with the subject naïve as to the purpose of the experiment (single-blind), the second experimenter was also naïve as to whether a particular word was taboo or neutral (double-blind), and in this way experimenter bias was greatly reduced.

Chapter 3 (Deregowski, 1972)

1 (*i*) BINOCULAR (Retinal) DISPARITY: because our eyes are (approximately) 6 cm. apart, they each receive slightly different retinal images, and the superimposition of these two images is *stereoscopic vision*. Convergence is related to this.
(*ii*) MOTION PARALLAX: this is the major *dynamic* depth cue, and refers to the speed of apparent movement of objects nearer or further away from us. Generally, objects further away seem to move more slowly than nearer objects.

2 (*i*) RELATIVE BRIGHTNESS: brighter objects normally appear to be nearer.
(*ii*) AERIAL PERSPECTIVE: objects at a great distance appear to have a different colour (e.g. the hazy, bluish tint of distant mountains) (see *Evaluation*: (ii)).
(*iii*) HEIGHT IN THE HORIZONTAL PLANE: when looking across a flat expanse (e.g. across the sea), objects which are more distant seem 'higher' (i.e. closer to the horizon) than nearer objects, which seem 'lower' and closer to the ground.
(*iv*) LIGHT and SHADOW: 3-D objects produce variations in light and shade (e.g. we normally assume that light comes from above).
(*v*) ACCOMMODATION: refers to the change in the shape of the lens of the eye depending on the distance of the object; it flattens for distant objects and thickens for closer ones.
(*vi*) CONVERGENCE: refers to the simultaneous orienting of both eyes towards the same object: when looking at a distant object (25 feet or more), the line of vision of our two eyes is parallel, but the closer the object, the more our eyes turn inward towards each other.

3 *Monocular* cues are those which can be detected with one eye only and so (*i*) are not primarily dependent on biological processes

(except accommodation) and (*ii*) are mainly *pictorial*, i.e. they are features of the visual field itself. (*Binocular* cues – retinal disparity and convergence – are *non-pictorial*.)

4 If the subject takes note of depth cues, and makes the 'correct' interpretation of the relationship between the parts when asked 'What is the man doing?' and 'What is closer to the man?', (s)he is judged to be a 3-D perceiver.

5 Subjects were asked to build a model of a drawing of two squares. Most 3-D perceivers (on Hudson's test) built a 3-D model, while most 2-D perceivers built a flat (2-D) model.

6 Concurrent validity.

7 There will be a significant positive correlation between subject's response to the Hudson pictures and the kind of model (3-D or flat) which they build of a drawing of two squares.

Chapter 4 (Searle, 1980)

1 According to weak AI, the main value of the computer is that it provides a very powerful tool for studying the mind; it enables us to formulate and test hypotheses in a more rigorous and precise way than is possible without the computer. (The 'computer analogy' as used in cognitive psychology is based on weak AI.)

   Strong AI claims that the computer is not merely a tool, but the appropriately programmed computer really is a mind, i.e. they literally understand and have cognitive states.

2 and 3 These could be debated in class using the arguments put forward by Searle and others in the *Commentary*.

4 For many years, the media have debated the issue of the threat to personal privacy and liberty posed by the 'all-knowing, all-powerful computer', and, at least in the UK, there has been legislation designed to protect the rights of the individual (Garnham, 1988). Weizenbaum (1976) believes that there are areas of our lives from which computers should be excluded, and that they encourage a mechanistic view of human beings which can be dehumanizing.

   Garnham (1988) wonders whether computers pose any more of a threat than any other product of technology which may be used for good or evil, depending on the motives of their users.

Chapter 5 (Craik & Lockhart, 1972)

1 An algorithm is a procedure which guarantees a solution to a given problem by systematically testing every alternative in turn, until the correct response is produced and verified (e.g. a flow diagram or decision chart).

   By contrast, heuristics do *not* guarantee a solution, but drastically reduce the amount of 'work' that must be carried out by selecting the most likely options from a possible set.

2 Trace decay; interference.

3 Trace decay; Gestalt theory; prevention of consolidation; interference; motivated forgetting (repression); cue-dependent forgetting. (The last three all represent a failure to retrieve.)

4 It is a way of reducing a larger amount of unrelated items of information to a smaller number of meaningful items, e.g. letters into words/words into sentences/numbers into historical dates.

5 (*i*) Recall; (*ii*) recognition.

6 In the Hyde and Jenkins (1973) study, five orienting tasks were used:
(*i*) rating words for pleasantness (semantic/deep processing; (*ii*) estimating the frequency with which words are used in English (semantic/deep); (*iii*) detecting the number of 'e's and 'g's in the words (non-semantic/shallow); (*iv*) deciding the part of speech appropriate to each word (non-semantic/shallow); (*v*) deciding whether or not the word fitted various sentence frames (non-semantic/shallow).

7 Incidental learning takes place when the subject is not expecting to be tested on the learned material, i.e. they are not *trying* to remember, because they are not expecting to be given a memory test (but it is retained despite this).
    In LOP experiments, it is the *orienting task* which is being manipulated, and nothing else is meant to influence retention (such as the subject's deliberate attempts to remember).

Chapter 6 (Loftus, Miller & Burns, 1978)

1 To avoid *response set*, the tendency to respond in one way rather than another, because of the position occupied by the 'objects' the subject is choosing between. In this case, the tendency to choose the slide on the left, for example, (regardless of its content) or, on a questionnaire, the tendency to tick the middle point on the scale.

2 Experiment 1: 'University of Washington students'
Experiment 2: 'Subjects'
Experiment 3: 'University of Washington students' (for course credit or paid)
Experiment 4: 'Subjects'
Experiment 5: 'Subjects'

3 ANOVA is short for *Analysis of Variance*. This is one of the most useful and versatile statistical tests used in psychology today (Solso & Johnson, 1989), and is a parametric test which calculates the proportion of total variance due to each of the independent variables in a *factorial design* (more than one independent variable) plus the interactions between them (plus the proportion due to all other variables). The ANOVA statisic is F (see chapter 25, *Evaluation*).

4 To control for *order effects*, i.e. to prevent the order in which the sentences were presented from becoming a confounding variable (cause of constant error).

The independent variable was the mention/non-mention of the critical incorrect detail, *not* the order in which the sentences appeared.

5 Relevance to real-world situations.

Chapter 7 (Murstein, 1972)

1 The crucial variable is the sample size, i.e. the number of subjects: as this goes up, so the lower the value of the correlation coefficient needs to be in order to reach significance.

2 Males and females are likely to judge members of their own and the opposite sex differently. As the photos were of males and females, non-significant correlations might have resulted just from having unequal numbers of male and female judges.

3 A scale of 1 to 5 with indications of percentages of the population who obtain a particular score (e.g. 3 = average, obtained by about 50 per cent), suggests an *ordinal* scale. However, the averages of the male and female judged scores were found to be highly correlated (0.80) using Pearson's *r* (a parametric test, requiring *interval* data). But again, to assess overall reliability, the scores of all eight judges were pooled, and then separated into two random halves, producing an *r* value of 0.91 (using the *Spearman-Brown formula*; this tends to be used when calculating reliability according to the *split-half* method. This suggests an *ordinal* scale).

(Note the very high coefficient (0.91) required with very small sample size, i.e. eight scores divided into two random halves is four.)

Chapter 8 (Manstead & McCulloch, 1981)

1 Because the study was partly a replication, and the aim was to compare their results with the American study, so the same categories needed to be used.

2 Presumably Granada is fairly typical of IBA channels. July is as good a time of year as any, unlike, for example, December with all the Christmas build-up. 6 p.m. to 11.30 p.m. is a large slice of viewing time, with the advertisements mainly aimed at adults. 170 different advertisements seems like a substantial number.

3 Inter-judge.

4 A test of correlation.

5

	Male	Female	Both
Total number of central figures	177	92	269

Here we have a single variable (central figures) with just two categories or cells (male/female). If there is no bias in media portrayal, we would expect roughly half the central figures to be male and half female (i.e. $269/2 = 134.5$). This represents the *expected* frequency for each cell ($E = 134.5$). The calucation proceeds in the normal way, excluding Yates's correction (i.e. subtracting $\frac{1}{2}$ for 1 degree of freedom). This represents a special case of χ^2, as a test of *goodness of fit*, i.e. it can be used to decide whether or not a large sample closely approximates a normal distribution. It compares proportions of the actual distribution (O) with the ideal proportions (z-scores) for a normal distribution (E).

Chapter 9 (Festinger & Carlsmith, 1959)

1 Independent groups (or independent samples).

2 Unrelated *t*-test. This is a parametric test which requires *interval* data. But were the rating scales true interval scales? The alternative would have been the Mann–Whitney U.

3 Hypothesis 2 says 'The *larger* the pressure . . . the *weaker* will be . . .'. This suggests a one-tailed (directional) prediction. (Hypothesis 1 just talks about a 'tendency to change', and so is two-tailed/non-directional.)

4 It removes experimenter bias, so that the interviewer cannot be influenced by knowledge of what condition the S was tested under as to how he *ought* to have rated the task. Since the S is also ignorant as to the purpose of the experiment, this represents a double-blind technique.

5 The independent variable = the size of reward ($1 or $20). The dependent variable = the degree of attitude change (how enjoyable the task was rated).

6 Correlation.

7 Yes: they were male, psychology students, who have to spend a certain number of hours participating as Ss (i.e. it is a course requirement).

8 When Ss believed the pill would relax them, the dissonance arising from the high-choice condition is still sufficient to produce attitude change (and it is contrary to what they expect to feel, so the 'discomfort/tension' must be due to their counter-attitudinal behaviour).

When given no information, the situation is no different from the Festinger and Carlsmith $1 situation.

But when told the pill would make them feel tense, the tension is attributed to the pill rather than the counter-attitudinal behaviour (and so the question of high/low choice becomes irrelevant).

Chapter 10 (Milgram, 1963)

1 (*i*) Proximity of the subject to the experimenter: when he left the room half-way through, the obedience rate dropped to zero; when he was never seen, but all instructions were given via a tape recorder, it was 22 per cent.
(*ii*) Proximity of the subject to the learner: when in the same room and 1½ feet away, obedience rate was 40 per cent, when the subject held the learner's arms down on the shock plate, it was 30 per cent.
(*iii*) The presence of another 'subject' who actually threw the switch: 92·5 per cent obedience.

2 I will let you sort this out for yourself. It is something which would lend itself well to a formal debate in class. [One point worth pursuing is whether it is an adequate defence for Milgram to say he didn't anticipate the results, however sincerely. Isn't it like pleading ignorance of the law; usually *not* an acceptable *legal* defence?]

3 They were volunteers, answering advertisements in a newspaper and direct mail advertisements. Although clearly not random, Milgram claims they represented a wide range of occupations (postal clerks, high-school teachers, salesmen, engineers and labourers), and they had a wide range of educational experience. However, those that went on obeying up to 450 volts seemed to have a stronger authoritarian character and a less advanced level of moral development. But this was a matter of degree only. Rosenthal and Rosnow (1966), amongst others, have found that people who volunteer for experiments are considerably *less* authoritarian than those who do not.

Chapter 11 (Piliavin, Rodin & Rodin, 1969)

1 Independent variables: (*i*) type of victim (drunk/ill); (*ii*) race of victim (white/black); (*iii*) presence/absence of model; (*iv*) number of observers.
Dependent variables: (*i*) latency of helping response; (*ii*) race of helper; (*iii*) number of helpers; (*iv*) movement out of the 'critical area'; (*v*) spontaneous comments.

2

	Advantages	Disadvantages
Field experiments	1 Results can much more easily be generalized (high ecological validity). 2 Subjects not normally aware of participating in an experiment and so 'demand characteristics' not a problem.	1 Much more difficult to control extraneous variables. 2 Much more difficult to replicate. 3 More time-consuming and expensive. 4 Ethical issues associated with 'unsolicited' subjects.
Laboratory experiments	1 Much greater control over extraneous variables. 2 Much easier to replicate. 3 Less time-consuming and expensive. 4 Subjects can easily be de-briefed.	1 Problems in generalizing to real-life situations, because of their artificial nature (low ecological validity). 2 Subjects' behaviour likely to be influenced by 'demand characteristics'.

3 Natural and quasi (the latter sometimes being called 'pseudo' or '*ex post facto*' experiments; the important point here is that the independent variable has not been manipulated as in 'true' experiments. When subjects are chosen because of their gender, race, intelligence, etc., they cannot be randomly allocated to control/experimental groups which characterize 'true' experiments. See Coolican, 1990).

4 The level of measurement is *nominal*, i.e. each time someone helped, they were *either* of the same race as the victim *or* of a different race; the victim was *either* cane *or* drunk, etc. So 'events' were being put into one category or another. The design was independent groups.

5 If you look at the results for black victims (table 11.3), the numbers are very small (0), making it likely that the expected frequencies (E) will be below 5 in two or more cells. This means that the ordinary χ^2 cannot be used, and so Fisher's exact is used instead. The test is also known as the Fisher–Yates test. (Yates is the person responsible for 'Yates's correction' as used in a 2×2 Chi-squared test and wherever there is one degree of freedom.)

Chapter 12 (Garcia & Koelling, 1966)

1 See the final paragraph of the *Summary*. (In fact, the last sentence.)

2 Aversion Therapy (used in the treatment of alcoholism, for example, and other addictions).

3 (*i*) Mann–Whitney U (independent groups design; ordinal data).

4 (*ii*) The dependent variable is fluid intake, measured in mls, which

represents an interval/ratio scale, so an independent *t*-test *could* have been used.

4 There is a zero correlation between (*i*) reduction in amount of saccharine drunk and (*ii*) interval between drinking and receiving the injection (at least for intervals of between five and 22 minutes).

Chapter 13 (Bennett-Levy & Marteau, 1984)

1 It is one-tailed and positive: the *more* rapid or abrupt the movements of the animals and the *more* they depart from the human form, the *greater* will be the fear ratings of these animals.

2 It is otherwise known as the Variance-Ratio test. It is used when the statistical hypothesis is concerned with the relative dispersions of scores under two conditions, as opposed to their means. It is a parametric test of difference. It is also used for checking the homogeneity of variance assumption of a parametric test.

3 Yes. Correlations usually involve obtaining two sets of scores from the *same* group of subjects (i.e. both variables are measured using only one group of subjects). No reasons are given for this unusual arrangement.

4 Yes. Counterbalancing or randomization of the questionnaires would be needed to reduce order effects.

5 (*i*) Randomly, at least from among the adult patients.
(*ii*) They were attending the health centre and so, presumably, were in need of medical care of some kind. We know that many patients seek help for psychsomatic illness, or use physical symptoms as a pretext for discussing psychological/emotional problems. It would be very difficult to ensure 'normality' (i.e. to exclude absence of phobias) for such a sample.

6 People are usually quite anxious while waiting to see the doctor, especially if they are feeling unwell. Of course, they could have refused, but it may have been difficult for them to 'escape' (unlike the situation where a market researcher approaches you in the street). They may have felt obliged in some way, because of where the study was being held.

Chapter 14 (Gardner & Gardner, 1969)

1 The tendency to attribute human characteristics (motives, feelings, etc.) to non-human things (animals, objects, etc.).

2

Washoe	Children
1 She was relatively old when the training began.	1 They are exposed to language from birth.
2 She was raised in an unnatural environment.	2 They are raised in natural environments.
3 She was deliberately taught to sign, something chimps don't spontaneously do (i.e. language training).	3 They don't have to be deliberately taught language, because it is spontaneous (i.e. language acquisition).
4 Only signs were taught (not grammar). The debate is about whether chimps sign 'grammatically'.	4 Neither words nor grammar are taught; *both* are spontaneously acquired.

3 Deaf children learning ASL (Carroll, 1986).

4 Direct comparisons between studies can only be made if the same (or very similar) methods are used. For example, it's much easier to use signs spontaneously than, say, plastic symbols, and so when evaluating a study's data regarding spontaneity (compared with children's spontaneous speech), this must be taken into account.

5 To some extent this is a matter of opinion; I'll let you think about this one.

6 It could be argued that, in some ways, rearing chimps 'as children' and training them to use language (usually in isolation from other chimps) is as unacceptable as raising them in laboratories. Is it 'mental or emotional cruelty' for the sake of 'science' or for the sake of meeting some need in the scientist regarding his/her human nature?

Chapter 15 (Salzen & Sluckin, 1961)

1 (*i*) Nominal.
(*ii*) The numbers in each cell are quite small: 3/16, 6/14, 6/14, 7/8, 0/6, 0/8, 2/3, making it highly likely that expected frequencies (E) will fall below 5 in two or more cells. This means that the normal χ^2 cannot be used. Fisher's Exact test (or the Fisher–Yates test) is used instead.

2 According to Lea (1984), there are three major reasons:
(*i*) There have been many attempts to explain human behaviour in terms of the evolutionary history of the human species, and so psychologists should take account of such explanations.
(*ii*) An evolutionary explanation is often a good place to begin; it helps us to understand the functions and mechanisms involved, which can then provide hypotheses to be tested with human subjects.

(*iii*) We cannot properly understand what it is to be human unless we understand what it is to be non-human. [See the *Exercises* for chapter 16.]

3 Altricial, which includes human beings, in which newborns are incapable of mobility, and are totally dependent on others.

4 (*i*) Attachment (e.g. Bowlby, (1951): for most children up to one year, but can extend to 2½ to three years);
(*ii*) Language (e.g. Lenneberg, (1964): up to puberty (i.e. ten to 11 years);
(*iii*) Gender identity (e.g. Money & Ehrhardt, (1972): 2½ to three years);
(*iv*) Personality development (e.g. Freud: the first five years).

Chapter 16 (Rawlins, 1979)

1

	Cayo compared with Field studies	Cayo compared with Laboratory studies
Advantages	1 Cayo is self-contained, easy to get around. 2 Animals generally visible. 3 All animals known and identified.	1 Cannot study social behaviour under laboratory conditions (for practical reasons). 2 The laboratory is an artificial environment. 3 Behaviour in Cayo is natural, not restricted/distorted by equipment, etc.
Disadvantages	1 There is interference on Cayo: food, tattoos, blood samples. 2 The animals were 'exported' there originally from India for medical research.	1 Poor control over the causes of behaviour on Cayo; no manipulation of variables is possible. 2 It is much easier to study one or two animals at a time than (up to) 600 or so (on Cayo).

2 [See *Answers to Exercises*, chapter 15.] An important point to add is that while all species have evolved *biologically*, human beings have gone beyond this and have evolved *socially* as well. This may limit the usefulness of comparative studies.

3 There is quite a lot of agreement that early *homo sapiens* was a 'hunter–gatherer' (like present-day Eskimos, Pygmies of the Ituri forest, Aborigines, Kalahari Bushmen, Punan of Borneo, etc.). These people live in small clans which hardly ever come into contact with other groups of people (Siann, 1985).
   But humans inhabit a tremendous range of climates, ecologies, etc. and it is the multiplicity of physical, social and cultural

environments which make human beings unique amongst the animal kingdom, and make generalizations so difficult.

4 By focusing public and scientific attention on them, we may become alerted to what we are doing to endanger them, which may then ensure their long-term survival.

Chapter 17 (Sperry, 1968)

1 The techincal material is almost exclusively logical, but in stories many things happen at once; the sense of a story emerges through a combination of style, plot and evoked images and feelings. So language *in the form of stories* can stimulate the right hemisphere (Ornstein, 1986).

2 Mentally rotating the object in space: right hemisphere (spatial abilities). Counting the boxes: left hemisphere (numerical/ mathematical/symbolic/analytic abilities).

3 Not only have they undergone the commissurotomy, but they have had intractable epilepsy (i.e. it could not be cured by any less drastic treatment, such as drugs, which they have probably been taking for many years).

4 Split-brain patients have not been randomly allocated to the 'commissurotomy condition'; it's difficult to find volunteers for such studies! So subjects are chosen because they already have a split brain.

Chapter 18 (Olds & Milner, 1954)

1 (*i*) The period during which lever pressing produced ESB.
(*ii*) The period during which it didn't.

2 When the acquisition score was *above* the extinction score, this was reward.
When the acquisition score was *below* the extinction score, this was punishment [see *Testing* in the Summary].

3 Periods when the rat was pressing the lever at least once every 30 seconds, i.e. intervals of 30 seconds or longer without a response were counted as a period of no responding.

Chapter 19 (Schachter & Singer, 1962)

1 Ordinal: 4 is higher than 3, but not necessarily to the same degree as 2 is higher than 1, as would be the case on an interval scale. It would be difficult to justify the claim that the difference between 'a little irritated and angry' and 'quite irritated and angry' is equivalent to the difference between 'very irritated and angry' and 'extremely

irritated and angry'. An interval scale has to be much more precise than this.

2 Mann–Whitney *U*: a test of difference, using independent samples and ordinal data.

3 Perhaps being told about side-effects (the wrong ones) produced a higher level of arousal, which made them more sensitive to environmental cues about the meaning of their arousal. This is, of course, quite consistent with the hypotheses.

4 The kinds of variables which would need to be taken into account are:
(*i*) general susceptibility to the influence of other people; (*ii*) general sensitivity to drugs such as epinephrine; (*iii*) appropriateness of the stooge's behaviour *re* sex roles; (*iv*) perceived attractiveness of the opposite-sex stooge, and its effect on the general level of arousal.

5 It means that the *direction* of the results is *not* being predicted. But from the three propositions, it would seem quite reasonable to make one-tailed (directional) predictions.

6 As a general principle, deception is to be discouraged. But this experiment depended on it. What is perhaps more worrying is the (apparent) lack of any medical checks/precautions given when an injection was actually being given.

Chapter 20 (Dement & Kleitman, 1957)

1 Although there is no particular reason for thinking that there are sex differences regarding REM/NREM sleep, it is always desirable to have roughly equal numbers of males and females. Perhaps more important is the very small number of subjects; individual differences were found *re* ability to recall dreams, for example, so much larger samples (or replications) are needed before any generalizations can be made.

2 These drugs are known to affect normal sleep activity, e.g. alcohol suppresses REM sleep without affecting NREM sleep.

3 With such a wide range of scores, the mean could be distorted (by the high and low scores). So the *median* might have been more appropriate.

4 This information may have influenced their dream reports; if they (through 'demand characteristics') believed that they were 'meant' to report 'proper dreams' after REM sleep, they could not have given honest and 'objective' accounts of their dreams.

5 This was a way of ensuring that the differential dream reports for REM/NREM sleep were not 'contaminated' by the sequence of awakening. If a common pattern emerged even when, for example, one subject had been told they had only been woken from REM sleep, this would be a better test of the genuine difference between the two kinds of sleep.

6 Sign Test: looking for a difference (e.g. between REM and NREM periods), repeated measures design (all subjects were woken from REM and NREM sleep), nominal data (recalled dream/didn't recall dream).

7 (*i*) Pearson's Product Moment (interval data, parametric test).
(*ii*) No, they were all $p = 0.05$ or below.

Chapter 21 (Orne, 1966)

1 (*i*) 'Correlate'. (*ii*) A test of correlation (either Pearson or Spearman).

2 They are used to assess the *reliability* of the Scale ('Alternative or Parallel Forms'), i.e. the consistency with which the test measures whatever it is measuring. There should be a significant positive correlation between scores on the different Forms if the test is reliable.

3 See the answer to 2 (chapter 1).

4 Some of the questions you may want to consider are:
(*i*) Is the experimenter displaying gratuitous sadism?
(*ii*) Does it serve a valid scientific purpose?
(*iii*) Does it contribute towards the clinical use of hypnosis?
(*iv*) Are subjects properly debriefed?
[Your answers to these questions may, of course, depend on whether you adopt a state or non-state view.]

Chapter 22 (Watson & Rayner, 1920)

1 It can be thought of as a whole series of *repeated measures*, and any one measure may depend, in subtle or complex ways, on the measures previously taken. If we know that the successive scores obtained from a subject are independent of each other, then there is no *statistical* objection to single-subject designs (Robson, 1973).

2 (*i*) 'In the 1920s' should be '1920'.
(*ii*) 'J.B. Watson' should be 'J.B. Watson and R. Rayner'.
(*iii*) 'did a series of experiments with children' should be 'initiated some laboratory experiments with an infant, Albert B'.
(*iv*) 'how emotional responses can be conditioned and deconditioned': no mention of 'deconditioning' in the original (the emphasis very much on conditioning).
(*v*) 'an eight-month-old orphan, Albert B.' should be 'nine-month-old Albert B., whose mother was a wet-nurse in a children's hospital'.
(*vi*) 'who happened to be fond of rabbits, rats, mice and other furry animals' should be 'none of these induced a fear response'.
(*vii*) 'toy rabbit' should be 'white rat' (a real one).
(*viii*) 'Then the rabbit was displayed to Albert, and, half a second or so later, Watson made a sudden loud noise' should be 'joint

presentations' (of the rat and hammer on steel bar).

(*ix*) 'crashing metal plates together' should be 'hammer on steel bar'.

(*x*) '. . . it spread to other stimuli . . . such as a glove, a towel, a man's beard, a toy and a ball of wool' should be 'rabbit, dog, fur coat, cotton wool, Watson's hair, and a Santa Claus mask'.
(You can work out the others for yourself.)

3 Stimulus Generalization.

4 Discrimination.

5 Extinction and Spontaneous Recovery.

Chapter 23 (Hodges & Tizard, 1989)

1

	Cross-sectional	Longitudinal
Advantages	1 Relatively simple and quick: it's a short-term study, so is relatively inexpensive. 2 Requires no continuity of the research team. 3 Data needn't be 'frozen' over long time period until subjects have completed their development. 4 Provides age-related norms.	1 No cohort problem (same subjects are being compared with themselves). 2 Smaller number of subjects required. 3 Sensitive to changes in behaviour which occur quickly (assuming the intervals between successive observations are fairly short). 4 Provides individual growth curves (as well as age-related norms).
Disadvantages	1 *Cohort* effect: if widely different age-groups/cohorts compared, any differences could be due *either* to actual change in the variables being studied *or* the fact that they represent different generations. 2 Subjects need to be matched on relevant variables, which is expensive and time-consuming. 3 Larger number of subjects required. 4 Can *describe* behaviour changes over time, but *not* explain them.	1 Time-consuming and expensive. 2 Requires continuity of research team. 3 The subjects who 'survive' may be affected in some way by repeated testing over the years; this may make them a less representative sample than they originally were.

2 (*i*) The natural experiment takes place in the normal course of events, and is not due to any kind of interference on the psychologist's part; the changes which occur would have occurred anyway.

(*ii*) The subjects in a natural experiment are not aware that they are part of an 'experiment'.

(*iii*) Because the psychologist is not randomly allocating subjects to the experimental/control conditions, there is no control over subject variables (and so the experiment is not a true, but a 'quasi' experiment).

[See answers to 3, chapter 11.]

3 The original 30 London working-class children no longer seemed appropriate for the mainly middle-class adopted group or the restored group who lived in mainly disadvantaged homes. A comparison 16 year old was found, therefore, for each of the ex-institution adolescents, matched on sex, one- or two-parent family, occupational status of main breadwinner, and position in family.

4 Without it, it would be impossible to know if it was the institutional experience, rather than something else, which affected the adolescents' relationships (e.g. 'they might have turned out like that anyway'). This is the basic principle of *all* control (comparison) groups.

Chapter 24 (Freud, 1909)

1 The investigator has little or no control over variables (making it impossible to infer cause-and-effect), it involves an individual (or family), and so cannot be replicated, it often involves the interpretation of the subject's behaviour from a particular theoretical perspective, and the investigator cannot be objective due to his/her role as a therapist/psychiatrist etc. in a helping role (as opposed to scientist role).

[All these points are a matter of degree, especially 'objectivity'. See, for example, Gross (1987).]

2 The case study is really Freud's interpretation of Hans' father's interpretation of his son's phobia; not the most direct connection between Freud and his patient (whom he actually saw on only one or two occasions). But Freud and the father were of one mind anyway regarding the Oedipal theory, and so would have probably reached the same interpretation, but the 'price' paid for this agreement is fitting Hans' behaviour etc. *into* the theory (i.e. a drastic reduction in objectivity).

3 Qualitative data = non-statistical, not involving measurement, involving much more description and interpretation.

Quantitative data = statistical, based on (precise) measurement. Can much more easily be 'checked out' by another investigator.

4 This is one you might want to debate in the class. Remember, Bowlby's interpretation, like Freud's, is made from a particular theoretical perspective, i.e. Attachment theory; Fromm's is more objective in this sense.

Chapter 25 (Samuel & Bryant, 1984)

1 (*i*) Counterbalancing.
(*ii*) To reduce the impact of order effects (e.g. practice or fatigue as a result of doing one task before another). This is an inherent problem in a repeated measures design.
(*iii*) Using the initial letter of each material (M = mass, N = number, V = volume), the following could have been used: MNV, NVM, VNM, such that one third of the subjects within each age group and within each condition were tested in each of these three, pre-determined, orders.

2 As Samuel and Bryant say, it was used to check that subjects who answered the post-transformation question correctly in the other two conditions did so by bringing over information from the pre-transformation display. It was, therefore, serving as a *control* condition.

Chapter 26 (Rees, 1971)

1 If standardized questions had all been asked in the same order for all interviewees, with concentration on hallucinations, they might have talked much less freely about the deceased and their feelings, and may have been much more inhibited about 'admitting' to hallucinations. This, then, would have been self-defeating as far as the study is concerned.

2 If subjects rationalized their experience (e.g. 'in my mind's eye'), or expressed any doubt about the reality of the experience, then the experience was not counted as an hallucination. Also, any experiences in bed at night were counted as dreams *unless* they happened immediately after retiring.

3 (Probably) all widowed people in Britain.
They were an opportunity sample: all widowed people living in Llanidloes, and all attending the same group practice.

4 Chi-squared.

5 Formula = (Rows − 1) × (Columns − 1):
Table 26.11: $(2 - 1) \times (6 - 1) = 1 \times 5 = 5$

6 Regression Analysis permits the prediction of unknown values of dependent variables based on knowledge of corresponding values of independent variables. Both must be measured on an interval scale. 'Linear' refers to the straight-line relationship between two variables. A correlation coefficient can be thought of as a statistical technique for drawing the best fitting straight line through a scattergram.

Chapter 27 (Bouchard & McGue, 1981)

1 The view that many pairs of genes are involved in the inheritance of intelligence (not just a single pair, as in eye-colour for example).

2 Some genes are more powerful than others; e.g. the brown-eye gene is dominant over the blue-eye gene, such that if someone inherits one of each (genotype) they will actually have brown eyes (phenotype).

3 The tendency for organisms – including human beings – to select as mates/sexual partners those with characteristics similar to their own.

4 If a range of values includes some scores which are extreme in one direction only, then the mean will be distorted and the median will be a more 'typical' score.

5 (*i*) A figure which takes sample size (the number of pairings) into account as a weight, which makes the different studies more comparable.

(*ii*) A measure of heterogeneity (dissimilarity) between the median correlations within each category. d.f. is, of course, determined by the number of studies in a set.

(*iii*) χ^2 divided by its d.f. has an expectation of 1.0 under the homogeneity (similarity) hypothesis, and can be used to compare the relative heterogeneity of different categories (i.e. between categories).

6

Individual tests	**Group tests**
1 Used primarily as diagnostic tools in a clinical setting (e.g. disruptive behaviour at school).	1 Used primarily for purposes of selection and research (e.g. the 11-plus exam in England and Wales).
2 Involves a 1:1 situation between the psychologists and the person being tested.	2 As many people are tested at one time as is practical (e.g. the number of tables and chairs in the room).
3 Face-to-face situation, in which it is important to put the testee at his/her ease.	3 Presented in the form of written questions (like an exam).
4 No standardized instructions as such.	4 Standardized instructions.
5 May/may not be timed.	5 Timed.
6 Usually involves some *performance* items.	6 No performance items.
7 Some room for interpretation of answers.	7 No room for interpretation. They are objective tests (only one answer can be accepted as correct; usually marked by computer).
e.g. Stanford–Binet, Wechsler Intelligence Scale for Children (WISC).	e.g. Raven's Progressive Matrices Test, British Ability Scales.

Chapter 28 (Eysenck, 1952)

1 (*i*) Psychoneurotic cases are not usually committed to state hospitals unless in a very bad psychological state;
(*ii*) there were relatively few voluntary patients in the hospital group;
(*iii*) such patients do receive *some* degree of psychotherapy;
(*iv*) there were probably quite important differences between the two groups *re* economic, educational and social status.
Denker's: his group was receiving no psychotherapy, came from all over the USA, displayed a wide range of neuroses and had a higher socio-economic status. *But* they were probably more incapacitated than the psychotherapy group.

2 The baseline represents the rate of spontaneous recovery (recovery without any treatment); if psychotherapy works, it must aid recovery *beyond* the baseline.

3 (*i*) Dream interpretation;
(*ii*) free association;
(*iii*) transference.

4 (*i*) Systematic Desensitization (S.D.) involves a step-by-step exposure to the phobic object (usually by imagining it), while simultaneously relaxing.
(*ii*) Implosion involves exposing the patient to what, in S.D., would be at the top of the hierarchy (a list of least to most feared contact with the phobic object), without any relaxation.
(*iii*) Flooding is exposure which takes place *in vivo* (e.g. with an actual spider, rather than imagining it), but is otherwise more like Implosion than S.D.

5 This refers to the replacement of a removed symptom (e.g. phobia) by another symptom (e.g. another phobia). It is what psychoanalytic theorists believe happens when *only* the behaviour itself (i.e. the fear), and not the underlying conflict, is dealt with (as in behaviour therapy). (See *Context and Background* section of the Commentary.)

Chapter 29 (Rosenhan, 1973)

1 In order to be able to generalize the results, i.e. the hospitals used should be representative of US psychiatric hospitals in general.
They were in different States, on both coasts, both old/shabby and new, research-orientated and not, well staffed and poorly staffed (staff:patient ratio), 11 state, one private, federal or university funded.

2 Psychiatrists are more likely to call a healthy person sick (a false positive) (Type-two error) than a sick person healthy (a false negative, Type-one error).
In psychology, we make a Type-one error when we incorrectly reject the Null hypothesis (i.e. we should have accepted it), and a

Type-two error when we incorrectly accept the Null hypothesis (i.e. we should have rejected it).

3 e.g. (*i*) Pseudopatients trying to gain admission but *without* complaining of hearing voices, or with different symptoms.
(*ii*) Telling staff the results of the first experiment, but not telling them to expect any pseudopatients.

4 'However distasteful such concealment is, it was a necessary first step . . . Without concealment, there would have been no way to know how valid these experiences were; nor was there any way of knowing whether whatever detections occurred were a tribute to the diagnostic acumen of the staff or to the hospital's rumour network . . .
I have respected their [individual staff and hospitals] anonymity, and have eliminated clues that might lead to their identification'. (Rosenhan, 1973: Notes)

Chapter 30 (Bem, 1974)

1 The criterion for selecting an item was that it should be independently judged, by males and females, to be significantly more desirable for men or for women. The implication is that males and females will have different ideas about what's desirable for the same and opposite sex, so that only where they do agree can an item be reliably considered sex-typed (and, hence, included).

2 It comprises a seven-point scale, each with a verbal description. It is taken to represent an *interval* scale because a *t*-test is used, which is parametric and requires an interval scale. (The androgyny score is expressed as a *t*-ratio, i.e. the *t*-test statistic.)

3 It is a measure of the test's *reliability*. Each item should be measuring the same variable and to the same extent, i.e. all items should contribute equally to the overall score. A common method for assessing internal consistency is the Split Half method. (Bem expresses the internal consistency of the BSRI as a coefficient alpha: α.)

4 Because if they had, it wouldn't have been a measure of the *reliability* of the test, but of the subjects' memory.

5 (*i*) Parametric. (*ii*) Spearman's rank-order correlation.

6 (*i*) Concurrent. (*ii*) Face/predictive/construct.

7 Eysenck Personality Questionnaire (EPQ); the Social Desirability scale is known as the 'Lie Scale'.

8 A test must be properly standardized, i.e. tried out on a large, representative sample of the population for whom it is intended, in order to establish a set of norms for that population, so that any individual's score can be compared against those norms.

Chapter 31 (Thigpen & Cleckley, 1954)

1 and 2 These can both be debated (perhaps together) in your psychology class.

3 (*i*) They have no particular theoretical 'axe to grind', so there is much less chance of bias in their interpretations.

(*ii*) They asked independent experts to give a variety of tests: psychological and neuro-physiological, objective and projective.

(*iii*) Thigpen and Cleckley could reach a diagnosis and interpretation etc. together, while Freud had no co-worker with whom he could discuss his cases. (A noteworthy exception was, of course, Little Hans' father, but he was a 'Freudian' already; see chapter 24, Commentary.)

(*iv*) Thigpen and Cleckley involved Eve's relatives to help verify certain recollections, and to add information, and in this way throw light on the case. (By contrast, Hans' father was also his major *psychoanalyst!*)

4

Multiple personality	**Schizophrenia**
1 Hearing voices is the only kind of hallucination, but is not a major symptom.	1 Auditory hallucinations are not the only kind, and are usually a major symptom.
2 Involves fugue and amnesia.	2 Does not involve fugue and amnesia.
3 Is a form of (dissociative) neurosis.	3 Is a form of (functional) psychosis.
4 Usually treated psychologically (psychotherapy).	4 Usually treated physically (major tranquillizers).
5 The different personalities are 'self-contained', although some are very specific/superficial. Each represents a 'part of the whole'.	5 The personality as a whole is split, e.g. there is a breakdown between self/reality, self/other, emotion/cognition.

References

Abramson, L. Y. and Martin, D. J. (1981) Depression and the causal inference process. In J. H. Harvey, W. J. Ickes and R. F. Kidd (eds), *New Directions in Attitude Research*, Vol. 3, Hillsdale, N.J.: Lawrence Erlbaum.

Abse D, (1974) The dogs of paradise, cited in S. Milgram (1974) *Obedience to Authority*, New York: Harper and Row.

Ainsworth, M. D. S., Blehar, M. C., Waters, E. and Wall, S. (1978) *Patterns of Attachment: a Psychological Study of the Strange Situation*, Hillsdale, N.J.: Lawrence Erlbaum.

Aitchison, J. (1983) *The Articulate Mammal*, 2nd ed., London: Hutchinson University Library.

Alba, J. W. and Hasher, L. (1983) Is memory schematic? *Psychological Bulletin*, 93, 203–31.

Allison, R. B. (1974) A new treatment approach for multiple personalities. *American Journal of Clinical Hypnosis*, 17, 15–32.

Allison, R. B. (1977) Diagnosis and treatment of multiple personality. Paper presented at American Psychiatric Association, Toronto, July 1977. Cited in J. Altrocchi (1980) *Abnormal Behaviour*, New York: Harcourt Brace Jovanovich.

Allport, G. W. (1955) *Becoming-Basic Considerations for a Psychology of Personality*, New Haven: Yale University Press.

Allport, G. W. and Pettigrew, T. F. (1957) Cultural influences on the perception of movement: the trapezoidal illusion among Zulus. *Journal of Abnormal and Social Psychology*, 55, 104–13.

Altrocchi, J. (1980) *Abnormal Behaviour*, New York: Harcourt Brace Jovanovich.

American Psychiatric Association (1980) *Diagnostic and Statistical Manual of Mental Disorders*, 3rd ed., Washington, D.C.: American Psychiatric Association.

Anderson, J. R. and Reder, L. (1979) An elaborative processing explanation of depth of processing. In L. S. Cermak and F. I. M. Craik (eds), *Levels of Processing in Human Memory*, Hillsdale, N.J.: Lawrence Erlbaum.

Archer, J. and Lloyd, B. (1985) *Sex and Gender*, Cambridge: Cambridge University Press.

Aronfreed, J. M., Messick, S. A. and Diggory, J. C. (1953) Re-examining emotionality and perceptual defence. *Journal of Personality*, 21, 517.

Aronson, E. (1988) *The Social Animal*, 5th ed., New York: Freeman.

Aronson, E. and Carlsmith, J. M. (1963) Effect of the severity of threat on the devaluation of forbidden behaviour. *Journal of Abnormal and Social Psychology*, 6, 584–8.

Atkinson, R. C. and Shiffrin, R. M. (1968) Human memory: a proposed system and its control processes. In K. W. Spence and J. T. Spence (eds), *The Psychology of Learning and Motivation*, Vol. 2, London: Academic Press.

Atkinson, R. C. and Shiffrin, R. M. (1971) The control of short-term memory. *Scientific American*, 224, 82–90.

Bailey, C. L. (1979) Mental illness – a logical misrepresentation? *Nursing Times*, May, 761–2.

Barber, T. X. (1969) *Hypnosis: a Scientific Approach*, New York: Van Nostrand.

Barber, T. X., Spanos, N. P. and Chaves, J. F. (1974) *Hypnotism: Imagination and Human Potentialities*, New York: Pergamon.

Barry, H., Bacon, M. K. and Child, I. L. (1957) A cross-cultural survey of some sex differences in socialization. *Journal of Abnormal and Social Psychology*, 55, 327–32.

Bar-Tal, D. and Saxe, L. (1976) Perception of similarity and dissimilarity in attractive couples and individuals. *Journal of Personality and Social Psychology*, 33, 772–81.

Bartlett, F. C. (1932) *Remembering*, Cambridge: Cambridge University Press.

Bateson, P. P. G. (1964) Effect of similarity between rearing and testing conditions on chicks' following and avoidance responses. *Journal of Comparative and Physiological Psychology*, 57, 100–3.

Baumrind, D. (1964) Some thoughts on ethics of research: after reading Milgram's behavioural study of obedience. *American Psychologist*, 19, 421–3.

Beaumont, J. G. (1988) *Understanding Neuropsychology*, Oxford: Blackwell.

Beier, E. G. and Cowen, E. L. (1953) A further investigation of the influence of 'threat expectancy' on perception. *Journal of Personality*, 22, 254.

Bekerian, D. A. and Bowers, J. M. (1983) Eye-witness testimony: were we misled? *Journal of Experimental Psychology: Learning, Memory and Cognition*, 9, 139–45.

Bem, D. J. (1965) An experimental analysis of self-persuasion. *Journal of Experimental and Social Psychology*, 1, 199–218.

Bem, D. J. (1967) Self-perception: an alternative interpretation of cognitive dissonance phenomena. *Psychological Review*, 74, 183–200.

Bem, S. L. (1975) Sex role adaptability: one consequence of psychological androgyny. *Journal of Personality and Social Psychology*, 31, 634–43.

Bem, S. L. (1977) On the utility of alternative procedures for assessing psychological androgyny. *Journal of Consulting and Clinical Psychology*, 45, 196–205.

Bem, S. L. (1979) Theory and measurement of androgyny: a reply to the Pedhazur-Tetenbaum and Locksley-Cotten critiques. *Journal of Personality and Social Psychology*, 37, 1047–54.

Bem, S. L. (1984) Androgyny and gender schema theory: a conceptual and empirical integration. In R. A. Dienstbier (ed.), *Nebraska Symposium on Motivation*, Lincoln: University of Nebraska Press.

Bem, S. L. and Lenney, E. (1976) Sex-typing and the avoidance of cross-sex behaviour. *Journal of Personality and Social Psychology*, 33, 48–54.

Berelson, B. (1952) *Content Analysis in Communication Research*, Glencoe, Illinois: Free Press.

Berger, M. (1973) Early experiences and other environmental factors – an overview. In H. J. Eysenck (ed.), *Handbook of Abnormal Psychology*, 2nd ed., London: Pitman.

Bergin, A. E. (1971) The evaluation of therapeutic outcomes. In A. E. Bergin and S. L. Garfield (eds), *Handbook of Psychotherapy and Behaviour Change: an Empirical Analysis*, New York: Wiley.

Bergin, A. E. and Lambert, M. J. (1978) The evaluation of therapeutic outcomes. In A. E. Bergin and S. L. Garfield (eds), *Handbook of Psychotherapy and Behaviour Change: an Empirical Analysis*, 2nd ed., New York: Wiley.

Berscheid, E., Dion, K., Hatfield, E. and Walster, G. W. (1971) Physical attractiveness and dating choice: a test of the matching hypothesis. *Journal of Experimental and Social Psychology*, 7, 173–89.

Bersheid, E. and Walster, E. M. (1974) Physical attractiveness. In L. Berkowitz (ed.), *Advances in Experimental Social Psychology*, Vol. 7, New York: Academic Press.

Bitterman, M. E. and Kniffin, C. W. (1953) Manifest anxiety and perceptual defence. *Journal of Abnormal and Social Psychology*, 49, 178–82.

Blau, P. M. (1964) *Exchange and Power in Social Life*, New York: John Wiley and Sons.

Boas, F. (1927) Primitive art, cited in R. Serpell (1974) *Culture's Influence on Behaviour*, London: Methuen.

Bogen, J. E. (1969) The other side of the brain. In R. Ornstein, *The Psychology of Consciousness*, 2nd revised edition, Harmondsworth: Penguin.

Bogen, J. E. and Gazzaniga, M. S. (1965) cited in J. E. Bogen (1969).

Bolles, R. C. (1980) Ethological learning theory. In G. M. Gazda and R. J. Corsini (eds), *Theories of Learning: a Comparative Approach*, Itaska, Illinois: Free Press.

Bootzin, R. R. and Max, D. (1982) Learning and behavioural theories of anxiety and stress. In I. L. Kutash and B. Schlesinger (eds), *Pressure Points: Perspectives on Stress and Anxiety*, San Francisco: Jossey-Bass.

Botwinick, J. (1984) *Ageing and behaviour*, 3rd ed., New York: Springer.

Bouchard, T. J. (1984) cited in Smith *et al.* (1986) *Psychology – The Frontiers of Behaviour*, New York: Harper and Ross.

Bower, G. H. and Miller, N. E. (1958) Rewarding and punishing effects from stimulating the same place in the rat's brain. *Journal of Comparative and Physiological Psychology*, 51, 669–74.

Bowers, K. S. (1983) *Hypnosis for the Seriously Curious*, New York: Norton.

Bowlby, J. (1951) *Maternal Care and Mental Health*, Geneva: World Health Organization.

Bowlby, J. (1969) *Attachment and Loss*, Vol. 1: Attachment, Harmondsworth: Penguin.

Bowlby, J. (1973) *Attachment and Loss*, Vol. 2: Separation-Anxiety and Anger, Harmondsworth: Penguin.

Bransford, J. D., Franks, J. J., Morris, C. D. and Stein, B. S. (1979) Some general constraints on learning and memory research. In L. S. Cermak and F. I. M. Craik (eds), *Levels of Processing in Human Memory*, Hillsdale, N.J.: Lawrence Erlbaum.

Brislin, R. W. and Lewis, S. A. (1968) Dating and physical attractiveness: a replication. *Psychological Reports*, 22, 976.

Broadbent, D. (1958) *Perception and Communication*, Oxford: Pergamon.

Bromley, D. B. (1988) Human Ageing – An Introduction to Gerontology, 3rd ed., Harmondsworth: Penguin.

Bronfenbrenner, U. (1979) *The Ecology of Human Development: Experiments by Nature and Design*, Cambridge, M.A.: Harvard University Press.

Broverman, I. K., Vogel, S. R., Broverman, D. M., Clarkson, F. E. and Rosenkrantz, P. S. (1972) Sex-role stereotypes: a current appraisal. *Journal of Social Issues*, 28, 59–78.

Brown, R. (1970) The first sentences of child and chimpanzee. In R. Brown (ed.), *Psycholinguistics*, New York: Free Press.

Brown, R. (1973) *A First Language*, London: Allen and Unwin.

Brown, R. (1986) *Social Psychology*, 2nd ed., New York: Free Press.

Buber, M. (1937) *I and Thou*, Edinburgh: T. and T. Clark.

Burks, B. S. (1928) The relative influence of nature and nurture upon mental development: a comparative study of foster parent–foster child resemblance and true parent–true child resemblance. *Yearbook of the National Society for the Study of Education*, 27, 219–316.

Byrne, D., Ervin, C. R. and Lamberth, J. (1970) Continuity between experimental study of attraction and real-life computer dating. *Journal of Personality and Social Psychology*, 16, 157–65.

Caine, T. M. and Hope, K. (1967) *Manual of the Hysteroid–Obsessoid Questionnaire*, London: University of London Press.

Campbell, D. T. (1964) Distinguishing differences of perception from failures of communication in cross-cultural studies. In F. S. C. Northrop and H. H. Livingstone (eds), *Cross-cultural Understanding*, New York and London: Harper and Row.

Campbell, H. J. (1973) *The Pleasure Areas*, London: Eyre Methuen.

Cannon, W. B. (1927) The James-Lange theory of emotions: a critical examination and an alternative theory. *American Journal of Psychology*, 39, 106–24.

Carlsmith, J. M., Collins, B. E. and Helmreich, R. L. (1966) Studies in forced compliance: 1. The effect of pressure for compliance on attitude change produced by face to face role playing and anonymous essay-writing. *Journal of Personality and Social Psychology*, 4, 1–13.

Carroll, D. W. (1986) *Psychology of Language*, Monterey, C.A.: Brooks/Cole Publishing Company.

Chance, M. R. A. (1959) What makes monkeys sociable? In G. Ferry (ed.), *The Understanding of Animals* (1984), Oxford: Blackwell and New Scientist.

Chomsky, N. (1957) *Syntactic Structures*, The Hague: Mouton.

Chomsky, N. (1965) *Aspects of the Theory of Syntax*, Cambridge, M.A.: MIT Press.

Chomsky, N. (1980) *Rules and Representations*, Oxford: Blackwell.

Claridge, G. (1987) Schizophrenia and human individuality. In C. Blakemore and S. Greenfield (eds), *Mindwaves*, Oxford: Blackwell.

Clarke, A. D. B. (1972) Comment on Koluchova's 'Severe deprivation in twins: a case study'. *Journal of Child Psychology and Psychiatry*, 13, 103–6.

Clarke, A. M. and Clarke. A. D. B. (1976) *Early Experience: Myth and Evidence*, London: Open Books.

Clutton-Brock, T. (1974) Why do animals live in groups? In G. Ferry (ed.), *The Understanding of Animals* (1984), Oxford: Blackwell and New Scientist.

Cohen, G. (1975) Cerebral apartheid: a fanciful notion? *New Behaviour*, 18 (September), 458–61.

Cohen, G. (1986) Everyday memory. In G. Cohen, M. W. Eysenck and M. E. Le Voi, *Memory: A Cognitive Approach*, Milton Keynes: Open University.

Colligan, M. J., Frockt, W. and Tasto, D. L. (1978) Frequency of sickness, absence and worksite clinic visits as function of shift. *Journal of Environmental Pathology*, 2, 125–48.

Condon, W. S., Ogston, W. D. and Pacoe, L. V. (1969) Three faces of Eve revisited: a study of transient microstabismus. *Journal of Abnormal Psychology*, 74, 618–20.

Constantinople, A. (1979) Sex role acquisition: in search of the elephant. *Sex Roles*, 5, 121–33.

Coolican, H. (1990) *Research Methods and Statistics in Psychology*, Sevenoaks: Hodder and Stoughton.

Cooper, J. E. (1983) Diagnosis and the diagnostic process. In M. Shepherd and O. L. Zangwill (eds), *Handbook of Psychiatry: 1. General Psychopathology*, Cambridge: Cambridge University Press.

Cooper, J. and Fazio, R. H. (1984) A new look at dissonance theory. In L. Berkowitz (ed.), *Advances in Experimental Social Psychology*, Vol. 15, New York: Academic Press.

Cornwell, D. and Hobbs, S. (1976) The strange saga of Little Albert, *New Society* (March), 602–4.

Cowen, E. L. and Beier, E. G. (1954) Threat expectancy, word frequencies and perceptual prerecognition hypotheses. *Journal of Abnormal and Social Psychology*, 49, 178–82.

Cox, T. (1978) *Stress*, Basingstoke: Macmillan.

Craik, F. I. M. and Tulving, E. (1975) Depth of processing and the retention of words in episodic memory. *Journal of Experimental Psychology: General*, 104, 268–94.

Croyle, R. T. and Cooper, J. (1983) Dissonance arousal: physiological evidence. *Journal of Personality and Social Psychology*, 45, 782–91.

Curtiss, S. (1977) *Genie: a Psycholinguistic Study of a Modern-day 'Wild Child'*, London: Academic Press.

Davis, K. (1940) Extreme social isolation of a child. *American Journal of Sociology*, 45, 554–65.

Davis, K. (1947) Final note on a case of extreme isolation. *American Journal of Sociology*, 52, 432–7.

Dement, W. (1960) The effect of dream deprivation. *Science*, 131, 1705–7.

Denker, R. (1946) Results of treatment of psychoneuroses by the general practitioner. A follow-up study of 500 cases. *New York State Journal of Medicine*, 46, 2164–66.

Deregowski, J. B. (1968b) Pictorial recognition in subjects from a relatively pictureless environment. *African Social Research*, 5, 356–64.

Deregowski, J. B. (1969b) Preference for chain-type drawings in Zambian domestic servants and primary school children. *Psychologica Africana*, 82, 9–13.

Deregowski, J. B. (1970) A note on the possible determinants of split representation as an artistic style. *International Journal of Psychology*, 5, 21–6.

Deregowski, J. B., Muldrow, E. S. and Muldrow, W. F. (1972) Pictorial recognition in a remote Ethiopian population. *Perception*, 1, 417–25.

Devlin Report (1976) *Report on the Secretary of State for the Home Department of the Departmental Committee on Evidence of Identification in Criminal Cases*, London: HMSO.

Dixon, N. F. (1971) *Subliminal Perception: The Nature of the Controversy*, London: McGraw-Hill.

Dixon, N. F. (1981) *Preconscious Processing*, London: Wiley.

Dreyfus, H. L. (1987) Misrepresenting human intelligence. In R. Born (ed.), *Artificial Intelligence: the Case Against*, Beckenham: Croom Helm.

Duncan, H. F., Gourlay, N. and Hudson, W. (1973) *A Study of Pictorial Perception among Bantu and White Primary School Children in South Africa*, Johannesburg: Witwatersrand University Press.

Durkin, K. (1985) *Television, Sex Roles and Children*, Milton Keynes: Open University.

Durkin, K. (1986) Sex roles and the mass media. In D. J. Hargreaves and A. M. Colley (eds), *The Psychology of Sex Roles*, London: Harper and Row.

Eagly, A. H. (1987) *Sex Differences in Social Behaviour: a Social-Role Interpretation*, London: Lawrence Erlbaum.

Ebbinghaus, H. (1885) *Über das Gedachtnis*, Leipzig: H. Ruyer and C. E. Bussenius. Published in translation (1913) as *Memory*, New York: Teachers' College Press.

Eiser, J. R. and van der Pligt, J. (1988) *Attitudes and Decisions*, London: Routledge.

Elms, A. C. (1972) *Social Psychology and Social Relevance*, Boston: Little, Brown.

Endicott, J. and Spitzer, R. L. (1978) A diagnostic interview: the schedule for affective disorders and schizophrenia. *Archives of General Psychiatry*, 35, 837–44.

Erdelyi, M. H. (1974) A new look at the new look: perceptual defence and vigilance. *Psychological Review*, 81, 1–24.

Erikson, E. H. (1963) Childhood and Society, 2nd ed., New York: Norton.

Erikson, M. (1968) The inhumanity of ordinary people. *International Journal of Psychiatry*, 6, 278–9.

Erlenmeyer-Kimling, L. and Jarvik, L. F. (1963) Genetics and intelligence: a review. *Science*, 142, 1477–9.

Etzioni, A. (1968) A model of significant research. *International Journal of Psychiatry*, 6, 279–80.

Eysenck, H. J. (ed.) (1960) *Behaviour Therapy and the Neuroses*, Oxford: Pergamon.

Eysenck, H. J. (1973) *The Inequality of Man*, London: Temple Smith.

Eysenck, H. J. (1976) The learning theory model of neurosis – a new approach. *Behaviour Research and Therapy*, 14, 251–67.

Eysenck, H. J. and Rachman, S. (1965) *The Causes and Cure of Neurosis*, London: RKP.

Eysenck, M. W. (1979) Depth, elaboration and distinctiveness. In L. S. Cermak and F. I. M. Craik (eds), *Levels of Processing in Human Memory*, Hillsdale, N.J.: Lawrence Erlbaum.

Eysenck, M. W. (1984) *A Handbook of Cognitive Psychology*, London: Lawrence Erlbaum.

Eysenck, M. W. (1986) Working memory. In G. Cohen, M. W. Eysenck and M. E. Le Voi, *Memory: A Cognitive Approach*, Milton Keynes: Open University.

Faris, J. C. (1972) *Nuba Personal Art*, London: Duckworth.

Fazio, R. H., Zanna, M. P. and Cooper, J. (1977) Dissonance and self-perception: an integrative view of each theory's major domain of application. *Journal of Experimental and Social Psychology*, 13, 464–79.

Feighner, J. P., Robins, E., Guze, S. B., Woodruff, R. A., Winokur, G. and Munoz, R. (1972) Diagnostic criteria for use in psychiatric research. *Archives of General Psychiatry*, 26, 57–63.

Ferry, G. (1984) A sense of purpose: behaviour and evolution. In G. Ferry (ed.), *The Understanding of Animals*, Oxford: Blackwell and New Scientist.

Festinger, L. (1957) *A Theory of Cognitive Dissonance*, New York: Harper and Row.

Fiske, S. T. and Taylor, S. E. (1984) *Social Cognition*, Wokingham: Addison-Wesley.

Flanagan, O. J. (1984) *The Science of the Mind*, London: MIT Press.

Fontana, D. (1982) Intelligence. In D. Fontana (ed.), *Psychology for Teachers*, London and Basingstoke: BPS and Macmillan Press.

Freedman, J. (1963) Attitudinal effects of inadequate justification. *Journal of Personality*, 31, 371–85.

Freedman, J. (1965) Long-term behavioural effects of cognitive dissonance. *Journal of Experimental and Social Psychology*, 1, 145–55.

Freud, S. (1905) *Three Essays on the Theory of Sexuality*, Pelican Freud Library, Vol. 7, Harmondsworth: Penguin.

Freud, S. (1922) *Postscript (to the Case of Little Hans)*, Pelican Freud Library, Vol. 8, Harmondsworth: Penguin.

Fromm, E. (1970) *The Crisis of Psychoanalysis*, Harmondsworth: Penguin.

Garcia, J. and Koelling, R. A. (1966) Relation of cue to consequence in avoidance learning. *Psychonomic Science*, 4, 123–4.

Gardner, B. T. and Gardner, R. A. (1971) Two-way communication with an infant chimpanzee. In A. Schrier and F. Stollnitz (eds), *Behaviour of Non-Human Primates*, Vol. 4, New York: Academic Press.

Gardner, B. T. and Gardner, R. A. (1975) Evidence for sentence constituents in the early utterances of child and chimp. *Journal of Experimental Psychology: General*, 104, 244–67.

Gardner, B. T. and Gardner, R. A. (1980) Two comparative psychologists look at language acquisition. In K. Nelson, *Children's Language*, Vol. 2, New York: Gardner Press.

Gardner, R. A. and Gardner, B. T. (1978) Comparative psychology and language acquisition. In K. Salzinger and F. Denmark (eds), *Psychology: the State of the Art, Annals of the New York Academy of Sciences*, 309, 37–76.

Gardner, H. (1985) *The Mind's New Science*, New York: Basic Books.

Garfield, S. L. (1982) Eclecticism and integration in psychotherapy. *Behaviour Therapy*, 13, 610–23.

Garnham, A. (1988) *Artificial Intelligence: an Introduction*, London: RKP.

Geer, J. H. (1965) The development of a scale to measure fear. *Behaviour Research and Therapy*, 3, 45–53.

Geis, F. L., Brown, V., Jennings (Walstedt) J. and Porter, N. (1984). Television commercials as achievement scripts for women. *Sex Roles*, 10, 513–25.

Gibson, J. J. (1950) *Perception of the Visual World*, Houghton: Mifflin.

Gombrich, E. H. (1960) *Art and Illusion*, London: Phaidon.

Gough, H. G. (1952) Identifying psychological femininity. *Educational and Psychological Measurement*, 12, 427–39.

Graham, P. and Rutter, M. (1985) Adolescent disorders. In M. Rutter and L. Hersov (eds), *Child and Adolescent Psychiatry: Modern Approaches*, 2nd ed., Oxford: Blackwell.

Gray, J. A. (1987) The ethics and politics of animal experimentation. In H. Beloff and A. M. Colman (eds), *Psychology Survey*, No. 6, Leicester: British Psychological Society.

Green, S. (1980) Physiological studies, I and II. In J. Radford and E. Govier (ed.), *A Textbook of Psychology*, London: Sheldon Press.

Greenwald, A. G. (1975) On the inconclusiveness of 'crucial' cognitive tests of dissonance versus self-perception theories. *Journal of Experimental and Social Psychology*, 11, 490–9.

Gregor, A. J. and McPherson, D. (1965) A study of susceptibility to geometric illusions among cultural out groups of Australian aborigines. *Psychologica Africana*, 11, 1–13.

Gregory, R. (1987a) In defence of artificial intelligence – a reply to John Searle. In C. Blakemore and S. Greenfield (eds), *Mindwaves*, Oxford: Blackwell.

Gregory, R. (ed.) (1987b) *Oxford Companion to the Mind*, Oxford: Oxford University Press.

Gross, R. D. (1987) *Psychology: The Science of Mind and Behaviour*, Sevenoaks: Hodder and Stoughton.

Gubrium, J. (1973) *The Myth of the Golden Years: a Socio-Environmental Theory of Ageing*, Springfield, Ill.: Thomas.

Guilford, J. P. and Guilford, R. B. (1936) Personality factors, S. E. and M. and their measurement. *Journal of Psychology*, 2, 109–27.

Guiton, P. (1958) The effect of isolation on the following response of brown leghorn chicks. *Proceedings of the Royal Physical Society, Edinburgh*, 27, 9–14.

Gunter, B. (1987) The psychological influences of television. In H. Beloff and A. M. Colman (eds), *Psychology Survey*, No. 6, Leicester: British Psychological Society.

Guntrip, H. (1968) cited in M. Jacobs (1984), Psychodynamic therapy: the Freudian approach. In W. Dryden (ed.), *Individual Therapy in Britain*, London: Harper and Row.

Hall, C. S. (1966) *The Meaning of Dreams*, New York: McGraw Hill.

Harcourt, A. H. and Stewart, K. J. (1974) Apes, sex and societies. In G. Ferry (ed.), *The Understanding of Animals*, Oxford: Blackwell and New Scientist.

Hardy, G. R. and Legge, D. (1968) Cross-modal induction of changes in sensory thresholds. *Quarterly Journal of Experimental Psychology*, 20, 20–9.

Hargreaves, C. D. (ed.) (1987) *Preventing Adolescent Pregnancy: an Agenda for America*, Washington, D.C.: National Academy Press.

Hargreaves, D. J. (1986) Psychological theories of sex-role stereotyping. In D. J. Hargreaves and A. M. Colley (eds), *The Psychology of Sex Roles*, London: Harper and Row.

Hargreaves, D. J., Stoll, L., Farnworth, S. and Morgan, S. (1981) Psychological androgyny and ideational fluency. *British Journal of Social Psychology*, 20, 53–5.

Hathaway, S. R. and McKinley, J. C. (1943) *The Minnesota Multiphasic Personality Inventory*, New York: Psychological Corporation.

Hayes, C. D. (ed.) (1987) Preventing adolescent pregnancy: an agenda for America, cited in M. Rutter (1989), Pathways from childhood to adult life. *Journal of Child Psychology and Psychiatry*, Vol. 30, No. 1, 23–51.

Hayes, K. H. and Hayes, C. (1951) Intellectual development of a house-raised chimpanzee. *Proceedings of the American Philosophical Society*, 95, 105–9.

Hayslip, B. and Panek, P. E. (1989) *Adult Development and Ageing*, New York: Harper and Row.

Heather, N. (1976) *Radical Perspectives in Psychology*, London: Methuen.

Hebb, D. O. (1949) *The Organization of Behaviour*, New York: Wiley.

Hefner, R., Rebecca, M. and Oleshansky, B. (1975) Development of sex-role transcendence. *Human Development*, 18, 143–58.

Heider, F. (1958) *The Psychology of Interpersonal Relations*, New York: Wiley.

Hendricks, J. H. and Hendricks, C. D. (1977) *Ageing in Mass Society: Myths and Realities*, Cambridge, M.A.: Winthrop.

Herman, J. H., Ellman, S. J. and Roffwarg, H. P. (1978) The problem of NREM dream recall re-examined. In A. M. Arkin, J. S. Antrobus and S. J. Ellman (eds), *The Mind in Sleep: Psychology and psychophysiology*, Hillsdale, N.J.: Lawrence Erlbaum.

Herrnstein, R. J. (1982) IQ testing and the media. *Atlantic Monthly* (August), 68–74.

Hilgard, E. R. (1974) Toward a neo-dissociationist theory: multiple cognitive controls in human functioning. *Perspectives in Biology and Medicine*, 17, 301–16.

Hilgard, E. R. (1977) *Divided Consciousness: Multiple Controls in Human Thought and Action*, New York: Wiley.

Hilgard, E. R. (1978) States of consciousness in hypnosis: divisions or levels? In F. H. Frankel and H. S. Zamansky (eds), *Hypnosis at its Bicentennial: Selected Papers*, New York: Plenum.

Hilgard, E. R. (1979) Divided consciousness in hypnosis: the implications of the hidden observer. In E. Fromm and R. E. Shor (eds), *Hypnosis: Developments in Research and New Perspectives*, 2nd ed., New York: Aldine.

Hilgard, E. R., Atkinson, R. L. and Atkinson, R. C. (1979) *Introduction to Psychology*, 7th ed., New York: Harcourt Brace Jovanovich.

Hilgard, E. R. and Hilgard, J. R. (1984) *Hypnosis in the Relief of Pain*, New York: Kaufmann.

Hilgard, E. R., Hilgard, J. R., Macdonald, J., Morgan, A. H. and Johnson, L. S. (1978) Covert pain in hypnotic analgesia: its reality as tested by the real-simulator. *Journal of Abnormal Psychology*, 87, 655–63.

Hinde, R. A. (1982) *Ethology*, London: Fontana Paperback.

Hinde, R. A. (1987) *Individuals, Relationships and Culture: Links between Ethology and the Social*

Sciences, Cambridge: Cambridge University Press.

Hinde, R. A. and Stevenson-Hinde, J. (eds) (1988) *Relations within Families: Mutual Influences*, Oxford: Clarendon Press.

Hochberg, J. and Gilper, R. (1967) Recognition of faces (1): an exploratory study. *Psychonomic Science*, 12, 619–20.

Hockett, C. D. (1960) The origin of speech. *Scientific Amerian*, 203, 88–96.

Hofling, K. C., Brotzman, E., Dalrymple, S., Graves, N. and Pierce, C. M. (1966) An experimental study in the nurse–physician relationship. *Journal of Nervous and Mental Disorder*, 143, 171–80.

Hohmann, G. W. (1966) Some effects of spinal cord lesions on experienced emotional feelings. *Psychophysiology*, 3, 143–56.

Holmes, T. H. and Rahé, R. H. (1967) The social readjustment rating scale. *Journal of Psychosomatic Research*, 11, 213–18.

Homans, G. C. (1961) *Social Behaviour: Its Elementary Forms*, New York: Harcourt Brace Jovanovich.

Horn, J. M., Loehlin, J. L. and Willerman, L. (1979) Intellectual resemblance among adoptive and biological relatives: the Texas adoption project. *Behaviour Genetics*, 9, 177–207.

Howes, D. and Solomon, R. L. (1950) A note on McGinnies' emotionality and perceptual defence. *Psychological Review*, 57, 229–34.

Howie, D. (1952) Perceptual defence. *Psychological Review*, 59, 308–15.

Hudson, W. (1960) Pictorial depth perception in sub-cultural groups in Africa. *Journal of Social Psychology*, 52, 183–208.

Hudson, W. (1962) Pictorial perception and educational adaptation in Africa. *Psychologica Africana*, 9, 226–39.

Hugdahl, K. (1978) Electrodermal conditioning to potentially phobic stimuli: effects of instructed extinction. *Behaviour Research and Therapy*, 16, 315–21.

Hugdahl, K. and Ohman, A. (1977) Effects of instruction on acquisition and extinction of electrodermal responses to fear-relevant stimuli. *Journal of Experimental Psychology: Human Learning and Memory*, 3, 608–18.

Hugdahl, K., Fredrickson, M. and Ohman, A. (1977) 'Preparedness' and arousability as determinants of electrodermal conditioning. *Behaviour Research and Therapy*, 15, 345–53.

Hull, C. L. (1943) *Principles of Behaviour*, New York: D. Appleton-Century.

Hyde, J. S. and Phillis, D. E. (1979) Androgyny across the life span. *Developmental Psychology*, 15, 334–6.

Hyde, T. S. and Jenkins, J. J. (1973) Recall for words as a function of semantic, graphic and syntactic orienting tasks. *Journal of Verbal Learning and Behaviour*, 12, 471–80.

Immelman, K. and Suomi, S. J. (1981) Sensitive phases in development. In K. Immelman, G. Barlow, M. Main and L. Petrinovich (eds), *Issues in Behavioural Development: The Bielefelt Interdisciplinary Conference*, New York: Cambridge University Press.

Immelman, K. and Wolff, J. R. (1981), cited in S. J. Suomi, Biological foundations and development psychobiology. In C. B. Kopp and J. B. Krakow (eds) (1982), *The Child – Development in a Social Context*, Reading, M.A.: Adison-Wesley.

Jackson, J. H. (1864) cited in J. E. Bogen (1969) The other side of the brain. In R. Ornstein (1986), *The Psychology of Consciousness*, 2nd revised ed., Harmondsworth: Penguin.

Jacobs, M. (1984) Psychodynamic therapy: the Freudian approach. In W. Dryden (ed.), *Individual Therapy in Britain*, London: Harper and Row.

Jacoby, L. L. and Craik, F. I. M. (1979) Effects of elaboration of processing at encoding and retrieval: trace distinctiveness and recovery of initial context. In L. S. Cermak and F. I. M. Craik (eds), *Levels of Processing in Human Memory*, Hillsdale, N.J.: Lawrence Erlbaum.

Jahoda, G. (1966) Geometric illusions and environment: a study in Ghana. *British Journal of Psychology*, 57, 193–9.

James, W. (1884) What is an emotion? *Mind*, 188–205.

James, W. (1890) *Principles of Psychology*, New York: Holt.

Jensen, A. R. (1969) How much can we boost IQ and scholastic achievement? *Harvard Educational Review*, 39, 1–123.

Johnson, R. F., Maher, B. A. and Barber, T. X. (1972) Artifact in the 'essence of hypnosis': an evaluation of trance logic. *Journal of Abnormal Psychology*, 79, 212–20.

Jones, M. C. (1924b) The elimination of children's fears. *Journal of Experimental Psychology*, 7, 382–90.

Jones, M. C. (1974) Albert, Peter and J. B. Watson. *American Psychologist*, 29, 581–3.

Jones, R. A., Linder, D. E., Kiesler, C., Zanna, M. and Brehm, J. W. (1968) Internal states or external stimuli: observers' attitude judgements and the dissonance theory–self persuasion controversy. *Journal of Experimental and Social Psychology*, 4, 247–69.

Joynson, R. B. (1974) *Psychology and Common Sense*, London: RKP.

Joynson, R. B. (1989) *The Burt Affair*, London: Routledge.

Juel-Nielson, N. (1965) Individual and environment: a psychiatric and psychological investigation of monozygous twins raised apart. *Acta Psychiatrica et Neurologica Scandanavica*, Supplement 183.

Kagan, A. (1975) Epidemiology, disease and emotion. In L. Levi (ed.), *Emotions, their Parameters and Measurement*, New York: Raven Press.

Kagan, J. (1984) *The Nature of the Child*, New York: Basic Books.

Kalish, R. (1985a) The social context of death and dying. In R. Binstock and E. Shanas (eds), *Handbook of Ageing and the Social Sciences*, New York: Van Nostrand Reinhold.

Kamin, L. J. (1977) *The Science and Politics of I.Q.*, Harmondsworth: Penguin.

Kay, H. (1972) Psychology today and tomorrow. *Bulletin of the British Psychological Society*, 25, 177–88.

Kellogg, W. N. and Kellogg, L. A. (1933) *The Ape and the Child*, New York: McGraw-Hill.

Kelly, G. A. (1955) *A Theory of Personality – The Psychology of Personal Constructs*, New York: Norton.

Kendell, R. E. (1983) The principles of classification in relation to mental disease. In M. Shepherd and O. L. Zangwill (eds), *Handbook of Psychiatry: 1. General Psychopathology*, Cambridge: Cambridge University Press.

Kety, S. S. (1974) From rationalization to reason. *American Journal of Psychiatry*, 131, 957–62.

Kihlstrom, J. F. (1980) Post hypnotic amnesia for recently learned material: interactions with 'episodic' and 'semantic' memory. *Cognitive Psychology*, 12, 227–51.

Kilbride, P. L., Robbins, M. C. and Freeman, R. B. (1968) Pictorial depth perception and education among Baganda school children. *Perceptual and Motor Skills*, 26, 1116–18.

Kimura, D. (1961) Some effects of temporal-lobe damage on adult perception. *Canadian Journal of Psychology*, 15, 156–65.

Kimura, D. (1964b) Left-right differences in perception of melodies. *Quarterly Journal of Experimental Psychology*, 16, 355–8.

Knox, J. V., Morgan, A. H. and Hilgard, E. R. (1974) Pain and suffering in ischemia: the paradox of hypnotically suggested anaesthesia as contradicted by reports from the 'hidden observer'. *Archives of General Psychiatry*, 30, 840–7.

Koluchova, J. (1972) Severe deprivation in twins: a case study. *Journal of Child Psychology and Psychiatry*, 13, 107–14.

Koluchova, J. (1976) The further development of twins after severe and prolonged deprivation: a second report. *Journal of Child Psychology and Psychiatry*, 17, 181–8.

Kraepelin, E. (1913) *Psychiatry*, 8th ed., Leipzig: Thieme.

Kreitman, N. (1961) The reliability of psychiatric diagnosis. *Journal of Mental Science*, 107, 876–86.

418 *References*

Lacy, D. W., Lewinger, N. and Adamson, J. F. (1953) Foreknowledge as a factor affecting perceptual defence and alertness. *Journal of Experimental Psychology*, 45, 169.

Lahey, B. B. (1983) *Psychology – An Introduction*, Dubugue, Iowa: Wm. C. Brown Co.

Laird, J. D. (1974) Self-attribution of emotion: the effects of facial expression on the quality of emotional experience. *Journal of Personality and Social Psychology*, 29, 475–86.

Landis, C. (1938) Statistical evaluation of psychotherapeutic methods. In S. E. Hinde (ed.), *Concepts and Problems of Psychotherapy*, London: Heineman.

Larson, P. C. (1981) Sexual identification and self-concept. *Journal of Homosexuality*, 7, 15–32.

Lazarus, R. S. (1976) *Patterns of Adjustment*, New York: McGraw-Hill.

Lazarus, R. S. and McCleary, R. A. (1951) Automatic discrimination without awareness: a study of subception. *Psychological Review*, 58, 113–22.

Lea, S. E. G. (1984) *Instinct, Environment and Behaviour*, London: Methuen.

Leahy, A. M. (1935) Nature–nurture and intelligence genetic. *Psychology Monographs*, 17, 235–308.

Lefrancois, G. R. (1983) *Psychology*, Belmont, C.A.: Wadsworth.

Legge, D. (1975) *An Introduction to Psychological Science*, London: Methuen.

Leventhal, H. (1980) Toward a comprehensive theory of emotion. *Advances in Experimental Social Psychology*, 13, 139–207.

Levy-Agresti, J. and Sperry, R. W. (1968) Differential perceptual capacities in major and minor hemispheres. *Proceedings of National Academy of Sciences*, 61, 1151.

Liben, L. S. and Signorella, M. L. (1980) Gender-related schemata and constructive memory in children. *Child Development*, 51, 11–18.

Light, P. H., Buckingham, N. and Robbins, A. H. (1979) The conservation task as an interactional setting. *British Journal of Educational Psychology*, 49, 304–10.

Lindemann, E. (1944) The symptomatology and management of acute grief. *American Journal of Psychiatry*, 101, 141–8.

Linder, D. E., Cooper, J. and Jones, E. E. (1967) Decision freedom as a determinant of the role of incentive magnitude in attitude change. *Journal of Personality and Social Psychology*, 6, 245–54.

Lindsay, W. R. (1982) The effects of labelling: blind and non-blind ratings of social skills in schizophrenic and non-schizophrenic control subjects. *American Journal of Psychiatry*, 139, 216–19.

Loftus, E. F. (1979) Reactions to blatantly contradictory information. *Memory and Cognition*, 7, 368–74.

Loftus, E. F., Freedman, J. L. and Loftus, G. R. (1970) Retrieval of words from subordinate and superordinate categories in semantic hierarchies. *Psychonomic Science*, 21, 235–6.

Loftus, E. F. and Palmer, J. C. (1974) Reconstruction of automobile destruction: an example of the interaction between language and memory. *Journal of Verbal Learning and Verbal Behaviour*, 13, 585–9.

Loftus, E. F. and Zanni, G. (1975) Eyewitness testimony: the influence of the wording of a question. *Bulletin of the Psychonomic Society*, 5, 86–8.

Lorenz, K. Z. (1935) The companion in the birds' world. *Auk*, 54, 245–73.

Lubinski, D., Tellegen, A. and Butcher, J. N. (1981) The relationship between androgyny and subjective indicators of emotional well-being. *Journal of Personality and Social Psychology*, 40, 722–30.

Lubinski, D., Tellegen, A. and Butcher, J. N. (1983) Masculinity, femininity and androgyny. *Journal of Personality and Social Psychology*, 44, 428–39.

Luborsky, L., Singer, B. and Luborsky, L. (1975) Comparative study of psychotherapies: is it time that 'everyone has won and all must have prizes?' *Archives of General Psychiatry*, 32, 995–1008.

Ludwig, A. M., Brandsma, J. M., Wilbur, C. B., Bendfeldt, F. and Jameson, D. H. (1972) The objective study of a multiple personality: or, are four heads better than one? *Archives of General Psychiatry*, 26, 298–310.

MacFarlane, A. (1975) Olfaction in the development of social preferences in the human neonate. In R. Porter and M. O'Connor (eds), *Parent–Infant Interaction*, Amsterdam: Elsevier.

MacKay, D. (1975) *Clinical Psychology: Theory and Therapy*, London: Methuen.

MacKay, D. (1978) cited in D. MacKay (1987).

MacKay, D. (1987) Divided brains – divided minds? In C. Blakemore and S. Greenfield (eds), *Mindwaves*, Oxford: Blackwell.

MacKay, D. M. and MacKay, V. (1982) cited in D. MacKay (1987).

Mackintosh, N. (1984) In search of a new theory of conditioning. In G. Ferry (ed.), *The Understanding of Animals*, Oxford: Blackwell and New Scientist.

MacNamara, J. (1982) *Names for Things*, Cambridge, M.A.: Bradford MIT Press.

Mandler, G. (1984) *Mind and Body: The Psychology of Emotion and Stress*, New York: Norton.

Marañon, G. (1924) Contribution à l'étude de l'action émotive de l'adrenaline. *Revue Française Endocrinol*, 2, 301–25.

Marcel, T. and Patterson, K. (1978) Word recognition and production. In J. Requin (ed.), *Attention and Performance*, 7 Hillsdale, N.J.: Lawrence Erlbaum.

Marshall, G. (1976) cited by E. R. Hilgard, R. L. Atkinson and R. C. Atkinson (1979), *Introduction to Psychology*, 7th ed., New York: Harcourt Brace Jovanovich.

Marshall, G. D. and Zimbardo, P. G. (1979) Affective consequences of inadequately explained physiological arousal. *Journal of Personality and Social Psychology*, 37, 970–88.

Maslach, C. (1979) Negative emotional biasing of unexplained arousal. *Journal of Personality and Social Psychology*, 37, 953–69.

Maslow, A. M. (1954) *Motivation and Personality*, New York: Harper and Row.

Mason, M. K. (1942) Learning to speak after six and one half years of silence. *Journal of Speech and Hearing Disorders*, 7, 295–304.

McArthur, L. Z. and Resko, B. G. (1975) The portrayal of men and women in American television commercials. *Journal of Social Psychology*, 97, 209–20.

McCarley, R. W. (1983) REM dreams, REM sleep and their isomorphism. In M. H. Chase and E. D. Weitzman (eds), *Sleep Disorders: Basic and Clinical Research*, Vol. 8, New York: Spectrum.

McGarrigle, J. and Donaldson, M. (1974) Conservation accidents. *Cognition*, 3, 341–50.

McGinn, C. (1987) Could a machine be conscious? In C. Blakemore and S. Greenfield (eds), *Mindwaves*, Oxford: Blackwell.

McNally, R. J. and Reiss, S. (1982) The preparedness theory of phobias and human safety-signal conditioning. *Behaviour Research and Therapy*, 20, 153–9.

Mehler, J., Bertoncini, J., Barrière, M. and Jassik-Gerschenfeld, D. (1978) Infant recognition of mother's voice. *Perception*, 7, 491–7.

Milgram, S. (1974) *Obedience and Authority*, New York: Harper Torchbooks.

Miller, E. and Morley, S. (1986) *Investigating Abnormal Behaviour*, London: Lawrence Erlbaum.

Mischel, W. (1968) *Personality and Assessment*, New York: Wiley.

Mischel, W. (1969) Continuities and change in personality. *American Psychologist*, 24, 1012–18.

Moltz, H. and Stettner, L. J. (1961) The influences of patterned-light deprivation on the critical period for imprinting. *Journal of Comparative and Physiological Psychology*, 54, 279–83.

Moore, C. and Frye, D. (1986) The effect of the experimenter's intention on the child's understanding of conservation. *Cognition*, 22, 283–98.

Moore-Ede, M. C. and Czeisler, C. A. (eds) (1984) *Mathematical Models of the Circadian Sleep–Wake Cycle*, New York: Raven Press.

Morris, C. D., Bransford, J. D. and Franks, J. J. (1977) Levels of processing versus transfer appropriate processing. *Journal of Verbal Learning and Verbal Behaviour*, 16, 519–33.

Morrison, A. R. (1983) A window on the sleeping brain. *Scientific American*, 248, 94–102.

Mundy-Castle, A. C. and Nelson, G. K. (1962) A neuropsychological study of the Knysma forest workers. *Psychologia Africana*, 9, 240–72.

Murphy, J., John, M. and Brown, H. (1984) *Dialogues and Debates in Social Psychology*, London: Lawrence Erlbaum/Open University.

Murray, E. J. and Foote, F. (1979) The origins of fear of snakes. *Behaviour Research and Therapy*, 17, 489–93.

Newman, H. H., Freeman, F. N. and Holzinger, K. J. (1937) *Twins: A Study of Heredity and Environment*, Chicago: University of Chicago Press.

Newton, N. (1988) Machine understanding and the Chinese room. *Philosophical Psychology*, 1(2), 207–15.

Oatley, K. (1984) *Selves in Relation: An Introduction to Psychotherapy and Groups*, London: Methuen.

O'Grady, M. (1977) Effects of subliminal pictorial stimulation on skin resistance. *Perceptual and Motor Skills*, 44, 1051–6.

Öhman, A., Eriksson, A. and Olofsson, C. (1975a) One-trial learning and superior resistance to extinction of autonomic responses conditioned to potentially phobic stimuli. *Journal of Comparative and Physiological Psychology*, 88, 619–27.

Öhman, A., Erixon, G. and Lofberg, I. (1975b) Phobias and preparedness: phobic and neutral pictures as conditioned stimuli for human autonomic responses. *Journal of Abnormal Psychology*, 84, 41–5.

Öhman, A., Fredrikson, M., Hugdahl, K., and Rimmo, P. (1976) The premise of equi-potentiality in human classical conditioning: conditioned electrodermal responses to potentially phobic stimuli. *Journal of Experimental Psychology: General*, 105, 313–37.

Olds, J. (1956) Pleasure centres in the brain. *Scientific American* (October), 105–16.

Olds, J. (1958) Self-stimulation of the brain. *Science*, 127, 315–23.

Olds, J. (1962) Hypothalamic substrates of reward. *Physiological Review*, 42, 554–604.

Olds, J. and Sinclair, J. (1957) Self-stimulation in the obstruction box. *American Psychologist*, 12, 464.

Orne, M. T. (1959) The nature of hypnosis: artifact and essence. *Journal of Abnormal and Social Psychology*, 58, 277–99.

Orne, M. T. (1962) On the social psychology of the psychological experiment: with particular reference to demand characteristics and their implications. *American Psychologist*, 17, 776–83.

Orne, M. T. (1966) Hypnosis, motivation and compliance. *American Journal of Psychiatry*, 122, 721–6.

Orne, M. T. (1970) Hypnosis: motivation and the ecological validity of the psychological experiment. In W. J. Arnold and M. M. Page (eds), *Nebraska Symposium on Motivation*, Lincoln, Nebraska: University of Nebraska Press.

Orne, M. T. (1979) On the simulating subject as quasi-control group in hypnosis research: what, why and how? In E. Fromm and R. E. Shor (eds), *Hypnosis: Research Developments and Perspectives* 2nd ed., New York: Aldine.

Ornstein, R. (1986) *The Psychology of Consciousness*, 2nd revised ed., Harmondsworth: Penguin.

Osgood, C. E. and Luria, Z. (1957) Case Report: a blind analysis of a case of multiple personality using the semantic differential. In C. H. Thigpen, H. Cleckley, *The Three Faces of Eve*, New York: McGraw-Hill.

Osgood, C. E. and Tannenbaum, P. H. (1955) The principle of congruity in the prediction of attitude change. Psychological Review, 62, 42–55.

Otto, L. B. (1979) Antecedents and consequences of marital timing. In W. R. Burr, R. Hill, F. I. Nye and I. L. Reiss (eds), *Contemporary Theories about the Family*, Vol. 1, New York: Free Press.

Parfit, D. (1987) Divided minds and the nature of persons. In C. Blakemore and S. Greenfield (eds), *Mindwaves*, Oxford: Blackwell.

Parkin, A. J. (1987) *Memory and Amnesia: An Introduction*, Oxford: Blackwell.

Parkinson, B. (1987) Emotion – cognitive approaches. In H. Beloff and A. M. Colman (eds), *Psychology Survey*, No. 6, British Psychological Society.

Parsons, T. and Bales, R. F. (1955) *Family Socialization and Interaction Process*, Glencoe, Ill.: Free Press.

Patterson, F. G. (1978) The gestures of a gorilla: language acquisition in another pongid. *Brain and Language*, 5, 72–97.

Patterson, F. G. (1980) Innovative uses of language by a gorilla: a case study. In K. Nelson (ed.), *Children's Language*, Vol. 2, New York: Gardner Press.

Pavlov, I. P. (1927) *Conditioned Reflexes*, London: Oxford University Press.

Pedhazur, E. J. and Tetenbaum, T. J. (1979) Bem Sex Role Inventory: a theoretical and methodological critique. *Journal of Personality and Social Psychology*, 37, 996–1016.

Penrose, R. (1987) Minds, machines and mathematics. In C. Blakemore and S. Greenfield (eds), *Mindwaves*, Oxford: Blackwell.

Petitto, L. A. and Seidenberg, M. S. (1979) On the evidence for linguistic abilities in signing apes. *Brain and Language*, 8, 162–83.

Piaget, J. (1926) *The Language and Thought of the Child*, London: Routledge and Kegan Paul.

Piaget, J. and Szeminska, A. (1952) *The Child's Conception of Number*, London: Routledge and Kegan Paul.

Piliavin, J. A., Piliavin, I. M., Loewenton, E. P., McCauley, C. and Hammond, P. (1969) On observers' reproductions of dissonance effects: the right answers for the wrong reasons? *Journal of Personality and Social Psychology*, 13, 98–106.

Plutchik, R. and Ax, A. F. (1967) A critique of determinants of emotional state by Schachter and Singer (1962). *Psycho-physiology*, 4, 79–82.

Porpodas, C. D. (1987) The one-question conservation experiment reconsidered. *Journal of Child Psychology and Psychiatry*, 28(2), 343–9.

Postman, L., Bronson, W. C. and Gropper G. L. (1953) Is there a mechanism of perceptual defence? *Journal of Abnormal and Social Psychology*, 48, 215.

Postman, L., Bruner, J. S. and McGinnies, E. (1948) Personal values as selective factors in perception. *Journal of Abnormal and Social Psychology*, 43, 142–54.

Potter, M. C. (1966) On perceptual recognition. In J. S. Bruner *et al.* (eds), *Studies in Cognitive Growth*, London: Wiley.

Premack, D. (1971) On the assessment of language competence in the chimpanzee. In A. M. Schrier and F. Stollnitz (eds), *Behaviour of Non-human Primates*, Vol. 4, New York: Academic Press.

Price, R. A. and Vandenberg, S. G. (1979) Matching for physical attractiveness in married couples. *Personality and Social Psychology Bulletin*, 5, 398–400.

Price-Williams, D. (1966) Cross-cultural studies. In B. M. Foss (ed.), *New Horizons in Psychology*, 1, Harmondsworth: Penguin.

Rachman, S. (1977) The conditioning theory of fear-acquisition: a critical examination. *Behaviour Research and Therapy*, 15, 375–87.

Rachman, S. (1978) *Fear and Courage*, San Francisco: Freeman.

Rachman, S. and Wilson, G. (1980) *The Effects of Psychological Therapy*, Oxford: Pergamon.

Ramsay, A. O. and Hess, E. H. (1954) A laboratory approach to the study of imprinting. *Wilson Bulletin*, 66, 196–206.

Rivers, W. H. R. (1901) Visual spatial perception. In A. C. Haddon (ed.), *Reports of the Cambridge Anthropological Expedition to the Torres Straits*, Vol. 2(1).

Robson, C. (1973) *Experiment, Design and Statistics*, Harmondsworth: Penguin.

Roediger, H. L., Rushton, J. P., Capaldi, E. D. and Paris, S. G. (1984) *Psychology*, Boston: Little, Brown and Co.

Rogers, R. W. and Deckner, C. W. (1975) Effects of fear appeals and physiological arousal upon emotion, attitudes and cigarette smoking. *Journal of Personality and Social Psychology*, 32, 222–30.

Rose, S. (1976) *The Conscious Brain*, Harmondsworth: Penguin.

Rose, S., Lewontin, R. C. and Kamin, L. J. (1984) *Not in Our Genes: Biology, Ideology and Human Nature*, Harmondsworth: Penguin.

Rose, S. A. and Blank, M. (1974) The potency of context in children's cognition: an illustration through conservation. *Child Development*, 45, 499–502.

Routtenberg, A. and Lindy, J. (1965) Effects of the availability of rewarding septal and hypothalamic stimulation on bar-pressing for food under conditions of deprivation. *Journal of Comparative and Physiological Psychology*, 60, 158–61.

Rowland, K. (1977) Environmental events predicting death for the elderly. *Psychological Bulletin*, 84, 349–72.

Rumbaugh, D. M. (ed.) (1977) *Language Learning by a Chimpanzee: The LANA Project*, New York: Academic Press.

Rumelhart, D. E. and Norman, D. A. (1983) Representation in memory. In R. C. Atkinson, R. J. Herrnstein, G. Lindzey and R. D. Luce (eds), *Handbook of Experimental Psychology*, New York: Wiley and Sons.

Rutter, M. (1981) *Maternal Deprivation Reassessed*, 2nd ed., Harmondsworth: Penguin.

Rutter, M. (1987a) Continuities and discontinuities from infancy. In J. Osofsky (ed.), *Handbook of Infant Development*, 2nd ed., New York: Wiley.

Rutter, M. (1989) Pathways from childhood to adult life. *Journal of Child Psychology and Psychiatry*, 30(1), 23–51.

Ryan, J. (1972) IQ – The illusion of objectivity. In K. Richardson and D. Spears (eds), *Race, Culture and Intelligence*, Harmondsworth: Penguin.

Sarbin, T. R. and Mancuso, J. C. (1980) *Schizophrenia: Medical Diagnosis or Moral Verdict?*, New York: Pergamon.

Savage-Rumbaugh, E. S., Rumbaugh, D. M. and Boysen, S. L. (1980) Do apes use language? *American Scientist*, 68, 49–61.

Scarr, S. and Weinberg, R. A. (1977) Intellectual similarities within families of both adopted and biological children. *Intelligence*, 1, 170–91.

Scarr, S. and Weinberg, R. A. (1983) The Minnesota Adoption Studies: genetic differences and malleability. *Child Development*, 54, 260–7.

Scarr-Salapatek, S. (1976) An evolutionary perspective on infant intelligence: species patterns and individual variations. In M. Lewis (ed.), *Origins of Intelligence*, New York: Plenum.

Schachter, S. (1964) The interaction of cognitive and physiological determinants of emotional state. *Advances in Experimental Social Psychology*, 1, 49–80.

Schachter, S. (1966) The interaction of cognitive and physiological determinants of emotional state. In C. D. Spielberger (ed.), *Anxiety and Behaviour*, New York: Academic Press (originally, (1964) *Advances in Experimental Social Psychology*, 1, 49–80).

Schlenker, B. R. (1982) Translating action into attitudes: an identity-analytic approach to the explanation of social conduct. In L. Berkowitz (ed.), *Advances in Experimental Social Psychology*, Vol. 15, New York: Academic Press.

Schneider, K. (1959) Primary and secondary symptoms in schizophrenia. In S. R. Hirsch and M. Shepherd (eds) (1974), *Themes and Variations in European Psychiatry*, New York: John Wright.

Schreiber, F. R. (1973) *Sybil*, Harmondsworth: Penguin.

Schulz, R. (1978) *The Psychology of Death, Dying and Bereavement*, Reading, M.A.: Addison-Wesley.

Searle, J. R. (1987) Minds and brains without programs. In C. Blakemore and S. Greenfield (eds), *Mindwaves*, Oxford: Blackwell.

Segall, M. H., Campbell, D. T. and Herskovits, M. J. (1963) Cultural differences in the perception of geometrical illusions. *Science*, 139, 769–71.

Seligman, M. E. P. (1970) On the generality of the laws of learning. *Psychological Review*, 77, 406–18.

Seligman, M. E. P. (1975) *Helplessness: On Depression, Development and Death*, San Francisco: Freeman.

Serpell, R. S. (1976) *Culture's Influence on Behaviour*, London: Methuen.

Shapiro, D. A. and Shapiro, D. (1982) Meta-analysis of comparative therapeutic outcomes: a replication and refinement. *Psychological Bulletin*, 92, 581–604.

Sheridan, C. L. and King, R. G. (1972) Obedience to authority with an authentic victim. *Proceedings, Eightieth Annual Convention, American Psychological Association*, Washington, D.C.: American Psychological Association.

Shields, J. (1962) *Monozygotic Twins Brought Up Apart and Brought Up Together*, London: Oxford University Press.

Shotter, J. (1975) *Images of Man in Psychological Research*, London: Methuen.

Sigall, H. and Landy, D. (1973) Radiating beauty: effects of having a physically attractive partner on person perception. *Journal of Personality and Social Psychology*, 28, 218–24.

Silverman, I. (1971) Physical attractiveness and courtship, cited in E. Berscheid and E. Walster, Physical attractiveness. In L. Berkowitz (ed.) (1974), *Advances in Experimental Social Psychology*, Vol. 7, New York: Academic Press.

Sinnott, J. D. (1982) Correlates of sex roles of older adults. *Journal of Gerontology*, 37, 587–94.

Sizemore, C. C. and Pittillo, E. S. (1977) *I'm Eve*, Garden City, New York: Doubleday.

Skeels, H. M. (1966) Adult status of children with contrasting early life experiences: a follow-up study. *Monographs of Society for Research of Child Development*, 31, No. 103, 3.

Skuse, D. (1984) Extreme deprivation in early childhood – I Diverse outcomes for three siblings from an extraordinary family. *Journal of Child Psychology and Psychiatry*, 25(4), 523–41.

Skuse, D. (1984) Extreme deprivation in early childhood – II Theoretical issues and a comparative review. *Journal of Child Psychology and Psychiatry*, 25(4), 543–72.

Sluckin, W. (1965) *Imprinting and Early Experience*, London: Methuen.

Smith, M. L. and Glass, G. V. (1977) Meta-analysis of psychotherapeutic outcome studies. *American Psychologist*, 32, 752–60.

Smith, M. L., Glass, G. V. and Miller, R. L. (1980) *The Benefits of Psychotherapy*, Baltimore, M.D.: John Hopkins University Press.

Smith, R. E., Sarason, I. G. and Sarason, B. R. (1986) *Psychology – The Frontiers of Behaviour*, 3rd ed., New York: Harper and Row.

Solomon, R. L. and Howes, D. W. (1951) Word frequency, personal values and visual duration thresholds. *Psychological Review*, 58, 256.

Solso, R. L. and Johnson, H. H. (1989) *Introduction to Experimental Design in Psychology*, 4th ed., New York: Harper and Row.

Sonderegger, T. B. (1970) Intracranial stimulation and maternal behaviour. *American Psychological Association Convention Proceedings 78th Meeting*, 245–6.

Spanos, N. P. (1982) A social psychological approach to hypnotic behaviour. In G. Weary and H. L. Mirels (eds), *Integrations of Clinical and Social Psychology*, New York: Oxford University Press.

Speisman, J. C., Lazarus, R. S., Mordkoff, A. M. and Davidson, L. A. (1964) The experimental reduction of stress based on ego defence theory. *Journal of Abnormal and Social Psychology*, 68, 367–80.

Spence, J. T. (1983) Comment on Lubinski, Tellegen and Butcher 'Masculinity, femininity and androgyny viewed and assessed as distinct concepts'. *Journal of Personality and Social Psychology*, 44, 440–6.

Spence, J. T. and Helmreich, R. L. (1978) *Masculinity and Femininity. Their Psychological Dimensions, Correlations and Antecedents*, Austin: University of Texas Press.

Spence, J. T., Helmreich, R. L. and Stapp, J. (1975) Ratings of self and peers on sex role attributes and their relation to self-esteem and concepts of masculinity and femininity. *Journal of Personality and Social Psychology*, 32, 29–39.

Sperry, R. W. (1966) cited in D. MacKay (1987), Divided brains – divided minds? In C. Blakemore and S. Greenfield (eds), *Mindwaves*, Oxford: Blackwell.

Spies, G. (1965) Food versus intracranial self-stimulation reinforcement in food deprived rats. *Journal of Comparative and Physiological Psychology*, 60, 153–7.

Spitzer, R. L. (1976) More on pseudoscience in science and the case for psychiatric diagnosis. *Archives of General Psychiatry*, 33, 459–70.

Spitzer, R. L., Endicott, J. and Robins, E. (1978) Research diagnostic criteria: rationale and reliability. *Archives of General Psychiatry*, 35, 773–82.

Stein, B. S., Morris, C. D. and Bransford, J. D. (1978) Constraints on effective elaboration. *Journal of Verbal Learning and Verbal Behaviour*, 17, 707–14.

Storms, M. D. (1979) Sex-role identification and its relations to sex-role attributes and sex-role stereotypes. *Journal of Personality and Social Psychology*, 37, 1779–89.

Storr, A. (1966) The concept of cure. In C. Rycroft (ed.), *Psychoanalysis Observed*, London: Constable.

Storr, A. (1987) Why psychoanalysis is not a science. In C. Blakemore and S. Greenfield (eds), *Mindwaves*, Oxford: Blackwell.

Stratton, P. and Hayes, N. (1988) *A Student's Dictionary of Psychology*, London: Edward Arnold.

Strong, E. K. (1943) *Vocational Interests of Men and Women*, Stanford, C.A.: Stanford University Press.

Suomi, S. J. (1982) Biological foundations and development psychobiology. In C. B. Kopp and J. B. Krakow (eds), *The Child-Development in a Social Context*, Reading, M.A.: Addison-Wesley.

Szasz, T. (1972) *The Myth of Mental Illness*, London: Paladin.

Taylor, A. (1986) Sex roles and ageing. In D. J. Hargreaves and A. M. Colley (eds), *The Psychology of Sex Roles*, London: Harper and Row.

Taylor, M. C. and Hall. J. A. (1982) Psychological androgyny: theories, methods and conclusions. *Psychological Bulletin*, 92, 347–66.

Tedeschi, J. T. and Rosenfeld, P. (1981) Impression management theory and the forced compliance situation. In J. T. Tedeschi (ed.), *Impression Management Theory and Social Psychological Research*, New York: Academic Press.

Tedeschi, J. T., Schlenker, B. R. and Bonoma, T. V. (1971) Cognitive dissonance: private ratiocination or public spectacle? *American Psychologist*, 26, 685–95.

Teichman, J. (1988) *Philosophy and the Mind*, Oxford: Blackwell.

Terman, L. M. and Miles, C. C. (1936) *Sex and Personality*, New York: McGraw-Hill.

Terrace, H. S. (1979) *Nim*, New York: Knopf.

Terrace, H. S. (1979a) How Nim Chimpsky changed my mind. *Psychology Today* (November) 65–76.

Terrace, H. S. (1987) Thoughts without words. In C. Blakemore and S. Greenfield (eds), *Mindwaves*, Oxford: Blackwell.

Tesser, A. and Brodie, M. (1971) A note on the evaluation of a 'computer date'. *Psychonomic Science*, 23, 300.

Thibaut, J. W. and Kelley, H. H. (1959) *The Social Psychology of Groups*, New York: Wiley.

Thigpen, C. H. and Cleckley, H. (1957) *The Three Faces of Eve*, New York: McGraw-Hill.

Tinbergen, N. and Perdeck, A. C. (1950) On the stimulus situation releasing the begging response in the newly-hatched herring-gull chick (*Larus argentatus Pont*). *Behaviour*, 3, 1–39.

Torrance, S. (1986) Breaking out of the Chinese room. In M. Yazdani (ed.), *Artificial Intelligence: Principles and Applications*, London: Chapman and Hall.

Tulving, E. (1972) Episodic and semantic memory. In E. Tulving and W. Donaldson (eds), *Organization of Memory*, London: Academic Press.

Turing, A. M. (1950) Computing machinery and intelligence. *Mind*, 59, 433–60.

Turner, E. A. and Wright, J. (1965) Effects of severity of threat and perceived availability on the attractiveness of objects. *Journal of Personality and Social Psychology*, 2, 128–32.

Tyrer, P., Lewis, P. and Lee, I. (1978) Effects of subliminal and supraliminal stress on symptoms of anxiety. *Journal of Nervous and Mental Disorders*, 166, 611–22.

Udry, J. R. (1971) cited in E. Berscheid and E. Walster (1974), Physical attractiveness. In L. Berkowitz (ed.), *Advances in Experimental Social Psychology*, Vol. 7, New York: Academic Press.

Valins, S. (1966) Cognitive effects of false heart-rate feedback. *Journal of Personality and Social Psychology*, 4, 400–8.

Vernon, M. D. (1962) *The Psychology of Perception*, Harmondsworth: Penguin.

Wagstaff, G. F. (1981a) Hypnosis, compliance and belief, cited in H. Beloff and A. M. Colman (eds), *Psychology Survey No. 6*, Leicester: British Psychological Society.

Wagstaff, G. F. (1982b) Hypnosis and witness recall: a discussion paper. *Journal of Royal Society of Medicine*, 75, 793–8.

Wagstaff, G. F. (1982c) Recall of witnesses under hypnosis. *Journal of Forensic Science Society*, 22, 33–9.

Wagstaff, G. F. (1983) A comment on McConkey's 'Challenging hypnotic effects?' The impact of conflicting influences on responses to hypnotic suggestion. *British Journal of Experimental and Clinical Hypnosis*, 1, 11–15.

Wagstaff, G. F. (1984) The enhancement of witness memory by 'hypnosis': a review and methodological critique of the experimental literature. *British Journal of Experimental and Clinical Hypnosis*, 2, 3–12.

Wagstaff, G. F. (1986) cited in Wagstaff, 1987.

Wagstaff, G. F. (1987) Hypnosis. In H. Belof and A. M. Colman (eds), *Psychology Survey No. 6*, Leicester: British Psychological Society.

Walker, S. (1984) *Learning Theory and Behaviour Modification*, London: Methuen.

Walster, E. (1970) The effect of self-esteem on liking for dates of various social desirabilities. *Journal of Experimental Social Psychology*, 6, 248–53.

Walster, E., Aronson, V., Abrahams, D. and Rottmann, L. (1966) Importance of physical attractiveness in dating behaviour. *Journal of Personality and Social Psychology*, 4, 508–16.

Walster, E. and Walster G. W. (1970) *The Matching Hypotheses*. Unpublished manuscript, University of Wisconsin.

Warr, P. (1987) *Work, Unemployment and Mental Health*, Oxford: Clarendon Press.

Watson, J. B. (1913) Psychology as the behaviourist views it. *Psychological Review*, 20, 158–77.

Watson, J. B. (1924) *Behaviourism*, 2nd ed. 1931, New York: Norton.

Waugh, N. C. and Norman, D. (1965) Primary memory. *Psychological Review*, 72, 89–104.

Webb, W. B. and Bonnett, M. H. (1979) Sleep and dreams. In M. E. Meyer (ed.), *Foundations of Contemporary Psychology*, New York: Oxford University Press.

Weizenbaum, J. (1976) *Computer Power and Human Reason*, San Francisco: Freeman.

Wilson, S. C. and Barber, T. X. (1983) The fantasy-prone personality: implications for understanding imagery, hypnosis and parapsychological phenomena. In A. Sheikh (ed.), *Imagery: Current Theory, Research and Application*, New York: Wiley.

Wing, J. K., Birley, J. L.T., Cooper, J. E., Graham, P. and Isaacs, A. (1967) Reliability of a procedure for measuring and classifying 'present psychiatric state'. *British Journal of Psychiatry*, 113, 488–515.

Wing *et al.* (1979) cited in E. Miller and S. Morley (1986), *Investigating Abnormal Behaviour*, London: Lawrence Erlbaum.

Wohlwill, J. F. (1965) Texture of the stimulus field and age as variables in the perception of relative distance. *Journal of Experimental Child Psychology*, 2, 163–77.

World Health Organization (1978) *Mental Disorders: Glossary and Guide to their Classification in Accordance with the Ninth Revision of the International Classification of Diseases*, Geneva: World Health Organization.

Yarrow, L. J. (1961) Maternal deprivation: toward an empirical and conceptual re-evaluation. *Psychological Bulletin*, 58, 459–90.

Yin, R. (1969) Looking at upside-down faces. *Journal of Experimental Psychology*, 81, 141–5.

Zajonc, R. B. (1980) Feeling and thinking: preferences need no inferences. *American Psychologist*, 35, 151–75.

Zangwill, O. L. (1961) cited in J. E. Bogen (1969), The other side of the brain. In R. Ornstein (1986) *The Psychology of Consciousness*, 2nd revised ed., Harmondsworth: Penguin.

Zanna, M. P. and Cooper, J. (1974) Dissonance and the pill. An attributional approach to studying the arousal properties of dissonance. *Journal of Personality and Social Psychology*, 29, 703–9.

Index

Author(s) of key studies are listed in the contents and not in the index.